Key Changes

Key Changes

The Ten Times Technology Transformed the Music Industry

HOWIE SINGER AND BILL ROSENBLATT

OXFORD
UNIVERSITY PRESS

OXFORD
UNIVERSITY PRESS

Oxford University Press is a department of the University of Oxford. It furthers
the University's objective of excellence in research, scholarship, and education
by publishing worldwide. Oxford is a registered trade mark of Oxford University
Press in the UK and certain other countries.

Published in the United States of America by Oxford University Press
198 Madison Avenue, New York, NY 10016, United States of America.

Library of Congress Cataloging-in-Publication Data
Names: Singer, Howie, author. | Rosenblatt, Bill, author.
Title: Key changes : the ten times technology transformed the music industry /
Howie Singer and Bill Rosenblatt.
Description: [1.] | New York : Oxford University Press, 2023. |
Includes bibliographical references and index.
Identifiers: LCCN 2023008575 (print) | LCCN 2023008576 (ebook) |
ISBN 9780197656907 (paperback) | ISBN 9780197656891 (hardcover) |
ISBN 9780197656921 (epub)
Subjects: LCSH: Music trade—History. | Sound recording industry—History. |
Music trade—Technological innovations. | Music and the Internet.
Classification: LCC ML3790 .S563 2023 (print) | LCC ML3790 (ebook) |
DDC 338.4/778—dc23/eng/20230306
LC record available at https://lccn.loc.gov/2023008575
LC ebook record available at https://lccn.loc.gov/2023008576

DOI: 10.1093/oso/9780197656891.001.0001

Paperback printed by Marquis Book Printing, Canada
Hardback printed by Bridgeport National Bindery, Inc., United States of America

To Sandy, no passing fancy; our love is here to stay.
– Howie Singer

To Jessica, who kept telling me "You have one more book in you" until
I believed her.
– Bill Rosenblatt

Contents

Acknowledgments

From the Authors

We have each had our own journey through music and technology that brought us to the point of writing this book, but the rest of the journey—to the product that you hold in your hands or see on your screen—has required a lot of research, help, and companionship along the way.

Many current and former music-industry executives were generous with their time with us, including Elektra Records founder Jac Holzman; Ralph Simon (cofounder of Zomba Records); former Warner Music Group executives Paul Vidich, Jacob Key, George Lydecker, and Jordan Rost; former Sony Music lawyer and former Napster General Counsel Gene Rhough; former Columbia Records executive Paul Rappaport; former CBS Records executive and NBC Friday Night Videos producer David Benjamin; former Sony Music executive Rich Appel; former Sony executive Marc Finer; Tucker McCrady of The Orchard (ex-WMG); Ted Cohen of TAG Strategic (ex-EMI); MQA executive Mike Jbara (ex-WMG); former UMG executive and CEO of presssplay Mike Bebel; Matthias Röder of the Herbert von Karajan Foundation; RIAA data guru Josh Friedlander; and Jonathan Taplin (Director Emeritus, Annenberg Innovation Lab at USC; former Bob Dylan and The Band manager; Oscar-nominated film producer). We also talked to several music technologists and studio people, including former RIAA Chief Technology Officer David Hughes, Bob Stuart of Meridian and MQA, Isabel Garvey of Abbey Road Studios, Niclas Molinder of Session, and Bill Klinger of the Association for Recorded Sound Collection.

We were privileged to be able to talk to several Grammy-winning recording artists and producers, including Jerry Casale of Devo, Nick Rhodes of Duran Duran, Imogen Heap, Arabian Prince of N.W.A., Peter Asher, Rob Fraboni, and Albhy Galuten. From the world of radio, we spoke with Jim McKeon (KWST Los Angeles, various Detroit stations, and various record labels), John Platt (WXRT Chicago, WNEW New York, and WFUV New York), and Sean Ross (Ross on Radio and Edison Research). Dr. Todd Boyd of USC was

kind enough to share his expertise on the issues surrounding race and popular culture.

Finding historical information about (and usable photos of) consumer audio electronics from the mid-twentieth to early twenty-first century turns out to be surprisingly difficult; this subject tends to fall into the
cracks between museums and current information. Luckily there are several online sources curated by passionate people who have filled in the
gaps, including WorldRadioHistory.com (a goldmine of searchable PDFs
of old audio magazines, consumer electronics retailer catalogs, and much
more), RadioShackCatalogs.com, JukeBoxHistory.info, WikiBoombox.
com, RadioMuseum.org, Reel-Reel.com, 8trackheaven.com, and
Tonbandmuseum.info. Flickr is also a rich source of photos of gadgets going
back decades. And let's not forget the Internet Archive Wayback Machine,
which is one of the true miracles of our age.

We'd also like to thank various people and institutions for all kinds of
help, including but not limited to, and in no particular order: Karl Sluis for
the graphics; Lisa Shaftel of Shaftel s2do for help with photo clearances;
Dave Hermann for old Schwann catalogs of commercially available
recordings; Jedi Master Librarian Gary Price for help in finding research
sources on old consumer electronics; Max Poser of My Radio Berlin
for boombox history expertise; Brian Wallace, Curator of the Sarnoff
Collection; Regan Smith of the US Copyright Office for pointers to copyright legislative history; Mike Lupica and Dante Sudilovsky of WPRB;
Louise Barder of Glossophilia.org; Viberate for its data analytics platform;
the NYU Bobst Library; the New York Society Library; and last but definitely not least, the amazing people and resources of the New York Public
Library for the Performing Arts.

Finally, much gratitude to our agent, Pamela Malpas of the Jennifer Lyons
Literary Agency, as well as to Norman Hirschy, Sean Decker, Egle Zigaite,
and everyone else at Oxford University Press.

From Howie Singer

If you had told me at the start of my career that I'd be discussing the future of
the music business with Neil Young or Robert Plant, I would have thought
you were crazy. I would never have reached that point if not for a PhD in
Operations Research and a successful career at Bell Labs, which depended

upon the support of Ben Operowsky, Alan Tucker, Jack Muckstadt, Janet Nici, Dave Menist, John Sheehan, and many others. My transition to the music industry would have been impossible without Larry Miller, Tony Grewe, Sandy Fraser, Tsvi Gal, Paul Vidich, and the entire a2b music team. My fifteen years at Warner Music Group gave me a ringside seat to how the music business handles disruption and provided the background needed to create this book. There are far too many people across the industry who helped to educate me to list here, but special thanks to Alex Zubillaga, George White, Michael Nash, Paul Sinclair, Laird Popkin, Mike Elias, Bill Ardito, Mike Jbara, Ron Wilcox, Craig Kallman, Edgar Bronfman, Jr, and Jac Holzman for their generosity and guidance. And thank goodness Bill Rosenblatt offered to join me on this journey. Without him, this project would have taken far longer and the result would have been far poorer.

Neither my career nor this book would have happened without the sacrifices, support, and love of my family. I know my parents, Bernie and Rhoda, would have shown off this volume with great pride and I expect that my sister Helene will do the same. My sons, Matt and Doug, and their respective spouses, Melissa and Camilla, were all cheerleaders for this project. My granddaughters Riley and Eloise pitched in by demonstrating that even the youngest music fans can now use voice assistants to play their favorite tracks. The final and most heartfelt thank you to my wife Sandy: my love, my best friend, and my number one fan. Here's to many more adventures together.

From Bill Rosenblatt

The path that I've taken into music technology might seem inevitable in hindsight, given that both of my parents were musicians, I played a few instruments myself, and I was a math nerd who liked to tinker with electronics. But the die was truly cast the summer after my senior year of high school in Philadelphia, when I learned that the radio station I loved to listen to, WPRB in Princeton, New Jersey, was the student-run station at the college I was going to attend; thus began an association that led to 12 years in radio and that continues to this day. It took a while to make my way from there into the music industry proper, but I'm here, and I'm home. People I'd like to especially thank for my journey into the music industry over the years include, certainly without limitation, Dan Harple, Chris Harrison, George Howard,

Adam Kidron, Larry Miller, Panos Panay, Bruce Rich, Rajan Samtani—and Howie Singer.

Howie and I have known each other for roughly 20 years. After I wrote a book on digital rights management in the early 2000s, his introduction led me to a heady three-year stint at a digital-music startup, which in turn led to a number of consulting projects with record labels, digital music services, and music tech companies. Howie and I have worked on various projects together, at Warner Music Group and elsewhere, most recently teaching different sections of the Data Analysis in the Music Industry class at NYU. When Howie approached me with his idea for a book during the lockdown in the summer of 2020, I saw immediately that it held much more appeal than the rather pedantic ideas for books on copyright and technology that I was toying with at the time. My partnership with Howie during this endeavor has been the second-best I've ever had—the first-best being the one I have with my wife Jessica Lustig, who has been a life partner in every sense of the phrase as well as an unstinting cheerleader for me and for this book.

1

Introduction

Whole Lotta Shakin' Goin' On—Jerry Lee Lewis

On April 3, 2018, Spotify began trading its shares publicly for the first time. Since its October 2008 launch, Spotify has added more than 200 million paid subscribers and a half a billion total users, including those who use its ad-supported tier. The largest technology companies in the world—Apple, Amazon, and Google—all offer streaming music as well. And around the world, other services—such as Deezer in Europe and Tencent in China—provide access to an enormous catalog of songs to millions more music fans at the touch of a finger to a smartphone.

This explosion in streaming has brought growth to a music business that had basically been treading water since the massive declines of the Napster era. Selling music downloads generated billions in revenues but never made up for consistently declining Compact Disc (CD) sales. Apple dominated the era of digital downloads with the iTunes store, and Steve Jobs often voiced his opposition to the streaming business model.[i]

He famously said, "People have told us over and over and over again, they don't want to rent their music." But the realities of the mass-consumer adoption of streaming finally drove Apple to abandon its founder's views—after his passing in 2011—and ride the next wave. At this writing, Apple Music is now estimated to have about 80 million music fans paying for access to its streaming service.

People "renting" music by the millions required the melding of a range of technologies. It represents a seismic shift in the industry, not just in terms of the innovations that create a viable alternative to what was the dominant music format of the day, but in the aftershocks that altered fans' expectations, the birth (and sometimes death) of the distribution channels to reach those fans, the methods that artists use to create their music, the legal framework around copyright, and the business models that ultimately fuel creators and rights holders.

Key Changes. Howie Singer and Bill Rosenblatt, Oxford University Press. © Howie Singer and Bill Rosenblatt 2023.
DOI: 10.1093/oso/9780197656891.003.0001

The music industry has existed on the fault lines of evolving technologies for more than a century. In the late nineteenth century, two competing formats for recorded music—the cylinder and the disc—altered the experience of listening to music and established the foundation for a new business. Phonographs were followed by radio, the long-playing record and the 45-rpm single. Then came 8-track tapes, cassette tapes, and MTV. Analog audio became zeros and ones, and the CD took over the music business and drove it to new heights of financial success. But those same digits seeded the conditions for the industry's eventual decline. With the adoption of the MP3 standard and advancements in computer technology, music could be compressed, and the resulting audio files could be sold—or shared—over ever-faster networks. And now downloading those files seems antiquated as streaming, whether on Spotify, Amazon, or Apple, drives listening to unprecedented levels. Fans have become more active participants in creating and distributing music through videos on YouTube or TikTok.

Format changes in recorded music are the best lens through which to view the evolution of the music industry; that's because changes in formats have pervasive effects on the rest of the industry. Every time the format changes, the foundations of the music business shake. Nikki Sixx, cofounder and primary songwriter of the band Mötley Crüe, said, "Formats are going to change because this is what the people want. It's not what the labels want."[ii]

For each of the formats in which recorded music has been distributed, this book will review how technological advancements came together to enable new experiences for fans. The first version of the new product was often not quite good enough to drive mass-market adoption. In today's terminology, that first release represented a "Minimum Viable Product," or MVP—that is, a version of the product that enticed early adopters with a somewhat compromised and limited feature set that was not quite good enough to attract a mass audience. But those early users provided the feedback that helped to point the way to the enhancements that broadened the product's appeal.

Once the technology advanced to make the format attractive to a large audience, the resulting mass-market adoption had wide-ranging impacts on business models and ways of garnering revenues. As we'll show in this book, the changes reach far beyond consumer experiences. Artists change their creative processes and musical styles to take advantage of the new formats. New distribution strategies emerge, as do new ways for artists to get paid. Rights administration, rights enforcement, and even copyright law itself may shift to reflect the realities of the new formats.

Although technology is constantly evolving, the history of the music industry makes it clear that certain sets of technological elements coalesced at specific times to create the distinct pivot points that we focus on. And as we will show, most of the important developments in the industry—from artists' creative processes through the ways in which people enjoy music and engage artists as well as artists' compensation and career trajectories—arise out of these distinct pivot points.

Conversely, there have been many technological developments that changed the way music is produced, distributed, and consumed but haven't risen to the level of the pivot points that we've identified in terms of their impact. (Just to name a few: four-track cassette recorders like the TASCAM 124; digital audio workstations such as GarageBand and ProTools; minor physical formats such as LaserDisc, MiniDisc, and SACD; and background/ foreground music services such as Muzak and DMX.) Technology has also contributed incalculably to the creation of music and increased its supply, but innovations such as electric guitars, synthesizers, and digital sampling haven't materially affected the structure of the industry the way format changes have.

We'll begin by rewinding the clock to the late nineteenth century when a group of inventors, led by Thomas Edison, made the recording of the human voice and instruments a reality. Edison's early phonographs (Chapter 2) recorded sound onto tinfoil or some other thin sheet of metal. These recordings degraded significantly with each playing and were not easily duplicated. His early machines were simply novelties. Calling them "minimally viable" may have been stretching the definition of viable. But they did represent the kernels of the modern recording industry: once others perfected the use of wax cylinders and discs that could be recorded more easily, reproduced in volume, and played back more frequently, the technology foundation was ready to construct a new business, complete with the first worldwide recording stars.

Advances in vacuum-tube technology made it possible for a family to listen to broadcast radio together instead of using earphones; affordable models with loudspeakers were introduced in 1927. The electronics essential to radio also found their way into a new generation of phonographs. The Great Depression after the market crash of 1929 made it more burdensome to purchase all the latest recordings. The disruption of listening to free broadcasts on a more affordable, one-time-purchase gadget won the day even if consumers had no choice but to listen to whatever music the radio programmers selected. By 1932, just a few short years after the crash, US record sales dropped over 90 percent to 6 million units. Music fans chose convenience and price over quality in what would turn out to be a recurring theme as music technology and formats evolved through time.

The broad reach of radio (Chapter 3) into a majority of US homes helped to create the first multimedia stars. Bing Crosby leveraged his enormous popularity on the radio in the 1930s to become not only one of the largest sellers of recorded music but also a huge box-office draw in Hollywood movies. The improvement of microphone technology itself helped to make his crooning, intimate style a success. AT&T's telephone lines enabled the creation of the national broadcast network, which, in turn, enabled advertising to thrive as a mechanism to support the music business. And the radio quickly made its way into the car as technology advances in electronics shrank the required form factor sufficiently.

The recorded music industry standardized on 78 revolutions per minute (rpm) in the 1920s. That limited the 12-inch diameter record—first made of shellac, then vinyl—to less than five minutes of music per side. If you wanted to hear the original Broadway cast recording of "Annie Get Your Gun," you had to listen to all 12 sides of the 6 records that were bound together as a "record album."

This was the case until after World War II: Peter Goldmark of Columbia Records introduced the new 12-inch "long playing" (LP) vinyl record spinning at 33 1/3 rpm in 1948. With LPs, listeners only needed to get up once to flip their record to enjoy more than 40 minutes of music. That was enough time to hear classical concertos in their entireties, or all the songs from a Broadway musical. Even though only one disc was needed, the album terminology stuck. The individual vinyl disc became known as the "album," and it drove decades of financial and artistic achievements for the music business. In fact, even in today's world of music streaming, the term album lives on. Billboard charts that report sales and streams together measure "stream equivalent albums" (SEA), and artists still make album releases into media events. Not to mention that vinyl albums have now become the fastest-selling physical format.

In 1949, RCA Victor introduced the 7-inch, 45-rpm format to compete with the LP, but fans were not particularly interested in purchasing groups of 45s to represent a collection of related works. The LP and the 45 (Chapter 4) quickly became the dominant formats for music collections and single songs, respectively. As baby boomers became teenagers, their love of rock & roll drove their parents crazy. And their ability to buy 45s with their allowance or babysitting money was the fuel that propelled that segment of the music business, along with the pocket-size transistor radios that appeared in the 1950s, which those teenagers could afford as well. The LP also provided bands and songwriters with a new creative canvas for the album as a unified artistic concept.

Vinyl was virtually the only format for recorded music products for several decades, although prerecorded reel-to-reel tapes had a small presence in the market, particularly for classical music aficionados, starting in the 1950s when "high fidelity" (hi-fi) listening equipment first appeared. Figure 1.1 shows how different formats—physical and then digital—began to proliferate after that (the RIAA began tracking annual revenues per format consistently in 1973).

More user-friendly tape formats began to appear in the 1960s. The cassette tape (Chapter 5) was introduced to the US market by Philips in 1964. The sound quality of those first tape cassettes was poor, but they were far easier to use than reel-to-reel. And the freedom they provided to listen to

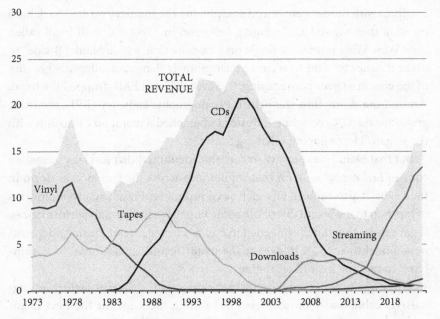

Figure 1.1 A half century of recorded music revenues by format, 1973-2022 (billions of dollars, adjusted for inflation). Source: RIAA.

the music you wanted to hear on the go and to make copies for your friends were major improvements. Shortly after that, 8-track tape players appeared, starting in certain Ford automobile models. The format was derived from tape cartridges used in radio stations. The 8-track was designed specifically for use in cars, where the driver could simply "plug and play."

At first, 8-tracks were better suited for use in cars than cassettes because of their superior sound quality, durability, and ease of use while driving. But in the early 1970s, consumer electronics and tape makers introduced home cassette recorders and blank tapes with sound quality that began to approach vinyl. By 1979, Sony had introduced the iconic Walkman, the first cassette player that was not only as portable as those transistor radios but also offered excellent sound through headphones, making cassettes desirable on both the road and the sidewalk. These developments brought the dominance of 8-tracks as a "music on demand and on the go" format to a rapid end.

The cassette was also the first format that enabled easy recording of music at home—another factor that contributed to the format's success over 8-tracks. Copying albums onto cassettes at home and sharing them with friends became common, and the technology had evolved by the late 1970s to enable fans to make cassette copies of LPs that sounded almost as good as the originals with moderately priced equipment. The industry pushed back hard on what they viewed as damaging behavior. In 1980, a British band called Bow Wow Wow released a single on a cassette tape with a blank "B-side" to make it easier for fans to record music. Shortly thereafter, allegedly because of the concerns over home taping, their record label EMI dropped the band. Around the same time, the British Phonographic Industry (BPI), the trade group for the UK recording industry in launched a major ad campaign with the slogan "Home Taping is Killing Music."

But that blank, inexpensive, recordable medium didn't just let you make a copy of *Led Zeppelin IV* for that sophomore across the hall in your dorm in the 1970s. It also enabled DJs such as Grandmaster Flash and other pioneers of hip-hop to make and distribute recordings of their live club performances. It gave them the tool they needed to create a new genre of music and a business model to support it, despite the major record labels' initial lack of interest in rapping instead of singing.

While hip-hop was burgeoning in the streets, the delivery of television signals via cable under those streets was setting the stage for the next major game-changer for the music industry. Sixteen million US households were receiving cable television and choosing among 28 channels in 1980. The

Cable Act of 1984 loosened regulatory constraints and unleashed a rapid period of growth. Soon a new wave of US teenagers were saying "I Want My MTV." And by the end of the decade, MTV was one of almost 80 channels being broadcast over cable into more than 50 million US households.

Though not a physical format like the vinyl record or the cassette tape, there is no doubt that the music video and the 1981 launch of MTV (Chapter 6) drove significant changes in the music business. The creative palette expanded so much that when you see a song title such as "Beat It" or "Material Girl" you think of the images from the videos as quickly as you recall the melody. For top musical artists of the 1980s such as Michael Jackson and Madonna, it is impossible to separate their iconic dance moves and visual imagery from the songs themselves.

The heyday of the cassette was relatively short lived compared to the decades of vinyl popularity. That's because Philips and Sony Electronics introduced the CD format in 1982 (Chapter 7). The first CD players cost up to $1,000 in the US but still sold several hundred thousand units in the first couple of years in the market. Within a decade, volume drove player costs down, and performance improvements made portable players a reality. CDs zoomed past both vinyl records and cassettes in total volume and became the choice of the mass market of music fans by the end of the 1980s. Unlike those earlier formats, the reproduction of the sound rendered from the digital bits placed on the CD did not degrade over repeated plays. And the perceived quality advantage of the CD motivated millions of baby boomers to repurchase their music collections, leading to the greatest financial success the music industry had ever experienced, as Figure 1.1 shows.

The seeds of the music industry's massive decline that was to come at the end of the century were planted with the ones and zeros embedded on those CDs. Compact Discs usually held 700 megabytes of data. The typical personal computer of the mid-1980s contained 20 megabytes of hard disk memory. The limitations of technology in terms of storage and processing power meant that you listened to CDs on CD players and only on CD players. But the fledgling personal computer industry was hard at work leveraging Moore's Law to drive massive improvements in computer performance, and CD drives for personal computers also became available in the mid-1980s.

As CDs were propelling the industry to unprecedented revenues, audio experts at Bell Labs and the Fraunhofer Institute of Germany were innovating with "Perceptual Audio Coding" algorithms. They could soon discard 90 percent of the data on the CD and create a far smaller audio file with an adequate audio experience that could be distributed over networks. Those techniques were standardized by the Motion Picture Experts Group (MPEG), and the resulting file was known as an "MP3" (Chapter 8). America Online (AOL) was the leader in providing Internet access to millions of homes via dialup modems, and it took more than 10 minutes to download one of those compressed song files.

In June of 1999, Shawn Fanning released a beta version of Napster at Northeastern University that ultimately triggered epic shockwaves across the music industry. Those small MP3 files were ideally suited for the "peer-to-peer" (user-to-user) exchange over the Internet, particularly over university networks that were much faster than the typical residential dialup connections at that time. But as broadband connectivity replaced dialup modems in homes, the unfettered copying of the most popular songs became an everyday occurrence across the globe.

The rapid declines in the music industry caused by Napster and its successors created a sense of desperation in the industry as millions of people simply stopped paying for music on CDs. Internet file-sharing went beyond home cassette taping in three major ways: while blank tapes cost money to buy and to send, digital files cost almost nothing; while tape copying had to be done in real time (or close to real time), copying digital files via broadband was instantaneous; and while cassette copies of LPs or CDs had degraded sound quality (even if only slightly), copies of digital files sounded like the originals.

The industry needed to find a way to attract millions of fans to pay for music obtained online. Universal Music Group and Sony Music launched an online music store called pressplay in late 2001 to compete with Napster, while other major labels partnered with streaming audio technology pioneer RealNetworks to launch MusicNet. The limited catalog and compromised user experience of these services were not comparable to the simplicity and price of the pirate services. In 2003, Steve Jobs and Apple created the first viable competitor to free; the easy-to-use combination of the iPod and the iTunes Music Store was soon selling billions of songs and albums—though not enough to offset those cratering CD revenues.

By the beginning of the 2010s, advances in computing and networking technologies enabled hundreds of millions of fans to pay $10 per month for on-demand streaming from a huge song catalog on their mobile phones, tablets, or PCs. These numbers continue to grow at a rapid rate around the world (Chapter 9), now that paying for access to music as a service rather than purchasing music as a product has become the preeminent music experience. That growth led, starting around 2015, to the first increases in overall recorded music revenues in almost 20 years. And that growth is expected to continue for a long time: In the 2022 edition of the Goldman Sachs "Music In The Air" report, they predict that the worldwide revenues for recorded music will exceed $50 billion, more than doubling the 2021 industry level, with over 85 percent of that total attributed to streaming revenues.[iii]

Music videos evolved as the Internet provided the two-way communications channel that cable TV lacked. You can still watch the very first video ever uploaded to YouTube in April 2005. It is titled "Me at the zoo" [sic] and shows one of the three founders of the company, Jawed Karim, at the San Diego Zoo. YouTube created a home for "User Generated Content" (UGC) that enabled anyone to share videos with what would soon become a massive, worldwide audience (Chapter 10). Creators generated revenues by leveraging the advertising capabilities that are also part of YouTube's platform. If you search for the most viewed videos of all time on YouTube, you find a list that is dominated by music videos featuring major artists, with "Despacito" by Luis Fonsi and Daddy Yankee at no. 2, with more than 8 billion views at this time of writing.[1] User creativity has become even more crucial to newer, short-form video platforms such as TikTok, where individuals complement popular songs with their own singing or dance moves.

The popularity of smart speakers, particularly the Amazon Echo and Google Home, has made it easy for a whole new group of users to discover and to enjoy music streaming services controlled via voice command. Though we are still at the early stages of this technology, it is already clear that it will have profound effects on how people discover and engage with music and how the distribution platforms and artists optimize what they do to leverage this new mode of interacting with music. Artificial Intelligence (AI) techniques make voice response ever more accurate; they are being deployed to improve music services' playlists and personalization and to find the most promising new artists. Creative AI tools that can generate music appropriate for specific needs, such as synching to a video or new songs in the style of famous artists, are already emerging as well. "Generative AI" is clearly going to have major repercussions throughout the industry in the coming years (Chapter 11).

What is the next set of technologies that will alter the structure of the music industry? As we write this in 2022, we are reasonably certain that the answer is "Web3." As we explain in our Afterword, Web3 is a catch-all term of distributed ledger or blockchain and related technologies; it should usher in significant changes to the ways in which music is distributed to fans and rights holders are paid. For example, nonfungible tokens (NFTs) have captured the imaginations of fans and artists alike as attempts to meld the advantages of digital and Internet technology with the scarcity and ownership attributes of physical media. Although it's too early to tell exactly how—and to what extent—the industry will change in response to Web3, we offer some observations.

As we said before, format changes are a powerful lens for viewing the development of the music industry because they cause many follow-on effects. We have identified six distinct categories of change in the industry, all of which are related to evolutions in formats. We call these the 6C Framework. They are shown in Figure 1.2.

We'll be referring to these icons in each chapter, but generally the categories of change are as follows:

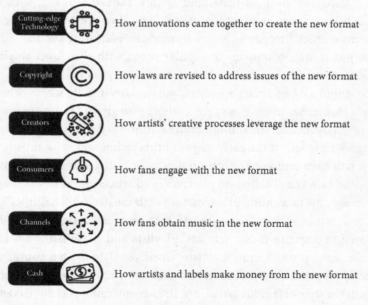

Cutting-edge Technology	How innovations came together to create the new format
Copyright	How laws are revised to address issues of the new format
Creators	How artists' creative processes leverage the new format
Consumers	How fans engage with the new format
Channels	How fans obtain music in the new format
Cash	How artists and labels make money from the new format

Figure 1.2 The 6C Framework. Graphics by Karl C. Sluis.

Cutting-Edge Technology

The innovations that converged to enable new ways to enjoy and to distribute music. Several separate technological innovations typically come together at a given time to enable the new format. For example, interactive streaming relied on streaming audio technology but didn't become mainstream until other innovations emerged: mobile devices with powerful processors and ample memory, mobile apps, and high-speed mobile Internet access.

Creators

The changes artists and songwriters have made to their creative processes and their creative outputs in response to the new format. New technologies lead to new ways for artists to create music, ranging from the electric guitar to the digital sample library. But new formats also lead to changes in styles and genres of music. For example, the LP was originally created in the late 1940s to hold classical concertos and Broadway musicals on single albums. But by the mid-1960s, LP players had become affordable for young pop music fans, and this created an opportunity for pop artists to consider the LP as more than a collection of singles; they turned the format into a canvas for albums that held together as cohesive artistic wholes.

Channels

The places—real and virtual—that labels and artists use to provide fans access to their music. Our definition of channels has three components: distribution, or the ways in which music is packaged and sent to the places where fans access it; merchandising, or the ways in which the channel presents the music to fans for discovery and selection; and consumption environment, or the ways in which consumers can play the music distributed through the channel. For example, labels manufacture vinyl records and distribute them to retailers; retailers choose which items to stock and how to display and promote them; consumers buy records and take them home to play on turntables and read the liner notes.

Consumers

Fans' expectations in terms of music acquisition and listening experience, relationships to artists, and the genres or styles of music they prefer. Channels determine how consumers can choose and listen to music, but consumers ultimately decide how they like to use the channels' discovery and consumption features. Consumers also decide how to engage with artists. For example, cassette tapes were arguably the first consumer-driven music format: in addition to purchasing prerecorded tapes, consumers made cassette copies of LPs; subsequently artists created mixes on cassettes and distributed them directly to consumers to usher in the hip-hop era.

Cash

Business models, royalty rates, and other industry practices that are in place to gather money and to distribute it to artists and songwriters. Often these models and practices are quite complex and take time to stabilize. For example, radio stations pay royalties to songwriters and music publishers through collecting societies such as ASCAP and BMI, which estimate airplay of individual compositions through combinations of monitoring, sampling, and self-reporting by stations; these practices evolved over the course of decades and were improved by technological innovations such as automated music recognition and large-scale databases.

Copyright

The music business is fundamentally based on legal copyright protection for both musical compositions (for songwriters) and sound recordings (for recording artists). Anyone who wants to make copies of, distribute, or publicly perform music needs licenses from copyright holders. Governments pass laws to facilitate copyright's applicability to different formats. But laws designed to meet the needs of older formats often become barriers to smooth-functioning markets for newer formats, creating the need for copyright laws and administration practices to evolve, which can take many years. Meanwhile, other formats owe their existence to gaps in copyright laws. As an example of the latter, one reason radio flourished as a medium for recorded music was that copyright law does not include a performance right in sound recordings; this meant that radio stations could play records on the air without having to pay royalties to labels. As an example of the former, the Digital Millennium Copyright Act (DMCA) of 1998 limited the legal responsibilities that online technology platforms bore for the actions of their users (such as uploading music files without permission). It provided the legal framework for YouTube to launch in 2005 and ultimately to become the world's largest music streaming site. Various other digital content services have flourished since 1998 by exploiting loopholes in the DMCA. This has prompted many in the music industry to complain that the law should be revised because it hasn't achieved the balance of interests between tech and content businesses that Congress originally intended in passing it.

Legal and regulatory frameworks beyond copyright, such as antitrust law and broadcast regulations, have also contributed to structural changes in the music industry. We touch on these as well when appropriate.

We use the 6C Framework to analyze each of these formats (phonographs, LPs, streaming, etc.) in the ensuing chapters. For each one, we start with the background story of the technologies that were on the cutting edge at the time and the ways in which they coalesced to enable meaningful innovation for the mass market of music fans. We follow up with discussions of how the other parts of the business—the rest of the 6Cs—morphed in reaction to this new reality. Sometimes these shifts occurred quickly, or at least they appeared so with the hindsight of history. Other times the music industry was reluctant to change course and dragged its feet for years before adapting.

It's the same old song again and again as the established order of the music industry gets "all shook up." Advancements in technologies converge to enable new ways to distribute and to enjoy music. Often the first market entries are simply "proofs of concept," and feedback from the early adopters helps to guide innovators to improve their products until they meet the needs of a mass market. Those successful new formats not only give fans new music experiences but also cause upheavals in the rest of the industry landscape. The business models that remunerate creators for their work need to be redefined to address the characteristics of the new format. New distribution outlets emerge that are better suited to the new format, while old channels change or disappear. Fans change how they interact with artists and their music based on the new product configurations. Often there are demographic shifts that coincide with these changes as younger people move first to join the next wave, which can result in new genres of music coming to the fore. Artists modify their creative processes to maximize the value they can now extract and to connect with their fans more effectively. And although it often takes years, the law eventually catches up with what the format has wrought.

Judge Sidney Thomas, in his ruling in an important file-sharing sharing case before the Ninth US Circuit Court of Appeals (the *Grokster* case; see Chapter 8) wrote:

> The introduction of new technology is always disruptive to old markets, and particularly to those copyright owners whose works are sold through well-established distribution mechanisms. Yet, history has shown that time and market forces often provide equilibrium in balancing interests, whether the new technology be a player piano, a copier, a tape recorder, a video recorder, a personal computer, a karaoke machine, or an MP3 player.

Once that equilibrium is in place, all the parts of the industry have adjusted to the "new normal." The resulting stability enables the players to thrive, but only for a limited time. Scientists, engineers, and entrepreneurs are always working to come up with yet another innovation that can unsettle the foundations of the music business. Learning how this cycle has recurred through the history of the music business helps us to be better prepared for the next go-around. As William Faulkner wrote, "The past is never dead. It's not even past."

In the concluding chapter, we reexamine each of the 6Cs to consider the effect it had across the entire recorded music timeline. We'll also show how each of the 6Cs affected another industry in analogous ways.

Who This Book Is For

This book will appeal to anyone who is curious about an industry that touches the lives of billions every day, from casual music fans to industry insiders as well as those who want to understand the aftereffects of technology disruption in other businesses.

This book is designed for music industry professionals who seek to deepen their understanding of the business, are considering the future of the industry, or may not be aware of its history or how it came to be the way it is today. It's also designed for journalists and industry analysts to help them place current developments or consider the implications of strategic decisions in a broader industry context. And it's intended for instructors of courses in music business or the history of business and technology, as well as researchers in those fields.

Finally, the book is for professionals in other industries where product innovations regularly disrupt their established practices. The 6C Framework and the lessons learned by the music industry provide ways to think about the changes they are facing. Although there are many excellent books on how the music business works today or its history—some of which are listed in the Bibliography—we aren't aware of any that view the history through a framework that enables understanding of the present and future. In that sense, we believe that this book is a novel contribution to an already rich body of work.

How This Book Came to Be

There are almost as many books about the music industry as there are cover versions of "Yesterday." Some concentrate on a single era, such as the birth of rock & roll or hip-hop. Others dive deeply into how the industry reacted to a specific disruptive technology; for example, we've read at least a half-dozen books about Napster's origins and how the industry dragged its feet while the CD business collapsed. Other books take a longer historical view, but only from a single perspective, such as how radio broadcasting or copyright law has evolved over the decades. No one has examined this long line of format changes with a consistent analytical framework that encompasses the technology, the artists, the fans, the channels, the cash, and the law.

This book originated as an idea that Howie had for a class in the Music Business program at NYU, where he teaches the Data Analysis in the Music Industry course for graduate students. He had a front row seat to the enormous shifts in the music business after Napster through the dominance of streaming by working for a start-up as well as for one of the largest music companies in the world. But as he started to map out a course on technology and its impact on music, he realized that the changes he had lived through were not unique to the Internet era. Instead this was a theme that had repeated itself again and again across the history of recorded music.

Howie mentioned the idea to Bill, a longtime colleague, who teaches the undergrad version of the Data Analysis in the Music Industry course and has worked in book publishing as well as in music and radio. Bill had come to a similar conclusion about the structural history of the music industry in an article he wrote for Forbes in May 2018,[iv] on the occasion of interactive streaming passing the milestone of bringing in the majority of the total US recorded music revenue. Bill's article, which included a version of the chart shown in Figure 1.1, divided the industry into five eras according to the dominant format by industry revenue at each time. The difference between Bill's and Howie's views was that Howie considered music videos, radio, and current emerging technologies as "formats" even though they don't necessarily contribute directly to industry revenue. Bill readily acceded to Howie's view and suggested that this idea would make an interesting book for a general audience.

2

Phonograph

Put Your Records On—Corinne Bailey Rae

Around the turn of the century, people used novel technology to experience music in a completely new way. They said the name of a particular song, then inserted their earpieces, and were amazed when they heard the track they had requested. Typically, they had to pay for this privilege, but some opted to hear an audio ad either before or after the song instead and then enjoy their selection for free.

That experience resembles what we have become accustomed to with the proliferation of smart digital assistants controlling streaming music applications. But the scenario just described was in place at the end of the nineteenth century. It was enabled in the 1890s by the ground-breaking development of the phonograph. If you lived in a major city, you could visit an "Automatic Phonograph Parlour" equipped with "nickel-in-the-slot" machines. You would use a speaking tube to tell an attendant which of the hundreds of available songs you wanted to hear. Once the recording was mounted on the talking machine, you inserted a pair of rubber tubes in your ears to hear it. Some songs were free if you listened to an ad, but most required the listener to insert a token first. The novelty of hearing a recorded human voice at these locations was a big draw initially, though it failed to become a sustainable business.[i] This is the first of the many examples of commonalities that turn up across the history of recorded music.

Thomas Edison, often referred to as America's greatest inventor, saw the phonograph's most promising and immediate application as a dictation machine for businesses. The early devices were difficult to use and the quality of the recordings often less than satisfactory. That limited their viability in offices and made them more suitable as proto-jukeboxes for "parlours" with trained staff. Edison, and other inventors, including Alexander Graham Bell and Emile Berliner, competed to refine their new machines until they were simple to operate and inexpensive enough to become mass-market products purchased by millions. Each of their "talking machines" had different names,

Key Changes. Howie Singer and Bill Rosenblatt, Oxford University Press. © Howie Singer and Bill Rosenblatt 2023.
DOI: 10.1093/oso/9780197656891.003.0002

but they were soon uniformly referred to as "phonographs" that played "records." Collectively, they set the stage for the creation of the music business that has influenced commerce and culture for more than a century.

Cutting-edge Technology

Though Edison was ultimately successful in his search for a filament for the electric light, his repeated failures would have deterred most people. Instead, the "Wizard of Menlo Park" famously said, "I have not failed. I've just found 10,000 ways that won't work." This determined and systematic approach proved unnecessary when it came to the phonograph. When searching for a way to record telephone messages, Edison found that speech caused a diaphragm to vibrate which, when connected to a stylus, made indentations in the wax-coated paper underneath. When that indented paper was run under the stylus again, one could hear a faint reproduction of the original sound.

Relying on those findings, Edison sketched out a machine designed to record and to play back the human voice on November 29, 1877. He turned that drawing over to one of his workmen, John Kruesi, who returned a day-and-a-half later with the first version of the machine. Instead of paper, the device now used tinfoil as the recording medium. Edison set the stylus against the tinfoil wrapped around the cylinder and yelled, "Mary had a little lamb" into the mouthpiece containing a diaphragm while turning the crank. When the stylus later ran over the indented foil, Edison's voice could be heard reciting the poem. Unlike the incandescent light, this prototype device worked on the very first attempt. Edison said later that he was never so taken aback in his life. He foresaw a wide range of uses for the phonograph, including recording speeches and music as well as enabling talking clocks and toys. However, he viewed the feature of making recordings as essential to fulfill its primary mission as a business dictation machine.

The next month, Edison filed for a US patent for his invention and took the train from New Jersey into New York City to demonstrate his invention to the staff at *Scientific American*. As the December 27, 1877 issue reported, "Mr. Thomas A. Edison recently came into this office, placed a little machine on our desk, turned a crank, and the machine inquired as to our health, asked how we liked the phonograph, informed us that it was very well, and bid us a cordial goodnight." Edison's ability to capture and replay speech was seen as

Figure 2.1 Thomas Edison with tin-foil phonograph, 1878. Edison National Historic Site, National Park Service. Public Domain, Edison National Historic Site, National Park Service. Reproduced with permission.

remarkable, and his new machine garnered attention in both the New York and national press.[ii]

Seeking to capitalize on the publicity, Edison sold the rights to manufacture and sell his phonograph to Gardiner Hubbard for $10,000. Hubbard, an investor in the new Bell Telephone Company in Boston, formed the Edison Speaking Phonograph Company in 1878 and became its President. The initial plan was to build 30 machines and sell them to the public at a retail store in New York City. However, the new units failed to work properly. At this point, Edison's phonograph was unquestionably a "Minimum Viable Product" (MVP). The device was difficult to operate properly. If the stylus was not set correctly or the crank was not turned steadily, the resulting recordings would be garbled. That's why Edison used a prerecorded message that could be checked in advance for intelligibility before the *Scientific American* demonstration.[iii]

To create a meaningful business centered on the phonograph, the MVP needed improvements in several dimensions. Turning the cylinder via hand crank yielded a wide variation in speeds and unreliable performance. The tinfoil used as the recording medium tore easily and was rendered unusable after just a few plays. Each recording lasted for two minutes at most. And there was no process to duplicate recordings for the mass market.

Because of his other contractual obligations, Edison's focus turned away from the phonograph to perfecting the electric light in 1879. Fortunately, there were other inventors who saw the potential for the talking machine and had both the technical expertise and the financial resources to advance the product. Alexander Graham Bell had been awarded the Volta Prize by the French government for his invention of the telephone in 1880. With that $10,000, equivalent to more than $250,000 today, he created Volta Labs in Washington, DC. Bell, together with fellow scientist and inventors Charles Sumner Tainter and Bell's cousin Chichester Bell, improved upon Edison's device. They introduced their own version of the phonograph, with the inverted name of "Graphophone"[1] and developed a version targeting business applications: the first "Dictaphone."

The Graphophone did away with tinfoil as the recording medium. Instead, in a literal example of "cutting-edge technology," the stylus "engraved" grooves into a cylinder coated with wax. The cylinders were far easier to change and to replace. The wax lasted longer than foil, and it could be shaved down and reused to make a fresh recording (although the resulting slight variation in diameter did make it tricky to adjust the stylus). A large funnel or horn was added for both recording and playback. A foot treadle, similar to the one used on sewing machines at the time, provided steadier rotation for the cylinders than the hand crank.[iv]

Bell's company approached Edison' London representative about joining forces on commercializing talking machines. Edison declined with a caustic dismissal of the proposal writing, "Under no circumstances will I have anything to do with Graham Bell [or] with his phonograph pronounced backward."[v]

The Columbia Phonograph Company, which built machines based on Bell's innovations, would become Edison's largest competitor, using cylinders to record music. Edison turned his own energies back to the phonograph, renewing the rivalry with the Graphophone. By 1888, he had launched what he labeled the "perfected phonograph." Edison followed Bell's lead and relied on wax as the recording medium, although he improved the reproduction quality even further by mixing paraffin with resin. He added a motor and battery to drive the cylinder at a steady rate. In the late 1880s, Edison, Columbia, and other manufacturers agreed on a standard size for cylinders with about two minutes of playing time to foster compatibility across companies.

Even with these advancements, making recordings was still a dicey proposition for untrained users. Leasing the machines to businesses as dictation devices was not successful. Many of the subsidiary companies that had been established in local markets to offer the machines for "mechanical stenography" were struggling financially. By 1891, only about 3,000 machines were in use. A similar fate befell an attempt in 1887 to use tiny cylinder phonographs inside of dolls to make them talk: the Doll & Toy Phonograph Company ceased operations after the market rejected that idea too.[2]

The one application that gained traction was using the devices to entertain the public. People were excited to experience the newfangled invention that could reproduce human speech or music. In November 1889, Louis Glass, the head of West Coast distribution for Edison's company, used a variety of cylinders and several of the battery-operated machines to create the first coin-operated phonograph "parlour" in San Francisco. Every machine had four sets of listening tubes, each with its own coin slot. In six months of operation, two machines each brought in $1,000 (equal to $60,000 today). That success was soon copied by other distributors across the country using phonographs that they leased for $125 per year. The "parlour" in New York City's Union Square contained 100 coin-operated machines. In Cleveland, the machines became an attraction for The Arcade, one of the first shopping malls in the United States.[3]

As lucrative as the coin-operated machines were at first, consumer interest was short-lived. The consensus view at the time was that the phonograph would never amount to more than a novelty. The player piano, on the other hand, was seen as a revolutionary musical instrument. To be successful, the phonograph would need to compete with the already-existing player piano as a home entertainment product.

Various versions of the player piano had been around for decades when Aeolian introduced the Pianola in the United States in 1898. The operator used foot pedals to generate suction that powered mechanisms that caused the hammers to strike notes encoded as perforations on the piano roll. This specific product was so successful that "Pianola" soon became the generic name for player pianos. Between 1919 and 1925, more player pianos were manufactured than standard pianos. However, the $250 retail price—equivalent to more than $8,000 today—put the player piano out of reach for most households. The same was true even when models with modestly lower prices were introduced. The ability to manufacture low-cost phonographs ultimately gave that device the edge in the home market.

In 1893, Edison introduced the Type M phonograph, which was specifically designed to serve the consumer market. The battery and electric motor that served the needs of businesses were replaced with a clockwork mechanism that reduced three things: the manufacturing cost, the weight of the machine, and the need for maintenance. However, the $150–$200 price (equal to around $5000 today) meant that the phonograph, like the player piano, still remained too expensive for the average household. The machine had only two controls: a switch to activate the drive that turned the cylinder and a screw to adjust the speed of rotation to deliver the correct pitch.

To lower the price further, Edison moved away from his commitment to office dictation as the primary use case and made the recording mechanism an option rather than including it on every model. The simpler playback-only version could be sold for $100. Columbia, the manufacturer of the Graphopone, went back and forth with Edison's company, each trying to outdo the other with ever-simpler designs and manufacturing improvements. Home phonographs marched down the price curve to $10 for the Edison "Gem" model in 1899, paving the way for millions of households to afford the machines. However, mass-market acceptance required not only less expensive players but also affordable recordings. The ability to make high-quality copies of recordings at scale was essential.

At first, making multiple cylinders of the same performance was about as low tech a process as one could imagine. The singer or musician performed into the recording horns of a bank of several phonographs, each one cutting the sound into its own cylinder. To make more copies, the artist simply repeated their performance. This approach was obviously neither scalable nor consistent in terms of quality. A mechanical improvement soon helped to provide somewhat more efficiency: a phonograph for making copies was created, with two cylinders that operated in a coordinated manner. One cylinder held the original to be copied and the other held a blank. As the grooves were "read" on the original recording, a mechanism copied them to the blank cylinder that was running in tandem. The recording material on the original wore down every time it was played; it could be used to make 100 copies at most. The duplicates created by this method were relatively poor quality that only declined further as the original became more worn.

Edison and others experimented with a plating and molding process to reproduce cylinders that delivered superior sound quality. The original cylinder was plated with metal and then turned into a durable mold through a series of additional plating steps. That mold was then filled with heated material to create the duplicate recording, and when the material cooled and was removed from the mold, it contained a copy of the indentations in the original cylinder. A reliable molding process required a material that was suitably malleable when melted yet got very hard after cooling. It took several years to perfect that material, and by 1901, Edison was able to introduce Gold Molded cylinders, and molding became the primary means of duplication.

The cylindrical shape of the mold created difficulties in extracting intact copies. The alternative form factor of the disc proved to be far more amenable to stamping out duplicate records.[4] There was yet a third talking machine that, unlike the phonograph and the Graphophone, used a disc as the recording medium. Its inventor, Emile Berliner, gave it another similar sounding name: the Gramophone.[5]

Berliner emigrated from Germany to the United States in 1870. His first major invention was a new microphone that could be used as a telephone transmitter. It became embroiled in a lengthy patent fight with Edison, who ultimately prevailed in court in 1901. Berliner's first patent for his Gramophone in 1887 used a cylinder but he quickly shifted his efforts to recording music on a flat disc.

Berliner made the entertainment market his primary focus from the start. He was remarkably prescient in understanding the key success factors for players and records that would in turn form the foundations of the modern record business. After presenting a demonstration of his Gramophone at the Franklin Institute in Philadelphia in 1888, he proceeded to offer his expansive view of the future. He foresaw that recorded discs would become standardized so that music fans would be able to listen to them on a player. He predicted that there would be a manufacturing process capable of producing millions of copies from a single original disc. He also stated that "prominent singers, speakers or performers may derive an income from royalties" for sold recordings and that those performance would be "registered to protect against unauthorized publication."[vi] Berliner's ambitions to serve the consumer market were reflected in his design choices. Gramophones were playback-only machines unencumbered with the complexity and cost of recording functionality. The discs were made of materials such as rubber or metal, making them far more durable than wax cylinders for multiple plays. Rather than carving the grooves in the up-and-down (known as "hill and dale") recording pattern used on cylinders, the stylus of Berliner's recording mechanism moved laterally, creating a spiral groove representing frequency and amplitude that started at the exterior edge and moved toward the middle of the disc. Because the turntable rotated at a constant speed, the stylus made its way around the disc more quickly as it approached the center, unlike the cylinder where the speed of the stylus remained constant throughout.[6] That increasing speed caused sound quality issues as the needle neared the center, and louder sounds could cause the needle to jump out of the groove. A paper label was placed at the center of the record so that the recording would end before the needle ever got too close to the middle. That contrivance provided a perfect place to include information about the recording, including the song and artist name along with the company issuing the disc. That last piece of data ultimately gave rise to the record companies being referred to as "labels." Having that information placed on the center of every disc proved far more user-friendly than the label on the end of the cylinder package.[7] In addition, discs provided louder sounds than cylinders, and their shape made them cheaper and easier to manufacture. Consumers found them easier to handle, and discs in sleeves took up far less storage space than a comparable number of cylinders in their boxes.[vii]

Given that discs ultimately prevailed over cylinders as the recorded music format of choice, there is a misperception that, in addition to these other advantages, they provided superior sound as well. This was simply not the case. Berliner's first hand-cranked Gramophones sounded even worse than the cylinder-based machines. The early Gramophones (which were offered in Europe only) were considered, like Edison's first versions, a mere curiosity rather than the foundation for a meaningful business. The duplication process was similar to the plating and molding approach Edison had developed, although it used acid to etch the grooves into a zinc disc. Unfortunately, that could erase some of the audio information, which, together with the hiss of the steel stylus on the record, delivered an audio experience that was decidedly inferior to cylinders. Eldridge Johnson, who was to become Berliner's partner in the United States, said that the Gramophone sounded like "a partially educated parrot with a sore throat and a cold in the head."[viii]

Berliner first approached Johnson, an American engineer and machinist, in 1895 to craft a spring-driven motor for the Gramophone to compete more effectively with the already motorized cylinder machines. Johnson met the design challenge of providing enough torque when the needle was at the outer edge of the record while maintaining a constant rotational speed. Johnson undertook a series of follow-on projects to enhance the sound quality of the machines. He designed an improved soundbox that held the diaphragm. He perfected the duplication process by following Edison's lead and using wax for the original recording instead of zinc and then electroplating multiple layers to make the mold. (He actually melted down some of Edison's cylinders to obtain the wax he needed for his experiments.) A shellac-based material that included pulverized minerals such as slate and cotton fibers for strength soon became the standard for the duplicate discs.[8] These refinements yielded discs that could compare more favorably with cylinders in quality; these were commonly referred to as "shellac" records. But they had an unappealing grayish color, so carbon black was added to the mix to provide the color that became emblematic of records. By the turn of the twentieth century, both Edison and Johnson were ready to mass produce recordings. That capability, combined with the lower-cost players, led many middle-class families to invest in this new form of home entertainment.[ix]

In 1901, Johnson and Berliner formalized their working relationship by combining their interests to form the Victor Talking Machine Company in Camden, New Jersey. That same year, they introduced 10-inch records, followed two years later by ones measuring 12 inches. The play time of these new formats exceeded three and four minutes, respectively, giving discs a major competitive advantage over two-minute cylinders. This scenario existed for several years as it took Edison time to find a new compound that could close the capacity gap while still meeting the demands of mass production.

The Victor company found another way to double the amount of music pressed onto the records they were selling to the public. In 1904, it improved its manufacturing process to allow songs to be recorded on both sides of the discs. The company increased the retail prices of these new double-sided records to reflect their greater entertainment value.[x] That same year, the Louisiana Purchase Exposition, better known as the St. Louis World's Fair, attracted almost 20 million visitors who could view the Victor and Columbia companies' latest phonographs and hear their records.

While the battle over playing time and sound quality continued, the Victor Company also innovated in a completely different direction. They came up with a new physical design that was distinctive from all the talking machines that had preceded it. Instead of a large protruding horn on top of a rectangular base, the horn and turntable were concealed within a wooden cabinet designed to resemble a piece of furniture. There was no volume control on early phonographs, but with a cabinet, the door could be opened for louder sounds or kept closed to muffle the output. The "Victrola" was introduced in September 1906, and the less obtrusive, more fashionable style was an immediate hit.[9] The Victrola designers combined form and function in a way that resonated with consumers almost a century before the renowned Apple designers did the same for the iPod.[xi] As you can see in Figure 2.2, the sales pitch for the Victrola was aspirational, with the new configuration being an integral—or even "inevitable"—part of a stylish, more upscale lifestyle.

Edison finally brought his format up to parity with the disc in playing time in 1908 by introducing the "Amberol" cylinder. There was no backward compatibility: a new Amberola phonograph was required to play the new cylinders, and the name and style were both modeled after the Victrola with its wooden cabinet. Bell's Columbia company had already introduced the similarly styled "Grafonola." The synthetic wax being used was hard enough to allow finer grooves to be cut into the cylinder, which provided increased audio capacity. The harder material also permitted the stylus to exert more pressure during playback, which produced greater volume. Unfortunately, the synthetic material had a short useful life and sometimes cracked during playback, shattering into many pieces. To correct these flaws, Edison soon adopted the new material that was making its mark in all manner of household goods: plastic. He tinted the material blue, to distinguish it from its predecessor, and introduced the new and improved version as the "Blue Amberol" cylinder in 1912. Thomas Lambert had been granted a patent for celluloid cylinders built around a core made of plaster of Paris. Edison took Lambert's company to court for copyright infringement

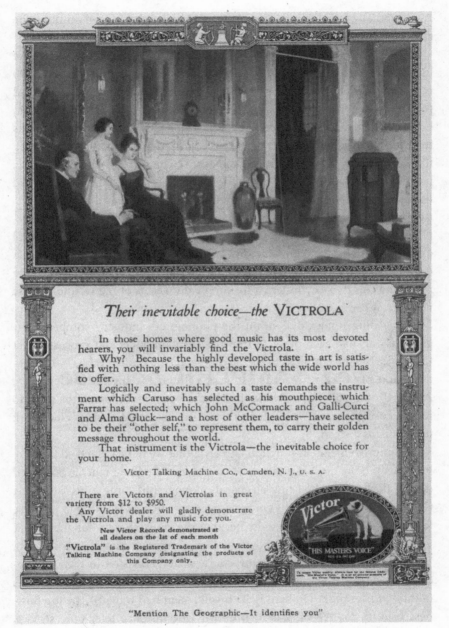

Figure 2.2 Victrola advertisement. Courtesy of the Hagley Museum & Library. Reproduced with permission.

and eventually forced it into bankruptcy, at which point Edison acquired the rights to Lambert's innovations.

In 1912, Edison introduced his Diamond Disc player and records. Unlike his immediate success with the tinfoil prototype, he had to test over 2,300 materials exhaustively until he found one he could use for a stylus that could pick up the recorded music patterns on the disc accurately. Up to that point, Edison had adamantly stuck with cylinders alone, relying on what he saw as their technical superiority, yet even he recognized that the disc was winning the "format war." Although Edison appeared to be surrendering to the disc, he could not bring himself to concede completely. His Diamond Discs did not use the same lateral recording method of Gramophone discs. This decision prevented any buyers of his new players from listening to any already-released records. Furthermore, Edison continued to produce Blue Amberol cylinders until his company shut down in 1929. However, from 1915 on, in a clear indication of the relative importance of the formats in the market, the recordings on those cylinders were simply duplicates of the Diamond Disc versions.

The leading innovators within the phonograph industry competed aggressively against each other to improve their products and processes. Yet these efforts were confined to the field of "acoustic phonographs"—the creation and playback of recorded sounds without the benefit of electricity. Although some talking machines had battery-powered motors, the drive to reduce costs, size, and weight led all the manufacturers to deploy clockwork mechanisms instead.

The improvements in function and style that we've described so far were incremental; the most significant advancement to talking machines arrived during the 1920s, when the "electrical phonograph" came onto the scene. Once again, the innovations emerged from researchers working to improve telephony. Volta Labs eventually became the research arm for the AT&T Corporation. Initially housed within that company's manufacturing arm, Western Electric, it was reconfigured as a separate division in 1925 and became known by its far more recognizable name: Bell Telephone Laboratories (although Alexander Graham Bell's involvement had waned). The top business priority for AT&T was to improve long-distance telephone service, and its Labs' research agenda was directed toward achieving that goal. Their scientists believed that electronic amplification was key to that improvement.

E. C. Wente invented a new condenser microphone at Western Electric in 1917. The rights to the three-element triode, a type of vacuum tube, had been purchased by AT&T in 1917; it was used to develop a tube that could reliably amplify a microphone signal. To run meaningful experiments, the engineers needed to replicate their test conditions to evaluate performance. And that meant using the exact same audio input each time.

Rather than trying to improve the acoustic phonographs already in the market to meet their requirements, they decided to use the innovations at their disposal to record sound electronically. The sound entering the microphone was turned into a series of electrical currents. The vacuum tube amplifier increased these currents to make them strong enough to create grooves in the recording medium. The cutter operated within a magnetic field and made grooves that represented the varying currents. The microphone's electrical diaphragm moved an infinitesimal amount compared to the previous acoustic diaphragm, which allowed it to capture a much broader range of frequencies with far less distortion. The engineers' efforts to improve the inputs for their long-distance tests had the unintended consequence of improving the phonograph.[xii]

By 1924, the Western Electric team was ready to produce demonstration records for Edison, Columbia, and Victor, the Big Three phonograph companies of the time. At first, none of them were interested in helping to commercialize this new technology despite the promise of much improved sound quality. The incumbents did not want to abandon their substantial investments in the older generation of machines and the products and profits they were already generating. However, radio's growth, which had already begun to erode the revenues of the record business, was gathering momentum. The weakness in their business soon became evident, and the Columbia and Victor companies decided to bring the Western Electric engineers into their respective recording studios to perfect this new approach as a response to the radio threat. After months of experimentation, the Western Electric solution became a commercial reality in May 1925, when Bessie Smith stood in front of a microphone rather than an acoustic horn to record her newest release, "Cake Walking Babies (From Home)."[xiii]

Though the first electrical recordings were issued in the spring of 1925, Victor and Columbia agreed to make no public announcements about these improved discs until the end of the year, to allow them to sell off their inventories of older acoustic recordings. In the fall of that year, Victor announced its new "Orthophonic Victrola,"[10] which was specifically designed to play the higher fidelity electrical recordings. A magnetic pickup in the arm moved across the record and turned the amplitudes and frequencies embedded in the grooves back into electrical current. The lower frequencies that had been so difficult to capture acoustically were now re-corded in the grooves of these new records. To play those bass tones back accurately, a nine-foot acoustic horn was required; the engineers twisted the horn into a spiral shell-like shape to reduce the total space required. That allowed the manufacturers to use the same expensive cabinets sitting in their inventory.

The *New York Times* front page on October 7, 1925 reported on the first public test of the new Victrola with the headline: "New Music Machine Thrills All Hearers." John Philip Sousa, the composer and band leader, had disliked the quality of his recordings on cylinders, despite their robust sales, using the derogatory phrase "canned music."[11] He had a much more enthu-siastic reaction to this new device, saying, "Gentleman [sic], that is a band. That is the first time I have ever heard music with any soul produced by a me-chanical talking machine."[xiv]

Brunswick, one of the smaller manufacturers, was the first company to go completely electric. Brunswick's new player had a motorized turntable, an amplifier, and a loudspeaker. By the end of the decade, most new record players were fully electric. Edison doggedly tried to improve his acous-tical machines; he was the last of the larger companies to make the change. But even he conceded the superiority of the electrical machines when he introduced his "Edisonic" models.

Early acoustic phonographs had rotation speeds that varied from 60 to 130 revolutions per minute (rpm). Cylinders typically turned at 150 rpm or more. By 1910, the record players had settled into the range of 78 to 80 rpm. Beginning in 1897, regulators or "governors" were added to the machines to ensure that as the machine was cranked, a steady speed was maintained. The shift to electrical motors provided the opportunity for a more precise solu-tion, and 78.26 rpm became the standard because it worked well for most of the existing records: that number of turns was the result of using a standard 3600-rpm motor to turn a 46-tooth gear.[12] The new discs proved popular and, before long, all records came to be referred to as "78s."[xv]

Volume control in acoustic phonographs was decidedly low tech. The Victrola's horn pointed toward louvered doors in the cabinet that were opened or closed to increase or decrease the volume. The owners of ta-bletop machines with an exposed horn resorted to an even less precise tech-nique: they kept a rolled-up piece of soft cloth nearby and shoved that into the horn when they wanted to muffle the sound—giving birth to the phrase "put a sock in it."[xvi] The loudspeaker in electrical phonographs meant that the product could have a small knob that adjusted the volume, providing a huge improvement in the user experience.

Further innovations were yet to come for the phonograph record, and we'll describe the LP and the 45 in Chapter 4. However, despite the many advances in electronics and digital technologies that were yet to come, one aspect of early phonograph technology has persisted right through the current resurgence of vinyl records: the industry still manufactures records by creating a "negative" mold from an original recording using metal plating and then employing that mold to stamp out duplicate discs.[xvii]

Over roughly 50 years, inventors and their companies improved the quality and manufacturability of the phonograph and recordings from primitive prototypes to products with mass-market appeal. The products themselves were necessary but far from sufficient to build a meaningful new business. The entire infrastructure for the industry had to be created, including how to decide what music to record, how record companies and artists should be compensated, and what laws were needed to protect their financial interests. Taking a cue from the most successful businesses of the day, run by moguls such as Rockefeller and Carnegie, the phonograph companies opted to integrate their operations vertically. They extended their business upstream to identify the talent to record as well as downstream to manage the distribution and sales of their products to consumers.

The phonograph companies understood all too well the limitations of the technologies they had invented. These limitations constrained the types of music and sounds that could be recorded most accurately. The companies and their executives were in the best position to select both the repertoire and the artists to record it, and then to manage the recording sessions carefully to provide the best results possible.

The time limit for recording on any cylinder or disc was the most obvious restriction imposed by technology. As materials improved, the duration of recordings increased from two minutes to four, and one-sided discs were replaced by those that carried music on both sides. Though the increases were significant on a percentage basis, the absolute length remained fundamentally incompatible with symphonies that often lasted an hour. Many popular songs from the stage or vaudeville were much shorter, but even that material often needed to be edited for length. Recognizing this, creators began to watch the clock when crafting new works. For example, Igor Stravinsky structured his "Serenade in A" to fit onto two two-sided discs, with each of the four movements lasting less than three minutes.[xviii] The recording medium had, in effect, circumscribed the music into a three-minute single, a market reality that constrained songs for decades.[13]

For longer artistic works, the solution was to issue a collection that consisted of many short selections on separate discs. Verdi's *Ernani*, the first opera recorded in its entirety in 1903, required forty discs. To hold all these discs safely, "record albums" were sold, consisting of empty sleeves and a hard cover mimicking the construct of a photo album. Eventually, the record companies assembled and sold multiple 78-rpm discs in their own albums as single products. The record albums offered in this way included symphonies, Broadway shows, or simply collections of songs from single artists. The "record album" has remained part of the industry's lexicon ever since, even when technology enabled a single long-playing record, a compact disc, or a group of digital files to embody a curated collection of songs.[xix]

In addition to the time limits inherent to the recording media, there were no recording studios and no editing capabilities whatsoever. Early acoustic phonographs often performed unreliably, and a skilled operator, a "recordist," was required to make quality recordings. If the stylus was positioned improperly or a musician played a wrong note or the vocalist sang an incorrect lyric, the recording was thrown away and the process needed to be started all over again.

Only those sounds within a few feet of the acoustic horn could be captured. Quiet passages required performers to position themselves right at the open end of the horn. If that soft section was followed by a loud high C, singers had to move back quickly to prevent distortion on the recording. If multiple performers were involved, they would all have to crowd around the horn. Placement was essential, as the closer musicians would drown out players standing further away. For ensembles, the vocalists would have to move out of the way so the instrumentalists could get to the horn for their part of the performance. In some more "choreographed" sessions, "pushers" maneuvered performers seated on rolling boxes around the room to ensure that the right people were in the right place at the right time. Broadway and vaudeville performers such as Al Jolson, who were well-practiced in projecting their voices to the back of the house, could do the same when singing into the recording horn.[xx]

Given these hurdles, it is not surprising that many recordings opted for simplicity and featured a single vocalist and accompanist. Creativity was required to make the recording process work. If the accompanying instrument was an upright piano, the back was removed and the entire piano was boosted up higher so that the sound could be at the same level as the horn. Even so, pianos still sounded somewhat coarse and tinny.

Other instruments were a poor acoustical "fit" for the recording process as well. Very loud sounds could cause the cutting stylus to jump out of its groove, so drums were often muffled or replaced by wooden blocks or cowbells. Soft sounds such as those from stringed instruments were also problematic to record. The lower-frequency double bass and cello were replaced by tubas and trombones to make better recordings. John Stroh, an electrical engineer, added a soundbox and horns to a violin to improve recordability, rather than substituting another instrument. The resulting instrument, known as the "Stroh violin," was much louder than the standard instrument, and its main horn could be directed right into the recording horn of the phonograph. (See Figure 2.3) A smaller, secondary horn was also added to make it easier for musicians to hear their own performance. Other sounds or instruments were by their nature more conducive to the early recording process; hence more records were made that featured the banjo, the xylophone, and even "artistic whistling."[xxi]

Dealing with the intricacies of acoustic recording had impacts beyond any individual track. Louis Armstrong was in the studio with his band, the Hot Five, to record a song called "Heebie Jeebies." Armstrong was singing when he dropped his lyrics sheets. Rather than stopping when the recording was going well, he started "scatting"—singing with improvised wordless syllables—and he was surprised that the take was not discarded. Armstrong was not the first to scat, but "Heebie Jeebies" turned out to be a hit and Armstrong was credited with popularizing what became an indispensable technique of jazz.[xxii]

Though not as culturally significant or popular as jazz, klezmer music was impacted as well. Originated by Eastern European Jews, klezmer absorbed many of their themes and religious melodies. If you know the genre well or are just familiar with the klezmer-influenced songs of *Fiddler on the Roof*, you are aware of the prominent role of the clarinet in the music. However, before 1900, the genre's primary instrument was the tsimbel, a dulcimer

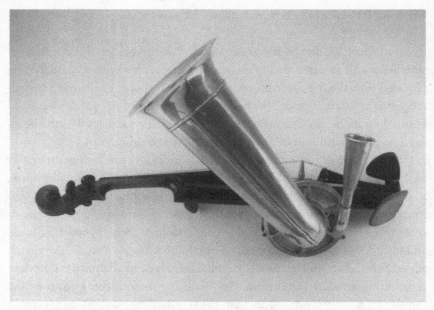

Figure 2.3 Stroh violin. © National Museum of American History, The Smithsonian Institute. Reproduced with permission.

played with hammers. When attempts were made to record klezmer music for the burgeoning immigrant population in the early twentieth century in the United States, the tsimbel's sound proved difficult to capture. To compensate, the lead melodic lines were given to the clarinet, cementing its plaintive notes as the trademark for the genre.[xxiii]

Given the constraints, the brass band turned out to be a good fit for early recordings, albeit with fewer pieces than one might find in a live concert to make the ensemble easier to locate in front of the horn. John Philip Sousa had reservations about the fledgling technology.[14] He thought that the convenience of listening to music in the home would deter people from coming to his concerts and from learning to play instruments themselves. His concerns notwithstanding, Sousa agreed to have Columbia record "The Stars and Stripes Forever," which became a resounding success. The company signed him to a recording contract, and the dozens of subsequent discs of his performances helped cement his position as "The March King."

At that time, Sousa was the exception, as most other recordings featured people of little prominence. Many of the major performing artists of the day steered clear of the phonograph because of the perception of the new device as little more than a novelty offering poor quality music. The Victor Company changed all that by recording music and artists with the cachet of high culture and then spending lavishly to advertise the results.

The American phonograph companies licensed their technology and provided expertise to enable Europeans to set up businesses in their domestic markets. Those European markets were viewed as the home for "good" music respected for its artistic ambitions. In 1897, the Gramophone Company was established in London. Fred Gaisberg, an American with experience at several of the US phonograph companies, was sent over by Victor Talking Machines to set up its recording studio in Britain. His role soon expanded from recording engineer to one of the very first and most successful A&R executives ever. His efforts to identify the "Artists & Repertoire" to record took him to cultural centers across Europe. His powers of persuasion were less than successful with higher profile artists until he broke through with the Imperial Opera in St. Petersburg. A Russian Gramophone dealer, wanting to cater to upscale customers, suggested that these new records be distinguished from the typical music that was already for sale. Instead of a black label on the discs, these would feature a red one; and they were priced higher to impress the public. This marketing tactic proved so successful that the practice spread, and soon many more well-known performers were featured on premium-priced "Red Seal" records, or their own distinctive label colors, to help their music stand out from the Sousa marches, instrumental solos, and duets that had constituted the bulk of the catalog.

Gaisberg's next stop was Italy. His visit to the La Scala opera house in Milan led him to sign the opera singer who became the foundational artist of the recorded music business. Enrico Caruso, approaching 30 years old, had a growing reputation for conveying emotion in his performances, but he was far from world-renowned. He had not yet performed in the United States. Unlike other "highbrow" artists, Caruso was not put off by the less-than-stellar quality reputation of the phonograph. Sopranos were the most popular operatic performers, but as with certain string instruments, their vocal qualities were difficult to capture accurately. The frequency range and tone of Caruso's tenor, on the other hand, were particularly well-suited to the early recording process. Furthermore, the singer was able to stand in front of the acoustic horn and provide take after take of consistent performances, even under the less-than-ideal conditions of recording in a Milan hotel room.[xxiv]

Caruso requested (or, according to some sources, demanded) to be paid £100 for that first two-hour recording session. Gaisberg sought approval from the home office in the United States to pay the tenor the equivalent of more than $17,000 today. The telegram he received in reply provided these explicit instructions: "FEE EXORBITANT FORBID YOU TO RECORD." Gaisberg went ahead anyway.[xxv]

The 10 Caruso performances recorded in Gaisberg's hotel room were "made in Italy by an American in the pay of the English branch of the gramophone company"[xxvi] and they paid off handsomely, both in terms of sales and in raising the cultural currency of the phonograph. According to Caruso's son, the recordings from those sessions ultimately earned $19,000, equating to more than $600,000 today. Other famous classical and popular performers followed in Caruso's footsteps by signing exclusive recording agreements for their "good" music, which was sold at a premium price. Having more culturally relevant artists helped convey that the phonograph was more than a toy or novelty.

Caruso blazed a trail for the career of a superstar musical artist. In an industry first, record sales became Caruso's calling card for even more high-profile live engagements. The Royal Opera brought him to London for appearances in eight different operas in 1902. The following year, he made his debut at the Metropolitan Opera in New York City, the first of more than 860 such performances over his career. Caruso was a pioneer as a multimedia performer as well. His performance of "Vesti la giubba," the now-famous aria from *Pagliacci*, was shown in Paramount Pictures film *My Cousin*. "Shown" is the operative word: *My Cousin* was a silent film and, not surprisingly, it tanked at the box office.[15] Elvis, Madonna, and the Beatles are among the dozens of musical artists who followed in Caruso's footsteps into films, though they managed to make far more successful movies with the benefit of sound.[xxvii]

Victor exploited Caruso's role as the top recording artist of the day by making him the embodiment of their brand to the public. They published ads that featured Caruso in costume as Radamès in Verdi's *Aida*, posing alongside a record of his performance with the headline "Both are Caruso." The copy said, "When you hear Caruso on the Victrola in your own home, you hear him just as truly as if you were listening to him in the Metropolitan Opera House."[xxviii]

Positioning the artist as the selling point for records, with Caruso leading the way, was effective for the Victor company but not universally accepted

across the industry. Edison understood that recordings could be more profitable in the long run than selling phonographs themselves; nevertheless he
preferred to emphasize the technical quality of the recordings and his appa-
ratus and to downplay the role of the performer. Edison's company offered
cylinders by volume and not by the subject of the recording, and he resisted
highlighting the performer's name or likeness on the packaging for cylinders.
Instead, his boxes prominently featured a photograph of Edison himself.

Downplaying the role of the performer on the product was consistent with
Edison's overall less-than-artist-friendly posture. Though the name of the selection was printed on the edge of his cylinders, the artist's name was omitted.
He complained that artists would jump to another company if offered even
a little more money, saying that for artists, "it is money, and money only
that counts." Rather than get into a bidding war for popular musicians, he
chose to seek out and record less well-known and therefore less expensive
local talent, including choirs in Newark and West Orange, New Jersey. Once
again, Edison's limited business acumen consigned his company to an inferior market position.[xxix]

We would be remiss if we did not consider the issue of race in discussing
creators and the phonograph. The history of the music business is riddled
with examples where Black artists led the way in creating and performing
new kinds of music but were pushed into the background in favor of white
artists. We will examine the repeated use of this practice in Chapter 12. There
was a perception that the majority white audience would simply not accept
music from people of color. This deprived black artists of the fame and fortune that they deserved.

"Alexander's Ragtime Band" provides a particularly instructive example.
Ragtime, an African American idiom, emerged in the 1890s and was featured prominently at the 1893 Chicago World's Fair. Ragtime was typically
composed as syncopated piano music, but ragtime recordings often featured
banjos because of the difficulties of rendering the piano's sounds accurately.
Ragtime's popularity had faded somewhat when the white, Jewish Irving
Berlin wrote his song. Music fans loved the recording by the American duo
of Arthur Collins and Byron G. Harlan; it was the top-selling recording in the
United States for 10 weeks in 1911.[xxx]

It became a signature song for Al Jolson, the most famous entertainer
of that time, who often performed in blackface. His vocal style when recording, and the idioms he used such as "the bestest band what am," were intended to convey the impression that the performer was African American.

The song's phenomenal success led the press to label Berlin "The King of Ragtime." However, that title had already been bestowed upon Scott Joplin, whose body of work was far more deserving of the appellation. Joplin, an African American composer and pianist, wrote over one hundred "rags" as well as a ballet and two operas. Yet Joplin's songs were rarely recorded. An even greater affront, at least to Joplin, was that he believed Berlin had plagiarized the melody of "Alexander's Ragtime Band" from him. Upon hearing Berlin's composition, Joplin said, "That's my tune." Berlin denied the accusation, though there is no debate that he reaped far greater rewards from ragtime than Joplin, who died penniless before turning fifty years old.[16] This, of course, was merely the first in a very long series of white artists achieving greater fame and remuneration with Black music styles than the originators did.

The shift from acoustic to electric phonographs in the 1920s brought fundamental change to the recording process and, as a consequence, to the most popular artists and music. Instead of selecting the content to suit the vagaries of the acoustic horn, the microphone captured subtleties of tone and dynamics and a broader range of frequencies that had only been available in live performances. Performances like Caruso's expansive tenor or Al Jolson's Broadway belting right into the horn were no longer necessary to create a quality recording. Big bands and larger orchestras became viable options, as it was no longer necessary to crowd a few individuals close to the horn. The result was a major expansion of the repertoire of music that was feasible to record. And the same microphone technology that enabled the crooning of artists such as Bing Crosby to dominate the radio waves captured his more subtle style for recordings.

For decades, phonographs and the recorded media were sold side-by-side in the same stores. Spiller Records of Cardiff, Wales was the first such outlet, offering phonographs along with cylinders and discs beginning in 1894. (It is still operating today, although its location has changed.)[xxxi] It wasn't until the 1930s, decades after the industry had standardized on the 78-rpm disc, that stores relying on record sales alone began to appear. In the United States, the first such store was George's Song Shop in Johnstown, Pennsylvania.[xxxii]

By then consumers understood the value of records, but that was not the case early on. Convincing people that this unfamiliar and perplexing device was worth having in their home was a challenge; it required hands-on demonstrations and education. To accomplish that, the phonograph companies exerted their influence "downstream" to shape how their products were explained, sold, and priced for consumers.

The companies preferred retailers that would maintain the manufacturer's suggested prices without discounting. They wanted stores where employees had the technical expertise to adjust and to demonstrate the product for potential purchasers and to repair the machines when required. Although the companies each sold some products at wholesale, they established outlets that were exclusive to their brand; this helped them avoid competition and ensure that employees had the expertise required.

In larger cities, department stores could devote significant floorspace to phonographs and records while offering multiple brands with discount prices to encourage traffic. Even upscale stores like Bloomingdale's sold records and players. Furniture dealers in smaller cities and towns were preferred options for distribution, as the wooden cabinets housing the talking machine proved popular. Hardware stores placed phonographs next to sewing machines and dry goods. For more rural markets, the Sears Roebuck and Montgomery Ward catalogs provided distribution. The 1900 Sears Catalog featured "The Wonderful Home Gramophone" for $5. By 1906, there were 25,000 stores selling records and phonographs.

The Victor company took the most active role in guiding disparate retailers to sell more professionally. Beginning in 1906, they published the *Voice of the Victor*, a monthly trade magazine for dealers. By 1916, more than six thousand dealers across the country received it. The magazine provided technical information on the products, guidance on effective sales techniques, advice on in-store displays, and advertising collateral. Victor even established a "Window Display Service" as a separate line of business to provide specific recommendations and goods such as pedestals to create more compelling and standardized in-store displays.[xxxiii]

Perhaps the greatest support that Victor provided to its retailers was the substantial investment it made in advertising. From 1901 to 1929, the company spent more than $50 million, or 8 percent of its revenues, on ads. Not only did Victor use artists such as Caruso to sell its machines, it flipped the script and used the machines to sell the experience of listening to realistic reproductions. And no image captured that idea better than the fox terrier cocking his head to listen to "His Master's Voice" emanating from the horn of a gramophone. The original painting by Francis Barraud showed his dog, Nipper, listening to a cylinder phonograph. The recording feature of those machines meant that Nipper could actually hear his master's voice being played back. However, Edison's London affiliate passed on the opportunity to purchase the rights to the image, and Barraud repainted it to contain a gramophone. Despite the fact that the slogan made little sense for Victor's machines that could not create recordings, the concept captured the public's imagination and became emblematic of "supreme musical quality." Periodical Publishers' Association rated that image as the world's most famous trademark in the 1920s, and it remains one of the most recognizable trademarks of all time.[xxxiv]

Though Edison eschewed the use of artists (or pets) in print advertising, even he saw the need to promote the listening experience and the technical superiority of his "Diamond Discs."[xxxv] "Tone tests" were recitals where artists would perform live at the same time their recordings were played. At the end of the show, the house lights were turned off, and the performer would leave the stage to demonstrate that the audience could not discern exactly when the recording was the only source of music. Audiences flocked to these recitals between 1915 and 1925.[xxxvi] Though the results impressed thousands with the quality of the reproductions, the artists were selected, in part, for their ability to sound like their own recordings thus biasing the tests in favor of the machines.[17]

Advertising fueled interest in buying phonographs, but even lowering the prices for some models to $5 represented a financial hurdle for many, as it is equivalent to $160 today. And, of course, models geared toward upscale consumers were even pricier. Extending consumer credit to purchase more expensive goods "on time" helped to overcome this obstacle. The vast majority of phonograph purchases were made via installment plans, and, by 1920, those purchases constituted 5 percent of consumer debt in the United States.[18]

Those credit arrangements established ongoing relationships between retailers and purchasers. The need to acquire additional music to enjoy once someone owned a record player added even more value to that relationship. Victor promulgated that message in its *Voice of the Victor* magazine, in an article titled "Are You Selling Music or Mechanisms?" in which it urged its retailers to encourage customers to build a music library. Many stores scheduled regular demonstrations to play new music they had received. They even recognized the importance of the music catalog by providing advice repeated by music marketers through the years: "The oldest music is new to the man [sic] who has never heard it."[xxxvii]

Larger stores often are willing to accept slimmer margins on a particular good in the hope of selling more items overall to customers. Retail stores, then and now, thrive on foot traffic, and price promotions have always been a surefire method to get people to come through their doors. Even in these early days, merchants considered reducing prices for music products as a "loss leader" as a tactic worth pursuing. As we will see, lowering the prices for music goods to attract a crowd who then purchase other items, from clothing to smartphones, is a recurring theme throughout the industry's history. The phonograph companies provided encouragement and advice to the retailers while protecting their parochial interests via strict contractual terms that forbade discounting and required maintaining professional standards. Breaching the terms would result in a write-up about the violation in the trade press, or even a suspended or canceled agreement. This economic arm-twisting did generate legal complications that will be discussed later in this chapter.

To build greater demand for their products, the phonograph companies encouraged their dealers to pursue one more market segment as a "civic" duty: schools. Educational reformers such as John Dewey were proponents of including music in schools, and what better way to experience it than to hear it played on a phonograph. Victor formed an Education Department to advocate for this and sent millions of brochures and letters to schools and superintendents. It created "musical memory contests" to encourage familiarity with certain compositions. Participating in this early version of "Name That Tune" required schools to have phonographs. The machines being purchased by schools represented incremental revenues in the short term, with the prospect that student familiarity with the device would lead them to lobby their parents to buy one for their home. Or taking an even longer-term view, students who enjoyed listening to music on phonographs would eventually become purchasers themselves once they were done with school.[19] These programs were hugely successful with more than ten thousand schools using Victor phonographs playing music into the ears of millions of impressionable schoolchildren.

Cash

The phonograph companies developed the products, processes, and policies that collectively laid the foundation for a successful business. They reduced the costs of talking machines to put them within reach of the mass market, with the help of installment plans. They created services to improve marketing in the distribution channels and placed tight controls on pricing to deter discounting. And they improved the materials and processes for mass production of recordings.

Their strategies proved successful, as the number of talking machines sold in 1909 grew to 345,000 units, a more than tenfold increase from the 30,000 units purchased in 1898. Five years later, in 1914, the industry hit the half a million mark, representing $37 million in revenues. And by 1919, the economic boom after World War I carried the industry to even greater heights, achieving sales of more than two million units. The growing sales attracted new entrants, and the Big Three—Edison, Columbia, and Victor—were joined by almost 20 other manufacturers. There might have been even more competitors, but the market leaders protected their intellectual property aggressively and took legal action against others that they believed were using their respective patents without licenses.

As the market grew, the manufacturers catered to different market segments with distinct products to increase their overall profits. They improved their manufacturing processes to enable the sale of machines that cost $10 or less to appeal to the growing number of middle-class households. At the same time, they crafted more expensive and higher quality phonographs encased in fine cabinetry that sold for $200 or more to smaller numbers of upscale customers.

Rather than the "music business discovering the phonograph, the phonograph business discovered the powerful, untapped commercial potential of music."[xxxviii] The phonograph companies soon realized that the sale of recordings represented an extremely profitable revenue stream that could continue for years following the purchase of a device. Sales of recordings paralleled the upward trajectory of talking machines. In 1900, the industry sold a total of four million cylinders and discs, and in 1914, industry volumes had reached 25 million units. By that point, discs were dominating cylinders by a factor of more than seven to one, and the cylinder was viewed as the "old-fashioned" product. That disparity helped persuade Edison to belatedly shift to making records.

The typical record cost roughly seven cents to manufacture and sold for 25–50 cents. Even with payments to artists and retailers, most recordings recovered their costs once sales reached 5,000 units. Victor's decision to distinguish records with higher quality music based on its Russian success increased that retail gross margin further. Red Seal and other records targeted toward upscale music fans sold for $2. Seventy million of those discs were sold between 1903 and 1925, though they never accounted for more than one-fifth of the total units sold. These premium-priced records featuring respected artists not only yielded incremental profits, they also increased the phonograph's cultural relevance. That relevance, along with more affordable prices and the ability to reproduce the human voice as well as a variety of instruments, provided the phonograph with a competitive edge over the player piano. By 1923, the phonograph dominated the home entertainment segment, outselling the player piano by a factor of five to one.[xxxix]

Revenue and profit growth in the industry impacted record companies' financial relationships with artists. Performers demanded larger and larger upfront payments for their contributions. Though some recordings earned back those payments many times over, other projects remained in the red. Rather than accepting the entire financial risk associated with a single large flat-rate payment, the labels reconfigured the business arrangements with the talent. Artists would receive royalty payments based on sales, but those payments would not commence until an advance payment was recouped, and given downstream royalties, these advances offered were more modest.

The success of Caruso's early recordings prompted interest in signing him from the other record companies. That gave him leverage to negotiate an overall set of terms, including royalties, that proved quite favorable compared to others. The Victor Company and Caruso concluded their first contractual agreement in 1904. Caruso would receive a royalty payment of 50 cents per 12-inch record once the advance he was to be paid had been recovered. These royalties would continue to be paid to his estate in the event of the tenor's passing. He was guaranteed a minimum of $10,000 in royalties in each year that he made three or more recordings. In addition, Victor acquired the exclusive right to record Caruso's performances in exchange for an annual payment of $2,000 each year of the term. If the company required Caruso's presence in New York for recording or any other business, he would be reimbursed a further $2,000 for his travel. Finally, Caruso had approval rights for recordings made under the agreement. If he was dissatisfied with the quality of the result, the product would not be released. This contract proved so lucrative for both parties that when it was revised in 1919, Caruso was guaranteed an annual minimum payment of $100,000 and a royalty of 10% of the price of the record rather than a fixed rate per disc.[xl]

These arrangements proved to be incredibly rewarding for the most successful artists. Over the course of 20 years, Caruso received more than $5 million from his record company, or $100 million in today's currency. In 1914 alone, he earned $220,000 or $6 million today. In many ways, this structure established the pattern for agreements between labels and recording artists that remains in use today. One element in such agreements is an advance that is recouped via a royalty payment set as a percentage of the price. Another is the artist demanding to renegotiate a higher royalty rate when sales climb significantly. Despite substantial payments to performers, these deals ensured that the labels retained the lion's share of the financial rewards as recompense for "fronting" the advance. As Enrico Caruso Jr. put it, his father earned a "small fortune" while his record company received a large one.[xli] The disparity between the outcomes for major labels and artists remains a major source of contention in today's music industry.

Government rationing to support the efforts in World War I reduced production of both record players and discs. Pent-up demand and the postwar economic recovery carried the music industry to new heights. Record sales eclipsed sheet-music revenues for the first time ever in the early 1920s. Victor sold 54 million records worldwide in 1921, surpassing their sales in any year to that point in time. Industry sales of records hit $110 million that same year, with overall revenues exceeding the equivalent of $5 billion in 2021 dollars.

The growth was, in part, fueled by shifts in patent protection. The phonograph patents that had blocked companies from entering the burgeoning business expired, leading to a tenfold expansion in the number of companies manufacturing phonograph-related products. Victor lost a court case involving its patents on flat disc technology; this allowed new, independent labels to offer a broader music selection. The resulting records fueled demand for players. Ironically, the legal loss ended up benefiting Victor as the market leader in phonographs.

Record sales began to drop after 1921 with the launch of commercial radio. The shift to electrical phonographs and recordings, using technologies from radio, halted the declines by the middle of the decade. Worldwide record sales began climbing again, reaching 200 million units by 1929, with half of that total in the United States. Yet that recovery was short-lived as the Great Depression brought the record industry to its knees. By 1932, US records sales dropped over 90 percent to 6 million units. To compete with radio—which, once purchased, delivered music for free—prices had to come down. Decca Records launched in 1934 and led the way. To drum up fan interest during difficult economic times, they offered records by big stars like Bing Crosby and Jimmy and Tommy Dorsey for only 35 cents, 30 percent less than the usual price. The other labels followed suit, but sales did not return to their former heights.[xlii]

Profits evaporated with reduced volumes and prices, and even the largest record companies were soon out of business or purchased by the now more successful radio companies. CBS bought Columbia and Brunswick. RCA snapped up Victor and acquired the rights to Nipper. And Edison's National Phonograph Company shut its doors, even as the NBC broadcast network, owned by the RCA subsidiary of Edison-founded General Electric, thrived.

Several efforts were made to support the record business through the Depression that did not rely upon the sale of phonographs to consumers. Jukeboxes, which allowed fans to select one of 20 records, were invented in 1927, and three years later, 12,000 of the machines were playing music in bars and restaurants. When Prohibition was repealed in 1933, the reopened bars needed music, and by the middle of the decade, despite the Depression, US jukebox operators were purchasing one-third of all the records sold to feed the 120,000 new jukeboxes purchased that year.[xliii] The now-renamed RCA Victor introduced the Duo, Jr. in 1934 to capitalize on the continuing sales. The Duo, Jr. consisted of a turntable that plugged into a radio and relied on that device for its amplifier and speaker to lower the manufacturing costs.[xliv] These moves helped to improve sales somewhat, but the era of the phonograph record as the dominant format had come to an end—at least until the invention of the LP and the 45.

The simple fact that phonographs could reproduce different instruments and the voices of famous performers provided music fans with an experience that had simply not existed before. The novelty alone was sufficient to generate consumer interest at first. But as the market for home use grew, the industry began to cater to different segments of the populace with distinctive products and music. Manufacturers offered different phonographs that addressed ranges of affordability and taste. Their advertising highlighted the wide range of price points available while emphasizing the "pleasure" that a talking machine could deliver (See Figure 2.4). Simple tabletop designs

Victor

Look for the dog on the horn and cabinet of every Victor, on the lid of every Victrola, and on every Victor record.

Victor I

$25

Other styles
$10 to $250

The world's greatest musical instrument.

Think of getting for $25 a musical instrument that brings to you the voices of the most famous singers, the music of the most celebrated bands and instrumentalists—the best entertainment of every sort.

Never has $25 bought so much pleasure.

The proof is in the hearing. Ask the nearest Victor dealer to play one of Farrar's newest records, "Vissi d'arte e d'amor" from Tosca (88192)—a beautiful record and one that well illustrates the wonderful advances recently made in the art of Victor recording.

See that he uses an **Improved Victor Needle** to play this record.

And while you are there **be sure to hear the Victrola.**

Victor Talking Machine Co., Camden, N. J., U.S.A.
Berliner Gramophone Co., Montreal, Canadian Distributors.

New Victor Records are on sale at all dealers on the 28th of each month

Figure 2.4 Victor I gramophone advertisement. Courtesy of the Hagley Museum & Library. Reproduced with permission

with lower manufacturing costs targeted those with less disposable income. For middle-class families, there were machines built into basic cabinets that could fit in with the rest of their furnishings. Cabinets crafted from fine woods in the Queen Anne or Chippendale style were offered to match the luxury appointments in the homes of consumers with the deepest pockets.

Music and performers with demonstrated popularity in live theaters and concerts were the first artists to be sought out for recordings, as exemplified by John Philip Sousa's Band with "The Stars and Stripes Forever." The vaudeville circuit provided stars such as Billy Murray, who recorded for almost every early record label with songs from George M. Cohan's Broadway shows such as "Yankee Doodle Boy" and "Give My Regards to Broadway." Songs with the broadest appeal were most desirable, but those that catered to sizable audiences with specific musical preferences also proved their worth quickly.

A focus on operatic music by artists like Caruso appealed to fans who already had exposure to performances of this repertoire in larger cities or had aspirations for more sophisticated "high art." Europe was not only the home for operas, it was also the birthplace of millions of immigrants arriving on the shores of the United States in the early twentieth century. More than 8 million people came to America between 1900 and 1910, representing more than 10 percent of the population. By 1910, more than three-quarters of the populations of New York, Boston, Chicago, and Detroit were either first- or second-generation immigrants.

Though many immigrants often arrived in abject poverty, they made rapid strides toward achieving some measure of economic security. That upward mobility enabled them to spend money on luxuries like music. Many yearned to hear songs that were sung in their native language or portrayed the immigrant experience and their desire for assimilation. The larger record labels were more focused on making records with mass appeal, which left opportunities for smaller independents like Okeh Records to step in and serve these more niche groups of music fans. Okeh made records in German, Yiddish, and Polish; they featured performers who used Irish brogues or Italian accents. Many of these songs were comedic and often relied on stereotypes or racist generalizations.

Billy Murray was the top-selling recording artist of the first decade of the century, and his recordings demonstrated this point.[xlv] He not only recorded George M. Cohan's Broadway compositions, he also sang "Twas Only an Irishman's Dream" and "My Cousin Caruso," appealing to ethnic music consumers. He sang the latter in a thick Italian accent that may have been unremarkable in 1909 but would certainly be considered insulting now. His song "If It Wasn't for the Irish and the Jews" highlighted the contributions that these groups were making to the American experience, including staging and writing plays as well as creating big department stores.[xlvi] Though recent immigrants appreciated the positive sentiments of that song, Murray also re- corded "The Whistling Coon." Though it is hard to fathom, the lyrics were even more virulently racist than the title. But this was not unusual for the time. The popularity of minstrel shows featuring white performers in black- face using exaggerated African American jargon carried over into the early days of the recording industry. The genre was referred to at the time as "Coon Songs," and the majority of such songs were penned by whites.

The nonoperatic song that proved most popular with consumers in the 1900s fell into that category. "The Preacher and the Bear," performed by Arthur Collins, was recorded in 1905, and it ultimately sold more than a mil- lion copies. Collins recorded for every one of the major labels over his almost 30-year career, with racist and stereotypical tropes about Black people as a recurring theme.

Acceptance of these stereotypes was so prevalent that even Black performers had little choice but to participate in these racist practices. The first African American recording star was George Washington Johnson. His popularity as a street performer whistling the tunes of popular songs in NYC brought the labels to his door to produce cylinders for the coin-operated machines of the 1890s. Given the cylinders' limited durability, Johnson's ability to perform the same song fifty times in a day to create numerous copies was valued. The song that proved to be his best-seller was "The Whistling Coon," which was no less racist when performed by an African American than when Billy Murray sang it.

The Great Migration of millions of Blacks from Southern states to the industrialized cities of the North had far-reaching effects on American so- ciety in general and on the music industry specifically. The market poten- tial for African Americans as a consumer segment was much more apparent to the people running the major music companies when that audience was located in the same cities they themselves lived in, such as New York and Chicago. Many of these new Northerners were already fans of jazz. Originating in New Orleans before spreading across the South, "Jass" music, as it was first known, built on African rhythms, ragtime, and blues. Leading jazz musicians such as Jelly Roll Morton and Kid Ory moved from New

Orleans to Chicago; once there, they attracted large audiences to their live performances, though the music industry initially declined to record them.

Instead, jazz was repackaged to increase its perceived commercial appeal to white audiences, pushing Black creators into the background yet again. In 1917, the Victor company brought the Original Dixieland Jazz Band (ODJB) into its New York studios to make the very first jazz recording of a song called "Livery Stable Blues." ODJB was formed in New Orleans with a completely white roster of musicians. To accommodate the constraints of time and volume, recorded jazz eliminated the lengthy improvisations and muffled the heavy percussion. Those changes along with more structured and ornate orchestrations "toned down" the more raucous aspects of the new genre in the hopes of increasing its acceptance by white audiences.

Paul Whiteman and his Orchestra epitomized that approach with their "Symphonic Jazz." Whiteman was the most popular band leader of his day, and his syncopated arrangements sanded down the rougher elements of jazz to the point where some detractors did not even consider it worthy of that label. However, his "jazzy" renditions of songs like "Whispering," played by his highly talented but all-white ensembles, were top-sellers. As with ragtime, this was yet another example of a historical pattern of the industry "white-washing" Black artistry for white audiences while reaping the financial rewards.

By the 1920s, more jazz and blues recordings did feature African American artists such as The Original Creole Orchestra and Bessie Smith. Their releases, initially known as "race records,"[20] were created expressly to appeal to African American consumers and advertised exclusively in newspapers owned by Blacks. African Americans' response to the music was positive, and white-owned record companies jumped on the opportunity and created new units to focus specifically on this segment of consumers. For example, General Phonograph's Okeh label launched an entire series of "Original Race Records." The line included 50 recordings featuring Louis Armstrong and his band, which cemented his position as a jazz virtuoso and a seminal figure in American popular music. Over the ten years from 1922 to 1932, over 20,000 of these "race records" were produced, with sales reaching five million units annually. This success paved the way for Black entrepreneurs to launch record companies of their own. Harry Pace founded Black Swan,[21] the first label marketing to African Americans owned and operated by Blacks.[xlvii] The company's slogan was "The only genuine colored record. Others are only passing for colored." The label had some measure of success and ended up being bought by Columbia in 1926.

Swing music evolved as a subgenre of jazz and became a fan favorite in the 1930s. Swing was more rhythmic, making it easier to dance to. The financially strapped Depression-era consumers who were unable to afford phonographs and records flocked to nightclubs and bars to enjoy the swing music they were hearing on the radio. In addition to hiring live bands, many of those venues purchased jukeboxes to provide musical entertainment, which drove a significant share of record purchases. The big bands of swing were led by musicians like Earl "Fatha" Hines, Duke Ellington, and Benny Goodman. Swing's popularity would span the Second World War until the introduction of the vinyl record in 1948 made it possible to record the newer bebop style of jazz, as we'll see in Chapter 4.

Urban music consumers, both Black and white, might have preferred jazz, but those in rural areas were bigger fans of "hillbilly music." Ralph Peer, the recording director of Okeh Records, heard the term in the South, and he used it to refer to a genre that included bluegrass, gospel, and country and western songs.[22] Okeh issued the first country record that included lyrics and vocal performances in 1923. It featured "Fiddlin" John Carson, who followed up that release with a series of others that sold well. The big labels, seeing how many consumers were interested in these country tunes, jumped on the opportunity that Okeh had identified. Victor followed suit with its own country artist, Vernon Dalhart, whose rendition of "The Prisoner's Song/Wreck of the Old '97" became the first million seller in the genre. By the 1930s, country fans were buying millions of copies of records by artists like The Carter Family and Jimmie Rodgers, and "hillbilly" music constituted a quarter of all sales.

Consumers were not only interested in the music itself: they were fascinated by the people who made that music, and the most popular artists became worldwide celebrities. Once again, Caruso paved the way. He was the first recording star who had to deal with the downside of fame that offset the enormous financial rewards. A century before Facebook and Twitter, the details of Caruso's life—both mundane and salacious—became tabloid fodder. News stories about Caruso featured him shaving his mustache, the theft of his wife's jewelry, and blackmail threats by an Italian organized crime group. The most sensational Caruso story was undoubtedly his arrest for allegedly molesting a woman in the monkey house at the Central Park Zoo.[xlviii] His trial was featured on the front pages of the New York newspapers for weeks. Despite challenges to the credibility of the accounts, Caruso was found guilty. However, the judge imposed the minimum fine allowed in New York courts, a mere $10. Caruso appealed, lost, paid the fine, and left America for Paris. The scandal set the precedent for many other artists who would run afoul of the law for sexual misconduct or addictions: it had little or no effect on Caruso's subsequent career.

The US copyright law in effect when the phonograph was invented was enacted in 1831. That statute explicitly covered musical compositions; it provided composers and music publishers exclusive rights to the reproduction of sheet music. However, that law did not contemplate copying a music performance onto a cylinder or disc, nor did it cover encoding notes played on a piano onto a perforated paper roll. However, soon after the turn of the twentieth century, it was quite clear that "piracy"—the unauthorized reproduction of records—was an issue for the industry.[xlix]

The fact that the law did not expressly address these new music formats did not deter rightsholders from going to court to address that piracy and to seek compensation. Stern & Company, a Tin Pan Alley music publisher, saw recordings as a way to "plug" songs to potential buyers of sheet music and founded the Universal Phonograph Company to manufacture cylinders for Edison's machines. It soon realized that the sale of those cylinders was itself a viable business and not simply a vehicle for promotion. George "Rosey" Rosenberg recorded and released cylinders with his versions of songs written by Stephen Porter, the composer and vaudeville performer. Stern had purchased those compositions, but the publisher sued because it viewed Rosey's recordings as infringing on its copyrights and damaging to its financial interests. In 1901, the District of Columbia federal appellate court dismissed the case of *Stern v. Rosey* summarily. Though Justice Seth Shepard agreed that the issue itself was novel because of the newness of the phonograph, he ruled that cylinders were not a substitute for sheet music. Furthermore, he ruled that the cylinders were not even copies as defined under the law. As Justice Shepard wrote, "We cannot regard the reproduction, through the agency of a phonograph, of the sounds of music instruments playing the music composed and published by the appellants, as the copy or publication within the meaning of the act."[l]

This legal ruling was simply following the precedent established for piano rolls some twenty years earlier. William Kennedy and the Automatic Music Paper Company had sued John McTammany, who proclaimed himself inventor of the player piano, for copyright infringement. McTammany had made an unauthorized piano roll of a song that Kennedy had licensed exclusively to the Company. The court found for McTammany and ruled that no infringement had occurred because, under the law, a piano roll was not a copy; it was simply a part of a machine. It could be rendered as a recognizable song by the mechanism, but, unlike sheet music, it could not be deciphered by a person. In 1892, the US Supreme Court declined to hear the appeal of this case.[li]

Many music publishers accepted the legal situation where there were no royalties for piano rolls and recordings because of their promotional value in increased sales of sheet music. The Automatic Music Paper Company merged with Mechanical Orguinette Company and was renamed the Aeolian Organ and Music Company. Aeolian became the largest producer of player pianos and rolls. Though it seemed contrary to their financial interests, the company favored a legal regime that required royalty payments to publishers for those piano rolls. Aeolian's plan was to corner the market by licensing the most popular songs from publishers on an exclusive basis and then to sell the piano rolls to their customers. Even without any retroactive payments and a 35-year term for the exclusivity, the prospect of royalties for piano rolls had 80 publishers signing on the dotted line.

However, the deal was dependent on having a copyright system that would prevent others from making their own piano rolls of these popular songs and undermining the value of exclusivity. Behind the scenes, Aeolian maneuvered to initiate a case that could establish that piano rolls were indeed copies deserving of copyright protection. In May 1902, White-Smith Music Publishing filed suit against the Apollo Company for infringing their copyrights by making unauthorized piano rolls. It argued that protecting creators against any form of piracy, including piano rolls, was the very purpose of copyright law.

Aeolian spent heavily to help White-Smith demonstrate that *Stern v. Rosey* had been decided wrongly and that piano rolls should be treated as copies. Aeolian's lawyers gathered evidence to support two arguments. First, they tried to show that a piano roll was simply an alternative type of music notation that could indeed be read by a pianist with practice. However, when they tried to demonstrate this "fact," the results were less than successful. Second, they claimed that piano rolls were a commercial substitute for sheet music. This argument was undercut by the existence of numerous letters from publishers to Victor, Edison, and Columbia asking them to promote their songs by producing piano rolls for promotion.[lii]

The focus on the publishers' commercial practices opened the door for the exclusive contracts crafted by Aeolian to be considered as part of the case. Apollo argued that long-term exclusive rights to the best music would enable Aeolian to put their competitors out of business. This proved to be a potent argument, given the climate engendered by President Teddy Roosevelt's public posture as a "trust-buster."

Before *White-Smith v. Apollo* was decided, the Librarian of Congress, Herbert Putnam, convened the first of three planned conferences to discuss revisions to the Copyright Law. President Roosevelt was far more supportive of enacting a law to cover these new, modern methods of reproduction than he was of anticompetitive practices. His message to Congress that year stated, "Our copyright laws are urgently in need of revision." Putnam invited organizations representing authors, artists, photographers, and others in the creative community, but he did not include any representatives of the phonograph or piano roll manufacturers. The only group from the music industry that received an invitation was the Music Publishers Association. Despite the concerns of popular composers like Victor Herbert, who felt that royalties should be paid for records and piano rolls made without his permission, the Association's representatives at the conference were notably reserved on the issue of such payments. They were under explicit orders to steer clear of any issue that might compromise the Aeolian contracts while the case was still pending.

That strategy proved less than fruitful. Despite the time and resources invested by Aeolian, the federal district court ruled for Apollo in June of 1905. Once again, the judge found that copyright law dictates that a copy of a musical composition must be a "tangible object that appeals to the sense of sight." Having failed in the courts, the path to protecting piano rolls and phonograph records as copyrighted works would indeed have to go through Congress.

When the Library of Congress held the remaining sessions on revisions to the copyright law beginning in November 1905, Nathan Burkan, a young attorney who would become one of the most influential advocates for songwriters as a founder of ASCAP, led the preparations for the Music Publishers Association. The publishers now argued for a "mechanical reproduction" right that would cover both records and piano rolls going forward. The attendees reached consensus on this and a wide variety of other issues including lengthening the copyright term and strengthening the civil penalties for infringement. This commonality of views led the participants to believe that the revised Copyright Act would sail through to legislative approval.[liii]

Yet the first congressional hearing on the draft bill in May 1906 quickly disabused them of that notion. The publishers were so confident that they had chosen celebrities rather than experts as their witnesses. The committee members handled John Phillip Sousa and Victor Herbert with kid gloves, but the two composers failed to lay out a compelling case for the benefits of the mechanical right. They did not explain how the compensation would encourage creators and thus benefit the public with more music.

The manufacturers of players and recordings, on the other hand, who had been surprised by the fast-tracking of the bill, presented a much more compelling case at the hearing. They built upon many of the same arguments that had proved persuasive in the Apollo ruling just a few months earlier and had been affirmed in appellate court just before the hearing. The manufacturers asserted that the courts' rulings that records and cylinders were not copies because they were not readable by people meant that they should not be considered "writings." Therefore, Congress did not even have the authority to craft a law providing copyright protection for these new products because the Constitution defined copyright as providing *authors* exclusive rights to their respective *writings*.

The exclusive contracts between Aeolian and the music publishers proved to be even more damning when scrutinized by Congress. The mechanical right was portrayed as an essential element of a monopolistic plan that greedily took money from the public to line the pockets of a few music publishers. The hearings went so poorly that striking the mechanical right from the proposed bill completely and proceeding without it was considered as a possible strategy. Burkan kept the literary groups—who might have chosen to leave the music industry to their own devices—on board by extending the mechanical right beyond musical compositions to their artistic outputs. The next time he showed up for hearings on a new copyright bill, in December 1906, he was joined by Sousa and Herbert along with authors William Dean Howells, known as the "Dean of American Letters," and Samuel Clemens, better known as Mark Twain.

This time Burkan was well prepared both for the political realities of Washington and the intricacies of copyright law. Herbert and Sousa joined him for meetings to schmooze with DC power brokers, including a courtesy call on President Roosevelt himself. At the hearing, Burkan presented a carefully researched and masterful rebuttal to the claim that Congress had no authority to create a mechanical right. He argued that "writing" could be applied to a "perforated roll or a phonographic disc" as they both made the author's ideas perceptible to the mind as opposed to the eye. Burkan argued that the exclusive right to public performances of written works—where the public would perceive the works with ears, not eyes—was a precedential example of the law protecting creators from unauthorized uses.

The members of the committee bought into Burkan's logic, but there was still the matter of those Aeolian contracts and their poor optics with Congress. The phonograph and player piano industries had become political forces responsible for thousands of jobs for workers and for millions in economic activity. They used that increased clout to push Congress to remove the mechanical right from the bill.

They got their wish when, in January 1907, the drafts from the respective Patent Committees emerged and the House omitted the mechanical right entirely. The *White-Smith* case had been appealed to the US Supreme Court, and Congress was willing to wait for that decision to provide guidance. The Senate committee, albeit by just a one-vote majority, included a version of the mechanical right that met with the approval of Burkan and the publishers. This fundamental difference between the two versions of the bill doomed any prospects for passage before the end of the session.

The impasse in Congress moved the Supreme Court case back to the forefront. Copyright was on the judicial agenda for the session, which commenced the first Monday of October in 1907; oral arguments were heard at the start of the new year. Burkan advanced the same arguments defining "copy" to include both piano rolls and phonograph records that the Congressional committees had found compelling. But the justices were unconvinced. They were willing to maintain the precedents, given that highly profitable businesses had thrived under those rulings. The Court's unanimous decision issued on February 28, 1908 stated unequivocally that a copy was defined as "a written or printed record in intelligible notation." Justice Oliver Wendell Holmes was unwilling to dissent given the precedents, but he was sympathetic to the composers' plight. In his concurring opinion, he wrote, "On principle, anything that mechanically reproduces that collocation of sounds ought to be held a copy, or, if the statute is too narrow, ought to be made so by a further act." The Aeolian contracts included a clause that the deal would take effect only if there were a favorable decision creating an enforceable mechanical right. The Supreme Court ruling put an end to Aeolian's hopes of creating an exclusive arrangement with the publishers.[liv]

The prospects for getting the mechanical right enacted in Congress were growing dimmer as well. The Senate Patent Committee was now led by Senator Reed Smoot of Utah, who had previously sided with the manufacturers. He reintroduced a bill stating that there would be no liability for copyright infringements from mechanical copies. On the House side, Patent Committee Chair Frank Currier of New Hampshire and other members were concerned about the potential for a monopoly in music rights. The terms of the Aeolian contracts and their exclusivity clauses provided valid cause for such fears.

Currier introduced a new House bill that adhered to the same hard line on mechanical rights that the Senate had put forward. The message to the publishers was clear: you can be remunerated for the copies of your songs used on piano rolls and records, but only if you give up the ability to control those uses explicitly. This "compulsory license" was a new concept for copyright law and, in the final joint Congressional committee hearing, Burkan argued strenuously on behalf of the publishers that the entire concept was unconstitutional. But without it, the manufacturers would challenge any mechanical royalty whatsoever. The publishers and the manufacturers agreed that a compromise needed to be struck.

The parties agreed to stay in Washington to work out the details and, of course, the rate for those mechanical copies was the core issue. A two-cent rate had been suggested at a previous hearing. The number rounded up the one-and-a-half-cent charge for each sheet-music copy that had proved small enough to avoid excessive economic harm to consumers. Two cents became part of the draft agreement among the parties even though many publishers felt the payment was insufficient. On the other hand, some manufacturers thought that even this amount was exorbitant. Though the parties did not formally agree before leaving town, the parameters of the final result had become clear.

A subcommittee was empowered to finalize the legislation when the lame-duck session of Congress convened in December 1908; it settled the remaining open items in the bill. The final bill was passed by both houses of Congress during the closing hours of the lame-duck session. It went to the White House on March 3, 1909, and in one of his final acts as President, Roosevelt signed it into law. The final bill extended the term for copyright protection to 56 years, consisting of initial and renewal terms of 28 years each. The mechanical royalty was indeed fixed at two cents. Once a composer or publisher allowed an initial mechanical reproduction of their work, any other party could avail themselves of the compulsory mechanical license, make copies, and pay that fixed rate. This gave rise to "cover versions": once there is a recording of a song, anyone else can record and sell their own version. This practice has given us both great recordings as well as some that proved lucrative but poor imitations of the original.[23]

The political machinations and maneuvering that led to the compulsory mechanical license gave credence to the cliché that enacting laws was like making sausage. That's why it took nearly 70 years for another major revision of US copyright law. Over that time, the mechanical rate increased to the current level of 9.1 cents (or 1.75 cents per minute of playing time for the song). Though it created a steady, reliable flow of funds to publishers, this statutory rate consigned them to a small share of the revenues for the millions upon millions of copies that would be sold over the next century.

The Aeolian agreements showed that publishers were willing to engage in anticompetitive practices to increase their bottom lines. Those tactics provoked the phonograph manufacturers to push hard for a compulsory license to ensure that there would be no exclusivity whatsoever on compositions. However, those same companies were not averse to exploiting their own market power when it served their own financial interests.

As discussed earlier, the phonograph companies tried to control their distribution channels through both direct and indirect means. They provided training and information to retailers to assist their educational efforts with potential buyers. They were particularly concerned that department stores and other large retailers would discount phonographs and then make up for the lost margins selling other goods. Victor's price schedule was included in its contracts with distributors, and violating the terms could result in suspension or cancellation.

Although many retailers bought into compulsory pricing, others objected. The Fair Store sued Victor over their efforts to set retail prices for phonographs. In *Victor Talking Machine Company v. The Fair* in 1903, the US Court of Appeals for the Seventh Circuit ruled in favor of the Victor Company, setting a legal precedent for price regulation. When later rulings restricted setting the actual sales prices, Victor and other manufacturers shifted to a "license" arrangement with retailers. Rather than selling their products, they licensed them for use by the retailers, thereby retaining pricing control for the term of their patents. Victor used its own dealers as part of their lobbying campaign against legislation that would ban its pricing regime.

But gradually the tide turned. The Department of Justice began to prepare an antitrust suit against Victor for using illegal tactics including bribery and coercion against its distributors. When Macy's Department Store failed to uphold the pricing schedule under the "license" agreement, Victor sued it for patent infringement. Victor's price maintenance practices became a centerpiece of Congressional hearings in 1917. And in April of that year, the US Supreme Court, in a 6–3 decision in *R.H. Macy & Company v. Victor Talking Machine Company*, found that these licensing agreements were simply a subterfuge to fix prices and that they were illegal and void; this foreclosed the need to bring any antitrust action. Of course, this would not be the last time that the record companies would be taken to task for yielding their power over the distribution, marketing, and pricing of music.[lv]

Conclusion

At the risk of oversimplification, the phonograph era can be characterized as the combined inventiveness of three men: Edison, Berliner, and Victor. Edison created the breakthrough concept of a talking machine. Berliner developed the mass production and duplication of discs. And Victor crafted the business processes covering everything from artist agreements to marketing and sales.[lvi]

Many foundational elements of the business that we still recognize today were established during the era of the phonograph. The length of a "single" song, referring to a collection of songs as an album, the molding method to manufacture millions of discs, royalty-based artist agreements, mechanical licenses for copies of records, and even fans' prurient interests in artists' personal lives all became reality then. For some, the record player's success led to the belief that the good times would never end. In 1922, Edison said, "I don't think the radio will ever replace the phonograph."[lvii] That optimism was unwarranted. In what would prove to be the first of many such transitions, new technologies were poised to disrupt the best laid plans of record companies and artists.

3

Radio

We Want the Air Waves—Ramones

As a means of distributing music, radio is almost as old as records, though its longevity has been much more robust. At a minimum, that's because it's the medium most accessible to the public: receivers are cheap, and reception requires only electricity. It's also arguably because the government has regulated the medium (to greater or lesser degrees) to ensure that the limited resource of radio bandwidth is available to a variety of broadcasters.

On the other hand, radio was not really a medium for recorded music for the first few decades of its existence. During the early days of radio, from the 1920s through World War II, music predominated; but the majority of it was performed live. The national radio networks had their own resident performing artists, even including orchestras such as the NBC Symphony under the direction of New York Philharmonic conductor Arturo Toscanini.[1] Records were played on air mainly to fill time between live segments or because phonograph makers or dealers were sponsoring segments of programming. Sound quality was poor: records were played on the air by placing a microphone in front of a speaker.

The first well-known radio program that featured recorded music was Martin Block's Make-Believe Ballroom, which started on WNEW-AM in New York in 1935. Block's show spawned imitators throughout the country, but many years would pass until recorded music became ubiquitous on radio. Apart from audio quality, regulation was a barrier. At various points during the 1920s and 1930s, regulators (first the Commerce Department, then the FCC) required announcements that the music was prerecorded, sped up the license approval process for stations that would agree not to play any recorded music for their first three years of operation, and even forbade larger stations from playing records on the air.[i]

The other barrier to radio play of recorded music was royalties. The American Society of Composers, Authors, and Publishers (ASCAP), founded in 1914 to collect royalties for songwriters, began charging radio stations for

Key Changes. Howie Singer and Bill Rosenblatt, Oxford University Press. © Howie Singer and Bill Rosenblatt 2023.
DOI: 10.1093/oso/9780197656891.003.0003

playing compositions in its catalog—with the implicit threat of lawsuits for copyright infringement if stations didn't pay. Through the 1930s, ASCAP increased the royalties it charged radio stations by over 400 percent.[ii] In 1941, when ASCAP hiked radio royalties by another 70 percent, radio stations had enough: they organized widespread boycotts of the popular music that dominated ASCAP's catalog. The following year, the American Federation of Musicians staged a strike against recording, to protest what they (correctly) saw as the inevitability of radio playing all recorded music.

These disputes were finally resolved in 1944, just as radio was expanding from AM to FM, and just before the LP and the 7-inch single were introduced. By the late 1940s, radio stations were starting to play much more recorded music. Standardization of television technology led to the creation of the first nationwide television networks; performing artists left radio in droves for the new medium. Regulations against playing recorded music on radio were loosened. But the big change in radio's role in the recorded music industry didn't come until several years later.

The disruptive factor that brought radio fully into the sphere of the recorded music industry was not a station, network, program, or regulation: it was a product that weighed about a pound and fit handily in a pocket or purse. The Regency TR-1 from Regency Electronics and Texas Instruments, the first transistor radio, appeared in November 1954. Pocket-size (or almost pocket-size) vacuum tube radios existed, but they suffered from long warm-up times, short battery life, heat from tubes, and poor sound quality. Transistor radios were smaller and lighter, they turned on instantly, and their batteries lasted for weeks.

The TR-1 sold for $50 ($480 in today's dollars) and received poor reviews for its performance. But it was quickly eclipsed by other models from Raytheon, Zenith, and several companies from the newly revitalized Japan, including Sony. These sold—for prices around $15–$20 (about $150–$200 today)—in the millions by the end of the 1950s to the growing number of baby boomers who were becoming teenagers then.

Transistor radios were among the most important reasons why rock & roll became big business. For the first time, teenagers didn't have to listen to their music on the big console set in the living room that families of the 1940s would gather around to hear dramas, variety shows, news, or presidential fireside chats. Instead they could listen on their own, outside of the house, with their friends, without having to be, as Chuck Berry put it, "Cruisin' and playin' the radio / With no particular place to go."

The vast majority of those pocket transistor radios only played AM. Although FM radio appeared in the late 1930s, it wouldn't be particularly relevant to the music industry until well into the 1960s. FM traded off audio quality for signal range. AM signals could be transmitted for hundreds or even thousands of miles, and a few early AM stations were given nationwide "clear channels" with no interference from stations on the same or adjacent frequencies. But the sound quality of AM was considerably inferior to the "hi-fi" recording formats that appeared after World War II, namely the LP (see Chapter 4) and magnetic tape (see Chapter 5). FM, in contrast, offered sound quality approaching that of LPs, as well as lower interference, but at much shorter transmitting distances; an FM signal typically covers a single city or metropolitan area.

Stereo FM emerged in the late 1950s, a few years after the appearance of stereo records. The FCC adopted a standard for FM stereo, based on technologies from GE and Zenith, in April 1961. The technique involved multiplexing (piggybacking) two signals: an L + R (left-plus-right audio channels) signal at the normal audio frequencies and an L − R (left-minus-right) signal "hidden" at frequencies above the audible range. This enabled backward compatibility with existing mono receivers: they would just play the L + R signal and ignore the higher frequencies. Stereo receivers, meanwhile, would detect and decode the L − R signal, then add the two signals together to create the left channel (L + R + (L − R) = 2L) and subtract them to get the right channel (L + R − (L − R) = 2R). The first stations to broadcast in stereo, two months after the standard was adopted, were GE-owned WGFM in Schenectady, NY, and WEFM in the Chicago suburbs.[iii]

Other innovations in radio technology in the predigital era increased the ease of changing stations. The first car radio appeared in 1929 from Automatic Radio Corp. The following year, Galvin Manufacturing Company of Chicago introduced its first car radio. Galvin introduced the iconic row of push buttons for mechanical station presets a mere six years later, so that drivers could change stations easily without taking their eyes off the road. Then in 1947 the company renamed itself after its radio, as Motorola (a telescope-word for "Motor" and "Victrola"). Figure 3.1 shows an ad for the Motorola Model Eight-Sixty from the late 1930s.

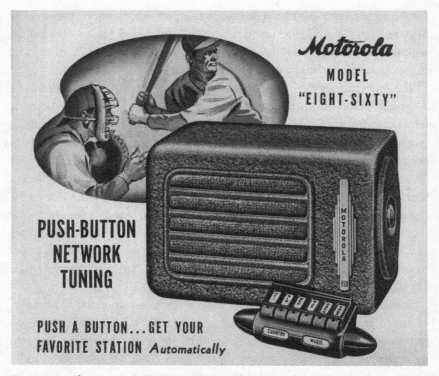

Figure 3.1 The Motorola Eight-Sixty car radio from the late 1930s featured pushbutton station presets. © Motorola, Inc., Legacy Archives Collection. Reproduced with permission.

Station-switching technology took its next leap forward in the early 1980s with the invention of phase-locked loop (PLL) electronic tuning. PLL tuning enabled a frequency to be set fully electronically, without requiring a mechanical action to turn a tuning capacitor. With PLL, a radio could have arbitrarily many presets and could "seek" and "scan" to other stations.

Streaming audio technology brought radio into the digital age in the mid-1990s, with technology introduced by the Seattle-based startup Progressive Networks (later RealNetworks) and a few others. By then, the technology for storing music in digital files was well understood (see Chapter 8); streaming audio involved breaking up audio files into small packets, transmitting a packet at a time, and reassembling the packets at the receiving end into a continuous stream of audio. Versions of codecs (digital audio encoding schemes) such as MP3 and MP4-AAC suitable for streaming were invented. Bitrates for streaming audio had to be chosen to suit the network bandwidth available. By 1995, Progressive Networks' RealAudio was capable of streaming stereo music with adequate sound quality over the 28.8 kbps dialup Internet connections that were common at the time. Microsoft and America Online (AOL) introduced or acquired their own streaming audio technologies in the ensuing years.

The first several uses of streaming audio for music transmission fell into two categories: simulcasts of AM or FM stations and "pure play" Internet radio. Early examples of the latter included NetRadio (125 channels of mostly rock music), HardRadio (over 50 hard rock channels), Sonicwave, and TheDJ, later renamed Spinner and sold to AOL. Live365 enabled users to post their own "stations," with fixed music playlists, for anyone to listen to.

But networks such as the Internet weren't useful just for sending preselected audio programs to remote users. Streaming audio services could send different streams to each user. Entrepreneurs also figured out quickly that the networks could also be used for listener input that would cause changes to the programming. They began to experiment with various types of input schemes. These fell into two categories: those that enabled users to pick the specific music they wanted to hear, and those that didn't. The former became known as interactive or on-demand streaming; we'll talk about those services in Chapter 9.

Simpler feedback mechanisms came first. Imagine Radio, which launched in 1998, enabled users to start stations based on music genres and artists. It also enabled users to rate both artists and songs on a 0-to-10 scale, which would determine how often they heard the particular music. LAUNCHCast, shown in Figure 3.2, started the following year. LAUNCHCast also enabled users to rate tracks; in addition, it let users "subscribe" to other users so that the other users' ratings influenced the subscribing users' playlists; and it introduced a "skip" feature. These were all precursors to features of later services like Pandora and iHeartRadio (such as thumbs-up and thumbs-down) and the concept of "following" users in social media. Imagine Radio and LAUNCHCast were eventually acquired by MTV and Yahoo!, respectively.

Another innovation in streaming radio was aggregation services. By the early 2000s, hundreds of AM/FM stations had started Internet simulcasts, and many pure-play Internet radio stations found audiences for certain niche musical genres (such as Soma FM for ambient music and Aural Moon for progressive rock). The next logical step was to compile databases of all

Figure 3.2 The LAUNCHcast Internet radio player enabled users to rate songs, artists, and albums.

these stations and deploy those databases as tuning guides. RealNetworks did this with its Real Guide, as did the startups RadioTime (later TuneIn) and Reciva. These databases were intended to power a new generation of tabletop and component Internet radios, such as the Kerbango model shown in Figure 3.3, which appeared on the market but never became very popular. Today, TuneIn's database holds over 120,000 stations from all over the world and is available through TuneIn's mobile apps and website.

The next step in the evolution of streaming radio was to get better at automated music selection to suit users' tastes. This involved the difficult task of describing the characteristics of music in metadata that could be crunched to produce customized playlists in real time.

The ideal way to do this would have been to get record labels to agree to a standard set of metadata attributes for describing music and to create that metadata as part of the process of releasing records. But that wasn't going to happen—at least not in the 2000s (we'll return to this in Chapter 10). Metadata had to be created by others after the fact.

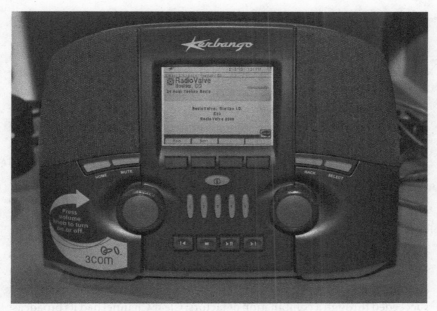

Figure 3.3 The Kerbango Internet radio by 3Com, the first tabletop Internet radio, on display at the Consumer Electronics Show in Las Vegas in January, 2001. REUTERS/Alamy Stock Photo.

Startups took two different approaches to this task. The first was based on the idea that users would contribute this metadata by what we now call "crowdsourcing." Last.fm, which launched in 2002, was based on technology called the Audioscrobbler. This enabled users to assign "tags" (metadata values) to songs, which would be shared with other users and used to inform automated musical selection.

The other approach was to pay trained musicologists to assign the metadata. That was the approach of the Music Genome Project (MGP), which had begun by the time Last.fm launched. MGP hired hundreds of musicologists to listen to songs and assign hundreds of metadata attributes to each one.[2] Pandora, based on the MGP, launched in 2005. MGP produced metadata that was better quality than crowdsourcing efforts such as Last.fm, leading Pandora to become the most popular streaming music service for a while. But the technique was expensive and didn't scale very well: after several years, Pandora's music catalog was "only" 1–2 million tracks, while the catalogs of iTunes and various interactive streaming services, not to mention streaming radio competitors such as Last.fm and Slacker, went into the tens of millions.

Pandora eventually augmented MGP with automated means of metadata creation to grow its catalog.

Meanwhile, large AM/FM station owners started to experiment with aggregating their own stations into online brands. This wasn't a strategy that seemed likely to succeed. As we'll see later in this chapter, FCC rules prevented single companies from owning very many stations; an online radio service featuring only a few hundred stations—many of which offered similar programming and all of which featured localized ads and DJ banter—was not a compelling proposition. CBS had modest success in its partnership with AOL: in 2008, it formed AOL Radio, featuring Internet simulcasts of its 200 broadcast stations and an equal number of pure-play Internet radio stations.

Yet the largest AM/FM broadcast chain in America tried this strategy and rode it to considerable success. Clear Channel Communications, which owned about 850 stations (roughly 6 percent of all commercial stations in America), launched the online radio service iHeartRadio in 2008. iHeart succeeded through a combination of factors: Clear Channel had its broadcast stations promote the new online service heavily on-air; it had the resources to sell ads and launch huge marketing campaigns, such as a major annual music festival.

iHeartRadio also added new features constantly. It added Pandora-style customizable pure-play Internet radio channels, complete with thumbs-up and thumbs-down buttons. It even made thumbs-up and thumbs-down work with simulcasts of some AM/FM stations to collect feedback to influence future programming. The company eventually convinced competitors such as Cumulus Media to make their stations available on iHeartRadio, and it blocked its own stations from being playable through TuneIn. More recently, iHeartRadio added podcasts and has become one of the leaders in that market. iHeartRadio became so important to Clear Channel's radio business that the company renamed itself iHeartMedia in 2014.

By the early 2010s, Pandora and iHeartRadio were number one and number two in streaming music respectively. As we'll see later on, interactive streaming existed but hadn't taken off yet. Pandora emphasized its MGP-based personalization algorithms, while iHeartRadio touted its connection to "real" radio. Apple eventually joined the fray with the Pandora-like iTunes Radio.

Even today, Pandora is still among the most popular online music services, although its user base has declined since it was purchased by SiriusXM in 2018.[iv] iHeartRadio and TuneIn represent traditional broadcast radio's connection to the present day, along with NPR's public radio apps. Today, whenever you ask Google or Alexa to play a radio station, your voice response system will play the station on whichever of those apps lists the station you want.

There are two other primary digital radio technologies: HD Radio and satellite radio. HD Radio is a type of "in-band-on-channel" (IBOC) digital transmission, in which a digital signal piggybacks onto a standard AM or FM signal with minimal degradation to the analog signal. Depending on how it is configured, an AM or FM station can have up to four HD signals, one of which (by FCC regulation) must be an HD version of the analog signal. Consumers need radios with HD capability to receive the signals; many current car audio systems have HD receivers. HD Radio's primary purpose is to increase the number of unique terrestrial radio stations in the country without allocating new frequencies for them.

Experiments in IBOC transmission began in the early 1990s around the same time as the first streaming audio experiments, but the technology was slow to take off. A company called iBiquity received FCC approval in 2002 to launch its technology, which it patented and branded as HD Radio, for commercial use. Currently there are over 4,500 HD Radio channels available throughout North America.

The other primary digital radio technology is satellite radio: digital signals transmitted from a satellite in geosynchronous orbit, meaning that it follows the earth's rotation and effectively sits over the same geographic position in the middle of the United States all the time. Satellite radio reaches—with a little help from terrestrial repeaters in valleys, big cities, Alaska, and Hawaii—the entire United States and Canada with CD-quality audio.

The FCC auctioned off frequencies for Satellite Digital Audio Radio Services in the mid-1990s. The two winning bidders, American Mobile Satellite Corp. and Satellite CD Radio, were given frequencies and launched—literally—in 2001 and 2002 as XM Satellite Radio and Sirius Satellite Radio, respectively. The two systems still exist, but the two companies merged to form Sirius XM Satellite Radio in 2007. The company is now owned by Liberty Media, which also owns Pandora as well as a chunk of iHeartMedia.

Most of satellite radio's channels are commercial-free, and users pay monthly subscription fees for the service. As with HD Radio, satellite radio's primary market is in cars. The vast majority of Sirius XM's subscribers—34 million at this writing—start their subscriptions when they buy a new car: many car models have factory-installed Sirius XM receivers, and new cars typically come with three-month free trial subscriptions. In addition to dozens of music channels, Sirius XM also features live sports, Howard Stern, and other exclusive programming.

Apart from the prevalence of live music in the early days of radio, the history of the relationship between radio and the music business is best understood through the history of radio music formats. Formats provide a top-down view of radio that the music industry can use to help it promote music.

The first recognizable "music format" on radio was Top 40. Top 40 came into existence before the transistor radio; it started in 1951 at Todd Storz's KOWH in Omaha. But the little device turbocharged the format's popularity; it expanded to hundreds of stations nationwide by the end of the 1950s. The first rock & roll stars—Elvis, Bill Haley, Chuck Berry—came on the scene in the years immediately following the introduction of the TR-1. Country radio stations also proliferated throughout the South and Midwest around the same time.[v]

Radio became an integral part of the recorded music industry with the advent of Top 40. Yet record labels understood the value of radio airplay in promoting sales long before then. The formula for labels was simple: get radio airplay; sell records; get more airplay; sell more records. It was a virtuous cycle: radio station asks the local record store what's selling; record store provides a list, often in exchange for a free ad on the air; station plays the hot-selling records and tells listeners where to buy them; sales increase; and the feedback loop continues.

Radio began to target young baby-boom teenagers as television was displacing radio as the dominant medium for families sitting together in the living room. As those teens grew older and got jobs and pocket money, the labels began to understand that they could use the virtuous cycle to their advantage: to promote musical performers who would benefit from that cycle and become disproportionately popular. That is, to create pop stars. Record labels started to figure this out around the outset of the 1960s, leading Top 40 radio and the record industry to grow symbiotically.

Later in the 1960s, two changes affected the relationship between record labels and radio. One was the separation of FM from AM. In its early days, FM suffered from a Catch-22 situation: signal ranges were limited, FM receivers were more expensive, and portable FM radios weren't available (until the early 1960s), so consumers didn't adopt FM; the lack of demand discouraged investment in FM transmitters and programming, which in turn inhibited demand even further. So the FCC allowed broadcasters that owned both AM and FM stations to simulcast their AM signals on FM, to help encourage adoption. But then as FM started to catch on through the mid-1960s, the FCC decided to curtail simulcasting in order to increase programming diversity. It passed a regulation in 1964 that required AM/FM station owners in markets larger than a population of 100,000 to limit simulcasting; the regulation went into effect at the beginning of 1967.[vi] FM stations had to start coming up with their own programming.

The other big change around the same time was pop music artists starting to think of LPs instead of singles as the primary canvases for their output, as we discuss in the next chapter. LPs were no longer to be thought of as collections of a few hit singles plus some filler tracks; they were conceived as integrated artistic creations. And with its superior sound quality and limited commercial expectations at the time, FM was the natural place to play groundbreaking albums from artists like the Beatles and Bob Dylan.

Progressive FM radio was born. DJs would play the latest rock records along with jazz, soul, folk, world music, and spoken word records; and they would organize the music into thematic sets—by topic, musician, songwriter, mood, or whatever. WOR-FM in New York and KMPX in San Francisco started the Progressive FM trend, and it expanded nationwide.

At the same time, the far-less controversial Beautiful Music format (later called Easy Listening) started to flourish: stations that played light orchestral music from the likes of Ray Conniff, Mantovani, and Percy Faith, with minimal announcements or other interruptions, intended for background listening and inexpensive to produce. Beautiful Music as a format predated FM, but—as pioneered by Marlon Taylor's WDVR in Philadelphia and then syndicated nationally by Jim Schulke's Stereo Radio Productions—it was another natural for the high-fidelity medium. Although Beautiful Music didn't attract as much attention from record labels, it was important to the growth of FM as a commercial proposition because of its higher ad revenue potential.

Both Beautiful Music/Easy Listening and Top 40 AM radio continued into the 1970s much as they had been in the 1950s and 1960s. But FM rock radio began to move away from the Progressive FM format. Playlists began to be restricted. Non–rock music went by the wayside, as did thematic sets. FM began to take on tight formats of its own.

Chicago DJ Lee Abrams is widely considered the father of formatted FM rock radio, though the practice had begun at WPLJ in New York and KLOS in Los Angeles before his ascendancy. Abrams pioneered various audience research techniques, such as polling concert attendees and including survey cards with records at record stores. Through his research, he found that FM rock stations could increase their audiences by focusing on more familiar artists. By 1971 he had systematized these techniques and packaged them for other stations. His central idea was to build audience familiarity around artists instead of songs, to create a canon of rock artists that would form the basis of a station's air sound.

The result was the Superstars FM radio format, the first iteration of the commercial rock format that Mike Harrison of *Radio & Records* (R&R) magazine dubbed Album-Oriented Rock (AOR). Abrams initiated Superstars at WQDR in Raleigh, NC in 1973; subsequently he and his partner Kent Burkhardt packaged the format for other stations and branched out into other formats. Eventually over 300 stations adopted the Superstars format. Other consultants, such as Jeff Pollack from WMMR in Philadelphia, began to create rival methodologies, leading even more rock stations around the country to adopt tighter formats.

FM stations also took advice on which songs to play from subscription tip sheets like Bill Hard's *Hard Report*, Bill Gavin's *Gavin Report*, George Meier's *Walrus!*, and Kal Rudman's *Friday Morning Quarterback* (FMQB), which had varying degrees of editorial independence and credibility.[vii] These collected information about tracks played, reported them as "consensus tracks," and made recommendations. As labels released albums, many stations played what the tip sheets advised rather than what the labels might have wanted them to play.

The labels started trying various strategies to exert more influence over radio stations' choices for airplay. Labels' objectives were not merely to use FM radio airplay to sell albums. They wanted to get stations to play tracks that they thought had potential to cross over to Top 40, which meant much higher album sales. By the mid-1970s, a successful album could sell a million copies through FM airplay alone; but if that album yielded a single that crossed over to Top 40, it could sell several million.

Apart from creative considerations that we'll discuss later in this chapter, labels found that they could maximize airplay by paying attention to the "burn factor"—the length of time that radio would play a song before listeners got tired of it ("burned out"). They would time their efforts to promote selected tracks on a new album so that by the time one track burned out, they would already have started pushing another track to radio. A sustained effort of track-by-track radio pushes could result in albums lingering on the charts for as much as a year, leading to multiplatinum album sales.[viii]

The precursors of this promotional tactic were 1976–1978 blockbusters like the Eagles' *Hotel California*, Fleetwood Mac's *Rumours*, and the Rolling Stones' *Some Girls*. When albums like these came out, FM rock stations tended to put multiple tracks into heavy rotation at the same time, while singles were released to Top 40 in sequence. For example, you'd hear four tracks from *Hotel California*—"Life in the Fast Lane," "Victim of Love," "New Kid in Town," and the title track—all in simultaneous heavy rotation on FM rock stations, even as the latter two tracks were being pushed to Top 40 sequentially (both hitting no. 1). Album airplay charts in R&R listed as many as four tracks from each charting album, though albums with that many tracks getting heavy airplay were rare.

This was just what Lee Abrams had in mind with the Superstars format: focus on artists, not individual songs. But by that point in time, labels were hoping to stretch out albums' runs on FM rock radio by sequencing track-by-track promotion just as they did on Top 40 AM. For example, *Hotel California* was off the R&R album charts by July 1977, seven months after it was released. The rule of thumb in the industry at the time was that a hit single would last a maximum of 12 weeks on the radio. So if *Hotel California* contained four songs that got heavy airplay, the album could have lasted a year on the charts if the songs had been released sequentially.[3]

Of course, labels couldn't really control which tracks AOR stations played from an album and when. So they invented various tactics to get DJs' attention and maximize each album's run on radio. Some labels sent prerelease records to radio stations, sometimes in exchange for airplay for other acts on their rosters. United Artists distributed 7-inch EP-format "mini-albums" containing four songs—the tracks that the label wanted to push to radio—in packaging that resembled that of the 12-inch LPs.[ix] In the early 1980s, Columbia started prereleasing lead-off singles from new albums to radio in 12-inch single format. A tactic used to stretch out an album's radio presence was to release a less "pop" track as a single first, to establish credibility, and then release Top 40 tracks as the second or third singles.[x]

By the mid-1980s, as FM rock radio's popularity started to peak, tight formats and consultants had taken over. And the structure of the radio industry began to change in ways that would affect music formats even further. As we'll discuss shortly, in 1984, the FCC began relaxing station ownership caps and indicated that it would loosen them further in the future. This led companies like Clear Channel to bulk up on station ownership. This in turn led to more homogenous management practices, including tighter playlists.

In other words, by that time FM was completing its journey from freeform Progressive to being as tightly formatted as AM since the Todd Storz days. At the same time, consolidation did lead to a proliferation of music formats that the industry recognized, even though each of those formats featured tighter and tighter playlists. As the big chains started buying multiple stations in the same markets, it made sense to differentiate their formats instead of having them compete with one another in the same format. As the 1980s wore on, computers and listenership data enabled stations to focus more narrowly on certain demographics more effectively.

Although music formats and selection schemes varied, sometimes subtly, across the thousands of commercial radio stations in the United States, the music industry recognized only a small number of formats on a nationwide scale. The arbiter of those formats was R&R, which was the radio industry Bible from 1973 to 2009. R&R published weekly radio play charts for each format, based on data collected by Mediabase and subsequently Broadcast Data Systems, services that monitored broadcast signals and noted the songs they played.[4]

R&R played a major role in determining which music formats were important by deciding which charts to define and publish. If R&R published a music format chart, it meant both that the format was important to the music industry and that there were a significant number of stations playing that format nationwide. Thus, R&R music format charts represented the nexus of the relationship between the music industry and radio as it evolved over time.

Figure 3.4 shows all of the charts that R&R published throughout its 36 years of operation. When R&R started in the mid-1970s, the only charts were National Airplay, Country, and Album Airplay (plus the short-lived Pop 40). National Airplay was essentially the radio Top 40 chart. Album Airplay covered FM Progressive and then AOR. Country radio had always existed in

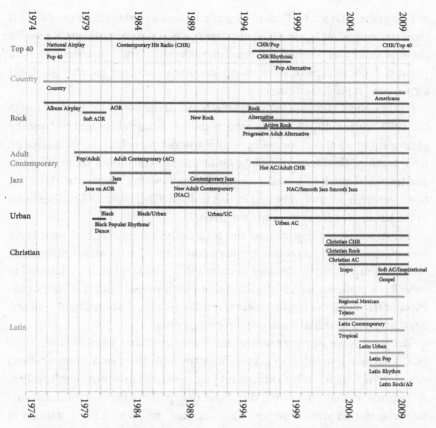

Figure 3.4 Radio station music format charts that appeared in *Radio & Records* from 1975 to 2009. Bill Rosenblatt.

its own world relative to rock and other genres; the Country chart persisted untouched for the entire 36-year run.

The Album Airplay chart, renamed AOR in 1981, continued intact through the heyday of the AOR format until 1988. The creation of the New Rock chart in that year reflected two developments in rock radio during the 1980s. One was the influence that college radio had been building up for several years. Many college radio stations had been playing punk and new wave, music that very few commercial rock stations were playing; yet the records were selling. Thanks to another industry publication called *College Media Journal* (CMJ), the labels figured out that those sales were coming through college radio airplay and started paying attention.

Bob Haber started CMJ in 1978 while he was a student at Brandeis. CMJ (later renamed *CMJ New Music Report*) enabled college radio stations—for the first time ever—to get information on what music other stations were playing. It got dozens of subscribing stations around the country to report airplay, and it published charts.

CMJ's importance rose in tandem with that of the new rock music through the 1980s. Eventually the CMJ charts and other editorial content became the equivalent of tip sheets for college radio programmers looking for advice on what was hip. The idea of a "college radio sound"—including amateurish DJs and technical glitches, as well as the music—emerged; college radio started to homogenize in its own way, and in this fashion, CMJ delivered college radio to the labels (insofar as it could be delivered).

The other factor that caused the bifurcation of commercial rock radio formats was AOR's increasing emphasis on older "classic rock"[5] material in order to court the baby-boomer demographic. Younger listeners defected to New Rock stations, which attracted them with music from the likes of the Psychedelic Furs, the Replacements, and the Jesus and Mary Chain—all artists that got their initial audiences on college radio.

The next wave of expansion of R&R format charts coincided with the FCC's further loosening of ownership caps with the Telecommunications Act of 1996, which was introduced into Congress the previous year. The 1996 Act eliminated national ownership caps but kept them in place for individual markets, so that station owners were "limited" to owning eight stations in each of the largest markets (New York, Los Angeles, etc.), with lower limits for smaller markets.

The big chains moved quickly to expand ownership based on these new limits. In doing so, they took on massive amounts of debt that required aggressive revenue growth to repay; this made them even more conservative and ratings-focused than they had been. Broadcast chains proliferated their stations' formats in efforts to reach ever-narrower demographics with ever-tighter playlists.

In response, R&R initiated several new charts between 1994 and 1996. By then, R&R had renamed Top 40 as Contemporary Hit Radio (CHR). CHR bifurcated into CHR/Pop (Hootie and the Blowfish, Bryan Adams, Dave Matthews Band) and CHR/Rhythmic (Boyz II Men, TLC, Janet Jackson). Adult Contemporary (AC) spun off Hot AC/Adult CHR (Melissa Etheridge, Elton John, Sting). Rock (formerly AOR) spun off Progressive (Soul Asylum, Natalie Merchant, Tears for Fears), which was renamed Adult Alternative, a.k.a. AAA or Triple-A for Adult Album Alternative. Rock also spun off Active Rock (metal and grunge). Americana was a short-lived chart that spun out of AAA and incorporated roots-rock acts (Steve Earle, Delbert McClinton) with a smattering of country and alt-country artists (Uncle Tupelo, Dwight Yoakam) who weren't commercial or traditional enough for the Country charts.

Industry racism rendered Black radio virtually invisible during the early years of R&R. The industry had long referred to R&B, soul, and gospel music as "race records." A parallel, de facto segregated industry of African American labels and radio stations existed through the 1940s, after which white label owners such as Ahmet Ertegun (Atlantic) and Leonard Chess (Chess) started signing Black artists. *Billboard* changed the name of its Race Records chart to Rhythm & Blues in 1949 and then to Soul in 1969, but R&R did not include a chart for that music during its first several years.

Black stations were the lifeblood of so much of that music at that time; they broke many Black artists and hits before they crossed over to Top 40. Yet they did not gain representation in R&R charts until the height of the disco boom in the late 1970s.[6] R&R started to track disco-format radio stations largely because of the phenomenal success of the 1977 movie *Saturday Night Fever*, which crossed disco over to white audiences and whose double-LP soundtrack became one of the top-selling albums of all time. The first disco radio charts were called, euphemistically, "Black Popular Rhythms" and then "Dance." It wasn't until 1983 that Black music stations in general—quickly renamed "Urban"—got their own charts. (*Billboard* renamed its Soul chart to Black in 1982.)

R&R didn't add Latin charts until 2003. It had acquired the Latino trade publication *Radio y Musica* in 2000, and it incorporated that magazine's charts and content into its own three years later. It experimented with several different music format charts for Latino radio, then gave up in early 2009 and stopped publishing them entirely. (R&R went out of business shortly thereafter.)

While racism may well have contributed to R&R's lack of Latin chart coverage until the early 2000s, other factors were involved. A music format would have to have a national footprint to merit a chart in R&R. Yet Spanish-language radio resists simple categorization at a national level. Hispanic populations (both Spanish- and English-speaking) are quite diverse across different American cities. For example, according to data from the 2009

American Community Survey, at that time the Hispanic populations of Northeastern US cities as well as Central and Gulf Coast Florida were largely Puerto Rican; South Florida (Miami) was majority Cuban; the Washington, DC area was primarily Salvadoran; Boston had a significant share of Dominicans; the Southwest and California skewed heavily Mexican; and these groups of people varied widely as to whether they were born in or outside the United States.[xi] And each of those groups has its own set of musical and cultural preferences.

Radio play is still reflected in *Billboard* charts today: it factors airplay into its calculations of positions in the many charts it publishes. In addition, Broadcast Data Systems and MediaBase still publish radio airplay charts, but far fewer of them than R&R published before it shut down and fewer still than those that Billboard publishes. In contrast, today *Billboard* publishes over 150 charts in a wide variety of genres.

With all these formats, labels' strategies for radio airplay are no longer just to cross over from Rock, Urban, or Country to Top 40 but to maximize exposure of artists and albums on as many radio formats as possible. The result is a sort of cat-and-mouse game that continues to this day: radio continues to slice up listenership into more precise demographics through narrower formatting, the better to deliver those audiences to advertisers; the music industry continues to try to maximize exposure by signing artists who can make it onto rotations in several formats. A quintessential example of this strategy today is Lady Gaga, who leaps from the top of one format chart to another: Rhythmic ("Bad Romance"), Adult Contemporary ("Shallow"), Latin ("Alejandro"), Rock ("You and I" with Queen's Brian May), and Jazz ("Anything Goes" with Tony Bennett).

The proliferation of radio delivery media at the end of the 1990s served to counteract the increasing narrowness of AM/FM formats. As discussed earlier in this chapter, Internet and satellite radio appeared at the end of the 1990s and early 2000s. Most Internet radio services of that period were either simulcasts of AM/FM stations or fixed-playlist pure-play channels of arbitrary genres.

Meanwhile, satellite radio created a space for fans of genres that aren't commercial enough for terrestrial broadcast radio. Fans of classical, jazz, blues, reggae, jam bands, and numerous other genres have stations for them on Sirius XM. Fans of the Beatles, Elvis, Michael Jackson, Bruce Springsteen,

Bob Marley, Miles Davis, and other artists have channels that play their music 24/7.

Copyright ©

Radio achieved its position of power and influence in the music industry because it was by far the most efficient way to promote recorded music for a long time. Yet its ability to do that has rested largely on a couple of quirks in US copyright law.

It's important to bear in mind that each music track normally has two copyrights: one for the musical composition, typically owned by songwriters and music publishers; the other for the sound recording of the composition, typically owned by labels or artists. Copyright law says that copyright owners have certain exclusive rights to their creations, but copyrights in sound recordings are more limited than copyrights in musical compositions. (In the next chapter, we'll see how and why this came to be.) Specifically, songwriters and music publishers have exclusive rights to public performances of their compositions, but recording artists and labels don't have exclusive rights to public performances of their records. Radio broadcasts are considered to be public performances.

The lack of a performance right in sound recordings means that radio stations have never had to license records to play them on air. They have only had to license the musical compositions.

As saw in Chapter 2, arguments over whether copyrights should exist for sound recordings date back to the age of wax cylinders and player pianos; those rights include the right of public performance on radio. Those arguments continued for decades. For example, the president of the musicians' union, the American Federation of Musicians, had this to say at a 1961 congressional hearing:

"[I]t is a shocking crime that people like Mr. Leopold Stokowski or Leonard Bernstein, or Louis Armstrong, or whoever the artist may be, are denied the right to receive additional fees, when money is made with his product. All you have to do is put a radio set into this room today and you can listen for hours and hours to canned music here, records received free by the broadcaster, if you please, while the men who made them are sitting home trying to figure out how to pay for their children's education."[xii]

As we'll see in the next chapter, when Congress finally enacted copyrights in sound recordings with the Sound Recording Act of 1971, it didn't include a public performance right, despite recommendations from the US Copyright Office that it be included.

As far as musical compositions are concerned, court decisions in 1940 established that radio stations could purchase records and play them on the air as many times as they wanted without having to seek permission from either labels or music publishers.[xiii] In other words, radio stations have a compulsory license to the musical compositions performed on the records they play, analogous to the compulsory license for mechanical reproductions of compositions that we saw in Chapter 2. Stations do have to pay royalties on musical compositions, but that is simple to do through PROs (performance rights organizations), which license public performance rights to musical compositions on behalf of large numbers of songwriters and music publishers.

As we've seen, ASCAP, the first PRO, formed before the start of radio. Next was BMI (Broadcast Music Inc.), which focused primarily on licensing music for radio. BMI was formed in 1939 by the National Association of Broadcasters (NAB), the radio industry's trade association, to inject price competition as ASCAP kept raising its royalty rates. ASCAP and BMI received antitrust consent decrees from the Department of Justice in 1941; these are essentially government permission slips to operate a duopoly. (There was a third PRO, SESAC, which focused on gospel music and European composers at that time; its market share was negligible compared to ASCAP and BMI.)

Today, ASCAP and BMI cover most of the market with roughly equal-sized catalogs, but there are other smaller PROs that also collect royalties from radio. SESAC has broadened its catalog to include compositions by the likes of Bob Dylan, Neil Diamond, and Rush. A PRO that licenses broadcast radio with an even smaller catalog is Global Music Rights (GMR). Veteran artist manager Irving Azoff founded GMR in 2013 by convincing a group of big-name songwriters that they could get higher royalties through a separate PRO than they were getting through ASCAP or BMI. GMR's current catalog includes only 90 songwriters, compared to over a million for BMI, but they include the likes of Bruce Springsteen, Bruno Mars, Prince, Pete Townshend, and John Lennon. And a new fifth PRO called Pro Music Rights, which licenses a catalog of mostly hip-hop compositions, has been recognized by some radio broadcasters.

PROs offer *blanket licenses*, meaning that a radio station just has to pay each PRO a license fee and it gets a license to all of the compositions in the PRO's repertoire. The PRO then figures out whom to pay for airplay and how much. (We'll talk about that in the Cash section later in this chapter.)

In other words, radio stations—unlike streaming services, as we'll see—have had an easy path to licensing music, enabling them to play whatever music they want whenever they want.

Congress had reopened the question of performance rights in sound recordings in 1978, just two years after the major 1976 revision of the Copyright Act had been signed into law, but nothing came of it,[xiv] and the matter was dropped for a while. But the advent of digital radio in the 1990s brought the subject back yet again. Although labels had long viewed radio airplay as promotional, they weren't inclined to view the new digital radio formats that way. On the contrary: they were afraid that digital audio technology, with its ability to make perfect copies, would lead to services that cannibalized record sales.

So the labels got the Copyright Office to open inquiries on the effects of digital audio transmission on music piracy in 1991, which led to Congress passing the Digital Performance Right in Sound Recordings Act (DPRA) in 1995. The DPRA established the performance right for sound recordings, but only for digital radio; it left intact the lack of a performance right in sound recordings for traditional AM and FM. The DPRA established a procedure for setting statutory royalties (i.e., rates set by law instead of by negotiation) for digital radio services, processes that the US Copyright Office runs every five years and which resemble litigations in court; we'll talk more about this shortly.

The DPRA also established certain rules for AM/FM terrestrial broadcast stations that simulcast online (most FCC-licensed broadcast stations do) to prevent people from using them to make digital copies of music. These stations weren't allowed, for example, to play more than four songs by the same artist in a three-hour period, or to preannounce any specific songs.[7] The DPRA also established that interactive streaming services—which wouldn't be in existence until several years in the future—would need to negotiate licenses with record labels and wouldn't get statutory royalty rates.

The result of the DPRA was that all types of digital radio services—Internet pure-play, AM/FM simulcast, satellite, the music channels on cable TV services, and Muzak—got compulsory licenses to play any sound recordings they wanted as long as they pay the statutory royalties. Separate royalty rates were eventually set up for the various types of digital radio.

However, as Internet radio services got more customizable, rightsholders began to argue that they had become tantamount to interactive services. In 2001, a group of record labels sued LAUNCH Media, the company that operated LAUNCHcast (which was offered through Yahoo!). Recall that LAUNCHcast offered features for users to customize their music feeds, such as by rating music and following other users; but it stopped short of enabling users to select specific tracks or artists. The labels claimed that this feature set was "interactive" and therefore that LAUNCHcast should have to negotiate license terms rather than get a compulsory license with statutory royalties. The Second Circuit appeals court found for LAUNCH Media in 2009. That decision paved the way for later customizable Internet radio services like Pandora and iHeartRadio, which were able to offer any recorded music track through compulsory licenses and pay statutory royalty rates.

Another loophole regarding sound recording copyrights in digital radio remained for many years afterwards. The DPRA established copyright protection for digital broadcasts of sound recordings, but only as far back as 1972—because the Sound Recording Act of 1971 did not make it retroactive to older recordings. Sound recordings made before February 1972 were subject to a patchwork of state copyright laws. This meant that digital radio services technically could not rely on statutory licenses and needed to negotiate licenses with labels for playing much of the music featured on oldies, classic rock, jazz, and classical stations—though of course this never happened. A series of lawsuits were filed by the likes of Flo & Eddie (lead singers of the Turtles as well as solo artists) and ABS Entertainment (label of Sam Cooke, Jackie Wilson, and other classic artists).

This loophole was finally closed in 2018 with the passage of the Music Modernization Act (MMA), although only for digital radio. The MMA was primarily focused on fixes to mechanical licensing of musical compositions for interactive streaming, as we'll see in Chapter 9. But it also included a provision that was originally called the CLASSICS Act (Compensating Legacy Artists for their Songs, Service, and Important Contributions to Society), which established a performance right in pre-1972 sound recordings for digital radio.

The final loophole wasn't closed: there is still no performance right in sound recordings (of any vintage) for terrestrial radio. The United States continues to be one of only a handful of countries in the world without this right; others include Iran, North Korea, and Rwanda.[8] AM and FM broadcasters still don't have to pay royalties to record labels or recording artists.

Arguments over whether radio should pay royalties to labels and artists have taken place numerous times since the 1930s. Recent arguments turn on whether radio still has the promotional value for recorded music that it did in the predigital era. Whenever this issue comes up inside the Beltway, both sides—the RIAA for record labels, the NAB for broadcasters—unleash economists armed with studies purporting to show that it does or doesn't. But the real reason why there is still no general performance right in sound recordings has to do with lobbying at the state level. And that takes us from copyright law to the FCC.

Radio frequencies are a limited resource, like land and water; so the government has regulated their use through the FCC (originally the Federal Radio Commission), which was established with the Communications Act of 1934. As radio stations proliferated around the country, the FCC moved to establish ownership limits: a single company could not own or operate more than seven stations nationwide, and no more than one in any given market. Although ownership caps were eventually relaxed in the 1980s (along with requirements for public-service programming and other regulations), they helped shape a market for radio stations that had no nationally dominant players. As we mentioned previously, national ownership caps were eliminated with the Communications Act of 1996. But by that time no more new frequencies were available, so if you wanted to own a radio station, you had to buy the license from someone else, which cost into the tens of millions for powerful stations in major markets.

When the 1996 Act passed, the big broadcast chains went on buying sprees, and by the mid-2000s, four chains (Clear Channel, Citadel, Viacom, and Cumulus) had an aggregate dominant share of audience and revenue, and the total number of station owners had decreased by one-third.[xv] But the total number of stations that those four chains owned was less than one-fifth of the total number of FCC-licensed stations. Even at its peak in 2003, Clear Channel owned around 1,200 stations out of about 15,000. (Now iHeartMedia owns about 850.)

As a result, most broadcast stations are owned by small-to-medium-sized businesses that are based all over the country. In contrast, the recorded music industry is concentrated heavily in three states: New York (NYC), Tennessee (Nashville), and California (Los Angeles/Santa Monica/Burbank). This means that whenever Congress considers legislation that pits the interests of radio against those of the music industry, there are members of Congress in three states being lobbied by the RIAA, while members of Congress in many of the other states are being lobbied by the NAB. NAB's nationwide reach gives them the clout to portray any royalty as a "performance tax," and raising taxes tends to be anathema for many politicians.

That's why there is no performance right in sound recordings today, and radio pays no royalties to labels or artists. The clash between the labels and the broadcasting industry over this issue continues to this day. At this writing, yet another attempt to plug this legislative hole is making its way through Congress: the American Music Fairness Act, introduced by senators and representatives from—you guessed it—New York, California, and Tennessee.[9]

At the same time, as Internet radio becomes less important with the rise of interactive streaming services (which have all subsumed Internet radio features), attention in radio is turning to podcasts. And as we'll see, copyright issues attending podcasts could cause radio's relationship with the music industry to become more distant.

Podcasts are an increasingly popular media format; currently over 100 million Americans listen to podcasts on at least a monthly basis.[xvi] Podcasts can be thought of as "talk radio on demand." Indeed, two of the most popular publishers of podcast content are two large sources of produced spoken-word radio programming: National Public Radio (NPR) and iHeartMedia. Both companies started in podcasting by simply taking their syndicated radio shows—Rush Limbaugh, Dr. Laura Schlessinger, and Glenn Beck in the case of iHeart; "Fresh Air," "Wait, Wait, Don't Tell Me," and "Planet Money" in the case of NPR—and releasing them as podcasts. Both have added many shows as podcasts since then.

But there's a problem with this regarding music licensing. When you make a broadcast program available on demand, you subject it to all the rules for licensing music for interactive services, which we'll discuss later in this book. For example, let's say you produce a public affairs show that has theme and background music. If your show airs once a week on an FM station, you don't need any specific music licenses; the musical compositions are covered under the station's blanket licenses with the relevant PROs,[10] and no licenses are necessary for the sound recordings. But if you make your show available for download or streaming online, you need several licenses. That means negotiating with record labels, obtaining licenses for compositions from music publishers, and generally doing more paperwork and paying more royalties. Unfortunately, there is neither a simple licensing mechanism for podcast use nor a statutory or other published royalty rate: every license has to be negotiated by hand, and the publishers and labels can refuse to license at all.[xvii]

As a result of this, not much music is used on podcasts, and there are few podcasts about music that have music in them. (That's why, for example, there is no podcast for iHeartRadio's "American Top 40" syndicated show.) As for background or theme music, many podcasters will commission their own or go to various online sources of royalty-free production music.

The further the radio industry migrates into podcasting, the less it will rely on music—unless and until changes are made to the way it's licensed for that purpose. Podcasting brought in $1.4 billion in ad revenue in 2021 and is projected to exceed $2 billion in 2022 and $3 billion in 2023.[xviii] The more it turns away from licensing commercial music, the more opportunity for labels and music publishers will be lost. This is a "brave new world" area of copyright law and is evolving fast.[11]

Copyright law determines the frameworks for royalty payments from radio. The magnitude—and even the direction—of those payments are another matter.

In the early days of radio, music publishers and record labels had diametrically opposite reactions to radio airplay of recorded music. Music publishers saw it as cannibalizing sales of sheet music: you could hear a professional performance of the music for free instead of having to play it yourself or pay to attend a live performance. On the other hand, record labels, as we've discussed, figured out fairly quickly that airplay was a potent way to promote record sales. The Top 40 format that began in the early 1950s created a winner-take-all situation that put a lot of pressure on labels to get airplay. In that respect, it would have been stranger if payola *didn't* exist than if it did.

Payola was the term given to payments of cash (and other types of gifts) to DJs in exchange for airplay. It also took other forms. One was DJs insisting on songwriter credit so that they could share in the composition royalties. The best-known example of this was legendary DJ Alan Freed's songwriting credit on Chuck Berry's "Maybellene." Other forms included forcing labels to buy advertising on stations and forcing bands to play free concerts sponsored by stations.

Payola didn't start in the Top 40 era; the payola-like practice of "song plugging"—paying bandleaders to play musical compositions live on the air—existed in the earliest days of radio. But the practice came into public view through its association with pop music radio in the late 1950s.

The story of the payola scandals of the late 1950s is well-known: Congress held hearings and passed a law making paying DJs for record airplay illegal. The hearings destroyed the career of Freed, arguably the creator of the term "rock & roll," while at the same time letting Philadelphia's Dick Clark of American Bandstand fame "skate." (Freed was defiant on the witness stand, saying that he only took payola for records that he would have played anyway; Clark denied taking payments and quickly divested his ownership stakes in dozens of songs and record labels.)

The 1950s payola scandals have been described on three levels. The most superficial explanation is that both DJs and record labels were corrupt, and it took Congress to put a stop to this evil practice that used bribery to sully the process of—what exactly? Art? Free expression? Serving the needs of listeners?

Deeper accounts of what happened around that time describe the payola scandals as an outgrowth of certain segments of society's revulsion to rock & roll as an insidious influence on youth, a revulsion that was rooted in racist attitudes. (Freed played a lot of music by Black artists on his shows.) But even that doesn't explain everything. The true root of the payola scandals was money: not just money paid to DJs, but also money that radio stations paid—or didn't pay—to music publishers and songwriters. And that leads to the deepest level of explanation of the payola scandals.

As we've discussed, broadcast radio stations didn't (and still don't) pay record labels royalties for sound recordings, but they do pay royalties on musical compositions. In the late 1950s, almost all such royalty payments were made through ASCAP and BMI. At that time, ASCAP's stable of songwriters and music publishers mainly included Tin Pan Alley writers of pop standards for the likes of Bing Crosby and Frank Sinatra, while BMI had the bulk of rock & roll songwriters in its catalog. Thus, radio stations that played Top 40 rock & roll were playing BMI compositions.

BMI was ASCAP's archrival, created by the radio industry itself to compete with ASCAP. ASCAP saw that if it could take down rock & roll, then radio would have to play compositions in its catalog, and it could dominate the radio market again. ASCAP figured that it could do this by capitalizing on the "rock & roll is evil" sentiment and lobbying Congress to go after rock & roll by going after payola.[xix]

ASCAP's gambit worked: Congress enacted a law making payola illegal in 1960. But it was a finger in the dike. The law defined payola narrowly as payments to DJs that weren't disclosed on the air and had the express purpose of getting specific records played. Its penalties were relatively mild: maximum fines of $10,000 (about $90,000 today) and maximum prison sentences of one year. Some have argued not only that the law was toothless but that its effects were insufficiently considered.[xx]

Payola has been around in one form or another ever since. In fact, it has been said that all that the law accomplished was to change where the payments went: instead of going to individual DJs, they went to station program directors, who then influenced or dictated the programming choices of all DJs on each station. This, ironically, was yet another step in the homogenization of music programming on radio that we discussed earlier in this chapter.[xxi]

The next attempt to enforce antipayola regulations, in the early 1970s, was to investigate record labels, the alleged sources of payola, instead of radio stations. In 1973, CBS abruptly fired and then sued the renowned record executive Clive Davis, claiming misuse of $94,000 for payola and "drugola."[12,xxii] The US Attorney's Office in Newark, NJ opened an investigation, code-named "Project Sound." Two senators, James Buckley of New York and John McClellan of Arkansas, called for further investigations.

The Project Sound investigations dragged on for two years, but they yielded convictions of only a handful of executives from CBS, including Davis, and the R&B label Brunswick Records—and for tax evasion, not payola violations.[xxiii] The prosecutors also investigated Gamble-Huff Record Co., owners of the Philly Soul label Philadelphia International, but ended up dropping charges when they couldn't get anyone to corroborate the evidence. Once again, this investigation had racist overtones, as most of its targets were connected to Black music.[13,xxiv]

Meanwhile, most broadcasters took steps to curtail payola, such as by making DJs sign no-payola verifications and setting hard limits on the value of gifts that DJs could accept from labels. Still, labels had various ways to curry favor with DJs. They would invite jocks to "listening parties" at fancy restaurants, where they would hear the latest releases over nice meals and open bars; or they would invite DJs to evenings built around artists' concerts or club gigs: nice dinner, limo ride to the venue, and after-party with the artist.

Even the DJs who refused drugs, stereos, plane tickets, or other enticements took part in these events.[xxv] Radio stations also get copies of new releases from record labels at no charge; this practice started during World War II[14] and became so routine that it's known as getting "service" from labels.

The labels' next steps were to insulate themselves from radio stations by hiring independent promoters. Labels would pay promoters to do "research"; the promoters would handle payments and other enticements to DJs, program directors, and music directors. As the argument went, labels couldn't be held liable because they were paying independent promoters flat fees and had no control over where the money was going after that. Independent promoters would charge labels tens of thousands of dollars to get a song added to major-market radio stations' playlists.[xxvi]

This led to another round of investigations in the mid-1980s, first in the House of Representatives, initiated by Rep. John Dingell of Michigan in 1984. A story that aired on *NBC Nightly News* in 1986 focused on a group of high-level indie promoters that called itself The Network and included notable figures such as Joe Isgro and Fred DiSipio, and insinuated that it had ties to organized crime.[xxvii] This prompted an investigation in the Senate, which featured two future political superstars: a young senator from Tennessee named Al Gore and a rising federal prosecutor from New York named Rudy Giuliani.[xxviii] The following year, a Los Angeles grand jury launched yet another investigation.[xxix]

Like the Project Sound investigations in the previous decade, these investigations focused on labels, and they followed on the heels of failed attempts to get the RIAA to launch its own investigation of labels' behavior. Yet none of them found much behavior that would be considered violations of the laws. The negative exposure from the NBC exposé led the major labels to stop using the promoters in The Network, though only temporarily.[xxx]

Labels cut down on independent promoters after the Napster era of the 1990s (see Chapter 8) as both the music and radio businesses began to decline, but then labels allegedly started paying radio stations directly again, and evidence emerged that labels were at least cognizant of payments that independent promoters made to individual stations.

The next wave of payola investigations started in 2002 under New York State Attorney General Eliot Spitzer, who was tipped off by a music business lawyer named Bob Donnelley.[xxxi] By June 2006, all of the then four major labels had agreed to settlements totaling over $30 million.[xxxii] The notoriety that Spitzer received from these investigations would help land him in the

New York Governor's office the following year. Around the same time, the FCC launched its own investigation of station owners, focusing on four of the largest: Clear Channel, CBS, Citadel, and Entercom. These resulted in fines totaling $12.5 million in 2007.[xxxiii] Labels as well as broadcast chains set up another round of new procedures designed to eschew payola as the law defined it.

The most recent attempts to rein in payola came in 2019, when the FCC launched an investigation on the major labels that was prompted by an article in *Rolling Stone*.[xxxiv] This time the intent of the inquiry was different because of the antiregulatory bent of the Republican-controlled FCC[15] when the investigation started: its focus appeared to be on the imbalance between payola regulations on broadcast radio and the lack of such regulations on digital music services. The result might have been a recommendation to Congress that it discontinue the anti-payola laws that it made sixty years ago. But after the presidency shifted to the Democratic Party in 2021, the investigation faded away.

The money flows on the songwriter and music publisher side are completely different for broadcast radio. As we discussed, radio pays public performance royalties on musical compositions; PROs handle those payments.

There are three steps to the process of paying radio royalties to music publishers and songwriters. First, stations pay PROs percentages of their revenue for blanket licenses to the PROs' repertoire. Each PRO negotiates the rates with an entity called the Radio Music Licensing Committee (RMLC), which represents radio broadcasters. Those negotiations generally turn on how much of the music that stations play is in each PRO's catalog. Each station is free to reject the blanket license and pay royalties per composition (and negotiate directly with the PRO), but the process would be a nightmare of paperwork. The PROs usually reach agreements with RMLC, but if they don't, the negotiations end up in court.

In the second step, each PRO pays songwriters and music publishers according to how much relative airplay their compositions are getting. BMI used to require all radio stations that took the blanket license to fill out separate music logs for two weeks out of each year. It would extrapolate those two weeks to the entire year and pay its rights holders proportionally. For loosely formatted stations that gave DJs freedom to play what they wanted, this system would invariably result in less popular "long tail" artists being paid nothing. Nowadays, the two major PROs use automated music recognition technology, which we'll discuss in more detail in Chapter 8, to analyze the signals of a subset of commercial radio stations in the United States, while other (mostly smaller) stations still need to send sample logs. For current popular music, automated recognition technology works about as well as reporting music selections directly from stations' computerized playout systems. But the current systems still tend to underrepresent nonmainstream artists, because they tend to be played on smaller radio stations that the PROs do not monitor.

Then there's the third step. Once the PRO identifies the sound recording being played, it has to identify the underlying composition. For mainstream repertoire, it will have composition information in its repertoire database. But then the PRO has to determine who the owners are and what their ownership shares ("splits") are. For example, let's say a song has ten writers (not an uncommon occurrence today). Six of them are ASCAP affiliates with collective splits adding up to 60%. Three are BMI affiliates with collective splits adding up to 30%. The remaining songwriter is in Sweden, is affiliated with STIM (the Swedish PRO), and claims 10%. For each radio play, ASCAP will calculate a royalty payment and apportion 60% of that payment across those six writers according to their splits. BMI will do the same thing and disburse 30% of its royalty payment among its three affiliate songwriters and their music publishers. Finally, STIM will pay 10% to its affiliated songwriter.[16] This will all work properly if all of the PROs involved have accurate ownership and split information—which is usually the case for mainstream repertoire but, once again, not necessarily for "long tail" compositions.

Music licensing for digital radio operates in a parallel universe from traditional broadcast radio. As we mentioned previously, digital radio services do pay royalties to record labels for sound recordings. Originally those were all handled by a PRO for sound recordings called SoundExchange. SoundExchange was founded in 2000 as a division of the RIAA and then spun out as an independent nonprofit in 2003. All digital radio services were required to feed their play data to SoundExchange,[17] which would pay out royalties to record labels and aggregators representing independent artists. Later on, some digital radio services—notably Pandora—started making direct royalty deals with record labels, though SoundExchange still handles the majority of those royalty streams.

Digital radio royalty rates for sound recordings are set by law in trial-like proceedings within the US Copyright Office that are similar to those for setting rates for mechanical reproductions of musical compositions. The PROs are supposed to negotiate composition performance royalty rates with digital radio services, but if the negotiations break down, federal courts determine the rates. The Music Modernization Act of 2018, which we'll discuss in more detail in Chapter 9, contains tweaks to this process that should result in higher royalty rates for songwriters and music publishers from digital radio.

In the early days of Top 40, radio airplay was so fundamental to record sales that tailoring songs for radio airplay was synonymous with tailoring them to be hits. This was especially true for producers. By the early 1960s, record producers became known for engineering records to be radio-friendly—which meant standing out on the portable transistor radios that were ubiquitous by then.

Two 1960s producers who were especially noted for radio-oriented sound were Phil Spector, of "wall of sound" fame, and Joe Meek, best known for producing the Tornados' 1962 instrumental "Telstar." But the true home of radio-friendly production was Motown. Many engineers and producers in New York and London looked to Motown and tried to emulate its sound. Noted producer Tony Bongiovi flew from New York to Detroit regularly for several years to learn his craft before deploying it on records by Jimi Hendrix, Gloria Gaynor, the Ramones, Talking Heads, Bon Jovi, Aerosmith, and a long list of others.[xxxv]

Sometimes artists got involved too: country music legend Buck Owens had producer Ken Nelson install small mono speakers in the control booth at Capitol Studios in Los Angeles to approximate AM radio sound quality.[xxxvi] Later on, it became standard practice to equip studios with low-power radio transmitters so that producers and artists could listen to mixes in their cars in studio parking lots.[xxxvii] The British rock band Def Leppard had producer Robert John "Mutt" Lange reach new heights of obsessive perfectionism to make their 1987 album *Hysteria* radio-friendly—including recording each note of each guitar chord on a separate track of analog tape. The album took three years to produce.[xxxviii,18]

By the 1990s, producers and engineers found themselves in competition with radio engineers and equipment makers to produce the loudest, brightest possible sound—the so-called Loudness Wars. In some cases, this led to perverse outcomes. For example, the Red Hot Chili Peppers' 1999 album *Californication* was produced by Rick Rubin and mastered by engineer Vlado

Meller. Meller's and radio stations' arsenals of effects cancelled each other out, with the result that the album's lead-off single, "Scar Tissue," ended up sounding softer than the surrounding material on the air.[xxxix]

Engineers embraced the Loudness Wars in the late 1990s and early 2000s despite the larger dynamic range afforded by the CDs of the day. Dynamic range has come back, to some degree, since then.[xl]

The other type of concession to radio airplay that producers and labels made was song length. As the 1960s wore on, questions started to arise about how longer or larger pieces could get radio airplay. An eventual answer— as we discussed earlier in this chapter—was FM, as opposed to Top 40 AM. But in the meantime, the first solution to this problem was simple: edit long songs to radio length.

The first "radio edit" was Bob Dylan's "Like a Rolling Stone." Columbia Records was reluctant to release the song at all because of its 6 minute, 13 second length,[xli] but a copy leaked to DJ Bill "Rosko" Mercer, then of KLBA in Burbank, who played it at a club in Los Angeles to a rapturous audience.[xlii] The song made it onto Dylan's classic album *Highway 61 Revisited*, released in August 1965. But a month earlier, Columbia released a promotional single to radio that had the first part of the song on side A, with a fadeout at the end, and the second part on side B.[19] At first, radio played only the A side of this single. But then it bowed to pressure from fans and played the single released to retail, which contained the full song on the A side (with "Gates of Eden" on side B). The song reached no. 2 on the *Billboard* charts.

On the other hand, there was "Light My Fire," from the Doors' self-titled debut album in April 1967. The song ran more than seven minutes long. DJ Dave Diamond of KHJ, a Top 40 station in Los Angeles, asked Elektra Records for an edited version for radio airplay; Elektra owner Jac Holzman responded with a 2 minute, 52 second version that cut the extended instrumental break in the middle of the song.[xliii] It was a no. 1 hit.

Radio edits became more and more commonplace as the years went on. A radio promotional rep at a major label once said, "We'll butcher it any way you like if it gets played."[xliv] In some cases, record labels fibbed about the length of singles, such as labeling a 3 minute, 8 second song as 2 minutes, 58 seconds to get it on the air.[xlv] In the early 1970s, Top 40 stations started creating their own edits, sometimes speeding songs up in earlier attempts to create a brighter sound and to be able to claim that they played more songs per hour than their competition.

The types of edits made for radio varied. The edit of the instrumental break out of "Light My Fire" was a precursor to the slashing of Iron Butterfly's 17-minute acid-rock marathon "In-A-Gadda-Da-Vida" (1968) down to the same 2 minutes, 52 seconds as "Light My Fire." Prog-rock epics such as Yes's "Roundabout" and Pink Floyd's "Money" got the same treatment in the early 1970s. Other types of edits involved cutting or shortening intros, as in Santana's "Black Magic Woman," Steely Dan's "Do It Again," and Parliament's "Tear the Roof Off the Sucker." Sometimes verses were dropped (as in Billy Joel's "Piano Man," the Eagles' "Lyin' Eyes," and Dire Straits' "Money for Nothing").

Yet at the same time, stations started making exceptions to the three-minute rule for certain songs—like the Beatles' "Hey Jude" and Richard Harris's "MacArthur Park," both of which were released in 1968 and ran past the seven-minute mark. By 1971, a few songs that got heavy airplay even went beyond eight minutes, such as Led Zeppelin's "Stairway to Heaven" and Don McLean's "American Pie." Even some radio edits exceeded 3 minutes, such as the Temptations' "Papa Was a Rollin' Stone" (1972), which ran almost 12 minutes on the album *All Directions*; the single was only cut down to 6 minutes, 54 seconds but still reached no. 1.

By the 1980s, some "radio edits" were made in the songwriting process. As electronic tuning became widely available, it became easier for listeners to change to a greater number of stations, making station-switching more frequent; this behavior showed up in Arbitron listenership numbers. This led to a drive to produce singles that got to the chorus or main hook faster—presaging the way TikTok is influencing songwriting today (see Chapter 10). And as technology made it easier, artists began releasing more radio edits: for example, Def Leppard released no less than five radio edits of songs from *Hysteria*.

Of course, other radio edits weren't for length—they were "clean" versions designed to clear the FCC's and radio station owners' rather amorphous indecency rules. The likely first "clean" version was Aretha Franklin's 1967 smash hit "Respect," which had the backing vocalists' "Sock it to me" chorus edited out for Top 40 radio.

Despite the rise of the Internet, radio has been amazingly resilient. Nielsen (formerly Arbitron) data shows that the monthly reach of radio only decreased from nearly 100 percent in mid-1990s pre-Internet days to 93 percent in 2021.[xlvi] The biggest reason why can be expressed in one word: automobile.

More than half of radio listening takes place in cars.[20] Cars are places where drivers can't be distracted in fiddling with audio equipment; more than one person is often listening, meaning that the choice of entertainment has to satisfy everyone; and the skill of weaving in the kinds of nonmusical information that car riders need (time, weather, traffic, news) has been refined over decades.

Two recent surveys confirm that radio listeners aren't tuning in for the music as much anymore. Radio listeners responding to Jacobs Media's annual Techsurvey answered questions about the main reasons why they like radio. The top three reasons say it all: no. 1 is "Easiest to listen to in car," no. 2 is "DJs/hosts/shows," and no. 3 is "It's free." Not until no. 4 do we get "Hear favorite songs/artists." After that, none of the reasons relate to music until no. 16, "Discover new music/new artists," and no. 17, "Music surprises." The other reasons have to do with news, talk, weather, emotional connections to radio, and force of habit. As Figure 3.5 indicates, past instances of the Techsurvey indicate that the appeal of on-air personalities overtook the appeal of music on the radio sometime between 2018 and 2019.[xlvii]

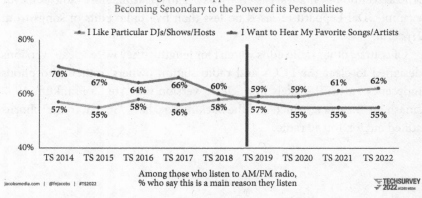

Figure 3.5 Percentages of radio listeners who cite music and on-air personalities as a main reason they listen to radio, 2014–2022. Jacobs Media, Techsurvey 2022.

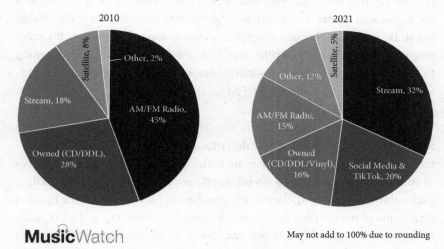

Figure 3.6   Share of weekly music listening hours among US Internet users ages 13 and above, 2010 versus 2020. MusicWatch Audiocensus Study.

Other survey data from MusicWatch indicates that Internet users are turning away from radio for music. As the Figure 3.6 shows, among the population of US Internet users ages 13 and up, the amount of time spent listening to music on AM/FM radio (including streams of stations) has plummeted from 45 percent to 15 percent from 2010 to 2020, a steeper drop than for "owned" music on physical media or downloads.

One reason why streaming has become so much more popular than radio is that it affords dedicated music fans the tools to select their own music so much more easily than buying and playing individual albums or songs. In contrast, radio can offer only a "lean-back" experience that appeals to casual music fans. At the same time, as we'll see in Chapter 9, streaming services have added plenty of lean-back features, further taking music listenership away from radio.

As a result, the reasons why people still listen to radio are things that only radio has and other forms of music distribution don't. Apart from the nonmusic content, ease of use is the biggest factor. Digital music (apart from CDs) is too complicated to listen to in cars if you're driving. That's even true today with the rise of Apple CarPlay and Google's Android Auto, so-called infotainment platforms that are designed to be seamless extensions of your iPhone or Android phone. Only 17 percent of respondents to a recent survey had Apple CarPlay installed in their vehicles; for Android Auto the figure was 11 percent. Forty-nine percent of respondents listen to digital audio in the car through their phones, compared to 73 percent for radio listening.[xlviii] And before CarPlay and Android Auto, the means for listening to digital music in cars were wonkier: Bluetooth, automakers' proprietary infotainment systems, audio cables, FM transmitters, and the dreaded cassette adapters (shown in Figure 3.7).

And the trajectory of people's relationships with cars does not bode well for radio in the long term. Streaming music users skew young, and they are more comfortable than their parents with connecting their mobile devices to automobile audio systems via Bluetooth or other methods. In the past, as each cohort of users aged, they would purchase vehicles and become the next generation of people spending their commute time listening to the car radio. However, car ownership has become less of an essential item for younger generations—who are also more frequent users of ride-sharing services. Accordingly, Spotify now provides functionality to allow passengers to select the music playing in Uber and Lyft vehicles.

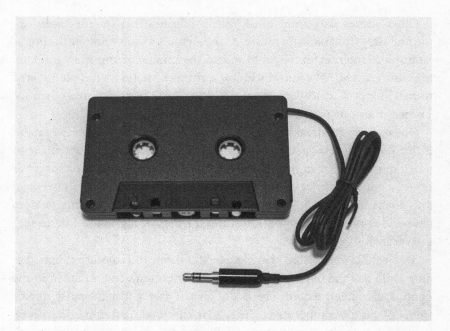

Figure 3.7 An adapter that enables portable audio devices to play through car cassette players via their headphone outputs. Bill Rosenblatt.

The fact that radio is free still matters too. Some digital music services are free, but very few have the equivalent of DJs or shows; Apple Music is the only major digital music service that features "personality" DJs. iHeartRadio is using AI-based technology, from a startup company called SuperHiFi that we'll see in Chapter 11, to create custom Internet radio feeds with tight segues from one track to the next, along with prerecorded announcements and other material between songs—all automatically, scalably, and in real time.

Conclusion

Nevertheless, radio's connection with the music industry is deteriorating. Radio has had a long history of helping to build connections with musical artists; it was the most effective way of doing this for decades. During the heyday of AOR in the 1970s and 1980s, radio forged bonds between artists and audiences in an annual cycle that ran like clockwork: Artist releases new album and announces tour. Tour date is set at local stadium. Local AOR station gets tickets and album copies to give away. Station plays artist in extra-heavy rotation[21] while asking for the 17th caller every hour. The day before the local stadium gig, artist drops by station to chat and maybe take listener calls. Artist plays gig to sold-out crowd at stadium, then moves on to next town. Repeat next year. (No new album? Release live album from last year's tour.)

In those days, certain DJs served as the glue between artists and audiences. Through labels' promotional efforts, key jocks would get to know the artists, in some cases "discovering" them, and champion them on the air—as Kid Leo Travagliante of WMMS in Cleveland did with Bruce Springsteen and Maxanne Sartori of WBCN in Boston did with the Cars, to name just two examples. The trust that the audiences placed in those jocks translated into receptivity to the new artists.

Those relationships are rare in today's radio, where programmers (not DJs) select music after major amounts of due diligence from tip sheets, focus groups, and other data sources including streaming activity. And commercial loads on broadcast radio remain much higher than on any type of digital music service: SNL Kagan measured the average ad load on broadcast radio in music formats as 14 minutes per hour in 2018,[xlix] compared to less than 3 minutes per hour on Internet radio.[l] Meanwhile, the job of building relationships with artists has largely migrated to social media—where the addressable audience is much larger and creators can communicate directly with fans.

Record labels still pay attention to radio, but that attention is diminished amid all of the promotional effort aimed at social media, not to mention streaming, and because radio—at least terrestrial broadcast radio—generates no direct revenue for labels. As a business, radio will continue to be gradually marginalized alongside other music distribution channels.

4

Vinyl

Spin the Black Circle—Pearl Jam

The 12-inch long-playing (LP) record has enjoyed the longest duration as the dominant recorded music format in the market—more than the 78s and wax cylinders that preceded it, and more than the cassettes and CDs that came later. Vinyl ruled for over 30 years, compared with just over 20 for both the 78 and the CD.

Why is that? It's because the LP put a combination of quality attributes and unique features together into a package with a value to consumers that remains unsurpassed, and almost all LP players are compatible with its close cousin, the 45 rpm single. This helps explain why vinyl has come back from oblivion. Vinyl brings in more than $1 billion to the music industry today, and consumer research from MusicWatch has found that more than 17 million Americans buy vinyl—fully a third as many as those who purchased digital downloads at the height of their popularity.[i] As we'll explain in this chapter, we're unlikely to see a revival in other physical music formats that rivals that of vinyl.

Attempts to create phonographic discs that played longer than 78s date back to 1904.[ii] In 1931, RCA Victor released a 12-inch disc that played for ten minutes a side at 33 1/3 rpm. But the product suffered from various problems, including poor durability: discs could only be played a few times before they wore out. Lack of durability and the Great Depression—players were expensive—killed it off in 1933. RCA Victor's arch-rival Columbia Records, which in 1938 became a division of the CBS broadcasting company that it co-founded in 1927, tried releasing 10-inch discs at 33 1/3 rpm around the same time and failed for similar reasons.[iii]

Key Changes. Howie Singer and Bill Rosenblatt, Oxford University Press. © Howie Singer and Bill Rosenblatt 2023.
DOI: 10.1093/oso/9780197656891.003.0004

Columbia succeeded when it tried again fifteen years later. It introduced the long-playing 12-inch "microgroove" record at a launch event at the Waldorf-Astoria Hotel in New York City in June 1948. It was the culmination of eight years of research led by Peter Goldmark, a Hungarian who fled the Nazis and emigrated to the United States in the mid-1930s.

Goldmark's team at Columbia found that polyvinyl chloride (PVC) had sufficient density and durability to hold grooves that were 0.001 inch (1 mil) wide, a third as wide as those in 78s. PVC had already been used for 78s during World War II due to shortages of (cheaper) shellac. 33 1/3 rpm was chosen as the speed; Columbia and other labels already had equipment for cutting discs at that speed for making "V-disc" records that were sent to soldiers overseas during the war. The combination of narrower grooves and slower speed enabled each side of a 12-inch disc to hold more than 22 minutes of audio, compared to four to five minutes for 78s.[1]

The increased capacity of the new format meant fewer record flips, no premature fadeouts, and less shelf space needed for recordings; it also meant lower prices. For example, a recording of a Tchaikovsky symphony that took up five 78s sold for $7.25, while a single-LP recording of the same performance cost a third less.[iv] PVC was also much more durable than shellac: it did not shatter, and the grooves required a stylus with a tracking force of only a few grams, leading to less wear over time.

More importantly, records cut in vinyl[2] had sound quality that was far superior to 78s and AM radio; it was even better than the FM radio that was in its infancy at the time (see Chapter 3). When processed through electronic equalization, vinyl records could reproduce roughly the entire range of human hearing, up to 20,000 Hz (or as they were called then, cycles per second). And vinyl itself introduced much less surface noise than the shellac used in most 78s.

Columbia introduced phonographs that played LPs in 1948. Shortly afterward, it released several albums on LP, starting with a recording of the Mendelssohn Violin Concerto by Nathan Milstein and the New York Philharmonic under the direction of Bruno Walter.[v]

Columbia offered an "upgrade path" to make the new format easy to adopt. It got Philco to make a turntable with amplifier that could connect to the loudspeaker of an existing 78 rpm–compatible phonograph or radio. As we'll see, this was before "high fidelity" (hi-fi) components became available. You'd take your radio or 78 player to an electronics store, they would install a jack for the speaker, and you'd plug your Philco LP player in. Columbia sold these for $30 (later reduced to $10) or gave them away with the purchase of several of their LPs.[vi] And they offered "starter libraries" of music with purchases of their more expensive record players.[vii]

Finally, Columbia offered to license the technology to both other record labels and electronics manufacturers, to forestall format wars and increase consumer confidence in the new format. But the tactic didn't quite work. While other electronics companies had record players that played LPs available at the launch in 1948, and almost every label took the license from Columbia, one didn't: RCA Victor. RCA expressed interest initially but decided to put out its own competing vinyl microgroove format: a 7-inch disc that played at 45 rpm and had a bigger spindle hole.

RCA Victor launched the 7-inch 45 in March 1949. RCA had actually started making 45s in December 1948; more than 100 titles were available to the public when the format launched.[viii] The first batch of 45s covered myriad genres, including R&B (Arthur "Big Boy" Crudup's "That's All Right, Mama"), country (Eddie Arnold's "Texarkana Baby"), Yiddish ("A Klein Melamedl (The Little Teacher)" by Cantor Saul Meisels), and children's records ("Pee-Wee the Piccolo" by Paul Wing). Initial 45s were pressed on colored vinyl until labels switched to black for cost reasons.

RCA initially positioned 45s as direct competitors to LPs, releasing classical music works on multi-45 sets. The 7-inch discs had sound quality that was actually superior to LPs, thanks to the higher speed and other factors. But their capacity was similar to that of 78s. RCA also sold a record changer for 45s, so that users could listen to the equivalent of an LP side without getting up—and if they were willing to put up with fadeouts and record-changing silences during classical concertos, symphonies, and other longer works.

RCA's creation of a format war caused confusion in the market, which put the brakes on sales. The record industry's revenue plummeted from $204 million in 1947 to $158 million in 1949—a drop of almost one-quarter in two years, the worst industry downturn since the Great Depression. Finally, in 1950, RCA gave in and licensed the LP technology from Columbia.[ix]

Of course, all labels eventually embraced both microgroove formats. The vast majority of record players could play all three speeds (33, 45, and 78)[3] and came with adapters so that 45s could fit the thin spindles for LPs and 78s. RCA designed a plastic adapter, known as the "spider," that you could buy cheaply at the record store and attach to 45s individually when you lost the adapter that came with your turntable (see Figure 4.1).

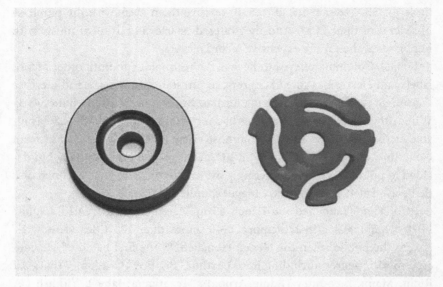

Figure 4.1 Adapters for playing 45-rpm singles on turntables: A metal adapter to use with your turntable (L) and a plastic "spider" meant to be attached to the records themselves (R). Bill Rosenblatt.

Unlike most format wars, which tend to end up with one (or neither) format succeeding and the other (or both) failing, each of the two vinyl formats eventually found its own niche: the 45 wasn't successful for classical music, but it became popular for pop music singles a few years later. Bill Haley's "Rock Around the Clock" was the format's breakout moment when it sold 3 million singles in 1955.

RCA also introduced the extended play (EP) format in 1952. The EP used the same form factor as the 45 but with narrower grooves and more compressed sound levels to achieve a capacity of 7.5 minutes per side, allowing for two songs on each side. EPs became more popular in Europe than in America, such as for Beatles records that are now valuable collectors' items.[4]

The accelerated release of high-quality titles on vinyl by many labels after 1948 was enabled by another technology developed around the same time: tape recording. As we'll see in Chapter 5, recording onto acetate tape coated with magnetic iron oxide was first developed in Germany in the 1930s and brought over to the United States after World War II.

Tape recorders had several major advantages over the disc-cutting technology then in use in recording studios. Unlike discs, tapes could have arbitrarily long recording times, limited only by the sizes of reels and by the recording speed, which, as always, traded off duration against sound quality. They could be edited easily with a razor blade and adhesive tape. They eventually had multiple tracks, which enabled multiple audio sources (instruments and vocals) to be recorded separately, yet in sync, and mixed down later to create a final recording.

Finally, tape recording setups cost much less than disc lathe setups. This led to an expansion of the recording industry as many entrepreneurs set up new labels. The list of labels that arose in the late 1940s through early 1950s includes Jac Holzman's Elektra, Ahmet Ertegun and Herb Abramson's Atlantic, Vivian Carter and James Bracken's Vee-Jay, Sam Phillips's Sun, Leonard and Phil Chess's Chess, and Bob Weinstock's Prestige. When Holzman started Elektra as a folk music label, he bought a Magnecord tape deck and a single Telefunken microphone for a few hundred dollars, built other equipment himself, and sent his tapes out to major labels for mastering and pressing. The major labels at that time (Columbia, RCA Victor, Decca, and Capitol) were eager to rent out their pressing plants to upstart labels: the shift from 78s to LPs meant that they had far fewer records to press and therefore had excess capacity.

The final piece of the format standardization puzzle fell into place in the mid-1950s: audio equalization. Record-cutting techniques included processing of audio signals that attenuated lower frequencies and boosted higher frequencies. This was done so that groove width could be reduced, leading to increased recording time, less hiss, lower bass distortion, and less risk of damage to the vinyl as the stylus traversed it. Equalization was the process of making those adjustments electronically at recording time and compensating for them on playback. The scheme for attenuating or boosting the audio signal by different amounts at different frequencies is called an equalization curve.

Different record companies originally used different equalization curves. To get the best sound quality, a consumer had to have playback equipment that switched among several curves and had to select the one used by the label of the record being played. For example, the Pilot HF-42 receiver from 1957,[5] shown in Figure 4.2, had a knob for choosing among five different equalization curves. To solve this problem, the industry formed a trade association, the Recording Industry Association of America (RIAA), in 1952. The RIAA designated a standard in 1954 based on RCA Victor's curve; this became known as "RIAA equalization." The RIAA curve became an

Figure 4.2 The Pilot HF-42 mono high fidelity receiver from 1957 featured five different equalization settings.

international standard by 1955,[x] and it was used for both LPs and 45s. Phono amplifiers made after the late 1950s supported only RIAA equalization and no longer had switches for selecting curves.

The last significant and successful innovation in vinyl technology was stereo. The move to stereo began soon after RIAA equalization became standard. As we'll see in Chapter 5, tape was the first consumer music format to go stereo in the mid-1950s. This led to a drive to implement it in vinyl. Recording tape in stereo was merely a matter of designing recording and playback heads that divided the tape up into tracks for left and right stereo channels. Cutting and playing records in stereo was a bigger technical challenge.

Yet it only took a few years for the industry to produce a standard stereo vinyl system. That's because a few different systems for cutting stereo discs had been developed, and it was only a matter of choosing one of them. One was the so-called binaural system, which used cutting heads spaced 1 11/16 (1.6875) inches apart, so that the left channel was recorded on the outer band and the right channel was recorded on the inner band.[xi] This required either two separate standard tonearms or special binaural tonearms, such as the model shown in Figure 4.3, and it cut in half the amount of recording time per side. The scheme was rejected as impractical.

Other systems used a single cutting head to record a stereo signal into a single groove, requiring only one tonearm and cartridge for playback. One such system, the Vertical-Lateral system, used up-and-down (vertical) motions for one channel and side-to-side (lateral) motions for the other. It suffered from differences in sound quality and crosstalk between the two channels, but it enabled easier compatibility with mono recordings. Another was the 45/45

Figure 4.3 The Livingston Electronic Corp. two-headed tonearm from 1951 for playing binaural records.

system, which was invented by Alan Blumlein at EMI in Britain in 1931 and developed into a commercial record-cutting system at Westrex, a division of AT&T. The system worked by making cuts at opposing 45-degree angles (one at 45 degrees from the top and the other 135 degrees from the top).[xii] With its superior sound quality, the Westrex 45/45 system won out and became standard in 1957.[xiii] By the following year, most labels had stereo recordings available.[xiv]

There was only one more attempt at major innovation in vinyl recording technology: quadraphonic, or four-channel, sound. It was one of the most notable technology market failures of the twentieth century.

Quad, introduced in the early 1970s, was an attempt to capture the three-dimensional ambiance of musical performances by adding a pair of rear speakers to the usual stereo left/right pair. There was a lot of hype around quad, but its launch was a chaotic mess compared to the relatively smooth launch of the LP in 1948.

The biggest problem was that there was no single standard: there were three competing quad systems for vinyl in the US market.[6] Two of them used standard tonearms and cartridges, while the third promised the best four-channel audio experience but required consumers to buy new equipment. None of the three systems was compatible with the others, and different labels released records in different quad systems. Some stereo amplifiers and receivers could play all three formats, while others could only play a subset.

It was a train wreck. Consumers were alienated, confused, and not seduced enough by the sound experience or by gimmicks in playback equipment—such as the joystick in the receiver shown in Figure 4.4—to lay out the money for new receivers, speakers, and possibly turntables. Quad evaporated by 1977–1978. Of course, multichannel audio lives on today in the form of surround-sound systems for home theater;[7] but few serious audiophiles used quad equipment or discs for music listening.

Otherwise, the technologies used to create vinyl records—Columbia's microgroove LP, RCA's 7-inch 45, RIAA equalization, and 45/45 stereo—were established by the late 1950s and have remained largely the same since. Apart from quad, other variations over the years have been minor, such as 12-inch 45 rpm singles or EPs with "hotter" sound quality released to radio stations and club DJs, and various types of high-quality manufacturing processes and vinyl substances for audiophiles.[8]

Figure 4.4 The Harman/Kardon 75 + quadraphonic receiver from the mid-1970s featured a joystick balance control. David Wolfson/Aural Pleasure Records.

Channels

The industry's transition to LPs and 45s caused a dramatic expansion of distribution channels to reach wider audiences beyond music aficionados and electronics hobbyists to the general public. One could almost say that the LP did for recorded music what big-box retail did for all sorts of consumer products starting in the early 1960s (when Target, Kmart, and Walmart all started).

The first new outlets were mass-market retail stores beyond the individually-owned record shops that sold 78s. Vinyl began to be sold in variety stores (a.k.a. 5 & 10 cent stores), drugstores, and supermarkets in the early 1950s. Independent subdistributors, or "rack jobbers," would select titles to fill racks at those stores and would handle payments and returns to record labels.

The first rack jobber to distribute records was Elliot Wexler's Music Merchants in Philadelphia in 1952; Music Merchants had been a distributor of sheet music. Next was David Handleman's Handleman Company, a distributor of drugstore items in Detroit. Handleman's business took off; the company kept going as a distributor of CDs as well as videos and computer software until it shut down in 2008.[xv]

Rack jobbers bought albums from labels, typically at 10 percent discounts, and handled sales and payments for the retailers. They initially focused on budget releases and later expanded to all releases. The volume of business they did enabled them to offer lower prices than traditional record shops. By the early 1960s, the volumes of sales through rack jobbers exceeded those of specialty record stores. Their high volumes enabled them to achieve 100 percent return privileges with labels, as opposed to the 10 percent that specialty retailers got.[xvi] Rack jobbers soon organized a trade association: the National Association of Recording Merchandisers (NARM), now known as the Music Business Association (a.k.a. Music Biz), started in 1958.

Rack jobbers were the primary logistical forces in expanding the market for recorded music to the mass market. And as the volume of sales they facilitated grew, so did their power in the industry. They occupied a link in the supply chain between the labels' own distributors (for those labels that did their own distribution; not all did) and the retail stores' own channels, a link that would eventually expand outward.

Retailers gave rack jobbers carte blanche to stock their racks with whatever product they thought would sell. Rack jobbers were more discerning about musical product than, say, department store buyers, but not necessarily by much—particularly as rock & roll came in and the age disparity widened between record company artists and repertoire (A&R) people and rack jobbers. A growing number of record labels gave rack jobbers more and more product to select and place in stores. So, inevitably, they began to place only records that were already hits or were by big-name artists. This accelerated the positive feedback loop that Top 40 radio engendered, which—as we saw in the last chapter—led to the creation of pop stars. In fact, some rack jobbers even supplied copies of new records to radio stations (as well as the usual "incentives" to play them on the air), instead of labels doing so; they would only push the most famous acts. As a result, the virtuous cycle spun even faster.

As rack jobbing grew more and more lucrative, the boundaries among record companies, rack jobbers, and retailers began to blur. Rack jobbers began to compete with labels' own distribution arms. The labels themselves built multitiered distribution systems around the country. Some labels' distribution arms began to act as rack jobbers (for other labels) on the side. Suppliers of records for jukeboxes, known as "one-stops," began to compete with rack jobbers. And as we'll see, rack jobbers eventually moved into retail themselves.

The labels soon found themselves at odds with rack jobbers, given their lack of cooperation in pushing the products that the labels wanted them to and the liberal return policies they negotiated on records that didn't sell.[9,xvii] Label executives would assail rack jobbers for their low risk tolerance for selling titles that weren't big hits by established artists.

One tactic that labels used to regain some measure of control was "cutouts": records that weren't selling well and that labels would delete from their catalogs. As hard as it may be to grasp today, with digital music services building up vast catalogs of "every record ever recorded,"[10] record labels started doing this routinely in the early 1970s. They would sometimes literally cut notches into the jackets of deleted albums and ship them into retail channels at deep discounts. This caused all sorts of logistical and bookkeeping headaches throughout the supply chain, not to mention the stigma that artists would feel when their albums were deleted.[xviii] Labels' other supply-chain tactics included throwing in titles by lesser-known artists for free along with supplies of hit records to rack jobbers, in addition to the kinds of inducements to rack jobbers that radio DJs and program directors were enjoying, as we saw in Chapter 3.[xix]

Soon after the rise of rack jobbers came discount record store chains. Sam Gutowitz started his Sam Goody store shortly after the launch of the LP as both a retail store on 49th Street in Manhattan and a mail-order business that took advantage of vinyl's lighter weight and smaller package size than 78s. Sam Goody sold records at 30 percent discount from retail prices, a move that enraged record labels.[xx] Courts ruled that the labels were powerless to dictate Goody's prices, so they tried to stop him through tactics such as refusing him return privileges and credit. Nevertheless, Gutowitz expanded to a chain of retail stores in the early 1950s; his business grew rapidly and soon accounted for 5 percent of the total record business.

The second discount chain was Grover Cleveland Sayre's Musicland, which opened its first store in Minneapolis in 1955. With their lower prices and big selection, the two chains expanded the market for vinyl even further, despite the labels' protestations. (The two chains would consolidate under the same ownership in 1978, using the Sam Goody name.)

The next new retail channel for vinyl was mail-order record clubs. Columbia Records started the Columbia Record Club in 1955; RCA Victor (partnering with both Reader's Digest and Book-of-the-Month Club) and Capitol followed with their own clubs soon thereafter.[xxi]

Labels had several reasons to start record clubs. The main one was to compete with emerging retail channels. Other entities besides labels had started record clubs by mail, such as the Music Appreciation Club, an offshoot of the Book-of-the-Month Club.[xxii] The clubs enabled labels to expand their retail distribution to rural areas and compete with the discounters' mail-order businesses. Otherwise, in a sense, labels set up record clubs to compete with their own existing wholesale channels—and to be able to charge full retail price while eliminating middlemen.

Record clubs became famous for their "twelve records for a penny" deals: you filled out a postage-paid postcard (which probably fell out of a magazine), taped a penny to it, and put it in a mailbox; a box of LPs arrived at your front door a couple of weeks later. But each month thereafter, for the next couple of years, you got another record in the mail, for which you were billed at full retail price, unless you wanted to pay for postage to return it. This wasn't the labels' original idea; Book-of-the-Month Club had started it in the 1920s.[xxiii] This practice, known as "negative option billing," became controversial and was outlawed in some countries outside the United States.

Each of the labels initially only made their own records available through the clubs, but the labels began—grudgingly—cross-licensing to one another's clubs in 1958 to stave off third-party competition. Cross-licensing increased through the 1960s until almost every club offered records from the other clubs' labels—with the notable exception that BMG Music Service (formerly RCA Victor Record Club) and Columbia House (formerly Columbia Record Club) did not cross-license their label siblings' music to each other.[11]

Record clubs were moderate successes for the labels for a long time, until the internet came along to replace them. By 1955, there were a dozen clubs with a million members among them.[xxiv] By the early 1960s, record club sales accounted for 15 percent of total industry sales volumes, compared to 27.4 percent through NARM-affiliated rack jobbers. By the mid-1970s, the clubs' membership had grown to 3 million, with their demographic skewing older than typical retail buyers.[xxv] RCA Victor and Columbia were the two largest clubs by far—large enough that the Federal Trade Commission, at the behest of the other major labels, started to investigate them for anticompetitive business practices.[xxvi]

In general, the expansion of record sales to the mass retail market led to a profusion of channels that filled the supply chain with various convoluted and contentious relationships—often to the benefit of consumers. Discounters drove prices down and led labels to seek ways to circumvent them; this led to budget releases. The discounters would also engage in a practice known as transshipping—buying unsold inventory from smaller retailers (who weren't allowed much in the way of return privileges with labels) at steep discounts and selling them to the public at their normal discount prices.

Meanwhile, some rack jobbers grew so large that they began to rival the major labels' distribution arms in size; for example, Transcontinental, a rollup of rack jobbers, had amassed 20 percent of the retail market by 1967.[xxvii] By the 1970s, rack jobbers had moved into retail themselves and had gotten control of 80 percent of the business.[xxviii] Musicland had started as a record distributor (Heilicher Brothers) in Minnesota. Russ Solomon, founder of Tower Records, started out as a rack jobber who sold records in his father's drugstore in Sacramento in 1960.

Around the same time as the labels started record clubs, jukeboxes that played 45s became available, making them the next major channel for vinyl. Jukeboxes existed before vinyl, but 45s expanded their market significantly. As we saw in Chapter 2, the first jukebox of the type that we recognize today—with a single turntable, a library of dozens of records, and a mechanism for delivering a selected record to the turntable—originated in the late 1920s and played 78s.[xxix]

The leading makers of jukeboxes were Automated Musical Instrument Co. (AMI), Wurlitzer, Seeburg, and Rock-Ola. (The name of the latter had nothing to do with rock & roll, which had yet to appear; the company founder was a Canadian named David Rockola, and the "-Ola" was a pun on "Victrola.") Seeburg introduced the first jukebox to play 45s, the M100B, in 1950; it had a capacity of 100 songs (both sides of 50 records). The HF100G shown in Figure 4.5, introduced in 1953, was a more durable model with metal replacing many of the wooden parts. Many subsequent 45-playing jukeboxes had capacities of 200 songs. This was much more than jukeboxes that played 78s, most of which had capacities of 40–48 selections.[xxx]

The advent of 45s led to major expansion in the jukebox market as smaller units with more music capacity became available. Collectively, the leading four makers shipped 213,000 jukeboxes that played only 78s during the period of the mid-1940s through early 1950s. Then, from the early 1950s through mid-1960s, the big four sold almost triple that amount—618,000 jukeboxes—that played only 45s. (Another 67,000 could play both 45s and 78s or could be configured for either.)[xxxi] In other words, on a year-by-year basis the installed base of jukeboxes roughly doubled in size once 45s became available.

Figure 4.5 The Seeburg HF100G jukebox, from 1957, at the Silverball Retro Arcade in Asbury Park, NJ. It was one of the first jukeboxes to play 45-rpm records. Bill Rosenblatt.

Much of the jukebox industry was controlled by mobsters during its heyday. David Rockola had mob connections; Sam Giancana took over ownership of AMI in 1949; Meyer Lansky owned a portion of Wurlitzer and controlled distribution of the company's machines in the New York City area.

Various other local jukebox distributors were run by mobsters. In addition to being lucrative themselves, jukeboxes were a convenient way to force venues that bought jukeboxes to play records by artists who had mob backing.[xxxii]

Ten years after vinyl's introduction, the market for phonograph records had recovered from the format-war slump and grown to nearly $400 million, almost double its size in 1947. 45s outsold LPs in unit volume, but LPs brought in more revenue: In 1958, LPs accounted for 24 percent of the market in unit volume, 45s did 68 percent, and EPs did 5 percent. But LPs accounted for 58 percent of the market by dollars spent while 45s accounted for 36 percent and EPs 4 percent. Sales of 78s had all but disappeared by then.[xxxiii]

As we'll see in Chapter 5, the vinyl market started to fade with the ascendancy of cassettes. Vinyl revenues continued a slow decline until their nadir in 2006, when the RIAA recorded rounding-error revenues of $26 million (compared with over $9 billion for CDs) and Tower Records closed its retail stores. But then, as we know now, vinyl slowly started to come back.

The rebirth of vinyl in the 2010s saved independent record stores from oblivion after the rise of big-box and online retail. The number of indie record stores is now growing again,[xxxiv] and vinyl record clubs are even back again.[xxxv] Many consumer electronics makers sell turntables, with newer companies like Pro-Ject and U-Turn joining established brands like Denon and Sony, and prices for audiophile models reaching up into the stratosphere.

The RIAA reported annual revenue from vinyl in 2022 as more than $1.2 billion, but the true figure is likely to be larger than that amount. Vinyl probably accounts for more than 10 percent of total US recorded music revenue. One reason for this is the used vinyl market. The RIAA doesn't keep track of this; no money from used record sales goes to labels or artists. But used vinyl is too big to ignore.

Most indie retailers also stock used vinyl. Our own research[xxxvi] has found that indie stores sell used vinyl that adds up to about 60 percent of the number of units that the RIAA reports as new vinyl sales. The two biggest online used vinyl marketplaces, Discogs.com and eBay, pull in about 40 percent of the sales numbers that the RIAA reports.[12] And we haven't even talked about flea markets or garage sales.

Also consider that the average sales price of used vinyl (in stores) is not far below new vinyl prices: $23 for used versus $25 for new.[xxxvii] (Some used LPs are priced very low, while others are expensive collector's items.) This all means that the total vinyl market by revenue could be as much as double the revenue that the RIAA reports.[13] In the United States, it's a $2 billion market in a $16 billion industry. Although the latest sales numbers indicate that vinyl sales growth slowed down in 2022 compared with their rapid rise through 2021,[xxxviii] that's still much bigger than anyone looking at the market in the late 2000s would have predicted.

Consumers' use of recorded music changed dramatically with the transition from 78s to vinyl. The biggest catalyst was audio quality. The breakthrough sound quality of LPs made it conceivable, for the first time ever, that recorded music could sound as good as live. It shifted the perception of prerecorded music from "Wow, we can hear a music performance!" to "Wow, we can hear a music performance that could sound like the real thing!"[xxxix] It also shifted preferences in the tone quality of phonographs from heavily colored ("soft, mellow, and flabby"[xl]) sound to sonic realism.

This shift coalesced with the postwar era's economic prosperity and flight from apartments in cities to houses in the suburbs, as well as with adults' increasing alienation from radio as it began to court the teenage Top 40 audience. The result was the hi-fi craze. Hi-fi equipment makers began to produce components—turntables, preamps, amps, and speakers—that consumers could select and combine into complete hi-fi systems. Entrepreneurs such as Saul Marantz, Sidney Harman, Bernard Kardon, and Avery Fisher started eponymous companies that made only hi-fi components, in contrast to electronics companies like Philco, GE, and RCA that made cheaper record players for the masses or big console systems for the living room. Hi-fi systems originally appealed mainly to classical music aficionados but eventually spread to fans of all music genres.

The market for hi-fi components exploded through the 1950s. One way to gauge how quickly this happened is to look at the catalogs of Lafayette Radio Electronics, a major retail and mail-order chain that ceased operations in 1981. Lafayette's 1947 catalog listed electronic parts, wooden cabinets for audio equipment, turntables designed to fit into the cabinets, and stand-alone record players; otherwise the only audio components it listed were PA systems for schools and churches. But by 1951, Lafayette's catalog listed 12 pages of component tuners, amplifiers, tuner/amp combos, turntables, tonearms, and speakers. And in 1959, when stereo had become available, stereo components took up 76 pages and were featured at the front of the catalog. Lafayette offered name-brand component stereo systems at prices up to $730 (about $7,300 today) for a phono system with preamp, power amp, a turntable, tonearm and cartridge, speakers, and speaker cabinets. Adding an AM/FM tuner would have brought the price up over $900 ($9,000 today).

With hi-fi components, there was more emphasis on sound quality than on furniture style, more knobs and dials, lighter tonearms, and heavier platters, as well as escalating price tags. Aficionados attended hi-fi trade shows and constructed listening rooms in their houses with optimal place-ment of speakers and chairs, and acoustic wall treatments. "Demonstration records" were released featuring sound recordings and effects that showed off hi-fi systems' capabilities. *High Fidelity* magazine debuted in 1951, followed by *Audio* (formerly *Audio Engineering*) in 1954 and *HiFi and Music Review* in 1958 (later *Stereo Review*). As explained in the previous chapter, transistors came along in the mid-1950s; they eventually replaced vacuum tubes in hi-fi equipment, although a faction of audiophiles insisted—and still insist to this day—that tubes sound better.

As Figure 4.6 shows, once the record industry recovered from the LP/45 format war in the mid-1950s, the hi-fi component industry was about half as large as recorded music by revenue and grew at about the same rate. It con-tinued to grow at more than 20 percent per year into the 1960s. The audio component industry continued in this vein until 1980, when it peaked at $1.8 billion,[xli] and then started to decline.

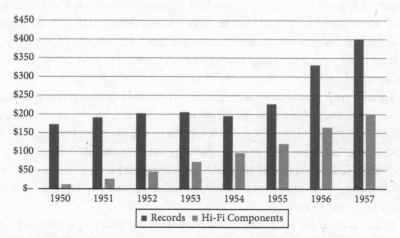

Figure 4.6 Annual revenues from recorded music and hi-fi components, millions of dollars, 1950–1957. Data sources: RIAA (recorded music), Institute of High Fidelity Manufacturers (hi-fi components). Bill Rosenblatt.

Although hi-fi turntables played 45s, consumers reacted very differently to 45s than to LPs. 45s were all about teenagers in the 1950s and 1960s; the catalysts for change were low prices and small, portable form factors.

The 45 was another contribution to teenagers' ability to listen to their music independently of their parents, the biggest—as we saw in Chapter 3— being transistor radios. They were cheap: prices of 45s started at 65 cents, equivalent to about $6.50 today, compared to LPs, which hovered around the $4 mark ($40 today) in the 1950s. And they were portable, in the sense that you could take a few 45s over to your friend's house to play them on their record player.

Transistors caused prices of consumer electronics to drop and sizes to shrink, so that teenagers could get their own record players; but the idea of a truly portable record playing experience remained elusive. It was impossible to play records in the car—though not for lack of trying: Columbia and RCA both tried to introduce shock-mounted under-dash automobile record players in the late 1950s, but they could not overcome the inherent mechanical problems of playing a record on a device attached to a vehicle moving down a road. By the 1960s, battery-operated portable record players began to appear, but they had limited uses: you could carry them around, but you had to stay in one place in order to listen to them, and you had to replace the batteries often. Transistorized record players that ran on AC power and were the size of briefcases, like the GE Wildcat shown in Figure 4.7, were introduced in the late 1960s and were more popular; but they were more likely to sit on a teenager's bedroom shelf than to be lugged over to friends' houses. As we'll see in the next chapter, the tape cartridge formats that were emerging around that time would supply portable music on demand.

Today's vinyl renaissance is definitely a consumer-driven phenomenon; it is not a product of technological breakthroughs, changes in economics, or quirks in copyright law. It began as a hipster trend, as one of many quests for post-ironic "authenticity" and "artisanality" that manifested themselves in revivals of fedora hats, craft-brewed beer, fixed-gear bikes, and farm-to-table donuts. But vinyl would not be a billion-dollar industry today if it were still confined to hipsters.

Reasons cited for vinyl's renewed popularity include its purported better sound quality than digital music. But that's largely a myth, at least today. It's true that the first generations of CDs and commercial digital downloads were made with immature encoding technology and/or at low bitrates, so they

Figure 4.7 GE Wildcat portable stereo record player, circa 1970. CC BY 2.0, Bradley Stemke.

didn't sound that great. But nowadays, encoding techniques have improved, bitrates have risen, and audiophile-grade digital–analog converters have been introduced. Digital data storage has become cheap enough so that users who care about sound quality can store large collections of digital music in "lossless" codecs such as FLAC on garden-variety PCs. In other words, digital files can sound superb today. And most young fans' playback equipment or earbuds aren't good enough to tell the difference anyway. Finally, much recent vinyl was recorded digitally in the first place and had to be converted back to analog to make LPs.

The factor that most likely explains the renewed interest in vinyl is that it restores a sense of ownership to music fans. In the 2016 book *The End of Ownership*, two legal scholars, Aaron Perzanowski of Case Western Reserve and Jason Schultz of NYU, explain that digital files bought online aren't really "owned" in the legal sense, and they advocate for reforms to establish ownership of digital content in law. They present consumer research suggesting that people expect ownership rights, even though they might not actually get them.[xlii]

The problem is that consumers don't feel a sense of ownership in digital files that merely take up space on their hard drives or stream to their portable devices—even if those files don't have restrictions on use through digital rights management (DRM; see Chapter 8). Despite record labels' efforts to create digital "packages" out of digital music downloads, piles of bits are impossible to touch, admire, manipulate, sell,[14] trade, and lovingly organize on your shelves. People didn't feel that they had built a collection of anything after spending 99 cents on iTunes hundreds or thousands of times, and they certainly don't feel ownership of music they listen to on streaming services. Time will tell whether the current nonfungible token (NFT) phenomenon, which we discuss in the Afterword, will replicate this sense of ownership in the digital realm convincingly enough for a critical mass of fans.

LPs, on the other hand, are often true physical art objects and collectibles. They also bring an almost ritualistic sense of occasion in playing them, including a modicum of skill necessary to place the tonearm without damaging the record (most turntables sold today are manual). They make for a more engaged listening experience than tapping a button on a phone to start an MP3 or Spotify playlist, or even than shoving a cassette into a deck or a CD into a slot. LP cover art is much more attractive than the packaging for cassettes and CDs. As Dave Grohl of Nirvana and Foo Fighters said, in a statement for Record Store Day 2015,[15]

> Nothing makes me prouder than watching my daughters spin that first Roky Erickson LP one of them picked out for their very own on one of our weekend trips to the record store. Or to watch the reverence they have as they handle their Beatles vinyl. How carefully they replace the albums into their sleeves, making sure they're placed back onto the shelf in the proper sequence. Watching them realize how crucial and intertwined every part of this experience is, I relive the magic of my earliest experiences with vinyl singles and albums, their artwork, liners notes etc. all over again and again.[xliii]

In fact, vinyl is far more popular than CDs in the used market, even though LPs' sound quality deteriorates with use a lot faster than CDs. Discogs, for example, lists over 46 million vinyl items in its marketplace at this time of writing, compared to 21 million CDs, and the average price of a used LP is considerably higher than the average price of a used CD. It also bears mentioning that many fans buy vinyl without even necessarily intending to play it: one study showed that only 50 percent of vinyl buyers in 2022 actually owned record players.[xliv]

Finally, it's worth noting that while the vinyl renaissance was originally mostly confined to classic rock and a bit of jazz, recent Discogs monthly sales charts have seen more current pop, R&B, and hip-hop titles. This also suggests that vinyl's renewed appeal is broadening beyond hipsters. Today's vinyl fans have already picked up their copies of *Dark Side of the Moon*, *Rumours*, and *Thriller*;[16] now they're ready for something new, and record labels are meeting that demand with new releases.[17] And the interest in vinyl has reached the mainstream: in 2022, Taylor Swift's *Midnights* sold 945,000 copies on vinyl, almost enough to go Platinum on vinyl sales alone.[18,xlv]

Creators

Recording studio technology such as multitrack tape recording, room-filling mixing consoles, and audio processing tools had, of course, incalculable effects on the creative output of musicians from the 1940s through 1980s; so did electronic instrument technologies. But the LP's format itself also unleashed a lot of musical creativity due to its length and sound quality.

Many people point to 1966–1967 albums such as the Beatles' *Sgt. Pepper's Lonely Hearts Club Band*, *The Who Sell Out*, and the Moody Blues' *Days of Future Passed* as exemplars of pop music artists using the 12-inch LP as a canvas for something greater than a collection of three-minute songs, although some critics point to even earlier examples such as the Beach Boys' *Little Deuce Coupe* (1963, songs about cars) and *The Ventures in Space* (1964, songs about outer space).

Yet record labels turned to various styles of music long before the mid-1960s to exploit the creative possibilities of the LP as a unit. Apart from classical music, the first of these were Broadway musicals and movie soundtracks. These existed as multidisc albums on 78s, but they were naturals for the LP—as natural as concertos or symphonies. Sales of movie musical soundtracks such as *Oklahoma!*, *The King and I*, and *The Benny Goodman Story* from the mid-1950s got labels interested in the genre, so they actually helped bring musicals to life to drive sales of albums.

By the early 1960s, soundtracks had become multimillion-selling albums, leading record labels to create more supply. CBS put up the money for the entire production costs of *My Fair Lady* in 1956 in return for a 40 percent ownership share. This kicked off a deluge of labels investing in musicals through the rest of the 1950s—although, just like pop music records, many of them bombed at the box office. (Everyone remembers *Fiddler on the Roof*; no one remembers the same writers' sequel *The Apple Tree*. CBS Records poured $450,000 into that one.)

But the first use of albums as creative canvases dates back much further. Frank Sinatra recorded a series of albums starting in the 1940s that featured common moods or themes. These started before the LP with *The Voice of Frank Sinatra* in 1946, issued as a set of four 78s and then as one of the first vinyl albums in 1948. Other Sinatra concept albums included *Christmas Songs* (1948), the torch song collection *Frank Sinatra Sings for Only the Lonely* (1958), and the travel-themed *Come Fly with Me* (also 1958).

The LP format was also ideally suited for the new jazz that was being created at the time. Bebop masters like Charlie "Bird" Parker and Dizzy Gillespie came up during the 1940s and played long improvisations on-stage at clubs and theaters, but they went into the studio and recorded three-minute selections onto 78s into the 1950s. (A few live albums, such as the all-star 1953 Toronto concert *Jazz at Massey Hall*, were released on LP.)

The next generation of jazz musicians took advantage of LPs' expanded length and created studio recordings that replicated—and went beyond—what they would do live. Miles Davis, for example, played in Parker's band and began to record as a leader in 1951. His first few albums, mostly for the upstart Prestige label, were on 10-inch LPs. His first release, *The New Sounds* (1951), featured track lengths beyond seven minutes. His classic 1956 sessions for Prestige with John Coltrane, released as *Cookin'*, *Workin'*, *Steamin'*, and *Relaxin'*, had tracks that went beyond the 10-minute mark.

Sonny Rollins recorded what is most likely the first nonclassical side-long studio track in 1957.[19] The album was a tribute to Parker, *Rollins Plays for Bird*. "Bird Medley" (Side 1) was a medley of pop standards associated with Parker that ran over 26 minutes long. Rollins followed it up with *Freedom Suite*, featuring his trio on the side-long title track, the following year. The free improvisation movement produced recordings that spanned *both* sides of an LP, such as Ornette Coleman's landmark *Free Jazz* from 1960. Charles Mingus's multi-part large ensemble work *The Black Saint and the Sinner Lady* (1963), rich with studio overdubs, took up an entire LP, as did Coltrane's iconic suite *A Love Supreme* in 1964.

The first rock albums with tracks that took up entire album sides appeared in 1966. Bob Dylan's "Sad Eyed Lady of the Lowlands" from the double LP

Blonde on Blonde was released in May of that year, followed by "The Return of the Son of Monster Magnet" on Frank Zappa's *Freak Out!* (another double LP) a month later. But these were only 11 and 12 minutes long respectively. The first true side-long rock track was "Revelation," a 19-minute jam on *Da Capo* by the LA psychedelic band Love, which followed in November. The first rock album with a track taking up both sides of an LP was an acid-soaked jam on the self-titled debut album by an obscure Southern California band called The Beat of the Earth, on the tiny Radish label, in 1967.

As the 1960s rolled into the 1970s, artists and record producers started focusing on constructing albums with the right songs in the right running order. Album-side sequencing began to take on a life of its own as a producer's art form. There were few iron-clad rules, though many 1970s rock albums had up-tempo rockers opening each side, followed by ballads. In addition, producers knew that the last tracks on each side couldn't have heavy bass, because the linear speed of a turntable decreases as the needle moves toward the center, meaning that the frequency response range would be limited and too much bass could cause the stylus to be knocked out of the groove.[20] One label head noted that it was common to include a long track on every LP "so that the radio DJ could get laid or go to the bathroom."

And then there was progressive rock, where bands would record heavily composed, suite-like tracks of album-side length. The first of these was the title suite of *Ars Longa Vita Brevis* by The Nice, featuring future ELP keyboard player Keith Emerson, in 1968. After that, album-side tracks became *de rigueur* in the early 1970s among prog-rock bands like Yes ("Close to the Edge"), ELP ("Tarkus"), and Pink Floyd ("Echoes"). The high point of the genre—or nadir, depending on your point of view—was Yes's 1973 *Tales from Topographic Oceans*, a double LP consisting of one track per side.

Finally, the use of the LP format in rock led to an explosion of creativity in album cover designs. One important step was to print song lyrics on the album cover; the first album to do that was the Beatles' *Sgt. Pepper*. The decision to print lyrics on album covers may seem obvious in hindsight, but it required overcoming objections from music publishers, who feared that doing so would cut into sheet music sales.

Another important step in the evolution of album covers was to hire "name" artists to do cover designs. *The Velvet Underground and Nico* from 1967, with the "banana" cover by Andy Warhol, is often cited as the first example of that (followed by his "zipper" cover for the Rolling Stones' *Sticky Fingers* in 1971). But Warhol had been designing album covers since 1949;

he had designed over a dozen covers, mostly of jazz albums, before doing the Velvet Underground's. The earliest instance of an already-famous artist doing an album cover is Salvador Dali's 1955 cover of Jackie Gleason's *Lonesome Echo*. Other early examples include ELP's *Brain Salad Surgery* (H. R. Giger) and Patti Smith's *Horses* (Robert Mapplethorpe), both from the mid-1970s.

The converse also happened, as a few artists became famous for their rock album cover designs. The pioneers here were Storm Thorgerson and Aubrey Powell of the British design firm Hipgnosis,[21] whose cover for Pink Floyd's *A Saucerful of Secrets* in 1968 led to hundreds of other covers for dozens of musical artists and many other projects beyond music. Roger Dean also started designing album covers in 1968; his iconic fantasy cover designs for Yes from 1971 onward led him to design work for dozens of album covers as well as video games.

As Chuck D of Public Enemy once said, "If you don't own the master, the master owns you." "Master rights" are rights to sound recordings, and as we'll see later in this chapter, sound recordings didn't carry copyrights until 1972—more than 20 years into the vinyl era. Yet it was almost unheard of for artists during the vinyl era to own their master rights; they assigned them to record labels in recording contracts. The reason was simple: when you made a deal with a label, the label advanced you the money to make the record and most likely owned the studio and the manufacturing plant. Later on, artists might record in independent studios, but the label still paid the artist an advance to cover the studio costs.

In other words, artists didn't have much leverage against their labels unless and until they became big stars—and as we saw in the previous chapter, there were very few big stars in recorded music until at least the late 1950s. Labels typically signed artists to contracts that required them to deliver a certain number of albums over a period of years.

Yet certain artists' leverage increased as they became famous. In the late 1960s, the major labels found a new way to keep their stars happy: give them subsidiary labels of their own. These became known as vanity labels.[22] The vanity label would typically do A&R and other creative work, while the parent label would handle manufacturing and distribution. The first of these were the Beach Boys' short-lived Brother, created by Columbia in 1966; Bizarre and Straight, created by MGM for Frank Zappa in 1967; and Apple, spun off from Capitol for the Beatles in 1968. This became more common practice as time went on. While most vanity labels were dedicated to the artists who founded them, a few of the early ones had their own successful signings of new artists, such as Straight's signing of Alice Cooper and Captain Beefheart, Apple's signing of Badfinger and James Taylor (plus all four Beatles as solo artists), and Led Zeppelin's Swan Song label (under Atlantic) signing Bad Company and Dave Edmunds. Vanity labels became even more successful in the 1990s, such as Maverick, which Madonna started within Warner Music Group in 1992, and Dr. Dre's Aftermath in 1996 within Universal/Interscope.

Otherwise, little happened during the vinyl era that would affect the industry's royalty structure for labels and artists. Two changes to the industry's royalty structure that took place in the 1970s involved public performances of sound recordings, but they resulted in new royalties for songwriters and music publishers only. As we'll see later in this chapter, these were for jukeboxes and cable television.

Apart from these changes to the *royalty* structure of the music industry, the *company* structure of the industry—specifically, the nature of the relationship between record labels and music publishers—changed substantially during the vinyl era. Put simply, labels got bigger than publishers and proceeded to eat up much of the music publishing industry.

Thanks to pop music and vinyl records as mass-market consumer products, recorded music became a major American industry during the vinyl period. Total annual revenue had grown from $157 million in 1949,[xlvi] the year after the introduction of the LP, to $2.2 billion by 1974,[xlvii] 25 years later. Even when adjusted for inflation, this was almost a sevenfold increase in sales.

It is likely that the recorded music industry had grown bigger than the music publishing industry by gross revenue by the early 1970s.[23] Record labels had taken over from music publishers in distributing and promoting music by then. As RIAA President Stanley Gortikov said at a congressional hearing on copyright reform in 1975, music publishers had become "heavily administrative and clerical; they are largely service entities, conduits for the processing of income and paper transactions. They don't promote as they used to. They don't advertise as they used to. They don't help create demand as they used to. They don't employ field representatives as they used to. These promotional functions necessarily have been taken over by recording companies."[xlviii]

The major labels started buying up music publishers in the 1960s and ended up owning many of the major ones. A few examples: Philips (later Polygram) bought Chappell publishing in 1968; Polygram sold it to private investors, who in turn sold it to Warner Bros. in 1987, creating Warner-Chappell Music, the publishing arm of Warner Music Group. MCA Records made its first of several publishing acquisitions with Leeds Music in 1964; MCA went on to merge with Polygram to become Universal Music Group, of which Universal Music Publishing—the largest music publisher in the world—is a subsidiary. Sony Music bought ATV Music from Michael Jackson in a multi-year process that began in 1995; ATV Music included the Beatles' song catalog, which Jackson had bought in 1984. The resulting Sony/ATV Music, the publishing arm of Sony Music Entertainment, was renamed Sony Music Publishing in February 2021. In fact, the big three major labels' publishing businesses account for over half of total music publishing industry revenue today.[xlix]

One of the reasons why record labels became bigger businesses than music publishers by the 1970s may be that they finally got copyrights on their sound recordings—although the economic implications of music recordings' lack of federal copyright protection until 1972 have been the subject of intense debate for decades. Nowadays it seems obvious that music recordings are copyrighted, but that was not at all the case when vinyl formats came into being. And it's not entirely the case today either: US copyright law still confers fewer rights on sound recordings than it does on musical compositions.

The better part of a century elapsed between the first audio recordings and copyright being established in sound recordings in US federal law. As we saw in Chapter 2, arguments over whether sound recordings should be eligible for copyright date back to the days of cylinders and piano rolls. During the period between the Copyright Act of 1909 and the 1960s, several litigations were brought, and more than a dozen separate bills were put forward in the House and the Senate, all in hopes of establishing copyright protection for sound recordings. None of these efforts succeeded.[l]

Myriad reasons were given for why sound recordings shouldn't get copyrights. In addition to those we encountered in Chapter 2, those reasons included that sound recordings weren't sufficiently creative compared to musical compositions or other copyrightable works,[24] that they were already protected under a patchwork of state copyright laws and by unfair competition law, and that copyright protection for sound recordings was just plain unconstitutional.

Even where there was general agreement that sound recordings ought to get copyright protection, the contours of that protection were unclear. Who should own the copyright—the record label or the performing artist? Record labels initially claimed that they should own the copyright, given that they engaged musicians to make records at their direction under work-for-hire agreements. Later on, when the industry produced big stars and that position became more tenuous, the labels would suggest that they get rights on copying and distribution while artists get rights on public performances, such as radio broadcasts.[25]

Then there was the question of what rights the copyright should cover: Simple reproduction of recordings? Recorded performances that sounded similar to existing records?[26] Radio broadcasts of recordings? Recordings made by radio stations for broadcasting later? Music recordings used in movies? It wasn't clear.

Yet another point of debate was whether sound recording copyrights should carry a compulsory license scheme like the one for mechanical reproductions of compositions. This brought up the issue of who would administer the royalties for such a license—the US Copyright Office, or a private-sector entity like the Harry Fox Agency? One possibility for the latter was the musicians' union, the American Federation of Musicians (AFM). Yet the AFM objected to sound recording copyrights. One reason was the potential for a compulsory license: they feared that a fixed statutory royalty would jeopardize musicians' bargaining power with labels. Another was a disparity in the union between members who made recordings and those who didn't. Others objected to the AFM administering the royalties out of fears that the union would engage in cronyism and not distribute the royalties equitably.

So many industry factions disputed the terms of sound recording copyrights in so many ways that nothing happened for decades. We discussed radio broadcasters' arguments against sound recording copyrights in the previous chapter. Music publishers and songwriters (to whom labels paid mechanical royalties), and performing arts organizations (PROs) like ASCAP and BMI, didn't like having to split up the pie with performers or labels. Jukebox makers didn't like it for the same reasons as radio broadcasters.

Bills repeatedly failed to advance in Congress; as a 1940 committee report put it, "thought has not yet become crystallized on this subject . . . and no way could be found . . . for reconciling the serious conflicts of interest arising in the field." A 1961 Copyright Office report would say the same thing, even using the word "crystallized" again.[li]

Yet by the mid-1960s, the various arguments—and those making them— had indeed "crystallized" around a set of ideas and compromises. It was decided that it wasn't unconstitutional to establish copyright in sound recordings. Once it was agreed that recorded performances were "writings," it made sense that the performing artist should get the copyright protection; labels could (and almost always did) assume ownership of those copyrights in contract terms anyway.

The labels found themselves focusing on copyright infringement with the rise of bootlegging in the late 1960s. While some bootlegs were designed as blatant imitations of commercial releases, others contained music that bootleggers released themselves because the labels weren't doing so. Among the most famous examples of the latter were 1967–1968 sessions by Bob Dylan released as the bootleg *Great White Wonder*, and *Live'r Than You'll Ever Be*, a bootleg of a Rolling Stones concert in Oakland in 1969.[27] The labels argued that it was much more effective to fight bootlegging through a single federal law than by relying on a patchwork of laws in 50 states.

Finally, international law had settled on copyrights in sound recordings with the Rome Convention for the Protection of Performers, Producers of Phonograms, and Broadcasting Organisations (known simply as the Rome Convention), which was ratified in 1961 by the United International Bureaux for the Protection of Intellectual Property, a UN agency that would later become the World Intellectual Property Organization (WIPO). The United States didn't sign on to the Rome Convention, but the Rome Convention created incentives for the United States to establish some sort of protection for performers—among other things, so that American record labels could recover royalties from foreign countries through reciprocity agreements. That is, the amount of money that the United States could get from other countries from exports of its rock & roll, soul, blues, and jazz was seen as economically significant.

Yet bootlegging of albums turned out to be the pivotal issue in getting the National Association of Broadcasters (NAB) to soften its objections to copyrights in sound recordings. As we'll see in Chapter 5, home taping of music from the radio wasn't considered a big issue in the late 1960s. So if bootlegging was the main concern, then copyrights on sound recordings could cover reproduction and distribution but not public performance, and this would mean—as we discussed in Chapter 3—that radio stations wouldn't have to pay royalties for the use of records.

With that obstacle out of the way, Congress passed the Sound Recording Act of 1971, which went into effect in February 1972. It established copyright protection for reproduction and distribution of sound recordings, but only on a prospective basis; older recordings would not get federal copyright protection. The Sound Recording Act did not include a compulsory license with a fixed royalty for sound recordings, so anyone who wanted to reproduce or distribute sound recordings had to negotiate a license with the record label, and the label could refuse to license at all (which happened, for example, with the record clubs we discussed earlier in this chapter).

Regardless of the economic impact of sound recording copyrights after 1972, the recorded music industry had gotten big enough before then to enable it to influence the momentum that led to the 1971 Sound Recording Act. The labels had built up a significant lobbying presence in Washington through the RIAA as well as through the American Record Manufacturers and Distributors Association (ARMADA), an older rival trade association formed in 1939 that became a home for independent labels.[lii,28]

By the early 1960s, the RIAA was more generally able to get its way in Washington.[29] The RIAA was able to align groups like performers' unions (SAG and AFTRA as well as AFM), record retailers, and even some music publishing interests behind it in its push for copyright protection. When music publishers tried to get Congress to repeal compulsory mechanical licensing because they felt that the fixed statutory royalties were too low, the RIAA was able to fend off those attempts (given that higher mechanical royalties would have reduced labels' shares of revenue from record sales).[liii] Still, as we explained in Chapter 3, the NAB proved an even more formidable lobbying force because of its nationwide influence on Congress compared to the concentration of the recording industry in just a couple of states.

As we mentioned earlier in this chapter, two other important changes to copyright law took place during the vinyl era after the Sound Recording Act. The first of these was the institution of statutory royalties paid by cable television. At first, cable TV was merely an extension of broadcast channels to rural areas that couldn't receive them; this led the Supreme Court to decide, in *Fortnightly v. United Artists Television* (1968), that cable operators weren't responsible for music copyrights in the broadcast signals they were carrying. This changed when cable operators began to offer their own programming; the 1976 Copyright Act included a compulsory license for musical compositions performances on cable TV. As we'll see in Chapter 6, music licensing for cable television would take on a whole new meaning a few years later.

The second change involved jukeboxes. Jukebox operators bought records for the machines but didn't pay royalties for their use. The PROs, the Copyright Office, and others had long argued that jukebox plays were public performances that enriched jukebox operators—which collectively took in $447 million in 1959[liv]—but paid nothing to the copyright holders. Those arguments failed for decades.[lv]

Congressman Emanuel Celler, from music-industry-heavy New York, started an effort to end the "jukebox exemption" and establish a levy on jukeboxes in 1952. Yet it wasn't until 1978 that jukebox operators had to pay performance royalties. At first, they paid $8 annually per machine for compulsory blanket licenses—flat one-time fees that covered all musical repertoire, administered by the Copyright Office. The Copyright Office collected over $100 million from more than 140,000 jukeboxes during the license's first full year of operation.[lvi] The fee was raised to $50 by 1984. In 1989, the compulsory license changed from one with flat rates to one that required jukebox operators to negotiate rates with each PRO. Jukebox operators set up the Jukebox Licensing Office in 1990 to handle these negotiations,[lvii] analogously to the Radio Music Licensing Committee that we saw in Chapter 3.

Yet this was largely a pointless exercise: by the time the levy was enacted, the jukebox industry had gone into a nosedive. Jukebox manufacturing had plummeted from 700,000 to 25,000 annually, and by 1980, there were fewer than 5,000 jukebox operators. The soda fountains and chrome dinettes of the 1950s had given way to jukebox-free fast-food chains.

Conclusion

The collapse of the jukebox market didn't hurt the music industry. On the contrary, it's best seen as part of a migration of music consumption to new and bigger use cases enabled by new devices. Vinyl helped recorded music become a multibillion-dollar industry, one that by the 1970s was led by large companies looking for growth. Growth would come from new ways to consume music, and those weren't going to come from bars and restaurants. Fans were happy for opportunities to listen to the music they wanted in the settings they wanted, whether those were at home, in the car, inside, outside, while traveling, or while hanging out with friends; and electronics companies were happy to supply gadgets and media formats to meet those occasions. As we'll see in the next chapter, the next phase of the music industry was one in which it used a format as old as vinyl to make that happen.

5

Tapes

Rhymin' and Stealin'—Beastie Boys

Until the advent of prerecorded tape, formats for distributing recorded music were introduced sequentially. LPs and 45s succeeded 78s; 78s—despite Thomas Edison's best efforts—succeeded cylinders. While those formats overlapped, the intent was for the new technology to supersede the old. Tape, in contrast, was the first format that existed side-by-side with another format for an extended period of time. The first prerecorded tapes distributed to consumers followed four years after the first vinyl LPs came out, and then vinyl and tape would go on to coexist for half a century before both of them faded away.

Consumers understood that there were tradeoffs among these formats: cartridge tape formats offered true portability, while LPs offered better random access and album cover art. Record labels were happy to sell consumers multiple versions of the same material, and electronics makers were happy to sell them multiple devices for different use cases. As for sound quality, while tape and vinyl started out on roughly equal footing, vinyl remained the gold standard while tape sound quality became secondary to portability.

Tape also gave consumers—for the first time, as a practical matter—the ability to make copies of recordings in the home. So while tape's portability would expand the market for recorded music dramatically by making it more ubiquitous, its recording capability may have made it less lucrative than it might have been for the music industry.

When we think of inventions made by and for the Nazis and exported to the United States after World War II, we usually think of rockets or Volkswagens. But another one was arguably just as important: magnetic tape. Two companies that would be associated with Nazi atrocities developed the

Key Changes. Howie Singer and Bill Rosenblatt, Oxford University Press. © Howie Singer and Bill Rosenblatt 2023.
DOI: 10.1093/oso/9780197656891.003.0005

technology, and its initial use was as a Nazi propaganda tool to record and broadcast Hitler's speeches over the German state broadcasting network.

Fritz Pfleumer, an Austrian-born engineer living in the German city of Dresden, invented a scheme for coating paper tape with magnetic particles in 1928 as a cheaper alternative to wire recording. He sold the rights to his invention to BASF, a division of the German chemical company IG Farben. The electric company AEG then produced the first commercially available magnetic tape recording device, the Magnetophon (see Figure 5.1), and demonstrated it at the Internationale Funkausstellung (International Radio Exhibition) in Berlin in 1935.[i]

The first known music recording on magnetic tape was made in 1936. A Magnetophon, with tape provided by BASF, was used to record a concert by the London Philharmonic Orchestra under the direction of Sir Thomas Beecham at the BASF-Feierabendhaus in Ludwigshafen, while the orchestra was on tour in Germany. Yet the sound quality of tape recordings made in the mid-1930s was markedly inferior to existing wire and disc technologies.

Three developments in magnetic tape technology through World War II made it more suitable for recording music.[ii] One was discovered by the RRG

Figure 5.1 AEG Magnetophon K4 reel-to-reel tape recorder, circa 1940. YLE Archives (public domain).

(Reichs-Rundfunkgesellschaft), the German state radio network. The RRG found that inserting a high-frequency AC "bias" signal before recording improved sound quality above the older technique of adding a DC current bias signal. BASF created the other two developments: the use of gamma ferric oxide (γ-Fe_2O_3) magnetic particles on the tape instead of the older Fe_3O_4 particles, and polyvinyl chloride (PVC) to replace the paper and cellulose acetate substrates. As we saw in the previous chapter, PVC was adopted for the microgroove disc formats in the late 1940s. For tape, PVC and acetate were eventually replaced by biaxially oriented polyethylene terephthalate, commonly known by the trade name Mylar.[iii]

At the end of the war, US Army Major Jack Mullin, a radar and electronics specialist, found Magnetophon machines at an RRG studio in Germany. He had two of the units shipped back to the States, along with schematics and other documentation.[iv] Mullin and his partner Bill Palmer created a version of the Magnetophon modified for American electronics and demonstrated it at a couple of audio engineering conferences. This led to a tiny startup called Ampex—in what is now Silicon Valley—producing the first American commercial tape recorder, the Ampex Model 200. Mullin also showed his design to Bing Crosby, who saw immediate potential as a means of recording his radio programs for later rebroadcast so that he wouldn't have to repeat live performances for different time zones. He hired Mullin to be chief engineer at Bing Crosby Enterprises, invested in Ampex, and bought several of their machines.[v,1]

Around that same time as tape flourished in studios as a superior alternative to recording direct to disc, as we saw in the previous chapter,[vi] tape began its spread into the home. In 1951, Ampex was one of a handful of companies that began releasing recordings on open-reel tape.[vii] Manufacturers such as Magnecord and Concertone marketed tape recorders specifically for home buyers, and Ampex began to produce lower-priced units for the home market. Although "lower" was somewhat relative: prices for professional studio tape recorders extended into the four figures, and while high-quality home tape machines sold for $400–$600 (about $4,000–$6,000 today), high-quality record-playing setups could be had for less than half that much.

Tape was the first recorded music format to go stereo. Unlike the complex process for recording stereo signals on to discs, recording in stereo on tape was straightforward: just divide the tape up into two parallel tracks for left and right channels and use dual heads to record and play the audio. Stereo tapes could play easily on mono tape machines: the single playback head simply read both tracks at once. (And vice versa: mono tapes could readily play on stereo machines.) For a while it was even thought that tape was the only practical stereo medium.[viii] Of course, dividing up recording tape into multiple tracks took on a life of its own in studios as multitrack recording came into being in the late 1950s.[ix]

The first prerecorded stereo tapes came in 1953, although the major labels didn't start to issue titles on tape in stereo until 1957, the year when vinyl records went stereo.[x] A standard format for commercially recorded tapes emerged in 1959: the tape was a quarter-inch wide and divided into four tracks, two left/right stereo pairs, analogous to the two sides of an LP.[xi]

The sound quality of tape is proportional to the area of tape that passes a playback head every second, which is a function of the width of the tape and the recording speed. The standard for commercial releases called for tape to be recorded at 7.5 inches per second (IPS). This was slower than the 15 or 30 IPS speeds typically used for mastering in recording studios, where the track widths were usually double that of consumer prerecorded tapes.[2] This meant that the amount of standard prerecorded tape passing a playback head was as little as one-eighth the area of the master tape. Sound quality is also proportional to tape speed in the sense that slower speeds are more susceptible to speed variations that cause distortions known as wow and flutter. Still, 7.5 IPS four-track stereo was considered sufficient for high-fidelity sound when played through quality home equipment. As the 1960s progressed, lower-cost prerecorded tapes with lesser audio quality became available at 3.75 IPS (using half as much tape) as well.

Magnetic tape also made recording more accessible to consumers at home. Disc-recording equipment was expensive, designed to be integrated into recording studios by professionals, and rarely used in homes. Magnetic tape recorders in the early 1950s came in complete packages with microphones, amps, and speakers included, at half the cost of disc setups. Disc recording equipment had disappeared from electronics retailers' catalogs by the end of the 1950s, while tape recording equipment got cheaper and models proliferated.

As far as sound quality was concerned, by the mid-1950s prerecorded open-reel tape was considered to have slightly better sound quality than vinyl because prerecorded tapes were closer copies of original master tapes.[xii] Tape also wasn't susceptible to scratches and dust as vinyl was, so it tended to hold its sound quality better over time.

Yet tape decks generally weren't advertised as standard hi-fi system components along with tuners and turntables; they were more like optional extras.[3] Open-reel tape was far less popular than discs for the same reasons that some future formats with superior audio quality would suffer in popularity: cost and convenience. Reel-to-reel tape decks were harder to use than turntables, and prerecorded tapes sold for at least 50 percent more than the same titles on LP.

Finally, just as reel-to-reel was the first format to go stereo, it was also the first format to jump on the quadraphonic bandwagon. Quad open-reel was easy to implement: just use the four tracks as a single set of quad tracks instead of two stereo pairs. Home four-track tape decks were available by the late 1960s; they just needed four-channel amps (or two stereo amps) to plug into. Commercial prerecorded quad open-reel tapes first appeared in 1969, three years ahead of quad LPs in the popular formats. But quad tape formats were even less popular than quad LPs.[4]

Attempts to make tape easier to use by enclosing it in cartridges came early on. The first tape cartridge system, introduced in 1952, was Bernard Cousino's Audio Vendor. It wasn't a complete solution: Audio Vendor cartridges used an endless loop, so that no rewinding was necessary, but they were designed to be placed onto standard open-reel tape machines, so the tape still had to be threaded.[xiii]

Audio Vendor was only modestly successful, but one of Cousino's employees developed a system that went much further: the Fidelipac, a cartridge that didn't require any tape handling at all. The Fidelipac was another endless-loop cartridge, invented by George Eash in 1954 (see Figure 5.2).[xiv] Fidelipacs used their own recording and playback equipment; no threading was necessary. They used quarter-inch tape and came in a variety of lengths. Fidelipac cartridges and machines became standard equipment in radio stations; they earned the imprimatur of the National Association of Broadcasters and came to be called "carts" in radio lingo.

Carts were the ultimate in ease of use. The only button a studio engineer or DJ had to press was Play; the tape would advance back to the beginning after playback and stop. They were also durable enough to withstand rough 24/7 handling in a studio. Carts were used most often for material produced in radio stations, such as commercials and station jingles. They were also sometimes used for songs, particularly on AM stations where sound quality wasn't as important. The Fidelipac cart had an incredible run of 40 years in radio

Figure 5.2 A Fidelipac tape cartridge used in radio stations (L) and a Stereo-8 a.k.a. 8-track tape cartridge (R). Bill Rosenblatt; Fidelipac cartridge courtesy WPRB.

stations before hard-disk-based digital audio devices finally replaced them in the 1990s.

The Fidelipac cartridge was also used in the first mainstream consumer tape format for recorded music. The primary motivation for cartridges in the consumer market was so that people could finally play recorded music on demand in cars. Recall from the previous chapter that a few failed attempts were made in the 1950s to make record players that worked in cars. Tape cartridges were a much more promising approach.

Accordingly, the man who introduced tape cartridges to the consumer market was someone who saw the opportunity from his vantage point in the land of freeways and car culture: Earl "Madman" Muntz. Muntz had been a car dealer in Southern California; then he went into consumer electronics, making radios and televisions in the 1950s. He hit upon the idea of making a tape player for cars in the late 1950s when his television business took a downturn.[xv]

Muntz started a business in the early 1960s to develop a consumer version of the Fidelipac system. He called his system Stereo-Pak and advertised the cartridges as "CARtridges." Like standard open-reel tape, the Stereo-Pak had four tracks configured as two stereo pairs. It ran at 3.75 IPS and had a total playing time of 40 minutes.[xvi]

The Stereo-Pak system debuted in 1962, but it didn't last very long as a commercial music format. It was eclipsed a few years later by another cartridge system, which was designed by Bill Lear of Lear Jet fame. Lear had gone into business distributing Muntz's Stereo-Pak players so that he could install them in his private jets. He developed relationships with Ampex, Motorola, Ford Motor Company, General Motors, and RCA Victor to create a new version called Stereo-8. Stereo-8 had four stereo pairs (eight tracks) instead of two, increasing playing time to a maximum of 80 minutes (20 minutes times four stereo programs), though some releases used only 10–11 minutes per track (for a total of 40–44 minutes). Stereo-8 became known simply as 8-track. As Figure 5.2 shows, the 8-track differed from the Fidelipac in certain ways, which enabled Lear to avoid having to license patents from Cousino and Eash[xvii] while also leading to cheaper and smaller players[5] and even more ease of use.[6]

Ford was the first automaker to install 8-track players (made by Motorola) into its cars; it did so in late 1965 as a factory-installed option for the 1966 model year. Lear also produced aftermarket auto as well as home and portable 8-track players under the Lear Jet brand. Third-party electronics makers followed with their own 8-track players the next year. Home component 8-track players (designed to be connected to amps or receivers) came in 1968 with the introduction of the TC-8 from Sony.[xviii]

For the first couple of years, units were available that played both 4-track Stereo-Pak and 8-track cartridges. But 8-tracks took over in popularity, because Lear made more arrangements with automakers, and because more music could fit onto 8-tracks. By 1970, Muntz had lost the format war and abandoned the Stereo-Pak.[7]

The 8-track format had its limitations. One was inferior sound quality. Like open-reel and carts, 8-tracks also used quarter-inch tape, but they had twice as many tracks and (like Stereo-Paks) ran at the slower 3.75 IPS speed. Cramming eight tracks onto quarter-inch tape not only meant less tape area per track, it also made the format susceptible to head misalignment problems: the playback head had to move up and down to switch tracks, and if it wasn't aligned exactly correctly, you'd hear an adjacent track in the background. Yet car audio systems of the late 1960s through 1970s never had great sound quality, so these issues weren't so important for most consumers.

Another limitation was track length, especially when the shorter 10–11-minute-per-track version was used. Songs would be chopped in half or reordered to fit. This was a particular problem for classical music, as well as for the side-long pop music tracks that were emerging in the 1970s. For example, Kraftwerk's "Autobahn" and Todd Rundgren's "A Treatise on Cosmic Fire" were each sliced up into *three* tracks on the 8-track versions of the albums *Autobahn* and *Initiation*.

The third problem with 8-tracks was that they didn't provide random access—the ability to start at specific points in a recording. Whereas it was at least possible to fast forward or rewind open-reel tape and navigate to values on tape decks' counters, 8-track players had nothing but a button to push to go to the next track. This made sense in the car (like pushbuttons on radios) but not in the home. In most cases, the next track in an 8-track tape was the next album side.

These limitations added up to ensure that 8-track was never a very popular music format anywhere other than the automobile.[8]

The next tape format to come along was by far the most successful of all: the Compact Cassette. It was invented at Philips in the Netherlands and introduced at the Internationale Funkausstellung Berlin in 1963; introduction in the United States under the Norelco brand came the following year.

The designer of the cassette was Lou Ottens, a Philips engineer who had designed Philips's first battery-operated portable reel-to-reel tape recorder a few years earlier. He based the design on a twin-sprocket tape cartridge that RCA had released (to little success) in 1958 and shrank the size so that it would fit in his jacket pocket. (Ottens would go on to lead the Philips team that worked with Sony in designing the CD.)[xix]

Philips quickly found itself in a format war with the German electronics company Grundig, then the largest manufacturer of tape recorders in the world. In 1965, Grundig introduced the DC-International, another two-sprocket cartridge design that was about 20 percent larger than Philips's Compact Cassette, yet smaller than the earlier RCA design. Philips won the format war, mainly by agreeing to license its intellectual property royalty-free to other electronics makers such as Sony and Panasonic.

So, the cassette was introduced two years before the 8-track. But it wasn't intended as a recorded music format; it was meant as a convenient pocket-sized medium for voice recording and dictation. Cassettes are less than half the size of 8-tracks. They use 0.15-inch tape at a speed of 1.875 IPS (half of 8-tracks' 3.75 IPS) in two-track mono or two-stereo-pair configurations. In the stereo configuration, this amounts to 60 percent of the amount of tape area passing the heads per second compared to 8-track. The original capacity of cassettes was 30 minutes on each side or 60 minutes total.[xx]

The first cassette machines were small portables that ran on batteries. Philips's first model, the EL 3300, was about the size of a thick paperback book, weighed about two pounds, and took five C batteries (see Figure 5.3).

Yet cassettes were used for music anyway, because of their small size and fast-wind random-access capabilities. The first prerecorded cassettes appeared in the United States in 1966, around the same time as the first prerecorded 8-tracks.[xxi]

The cassette ecosystem grew quickly. Consumer electronics makers were introducing under-dash cassette players for the car as well as home record/play cassette decks; component cassette deck models proliferated faster than component 8-tracks.[xxii] More labels began releasing titles in the format. Tape manufacturers designed thinner tape to increase capacity to 90 minutes total, enough for one complete LP on each side, with a tradeoff in

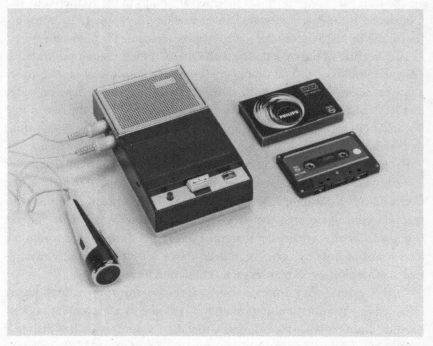

Figure 5.3 The Philips EL 3300, the first cassette recorder, from 1963. Used with permission of Koninklijke Philips N.V.

durability.[xxiii] Once again, and just as with 8-track over open-reel, convenience won out over quality: by 1968, cassette recorders were outselling both
open-reel and 8-track machines, a trend that would only accelerate in the
years to come.[xxiv]

Cassettes' fast-growing popularity motivated the industry to improve their
sound quality. Two technological innovations came together at the outset of
the 1970s to help make this happen.

The first of these was noise reduction to reduce the hiss that was endemic
to cassettes. A general technique for reducing noise is to compress certain
frequency ranges of the audio signal at recording time and then expand
them again on playback, a process known as compansion (a portmanteau of
*com*pression and ex*pansion*). The manufacturing facility uses a compression
scheme to make prerecorded cassettes, and then the user's player has to have
compatible expansion circuitry to play them back properly.

Ray Dolby brought audio compansion to tape recording. A media technology prodigy, Dolby worked with Ampex during his undergrad years at
Stanford to develop videotape in the mid-1950s. He started his eponymous
company in 1965; his first product was a compansion-based noise reduction system that he called Dolby A. It reduced high-frequency noise by 20
dB, which a listener would perceive as a 75 percent reduction. Dolby A came
into wide use in recording studios. But it required high degrees of precision
in matching the compression and expansion processes to work correctly—
precision that would be too expensive to build into low-priced consumer
players.

So Dolby designed a successor technology three years later, which he
named Dolby B. Dolby B traded off less noise reduction in favor of simpler
implementation and listenable sound quality in players that did not have the
decoding circuitry. Dolby B became the de facto standard noise reduction
scheme for cassettes. It provided 10 dB of noise reduction, meaning that it
cut the perceived volume of hiss in half.[9]

The other innovation was new types of magnetic particles for embedding
onto tape that had better signal retention properties, which would increase
the tape's frequency response range beyond that of standard ferric oxide.
The first and most successful of these new formulations was chromium dioxide (CrO_2).[10] Du Pont had developed a process for synthesizing CrO_2 in
1956. It began licensing the technology to tape makers in the early 1970s.
CrO_2, or "chrome," became the standard for premium-quality cassettes.[11]
Tape machines needed electronics that were adapted to these new tape

formulations to record and play them correctly, such as different bias frequencies for the different formulations.

Thus, by the outset of the 1970s, Dolby B noise reduction and CrO_2 tape had the potential to transform the small cassette from a pocketable medium for voice into one for music with sound quality to equal or exceed 8-tracks. The man who saw the potential and acted on it was Henry Kloss.

Kloss was another media technology whiz kid; he designed loudspeakers as a sideline while a student at MIT. He became a serial entrepreneur who specialized in innovations that made top-notch sound quality affordable. He was the coinventor of the acoustic suspension speaker, which provided smooth, full bass response in a small box and became the most widely used speaker design. He designed successful lines of speakers and electronics with his companies Acoustic Research and KLH (named for its founders Kloss, Malcolm Low, and J. Anton Hoffman). KLH produced the first consumer product with Dolby B noise reduction, the KLH Model Forty reel-to-reel tape deck, in 1968.

Around that same time, Kloss left KLH to start Advent Corporation. His original aim for Advent was to develop a projection TV system for the home. To raise funding for the project, he designed another acoustic suspension speaker simply called the Advent Loudspeaker. The Advent Loudspeaker was a milestone in audiophile-grade sound quality at a moderate price; it became so popular that it overshadowed everything else the company did— eventually including the first projection television system for home use, the VideoBeam 1000. Another such product was one that revolutionized home tape recording.

The Advent 200, launched in 1970, was the company's first cassette deck. Kloss designed it to be the first true high-fidelity cassette machine. It launched in 1970 and sold for $260, which was marginally more expensive than other quality cassette decks but far cheaper than high-end home reel-to-reel machines. It included both Dolby B noise reduction and chromium dioxide tape compatibility. *Stereo Review* rated it the best of that year's crop of cassette machines, better than cheaper models from Fisher and Harman-Kardon that also had Dolby B and chrome tape support.[xxv] Yet the 200 was plagued by mechanical reliability problems; Advent quickly replaced it in 1971 with the Advent 201, which had a different transport and improved electronics.

The Advent 201 was the game-changer. *Stereo Review* called it "*the* best cassette recorder we know of" and "the one that sets the standard for cassette recorders," and found that it held up favorably against several more expensive reel-to-reel decks. The magazine used it as a reference machine for measuring the audio quality of blank cassettes.[xxvi] The 201 stayed in Advent's product line for several years.[12] It wasn't the smash hit product that the Advent Loudspeaker was—it's more like a cult classic—but it put the industry on notice that hi-fi quality from cassettes was possible and reasonably affordable.

The next step in the "hi-fi-zation" of cassettes came in 1973. The Japanese company Nakamichi—which ironically had built the balky tape transport for the Advent 200—took the concept to an extreme with the introduction of the Nakamichi 1000. The idea of the 1000 was to create a cassette deck with audio quality to rival the best open-reel tape. In doing so, Nakamichi borrowed various features from studio-quality reel-to-reel machines[13] and added a few innovations of its own, including some that required users to record cassettes on the machine to have the best playback quality.[14] The 1000 achieved Nakamichi's goals, though at a price of four times that of the Advent 201.[xxvii] It set a benchmark for the legitimacy of cassettes as a high-quality medium for music—one that has arguably been exceeded only by the company's own subsequent top-of-the-line models. Though few could afford the Nakamichi 1000[15]—it sold for the equivalent of $8,000 in today's money—audiophiles knew about it and understood its implications.

The cassette was the last successful consumer tape format for commercial music reproduction. Subsequent successful tape formats were digital instead of analog, and as we'll see in Chapter 7, they weren't used as consumer audio formats.[16] Other analog tape formats continued to thrive for nonmusic applications such as telephone answering machines and children's toys.

Tapes were the first medium that enabled everyday consumers to make copies of recorded music products easily. Whether they *should* make those copies became a vexed question. Tape eventually became the medium that shifted the objects of the music industry's concerns about copyright infringement from bootleggers to ordinary consumers.

Hi-fi magazines of the 1950s contained articles instructing readers on how to make open-reel tape copies of their LPs and suggesting they do so to preserve the vinyl.[xxviii] Yet as we've discussed, open-reel tapes were never very popular, so this wasn't a major concern to record labels. Home 8-track recorders and blank tapes became available, but 8-track was never popular as a home recording format. Nevertheless, around 1967 some record label executives were known to have tried to block the availability of home component cassette and 8-track recorders for fear that home taping would cut into record sales.[xxix]

People could record music onto cassettes directly from radio broadcasts—without using microphones—starting in 1966 when the radio-cassette portable was introduced. That didn't particularly concern the record labels either. But then component cassette and 8-track decks, which enabled people to duplicate albums onto tape, finally came out in 1968. This led to questions about what was and wasn't legal to do, and the answers weren't exactly clear.

The reality at that time was that recording any copyrighted music at home—whether from the radio or your own records—was nominally a violation of copyright law in the United States.[17] But the practical advice given out in trade magazines was that you could tape off the radio or your own records and get away with it as long as you kept the tapes for your own personal use only.

For example, in its *Tape Recorder Annual 1968*, *HiFi/Stereo Review* magazine said:

> [T]he law is rarely applied against a non-commercial amateur. As a matter of everyday practice, what you do in your own home with no other people involved is still pretty much your own affair. However, the moment your acts assume a public nature, . . . so too can the law, for it is the business of that 'jealous mistress' to protect the interests of individuals with relation to the public insofar as it pertains to . . . the ownership of rights in intellectual creations, and the public distribution of artistic performances and productions.

Yet elsewhere in that same magazine, there was an article called "How to Record Off the Air" that offered the (then)[18] dubious advice that "it isn't illegal to record radio programs" as long as you don't "(1) play them before a public gathering, (2) charge admission to listen to them, or (3) copy them for resale purposes."[xxx]

At that point, the only way to make decent-sounding copies of LPs or radio broadcasts was on open-reel tape with an expensive deck. But by the late

1970s, it was possible to make copies that were very close to the originals with moderate-priced cassette decks[19] and premium-quality blank cassettes. In fact, it became fairly common practice for audiophiles to make cassette copies of LPs immediately after purchasing them, because cassettes held their sound quality a lot longer than vinyl (with typical handling).

The music industry's concern about home taping heightened at the end of the 1970s, when total industry revenues started to drop for the first time since the LP versus 45 format war of the late 1940s. Despite the huge increases in opportunities to play recorded music that portable cassette devices afforded, overall industry revenues plummeted from 1979 through the early 1980s and didn't recover until the introduction of the CD in the mid-1980s. Home taping was surely a factor in this.[20]

Yet the US recorded music industry didn't make the biggest noises against home taping; those came from the United Kingdom. The British music industry was galvanized into action by the arrival in Britain in 1981 of a new device that made home taping even easier: the dubbing cassette deck.

Dubbing decks contained two tape transports, typically one that recorded and played, and another that only played. Some models could be set up to duplicate a tape at double speed, meaning that it took half the playback time to create a copy (with a slight loss in sound quality). A few even had bidirectional double-speed dubbing functionality, so that an entire two-sided tape could be copied in a quarter of the playback time.[xxxi]

The dubbing deck was the brainchild of Alan Sugar, a self-made entrepreneur who grew up on a council estate in London and rose to become a billionaire, a media personality, and a baron, being named a life peer in 2009. His company Amstrad (for Alan Michael Sugar Trading) produced a line of consumer electronics and, eventually, personal computers. While on a visit to Toyko's Akihabara electronics district, Sugar saw a dubbing cassette recorder made by Sharp and designed for professional studios, and he decided to build a consumer version of the product.

The Amstrad TS55 wasn't an expensive audiophile product; it was a low-priced all-in-one stereo system with a dual cassette deck, turntable, tuner, amp, and two speakers. It debuted in October 1981. Advertisements for the system contained notices warning against duplicating copyrighted material. In his autobiography, Sugar admitted that he did this as a nudge-nudge-wink-wink to give people the idea to use it for just that purpose.[xxxii] The BPI (British Phonographic Industry, the United Kingdom's analog to the RIAA in the United States) tried suing Amstrad to keep the product off the market.

Although the BPI won its initial lawsuit, Amstrad appealed to the House of Lords and ended up prevailing in 1988.[21]

Around the same time that the TS55 was launched, the BPI launched a publicity campaign called Home Taping Is Killing Music, which included a skull-and-crossbones logo that it got some record labels to put on the inner sleeves of LPs, as shown in Figure 5.4. The campaign got a lot of exposure, including widespread ridicule and parody that probably did not help to drive home its message.

The BPI also tried to get Parliament to enact a levy of 1 penny sterling (about 2 cents) per minute on blank cassettes, which would have raised the price of a chrome C-90 (90-minute tape) by about 60 percent (based on a typical "street price" of $3 at the time).[xxxiii] This effort failed.[22]

On the other hand, a few artists and labels decided to use the growing fervor for home taping as a way of ingratiating themselves with fans. The indie rock bands Bow Wow Wow and the Dead Kennedys released cassette versions of their albums as C-90s with music on the A side and the B side

Figure 5.4 The Home Taping Is Killing Music logo on the inner sleeve of an album released in the United Kingdom. CC BY-ND 2.0, blondetpatrice.

left blank, with recommendations to use the B sides to record other albums. Island Records even launched a cassette series called One Plus One that featured the label's albums on both sides of a high-quality chrome tape with an invitation to record "whatever you like" on one of the sides; artists with albums in the One Plus One program included U2, Tom Petty, Robert Palmer, and Cat Stevens.

In the United States, meanwhile, evidence was mounting that home taping of music was increasing dramatically. The Copyright Royalty Tribunal, a body established by Congress in 1976 to administer compulsory licenses, carried out a study that found that 20 percent of the US population ages 10 and up taped music at home. Sales of blank cassettes skyrocketed from 1976 to 1978.[xxxiv] Dubbing decks began to appear in the US market after the Amstrad TS55 was introduced, including both high-end components (with prices to match) and portables.[23] By the mid-1980s most of the major Japanese audio brands had introduced moderately priced component dubbing decks.[xxxv]

Yet the music industry's options for legislative remedies were limited. In 1978, a California district court ruled that home videotaping of television broadcasts was fair use. This was in a case that pitted a Hollywood studio against Sony, which had been marketing a videocassette format called Betamax. The case was appealed all the way to the Supreme Court, in what became *Sony Corp. of America v. Universal City Studios*, known as the *Betamax* case. The Supreme Court agreed with the lower court[24] and found for Sony in 1984—though, ironically, by then Sony had lost a videocassette format war to JVC's VHS. *Betamax* was a landmark decision that would go on to be cited in virtually every subsequent case involving new technologies used for copying content.[25]

The RIAA did not launch a large-scale public propaganda campaign as the BPI did, nor did it facilitate a lawsuit to get dubbing decks pulled off store shelves. Instead, the music industry engaged in various behind-the-scenes tactics to quash unauthorized taping. Labels threatened to pull ads from radio stations that played albums in their entirety and from publications that put blank tape ads on the same pages as ads for music. They got into arguments with electronics makers and record retailers, both of which accused the labels of selling products that were inferior to home-recorded cassettes for the same prices as vinyl. In fact the majors' typical practice by that time was to use cheap ferric oxide tape in high-speed duplication processes that compromised sound quality, for unit costs that were lower than LPs.[xxxvi] Labels also sued retail chains such as Sam Goody for allegedly making and selling millions of unauthorized copies of commercial cassettes; Goody pleaded no contest and was fined $10,000, and one of its executives was sentenced to a year in prison.[xxxvii]

The US music industry did emulate the BPI in attempting to get a royalty on home taping enacted—with similar results. Bills that were introduced in the House and Senate in 1982 would have made home taping legal while imposing royalty fees on tape recorders of up to 25 percent of wholesale prices and a levy on blank tapes of a penny a minute (resulting in a price hike of about 30 percent on chrome C-90s).[xxxviii]

As these bills made their way through Congress, the music industry engaged in what may have been one of the most bizarre[26] quid-pro-quo political deals in its history. A group of women in Washington, including Tipper Gore (wife of Senator Al Gore) and Susan Baker (wife of Treasury Secretary James Baker), founded an organization called the Parents Music Resource Center (PMRC). The PMRC was concerned with what they considered to be a rising tide of harm to children from hearing explicit song lyrics. They pushed record labels to put warning stickers on album jackets with labels such as X for explicit sex or profanity, V for violence, D/A for drugs or alcohol, and O for occult content.

The PMRC used its influence to get hearings scheduled in Congress in September 1985. Witnesses included singer-songwriter John Denver, Dee Snider of the metal band Twisted Sister, and—most famously—Frank Zappa. In his withering testimony, Zappa accused the RIAA of agreeing to warning stickers in exchange for favorable consideration of its home-taping royalty in Congress. The bill ultimately failed, although several labels had already agreed to put stickers on album shrink wrap anyway.[xxxix] Zappa memorialized the events in the track "Porn Wars," from his 1985 album *Frank Zappa Meets the Mothers of Prevention*, which included snippets of speakers at the hearings.

In summary, none of the music industry's efforts—in the United States or elsewhere—had much impact on home taping during the heyday of the cassette.

Copyright also had implications for creators who used the cassette format to establish one of the most popular music genres in history, as we'll see later in this chapter.

Tape in its various forms coexisted with vinyl for the entirety of its 50-year aggregate run as a commercial music format. Schwann catalogs of recordings listed vinyl as the default format and noted where albums also came out on cassette or 8-track. And for the most part, they were sold in the same ways that vinyl was. This parallelism even extended to the LP/45 dichotomy: "cassingles" (cassette singles) were released, often with paper sleeves instead of plastic boxes, starting in 1980 with Bow Wow Wow's paean to home taping, "C·30 C·60 C·90 Go."

There were some differences in target markets among formats, such as by music genre. By 1971, the vast majority of pop music releases were made on both 8-track and cassette (in addition to vinyl), slightly more on the former than the latter. A very small number of releases came out on 8-track only, mostly compilations and greatest hits collections, with country music dominating (*Country Hits Parade, Queens of Country Music*, etc.).[xl]

Classical and jazz were a completely different story. In the early 1970s, at most about ten percent of classical albums were released on cassette, even fewer—unsurprisingly—on 8-track. Perhaps 15–20 percent of jazz albums were released on cassette, slightly more on 8-track. This situation changed somewhat by the mid-1970s, when good sound quality had made it to moderate-priced cassette equipment: jazz cassette releases had grown to cover about one-third of vinyl titles, where they stayed throughout that decade;[27] and classical releases on tape never made it past 20 percent or so of vinyl releases.[xli]

Retail outlets for prerecorded tapes were initially the same as for vinyl. But products that were much smaller than LPs and designed for portable listening engendered new retail outlets, which in turn led to new distributors getting into the business. Cassettes and 8-tracks appeared in drugstores, convenience stores, and various other types of retailers. Albums that were released on 8-track tape only, such as the country music compilations mentioned previously, were often sold at truck stops.

A key figure in the expansion of music retail to tape was Larry Finley, another entrepreneur in the land of the eternal freeway. Finley (born Lawrence Finkelstein) was the co-owner of a San Diego music venue, so he had a foot in the door of the music business. And as a radio broadcaster and station owner, he knew carts.

Finley got in on the ground floor of prerecorded tapes. He started his first label, International Tape Cartridge Corp. (ITCC), in 1965. He purchased a million blank cartridges and released titles in both Stereo-Pak and 8-track formats.[xlii] In addition to releasing his own material, Finley acquired tape rights to albums from dozens of record labels.

Finley saw the accretive effect that tapes had on overall music industry revenue and became a cheerleader for the entire tape segment of the industry; his "bully pulpit" was the Tape Cartridge Tips advertorial column that he wrote in *Billboard* magazine through 1968. Finley went on to start a trade association called ITA (International Tape Association) to set standards for things like tape length and manufacturing quality in prerecorded tape releases.[xliii] ITA subsequently branched out into videotape and then digital distribution.[28]

Yet cassette sales weren't limited to the same channels as vinyl. Because cassettes were originally a home recording format, they blurred the lines between creators and distributors to a greater extent than ever before. While major labels were using facilities with high-speed commercial tape duplication machines that sold for hundreds of thousands of dollars,[xliv] anyone with two cassette decks—or a dubbing deck—could get into the duplication business. Smaller-scale tape duplicators that handled up to four tapes at a time, at up to 16 times cassette speed, became available for a few hundred dollars or less. And manufacturing costs for cassettes in small volumes were reasonable, whereas they were prohibitively high for vinyl.

As a result, cassettes powered the rise of various independent music distribution networks that wouldn't have been possible without them. The earliest of these were tape-trading networks, in which fans would duplicate and swap tapes. Most of these were bootlegs of concerts and studio outtakes rather than dubs of commercial albums. The first was the First Free Underground Grateful Dead Tape Exchange, which Les Kippel started in 1971—using open-reel tape at first—for trading tapes of the Dead's epic live shows that the band allowed fans to make. The tape-trading ethos was to swap tapes for free (or only for "B&P" or blanks-and-postage charges) and to shun those who would sell the tapes for profit, although inevitably many of the tapes fell into the hands of for-profit bootleggers.

Two other independent cassette-based distribution networks arose directly from musical creators. One of these was based on the simple idea of cassettes as alternatives to vinyl for short-run releases.

The pioneer in this area was the New Jersey-based singer, songwriter, and multiinstrumentalist R. Stevie Moore. Moore is one of the godfathers of indie rock and one of the most prolific recording artists of all time, with over 150 studio albums. Releasing all that material to his modest-sized but dedicated fan base on vinyl would have been impracticable. Moore began releasing music on cassettes in 1973, just when hi-fi sound quality from the medium was starting to be available. In 1982 he started the R. Stevie Moore Cassette Club, a mail-order service for his albums. The vast majority of Moore's music is self-released.[29]

An informal movement known as the cassette underground emerged in the 1980s. Several tiny cassette-only labels were born, most of them specializing in various flavors of postpunk, indie rock, and experimental music. Some music magazines also distributed sampler cassettes of new artists with their issues. For many artists, the ability to record on cassettes and distribute in low volumes made the difference between not releasing music and releasing music.[xlv] Some of these labels didn't even distribute prerecorded cassettes; instead they asked fans to send them blank cassettes and returned them with albums recorded on them.[xlvi] The cassette underground produced a handful of "stars" such as Moore, avant-garde guitarist Eugene Chadbourne, and the British indie bands Cleaners from Venus and Danny and the Dressmakers.

But otherwise the cassette underground's activity generally took place in lieu of vinyl and other traditional aspects of recorded music distribution. Although the "lo-fi" movement in indie music was often associated with cassettes, the music on cassette-only releases was created in much the same way as music released on LPs and 45s.

The same cannot be said of the other sphere of creators' activity based on cassettes, one that helped usher in one of the biggest movements in popular music ever: hip-hop. It's no exaggeration to say that the cassette was to hip-hop as the transistor radio was to rock & roll; the genre probably would not have flourished without it.

Hip-hop got its start during the 1970s in the South Bronx. DJs and rappers like Kool Herc, Grandmaster Flash, Lovebug Starski, Grand Wizzard Theodore, and Afrika Bambaataa would entertain crowds at parties, armed with DJ rigs and PA systems. They would play records, repeat sections of songs that got people dancing, play records over each other, and rap over the music. They invented turntable scratching techniques that added spice to the mix. In other words, they used three basic tools—turntables, microphones, and mixers—in ways that were so innovative and distinctive that the results became a new form of audio expression.

These artists began to record their performances on cassettes. They would duplicate their party tapes, a.k.a. mixtapes, and sell them or give them away around the neighborhood, the city, and beyond. For more (sometimes a lot more) money, they would create personalized tapes by request with shout-outs to the requesters. As their mixtapes began to be heard in public on more boomboxes and "boom cars" (car stereos with powerful amps and massive woofers), their reputations grew. And grew.

The underground nature of early hip-hop was key to its survival, in part because—ironically—all those songs that DJs would play at parties became potential copyright violations when they were recorded onto mixtapes.[30] This became an issue when hip-hop artists began to sign to labels that were skittish about the copyright risks. The type of sampling used in hip-hop was so new that the rules for clearance and royalties were not certain—sometimes being made up as they went along. The process involved lots of effort and expense in contacting rights holders and paying royalties, as well as dealing with possibilities that rights holders could ask for too much money, refuse to license at all, or not be findable.

So the music changed as hip-hop made the transition from mixtapes sold on the street to major label releases. Artists started limiting the use of other records to scratches and other samples that obscured or transformed the source material.[31] They used techniques for avoiding sample clearance such as "completely chop[ping] it to pieces so it's unrecognizable"[xlvii] or even re-recording musical segments anew. A classic example of the latter was Afrika Bambaataa's "Planet Rock," from 1982, which recreated the melodic synth hook from Kraftwerk's "Trans-Europe Express."[32]

In general, the quantity of samples used in hip-hop declined over time.[xlviii] Hip-hop records began to emphasize rappers over DJs, and producers started to invent more creative ways to use sampling, even as emerging digital technology made it much easier to store, manipulate, and reuse samples in the studio. A prime example of this was the seminal rap group Public Enemy: rappers Chuck D and Flavor Flav got most of the attention, while DJ Terminator X stayed largely in the background, and the Bomb Squad (Hank and Keith Shocklee, Eric "Vietnam" Sadler, and Gary G-Wiz) became one of the most innovative production teams in music history. Public Enemy memorialized the sampling controversy on "Caught, Can We Get a Witness?" from the 1988 album *It Takes a Nation of Millions to Hold Us Back*.

The rules around sampling remained unclear until well into the CD era, when a series of court cases helped define them. The first important case was

Grand Upright Music v. Warner Bros. Records in 1991, in which the publisher of Gilbert O'Sullivan's 1970s soft-rock hit "Alone Again (Naturally)" sued the record label of rapper Biz Markie for his "Alone Again," which sampled the track; it was found to be infringing. Another important case was *Campbell v. Acuff-Rose* in 1994, involving the sampling of Roy Orbison's "Oh, Pretty Woman" on 2 Live Crew's "Pretty Woman," which was found to be fair use.

Still, mixtapes kept on going in the hip-hop underground, even retaining the word "mixtape" after the transition to CDs.

Yet to many everyday music listeners during the 1980s and 1990s, "mixtape" didn't mean hip-hop DJs and MCs. A mixtape was a selection of songs that you recorded onto a cassette to give to someone else—a friend, a lover, a would-be lover, or someone whom you wanted to educate about music. Unlike today's streaming music playlists, cassette mixtapes had the all-important element of effort involved in making them and personalizing them for the recipient.

Mixtapes were meant to be one-offs, not duplicated. You constructed your mixtapes in real time from your vinyl collection, and you created "cover art" and "liner notes" on J-cards (the paper inserts to cassette boxes) by hand. Just as radio DJs did in the days of progressive FM, you considered the order of and transitions between songs just as carefully as you did the songs themselves.

But mainly, consumers used cassettes to open up new spaces and use cases for music listening, and new devices emerged that enabled those new use cases.

One of those new use cases was music on demand in cars. The 8-track tape was invented for this, but cassettes began to overtake them there. By the end of the 1970s, the leading car audio systems included cassette rather than 8-track players, and automakers tended to include factory-installed cassette players in their cars. Auto-reverse—the ability to sense the end of the tape and reverse playback direction—came to cassette players in cars before it came to home players. Cassettes had also displaced 8-tracks in the home: although a few component 8-track record/playback decks were available, none of them were audiophile-grade machines, let alone ultrahigh-end equivalents of the Nakamichi 1000.

The other new use cases were about personal portability. Two new types of devices, introduced in close succession, significantly enhanced the cassette's value to users on the go in different ways.

The first of these was the boombox, the combination radio and cassette recorder/player. The boombox wasn't a technological breakthrough; it was a nickname given to an evolution of the combination radio-cassette recorder, which dated back to 1966. But these were compact devices with unimpressive sound quality. Portables that had more powerful amplifiers and stereo speakers with decent (or exaggerated) bass response, arguably the first true boomboxes, came from Japanese electronics makers and appeared in Western markets starting around 1978. Boomboxes offered "big" sound at prices considerably lower than home component stereo systems.

By the mid-1980s, boomboxes had metastasized into mammoth units the size of suitcases, some of which had detachable speakers. The unit that was supposedly the largest one-piece boombox ever produced was a Taiwan-manufactured unit, shown in Figure 5.5, that was marketed under various no-name brands and model numbers and known among boombox aficionados as the "Master Blaster."[33] It was almost 3 feet wide and 18 inches high; it included side carrying handles, rolling wheels on the bottom, dual

Figure 5.5 The Elta 6930 "Master Blaster" from the mid-1980s, also badged as various other brands and model numbers, the largest one-piece boombox ever made. Max Poser/My Radio Berlin.

cassette decks, a four-band radio, graphic equalizer, and speakers with 10-inch woofers.

The boombox's signature use case was sharing your music with a group of friends—and/or involuntary passers-by—in public, wherever you went. Boomboxes began to be associated—rightly or wrongly—with urban Black and Latino youth, who would carry them around on the streets. They would be used for impromptu parties. They were known as "ghetto blasters" before the more acceptable term "boombox" emerged. By the late 1980s, New York and other cities had banned their use in public places as part of "sweep laws" that some considered to be racially motivated.[xlix] Perhaps the pinnacle of the boombox's cultural significance was in Spike Lee's 1989 movie *Do the Right Thing*, where Radio Raheem uses it to blast Public Enemy's "Fight the Power" and the device becomes a catalyst for racial violence and police brutality.[34]

The next late-1970s innovative device addressed a different use case: listening to music with high-quality audio *in private* wherever you went. That product launched in July 1979: the Sony Walkman, one of the most iconic devices in the history of consumer electronics.

The Walkman was also an evolution—of previous Sony pocket-size cassette machines such as the TCM-100 (a.k.a. Pressman). But it was the first such device devoted solely to stereo playback, and the first to ship with high-quality stereo headphones.

The idea for the Walkman came from Sony cofounder Masaru Ibuka. An opera buff, Ibuka challenged his engineers to find a way for him to listen to operas with good sound quality on his many long plane rides. The engineers essentially took the TCM-100 design, removed the recording functionality, and added stereo playback to create the TPS-L2, shown in Figure 5.6.[35] The product, including lightweight headphones, sold for the equivalent of about $500 today; it did so in volumes beyond Sony's wildest expectations.

The Sony Walkman led to countless other personal portable cassette players from various manufacturers in ever-shrinking sizes. Sony's own WM-20, introduced in 1983, was the size of a cassette box. "Walkman" came dangerously (for Sony) close to becoming a generic for "personal portable cassette player," as "Kleenex" did for "facial tissue." (Sony would subsequently use the name "Discman" for its portable CD players.) Most other electronics makers simply used model numbers for their small portable cassette players rather than use Sony's trademark or make up their own names,[36] although searching for "Walkman" on eBay today yields vintage portable cassette players from other brands.

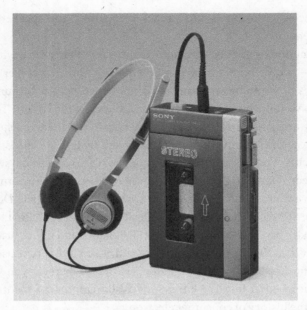

Figure 5.6 The Sony Walkman TPS-L2 portable cassette player, the first Walkman model, from 1979. Used by permission of Sony Electronics Inc. All Rights Reserved.

The boombox and Walkman together dramatically expanded the audience for recorded music by, in effect, introducing another paradigm beyond the transistor radio that had been introduced a quarter century earlier: not only could you listen to music while on the go, but you could choose the music you wanted to listen to.

Tape became the dominant format for recorded music for a while, but not until 30 years after it was first used for that purpose. And for the first half of that time, it was a minuscule part of the recorded music industry. By 1957, prerecorded open-reel tape was a $7 million market in the United States,[l] which was less than 2 percent of overall annual recorded music revenue at that time.[li] Not only were tapes harder to use than LPs (and required equipment that was more obtrusive in the living room), but they cost more too: in 1963, just before cassettes were introduced, typical retail prices for prerecorded open-reel tapes were $7–$9, versus $4–$6 for LPs and lower for budget releases.

The RIAA began tracking total annual US recorded music revenues consistently in 1973; Figure 5.7 shows how revenue from vinyl and tape formats changed from then until 1990, the peak year for tape sales. Sales of 8-track tapes were an order of magnitude higher than open-reel tape, but they never approached the level of vinyl sales, despite the availability of almost all pop music releases on 8-track. In 1973, as the figure shows, 8-track had become a mainstream format. Revenue from 8-tracks hovered around 40 percent of revenue from LPs through the late 1970s as the two formats grew in tandem. Then 8-track sales began plummeting in the late 1970s and disappeared entirely by 1982.

Cassettes eventually became the best-selling music format, but that took a while. Cassette sales lagged behind 8-tracks for several years. In 1973, they were only 16 percent of 8-track sales (and only 6 percent of LP sales), pulling in a mere $76 million. Cassettes gradually gained on both vinyl and 8-tracks through the mid-1970s, then continued growing as 8-tracks started to decline. In 1979, sales of prerecorded cassettes surpassed 8-tracks.

Cassette sales finally exceeded vinyl sales in 1984, despite the rise of home taping. The obvious reasons for this were cassettes' small size, exciting new devices that enabled portable use, and potential sound quality to rival vinyl.

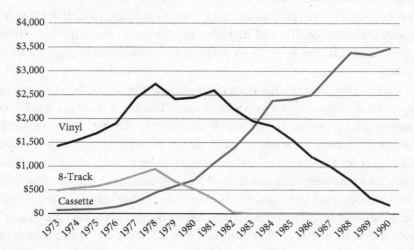

Figure 5.7 Recorded music revenue from vinyl, 8-track tapes, and cassettes, 1973–1990, millions of dollars. Data source: RIAA. Bill Rosenblatt.

But there was another important reason for the timing of cassettes' ascendancy: price.

When cassettes and 8-tracks first came out, their list prices tended to be a dollar or two higher than vinyl LPs, if lower than open-reel. But the price gap narrowed steadily through the 1970s and eventually disappeared. When labels raised mainstream LP prices from $5.98 to $6.98 in 1976, they raised cassettes and 8-tracks to $7.98 (and phased out open-reel). But then when the labels raised LP prices to $7.98 in 1978, they held tape prices steady. By the start of the 1980s, the big retail chains—which typically discounted everything and priced each type of item according to its own profit margin—were pricing LPs and tapes equally.[lii]

Cassettes leapt passed vinyl's peak revenue of $2.7 billion in 1987. They remained the dominant format by revenue for a short time until CDs overtook them in 1990. And although cassette revenues started to decline after that, cassettes continued to outsell vinyl until the early 2000s, when both formats faded away.

Cassette sales started up again in the mid-2010s. A catalyst for this was the 2014 Disney sci-fi film *Guardians of the Galaxy*. In the movie, the hero's dying mother gives him a mixtape of 1960s and 1970s hits, which he plays on a Sony Walkman to help him stay connected to his home on Earth. Disney created a soundtrack album based on the mixtape and released it on cassette, complete with faux-handwritten J-card, in an exclusive arrangement with indie record stores. It was the first cassette that the studio's record label had released since 2003. The soundtrack (which was subsequently released on CD and digitally) hit the top of the Billboard album charts that year. Prices for used original Sony Walkman models on eBay spiked.

But this phenomenon has been nowhere near the size of the vinyl renaissance we discussed in the previous chapter. The RIAA does not track new cassette sales anymore—other than to include it in the tiny "Other Physical" category,[37] which constitutes less than 0.1 percent of industry revenue. Discogs.com, the premier marketplace for used records, lists 1.4 million cassettes on its website at this time of writing, compared to over 46 million vinyl records. And the video for Adele's "Easy on Me," the first single from her long-awaited 2021 album *30*, featured a cassette as "product placement"; but the actual cassette of the album only sold 2,000 copies,[liii] compared to (at this writing) about two billion streams.

Conclusion

Still, unlike other tape formats, cassettes have a place in music fans' hearts. There has been enough new cassette activity since the mid-2010s that a few cultural commentators, particularly in Britain,[liv] proclaimed a revival and made various attempts to explain why it's happening.[38,lv] Many of these explanations could apply to vinyl as well, but not all of them. For one thing, unlike vinyl, no one thinks that cassettes sound superior to today's digital audio. Whereas various audiophile-grade turntables are being designed today with price tags reaching up into Rolex watch territory, the few cassette machines that are sold today are cheap portables and retro nostalgia models.

Instead, the special appeal of cassettes nowadays is that of the cassette underground of the 1980s. Artists who release cassette-only albums today could certainly put their music out faster and cheaper online. But to these artists' fans, cassettes evoke an era when they signified closer connections to the people whose music is on them—who may have been personally involved in loading blank tapes into duplicators, packaging the tapes in boxes with J-cards they designed, and sending them off in the mail. Never mind that some of the artists who used to do this in the 1970s and 1980s now say that they used cassettes because they had no other reasonable choices and despite their mediocre sound quality and poor capacity for cover art.[lvi] That's the DIY ethos that today's cassette artists embrace and seek to maintain.

Meanwhile, as the popularity of both cassettes and home taping began to rise and that of vinyl began to fall, the music industry plotted its next move. It decided to address tape's tradeoffs against vinyl by introducing a new format, one that combined the portability of cassettes with sound quality that was arguably better than vinyl but that didn't support duplicating records at home. As we'll see, this would work out extremely well for the industry—at least until the last of those attributes ceased to be true. Yet just before the CD hit the market, another set of outside forces came back in to disrupt the music industry as it did back in the 1930s: broadcast media.

6

Television

Television Rules the Nation—Daft Punk

When MTV launched in August 1981, its success was far from assured. In fact, the network had a list of substantial shortcomings. Its entire library of videos consisted of 125 songs. With 24 hours of airtime to fill seven days per week, every single track would need to be played three times per day, no matter the quality or popularity. That presented an issue, because many of those videos were from British new wave bands who were not particularly well-known in the United States at the time. And the ones from American artists included acts like Devo, who had developed a cult following but had not achieved mainstream acceptance. Very few households in the United States could experience the fledgling network because most cable networks simply chose not to carry it. And the networks that did offer MTV at first were in limited media markets such as Columbus, Ohio, and Tulsa, Oklahoma. This represented a total addressable viewership of only 1 million households at launch. With such a limited audience, advertisers were not lining up to purchase commercial time.

Given those constraints, the nascent MTV of 1981 could certainly be deemed a "Minimal Viable Product" for a music channel. Although they were not a format that was distributed to consumers in the same way as vinyl or tapes, music videos became so important to MTV's audience that devoted fans became known as the "MTV Generation." MTV unleashed a wave of creativity and turbocharged the popularity of superstars such as Michael Jackson and Madonna, whose videos were often as memorable as the melody or lyrics of their songs.

We'll review in detail how MTV overcame its initial deficiencies to become a cultural phenomenon and an enormous financial success. MTV did have one crucial asset right from the start that had been true for more than 50 years: people loved to watch, and not just listen to, recorded musical performances.

Key Changes. Howie Singer and Bill Rosenblatt, Oxford University Press. © Howie Singer and Bill Rosenblatt 2023.
DOI: 10.1093/oso/9780197656891.003.0006

The idea of combining audio and visual performances was not new; it dates all the way back to the early days of the phonograph, although that new invention did not play a role at first. Music publishers wanted to sell sheet music and needed to expose new songs to as broad an audience as possible. Getting a big name on the vaudeville circuit to perform a new song in their act was highly desirable, but there was no guarantee that a particular artist would like the tune. A surefire technique was to hire "song pluggers" to play the new material at cafes, restaurants, and even department stores.[1]

The pluggers would repeat their performances in the evenings in nickelodeons and movie theaters. Before the show and during the intermission, the pluggers would play the new song while hand-colored pictures on painted canvases or glass slides that related to the lyrics would be shown behind them. These "illustrated songs" were popular with audiences as additional free entertainment. They proved to be an effective promotional tool because they made popular songs into "visual spectacles" some 90 years before MTV.

The inventors of the day were pursuing a different path to meld music and images. In 1895, Edison introduced the Kinetoscope, which combined his cylinder phonograph with a motion picture player in a single physical cabinet. The two media were not synchronized, and the ability to exhibit films to an audience in a large screen soon superseded this "peep-show" approach that served only a single viewer at a time.

Efforts to perfect the audio-visual experience continued throughout the silent film era, and the age of the "talkie" arrived in October 1926. Al Jolson was already one of the most popular American musical artists when he starred in the first feature film with sound, *The Jazz Singer*. Jolson's musical performances were recorded on the set and the advertisements highlighted that "You'll See Him and Hear Him on Vitaphone," the latter being the technology that synchronized the audio with the film. The movie was a major box office hit earning a total of over $2.5 million, or almost $40 million in 2022 dollars, cementing the value of sound as more than a mere gimmick to the motion picture industry.

Movie musicals became a staple in cinema as the extravagant production numbers crafted by Busby Berkeley and the intricate choreography of Fred Astaire and Ginger Rogers entertained millions during the Great Depression. Musical numbers were so popular with the public that the Mills Novelty Company of Chicago updated Edison's Kinetoscope idea for the 1940s and created a "movie jukebox" called the Panoram. Each unit contained a projector and played an endless loop of eight three-minute films that consisted of musical numbers featuring singers, dancers, and bands. These forerunners of the music video were known as "Soundies." Patrons of bars, restaurants, and diners would put 10 cents into the Panoram and get to watch whichever film was next in the loop. They inserted so many dimes that the company soon earned millions per year.

Soundies featured a wide variety of music, including classical and big bands, highlighting artists such as Jimmy Dorsey, Lawrence Welk, and Gene Krupa. They provided an outlet for the creative output of many African American artists who were limited in the Hollywood system. Fortunately, many of the Soundies survived and constitute a valuable record of performances by Fats Waller, Duke Ellington, Count Basie, The Mills Bothers, and Sister Rosetta Tharpe, to name just a few.[2]

Despite the success of the Panoram, the production demands of World War II limited the availability of the materials needed to manufacture the machines. The company kept the business going by creating new short films. But without new hardware to expand to more locations, the growth of Soundies was constrained. Ultimately, the mass market adoption of television brought an end to the Panoram.[i]

As the postwar economy and the suburbs grew, television sets began to proliferate in US homes, and musical programs and artists that had proved popular on radio added images to their sounds. For 15 years, Your Hit Parade had offered performances on radio of the most popular songs each week from its stable of singers. A televised version of the program began in 1950. Counting down to the number one song of the week proved popular for TV audiences as well.[3] In 1957, the show covered hits by artists such as Debbie Reynolds and Pat Boone.[ii] Those singers were certainly popular with the generation who had grown up on radio, but that sort of music was not well suited to the young people weaned on TV who were discovering the new genre that they viewed as their own: rock & roll.

The movies were already beginning to cater to the tastes of the Baby Boom generation with films such as *Blackboard Jungle*. Released in 1956, the film focused on an inner-city school with teenaged protagonists, and it featured the first use of a rock song in a Hollywood film. "Rock Around the Clock" by Bill Haley & the Comets played while the opening credits ran. Teenagers going to the movie theater literally danced in the aisles. The song went to no. 1 on the *Billboard* charts.

Broadcast television took note of this success and of the growing and rabid fanbase of a certain young singer from Memphis. Both Steve Allen and Milton Berle invited Elvis Presley to appear on their shows. Ed Sullivan, who hosted the top-rated TV Variety program, was not a fan; he felt that Elvis was unfit for family viewing. But the ratings for the appearances on his rivals' shows were too large to ignore. Sullivan featured Presley on September 9, 1956 and sixty million people tuned in. To avoid offending anyone with the gyrations of Elvis's pelvis, they shot his performance from the waist up.[iii]

One year later, the same Baby Boomers who screamed for Elvis began tuning in every afternoon to a show that played just the hits they cared about: American Bandstand. Hosted by former radio DJ Dick Clark, the show featured artists such as Paul Anka and Chubby Checker lip-synching their hits while teenagers in the studio danced along. The program had started on a local Philadelphia station in 1950 as a TV version of the radio show "Bandstand." Though there were occasional studio guests on that local show, much of the airtime was filled by short films of prerecorded musical performances. By 1959, American Bandstand, propelled by rock & roll as the soundtrack of teen culture, reached an audience of 20 million each day.[iv,v]

The musical show that appealed to millions of older music fans in the early 1960s was considerably more sedate. Sing Along with Mitch, hosted by Mitch Miller, featured a male chorus performing pop standards with the lyrics included at the bottom of the screen.[4] The karaoke-style show of its day proved so popular that Miller recorded and produced albums with songs from the show complete with tear-out lyrics. The weekly show was canceled in 1964 as musical tastes shifted even more dramatically toward rock.

Before that seismic shift, the early 1960s brought one more attempt to build a business around the concept of a video jukebox. Scopitone machines, originally offered in Germany, were deployed in adult establishments, including cocktail lounges, to avoid competing with the jukeboxes that were popular with teens.[vi] These units improved on the Soundies by offering short films in color, and patrons could choose which one they wanted to watch rather than being restricted to watching the next one on a loop. Over 500 machines were installed by 1964, with films featuring performances by artists like Neil Sedaka and Bobby Vee. The business failed to convince many of the next wave of music superstars, including those who were part of the British Invasion, to include their songs; this fatally wounded one more video jukebox platform.

Of course, the band leading that invasion was the Beatles, who began dominating the US charts in 1964. On a trip to London, Ed Sullivan happened to be at the airport the same day as the Beatles returned to England from a European trip and witnessed their screaming fans first-hand. He booked the band for their first live TV appearance in the United States. On February 9, 1964, at 8 p.m., 60 percent of the households in the United States tuned in to watch the Beatles shake their mop-top haircuts and try to be heard over a crowd of screaming teenage girls. The Sullivan show had received 50,000 requests for the approximately 700 seats in their theater. The estimated 72 million viewers handily topped Elvis's record, and TV fueled Beatlemania and the British Invasion.[vii]

The broadcast networks, seeing the drawing power of rock & roll music on television, followed a tried-and-true business practice: create imitations. Shindig premiered on ABC in September 1964, and Hullabaloo followed on NBC in January 1965. Shindig had replaced Hootenany, another music-oriented show that focused on folk music, whose ratings had plummeted as rock & roll began to top the charts. The guest lists for the two shows read like the *Billboard* charts, including Sam Cooke, the Byrds, the Supremes, the Lovin' Spoonful, and Simon & Garfunkel. But the networks were truly broadcasters: they tried to balance appealing to younger viewers while attracting the Mitch Miller crowd as well. They featured the artists that would draw teens but added hosts like Jerry Lewis and Zsa Zsa Gabor who could make the show feel less risqué and more palatable for older viewers. This middle-of-the road combination proved less than compelling for either audience segment, and within two years both shows were off the primetime schedule.

NBC had much more critical success with the Monkees television show, which first aired in 1966. Clearly inspired by the successful Beatles film *A Hard Day's Night*, which captured the Fab Four's frantic lives chased by rabid fans, the producers chose to put together a TV-ready foursome who could portray an up-and-coming long-haired rock band. Davy Jones,[5] Peter Tork, Micky Dolenz, and Mike Nesmith were selected after a lengthy audition process. They sang catchy songs[6] but, at least initially, did not play the instruments on their recorded tracks. The combination of the comedic elements with cleverly filmed music numbers earned them the Emmy for Best Comedy series in 1967, and the band sold 8 million records in the first four months of the show.

During the 1970s, the programming of rock music on television shifted its focus from primetime to late night. The Midnight Special and Don Kirshner's Rock Concert both featured live performances, in contrast to the typical appearances on television of lip-synching to prerecorded tracks. To compensate for the monaural sound of broadcast TV, Rock Concert performances were recorded in stereo and then simulcast via FM stereo stations to create a superior audio experience. Although more diverse artists such as Earth, Wind & Fire were sometimes featured on these late-night programs, R&B and soul artists commanded the stage on Soul Train, a syndicated music program airing weekly beginning in 1971. At that time, it was the first commercial TV program aiming for a Black audience that was produced by Black people, led by the Chicago-based radio news reporter turned entrepreneur Don Cornelius. There were other syndicated variety shows that were geared towards fans of specific music genres: country fans watched Hee Haw while more traditional music (and polka) fans chose the Lawrence Welk Show.

Despite the well-established appeal for prerecorded audiovisual performances, there was no regular outlet for the short-form music videos being created as promotional tools for radio stations in the late 1970s. Bob Pittman, who later became one of the founders of MTV, cohosted a music video and news show that ran on some NBC stations in 1978. Mike Nesmith, the former member of the Monkees, crafted a new show produced by Jac Holzman, the founder of Elektra Records, to promote Warner Communications' records. Nesmith recognized that the short music videos, like the one for his song "Rio" that was produced as a marketing tool for other territories, could promote the song within the United States too. Calling his show "PopClips," after a similar program airing in Australia and New Zealand, he pitched his pilot to broadcast networks without success. In 1979, John Lack, an executive for the catchily named Warner-Amex Satellite Entertainment Company (WASEC), the entity charged with programming for Warner Communications' cable systems, met with Nesmith. Lack liked the PopClips idea and contracted for 13 episodes, which played several times per day on Nickelodeon, a channel that specifically targeted young audiences with its programming. Homes in Columbus, Ohio, that subscribed to Warner Communications' nascent QUBE network[7] watched those music videos over cable television. PopClips had comedians as announcers, including Howie Mandel, though Lack felt that they took away from the focus on music.[viii]

There is some dispute about how much the PopClips experience influenced the team that launched MTV. Lack hired Bob Pittman as head of Pay-TV at Warner Cable; Pittman brought his own broadcasting experience, which included the local NBC music video show. John Sykes, who was hired as MTV Promotion Director, thought that Nesmith did not deserve any credit and that he could "go jump in a lake."

Regardless of the exact heritage, it is clear that creating "radio on TV" by expanding from limited length programs to an entire channel built around music videos was the seed of an enormously successful franchise. Creating a platform for advertisers to connect with 25–34-year-olds who had become more and more difficult to reach via traditional TV was the important new element. The music videos themselves were not particularly innovative—at least at first.

MTV kicked off on August 1, 1981 by playing "Video Killed the Radio Star" by the Buggles. The prophetic title has become a popular music trivia question, but Steve Casey, an MTV programming executive, said that it was the second video they aired that really foreshadowed the effects on the music industry: "You Better Run" by Pat Benatar.

The founders of MTV did not view their network as a technology-driven enterprise. Instead, it was the packaging together of all the pieces that collectively constituted something new. As Bob Pittman said, "The network is the star." Regardless of that view, MTV rested on a foundation of innovation.

When the entire MTV team gathered for a launch party to watch the premiere of their new venture, one might have expected to find them in some fashionable and trendy spot in the heart of New York City. Instead they crossed the river to Fort Lee, New Jersey, a "bridge and tunnel" town not known for being particularly fashionable or trendy. But Fort Lee had one key characteristic that distinguished it from Manhattan or any of the other boroughs of NYC: a cable system that aired the new music video channel. In 1981, major metropolitan areas—with plenty of local broadcast channels—had not yet adopted cable television. Cable deployment was still constrained to the less urban markets that had spawned the technology in the first place rather than New York or Los Angeles.

Television signals broadcast over the air require a "line of sight" between the transmitter and the receiver. That allows the airwaves carrying the signal to reach the viewer's antenna. In the early days of television, the only broadcast stations were in cities, and people in more rural or mountainous locations often had difficulty picking up those over-the-air broadcast signals. To solve this problem, a single large and more expensive antenna was constructed in each of these more remote areas to receive the broadcast signal. Then, coaxial cables from that "community antenna" were run to individual homes to convey the programming via radio frequency signals. To compensate for the signals weakening as they traversed the cable, amplifiers were deployed along the way to boost the signals. This architecture became known as "Community Antenna Television" or CATV.

By the mid-1970s, several advances in technology improved both the quality of CATV service and the costs of delivery. Geosynchronous satellites were used to beam programming such as HBO to that master antenna or "cable headend," thereby eliminating the line-of-sight restriction. When fiber optics replaced coaxial cables, signal loss decreased, which reduced the number of amplifiers needed to maintain transmission quality. Those same fiber optic cables were capable of carrying much more data than the older coaxial cables. That higher bandwidth meant that fiber-optic cable systems could supply many more channels to their subscribers.

The greater channel capacity allowed companies like Warner Cable to focus on a variety of niche audiences rather than programming to appeal to as broad a population as possible, as was necessary with broadcast television. There was room for channels targeting golf enthusiasts, animal lovers, and bargain hunters who wanted to shop from their couches—and even one that showed music videos round the clock. *Fortune* magazine named MTV as one of its 1981 "Products of the Year," citing its ability to "serve up specific audiences for advertisers, as specialized magazines do."[ix]

When Warner surveyed potential MTV viewers prior to launch, 85 percent said they would watch music videos. An even higher percentage said that they owned stereo systems and that most of those systems were located in the same room as their television set (which could deliver only monaural sound). When a cable system agreed to carry the channel, MTV required it to purchase a "stereo transmission processor" from a company they recommended. The $1400 unit, developed by Dolby, modulated the stereo soundtrack and allowed it to be transmitted through the cable TV network along with the video signal. By connecting the cable-TV output to an FM receiver's antenna input and tuning the receiver to the right frequency, customers could listen to the stereo sound. Many cable operators were able to charge subscribers about $1.50 extra per month above their standard fees simply for providing the ability to listen to programming in stereo.[x] The FCC adopted a standard for stereo audio in television transmission in 1984, and manufacturers eventually built the capability to receive stereo into televisions.

We have all come to expect that every music video displays the name of the song and the artist. But the ability to overlay textual information on a video was invented not long before MTV's launch, by Systems Resources Corporation in the 1970s. This higher-tech process replaced filming decorative cards or cranking credit rolls by hand. The company was renamed Chyron, and "chyron" became the generic term for "text or graphics overlayed on video." MTV made it a policy to use a chyron to add the name of the song and the artist on every single music video at the beginning and the end to increase its promotional effectiveness.

Not only was MTV a channel in the programming sense, but it was the new distribution channel for the music video format. MTV did not create music videos, but it also had to persuade artists and labels to let the channel air them. They did not decide which cable operators would offer the channel to viewers, but they had to persuade businesspeople at those operators that MTV could attract a youthful fanbase.

MTV's leaders learned early on that convincing these gatekeepers was no small task. *Billboard* magazine held the first Video Music Conference in the fall of 1979. At that point, MTV's founders had not even decided on a name for their channel. Nevertheless, John Lack attended the event and, during one of the panels, he announced the plan for a new network showing music videos around the clock. Many of the label executives in the room found the concept, shall we say, less than compelling. Sidney Sheinberg, the President of MCA Records, stood up and declared, "We won't give you our fucking music."

Those sentiments exemplified the labels' reluctance to furnish their copyrights to establish a new format. Of course, that reluctance can sometimes be overcome through substantial upfront payments specified in licensing agreements. MTV's launch plans did not include making any such payments. Instead, they were asking the labels to offer their catalog of music videos for free. As Bob Pittman put it, "This was not a business model. That's chutzpah."[xi]

MTV's founders knew that one of the most common complaints about radio was that DJs could not be relied on to announce the details of the songs being played. How could radio play provide promotional value if they failed to declare who or what was being promoted? MTV's use of chyron technology to overlay the title of the song and the performer's name on each clip enabled the new network to argue that every single video would serve as a three-minute advertisement for the music. Addressing radio's weakness head-on was a positive for MTV, but it would not have been enough by itself to persuade the labels to take a chance on supplying their music videos.

Yet MTV's timing was propitious for it, if not for the music industry itself. As we saw in Chapter 5, in the early 1980s, the record business was in the midst of a multiyear slump. Over the ensuing four years, the number of units sold and associated revenues both dropped almost 20 percent from 726 million and $4.3 billion respectively. In addition to the reasons discussed in Chapter 5, the shift was also caused by demographic trends. Younger music fans had been the core of the economic engine through the rock era, but those Baby Boomers were aging out of their prime music purchasing years, and younger music fans were not picking up the slack. Fifteen-to-24-year-olds represented 45 percent of the industry's revenues from 1979 through 1981, but that number was heading downward toward 39 percent by 1982. Furthermore, the industry was broadly dissatisfied with radio's performance in breaking new artists because of increasingly restricted playlists.[xii]

Given the industry slump, many labels were willing to take a chance on MTV, although both MCA and Polygram remained on the sidelines. The record companies had a limited number of music videos on hand at that time, and giving them to MTV seemed like a risk worth taking. As Al Teller, then President of CBS and Columbia Records, explained, "The timing was perfect. The music industry was in the doldrums."[xiii] MTV, if successful, would boost those lagging results by activating a younger demographic. The thinking at the time was that once MTV had established itself as a viable channel (in both senses of the word), there would certainly be opportunities to revisit the financial arrangements and to extract payments for labels and artists.

It is worth noting that it is riskier than it might seem for the labels to accept terms that would never have been contemplated if not for the industry's declining fortunes. The more successful the channel becomes, the more dependent the industry becomes on its contributions. And that dependence gives the channel leverage even though it relies on the labels' content. Providing videos for free proved to be a "devil's bargain" as MTV came to exert tremendous power over the industry's fortunes down the road.[8]

Having the labels on board to offer their videos checked off one of the required items for MTV's launch. But it still needed cable operators to carry the station. Unlike the music labels, which at least saw the need to stay in touch with the latest trends in popular culture as an essential element for their success, the owners and operators of the cable networks in the early 1980s tended to be older, whiter, and more conservative businesspeople. And while other cable stations required operators to pay a "carriage fee," MTV was offered for free. Yet even at that price, the cable operators were not receptive to showcasing postpunk music from Britain even if MTV used the more acceptable name "new wave."

As gatekeepers, these cable operators were, in some sense, a reflection of the markets they served. Because of the technology's origins in extending television coverage to areas lacking line-of-sight access, cable households in the early 1980s were concentrated in the suburbs, smaller cities, and rural areas. The largest urban centers were simply not included. When MTV conducted surveys to determine the likely viewers in those addressable markets, they found that the channel would appeal to 23–34-year-olds who were well-educated and affluent. That audience's tastes matched up with the videos MTV had to broadcast from predominantly white rock musicians. That focus on white bands made sense demographically, but it eventually became a major issue in diversity for the channel and its relationships with some of the most popular artists in the world.

As part of a joint venture between Warner Communications and American Express, MTV had support in markets such as Columbus, Ohio, where the parent company controlled the cable operator. It was also able to persuade operators in markets such as Tulsa, Oklahoma, and Fort Lee, New Jersey, to provide carriage for the channel, which added up to that addressable market of one million households at launch. But MTV's efforts to convince the major cable operators with much larger audiences met with resistance. The largest cable network at the time was TCI, based in Denver, Colorado and led by CEO John Malone.[9] He wouldn't even take a phone call from John Lack to discuss MTV. Lack flew to Colorado and appealed to Bob Magness, the TCI founder and Chairman, who personally escorted Lack into Malone's office to make the pitch. Malone's response was presumably less colorful than

Sheinberg's of MCA, but the bottom line was the same. He escorted Lack to the door and threw him out.

To realize its full potential, MTV had to get Malone and other equally conservative cable operators—as well as the recalcitrant labels—to revisit their opposition. The initial video catalog may have been limited in size, but the young viewers who received the channel liked what they saw. Those fans became the catalysts to increase the size of both the video catalog and the addressable audience.

Bob Pittman's experience in radio made him a believer in using research to guide programming decisions. Based on a sample of the two million households that would be able to receive the channel at launch, the network gathered data about 150 different artists to determine the audience's preferences. They found that there was not a great overlap between the addressable market's desires and the videos that the channel had to offer. Going to market with this limited video catalog was less about serving that audience than it was about avoiding the costs of acquiring or funding videos starring the most desired artists. MTV cofounder Tom Freston admitted that the catalog of videos was so limited that they "would have played anything."

That selection had the unintended consequence of making the channel edgier than it might have been, thus boosting its appeal to younger audiences who wanted to find their own new artists.[10] Rock critic Robert Christgau pointed out that if the labels had videos of Air Supply or Linda Ronstadt, MTV would have been much more "middlebrow."[xiv] Including videos of artists of the Baby Boomer era might have seemed like a logical strategy. But that generation had already moved past the age when music was most central to their lives. Broadcast TV had already catered to them during their prime music years with shows from American Bandstand to the Monkees. Trying to get these older fans to change their music listening habits to the new medium of cable TV would have been a challenge.

Instead, the available catalog skewed "young." It featured emerging British pop artists like the Eurythmics and new wave bands like Duran Duran who, at that time, were less popular in the United States than in Britain. American artists with videos were rarer, and those who had them, such as Devo, were more cutting-edge and less mainstream. These acts chose to make avant-garde music videos to serve their own artistic purposes.

There were some concerns in the industry that fans would not enjoy watching music videos of bands simply lip-synching over prerecorded songs. The productions in the early 1980s already featured sounds, such as synths and drum loops, that were "manufactured" rather than played live. Recreating those recordings accurately during live performances required the use of those same techniques in venues. Fans had become accustomed to more "artificial" elements within performances of their favorite songs whether live or on TV.[xv]

As we've seen with the transistor radio and the personal tape player, younger, more passionate music fans are often the first to adopt new formats and to make them their own. MTV was no different: it quickly became "must-see TV" for the youthful, suburban fans in communities with access to the channel. By October of 1982, a Nielsen survey showed that 85 percent in the key demographic group for the channel were watching the station between four and five hours per week. In a survey of 600 high school students, 80 percent were watching MTV two hours per day on average.

Filling the network's schedule seven days per week and 24 hours a day required repeated plays of their constrained catalog. This had the unintended consequence of creating a limited playlist like most radio stations. And, just like those stations, the constant drumbeat of promoting a limited number of songs to viewers made an impression.

The new American fans of bands in heavy MTV rotation, such as A Flock of Seagulls and Duran Duran, bought those bands' albums at unprecedented levels. Columbia Records had very low expectations for sales in the United States for the Australian band Men at Work and pressed fewer than 8,000 copies of their debut album initially. The video of the band's single "Who Can It Be Now" cost $5,000. But once MTV started airing it, the album climbed to no. 1 and stayed there for several months, much to the surprise of the label.[xvi]

As one would expect, the increased popularity and sales volumes of the artists whose videos were being shown by MTV were concentrated in markets that aired the channel. Having some cable operators offer the station while others did not created a "natural experiment" that demonstrated the impact of the network's impact on sales. In October 1981, *Billboard* magazine surveyed record stores in those cities where MTV was being offered to viewers. Artists whose videos were being aired showed increased sales when compared to other cities and other artists.[xvii,xviii]

Another example of MTV's impact was Stray Cats, a rockabilly trio from Long Island that had no radio airplay and a low profile before a video of its song "Stray Cat Strut" went into heavy rotation on the channel. When the band's tour hit MTV markets, they sold out all the clubs where they appeared. As singer/guitarist Brian Setzer noted, "We'd go to a place like Des Moines and play for a thousand people." Fans purchased 200,000 copies of the band's album. They would have topped the charts if not for the even more successful record from Men at Work that was boosted by MTV as well. Tulsa, Oklahoma, was one of those MTV cities and, before long, Sound Warehouse, a local retailer with three locations, began to stock its shelves based on the videos in rotation.[xix]

Retailers were not the only ones noticing that fans were making buying decisions for tickets and albums based on the artists they enjoyed on MTV. The labels that had been withholding videos over the lack of payments from the channel overcame their reluctance. Jordan Rost, then VP for Research at the parent company Warner/AMEX, discussed the results and said, "It did not take a lot of convincing as this was a 3-minute ad. It was just better airplay."[xx]

The eagerness to build a motivated fanbase brought Polygram on board, followed shortly thereafter by Universal. And the marketing teams at all the record companies cited the economic impacts of being aired on MTV to justify the investment in new videos covering a broader array of priority releases. Video budgets increased and the promotional impact grew as well. The video for "Every Breath You Take" by the Police cost close to $100,000. Jeff Ayeroff, the Creative Director for Warner Brothers Records, pointed to the 5 million albums sold and labeled the returns as "phenomenal."[xxi] In May of 1981, only 23 of the top singles in the Hot 100 chart had videos. Two years later, that number was up to 59; and one year after that, more than three-quarters of the top tracks had videos.[xxii]

The labels expanded the flow of content to the channel to trigger more sales. But the cable operators who controlled access to a larger audience had a different set of priorities. According to Bob Pittman, advertisers were reluctant to be associated with "sex, drugs, and rock & roll," and without those ad revenues it was even more difficult to convince the cable operators of the channel's potential. MTV hired an ad agency to create a campaign that would send a message to their potential viewers in what Pittman referred to as a "Hail Mary pass to obtain the distribution the channel needed to survive." The first advertising message to explain the network to a broader audience was "Cable Brats," with a sub-tagline of "Rock 'n roll wasn't enough for them, now they want their MTV." Whenever the MTV executives would show up to make their case to the cable operators, they were referred to as the "cable brats."

Needless to say, that campaign did not last long; the message was soon boiled down to "I want my MTV."xxiii Commercials featuring that catch-phrase blanketed the airwaves in specific markets where the channel was not available. MTV ran the ads in Denver, and the fans began calling TCI, their cable operator, almost immediately. The number of calls climbed into the thousands by the second day, and soon the local newspapers were covering the story. John Malone, the executive who had once refused to even take calls from MTV, caved within a week and added the channel to the TCI lineup. And MTV would then move on to the next city and prompt the public there to besiege their cable operator with demands for "their MTV."

As a format, MTV changed the relationship between the industry and its fans. Every recorded music shift required mass-market acceptance to be successful. But in the case of music videos, the public's role was more than just enjoying their favorite songs in a new configuration. They played a far more active role by expressing their preferences loudly and repeatedly. The Generation X teens who loved the network even came to be referred to as the "MTV Generation." They believed their opinions mattered and that the entrenched business interests should pay heed to their collective voices. We'll discuss in Chapter 8 how improved network connectivity and the powerful software of the Internet era would prove to be even more potent catalysts in upending the business.

"I want my MTV" was certainly catchy, but the words themselves would not have been enough to persuade music fans to advocate for a channel they may have heard about but had never experienced personally. Motivating the public to take action required communication that commanded their attention. And no one could elicit a greater response from fans than their musical idols.

Despite the allure of substantial payments, many artists simply refused to "sell out" and to license their songs for commercials. Even fewer wanted to appear in ads personally. Neil Young is just one well-known example.[11] Many others would consent to such arrangements, but only for the right (very large) price. MTV's challenge was the fact that their talent budget for ads equaled their acquisition budget for music videos: zero. Getting even one superstar artist to make a commercial without writing a check with lots of zeros seemed like an impossible task.

Nevertheless, Les Garland, Executive VP of Programming for the channel, took on that mission and flew to France to meet with Mick Jagger of the Rolling Stones. Garland told Jagger that he wanted him to go on camera and say "I want my MTV" to promote the channel and its music videos. Jagger explained that the Stones did not make commercials. Garland pointed out that the Stones did indeed accept tour sponsorship from companies. Jagger agreed but said the Stones got "paid a lot of money for that." Of course, Garland had no such budget to draw on, and he told that to Jagger. Instead, Garland put a single dollar bill on the table. Surprisingly, Jagger agreed. The commercial was shot the next day.

Getting Jagger on board not only gave MTV a rock legend to pitch the channel to fans, it gave the entire advertising effort the credibility to attract other artists under the exact same arrangement: no compensation. The network reached out to Pat Benatar and told her Mick Jagger was doing the ads; she followed suit. The same argument worked for David Bowie, Pete Townshend, The Police, and Cyndi Lauper, to name just a few. Sony Music CEO Tommy Mottola said, "The campaign gave MTV integrity and credibility with the audience; their favorite band or icon was endorsing this brand and telling them this was the thing they should watch." The fans took those instructions to heart and loudly demanded their MTV in phone calls and letters. The cable operators complied. Group W, the operator covering the northern half of Manhattan, added MTV in time to air the 1983 New Year's Eve Rock n' Roll Ball. That same company also controlled the Southern California market; three weeks later, they flipped the switch there.[xxiv] Music fans in the major media centers in United States, along with millions of others nationwide, had done as their idols had commanded, and now they had their MTV.[xxv]

Although music videos are an essential element of virtually every record release today, at the start of the MTV era many artists resisted the pressure to appear in them. Billy Joel saw himself as a piano player and not an actor; he hated making videos. Elton John might have been the consummate showman on stage, but he felt that he photographed poorly, so he avoided shooting videos as well.

Van Halen was another band that held negative views about MTV. They felt that music videos were simply beneath them, but rather than refusing to participate, they elected to undermine the process. When they needed a video for their cover version of Roy Orbison's "Pretty Woman," the band chose to take on the characters of a cowboy, a samurai warrior, Tarzan, and Napoleon. That could have been the basis for an entertaining video. However, the band chose to build the story around two little people reaching up the skirt of a young woman whose hands were tied to two posts while the events were observed by a hunchback. Van Halen pushed the envelope further by ending the video with the girl removing her wig to reveal that she was a man. What was most surprising for the early 1980s is that the network actually aired that video once or twice before banning it completely.[12]

Bruce Springsteen wanted to focus on "writing songs, making records, and doing concerts," and there was no room within those three priorities for music videos. When his album *Nebraska* was released in 1982, Columbia Records put together a music video for "Atlantic City." The video met with Springsteen's approval because he did not appear at all in the roughly three-and-a-half-minute run time. By 1984, MTV's power to promote new songs became too potent to resist, even for the Boss, and he can be seen pulling a young Courteney Cox from the audience to join him on stage in the video for "Dancing in the Dark." That song became Springsteen's highest charting single up to that point in time.

Not all creators viewed making music videos as a burden or a process to be subverted. Some bands used the production budgets to live up to the rock stereotype. They enjoyed casting bikini models to appear as eye candy in the videos and made sure that everyone on set was well supplied with a variety of illegal substances. That's not to minimize the use of attractive women in music videos to appeal to much of the young and male MTV audience. Whitesnake furnished just such an example later in the 1980s. The British hard rock band had built a successful following in Europe, but it had been unable to achieve meaningful sales in the United States. The music video for "Here I Go Again" featured actress Tawny Kitaen—the future wife of singer/bandleader David Coverdale—doing front handsprings across several Jaguar XKEs. MTV put the video into heavy rotation, and the album featuring the song broke through in America. It made it to no. 2 on the *Billboard* charts and eventually went eight times Platinum.[xxvi]

Of course, there were other artists who saw videos as opportunities to make more meaningful artistic statements. Devo is a compelling case study of a band that embraced video as an extension of their musical sensibilities. Gerard "Jerry" Casale was one of the founders of the band. He composed much of their music and directed many of their music videos as well. He later became a director for other top-selling artists such as the Cars and Foo Fighters. From their start in the 1970s, Casale saw Devo as a "bridge between the art museum and the record store."[xxvii] He says that they were thinking visually from the start and that showing their short films at concerts helped to "prime their audience to start at full throttle" for their live performances. The record labels thought the band was foolish to spend unrecoupable dollars on videos rather than investing in in-store promotions or billboards, which they believed were more effective. When MTV launched, Devo was among the few American bands that had videos ready for the network, and Casale described the effect as a "booster rocket" for record and ticket sales. The band went from selling out 400-seat clubs to doing the same at theaters with ten times as many seats.

Dave Stewart of the Eurythmics created a storyboard for the video of "Sweet Dreams," drawing out every scene in advance. The label people were less than thrilled when they saw the result, with Annie Lennox's closely cropped orange hair and dressed in a suit and tie to match Stewart. The cow wandering through the video didn't make the executives any more comfortable. Yet MTV saw the creativity and the vibrant colors resulting from shooting on film and approved. The video and the song were both enormous hits. Thomas Dolby took on the "auteur" role by planning out in advance all the shots for the video of "Blinded By Science." He devised the entire visual concept before he wrote the song and then convinced the label to let him direct the video as well. Unlike virtually all other videos, Dolby crafted the music in service to the visuals and not the other way around.[xxviii]

The most natural complementary imagery to music is dance; that had been true for film from the days of Busby Berkeley and Astaire & Rogers. Filmmakers quickly saw the potential to promote dance-oriented segments of their movies to the youthful MTV audience. *Flashdance* was a 1983 film that told the story of a young woman, Alex Owens, who dreamt of becoming a ballerina while holding down two jobs: welder and exotic dancer. The dance performances within the film supplied numerous opportunities for choreography that was matched to the songs picked for the soundtrack. Despite (or perhaps because of) the lead character's somewhat unusual career choices, the movie and the soundtrack album were both surprise hits. Pauline Kael, film critic for the New Yorker, described the movie in her review as a series of "rock videos," and soon scenes were recut to become exactly that.[xxix] "Maniac," by Michael Sembello, featuring Alex in a training montage, was shown repeatedly on MTV; it climbed to the top spot on *Billboard*'s Hot 100 chart as well. From that point on, music videos based on songs from soundtracks became an integral part of MTV's on-air inventory. In addition, the advertisements for those same films became a major source of the network's revenues.

The one artist whose career epitomizes music videos that marry amazing vocal performances with ground-breaking choreography is Michael Jackson. Yet he, like many other Black artists, was rarely seen on MTV in its early years. Opinions differ on the cause of the channel skewing its airtime toward white acts. MTV executives denied any claims of prejudice. They pointed to their background in Album-Oriented Radio (AOR) and their reliance on audience research guiding the decision to focus on rock music, which excluded Black artists as a result. They believed that pushing the channel into R&B (or country or folk, for that matter) would alienate a significant portion of their audience that preferred rock. That was the rationale that Mark Goodman, one of the MTV on-air hosts (known as VJs), put forward when David Bowie turned the tables on him during an interview and asked why there was a paucity of Black artists on the channel.

Some artists were vociferous in their objections to MTV's decisions to pass on videos starring Black artists. After the network turned down the video for "Super Freak," Rick James complained publicly that excluding him and his peers such as Stevie Wonder, Smokey Robinson, and Earth, Wind & Fire was damaging to their record sales. He called the network "racist." Soundies had already demonstrated the appeal of short films of musical numbers featuring talented Black performers. But like the Hollywood studios of that earlier era, MTV chose not to take advantage of those artists.

Michael Jackson's *Thriller* was the top-selling album, and "Billie Jean" was dominating the singles charts, in 1982. Despite these impressive results, MTV refused CBS Records' requests to air the video for two full months after its release. The label had the contractual right to pull its music videos from the channel with 24-hour notice, and, according to David Benjamin, VP of Business Affairs for the label at that time, they decided to exercise that clause unless MTV changed its decision. With 25 percent market share, CBS Records possessed a big hammer. Both Pittman and Garland refused Benjamin's call, but he did get through to John Sykes, VP of Programming at MTV, and instructed him to remove all the label's videos. Benjamin immediately headed over to CBS Records CEO Walter Yetnikoff's office to inform him of the step he had taken. By the time he walked around the hallway and reached his boss's door, the secretary was waving him in. Yetnikoff was on the phone, and he told Benjamin that he was talking to his "best friend" Bob Pittman who had just said that MTV was going to start playing "Billie Jean."[xxx] MTV executives deny that this showdown ever occurred and say they always planned to add the video to their rotation. Regardless, Michael Jackson's "Billie Jean," followed by "Beat It," were both enormous successes for MTV. The popularity of Jackson's videos proved that the rock-centric focus was far too narrow. He cleared the path for other Black artists to be included on the channel, and despite its recalcitrance, MTV benefited enormously as well.

It was Jackson's next video, however, that demonstrated the artistic potential for the medium most clearly. Intrigued by John Landis's direction of *American Werewolf in London*, Jackson contacted him to make the video for the title track from *Thriller*. Jackson and Landis together crafted a nearly 14-minute-long musical horror film that required a budget of $900,000, far higher than any other music video up to that time. Yetnikoff begrudgingly agreed that CBS Records would help to fund the video but capped its contribution at $100,000. The creators decided to film a "Making of" documentary along with the video, creating a one-hour special that could be promoted as an event. They convinced the cable network Showtime to pay $300,000 for pay-cable rights; and MTV, in a significant exception to its policy of not paying for the creation of videos, kicked in $250,000 for exclusive rights on basic cable. Jackson covered the remaining budget personally.

Given those investments, the expectations for "Thriller" were high, yet the reactions managed to exceed them all. MTV and many other media outlets rate it as the greatest music video of all time. It created a template for music videos to become more sophisticated in terms of both storytelling and original choreography. The "zombie dance" became a cultural touchstone with fans and is still imitated around the world, particularly on Halloween. Sales of *Thriller* were reinvigorated after the video release, more than doubling to reach its current position as the top-selling album of all time worldwide.[13] Its sales were ultimately twice as large as those of *Saturday Night Fever*, another movie soundtrack whose sales were propelled by the disco craze and the videos of John Travolta dancing to the Bee Gees' music. The *Thriller* VHS tape, which combined the music video and the documentary, sold over a million copies. On the other hand, the acclaim for *Thriller* was not universal: the

National Coalition on Television objected to its violence, and Jerry Falwell of the Moral Majority viewed Jackson as a poor role model, though criticism from such sources may have helped with the MTV audience.

MTV certainly helped to cement Michael Jackson's dominant position as the "King of Pop." It is worth noting, however, that he came into the MTV era already established as an industry powerhouse. Jackson's *Off the Wall*, the last album with new material released before *Thriller*, was the third best-selling album of 1980 and nestled at no. 1 on the *Billboard* R&B charts for 16 weeks.

Madonna's eponymous debut album, on the other hand, was released in 1983 after the launch of MTV. It can be argued that her success in combining music, choreography, and visual imagery that complemented her ever-evolving persona is even more inextricably tied to MTV. The videos of the singles "Holiday," "Lucky Star," and "Borderline" from that first album established Madonna as a pop-dance phenomenon and a style icon for millions of teenage girls. Some industry experts predicted that Madonna's popularity would dissipate quickly and that her voice and style would limit her to fad status rather than establish the foundation for a long career. *Billboard* magazine, for example, said that "her image completely overshadows her music," which was perhaps the most negative critical assessment of a musical artist since *Newsweek* described the Beatles as a "catastrophe" in 1964.[xxxi]

By her second album *Like a Virgin*, Madonna was producing videos that not only maintained her pop/dance credibility ("Into the Groove") but demonstrated her ability to attract attention with more explicit sexual themes and imagery. Her style shifted from a punk street-wise aesthetic to lacy bustiers and low-cut gowns. The video for the album's title track cost $150,000 and featured Madonna singing and dancing on a gondola riding through the canals of Venice. Her performance of the song at the first MTV Video Music Awards, as she writhed on stage in a wedding dress, raised her profile as both performer and provocateur. The video for "Material Girl," another track from the album, was a clear homage to the movie *Gentlemen Prefer Blondes*, with Madonna taking on the Marilyn Monroe blonde bombshell character. Later videos such as "Papa Don't Preach" and "Like a Prayer" focused on controversial issues such as teenage pregnancy and incorporated religious imagery. The former managed to raise objections from both sides of the abortion debate, while the latter was declared blasphemous by the Vatican. Sexual and religious issues aside, Madonna collaborated with talented directors who had been limited to commercials and gave them a higher profile and bigger budget opportunities. "Express Yourself," with imagery inspired by the Fritz Lang film *Metropolis*, had a total budget of $5 million. It was the most expensive music video ever to that point in time (and remains, today, the third most costly music video ever). "Vogue," with its black-and-white fashion magazine glossiness and dance club vibe, cost only $5,000. David Fincher directed both and established his credentials as a directorial talent, which ultimately led to *Fight Club*, *The Social Network,* and three Oscar nominations.

Although we have focused on Michael Jackson and Madonna, many other artists expanded the boundaries of what could be expressed via music videos in genres from pop to hip-hop, including a-ha, Peter Gabriel, Jay-Z, Dr. Dre, and, of course, Beyoncé. Bob Pittman pointed out that the creativity embodied in music videos changed the live performance business as well as audiences. For the stars on MTV, a concert could no longer consist of the band members on some risers surrounded by speakers with a few spotlights and dry ice. Instead, they needed to lift the production values to a level where the concert experience compared favorably with the images ingrained in the audience's memory by the video.

Yet in spite of some artists' creativity, there was an underlying concern in some quarters that the growing importance of MTV emphasized surface appearance and style to the detriment of more "serious" musicianship. There were certainly artists such as Paula Abdul and Jennifer Lopez who initially relied more heavily on their dance skills rather than their musicianship as a calling card to build a reputation. Perhaps the most extreme example of style winning out over musical substance was when Milli Vanilli, with MTV's unstinting support of their single "Girl You Know It's True." The song won the Best New Artist Grammy in 1990, and the album sold millions of copies. It all came crashing down when the press reported that the photogenic duo had not recorded their own vocals on the record. It was the first and only time that the Grammys ever rescinded an award.

At its inception, the "cost of goods" for music videos, MTV's "raw materials," was ostensibly zero. (Although it did not pay the labels for the content, it did cost MTV about $1,000 for each track to clean up the audio and to transfer to the one-inch tape needed for broadcast.)[xxxii] The more successful MTV became, the greater the likelihood the labels would seek to alter what they increasingly believed were overly generous business terms. Yet it would take a couple of years for the right moment to come to seek changes.

By the beginning of 1983, with the NYC and LA markets finally covered, MTV garnered a new degree of respect and influence. At the end of January of that year, *Billboard* added music video plays to the industry metrics in its magazine, making it clear that the format was an important element in promoting and marketing music and artists. Like many Internet companies of a later era, MTV started out by building a recognizable consumer brand and cultural currency using unpaid content and did not reach profitability for quite some time. In its first two years, the network lost $34 million.

Several critical success factors fell into place in 1983. MTV came into the year reaching 18 million homes; that number, paired with those desirable youthful demographics, made advertisers sit up and take notice. Soon 140 companies were buying ads on the station pitching more than 240 different consumer products. (Sixteen of those companies were advertising jeans.) The tables had turned: instead of pleading with the cable operators to offer MTV, the parent company WASEC was now able to start demanding payments from those same operators for the right to carry the station.

Meanwhile, the music industry slump that began in the late 1970s subjected every expense to greater scrutiny. As we've discussed, improved sales driven by video play demonstrated that the labels could reach record buyers more cost-effectively via MTV than by supporting a tour. In addition, the labels had no influence over artists' performances on the road, but they could exert at least some control over the music video budget, content, and director.[xxxiii]

We've already cited several examples of videos that required extraordinary investments to realize a particularly creative vision; these were less cost-effective despite the huge sales numbers that the videos helped the songs pull in. As artists began to see what others were doing, even typical music videos grew more costly as they embodied more ambitious stories and relied on higher production values. In 1981, the average music video cost approximately $15,000 to produce. Two years later, that increased to $25–35,000 and yet again to $40–50,000 in 1984. And despite the rising costs, the labels were producing so many videos that MTV could become more selective and decide which tracks received the heaviest rotation and which ones did not air at all.

As the costs climbed, the labels found a way to reduce the bottom-line impact: they modified their accounting practices to treat video budgets as recoupable expenses, meaning that the costs were deducted from gross revenues before profits were paid to the band. This effectively raised the break-even point for any record release and delayed the time when royalty payments would reach artists. The bands that pushed for a party atmosphere at the video shoot were effectively footing the bill for their own entertainment.

Even with these accounting machinations and the positive returns from video play, the labels felt the bargain they had struck with MTV to display their content without compensation was fundamentally unfair. Tommy Mottola, former Chairman of Sony Music, said of MTV, "They built the biggest music enterprise in the history of the world off of our backs, off of our money, off of our sweat."[xxxiv] When the channel turned a profit in 1984, the labels demanded a new deal.

Larger corporate issues were motivating MTV to finalize deals for access to the music videos that were the lifeblood of its business. The Warner-Amex joint venture that owned MTV had lost close to $100 million in 1983. To raise more money, it needed to offer stock, and MTV's newly profitable posture had become a linchpin of a successful offering. To make Wall Street comfortable with its long-term prospects, MTV needed predictable economics—which translated to having a deal with the labels.[xxxv]

Pittman knew that with MTV's healthier financials, the free ride was over. The channel would have to pay the labels to air the videos that had become increasingly costly to produce. However, the network's demonstrated power in building artist brands and driving sales had made it invaluable to the marketing teams at the labels. The record companies had become addicted to the promotional value of MTV, and that gave the network significant leverage in the negotiations. MTV used that position of power to focus on garnering exclusive rights as a way to fend off any potential competitors.

The first proposed agreement with Capitol/EMI would have required MTV to pay the label $1.25 million over three years. In exchange, 35 percent of the label's videos shown on the network would be exclusive to MTV for 30 days. MTV would select two-thirds of the videos covered by the exclusivity clause, and Capitol would choose the remainder. This clause gave the channel the ability to ensure that the most desirable songs would be aired on MTV, and only MTV, for a month. At the same time, MTV's demonstrated promotional value made the labels anxious to have the right to select some of the videos that made it into MTV's rotation. The labels' own marketing priorities took precedence over following the preferences of the audience.

Cable television did not have the same type of payola landscape as radio did, as we saw back in Chapter 3.

Capitol/EMI ultimately rejected these terms, but they established the framework for later deals with the other record companies.[xxxvi] By September 1984, contracts had been signed with CBS, RCA, MCA, Geffen, Polygram, and the Warner Music labels. These provided exclusivity for "television exhibition" for one to two months covering 20–40 percent of each label's videos in exchange for differing cash amounts. For example, market share leader CBS received $8 million over two years, a sum that the label projected would cover the production expenses for the 200 videos they made per year. MTV Networks was incorporated as a separate entity, and that new company formally acquired both MTV and Nickelodeon from WASEC. Warner-Amex gave up some financial control through a successful stock offering while retaining 90 percent of the voting control.

Al Teller, then President of CBS and Columbia Records, had recommended to his boss, Walter Yetnikoff, that the label should pass, but he was overruled. The labels got the cash and secured the right to place some videos on MTV. In exchange, they gave MTV the exclusivity that would cement its market-leading position and make it even more powerful down the road. As Teller said, "The music industry has a long history of doing incredibly stupid things at important moments in its history."

MTV's clout would be reduced with competition. And the obvious popularity of music videos attracted interested parties. The creators of the Financial News Network, which included Wall Street powerhouse Merrill Lynch, started efforts to launch the Discovery Music Network (DMN) to air on cable stations nationwide. NBC launched the show *Friday Night Videos*, and WTBS, Ted Turner's Superstation, introduced a weekend show called *Night Tracks* in the summer of 1983. The success of the latter led Ted Turner to plan for a new station dedicated to music videos to go head-to-head with MTV named, unimaginatively, the Cable Music Channel (CMC). The channel would be offered for free to cable operators to undermine MTV's efforts to extract carriage fees from those same operators. All these initiatives saw MTV's narrow focus on a teen audience as an opportunity and intended to offer a broader range of music along with tighter standards on the display of sexuality and violence.[xxxvii]

CMC launched late in October 1984, and, in one of the quickest flame-outs in the history of media, it was shut down approximately one month later. Not enough cable providers signed up to carry the channel, and it was bleeding buckets of red ink. Many operators simply did not have room for yet another music video channel, while others resented what they felt were Turner's strongarm tactics in promulgating his cable news channel, CNN. Turner sold the assets of CMC to MTV's parent company for $1 million and a commitment to purchase $500,000 worth of ads on other Turner properties. The CMC assets included satellite bandwidth that gave MTV the technical platform to launch a second music channel. That new station was created in part to head off the competitors with a focus on a broader range of music for an older demographic. That sister station launched in January 1985 as Video Hits One, or VH-1 (shortened to VH1 in 1994). The other potential competitors were not much more successful in terms of market launches, but they were very active in the courts, as we will discuss later in this chapter.[xxxviii]

Despite a successful stock offering and MTV's momentum, Warner and American Express began looking for a way to sell their holdings in MTV Networks. Warner was in a deep hole because of the ill-advised purchase of the video game company Atari. AMEX's rationale for investing to get into interactive services had proved to be illusory in the 1980s, and they found cable programming to be an expensive proposition. In 1985, Viacom purchased the two companies' interests in MTV Networks in a complicated transaction for $525 million.[xxxix] The founders had been hoping for a leveraged buyout that would grant them major equity stakes in the company, but instead they simply became employees at another large media company. MTV, of course, continued to thrive, and its valuation climbed into the billions. Steve Ross, the head of Warner Communications said selling MTV was "the biggest regret of his career."[xl,14]

The strength of the MTV brand and the cultural cachet it held with young people were incredibly valuable assets that the network used repeatedly to its financial advantage. They allowed it to expand to international markets. As Bill Roedy, Chairman of MTV International, said, "'A-wop-bop-a-do-bop, a-wop-bam-boom' [sic] means the same in every language."[xli] The network created valuable, repeatable programming that was an extension of its brand, such as MTV Spring Break, Total Request Live, and the MTV Music Video Awards. Labels competed to get slots for their artists on these platforms.

The logical next step was to create programming that reached that same audience but did not rely on music videos. MTV could own the intellectual property itself and improve its margins. Reality shows such as Real World and animated programs such as Beavis and Butt-Head proved popular and did not require any payments to labels. The original premise of the network as music videos all the time disappeared. As Nick Rhodes of Duran Duran said, "At some point, the M in MTV changed from Music to Money."[xlii]

The copyrights associated with music videos are complicated and entail several different permissions and payments. Using music in a timed relationship with visual elements in a television show, motion picture, commercial, or music video requires a synchronization or "synch" license.[15] The license requirement covers both copyrights embodied in a particular rendition of a song: the recording and the composition. The performer on the recording, or the label holding the rights to that version, must authorize the new creation, as must the composer who wrote the song or the music publisher that holds those rights. When an entity performs that resulting creation publicly, including airing it on a cable station, it must pay a performance royalty to the songwriter or composer as compensation for that use.[xliii]

Synchronization rights are not covered by any blanket arrangements or statutory (government-set) licenses, nor are they even covered by any widely accepted industry conventions. As a result, synch licenses typically require separate negotiations with each of the rights holders whenever someone wants to create a new audio-visual work. Given the instant recognizability of a specific certain recording, getting the approval to use it for a film or a commercial can be an expensive and time-consuming proposition. For example, when Microsoft launched Windows 95, it decided that the company's very first television commercial should have music that emphasized the start of a new era as well as the start button on the launch screen. Bill Gates wanted to use the song "Start Me Up" by the Rolling Stones, and he negotiated the synch rights personally with Mick Jagger. It required a payment of $3 million for the 60-second commercial.[16] In cases like this, the hit song's inherent value created a "halo effect" for the advertised product.[xliv]

However, for a new release, even by an established artist, the music video was intended to create demand for a song that was not yet known. In this case, when the label decided to make a music video for an act on its roster, it treated the video as a "promotional" use. The label's contract with the artist typically included the authority to synchronize any recordings in that manner without additional compensation. Unlike a commercial use in an advertisement or a movie, that promotional designation obviated payments for the recording. These licenses were typically gratis or required minimal payments intended to cover the administration costs associated with the paperwork and nothing more. The rationale for this policy was an assumption that the rights-holders would receive benefits from the performance royalties associated with playing video on cable television and the downstream royalties from sales of recordings.

One might have expected this argument to fall by the wayside once MTV began to make multimillion-dollar payments to the labels for the right to show the music videos. However, the labels continued to treat the videos as promotional with regard to any pass-through payments to songwriters for synch rights. Although the labels treated these as recoupable expenses in artist agreements, there were no guarantees that any individual project would yield the income to cover those costs. The MTV payments were viewed as helping to defray those significant upfront costs to produce the videos.

Whether the music videos were promotional or not, when MTV (or any other station) aired them they also owed the songwriter performance royalties for that use. As we discussed with radio, these fees are not paid directly; they are paid to PROs such as ASCAP, BMI, and SESAC. MTV needed agreements with each of them. Contracts covering performance royalties for music videos are typically made at a company-wide level rather than for individual tracks or even networks. Instead, Viacom, on behalf of all its subsidiary networks including MTV, VH1, Nickelodeon, and so on, negotiated a single multiyear contract with each of the PROs that paid them for the performances of their respective compositions. Viacom also agreed to supply the detailed data that allows the PRO to distribute the funds to rights holders accurately.

The exclusivity clauses in MTV's major-label contracts that were intended to offer substantial advantages over competitors proved to be a far greater source of legal problems for MTV than any aspects of copyright law. MTV's early success attracted other players to offer alternative shows and services. The new entrants believed that broadening the rock-oriented teen focus would enable them to work around the exclusivity clauses and attract distinct audiences. Those clauses were limited to a relatively small percentage of all videos and covered only a month or two. However, even if its overall playlist was broader, fans still expected a music video channel to air at least some of the most popular videos. And, unfortunately for the potential competitors, at any point in time that list of "must-see" videos was short enough to be covered by the exclusivity restrictions.

These issues reached a boiling point beginning in August of 1984. First, the Antitrust Division of the US Department of Justice launched a preliminary inquiry to determine if there was sufficient evidence that MTV and the labels had illegally colluded to block competitors through their contractual arrangements. A few weeks later, even before its planned launch date, DMN filed suit against MTV in US District Court in Los Angeles. DMN charged that MTV was attempting to eliminate it as a competitor by creating a monopoly in violation of the Clayton and Sherman Antitrust Acts. The discovery process revealed that the one or two months of exclusivity in the agreements were not the complete picture. The exclusivity period actually extended to six months with regard to competitors who offered 24-hour-a-day music video programming. Given the ephemeral, hit-driven nature of music videos, that half a year covered virtually all of the peak demand period for any of the most popular songs. As the legal case dragged on, DMN shifted its plans to over-the-air UHF broadcast as it was unable to convince cable operators to carry their station. Its efforts to add some major muscle to their legal efforts failed as Ted Turner declined to join the case.

While the DMN case was pending and the Justice Department inquiry was still looming, yet another antitrust action was brought against both MTV and Warner Communications in October of 1985 in US District Court in Texas. Hit Video/TV5 was a music video station airing on broadcast channel five in the Houston market. The channel, owned and operated by Wodlinger Broadcasting Company, had a low-power transmitter with a geographic reach of 15 miles. One of the lawyers filing the case was a colorful Texan attorney known as Richard "Racehorse" Haynes. Not surprisingly, MTV's reaction to this entire endeavor could be summarized as "Who are these guys?" However, Constance Wodlinger, the owner of the company, had ambitious plans: she invested $4 million to rebrand the station as Hit Video USA and to take it national. However, like DMN, they struggled to get cable operators to sign up. Some people at MTV suggested that the lawsuit was simply a way to publicize the upstart channel.[xlv]

Ultimately, none of these efforts to compete more effectively with MTV by attacking the exclusivity clauses had any meaningful results. The Justice Department closed its inquiry without ever filing a single charge. DMN never launched its service and settled out of court in 1986 for a nominal payment that covered its legal expenses. Hit Video USA lasted for several years as the litigation dragged on. It continued to complain to the press about MTV's anticompetitive behavior, but it was never more than a minor irritant. Yet again, the case was settled out of court and, after buying out Wodlinger, Viacom closed Hit Video USA altogether.

Exclusivity with record labels was an ongoing source of concern to other channels offering music videos even when it was not the main focus for their programming. In 1991, Black Entertainment Television (BET) programmed music videos into its schedule but was frustrated by those clauses. It began a boycott of all MCA Records artists to protest MTV's exclusive rights to "Now That We've Found Love" by Heavy D and the Boyz. Though the terms were kept confidential, BET reached a settlement with MCA Records, and Heavy D's new video continued to be aired by MTV alone.

MTV was not done fighting antitrust battles, but when the next one arose in the early 1990s, it was the one complaining about unfair treatment. As in the United States, airing music videos in the United Kingdom and Europe required both rights to the videos and the payment of performance royalties. In the United Kingdom, Phonographic Performance Limited (PPL), owned by the major and independent record companies, licenses music to broadcasters on their behalf. As MTV began its international expansion in mid-1984, PPL formed a sister company called Video Performance Ltd (VPL) to license music videos for broadcast on television. It also had reciprocal arrangements with other European countries.

In the United States, MTV had started out without making any payments to the labels, and when the time came to change that posture, they had the advantage of "perfect information" on the deal terms with each of the labels. The labels had no intention of providing that same sweetheart deal to the now much more powerful MTV in Europe. Under UK law, the labels were permitted to empower VPL to negotiate as a single representative of all the member companies. VPL's deal with MTV required 20 percent of the channel's top-line revenues to be paid to the labels for the use of music videos; that does not include the payments for performance royalties. MTV reaped the benefits of its dominant market posture in the United States, but when the labels followed a similar playbook in Europe, the network did not appreciate being on the receiving end. The head of MTV Europe considered the label deals untenable and described them as a "holdup."[xlvi]

Despite concerted efforts to get just one of the labels to break rank and to negotiate individually, MTV was unable to do so. Ultimately, it decided it had no choice but to take legal action against what it called the labels' oligopoly. First, it lodged a complaint with the European Commission accusing VPL of monopolistic practices and overcharging for music video rights. The labels held firm, and MTV decided to file a lawsuit in the United Kingdom. A preliminary order from the European Commission required the major labels to negotiate separate deals and made it clear that this would be its final decision as well. The labels came to the table individually, and the court case was rendered moot. But while the legal battle was underway, four of the major labels created a local music video channel in Germany, called Viva, to compete with MTV's pan-European channel. The German-language Viva proved popular and created the first meaningful competition to MTV in Europe, which reacted by offering more targeted channels in the local language.[xlvii]

Conclusion

MTV did not fundamentally change how the industry made money, but it proved to be an accelerant. MTV's promotional value became an alternative to radio and touring in building an artist's image and brand. It boosted revenue streams from music purchases and ticket sales. In fact, including visuals helped to establish artists' careers more quickly and effectively than songs alone.

Nor did MTV directly cause any significant shifts in copyright law. But the business and legal dynamics between the labels and MTV had repercussions down the road. The music industry learned what it thought were valuable lessons, but they did not play out as hoped. This would not be the last time that the labels would enable a fledgling company to use their artists' music to build a powerful and valuable enterprise that could then use its newfound leverage to its advantage.

When the labels faced a similar scenario again, the MTV experiences led them to several major shifts in their approach. First, they decided that startups needing music licenses, even those with minimal financial resources, would be expected to pay artists from the start. Second, the labels expected those payments to include a substantial upfront guarantee to protect against any potential downsides. Third, they would request, and often receive, an equity stake in any new corporate entity.

However, these practices had unintended consequences. They created disincentives for investors in new companies that slowed down the development and growth of innovative copyright-respecting services. That, in turn, created openings for services that launched without licenses, following the oft-quoted mantra of Silicon Valley to seek forgiveness later rather than ask permission in advance. With MTV, fans played a very influential role in persuading the established cable operators to offer the channel. In the Internet era, innovative technologies would enable music consumers to become the source for unlicensed music and videos. As we'll see in Chapters 8 and 10, these actions upended the industry and caused reverberations in the legal underpinnings of copyright that continue to this day.

The Viva experience in Europe demonstrated that the labels could work together to establish a potent competitor to these new companies even though they were not first to market. When similar circumstances arose again, the labels tried to recreate that success by collaborating to launch their own services to take advantage of the emerging opportunities. However, the antitrust regime in the United States prevented any of these new services from including the full complement of the labels with their collective catalog, thereby stifling the quality and user experience of the offer to consumers.

MTV was the culmination of decades of combining music and images to delight music fans. Though the network lost much of its cultural currency, the value of that combination, including synchs for popular TV shows, continues to be an effective way to boost sales. The conclusion of the HBO series *The Sopranos*, which aired in June 2007, featured Journey's "Don't Stop Believin'" as it famously cut to black; digital sales for the track shot up 400 percent in a week. And when Kate Bush's song "Running Up That Hill" became a key element of the Netflix show *Stranger Things* in 2022, it became the most streamed song in the country 17 years after its release.[xlviii] Getting a slot on *Saturday Night Live* (SNL) remains a major marketing opportunity for new music. Some artists simply perform a live rendition of their song on SNL, while others, such as Billie Eilish dancing on the ceiling for "bad guy" and Taylor Swift's 10-minute film complementing "All Too Well," offer the live equivalents of music videos on the show.

Many of the shifts in business practices and legal infrastructure engendered by the music video would only come to fruition decades later. But one fundamental change was immediate and truly beneficial for artists and fans. David Geffen, the founder of Asylum Records in the 1970s and Geffen Records in the 1980s, summarized it well when he said MTV is "stimulating and encouraging recording artists to expand their creativity both visually and conceptually . . . music in video can monopolize the imagination of a new generation."[xlix] Geffen was referring to Gen Xers who came of age when MTV was in its heyday. But his remarks could accurately describe what is happening today as well. We will learn more about how younger people of Gen Z are using TikTok to fuel the creativity of videos with music in Chapter 10.

7

Compact Discs

Zero-Sum—Nine Inch Nails

The Audio Compact Disc (CD) is the biggest-selling audio format in terms of revenues—by a wide margin—of all time. That much is beyond dispute. But what's less clear is how it got its size and recording length. The CD's technical specifications are spelled out in the "Red Book" standard, one of a series of technical standards related to the format.[1] Sony and Philips collaborated to author that standard, which was issued in 1980. The document spelled out that the CD would have a 122 mm diameter and would contain a maximum of 74 minutes of music. Researching what led to this specification yielded multiple different versions of the "true" story. Like the Japanese film *Rashomon*,[2] the participants each have their own version of the events.

The "official" history on the Philips website explains that the Sony vice president in charge of the project, Norio Ohga, insisted on that length to guarantee that Beethoven's Ninth Symphony as conducted by Herbert von Karajan would fit on the disc in its entirety because that was his wife's favorite musical selection. According to Kees Immink, a key innovator in digital media who served as a leader on the Philips team, this account is a reminder not to believe everything you read on the Internet. In one article, Immink states the top Philips executives picked the size to be only marginally larger than the successful Compact Cassette to strengthen its appeal to consumers.[i]

Rather than putting the fans or the art first, two other explanations suggest that mundane business considerations ruled the day. Polygram, owned by Philips, already had an experimental manufacturing plant capable of producing large volumes of 115 mm discs containing up to an hour of music, that hour being the original target spec for the format. Sony lacked a similar production capability. By insisting on the longer playing time—which, in turn, required a larger disc—Sony effectively blunted Philips's competitive advantage in production capacity.[ii]

Marc Finer, who was part of the Sony Electronics communications team that supported the launch of the CD, recalls yet another explanation. Philips's

Key Changes. Howie Singer and Bill Rosenblatt, Oxford University Press. © Howie Singer and Bill Rosenblatt 2023.
DOI: 10.1093/oso/9780197656891.003.0007

preference was based on the 14-bit word for each digital sample of the analog audio because that was the capability of the digital to audio (D-to-A) converter they had available. Sony had a 16-bit D-to-A converter that provided superior quality but required additional data, and it insisted on a larger disc as a result. According to Finer, Sony's view won out and the larger disc was the result.[iii]

How the companies arrived at the final CD size may remain open to debate, but the exact number of minutes of music on the disc turned out to be far less crucial than it seemed at the time. Other factors led to the format's unprecedented success, and technology improvements eventually extended the disc capacity to achieve an 80-minute maximum.

The first 50 commercially released CDs reached the Japanese market in October 1982. The list of titles was led by Billy Joel's *52nd Street*, a chart-topping record that won the Grammy award for Best Album in 1980 and, not coincidentally, was issued by Columbia Records, a subsidiary of Sony Music. That introduction represented the dawn of the most popular physical music format ever. The financial rewards reaped by Philips, Sony, and every other music company were beyond anything that the industry had ever seen before or since. During the 1990s, as the CD format contributed billions to industry revenues, the struggle was not how to make money but simply how to count it all. That success may seem inevitable in hindsight, but it required a confluence of technological innovations and collaboration across the various players in the industry to make it happen.

Philips Electronics is headquartered in Eindhoven, a small city in the Netherlands near the Belgian border. Three hundred journalists traveled there on March 8, 1979 to listen to J. P. Sinjou, who demonstrated the prototype of Philips' new digital audio product, as shown in Figure 7.1. He explained the various elements that Philips had developed, ranging from the encoding of the music to the lasers reading the data off the disc to the manufacturing processes required for the media. And he made a point of comparing this new digital format to the vinyl record, to emphasize its smaller size and greater convenience. The reporters were impressed with the quality of the playback, especially the total lack of background noise during pauses in the music.

Figure 7.1 J. P. Sinjou Introduces the Compact Disc, March 1979. NBC News.

Several other electronics companies—including Sony Electronics, which had already prototyped a 30-cm disc—had similar efforts underway. The Philips team, wanting to avoid the format war that had proved so problematic for video recorders (a war that Sony lost) and to improve the audio coding technology in the prototype, met with a variety of companies including Sony, Hitachi, Pioneer, and Matsushita (the parent company that sold in the US under the brand Panasonic) to review the technology and to discuss the possibilities of collaborating. Following the Sony meeting, Sony chairman Akio Morita called his counterpart at Philips to say that they had decided that the two companies should work together. As we saw in Chapter 5, despite being competitors in many areas, Philips had licensed the intellectual property for the Compact Cassette freely to Sony in the 1960s.

By joining forces, the parties brought complementary technical skills to their joint endeavor: Sony with its greater digital audio expertise, and Philips with its laser know-how and a large patent portfolio related to optical discs based on its previous efforts on the LaserDisc (LD).

The LD was the first optical storage medium for consumer media. The concept was not new: recording sounds on a glass disc using a beam of light dates back to 1884, when Alexander Graham Bell and two colleagues accomplished this at their lab in Washington, DC.[3] Eighty years later, James T. Russell invented the first system that used high-powered light (though not a laser) to record digital video signals onto an optical medium.

Philips licensed the Russell patent as part of its efforts to create the LaserDisc, which it envisioned as a new movie format to replace both VHS and Betamax. Each LD consisted of a two single-sided aluminum disc covered with a layer of plastic. As the 30 cm (12 in.) LD spun, the laser "read" the information stored in the underlying material. Both the spacing and length of the "pits" in that material were used to encode the original analog video signal; that is, the pits didn't just represent 1s and 0s. In other words, the Laser Disc was not a "pure" digital product.

The LaserDisc was first made available in 1978. The image quality produced by the LD was superior to both Betamax and VHS tape, and the videophile community readily adopted the new format. But that community was very limited in size, and the low sales volume did not create the momentum to drive prices downward quickly. In addition, the vast majority of consumers valued the ability to record programs on the tape format of their choice—something that wasn't possible with optical discs. The ability to "time-shift" broadcast content allowed every user to create an inexpensive library of content to enjoy at a time of their own choosing. The studios made some films available as prerecorded LaserDiscs, but they were pricey. That limited and expensive selection meant that without a recording feature, typical consumers found little value in the product. In fact, half of the initial production of 400 LaserDisc players were returned when consumers realized that the product could not record programs.

The LaserDisc never advanced beyond a Minimal Viable Product because its original design could not easily accommodate the feature demanded by the vast majority of video consumers. Instead, it filled that valuable role as Sony and Philips crafted the requirements and plans for the CD and set it on a path to achieve the success never realized with the LD.

The core technology needed to make the CD a reality was a way of converting the analog music carved into the grooves of vinyl records, or stored on magnetic tape, into a series of equivalent 0s and 1s. The technique to accomplish that digitization is called Pulse Code Modulation (PCM). PCM was initially developed to encode voice signals for efficient transmission over communications networks. An analog sound wave is sampled at regular time intervals, and the amplitude of the sound at each point in time is recorded as a 16-bit number. Silence is encoded as 16 zeros, while 16 ones is the most powerful sound that can be registered without any distortion. For the CD, the audio is sampled 44,100 times per second (see Figure 7.2). The Nyquist Theorem establishes that half the sampling rate represents the maximum frequency that can be captured—meaning that the 44.1 kHz sample rate can handle tones up to 22.05 kHz. As we saw in Chapter 5, the human ear can't hear frequencies higher than 20 kHz, so this combination of parameters allowed the CD to capture the audible information necessary to recreate music that approaches the original sound in quality.[4]

All that sampled information is represented by a series of microscopic "pits" and "lands" on the disc. The pits are the tiny grooves on the disc and the lands are the spaces between the pits. One might have expected that the pits and lands correspond to the ones and zeros of digital information. Instead, they are used as an indicator to "flip the bit." A change from a pit to a land or vice versa is interpreted as a "0," and no change (land to land or pit to pit) is interpreted as a "1." To get a sense of the amount of binary data being managed, one hour of music would be equivalent to 6 billion bits encoded onto the disc in one continuous path that is two and half miles long.[iv]

To encode the zeros and ones that represent the audio onto the light-sensitive material for the master copy, a "write" laser creates pits that are 0.6

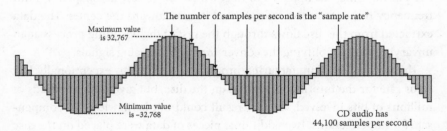

Figure 7.2 CD Audio Sampling. Source: Introduction to Ogg Vorbis. Used by Permission of Graham Mitchell.

microns wide, which is less than 1/100th the thickness of a human hair or 1/25th the width of the groove in an LP. Needless to say, controlling a laser so precisely was itself one of the engineering advances required to make optical media even feasible. The "write" laser is far more powerful than the laser included in every CD player. It must be capable of modifying the material to create the pits and lands, while the "read laser" simply bounces the light over the surface of the disc to detect them.

Manufacturing CDs in volume requires tightly controlled processes as well. Like vinyl records, the master copy is used to "stamp out" the final products. The high-grade plastic used for those final products needs to be exceptionally pure and the production facility clean enough to ensure that dust particles are not introduced. A reflective layer is added so that the laser bounces back when the data is later read off the disc. Then a lacquer layer is added to prevent oxidation and to allow for artwork to be printed on top.

The processes to extract the data at playback are just as carefully designed. The "read laser" included in each player must be precise in terms of locating the beam properly as the disc spins to obtain an accurate reading of the information. The beam comes from beneath the spinning disc and reflects straight back when it encounters a land but scatters when it sees a pit, which yields the binary information needed.

Playback of optical discs is, in many ways, the antithesis of the process of playing vinyl records. For optical discs, instead of starting at the edge and spiraling inward toward the spindle, the CD laser reads the data starting at the inside edge and moves outwards. And instead of rotating at a constant speed of 33 1/3 or 45 rpm, the CD spins at a dizzying speed of 500 rpm but then gradually decreases to 200 by the time the laser is reading the data from the outermost edge. That guarantees that the disc moves at a constant linear rate, which ensures constant frequency response throughout the entire playing time—as opposed to LPs, which, as we saw in Chapter 4, limit frequency response as the stylus makes its way toward the center. The data extracted from the disc flows through the rest of the decoding process at an unvarying rate, simplifying the conversion back to analog signals.

These stringent manufacturing procedures yielded an exceptionally low error rate for the information stored on the disc, but given the hundreds of millions of bits involved, the end result could not be flawless. To compensate for imperfections, two additional pieces of data were placed on the disc at every sampled instance. These bits could be examined at playback to determine the correct information when the audio information went missing or was damaged. In addition, the data was recorded out of exact chronological order to make the results robust to even larger defects, such as scratches. Sony contributed these sophisticated error-correction techniques, known as Reed-Solomon coding, to the project. Reed-Solomon coding was first deployed by NASA a few years earlier to ensure reliable communications with the Voyager spacecraft as it explored the outer planets of the solar system. The CD was the first consumer product to take advantage of these techniques.[v]

CDs initially targeted a one-hour playback time of audio, compared to two hours of audio and video for LDs. The smaller data capacity meant that the disc could fit comfortably in one hand, in contrast to the larger LP-sized platter of the LD. This choice meant that as technology improved, the sizes of players could be reduced to allow for automobile and portable players. As we saw in Chapter 5, the success of Sony's Walkman demonstrated how valuable portability could be to the music experience; Sony kept working quietly to miniaturize the electronics.

Sony released the first commercial CD player, the CDP-101, in Japan in November 1982; worldwide launch followed in March 1983. As Figure 7.3 shows, this was a stereo component, a bit smaller than cassette decks of the time, designed to be connected to a stereo amplifier or receiver.[vi]

The Sony D5, the first CD player that could be deployed in vehicles, hit the market late in 1985.[vii] It was only a little larger than the jewel case, though the external battery was the size of a shoebox. Further improvements meant that

Figure 7.3 Sony CDP-101, the first commercial CD player. Used by permission of Sony Electronics Inc. All Rights Reserved.

the CD would eventually be a viable competitor to the Compact Cassette for listening on the go as well as a replacement for the vinyl record at home. In fact, the Compact Disc name was selected to encourage consumers to see it as a successor to the highly successful Compact Cassette format.

Engineers appreciated the integration of so many advanced technologies, from miniaturized lasers to error correction, as a remarkable accomplishment. But it was an esoteric discussion to the average music fan. To avoid the debacle of the LD, this new format had to be marketed to consumers in ways that they could understand and appreciate. The CD offered a long list of advantages when compared to the vinyl record, and these were exploited to the fullest.

The CD logo did more than simply name the product. The logo conveyed that the product was more than "compact" like the cassette already familiar to music fans. It also highlighted that the product contained "Digital Audio." In the early 1980s, as the world experienced the burgeoning personal computer revolution, the word "digital" conveyed the idea of advanced technology and modernity all by itself. It also supported the superior quality message that was the core of the value proposition to the average music fan.

The tagline that accompanied the logo was "Pure, Perfect Sound Forever." That message targeted the precise pain points that the average music fan had become all too familiar with when dealing with their vinyl records or cassettes. The new format was not only about the perfection of sound but also about durability and robustness over the life of the product.

Listening on the go with a cassette on a Sony Walkman was convenient, but the quality of the sound was clearly inferior to vinyl. There were issues with the tape snarling or tearing, and rewinding loose tape back into the cartridge using a pencil placed in the hole in the cassette was a "fix" that most consumers found necessary on many occasions. Meanwhile, vinyl records skipped, warped, scratched, and broke. Simply listening repeatedly to the same album gradually degraded the sound because of the friction between the needle and the record. With the CD, the laser never touched the disc; it read the data encoded in the underlying material without physical contact. The laser performed the same way every time and did not wear down like the phonograph needle stylus that needed (though rarely got) frequent replacement. Every play produced the exact same sonic experience as the first listen.

Unlike vinyl, dirt on the disc did not interfere with the playback, though you did need to be careful about fingerprints. In addition, the physical structure of the disc, though not indestructible, was far more resistant to scratches and did not warp or break easily. Even the hissing sound present in magnetic tape or created by the needle moving over the surface of the grooves on a vinyl record was eliminated. The CD's ability to play all the tracks sequentially from start to finish eliminated the need to get up from the couch after 25 minutes or so to flip the vinyl from Side 1 to Side 2. For couch potatoes, this was the best enhancement to an entertainment product since the invention of the TV remote.

The zeros and ones that constitute the music on the CD are imprinted as a continuous stream of information from the first bit to the last. There are no physical breaks or spaces between the songs. Instead, the data begins with a "Table of Contents" (ToC), a set of metadata that includes the title of the disc as well as the length of every track. That allows consumers to play any track they choose in any order. The hardware uses the ToC data to find the exact spot for the laser to begin. Of course, you could play any song on a vinyl record if you were willing to make the effort—and had the skill—to drop the needle on exactly the right spot without damaging the record. Cassettes were even less amenable to random access: although making mixtapes from songs on the radio or your record collection was popular, it required a significant investment of time and effort.

Empowering fans to select the playing order of the songs they want to hear with the press of a button seems like just one more small selling point on a lengthy list of consumer benefits for the CD. Many fans didn't even care enough about this feature to bother using it. The fan always made the decision to choose the recording from their collection that they wanted to place on their turntable, in their Walkman, or in their CD player. But once they made that choice, the audio journey they took was, for all intents and purposes, pre-determined by the album's creative team.

Yet this new feature was a harbinger of the complete dismantling of the album as a unified entity controlled entirely by the creators. The ability to craft and to release an end-to-end thematic experience, as exemplified by the concept albums that we saw in Chapter 4, did not disappear. But the artist's control over the final experience had been compromised. The fan's ability to define their own preferred version of that audio experience was a fundamental change in the power dynamics of the music industry. Journalist Luke Dormehl put it well when he wrote that the CD "taught us that the modern unit of music is not the album, but the single track."[viii]

Taking all these differences into account led the average music fan to perceive the CD as superior to the previous music formats. Consumers wanted to experience the latest releases as well as all their favorite older albums on CD. This desire to upgrade all the music in one's collection became a key driver in the financial success of the format.

Sony's CDP-101 retailed for roughly $1,000 when it launched. Selling audio hardware at that price—equivalent to $2,800 today—meant that retailers needed to have the expertise to explain the product and its benefits to a clientele that could afford to spend that amount. Specialty audio retailers such as Listen Up in Denver or Eber in San Francisco were best suited to help establish a beachhead for the CD player; Although Best Buy and Circuit City existed then, neither of them had yet adopted the "superstore" concept to sell all manner of consumer electronics and prerecorded media. For vinyl records and cassettes, music fans went to their favorite independent record stores or outposts of national chains such as Sam Goody's or Trans World Entertainment's Record Land.

Seeing the need to "prime the pump" to make the CD a success, Sony and Philips established the Compact Disc Group in 1983 to coordinate marketing and communications with all the stakeholders, including hardware manufacturers, consumer electronics retailers, record stores, and the distribution arms of the major record labels. By agreeing on a common specification, Sony and Philips lowered the risks for the hardware providers, which responded by introducing a plethora of models.[ix] Many retailers were quite content with selling vinyl records and tapes and saw little need to accommodate yet another format. Jerry Shulman of CBS Records summarized retailers' reaction as follows: "We're carrying Michael Jackson in an LP and a cassette—and now you want us to carry it in a third version? Fuck you!"[x] Russ Solomon, the founder of Tower Records, had more foresight. He understood the potential for the CD quickly and was a key advocate for the new format and provided some early momentum for the group.

One of the first issues to resolve was the packaging for this new product. Record retailers had invested millions in display fixtures to show off those 12-inch vinyl records. They were not anxious to spend a substantial amount to change their shelves to fit the smaller size of a new unproven format. Not to mention that those 5-inch CDs would be much easier to pocket and steal, increasing inventory "shrinkage." After several months of negotiations among the labels and the retailers, a clever but wasteful compromise was reached: the "longbox" package, which measured 6 by 12 inches and was made of plastic and cardboard. It contained a space for the disc, stored in a "jewel case" in the lower half of the box, and another space for the booklet in the upper half. Two longboxes could sit side by side in the existing spaces for albums, making it easy for shoppers to look through the selection of discs available. And making the package much larger than actual physical media acted as a deterrent to theft.[xi]

The packaging created a public uproar because of the large amount of extra trash generated as CD sales climbed. To quell the uproar over the waste, the packaging eventually evolved to a plastic box of the same size that contained the CD-sized case, which was opened at the cash register and reused. Shoppers who were playing by the rules did not see the extra step of unlocking the case as a particularly friendly experience. Ultimately, record stores revamped their displays to fit the CD jewel case by itself and attached a magnetized detector to each one for security.

Enabling record stores to display the CD without a major investment was a good first step, but making potential buyers flip through longboxes did little to convey the benefits of the new format. At electronics stores, TVs and VCRs were the priorities while audio products were just not considered cool. Beginning in 1983 and carrying over into 1984, the Compact Disc Group put together a display program that featured Sony CD players and bundles of discs to demonstrate this new experience for potential buyers. In addition, it instituted a program for 50 radio stations around the country to promote the product. Every time these stations played a song from a CD on the air, they would announce that the music was coming from a Sony CD player. Of course, the music sounded exactly the same as it always had over the radio airwaves,[5] but the marketing message was delivered just the same.

As sales of players and CDs started to grow, the promotions to support the channels and to stoke interest scaled up as well. They obtained "product placement" in movies and TV shows to show off the new format. In 1985, the music companies and Bose worked with MTV to enable a giveaway that included hundreds of players and thousands of discs. MTV "VJs" were required to hype the giveaways, so there was extensive on-air coverage to a national audience of young consumers. The program was tied into live MTV broadcasts from Daytona Beach for Spring Break for the first time; it was so successful that the annual event became synonymous with the music network. And in echoes of Edison's phonograph demonstrations decades earlier, the CD proponents had bands surreptitiously shift from live performance to lip-synching to a digitally recorded performance to prove audiences could not hear the difference.[xii]

The early years of the CD coincided with the creation of the electronics superstore. Wards Company, which had started as a TV and appliance chain in Virginia, expanded its warehouse concept and morphed into Circuit City in 1981.[xiii] The Sound of Music, a small chain of high-end audio retail stores based in Minnesota, expanded its product line to include home appliances and VCRs, and in 1983 rebranded itself as Best Buy. As the CD's popularity grew, these stores found that popular new releases drew customers who might be persuaded to purchase other items. To fuel that traffic, the stores created advertising inserts in the weekend papers highlighting the extensive selection of CDs at discounted prices.

Circuit City and Best Buy were not alone. The draw of those discounted CDs was so compelling that other major retailers, such as Walmart and Target, which did not primarily focus on the sale of music, adopted the same approach. The CD became a loss leader for these retail chains: selling music for less than the wholesale price made sense if the CD shoppers filled up their carts with other items. The race to the bottom in CD pricing became an issue for the labels and ultimately led to a significant legal battle that we will discuss later in this chapter.

Before 1991, as we saw in Chapter 5, the cassette was the top revenue producer for the industry. But in that year, the sales of CDs made it the top-selling format, a position it would not relinquish for almost 20 years. However, an even more impactful change occurred at the cash registers of those stores in 1991: Soundscan, a New York-based research firm, began collecting data based on scanning the bar codes on CDs (and other music formats). Before then, *Billboard* compiled its charts based on phone calls to stores to find out which titles were the hot sellers; the process managed to be both inaccurate and subject to bribes and other forms of manipulation. Charts based on the Soundscan data revealed that genres such as hip-hop, country, and grunge were far more popular than the industry believed. This set the stage for artists as diverse as Garth Brooks, Ice Cube, and Nirvana to reach superstar status.[xiv]

Record stores tried to compete more effectively against these giant retail chains by enhancing their shopping experiences. One solution was to return to what had worked so well in the 1950s. At that time, record store patrons had the option of entering isolation booths to hear the latest singles to help them decide which songs to buy. The heyday of the CD revived the concept, as retail stores installed listening stations with selections as large as 14,000 CDs. Fans could once more get acquainted with new music they had not heard previously to help them to decide what they should purchase.[xv]

At the CD's launch in 1983, the catalog of available titles in the format in the United States numbered around 20. Rights issues hampered the list from matching the 50 unique items introduced in Japan. This was not the most auspicious beginning for the format that, as we know now, became the source of phenomenal growth.

Polygram Records was a subsidiary of Philips, and Sony/CBS was a joint venture between CBS Inc. and Sony Japan Records. Even with those relationships, getting all the labels on board required effort. Jan Timmer, the head of Polygram at the time, described the initial meetings as "Hostile. Very hostile." The industry was in the midst of a slump in both vinyl record and cassette sales. The labels had made significant investments in the production facilities for those formats, and the prospect of spending upwards of $20 million to set up a production line for the unproven CD because of the "clean room" conditions required for quality control seemed like a very risky proposition.[xvi] Several top executives at the labels, including Walter Yetnikoff of CBS Records, were adamantly opposed to the compact disc. In addition to the investment required, he saw the CD as providing a source for even higher quality bootleg cassettes than those that, as we saw in Chapter 5, had plagued the industry.

Meanwhile, Sony and Philips, after the respective failures of Betamax and LaserDisc, had a lot riding on the success of the CD. They were willing to invest resources and political capital to overcome the naysayers. Sony's Ohga went over Yetnikoff's head to the head of the CBS Corporation to ensure support. They put together a team to demonstrate the product to people throughout the labels, artists and fans.

Members of the Sony communications team representing the Compact Disc Group would visit label offices, product in hand, and announce, "This was the CD player you've been hearing about." They would click the remote, and the drawer holding Billy Joel's *52nd Street* disc would slide into the machine. When the silence was broken by the tinkling of the piano keys followed by Billy's voice, the resistance in the executive conference rooms began to dissipate, and interest started to pique, much like the press at the initial Philips demo.

With prices up to $1,000 per player, only 35,000 players were sold from March through December 1983—along with 230,000 CDs. Though barely noticeable compared to the more than half a billion vinyl records and tape cassettes sold that year, the fact that the average number of CDs sold per player averaged more than 6 was an extremely encouraging sign. Growing disc sales depended on increasing that base of players significantly.

As more hardware vendors entered the market, prices dropped to $600–$700 and volumes increased accordingly, reaching a cumulative total of 400,000 players in the US market by the end of 1984. Sony's roadmap included miniaturizing the components and improving the manufacturing processes significantly.

In late 1984, Sony introduced the first portable CD player: the Discman (renamed the CD-Walkman in 1999). The product was about the size of four CD cases stacked on top of one another. It faced some initial playback issues caused by movement, but additional buffering made the product more resistant to shocks. The CD player was no longer homebound. The improved product brought the manufacturing cost down as well. At $300 ($800 today), the next generation of hardware meant that the format was definitely on its way toward mass-market adoption.

As CD players marched down the cost curve, disc sales climbed accordingly. The volumes leapt from the hundreds of thousands in 1983 to 6 million units one year later. That total represented less than 1 percent of the industry volume that year. By 1988, CD sales had passed vinyl in units sold. In 1989, more than 200 million units were sold, representing more than 25 percent of the total US volume of recording music. Two years later, the CD left the cassette in the dust, heading toward a half a billion units in 1993 and amounting to more than half of the industry's volume. And by the turn of the twenty-first

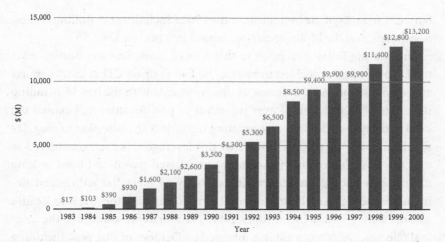

Figure 7.4 CD unit revenues by year, 1983–2000. Source: RIAA. Howie Singer.

century, CD volumes approached 950 million units and accounted for a remarkable 87 percent of the total album units sold in the US.

The revenue impact of the CD (see Figure 7.4) exceeded its volume impact, because each disc sale put more money in the cash register than the comparable album or cassette. LPs and cassettes were priced at $7–$12 on average in the 1980s. Retail prices for CDs were nearly double that at $15–$20 retail. The $100 million realized in 1984 was only 2.4 percent of the industry's annual revenue. In 1989, the CDs accounted for $2.6 billion, or about 40 percent of total revenues. Four years after that, almost two-thirds of total industry revenues were earned by the CD. More than 92 percent of revenues in 2000, or over $13 billion, were brought in by the CD. In the span of 17 years, CDs had gone from a footnote to being virtually the entire recorded music business.

LP sales dropped off from roughly 300 million units in the late 1970s to almost nothing by 1990. CD sales at their peak tripled the pre-CD vinyl numbers. (Cassette volumes remained relatively stable until the late 90s.) That growth in revenues from the CD was attributable to some of the best-selling artists of all time at the peak of their creativity, including Michael Jackson, Madonna, and Prince. But it also was caused by millions of fans preferring the sound quality, convenience, and reliability of the CD to the possibly scratched and worn vinyl records that they already had on their shelves. The labels observed this behavior and dug into their catalogs to release older albums that were past their peak but held special places in the hearts of music fans. CD reissues of the best music of the 1960s, including the Rolling Stones, Bob Dylan, and the Motown catalog, flowed into the market.

One glaring initial exception to this flow of music was the Beatles; EMI made news when it decided to release the Fab Four on CD at last.[6] Reports at the time suggested that financial disagreements with the band (including the estate of John Lennon) over payments of past royalties had caused the label to delay the release as a negotiating tactic. It is an indication of the CD's financial power by the late 1980s that this leverage was even considered as a factor. EMI denied this was the case and stated that it had been waiting until it had enough manufacturing capacity to meet the anticipated demand for the biggest selling band of all time. Regardless, the first four Beatles albums were reissued in February 1987—in monaural sound like the original releases. Eight more albums followed by October of that year, including *Help!*, *Revolver*, *Rubber Soul*, and *Abbey Road*.[xvii]

The enormous CD sales volumes drove top-line revenues to new heights for the labels. And the labels' royalty payments and practices ensured that the margins they obtained from each were in their favor as well. Manufacturing CDs was far more expensive than making cassettes when the product launched. In recognition of this disparity, the record companies used reduced percentages of the cassette royalty rate to calculate CD payments. This difference could have been 15–25 percent less depending on the specific artist and label. Even when CD volumes increased and manufacturing costs declined, this reduction in royalties for "new technology" persisted for several years.[xviii]

That was not the only way that the record companies structured their deals to maximize their profits on the CD. Most deals included a packaging deduction to reflect that the music itself should generate payments for the artist, but not the plastic case, cover art, or booklet. This deduction typically ranged from 20 to 25 percent on CDs; and yet again, these levels persisted even as the CD packaging costs declined with volume.

From the 1960s on, the music industry preferred the album over the single as the best way to experience an artist's creativity and for its superior economic returns. Most albums had just one or two hit singles if you were lucky. Michael Jackson's *Thriller* album released in 1983 changed that pattern: it set the record with seven top-ten singles from a single album, including "Beat It" and "Billie Jean." The sheer number of hits convinced fans they had to own a copy of the album; it sold 32 million copies by the end of the year.[7] Others followed suit with both Bruce Springsteen's *Born* in the USA and

Janet Jackson's *Rhythm Nation* matching the record of seven top-ten singles each in 1984 and 1989 respectively.

By the 1990s, the labels shifted gears and chose to cap the number of singles pressed or not to release certain singles at retail at all while promoting those songs on the radio. The aim was clear: persuade fans to buy that far more profitable album on CD. Instead of the purchase decision being driven by overall entertainment value, let a ubiquitous radio hit be the driver. For example, Chumbawamba's song "Tubthumping" never topped the Billboard Hot 100 chart despite its enormous popularity. The label manufactured only 100,000 singles, effectively limiting its performance on the chart.[xix] It is doubtful that anyone at Chumbawamba's labels was particularly upset with this outcome, as the album the song was on, *Tubthumper*, sold 15 million copies worldwide. That single song, in essence, generated close to $100 million in revenues from CD sales in the late 1990s. The so-called "War on the Single" yielded lucrative returns in the short term, though it fed the fans' frustration with paying a lot of money for a CD to get access to the one song they really cared about.[xx]

Creators

Although typical listeners were impressed with the quality of the sound, many artists, record producers, and engineers were somewhat less enamored with the CD. A group was formed called "Music Against Digital," and one of its main spokespeople was Neil Young.[xxi] In 1992, Young wrote an opinion piece for Harper's magazine entitled "The CD and the Damage Done."[8] He referred to the CD era as the "darkest time ever for recorded music"[9] and wrote that "listening to a CD is like looking at the world through a screen window."[xxii]

Young was not alone in his disdain for the CD. Many artists felt (and still feel) that vinyl records produce a "warmth" that is missing from the digital versions. Many audiophiles feel that way too, even though both CD mastering and playback technologies had advanced since the early days of the CD to ameliorate the "brittleness" of the sound. Nick Rhodes, a founding member of the New Wave band Duran Duran, recalls his reactions when the CEO of EMI played him a CD of the band's second studio album *Rio*, which had peaked at no. 2 on the UK album charts and no. 6 in the United States. Rhodes had mastered several of the tracks for that album in addition to writing and performing the songs with his bandmates. He said, "I almost wanted to cry hearing it. It was not my idea of progress." The sound was "cleaner" than the vinyl record, but he "liked all the noise" on the original because it offered the "atmosphere" the band wanted and had worked so hard to create in the studio. And he thought the "packaging was horrible" too. The broad canvas created by the vinyl album packaging with photographs, artwork, and lyrics had been reduced to a functional but far less compelling 4.75-by-4.75-inch booklet.[xxiii]

Peter Asher, Apple Records executive and famed producer of James Taylor and Linda Ronstadt, among many others, pointed out that the precision of the CD table of contents enumerating the start times for each song did not always serve the artistic goals of the creators. For example, Side 2 of the Beatles' *Abbey Road* contains the famous 16-minute suite of eight short songs blended together. The idea was Paul McCartney's, and it was an artistic landmark. But Asher said it caused a debate among those involved with the CD reissue: it was unclear whether and how these individual sections should be delineated in the ToC on the CD.

Rhodes took great pride in sequencing the tracks on Duran Duran records. He was conscious of the emotional journey, the tempos, and the keys as one song led to the next. For vinyl, one had to be conscious of selecting the last song on side A to entice the fan to get up and flip the record over to hear more. But one also had to deal with the time limitations and the greater likelihood of the needle jumping the track if the final song on the side had too much bass. Jac Holzman, the founder of Elektra Records, said "Sequencing was an art form, and I always reserved the right to do it on my records."[xxiv] Peter Asher remarked that, when he sequenced albums during the CD era, he would come to the middle of the album and think, "We should put something in here to fire everyone up"—realizing that he would be choosing the Side 2 leadoff track of a vinyl LP.[xxv]

Rhodes and Holzman both felt that the random access feature for tracks on the CD removed a valuable tool from their bag of tricks to create a great experience for fans. Using it now on *Abbey Road* randomizes those eight short songs that McCartney and producer George Martin so carefully assembled. Albhy Galuten, Grammy-winning producer of the Bee Gees, summed up the creative community's attitude toward this feature succinctly: "Shuffle is the devil."[xxvi]

As discussed in the opening to this chapter, how the 74-minute length of the recording time on the CD became *the* number is a subject of ongoing debate. However, those additional minutes represented 60 percent more playing time than the typical 45-minute total spread over the two sides of a vinyl LP. One would not have expected artists to run into issues fitting their creative output onto the more expansive CD. However, that tight timeframe on vinyl meant that many recordings had to be released as double albums to accommodate the amount of material. In 1988, DJ Jazzy Jeff & The Fresh Prince released *He's the DJ, I'm the Rapper*, the very first hip-hop double album. Rather than taking the risk of offering an expensive double CD, 13 minutes of content was removed to craft a single disc version. Releases from British progressive rocker Mike Oldfield (*Incantations*) and jazz great Chick Corea (*My Spanish Heart*) suffered a similar fate. Not everyone was forced to bastardize their original double albums to reduce the CD release price: the Beatles' eponymous 1968 double LP known as *The White Album* clocked in at over 90 minutes; it was reissued as a double CD set without any cuts.

Though the CD took away some of the control artists had in crafting the album experience, it also provided degrees of freedom that had been lacking on the vinyl record. Given the constant linear velocity against the grooves of the vinyl, the songs placed closer to the outside edge sounded better than they would toward the middle of an LP, as we saw in Chapter 4. That, in turn, influenced how the songs would be sequenced. As Galuten said, "The CD meant that you didn't have to worry how you put the tracks on the disc."

If fans listened to the same track at differing loudness levels, the conventional wisdom was that they preferred the louder one. Knowing that, artists and labels had been upping the volume of their records to make them stand out from the pack. Bob Ludwig, the eminent mastering engineer who has worked with everyone from Queen to Bruce Springsteen, said that everyone "wanted to have his 45 sound louder than the next guy's, so that when the program director at the Top 40 radio station was going through his stack of 45s to decide which two or three he was going to add that week, that the record would kind of jump out to the program director, aurally at least." (Meanwhile, as we saw in Chapter 3, radio stations themselves were compressing audio to produce the loudest sound possible so that they jumped out at listeners who were using their radios' Scan and Seek buttons.)

As more and more records followed this same approach, the dynamic range (the difference between the softest and loudest portions of the recording) decreased. This was discussed in more detail in Chapter 3. The CD was a key weapon in the "Loudness Wars," as the volume could be increased to levels beyond what vinyl records or even cassettes could tolerate. Although heavy metal had first emerged as a genre in the 1970s, the raw, raucous sound was well-suited to the CD's sonic capacity. Headbanging worked better when the sound was louder, and therefore it is not surprising that two of the best-selling albums of the decade were AC/DC's *Back in Black* and Guns N' Roses' *Appetite for Destruction.*[xxvii]

One challenge to the growth of CD revenues was that it did not require a criminal enterprise to make pirated copies. All it took was a CD owner deciding that the album they had purchased no longer deserved a spot in their collection. Music fans were quite familiar with the pristine sound emanating from the discs no matter how many times they had been played. They also were well aware that the CD was much more difficult to damage or to break than a vinyl record or a cassette. The characteristics that made CDs so valuable as a format to purchasers also made them ideal to sell as used items.

There had been a viable business in selling used vinyl albums for years, as we discussed in Chapter 4, which was enabled by the first sale doctrine embodied in copyright law. This says that objects such as photographs, books, and records are "staple articles of commerce," like clothing or cars or furniture, and can be "alienated" (resold, loaned, given away, etc.) without any involvement from the original seller. The US Supreme Court enumerated this doctrine in 1908, and it was codified in the Copyright Act of 1976 as Section 109 of the law.

Once a vinyl album or a CD has been sold lawfully or even transferred legitimately for free, the copyright owner's interest in that physical item is "exhausted."[10] The purchaser can decide to give that purchased item to a friend, sell it to a retailer, use it as a drink coaster, or simply throw it away. They can't make a copy of the work and then sell or give it away, as that would implicate the reproduction and distribution rights. Owners of CDs—as well as LPs and other sound recordings—are not permitted to rent them to anyone else. This last restriction is different from how books or movies are treated. The first sale doctrine allows rentals of those products, which enabled businesses such as Blockbuster Video to thrive renting VHS tapes in the 1980s and the original Netflix DVD-by-mail business to boom at the turn of the century.

The different policy between music and movies on rentals was established in the Record Rental Amendment of 1984. This exception to the first sale doctrine applies to sound recordings that contain only musical works. It does not apply, for example, to audiobooks or movie commentary tracks. This narrowly crafted section of the US Copyright law was implemented to prevent anyone from creating a music rental business. The record industry successfully lobbied for this change, during a period when home taping on cassettes was becoming widespread, because it believed that such rentals would encourage home copying without paying royalties to artists or labels.[11]

Independent record stores relied on the first sale doctrine to offer used CDs. The low prices of $2–$8 made them compelling alternatives to new discs that were priced about $10 higher for many shoppers. Though the industry and artists did not earn any royalties from these transactions, the losses were limited as long as sales were confined to the indie retail community. In 1992, the Hastings Books and Records chain based in Texas, with over 100 retail locations, began selling used CDs. Wherehouse Entertainment, with over 300 stores, followed suit.

Although used CDs sales represented less than one percent of the total industry sales, the record companies decided to take action before other major record store chains decided to undercut the enormously profitable new CD business. The distribution arms of Sony Music, Warner Music, Universal, and EMI, representing four of the six major record labels at the time, all withdrew advertising and promotional allowances from any retailer that sold used CDs.[xxviii]

The more restrictive policy hit the retailers hard, because these allowances represented a major portion of what chains spent to advertise CDs. The Wherehouse chain alone faced the loss of $5 million annually. Wherehouse had conducted test marketing of used CDs and found they had appeal in all of its markets, from suburban malls to college campuses. Rather than back down, Wherehouse, along with the Independent Music Retailers Association, representing small music stores, filed antitrust lawsuits against the labels in 1993 for acting in lockstep to end the practice of providing this valuable financial support.

The major labels blinked first and revised their policy. They restored the advertising and promotional dollars, but they stipulated that the money could not be used to support the used CD business. The used CD remained a niche offering, and the antitrust suit never came to fruition. (Of course, used CDs are still sold, though the market for used vinyl currently dwarfs that of used CDs.) But this was not the last time that the major labels would attempt to use their muscle to influence how retailers marketed CDs.

The CD specifications were expanded in the late 1980s to include writeable versions, in part to serve the need for inexpensive computer storage. There were two designs: the CD-R, which was recordable but could not be overwritten with new data, and the CD-RW, which could be rewritten with data after the initial use. Given the popularity and profitability of music CDs, it was obvious that these extensions could generate new ways to make more CDs outside of the authorized supply chain.[xxix]

Although selling unauthorized copies of CDs violated copyright law, the profitability of CDs made them an inviting target from the start. Authorized CD factories were monitored carefully to be sure that they were not producing overruns that could be fed into the black market. Setting up manufacturing lines to make counterfeit CDs, as with vinyl records, took a certain degree of technical skills and investment. The RIAA broadened its net to find and shut down music piracy in the CD format. In 1996 it seized more illicitly produced CDs than cassettes, with 1.2 million units seized, an increase of more than 1,300 percent from the previous year, though still miniscule compared to the almost 800 million CDs sold that year. However, each of these bootleg CDs contained the exact same set of 1s and 0s as the original, unlike the progressively degraded copies made from LPs or tapes.[xxx]

The same equipment that could support the burgeoning CD-ROM business could support a new, less capital-intensive bootleg music CD infrastructure as well. By 1998, $6,500 would get you a CD duplicator from Cedar Technologies that made dozens of music CDs at once. You could even print the needed labels for just another $1,000. Octave, another CD-R start-up, was selling up to 5,000 blank discs per day.[xxxi]

In 1997, the RIAA confiscated fewer than 500 unauthorized CDs that were on recordable media. One year later, the New York Police Department, with the cooperation of the RIAA, charged over 40 people in "Operation Copycat." The seizure claimed the largest CD reproduction facility ever shut down by law enforcement up until then—one that could produce over 75 CDs per hour, amounting to an annual production capacity estimated at $19 million from that single counterfeit ring.[xxxii]

That same year, Philips announced the first product intended for consumers to record their own CDs. It was priced at $700, which was too high for many consumers but would decline quickly to the $300–$400 range in just a couple of years as volumes increased. The unit accepted audio from any analog or digital source in the home as input and wrote the information onto a CD-R. As prices of CD burners declined with volume, the piracy threat expanded from commercial operators to individual consumers, who could now make duplicate CDs for their friends and family—or for sale.

This shift proved problematic for the traditional bootleggers as well: people making CD-R copies began "bootlegging the bootleggers." These new fan-generated copies were being sold for $10 less than traditional unauthorized CDs, disrupting this illegal business model too. At the same time, there were efforts to create new digital products such as Digital Audio Tape (DAT) and Minidisc (MD) that were even better suited for mobile applications than the CD, though neither of these formats succeeded for consumer applications.

To address the concerns arising out of these new products as well as the threat of home taping and CD burning, the music industry tried to convince consumer electronics companies to incorporate restrictions on their products' ability to make unlimited perfect digital copies. Songwriters and publishers also wanted some form of compensation for any copying performed by these devices. Music industry interests and consumer electronics companies reached a compromise in 1989 that enabled the launch of DAT recorders in the United States. The products would include a Serial Copyright Management System (SCMS): technology that permitted first-generation copies of an original DAT but included a "copy bit" that could be examined by compliant hardware to disable the making of any subsequent generations of copies.

This compromise formed the basis of the Audio Home Recording Act (AHRA), which passed in 1992. It applied specific rules to both "digital audio recording devices" and "digital audio recording media." The former covers devices that are designed or marketed primarily for the purpose of making copies of digital audio for private use, whether or not that device is included as part of a larger machine. A DAT player or a home CD recorder that is purchased and used as a peripheral to a home stereo unit would qualify. But a personal computer that includes a CD burner would not, because the applications for the CD burner were broader than just music. Any such recording product is required by the law to implement a SCMS comparable to the one agreed on for the DAT. (Given that the PC was to become the hub for digital music in the home by the turn of the century, this narrow definition of a digital recording device turned out to be very consequential.)[xxxiii]

"Digital audio recording media" is similarly defined as a material object that is used by consumers to make copies of digital audio recordings for use by individuals. A CD-R that is marketed for making back-up copies of photos or documents would not qualify, while a CD-R that is specifically targeted for making personal copies of music CDs would qualify.

Makers of devices and media that fit these definitions are required to pay levies of 2 percent on recording devices and 3 percent on blank DATs to the US Copyright Office. The law specifies how those funds are allocated and distributed to rights holders to compensate, in part, for the money that would have been paid for purchases of original recordings. There was actually no technical difference between the CD-Rs that were marketed as being suitable for music and those not so labeled. The music CD-Rs were priced higher, however, to cover the levy payments under the AHRA. If you searched for "CD-R Music" on Amazon or Walmart decades after the peak of the CD format, you could still find these discs.

Even with the law in place, CD-burning capabilities that cropped up in homes across the country worried the industry. This development raised questions about how strong a public posture the industry should take on the legality of such copying. The industry pushback against home taping, which we discussed in Chapter 5, had not yielded positive results. The bootleg businesses just described clearly fell outside the line of legality as they pursued profits at scale. But individuals making single backups of CDs that they had previously purchased presented a different set of facts. And the fact pattern was affected by whether the consumer put the copy in a drawer or gave it to their next-door neighbor as a gift.

The RIAA spelled out its views on permissible behavior with regard to CD-Rs on its website as follows:

- "It's okay to copy music onto special Audio CD-R's, mini-discs, and digital tapes (because royalties have been paid on them)—but not for commercial purposes.
- Beyond that, there's no legal "right" to copy the copyrighted music on a CD onto a CD-R. However, burning a copy of CD [sic] onto a CD-R, or transferring a copy onto your computer hard drive or your portable music player, won't usually raise concerns so long as:
  o The copy is made from an authorized original CD that you legitimately own.
  o The copy is just for your personal use. It's not a personal use—in fact, it's illegal—to give away the copy or lend it to others for copying.
  o The owners of copyrighted music have the right to use protection technology to allow or prevent copying.

o Remember, it's never okay to sell or make commercial use of a copy that you make."[xxxiv]

In other words, the RIAA takes the position that what you're doing if you copy music onto CD-Rs, or other blank digital media, is technically a violation of copyright law but admits the practicality that you're extremely unlikely to get caught if you're copying your own music and the copy stays in your possession (not to mention that such actions may be fair use).

As discussed earlier in this chapter, using the CD as a loss leader to drive retail traffic concerned the labels because the practice could devalue their product in the eyes of the average consumer. It certainly made it harder for smaller record stores to compete when they did not have the luxury of making up for losses on music with profits on other goods. Yet by law, the labels could not dictate the retail price of their goods. So instead they created a workaround called the "Minimum Advertised Price" (MAP) to encourage retailers to keep prices at what they considered to be reasonable levels. The labels contributed marketing dollars to help fund those weekly circulars if the retailer kept their CD prices above the MAP.

As with their earlier efforts to withdraw advertising funds from retailers that sold used CDs, these tactics landed the major labels in legal hot water. The Federal Trade Commission launched an inquiry in August 2000 as to whether marketing agreements such as MAP were intended to raise prices by putting an end to the price wars being pursued by Target, Best Buy, and others—in which case they would be unlawful restraint of trade. The FTC believed that the result of the program was that consumers had paid an extra $5 per CD, resulting in almost $500 million in overcharges over five years.

Shortly thereafter, Florida and New York led a coalition of 41 states in filing a price-fixing lawsuit against the record companies. A settlement was reached in 2002 that included the then five major labels (BMG, EMI, Sony, Universal, and Warner) and music publishers, as well as retailers including Tower Records, Trans World Entertainment, and Musicland. The parties admitted no wrongdoing, though they agreed to pay a fine of almost $70 million and distribute more than $75 million in CDs to nonprofit and public groups.[xxxv]

The legal issue was not really about the specifics of the MAP program itself. The retailers remained free to set retail prices at whatever levels they chose. However, the circumstances were evaluated under different antitrust legal standards if competitors discussed implementing these policies collectively and then the entire group put them into place in a unified and coordinated fashion. It was the horizontal agreement across the industry, which the FTC alleged amounted to restraint of trade, that created the much greater legal risk that led to the eventual settlement.

Conclusion

The CD was an unparalleled success for the music industry. Getting music fans to buy new music as well as copies of all their favorite older albums, at higher prices than vinyl or tape, drove revenues and margins to stratospheric levels. That money bankrolled big deals for executives and artists alike. (It also covered the costs of wrecked hotel rooms and a wide variety of illicit drugs.) The desire for more profits even compelled the labels to pull back on the release of singles to boost CD sales further. Though this was great for the bottom line, the business strategy fueled consumer frustration. Fans resented the need to buy an entire CD to get the one song they cared about.

The unprecedented prosperity and fan frustration from the CD were like plates under the Earth's surface rubbing against each other to form a fault line. The conditions were in place for a major earthquake triggered by technologies that were coalescing in the 1990s to create yet another music format. This time, the format enabled college students to vent their frustrations and to wrest control from the grasp of the industry movers and shakers who were loath to change their lucrative ways.

8

Downloads

Don't Download This Song—Weird Al Yankovic

Turning analog audio files into a collection of zeros and ones that could be embedded on a plastic disc was the fundamental innovation that led to the flourishing of the music industry in the late twentieth century. Every Compact Disc (CD) is a digital "master." With the right tools, which had become standard on every PC or laptop by the end of the last century, every song file on the CD could be copied, compressed, and then "shared" with a million "friends" over networks. Unlike the DVD, which was developed in the mid-1990s, the CD specification of the early 1980s contained no provisions for encrypting the content, nor were any other mechanisms to deter copying included.

With the benefit of hindsight, it is easy to criticize this omission, but it was more than just a simple oversight, because of the state of computer technologies in the mid-1980s. A typical personal computer at the time of the CD's introduction was equipped with a 10 Megabyte hard drive, while a typical CD contained over 700 Megabytes of data. There wasn't even enough space on that drive to hold the data from a single song, let alone an album. Not to mention that the removable memory slot on that PC was for a 360 kilobyte floppy disc.[i]

CD drives for computers did not become standard until a decade later. The sheer size of the data files on the CD created what appeared to be, at the time, an insurmountable security barrier to copying. Thus it is not surprising that Sony and Phillips chose not to address these issues when creating the CD.

There were some early downloadable music concepts that pointed the way for what was to come. As early as 1982, Frank Zappa proposed aggregating a catalog of tracks and distributing them over cable networks to fans who would record as many as they wished on tape for a flat monthly fee.[ii] Just over a decade later, the Internet Underground Music Archive (IUMA) launched to allow unsigned artists to share their music with fans via FTP sites.[1]

Key Changes. Howie Singer and Bill Rosenblatt, Oxford University Press. © Howie Singer and Bill Rosenblatt 2023.
DOI: 10.1093/oso/9780197656891.003.0008

In 1994, Jim Griffin, then the CTO at Geffen Records, distributed an Aerosmith track to ten thousand subscribers to CompuServe, a proprietary dial-up network that predated the commercial Internet. It took up to 90 minutes to download that single song as an uncompressed WAV file.[iii]

These experiments took advantage of innovations at the time that were improving the performance of computers and the speed of network connectivity. Yet even with these changes, the size of the music files on the CD would still have stood in the way of a sustainable business. What was needed was a method that could reduce the size of the music file while maintaining the quality of the playback. In the mid-1980s, research began to create just such an algorithm, one that would eventually give birth to the MP3 format.

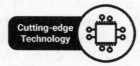

Karlheinz Brandenburg became interested in the problem of compression for music when his PhD thesis advisor in psychoacoustics had his patent application for a "digital jukebox" rejected.[iv] The patent examiner determined that there was simply no way to fit all the bits from a music CD through an ISDN connection, although this was considered a relatively high-speed telephone network at the time.[2] Although Brandenburg was skeptical at first, he became convinced that it would be possible to compress music by a factor of 12 to 1 or more. With that reduction in size, the jukebox became feasible. After completing his dissertation, he came to Bell Labs to collaborate with James D. (J. J.) Johnston to refine his approach. AT&T's research arm had a tradition of world-class experts in this area because it needed to reduce the amount of data necessary to send intelligible voice conversations over capacity-constrained telephone networks.[v]

Brandenburg returned to Germany in 1990 and joined the Fraunhofer Institute to continue his work. After an extensive testing and evaluation process, the Motion Picture Experts Group (MPEG) approved Brandenburg's compression algorithm as the MPEG-1 Layer 3 standard in 1993. The algorithm was soon referred to colloquially as MP3. A single musical artist and the qualities of a specific song played a critical role in the development of the format: Suzanne Vega is referred to as the "mother" of the MP3 because her song "Tom's Diner" was used repeatedly to assess the quality of the algorithms and to refine the results. The vocal quality and percussive elements in the track made it easier to identify imperfections created during the compression.[vi]

MP3 is a "lossy" compression scheme that relies on principles of psychoacoustic modeling. It is lossy in the sense that significant portions of the original data that constitute each digital music file are discarded and can't be recovered when the compression is reversed. Psychoacoustics uses knowledge of human hearing and perception to determine which parts of the file can be ignored because they are too high in frequency or rendered below the "noise floor." In other words, many components of sounds cannot be heard because they are masked by other often louder parts of the music.[vii] After discarding the data associated with the unhearable sounds, the remaining data is encoded efficiently using sophisticated mathematical techniques including Modified Discrete Cosine and Fast Fourier Transforms.[viii]

Given that almost all of us are listening to music that has been compressed using MP3 or one of its perceptual audio coding successors, we have become somewhat oblivious to its remarkable performance. MP3 effectively reduces the size of the file on the CD by 75 to 95 percent. A CD containing one hour of music is equivalent to 635 megabytes (MB) of data. Applying MP3 at a bitrate of 128 kilobits (kbit) per second to that collection of digital songs yields a file that is 57.6 MB, or less than one-tenth the size of the original.[3] Eight or nine out of every ten bits are thrown away, yet the resulting MP3 file offers an enjoyable experience for music fans. For many casual music fans, listening to the MP3 of a track at 256 kbits or higher is often indistinguishable from the original CD in a blind listening test.

During the decade of the CD's dominance, personal computers were evolving rapidly. By the mid-to-late 1990s, disk storage costs had decreased so quickly that 1 gigabyte (GB) hard drives had become a reality.[4] CD drives were under $100, and in 1997 rewritable discs were introduced. Modems operating over standard telephone lines providing connectivity to online services and the Internet had improved by a factor of ten, from 2.4 kbit/s in the mid-1980s to a rate of 28.8 kbit/s by the mid-1990s.

Moore's Law states that the number of transistors on an integrated circuit doubles every two years, which results in enormous increases in the power of the processor at the heart of every computer. The resulting horsepower could run the MP3 decoder and turn the compressed files back into music. The MP3 code was efficient to run, and PCs of the late 1990s could operate the encoder as well. They could read the data off the CD and turn it into an MP3 file one-tenth the size of the original.

If you put all those pieces together, you had the technology foundation for MP3-based music distribution. Music fans could create MP3s from their own CDs and store them on their machines and play them back later at adequate quality. They could download already compressed song files from online sites, save the bits on their hard drive, and then play them back whenever they wanted. Although it could take 15 minutes to download a single track using a modem, that was a lot quicker than driving to the record store. With a writeable CD drive, those decoded tracks could be burned back to a disc and be listened to on any CD player whether in the home or on the go.

It didn't take long for several startups to take these elements and integrate them together into what were, in essence, Minimum Viable Products (MVPs) for downloadable music e-commerce services. Liquid Audio and a2b music both developed such services that relied on software security to deter the copying of the digitally distributed songs. Liquid Audio was formed in 1996 in Redwood City, CA, by Gerry Kearby, Robert Flynn, and Phil Wiser to offer an end-to-end solution for secure downloadable music. At the same time, a2b music was formed as an internal venture at AT&T Labs by Larry Miller and Howie Singer. It used Advanced Audio Coding (AAC), a perceptual audio coding scheme like MP3 with improved sound quality at comparable bit rates. A2b music's security architecture was based on public/private key cryptography, which could also run in software on the more powerful PCs of the later 1990s.

The focus on security was essential to getting the record labels to consider these new platforms. The music companies had come to realize the threat posed by the music files on the CD being "in the clear," and they would not contemplate distributing music online without a stringent Digital Rights Management (DRM) solution being built-in. DRM gave rights holders the ability to set up policies or rules regarding the use of the music files even after they were stored on an end-user's computer. Those rules could include such things as "play this song a limited number of times only" or "play the song during a limited time window" or "this song may not be copied onto a CD." Songs were downloaded with encrypted licenses specifying these permissions and, before playing the music, the software decrypted and checked that the license contained the correct approvals for the action requested.

Even though these entrepreneurs had crafted their services to meet the needs spelled out by the major labels, the industry didn't embrace these new initiatives. They expressed mild interest, but given the gusher of cash that was flowing in from CD sales, none of the music companies was ready to jump in wholeheartedly. At one of the first meetings to discuss a2b music, one major label executive, after hearing the compressed digital files played through expensive speakers in his boardroom, said, "No one is going to listen to that shit." Other label meetings elicited even more colorful language.

There was more at work here than mere reluctance to abandon the enormously profitable CD. The top label executives were simply ill-equipped to wrestle with the upheaval of the late 1990s. No one exemplified this more than Doug Morris, then the CEO of Universal Music. A "record man" in the truest sense, he even wrote "Sweet Talkin' Guy," a 1966 hit song recorded by the Chiffons. When looking back at this era, Morris basically admitted that music business leaders were clueless: he said, "There's no one in the record company that's a technologist." Even that assessment was questionable, as he acknowledged in the same interview that he "wouldn't be able to recognize a good technology person."[ix] In fact, the major labels had people who understood the issues clearly, though their advice typically fell on deaf ears.[5]

At the same time these nascent businesses were attempting to address the major labels' security concerns, others were taking advantage of the unprotected CD files and the availability of MP3 software tools to feed the desires of music fans and indie artists directly. Justin Frankel, a teenage dropout from the University of Utah, developed the Winamp music management software for Windows PCs, shown in Figure 8.1, to make it simpler to create and to playback MP3 files.[x] Version 1 of the shareware program quickly became the Internet's most popular player for MP3-encoded tunes with over 3 million downloads. The controls to play and to skip files were straightforward, and there was even a graphic equalizer that allowed users to adjust the sound of the music. Though the software enabled songs to be imported from CDs and added to the users' collections, many people obtained the music files without authorization or payment via Internet Relay Chat (IRC), an early text-chat system that could be used to send and receive files.

With the MP3 encoder built in, Winamp and other similar programs were equipped to take all the digital data that constituted the songs on a CD and turn them into compressed music files. Unfortunately, there was a critical set of information that the CD lacked: the name of the disc, the artist's name, and the song titles. The CD specification did not consider the possibility that the audio tracks would someday need to be extracted as data files to be catalogued, so there was no metadata (data about the data that made up the songs) on the disc other than the human-readable text. The Compact Disc

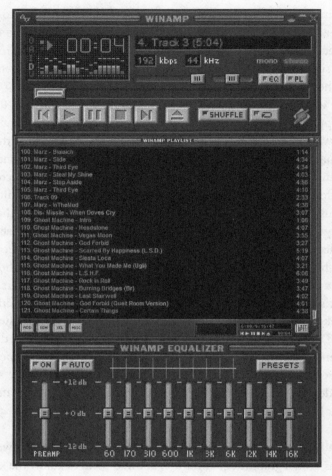

Figure 8.1 WINAMP user interface with graphic equalizer. Used by permission of Winamp Inc., All Rights Reserved.

Database (CDDB) was created to avoid relying on every person entering this detailed song data themselves. To use the CDDB, first an identifying code was calculated based on characteristics of the CD inserted into the PC's drive, including the number and length of tracks. That number was used to look up the other data about the disc in the database. If crowdsourced data was available, the title and artists fields would be populated automatically. If the particular CD was not yet in the database, the user entered all the relevant metadata, which then became available for all subsequent lookups. CDDB was initially created as an open-source project, but it eventually became a for-profit company called Gracenote.

There was no better domain name than MP3.com to attract users looking for music and information about this new format. Michael Robertson bought that name from the original owner after monitoring the traffic on his own filez.com site and seeing rapid increases in people searching for MP3 files. The surge in traffic helped support MP3.com's ad-based business, and soon it was providing news about MP3s as well as information and instruction guides about hardware and software that could manage MP3 files. It encouraged indie artists to post their songs on the site in MP3 format and split the profits 50/50. By 1999, MP3.com had over 56,000 songs from 11,000 artists, and when it raised over $370 million in an Initial Public Offering (IPO), it was the largest tech IPO ever until that point in time.[xi]

Using software on your computer to obtain music and then enjoying it through computer speakers was the perfect use case for many fans, particularly ones who lived in dorms. College students possessed three important attributes that made them the perfect demographic for file downloading: a passion for music, campus networks with some of the fastest Internet connections anywhere, and little in the way of disposable cash. But the technology of the day did not enable you to take your digital music files with you to listen to on the go, as so many were doing with their portable CD or cassette players. Fans could burn the songs on their computer back to a CD, but that seemed to be a step back from the promise of this new format. What was needed instead was a portable MP3 device that stored copies of the songs from the PC in memory and then played them back.

Right from the start, AT&T's a2b music's pitch to the record labels included a demonstration of a prototype portable player, shown in Figure 8.2, with an album's worth of music stored on a standard flash memory card. As Howie Singer, one of the founders, told music executives, "Which would you rather jog with? A disc player that skips when you nudge it, a tape player that bounces around on your belt, or a solid-state player the size and weight of a pager that never misses a beat?"[xii]

The first commercial version of such a portable MP3 player was introduced in Japan and Korea by a company called Saehan in May of 1998. Four months later, Diamond Multimedia launched the Rio PMP-300 Portable MP3 player in the United States. The Rio device cost $200 and was roughly the size of a deck of cards.

Figure 8.2 AT&T a2b music flash memory prototype. Courtesy of AT&T Archives and History Center.

The Diamond Rio PMP-300 had a small LCD screen that showed the name of the track being played and buttons for controlling playing, stopping, and skipping. It came with 32 MB of memory and a SmartMedia flash memory card slot to increase the storage space available. A single AA battery in the device powered 8 to 12 hours of playback. To get the music onto the device, you connected it to a computer's parallel port and transferred the files over. The product came with a copy of MusicMatch software, a competitor to Winamp, to manage the MP3 files on the PC. If your songs were compressed at a bitrate of 128 kbit/s, the device could hold only 30 minutes of music: not even enough songs to get through a typical workout without repetition. In addition, the device had several physical design problems that led to parts frequently breaking or falling off.[xiii] Yet Diamond Multimedia faced a bigger issue than a few defective parts: the RIAA sued it for copyright infringement (which we will discuss in more detail later in the Copyright section of this chapter).

Like the first digital music services, these initial products with their limited features would certainly be classified as MVPs. The Rio eventually sold over 200,000 units, which is significant for a new consumer electronics category but far from mass-market success. The Apple iPod was the MP3 player that broke through to mass-market popularity when it was introduced three years after the Diamond Rio. Many elements of the product reflected Steve Jobs's elegant design sensibility, such as the inclusion of a click wheel to make scrolling through thousands of songs and selecting the right one intuitively simple. But the product could not have contained thousands of songs without a major innovation from Toshiba. All the other MP3 players in the market used flash memory to store compressed music files. That storage technology was coming down in price rapidly but not quickly enough to achieve the "a thousand songs in your pocket" realized by the iPod at $399.[xiv]

Jobs's interest in developing a portable music player in 2000 had initially come to naught because the necessary components to build a product with the right combination of price and capability simply did not exist. Then Jon Rubinstein, the head of Hardware Engineering at Apple, visited Toshiba on a regular supplier visit in February 2001. Toshiba's engineers had developed a tiny 1.8-inch hard drive, but they were not sure how they could use it. Rubinstein knew immediately that the drive was the linchpin for Apple's music device. He asked Jobs for a $10 million check to purchase the drives, saying, "I know how to do it now."[xv]

The first iPod, shown in Figure 8.3, launched in October 2001. Users connected it to their Macs to transfer songs from iTunes, the music management application that Apple had launched earlier that year. Apple's ad campaign famously featured the slogan "Rip. Mix. Burn." which encouraged users to encode the music from their CDs and to make copies for others by burning CDs. This did not sit well with music executives, and adding music portability with the iPod did not make them any happier.

Eventually, Apple added the sale of downloadable music to its hardware and software suite. Elegantly integrating software and hardware, Apple gave music fans an end-to-end solution that made it simple to buy and download music and transfer it easily to an iPod. It needed to convince the labels, in spite of the objectionable iMac marketing message, that it would be a good partner and that licensing their catalogs to Apple for download sales made sense. Steve Jobs's powers of persuasion certainly played a role, but the labels were ready to listen—because of the impact of illegal file-sharing triggered by the launch of Napster.

Founded by Shawn Fanning and Sean Parker, who were respectively 19 and 20 years old in 1999, Napster used "peer-to-peer" (p2p) technology

Figure 8.3 First Generation Apple iPod. Apple Newsroom. Used by permission of Apple Inc. All rights reserved.

as the underpinnings for their file-sharing service. P2p meant that users' devices shared files directly among one another rather than going through a central server such as one operated by CompuServe or America Online (AOL), the dominant consumer online service providers of the time.

Yet Napster wasn't a pure p2p model: it had a central index that indicated which files could be found where. When someone installed Napster, it created a list of all the music files on that individual's machine that became part of the centralized Napster index. When another user wanted a song, they searched that index and selected the track they wanted. That user was then connected directly with the PC of the user who had the desired song, and a file transfer occurred from one "peer" or user directly to another.

Hundreds of college students at Northeastern University, where Fanning studied, were actively exchanging music just weeks after the beta launch. The small size of MP3 files and the high-speed networks in dorms were a perfect match. Form followed function. The early adopters were willing to live with a spreadsheet-like interface filled with text and numbers, as shown in Figure 8.4. The experience was geared toward tech-savvy users searching a database of tracks. There were no graphical elements related to artists or playback.

The music industry had dealt with unauthorized copying before with cassette tapes and CDs, but Internet file-sharing brought heightened challenges. In addition to the network effect of the service quality improving simply by adding more users, Napster had other advantages. The costs of the computer and connectivity were, in essence, fixed costs, and there was no need to buy blank tapes, nor were there any incremental shipping costs. Cassettes had to be recorded in real time (or perhaps half real time), but it took virtually no time to copy a digital file particularly if both parties were on a fast campus network. Finally, those digital copies sounded remarkably like the originals, while cassette copies had reduced sound quality.

A variety of Internet protocols, including Usenet, Hotline, and IRC, were being used to distribute MP3 files before Napster. Finding the content you wanted required searching through a variety of services and message

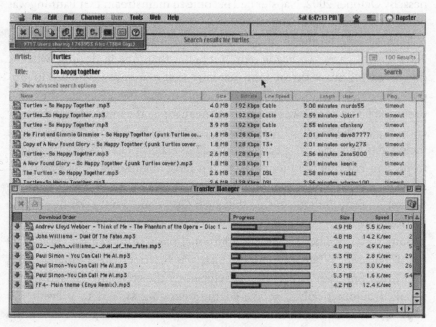

Figure 8.4 Napster user interface. Used by permission of Napster Inc. All rights reserved.

threads. It worked, but it was much simpler and far more effective to search via Napster's index. Furthermore, the more people who downloaded the software, the larger the catalog of music available became.[6] The more popular the song, the more likely that you could find a peer that had the file, which meant you could easily get your own copy. Napster went viral, spreading rapidly among universities and then to the broader population. By March 1999, MP3 files were more popular than sex—at least in terms of Internet searches.[xvi]

Napster's mainstream appeal was reflected in the media attention accorded to Shawn Fanning and his cofounder Sean Parker. Fanning appeared as a presenter at the MTV Music Awards in 2000. MTV News featured the cofounders in an interview, where Parker said, "We think that when music transitions to digital distribution, people will pay to receive music to their cellphones or to their portable devices."[xvii] That argument was not persuasive to the music establishment, as Napster usage peaked just five months after launch with 80 million users transferring approximately 2 billion files per month without paying for the privilege. Imputing a conservative price for each one of these songs, the estimated value of these copies was on a pace to exceed the annual revenues of the entire US recorded music business. By October 2002, Napster had become so mainstream that Fanning was pictured on the cover of *Time* magazine.

Sony and Bertelsmann created Sony BMG Music as a joint venture in 2004. In this case, two heads were not better than one in dealing with the downloadable music threat. One year later, that new entity managed to produce the greatest technology fiasco of the downloadable music era: the copy-protected CD. The CD was the fountainhead for all the music that ultimately ended up on the file-sharing networks because no copy protection had been included in the original specification. Labels experimented with technology to prevent copying the files on CDs, but most abandoned their efforts because of compatibility issues with the more than 2 billion CD players in the market. In fact, Philips asserted that such discs should not even display the CD logo.

Sony BMG decided to add an additional piece of software to every CD that it released. When one of these CDs was inserted in a computer drive, a software program called XCP, developed by the company First4Internet, installed automatically that altered the operating system to prevent CD copying. This software installed a "rootkit," a way of accessing low-level functionality in the PC operating system, as part of a layer of DRM technology for the CD where none had existed before. The rootkit created vulnerabilities to malware and was difficult to uninstall. This retroactive attempt to limit the CD's utility and deter file-sharing caused a consumer uproar, a class-action lawsuit, and a government investigation. Sony BMG eventually paid restitution to some affected users and abandoned the entire effort in 2007. The unprotected digital masters on CDs continued to serve as an essentially limitless supply of free music for anyone with the right software.[7]

As we've seen before, new formats and products test the boundaries of established copyright law and make it more difficult to enforce rights. The creation, copying, and transferring of digital music files triggered a variety of legal actions that were aimed at stopping these disruptions in their tracks.[8]

The first legal skirmish of the download era was over the Rio Portable MP3 Player. As discussed in Chapter 7, Congress passed the Audio Home Recording Act (AHRA) of 1992, which required that digital audio recording devices incorporate Serial Copy Management Systems (SCMSs), or technologies designed to ensure that only limited first-generation copies of digital audio recording could be made, and that royalties on those copies be paid to songwriters and recording artists. The AHRA was originally intended to apply to Digital Audio Tape (DAT), a putative successor to the standard audio cassette that never succeeded as a consumer media format, though it was used in recording studios and as a backup format for computer data.

The Recording Industry Association of America (RIAA) sued Diamond Multimedia, claiming that the new product did not employ a SCMS and therefore violated the AHRA. Digital audio recording devices as defined by that law were required to make payments to the industry. In essence, the industry did not want to allow MP3 songs on computers to be transferred to devices that did not pay compensation of artists and labels as part of their cost structure.

The lower court denied the RIAA's request for an injunction to stop the sale of these devices, and the labels lost the higher court appeal as well.[xviii] The court ruled that the Rio did not qualify as an audio recording device under the AHRA because the copies of songs on the device were transferred from a computer hard drive and not directly from a transmission of audio files. The limited functionality of the device and its reliance on the somewhat inconvenient step of loading the music from the PC had insulated the Rio from the law's requirements. The court also ruled that computer hard drives were not digital audio recording devices, because making digital audio recordings was not the primary purpose for the device. Finally, the court ruled that "space-shifting"—moving the music from one user device to another—facilitated fair use as intended by the law. Instead of enabling the music industry to receive payments for all manner of PCs, laptops, and solid-state music players, the courts had created fertile space for the consumer electronics business to thrive in digital music.[9]

The stakes in the Rio case were certainly significant, but they were dwarfed by those of the next major lawsuit in the MP3 era. The RIAA sent cease-and-desist letters to and sued several sites that offered downloads of free MP3 files from their servers. These sites either shut down immediately or did so as part of a settlement with the industry.

Napster's reliance on p2p technology meant that it was not providing the files itself, and this changed the legal arguments substantially. Nevertheless, the music industry viewed its "hockey stick" growth as an existential threat. If every fan could find and download any song for free, who would buy those $15 CDs that were funding the labels and their executives' bonuses? On December 6, 1999, just a couple of months after Napster launched, 18 record labels, all part of the "big four" major-label groups at the time (EMI, Sony Music, Universal Music Group (UMG), and Warner Music Group (WMG), filed a district court case alleging that the service was liable for copyright infringement. They requested a preliminary injunction to halt the exchange of copyrighted songs immediately.

It wasn't just the labels that thought Napster was taking money out of their pockets; many artists shared these concerns. The heavy metal band Metallica filed its own lawsuit against Napster in April 2000. Not only did it allege that Napster was liable for copyright infringement, it charged the company with racketeering under the RICO statute, which was most notably used by the FBI to take down the bosses of organized crime families. Metallica's suit even looped in several universities, including Indiana University, Yale University, and the University of Southern California, for allowing their networks to be used to steal their music via Napster.

At a rate of $100,000 per track downloaded illegally, Metallica requested at least $10 million in damages.[10] The band hired the consulting firm NetPD to gather detailed information about the more than 300,000 Napster users who were providing copies of their songs to others.[xix] The list came to 60,000 pages. Metallica's drummer, Lars Ulrich, delivered that list to Napster's office himself and requested removal of all these accounts from the service. The backlash from the Napster community was swift and fierce, as Ulrich began to receive death threats. Dr. Dre, the hip-hop pioneer, adopted a similar approach and presented his own list of 230,000 misbehaving users to Napster. Napster banned those accounts from the service, which only inflamed Napster users further.[xx]

In July 2000, Judge Marilyn Patel of the Federal District Court in San Francisco ruled that Napster was in violation of copyright law. Her ruling stated that Napster "knowingly encourages and assists" users to exchange copyrighted music and that this activity was not fair use. The earlier *Betamax* case, which we saw in Chapter 5, established a precedent that the maker of a technology that had "substantial non-infringing uses" could avoid copyright liability. Napster's lawyers tried to make the same argument, but the court didn't buy it because the infringing activities far outweighed the authorized uses. Furthermore, Napster's centralized index of the songs that were available demonstrated that it had knowledge of the infringements, thereby increasing its liability.[11] To stop the ongoing damage to the labels' business, Patel issued an injunction that compelled Napster to remove every copyrighted song from the service.[xxi]

Judge Patel's injunction, if upheld, would be exceedingly difficult to implement. Not only was there a vast number of infringing songs available through Napster, but identifying all of them accurately was a near-impossibility. And if the service could be cleansed of that material, it would effectively lose the very thing that was attracting fans. Napster quickly appealed to the Court of Appeals for the Ninth Circuit, and just two days later, that court issued an emergency stay pending its hearing of the case.

The stay gave Napster a window of opportunity. It started talking to technology companies about how to implement the changes that would be imposed if its appeal failed.[12] In addition, Napster tried to reach a settlement with the record companies that would allow it to stay in business in exchange for payments to enable the exchange of copyrighted songs. Those discussions led to Bertelsmann announcing in October 2000 that it would invest in Napster to support the shift to a licensed model. Bertelsmann—a large, privately-held German media company best known for its activities in book publishing—owned BMG Entertainment, which was one of the labels suing Napster. Because of the deal, Bertelsmann dropped out of the ongoing legal action against Napster. Bertelsmann Chairman Thomas Middlehoff said, "Napster has pointed the way for a new direction for music distribution, and we believe it will form the basis of new and exciting business models." The plan was to turn Napster into a secure, membership-based service with the participation of the other major labels.[xxii]

Mike Bebel was part of the Universal Music Group team that met with Napster executives to discuss transitioning to a legitimate offer. Napster's initial offer was five cents per downloaded track. UMG threw them out of the office.[xxiii] In February 2001, the press reported that Napster had upped their proposal to the industry to $1 billion to license music for the service and settle the legal actions.[xxiv] That "B" word makes it sound like Napster was making a very large offer, but it was not quite as rich as it sounded. The total covered five years of fees, equivalent to $150 million per year to each of the major labels and another $50 million to independent labels and artists. But the recorded music industry had just closed out a year with more than $14 billion in US revenues. Risking the majority of those revenues in exchange for an annual check that represented less than 15 percent of that total certainly represented a poor deal.

The conventional wisdom is that the music industry made a mistake by turning down Napster's entreaties. However, people directly involved with Napster at the time indicate that the company was never really committed to a legitimate model. Napster offered Ted Cohen the position of CEO, and when he declined, it hired him as a consultant to help negotiate with the labels. Cohen was a long-time entertainment executive who had worked at EMI Music, Warner Brothers Records, and Philips Media. He was (and is) well known as an evangelist for new technologies, gadgets, and the promise of digital distribution. He has confirmed that some of the Napster team were not serious about a settlement: it simply wanted to "slow walk" the discussions with the labels, because it had been convinced by their legal team, headed by heavyweight corporate lawyer David Boies, that Napster would ultimately prevail in court.[xxv]

On February 11, 2001, the record labels rejected Napster's settlement offer because, in their view, it proposed neither an adequate security solution for music nor a satisfactory business model.[xxvi,xxvii] The next day, the Ninth Circuit issued its ruling on the case, which essentially upheld all of Judge's Patel's key findings. The court said that "a preliminary injunction against Napster's participation in copyright infringement is not only warranted, but required."[xxviii]

That ruling rejected a variety of defenses that Napster had put forward. One of these was the AHRA. In exchange for the levies that the AHRA imposed on digital audio recording devices and blank media, it absolved makers of those products of copyright liability. Judge Patel ruled that the AHRA did not apply to the downloading of MP3s over the Internet.

Another defense that Napster had raised was a new piece of legislation called the Digital Millennium Copyright Act (DMCA). The DMCA was the first major update to copyright law since 1976, and it is the piece of copyright law that has had the biggest impact on the online world since its enactment in 1998.

The DMCA's roots date back to the early 1990s, when consumer-accessible digital communications networks started to go mainstream. Proprietary networks like CompuServe and AOL were on the rise, and the Internet was poised to expand from academic institutions and the military to ordinary users. Two industry factions—media companies and the telecommunications concerns that ran the networks—were at odds over the issue of protecting copyrighted material over these digital networks. Media companies were alarmed about digital networks' virtually unlimited capabilities for copying and distributing digital files, while phone companies and cable TV operators were concerned about being held legally liable for their users' infringing actions.

The two industry groups negotiated on legislation that would attempt to protect copyrights from rampant infringement on digital networks while shielding network service providers from what lawyers call secondary liability—in this case, liability for copyright infringements committed by end users. The first result of those negotiations was two treaties passed by the World Intellectual Property Organization (WIPO) in 1996, which individual countries would then implement in their own copyright laws. In the United States, legislation to implement the terms of the WIPO treaties was brought in a bill that was originally called the Online Copyright Infringement Liability Limitation Act (OCILLA). It was enacted as part of the DMCA; the DMCA has several components, but OCILLA became the most consequential piece.

The DMCA creates copyright safe harbors for online service providers. "Safe harbor" is a legal term for a way of avoiding legal trouble by following rules or meeting conditions. The DMCA provides safe harbors that enable online service providers to avoid liability for the copyright infringements of their users if they take certain steps that depend on the type of service provider they are. If they don't take those steps—or a court decides that they failed to do so sufficiently—they could be liable for vast sums of money in damages.[13]

Congress defined four DMCA safe harbors according to the types of online service providers that existed in the 1990s. Napster claimed that it qualified for two of these (the safe harbors for ISPs and online storage services); the court said no. Though the DMCA argument was not central to the Napster case, it would become one of the key factors in enabling future services such as YouTube to offer music uploaded by its users, as we'll see in Chapter 10.

Judge Patel's ruling did require the lower court to make some changes, including a requirement that as part of the process to remove works, the labels had to give massive amounts of data to Napster that would enable it to identify which of their songs were being infringed. As predicted, keeping all the copyrighted songs off the service, as required by the reinstituted injunction, proved impossible for Napster given its scale. In April 2001, the judge stated that Napster's efforts up to that point were "disgraceful."

Napster tried using a new technology called acoustic fingerprinting to find the infringing files. Acoustic fingerprinting is a way of identifying music files by their audible characteristics. An acoustic fingerprinting service analyzes a file of digital audio and outputs a series of numbers—the "fingerprint" of the file—that represent the file's musical characteristics as a human would perceive them. The way acoustic fingerprinting works, all files containing a specific song—no matter what codec or bitrate it is, and no matter how it is digitized—should yield the same fingerprint. The service then looks up the fingerprint in a database of fingerprints of copyrighted songs and sees if it matches any songs in the database. If so, the file is a copyrighted work and (in this case) should be removed from Napster. (We will revisit acoustic fingerprinting in Chapter 10, as it was key to YouTube's success.)

Although acoustic fingerprinting technology was relatively new and untested at scale at the time, the technology that Napster used achieved a 99.4 percent accuracy rate. Nevertheless, in July 2001, Judge Patel said this was not good enough and ordered the service shut down until it could keep all the copyrighted songs off. The case was partially settled in September when Napster paid $26 million to rights holders for unauthorized uses of their music—a tiny fraction of the billions in damages for which Napster could have been held liable under the theory of statutory damages for willful infringement.

Even after the shutdown, Bertelsmann remained convinced that Napster could form the basis of a legitimate offering. It pumped $85 million into the company in an attempt to build a "copyright respecting" version of the service that used acoustic fingerprinting to keep unlicensed songs off. But it was all in vain: Napster filed for chapter 11 bankruptcy in May of 2002. Bertelsmann offered to buy the assets out of bankruptcy for $8 million more, but a Delaware judge blocked the transaction in September after objections from rights holders. Sean Fanning's Napster was finally dead, although as we'll see, the brand name would be resurrected later for a licensed streaming service that still operates today and otherwise has nothing in common with the original file-sharing network.

Finally, in what can only be described as the crowning irony of this sordid legal tale, an alliance of publishers and music labels sued Bertelsmann and Napster's venture capital firm, Hummer Winblad, for the damages caused by their financial backing of the p2p service, to the tune of $17 billion. That case was settled for tens of millions of dollars several years later.

Napster was gone, but p2p technology was not; and the catastrophic impacts on the music business were not finished. In early 2001, attracted by Napster's enormous popularity, a whole new wave of p2p-based clients launched. These new services, including Morpheus, Grokster, and Kazaa, were considered the second generation of p2p technology. Judge Patel's ruling that a centralized index established knowledge of and responsibility for the infringements on Napster's service was essentially a roadmap for p2p developers. The protocols underlying these services, such as Gnutella and FastTrack, were designed without a centralized server. This meant less efficient searching for files from an engineering perspective while cleverly sidestepping the legal argument that had proved fatal to Napster in the US courts. Morpheus's parent company was based in Nashville, but Kazaa's main offices were in Amsterdam, and Grokster's on the island of Nevis in the Caribbean, thereby making any copyright litigation more difficult.

By August of 2001, over 3 billion files had been downloaded through these Napster "clones."[xxix] Regardless of corporate location, the RIAA decided to sue these next-generation services for copyright infringement.[xxx] This time, the record labels were joined by the Motion Picture Association of America (MPAA), as movies had become just one more "file type" in the catalogue of these services. Connectivity had advanced to the point where it had become feasible to download the very large files that constituted an entire compressed movie—roughly one gigabyte per hour of video. The lawsuit against Kazaa, Morpheus, and Grokster, filed in October 2001, was destined to make it all the way to the US Supreme Court—but not before some significant twists and turns along the way.

First, the US district court found in 2003 that file sharing software was not illegal, according to the "substantial non-infringing uses" standard established in the *Betamax* decision, even though some estimates found that 90 percent of the files downloaded via Grokster were copyrighted. Furthermore, the developers of these programs were held not liable for the copyright infringement committed by their users. Things did not go better for the RIAA and the MPAA in their appeal to the Ninth Circuit. A year later, that court ruled yet again that Grokster was not liable for contributory or vicarious copyright infringement.[xxxi]

Given the enormous threat represented by these file-sharing programs, rights holders were not prepared to give up. Not only did they appeal the case to the US Supreme Court, they also decided to make the most controversial legal move of the download era: suing individual users.[xxxii] The technology advocacy organization Public Knowledge, siding with the p2p software companies, supported "strategically targeted legal action against individual infringers," though they did not believe that large-scale suits would be effective.[xxxiii]

Public Knowledge was correct. In fact, the lawsuits turned into a public relations nightmare: teenagers and grandmothers were caught up in these cases, becoming liable for tens of thousands of dollars in damages, making it a "David versus Goliath" story that the press ate up with relish. The fact that the RIAA did not have access to personal details about the file-sharers before taking legal action did not assuage the criticism. But at the time the RIAA implemented its plan, the courts had ruled out meaningful action against the p2p software developers.

The US Supreme Court ruled on *MGM Studios, Inc. v Grokster, Ltd.* in June 2005. In a unanimous reversal of the lower court rulings, the Court found for the plaintiff labels and studios.[xxxiv] The decision did not turn on the *Betamax* test of whether or not p2p software was capable of substantial noninfringing uses. Instead, the ruling found that Grokster had "induced" their users to commit copyright infringement. The court pointed to several areas where Grokster took active steps to encourage its users, including targeting former Napster users to join Grokster and advertising and instructing how to infringe.[14]

The ruling took many in the industry by surprise, given the trajectory of recent copyright rulings, and the reaction was almost immediate. Grokster shut down and settled with the media industry, agreeing to pay an undisclosed amount to the movie studios and $100 million to the four major labels. The RIAA sent a copy of the decision to the other p2p services, emphasizing the new "inducement" standard established by the Court. Many services simply closed their doors. Some attempted to "go legit" by filtering unlicensed content from the service through the application of acoustic fingerprinting technology to identify copyrighted works. This proved to be as problematic as it had been for Napster—not so much because of the accuracy of the fingerprinting technology but more because filtering out copyrighted songs meant that afterward the remaining catalog was insufficient to retain many users. Even when some independent labels decided to allow these second-generation p2p services to offer their songs, it wasn't enough to build a user base.

A few second-generation p2p services tried various tactics to strike a balance between respecting copyright and offering access to major-label material. Kazaa, for example, tried to persuade their millions of users to switch to paid downloads by providing 30-second samples in response to song searches and then directing users to sign up for a fully featured licensed service. Two other startups, Weed and Peer Impact, tried to implement services in which users could sell DRM-encrypted files to each other over a p2p network, with rights holders getting a commission on each sale. Yet another startup called Bitmunk tried p2p file-sharing with digital watermarks embedded in music files that contained user IDs, presumably so that users would only share files with people they knew and trusted. None of these ideas resonated with either major labels or very many users. See Chapter 10 for more on this.

As other second-generation p2p networks ceased operating because of legal pressures or failed attempts to shift to licensed models, LimeWire continued to thrive and was ready to absorb the millions of users still on the hunt for a free option. NPD, a market research firm, estimated that at one point, LimeWire was responsible for 80 percent of all of the illegal downloads in the US. In August 2006, the RIAA filed a $1.4 billion copyright infringement suit against LimeWire. It took four years to resolve the case, but, relying on the inducement standard established in Grokster, the music industry won. LimeWire and the labels reached a settlement, and Mark Gorton, the founder of LimeWire, agreed to pay $105 million in damages.[xxxv]

The music industry's reaction to digital distribution was driven completely by the labels' financial circumstances. Before Napster, the funds flowing from CD sales led them to take an overly cautious approach toward the startups pitching them. Not to mention that the major-label bonus structure offered incentives tied to CD income rather than encouraging support of new, untested models. Winning the case against Napster did not stem their losses as a next wave of un-authorized distributors simply accelerated the trend toward free music.

The major labels saw the initial forays into digital distribution as a threat to their profits rather than as an immediate business opportunity. Some smaller labels, such as Creation Records in London, announced plans to release all new singles for free as MP3 files. Sony, which owned 49 percent of Creation, put a stop to those plans, preferring to work with the platforms that protected their songs.[xxxvi]

The labels were willing to license content to Liquid Audio and a2b music, but only on a very limited project-by-project basis. The focus was less on revenues from digital distribution at this point than on how these new channels could help to sell their traditional and far more profitable products. Val Azzoli, the CEO of Atlantic Records in the 1990s, promoted the Tori Amos album *From the Choirgirl Hotel* through the release of a new song called "Merman" that was not included on the album. Fans who preordered the album received a unique code to download the song using the a2b music technology. Tens of thousands of copies were downloaded, and the attention helped sell over 150,000 albums, making it no. 5 on the *Billboard* charts.[xxxvii]

In September 1997, Duran Duran's song "Electric Barbarella" was the first track to be offered for sale via digital download. The price was set at 99 cents for the radio track and $1.99 for a special remix, with Liquid Audio's DRM features constraining the ability to share and to copy the file. Capitol Records executive Robin Bechtel made it clear that this was merely a promotional ef-fort to garner attention and to promote album sales. These early efforts were essentially science experiments rather than the seeds of viable businesses.[xxxviii]

The labels did begin to invest more in digital distribution projects that were backed by larger, well-established companies. They set about control-ling the agenda for these efforts with the objectives of maintaining control of future channels or extending the value of the CD into the future even as digital distribution was becoming a reality. And they got together with many

of those established companies (as well as various startups) in a standards initiative called The Secure Digital Music Initiative (SDMI).

SDMI was formed in late 1998 to develop specifications and technology for
playing, storing, distributing, and performing digital music. More than 200
consumer electronics, communications, and IT companies joined the labels
and rights societies to create a standard to counter the growth of the inse-
cure MP3 format. The mood was "do or die," and the proposed timetable was
among the most aggressive of any technical standard ever attempted. Howie
Singer, then the CTO of AT&T's a2b music, said of the time pressure, "Every
day that ticks by, there's good news and there's bad news. The good news is
that the potential client base for secure digital distribution is growing. The
bad news is that they're also getting used to not paying."[xxxix]

The plan was to insert digital watermarks into songs to ensure that SDMI-
compliant players would detect the watermarks and play only music authorized for that device. The watermark needed to survive playing back the song
and then re-recording the sounds coming out of the speakers—the so-called
analog hole. The participants even persuaded Leonardo Chiariglione, the
Italian engineer who chaired MPEG when it established MP3 as a standard,
to lead the effort.

Months later, in February 1999, the major labels were in the news again,
this time announcing Project Madison along with IBM.[xl] The effort began
with a technology pilot serving 1,000 homes equipped with broadband cable
connections. IBM would enable entire digital albums (but not individual
songs) to be sent to these homes, where the albums could be burned onto
writable CDs. Digital booklets for printing were provided as well. The system
was designed to have end-to-end security with no leakage of music to people
outside of the pilot project.

These projects were ambitious, the technology challenges were significant, and ultimately neither one led to a standard or commercial offering
that achieved the goals.[xli] Designing a digital distribution system that met
the major labels' requirements for control and security while open and unprotected MP3 use was growing like wildfire was a major challenge. As
millions of music fans flocked to the post-Napster p2p networks, struggling
to reach consensus on technical standards and specifications though large
committees became a time-consuming luxury that the labels could no longer
afford.

Instead, music companies jump-started their efforts to sell music online
in the hopes of drawing fans away from the p2p platforms. Yet the plans they

pursued did not have much chance of success, for two main reasons. First, the major labels divided their efforts—and catalogs—between two incompatible services. Second, the labels codified a set of complicated and restrictive usage rules that would be enforced via DRM. Getting users to pay for the "privilege" of having a poor user experience simply could not compete with the unencumbered and free world of MP3 files.

Universal Music and Sony Music teamed up to create a joint venture called pressplay, which launched in December 2001. The other three major labels at the time, EMI, Warner Music, and BMG, did license some of their music to pressplay, but the catalog was far from complete. In a move that one could argue was ahead of its time, any song in the catalog could be streamed. However, the streams were low quality and were capped at 300 listens total per month. Buyers got 30 song downloads per month, but not every song in the catalog was available for this feature. In addition, the downloads all expired at the end of the month and were no longer playable. None of the streams or downloads could be transferred to any portable music player. Instead, to enable listening away from the PC, ten songs per month could be burned to a CD, but those ten songs could include no more than two tracks from the same artist—effectively preventing duplication of an album. Microsoft's Windows Media DRM technology ensured that all these rules were enforced. The service cost $9.95 per month.

One reason BMG, Warner Music, and EMI held back some of their songs from pressplay was that they wanted to support their own joint venture with streaming audio technology pioneer RealNetworks called MusicNet. While pressplay was a direct-to-consumer retail service, MusicNet was a wholesaler, a "white label" infrastructure that companies could use to offer retail services with their own brand names. AOL Time Warner (the corporate owner of Warner Music Group at the time) and RealNetworks were the first two companies to launch services based on MusicNet. Real Networks branded its service as RealOne, and it had access to over 100,000 tracks. MusicNet initially used a DRM technology from RealNetworks that ensured that files could not be burned to CDs or copied to portable MP3 players; it was incompatible with pressplay's Microsoft-provided technology. The user's music experience was capped on this service as well: the $9.95 per month price got you 100 downloads and 100 streams per month.[xlii]

Although pressplay and MusicNet were different services with different participants and different business models, there was some overlap between the two. EMI, the smallest of the major labels, licensed its content to both services. The other point of commonality had to do with the way that the musical compositions embedded in the sound recordings were licensed. At the time, the National Music Publishers Association (NMPA)—the equivalent of the RIAA for music publishers—owned the Harry Fox Agency (HFA), which was almost-but-not-quite a "one stop shopping" service for obtaining the so-called mechanical licenses to musical compositions that online music services needed. The RIAA made a deal with the NMPA in which all major label–owned services would license musical compositions through HFA.

But this first iteration of major label–affiliated services was doomed from the start. Even if you asked someone who had decided to pay for one of these services, chances are they could not have remembered all the rules and restrictions. That was the crux of the problem. There were suspicions at the time that major-label management set these complex, Byzantine rules to discourage adoption, to avoid cannibalizing the CD sales that their bonuses depended on. Meanwhile, the competition was just a "click away" using a p2p client; one could download any song (and we do mean any) for free, keep it forever, burn it to CD, and pay the bargain price of zero. In 2006, *PC World* rated MusicNet and pressplay as tied for ninth place on their list of the "25 Worst Tech Products of All Time" and described the features as "stunningly brain-dead."[xliii]

The music labels' joint efforts were compromised in terms of user experience, but the US Department of Justice (DoJ) became concerned about antitrust implications. Given that the labels constituted an oligopoly, it raised the possibility that they could work together to squeeze out others in the market even though neither of the two services involved all of the majors. The DoJ started an investigation, which Napster tried to use as evidence during its court battle. The argument did not succeed, but Judge Patel did observe that the labels coming together in that way "looks bad, sounds bad, and smelled bad." Pressplay and MusicNet didn't stand a chance—although as we'll see shortly, MusicNet did stick around for a while strictly as a wholesale service provider.[xliv]

The first truly successful commercial digital distribution effort didn't come until 2003. By then, the iPod was the most popular MP3 player in the world with over 700,000 units sold. Steve Jobs became convinced that an online store was needed to sell songs to fill up those miniature hard drives (and trade up to larger models when they were full). That same year, the music industry was staring at revenues declining 20 percent from the industry's peak, with no bottom in sight. The labels were ready to agree to terms with Apple that they would not have even contemplated a few years earlier.

By building commerce right into the music management software which already had the capability to transfer files to the iPod, Apple had created a solution that could compete with Napster on simplicity. Steve Jobs personally demonstrated a beta version of the iTunes Music Store to key executives at the labels to drive that point home and to persuade them to agree to financial terms that had a chance for success. Paul Vidich led the strategy team at Warner Music Group, which was the first major label to come to terms with Apple. He remembers seeing the demo and thinking, "This is so simple. It works. It's great."[xlv] Any song in the store could be purchased individually and not necessarily as part of an album. This represented a major shift in policy, but it was the only way to compete effectively with Napster, which already had broken up the album as a unified entity for distribution. Vidich says he suggested the $0.99 per single price, which Jobs accepted readily (and took credit for later), as it was far lower than the more than $3 price tag being proposed by Sony.[xlvi,xlvii] Digital albums were set at $9.99 each.

The labels all agreed to deals with Apple but kept it on a short leash. The terms were only for one year. They covered the United States only, and the store was limited to Mac computers. The files were compressed using the MPEG4-AAC codec, which Apple touted as providing superior quality to MP3. DRM was still needed to satisfy the labels' concerns about security. Apple bought a small startup called Veridisc, which had built a DRM technology called FairPlay, and Apple incorporated this into iPods' firmware and the iTunes software. FairPlay was (initially) much simpler technology than the Microsoft DRM used in pressplay and MusicNet, and Apple's implementation enforced looser rules: purchased tracks could be transferred to up to 5 iPods and burned onto an unlimited number of CDs.

Some people objected to the use of any DRM solution, but, despite that concern, the simplicity of the end-to-end solution carried the day. The store sold a million tracks in its first week, in April 2003. By the fall, the total had grown to 10 million, and the labels agreed to expand to a broader set of countries and to Microsoft Windows–based PCs. By the end of its first year in business, sales totaled 50 million tracks, and the industry finally had a successful digital distribution alternative to the p2p services.

The iTunes Store was the only place on the Internet to get music from major labels for the iPod legally. Apple's steady stream of iPod enhancements and upgrades, along with its masterful marketing, including the iconic and ubiquitous silhouette commercials featuring popular songs, made it the "must-have" music player. The good news for the labels and artists was that paying for downloadable tracks and albums had become a meaningful segment of their business. The bad news was that the revenues did not come close to offsetting the decline in CD revenues; and that a single company, Apple, was dominant in that space and could dictate terms going forward and resist changes the labels wanted, such as flexible pricing.

FairPlay DRM ensured that files purchased in the iTunes Music Store were playable only on iPods. Apple might have had philosophical concerns about DRM, but the technology "locked in" consumers, which gave clear advantages to the Apple ecosystem. MP3 files without DRM were playable on the iPod, but the labels had been reluctant to license other online retailers to sell them; a few startups such as eMusic sold MP3s that were playable on iPods but came from indie labels only. Apple could have offered the FairPlay DRM for use by others in the same way that Microsoft licensed Windows Media DRM, but it did not want to invest in the resources required to offer it as a licensed technology.[15] Apple's efforts to keep users within their ecosystem were not confined to DRM: for example, when the third-generation iPod was released in 2003, Apple dropped support for MusicMatch as a tool to manage your song library including transferring tracks to your device. Users had to use Apple's software to manage Apple devices.

By the mid-2000s, several other services sold music downloads at the magic $0.99/$9.99 prices for singles and albums respectively. Most of these used Microsoft's technology stack, including Windows and its proprietary codec (Windows Media Audio) and DRM technologies. In 2004, Microsoft introduced a new version of its DRM along with a technology called PlaysForSure. PlaysForSure was a scheme for securely transferring media files (audio or video) from PCs to compatible portable devices. Users could buy music and download it onto their PCs, then transfer it to portable music players made by a variety of manufacturers that signed on to the PlaysForSure program. Because it involved multiple companies and also supported different content access models (such as monthly subscriptions), the technology was considerably more complex than FairPlay. It inevitably suffered various technical glitches that made the user experience fall short of Apple's.

Most of the PlaysForSure-based music services were based on MusicNet's wholesale service, which had migrated from RealNetworks' technology to Microsoft's by that time. Companies that slapped their brands on the

MusicNet infrastructure included AOL, Virgin, Yahoo, HMV, Samsung, and MTV. None of these achieved significant market shares, and the dilution of brand awareness among several companies that offered essentially identical services didn't help. Another of these services was called Napster but had nothing in common with the file-sharing network: it was actually a rebadging of pressplay, which had been acquired by digital media software tools company Roxio in 2003.[16]

Microsoft tried a more Apple-like approach in 2006 with the introduction of the Zune. Zune was a line of Microsoft-branded portable music players (initially made in partnership with Toshiba) and a music service that offered streams as well as downloads. The Zune included some interesting features not present in the iPod that made the device more useful, such as an FM tuner and the ability to share tracks with other Zunes (that could then be played 3 times). But the physical design did not measure up to the iPod family, and the brown color was widely ridiculed. Microsoft's efforts were simply too little, too late.[xlviii]

Another heavyweight that tried to compete with Apple in the mid-2000s was Sony—the creator of the leading portable music players of both the tape and CD eras. Sony was in the unique position of owning a major label as well as its iconic consumer electronics business. It attempted to build a player-and-service ecosystem that offered cutting-edge technology while serving the interests of rights holders at the same time. As a company, Apple had modeled itself on Sony in many ways, including the idea of building products that attracted consumers with superior technical features and unique branding rather than through compatibility with other companies' products and technologies.

In May 2004, Sony Corporation of America (not the Sony Music label) launched an iPod/iTunes/iTunes Music Store competitor called Sony Connect. Sony had hired Jay Samit, EMI's digital chief, to run the service. Sony Connect was based on Sony's proprietary technologies, including a codec called ATRAC and a DRM called OpenMagicGate (OpenMG). Sony launched a line of portable music players that ran these technologies. It claimed that the ATRAC files sounded better than MP3 or AAC files, and it priced them above 99 cents. It also didn't succeed.

Through the mid-2000s, the major labels continued casting about for a retail partner that could compete with Apple meaningfully. By then, Amazon had emerged as the largest retailer of physical music, eclipsing brick-and-mortar stores such as Tower, HMV, and Virgin, all of which had suffered with the rise of Napster. Amazon was especially attractive to the labels because of its massive trove of customer and sales data. But Amazon needed something extra to be persuaded to sell digital music; it would not be yet another online store that sold $0.99 downloads that wouldn't play on iPods.

The solution was simple, even if it was a bit hard for the labels to swallow: Amazon would need to sell DRM-free files. In mid-2007, Amazon reached agreements with Universal Music Group and EMI to sell limited catalogs of DRM-free music. The AmazonMP3 store launched in September 2007, the other majors followed with licensing deals, and soon Amazon offered a catalog of DRM-free music from majors and indies that rivaled Apple's. Eventually the labels agreed to let Amazon offer free MP3 downloads of albums that users bought on CD; the so-called AutoRip feature became available for the vast majority of recent titles in Amazon's catalog.[xlix]

Some in the industry saw DRM-free as inevitable during the run-up to Amazon's September 2007 launch. One of those was Steve Jobs. In February 2007, he posted an "open letter" called "Thoughts on Music," in which he exhorted the industry to give up on DRM.[l] Many people took this at face value and praised Jobs for his vision, especially when it became reality a year later. But "Thoughts on Music" was really just another example of Jobs's legendary Reality Distortion Field: he saw the momentum for DRM-free coming down the tracks and decided to get on that train despite the value of consumer lock-in.[17]

In any case, the quest to create a secure digital distribution system that had begun more than a decade before was essentially over. The music industry finally conceded that for digital downloads the open MP3 and AAC file formats had won the day.[18]

The download era is a simple story when it comes to money. The industry gave back all the gains it had realized during the years of CD dominance. By 1991, CDs accounted for more than half of the total US recorded music revenues, which were $7.8 billion that year. With CDs fueling growth, the industry peaked at $14.6 billion in 1999. By 2009, revenues had fallen back to $7.8 billion again. That wasn't even the bottom of the trough, as revenues fell below $7 billion in 2014 and 2015.

It is worth considering the question of whether Napster and its successors caused revenues to plummet or if Napster's launch date simply coincided with the year of maximum dollars. There were certainly many arguments made about the economic value (or lack thereof) created for labels and artists by file-sharing. For example, some argued that the downloaders used the free files as a preview to help decide if they should lay out their hard-earned cash to buy the album. Others said that even if fans downloading for free would not have bought the music anyway, the exposure led to other purchases such as tickets or merchandise. There were even a few academic studies that purported to show that piracy did not impact record sales. However, after the volume of research papers published in the wake of Napster subsided, 25 of the 29 papers that used actual data found economic harm from piracy.[li] The evidence indicates that Napster was a cause of the industry's decline, but not the only one.

The enormously popular iPod combined with the iTunes Music Store created a successful digital sales channel for the industry after many failed attempts. When iPod sales hit their maximum in 2008, the iTunes store was the top music retailer in the United States. By February 2010, it was the biggest music store (of any kind) in the world. One might have expected that the transition from physical to digital distribution would have resulted in more stable revenues rather than the industry turnover being cut in half.

The labels would have preferred to continue the same limited single and album strategy from CD days into the download era. They released retail singles selectively (if at all) to encourage the purchase of the CD even if there was only one song driving interest. Yet the deals that the labels reached with Apple permitted the iTunes Music Store to sell the digital album as a collection side-by-side with every one of the individual tracks for the low price of 99 cents each. Given the need to compete with the file-sharing sites, there was little choice, as every song from every album was already available individually on the file-sharing platforms. Competing effectively with that free alternative demanded that the licensed services do the same despite the financial implications.

The record labels were of two minds with regard to the early financial success of the iTunes Store in terms of selling downloads. They were encouraged that they finally had a platform that could compete head-to-head with the p2p services and win over millions of customers. At the same time, they were worried that less lucrative single sales would displace more profitable album sales. The labels tried various approaches to protect album revenues even if it meant constraining downloadable single sales.

One example is Shakira's English-language album *Oral Fixation, Vol. 2,* which Epic Records released in 2005. Neither the album nor the first single "Don't Bother" lived up to expectations, with sales of 400,000 units in the crucial Christmas season. Epic decided in early 2006 that it needed a creative approach to get her career back on an upward trajectory. Shakira and Wyclef Jean went into the studio and came out with "Hips Don't Lie," which became the biggest hit of Shakira's career. The album was rereleased to physical stores with the hit single added, but not to the online retailers. No downloadable version of "Hips Don't Lie" was available for purchase. But CD sales did not take off despite the inclusion of the most played track on radio that year. However, when the single was finally released digitally in mid-June, it shot to no. 1 on the download chart and has sold over 13 million copies since then, with the album selling a million copies.[lii,liii]

The labels also tried adapting some of the same marketing and promotion techniques that had proved successful in the physical world to drive album sales. The album images on the main page or the Rock page of the iTunes Store became desirable real estate that helped to improve awareness and to increase sales. The labels worked their relationships with Apple to get these spots, just as they had previously lobbied retailers for album slots on the endcaps of store aisles. Revenue per square foot as a key measure effectively became revenue per pixel.

Brick-and-mortar stores that sold records wanted special edition albums that included bonus tracks exclusive to them as a way to drive foot traffic to their stores. Similarly, the labels created deluxe versions for iTunes that included tracks and other digital items that were designated as "album only" to encourage fans to pick the album over singles.[19] For example. Ace of Base released *Hidden Gems* in 2015; fans purchasing it on iTunes received two additional tracks and a 15-page "digital booklet."[liv]

A variation on the bonus track idea that was specifically geared toward the download environment was quite successful. When a release was made available for preorder before the official street date, there was the option to offer fans an "Instant Gratification" track (or tracks). When the user placed a preorder, they got immediate access to download that track before it was officially for sale.

Apple went even further and introduced a new album format called iTunes LP in 2009 to add bonus content like liner notes, lyrics, and videos to full albums. Typically priced at $1 more than the regular downloadable album, the objective of iTunes LP was to increase album sales by providing a richer multimedia experience. LP used common web technologies such as HTML, CSS, and JavaScript, although the overall "package" was proprietary to Apple. The labels were supportive and released several hundred titles in the format. However, the format never caught on, in part because the experience was limited to desktop platforms. A version accessible on tablets and phones was never released, and Apple discontinued ongoing support in 2018.[20]

These various approaches to improving revenues are all more complicated than the simplest option: raise prices. Steve Jobs felt strongly that the simplicity of $0.99 for a single and $9.99 per album was a major factor encouraging users to pay. When it was time to renegotiate the iTunes deals, the labels sought additional flexibility that would allow them to raise prices on the most popular new releases and to lower them on slower moving content, but Apple refused. After Amazon launched its download store offering DRM-free MP3 tracks, Apple requested similar treatment: it asked the labels to approve the removal of its proprietary FairPlay DRM on tracks they sold and indicated that it would agree to variable pricing in return. A deal was struck, and in 2009, Apple went DRM-free and implemented three price tiers for singles, at $0.69, $0.99, and $1.29.[lv] Initially, Apple made limited DRM-free tracks (with a higher bitrate for better sound quality) available at the higher price, but it eventually removed DRM for the entire catalog and eliminated the higher price for DRM-free.[lvi]

These efforts mitigated the album versus singles mix to some extent, but the overall economic consequences were still severe. In 2012, digital albums and digital single sales totaled $2.8 billion, the highest total for these formats. Digital album sales had climbed to almost 120 million units. That total was swamped by the 1.4 billion digital songs sold. But at the same time, CD sales had dropped to fewer than 200 million units from 940 million in 1999. This translated to a decline of over $10 billion in revenues. These declines can't be attributed completely to file-sharing or to the product mix in online stores. As CD sales declined, many record stores closed, while others devoted more shelf space to the movies and DVDs that were still increasing in sales. If there were fewer locations to buy CDs, there would obviously be fewer purchases. Making it simple and inexpensive to buy online yielded a far greater number of digital transactions. Overall, the industry had traded sales that put $10 to $15 in the till for ones that only yielded a buck each. On the tenth anniversary of the iTunes Store, CNN.com summed things up as follows: "A decade of iTunes singles killed the music industry."[lvii]

The precipitous declines in the CD business, even if offset to some degree by the legitimate download sales, painted a bleak picture for the long-term health of the major music companies. Increasing the size of the catalog of music that could be exploited while reducing personnel staffing and duplicative functions seemed like a logical approach to weathering the storm. Ownership of what had been enormously profitable assets became a negative on the balance sheets of their parent firms. This led to a dizzying wave of changes in control, mergers, and corporate consolidations starting in 1999.

At the start of 1999, the major labels were collectively referred to as the "Big Six": Warner Music, EMI, Sony Music, BMG, Universal, and PolyGram. Warner Music was part of Time Warner at that time, and Seagram was the corporate parent of Universal. These companies had become "major" labels by absorbing smaller entities: for example, Polygram purchased Island Def Jam, Casablanca, and A&M, while Warner Music Group represented the union of Warner Brothers, Atlantic, and Elektra Records.

PolyGram merged into Universal in 1999, making it a Big Five. One year later the French company Vivendi acquired the media assets of Seagram including the music company. Vivendi had owned Universal Studios; it sold 80 percent of that to GE, which merged it with NBC, but it kept its 80 percent stake in the music company. Vivendi later bought out the remaining 20 percent interest that was still held by Matsushita, the Japanese consumer electronics company best known for its Panasonic brand.

Sony Music and BMG had formed their 50-50 joint venture Sony BMG Music in 2004, and in 2008, Sony bought out BMG's stake for $1.2 billion, so the Big Five shrank further to a Big Four. The private equity firm Terra Firma Capital Partners bought EMI in 2007. Losses piled up, and in 2011, Citigroup, which held $4 billion in debt from the deal, took over ownership of EMI and promptly broke up the company into pieces and sold them off. Most of EMI's recorded music assets were picked up by Universal. EMI's Parlophone and Virgin Classics labels went to Warner to satisfy antitrust issues raised by the EU given Universal's size. The music publishing assets made their way to Sony.

Warner Music was included when Time Warner merged with AOL in 2000. To lower its debt load from that disastrous deal, Time Warner sold Warner Music to a group of investors led by Edgar Bronfman, Jr. in 2004. Bronfman had previously put the PolyGram and Vivendi deals together when he ran Seagram. The newly independent Warner Music went public in 2005 and then was privatized yet again in 2011 when Access Industries, owned by Ukranian-born billionaire Len Blavatnik, purchased the company. For the sake of completeness, WMG went public for the second time in 2020. Vivendi sold a minority stake in UMG to the Chinese firm Tencent Entertainment before it listed the music company separately on the Amsterdam Stock Exchange in 2021.

This litany of corporate machinations meant that by the time Spotify entered the US market in 2011, the number of major labels had been cut in half. The Big Six had become the Big Three: Universal, Sony, and Warner. These consolidations were intended to create efficiencies to help survive the industry's decline by exploiting larger catalogues while eliminating duplicative functions and cutting staff.

The labels hoped that despite the revenue pie shrinking, the shift to digital distribution represented an opportunity for a broader swath of artists to achieve success. The "Long Tail" theory, put forth by Chris Anderson in his 2006 book of that name, examined the implications of the Internet removing the constraints facing physical retailers such as Wal-Mart or Best Buy in determining which products should be displayed on their shelves and stocked in their storerooms. These brick-and-mortar stores could make only a limited product selection available, so it was no wonder that so few titles— whether albums, movies, or books—captured the vast majority of revenues. The theory predicted that the infinite shelf space of online stores would allow a much greater percentage of sales to go to a wider variety of goods created by a broader spectrum of artists.

The reality, however, did not live up to these expectations. A study conducted in 2008 found that 80 percent of the tracks available online sold exactly zero copies. Furthermore, 80 percent of the revenues garnered by the one-fifth of the tracks that did sell went to only 52,000 songs.[lviii] In music, the best-known artists continued to reap the majority of the rewards.[lix] This would not be the last time that smaller, independent artists would see Internet platforms as overpromising and underdelivering for them.

The artist reaction to the MP3 format and to Napster in particular was decidedly mixed. Instead of lawsuits, some musicians, with the support of their labels, tried to use file-sharing technology itself to push back on unauthorized downloading. They placed so-called "spoof files" on the networks. These files were crafted to look like full-length songs but instead contained only snippets that repeated over and over again. The hope was that by adding some friction to what was a very simple process, users would decide to pay instead.

For example, before Madonna's album *Music* was released, unfinished portions of the title song showed up on Napster. So as the clock ticked down to the release of her next album, *American Life*, Warner Brothers Records, Madonna's label, flooded the file-sharing networks with spoof files to deter piracy. These fake files contained no music, just Madonna saying, "What the fuck do you think you're doing!"[lx] The approach did not succeed, as copies of the new album still turned up online before the release date. In fact, some people were so upset with the tactics that they hacked Madonna's website and placed copies of those leaked tracks for download right there.

Unlike Metallica and Madonna, other musicians jumped onto the MP3 bandwagon despite the lack of compensation. The Beastie Boys made live tracks and unreleased songs available for free to promote the release of their album *Hello Nasty*. They Might Be Giants offered entire albums. Chuck D of Public Enemy saw MP3 files on the Internet as a path for artists to create direct relationships with their fans and disintermediate the labels. Free of his label deal with Def Jam Records, he told *Rolling Stone* that "digital distribution levels the playing field" for artists to maintain greater control over their work.[lxi]

In general, the labels pushed back on these artist-driven efforts even if they helped to promote new releases to a growing file-sharing community passionate about music. They felt that this group of fans was less likely to pay and that artists should not be encouraging greater adoption of the MP3 format before acceptable e-commerce solutions were in place.

Artists who examined royalty statements saw their income declining as less lucrative single-song downloads failed to compensate for the payments from the CDs they used to sell. Several very high-profile artists, including the Beatles, simply refused to allow their music on the iTunes store. In the case of the Fab Four, their reluctance related to the business model as well as outstanding trademark issues.[21] Seven years after launch, the parties resolved their differences and the Beatles' music finally became available on iTunes. Some other artists, like AC/DC and Garth Brooks, informed Apple they would hold out unless Apple offered their music on an "album-only" basis; no single tracks allowed. Apple refused to concede.

As a precursor to the current debate about the fairness of streaming payments, there were several disputes between artists and labels about whether those $0.99 purchases should be treated as sales or as licenses. Though the argument revolved around legal definitions, in actuality the dispute was really about how the revenue from a sale should be allocated. When a song is licensed, such as for use on a TV show, artists receive 50 percent of the royalty payment, while the percentage going to the creator for the sale of a CD is typically 10–15 percent depending on the details of the contract with the label.[22] The record companies treated download transactions as sales, invoking the lower royalty payment to artists.

Eminem, the Allman Brothers, the Youngbloods, and Cheap Trick were among those artists who said "not so fast" and filed class-action lawsuits against their labels. They argued that there was no transfer of a physical object when a song file was copied to the user's computer. Instead, the label had simply granted Apple permission to make copies and to authorize others to make their own copies for a fee. Furthermore, they argued, DRM restricted what the end user could do with that downloaded file, so did the user actually own the track they had "purchased"?[lxii] The parties in all of those cases eventually settled, and downloads continued to be paid out as "sale" transactions.[lxiii,23]

The shift to distributing MP3 files via the Internet had no impact on artist's creative processes initially, because artists, producers, engineers, and labels played absolutely no role in making millions of different songs available as an MP3 file. Unlike every other format that preceded it, the MP3 did not require any audio expertise to produce it, nor did it require expensive machines or factories to replicate it. Winamp and other similar music management tools, paired up with p2p software, did those jobs. Any artifacts or imperfections introduced into the MP3 file were beyond the control of the creator.

No matter how clever perceptual coding techniques may be, discarding large amounts of data from the original file has inherent limitations. Higher frequency information can be discarded or encoded with distortions. If there is a sharp transient burst of sound in a song, such as a percussive attack, the audio content may be "time-smeared," which results in echoes of that sound in the compressed file. The lower the bit rate, the more prevalent and perceptible these effects will be. And the bit rate setting is at the discretion of the person ripping the CD, not the creator. In addition, the PC running the compression algorithm can have performance issues that could result in silences or glitches in the resulting file: the record skip of the digital age.

As a result, musicians who spent countless hours in the studio to craft a recording that met their high standards were unhappy that fans were not hearing anything close to what they intended. Even those bands who worked with services such as Liquid Audio were well aware of the limitations. Nick Rhodes of Duran Duran said that "MP3s are junk food."[lxiv] The crisp snare drum or precise plucking of a guitar string ended up in a softer and smoother sound in the MP3 file. No artist expressed the dissatisfaction more clearly than Neil Young, who said "My goal is to try and rescue the art form that I've been practicing for the past 50 years. We live in the digital age, and unfortunately it's degrading our music, not improving."[lxv,24]

Yet once online stores such as the iTunes Music store became viable sales alternatives to the p2p networks, artists and labels could take back a measure of control over the end experience for fans. They instituted quality-assurance processes to ensure that the asset ultimately delivered to fans met their expectations. During the mastering process, artists would approve two versions of their album: one optimized for the CD format and one to be delivered as a compressed audio file to the online stores. The engineer in the studio adjusted the loudness and the filters to craft a version that sounded as good as possible after compression.

Alternatively, many artists simply delivered a higher quality master to the distributor, often at higher sampling rates and bits per sample than the CD. Having source material containing even more information than the CD improves the quality of the compressed version. Apple established its own set of specifications called "Mastered for iTunes" that instructed artists and labels on how to deliver a higher resolution file that enabled the best versions to be created for various listening environments.

As we've seen over the course of recorded music history, even when outside forces created a new way to experience music, the industry had the clout to decide whether or not their songs or artists would be used to support the new format, and the law would often help them to enforce those decisions expeditiously. The decisions to experiment with the early secure download start-ups on a very limited basis or to support SDMI were rooted in the belief that the levers they controlled would lead to positive results.

Yet relying on control in the era of MP3 files and p2p networks was like chasing a mirage. Licensed services with restrictive DRM rules appeared to preserve that control, but consumer uptake was limited. The widespread dissemination of MP3 encoding software meant that every fan could create a replica of their entire music collection and make it available to others. The labels no longer decided which tracks were offered up, the fans did. No need to complain about the need to buy the entire album to get the song or two you wanted. And if a user downloaded those songs using Morpheus, they were free. The labels' pricing power had evaporated, and leaks of newly released songs would upend the their label carefully laid marketing plans.[25]

In a CBS News survey conducted in 2003, 58 percent of Americans who were aware of file-sharing over the Internet considered it an acceptable practice, and that percentage went up if only people aged 19–29 were included.[lxvi] Even if people viewed the behavior as somewhat sketchy, the argument quickly turned to "who was being hurt." There was not much sympathy for artists and the elaborate lifestyles shown on MTV Cribs, or for the wealthy record company executives who appeared to be technology Luddites.

In general, fans were far less concerned than artists about the sound quality of downloaded songs. As with cassettes in the 1970s, convenience and price trumped audio quality. Users' view of quality related more to data errors in the file than to how the song itself sounded when played back. "Poor quality" files on the p2p networks could contain a burst of noise or a period of silence that was not in the original song because of issues introduced during encoding by individuals.[26] Apple and the other licensed stores put quality assurance processes in place to avoid these kinds of issues.

Jonathan Berger, a Stanford University Professor of Music, surveyed his incoming students each year to get their reactions to various music formats including MP3. In 2009, he noted "not only that MP3s were not thought of [as] low quality, but over time there was a rise in preference for MP3s." He believed that people came to like the sound of MP3 files as they became more familiar with it.[lxvii]

If you had asked a college student about the size of their music collection in the late 1980s, the answer might have been something like, "I have 200 albums," referring to vinyl records and CDs. After Napster, people started measuring their music collection in gigabytes rather than albums or tracks. That made it easier to determine how much of their music could fit on their portable MP3 player and if they needed to upgrade to the latest iPod with an even larger capacity.

The file-sharing experience raised consumers' expectations. Fans expected to easily find any song they desired. And any song they desired had to be available to download when they wanted it. To meet these heightened requirements, the catalogs of the online stores had to be enormous. Using these platforms had to be drop-dead simple. The timings of releases as part of carefully crafted marketing campaigns went out the window. Even when all those factors were considered, it was impossible for the legitimate options to match the file-sharing price of zero.

Paying for music had become completely optional. Fans could decide which music to buy and which to take for free based on their own sense of connection to the artist and a desire to support their creativity. They could decide to purchase concert tickets or merchandise as a means of support rather than paying cash for the content itself. One study conducted by American Assembly, a public policy forum associated with Columbia University, showed that file-sharers did purchase more music than non-p2p users.[lxviii] The study was interpreted incorrectly as supporting the narrative that consumers who shared files were creating additional value for the industry rather than hurting the business.[27]

Attempting to communicate the economic harm being done to artists was fruitless in the face of studies like that one and the headlines about suing file-sharers. The language used by both parties exemplified the gap in perceptions. The record labels referred to downloading music for free as "piracy," and strictly speaking, one definition of piracy in most dictionaries is the act of reproducing or disseminating copyrighted material. However, to people trading files online, this was simply "sharing," and weren't we all taught in kindergarten that sharing was good? When you share something you typically have less of the item afterward. In p2p file-sharing, you never gave up possession of any of the music that you started with.

To some degree, the language and attitudes were simply a rationalization for behavior that seemed less problematic when conducted online. People who would never dream of going into a record store and walking out with a CD they had not paid for had no issue with copying the entire catalog of Led Zeppelin using Napster or Kazaa. By the iPod's third generation in 2004, there were models that could hold 10,000 songs; using p2p networks to fill that hard drive at zero cost was a completely rational economic decision.

The openness of the MP3 format and the availability of the next file-sharing platform, even when your favorite software was found to be infringing copyrights, gave music fans the ability to decide, song by song and artist by artist, when to play by the industry's rules. As Michael Robertson, CEO of MP3.com said: "The consumer will have the last word. The real wild card is the Internet because it empowers consumers."[lix]

Conclusion

Downloadable music brought an abrupt end to the enormous sales and exorbitant profits of the Compact Disc. Though the number of music transactions climbed higher than ever before, the revenues from those sales marched steadily downward for the entire first decade of the twenty-first century. Reversing that decline was going to require a fundamental change in the music experience. The "celestial jukebox" had been predicted for years and it was poised to become a reality at last because of advances in technology.

9

Streaming

Islands in the Stream—Dolly Parton and Kenny Rogers

When the music industry suffered massive declines in revenues post-Napster, virtually no one would have predicted that a streaming music company would generate excitement for a Wall Street initial public offering (IPO). But that is exactly what happened in December 2018. An IPO raised over $1 billion, yielding a total enterprise value of over $21 billion for a company that offered music streaming. That value exceeded total worldwide music industry revenues for all of that year by more than $1 billion.

One might think that this valuation had to be based on serving one of the world's biggest recorded music markets, such as the United States, Japan, or perhaps the United Kingdom. But the company was Tencent Music, and this spinout from one of China's Internet giants offered incontrovertible evidence that streaming music was the engine powering growth in the music industry.[i,ii] At the time of its IPO, Tencent Music had over 700 million monthly active users on its QQ Music app, dwarfing the customer base of Spotify. It was the exclusive sublicensee of Universal, Warner, and Sony Music in China, and it held a 78 percent market share in the first quarter of 2020. The Chinese government put an end to those exclusive arrangements with an antitrust action in 2021, which generated fuel for Netease Music, the number two streaming service in China that year with more than 180 million monthly users, to file for its own IPO.[iii]

In 2013, China produced just over $80 million in music-related revenues despite having over a half a billion mobile internet users. That figure didn't even place China, the world's most populous nation, in the top 20 revenue-producing countries for the music industry. Unauthorized distribution of music in China was widespread, and the music industry's legal battles for fostering piracy against the Chinese Internet search leader, Baidu, had yielded little.

Yet by 2017, China had entered the top 10 list of countries for the music industry, with revenues closing in on $300M—growing almost 40 percent per

Key Changes. Howie Singer and Bill Rosenblatt, Oxford University Press. © Howie Singer and Bill Rosenblatt 2023.
DOI: 10.1093/oso/9780197656891.003.0009

year over four years. By 2022, China had continued its ascent to become the fifth largest music market in the world. During the second quarter of 2020, Tencent's revenues alone approached $1 billion as paying users grew more than 50 percent year on year.[iv,v] That growth—and the enormous valuation for Tencent Music—were driven by the shift to music streaming. Instead of buying music as a product, hundreds of millions of fans around the world now access "Music as a Service"[1] in exchange for a monthly subscription fee, and billions more stream for free in exchange for listening to ads.

Of course, in terms of *global* growth, the leader was not Tencent but Spotify. Its revenues in the final quarter of 2022 exceeded $3.4 billion on a base of 489 million active users and 205 million premium subscribers, dwarfing those of Tencent Music.[vi] That Swedish company established a successful beachhead in the Nordics and used that experience to negotiate the licenses needed to enter the US market in 2011. The successful public listing of its stock in April 2018 gave the company a valuation of almost $30 billion and no doubt encouraged Tencent to follow in their footsteps.[vii]

Spotify, Tencent, and a host of other streaming music services, including those from some of the most valuable companies in the world—namely Apple Music, Google Play/YouTube Music, and Amazon Music—serving music to more than a half a billion paying subscribers have led the music industry to six years of sustained revenue growth for the first time since 1999—the year Napster launched (see Figure 9.1). In 2022, the on-demand music streams in the United States alone exceeded 1 trillion.[viii]

Though the industry resurgence of the past several years has been driven by streaming adoption, the ability to offer a "Celestial Jukebox" was already part of the conversation around the turn of this century. In the December 2000 issue of the now defunct *INSIDE* magazine, Charles Mann wrote an article entitled "The Hot New Bad Idea." His thesis was summarized as follows: "What an amazing notion. Every song ever recorded, delivered to you digitally via any device, paid for with a simple subscription fee. Everyone from AOL to Vivendi is touting the 'Celestial Jukebox' as nirvana for an industry under siege from Napster. One small problem: It's not going to work."[ix] Fortunately for the music labels, the reality has proved to be closer to nirvana than this prediction.

A proof of concept already existed for that Celestial Jukebox. In April 1998, at roughly the same time that the early music download platforms were vying for customers and content, the Rock & Roll Hall of Fame and Museum in Cleveland opened an updated Hall of Fame section with signatures of

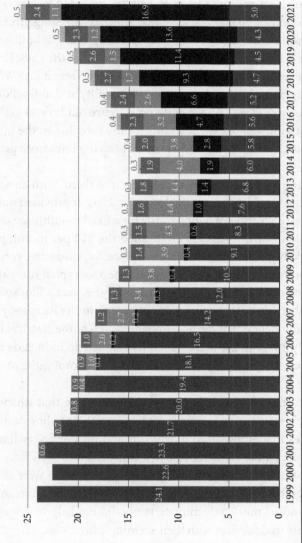

Figure 9.1 Global Recorded Music Industry Revenues 1999–2021 (US$ Billions). IFPI Global Music Report 2022. Used by permission of IFPI.

every inductee etched in glass surrounding a circular theater showing performances by music legends. As visitors exited the theater, they came face to face with several multimedia kiosks. Each kiosk had a touchscreen that enabled visitors to select any song from any album recorded by any of the inductees—a selection of 30,000 tracks. Once selected, the song streamed from a server in the basement at near CD quality. The system was built by the a2b music team at AT&T, which was a corporate sponsor of the Hall. Howie Singer led this project and said at the time, "Everyone who sees it says 'When can I get this in my house?' Would people pay for quality at that level of access. I think the answer is yes. All we gotta do is figure out how to get it to them." In fact, museum visitors spent so much time listening to the music, that the museum had to add additional kiosks to keep the lines from getting too long.[x]

The first company to fulfill that promise to "get it to them" with an actual commercial offering was Listen.com. In December 2001, it provided unlimited access to a large collection of digital music for a fixed monthly fee under the brand name Rhapsody. Rhapsody established the $10 per month price point that, remarkably, remains the reference price for streaming services 20 years later (despite it being worth $17 today). The apocryphal story at the time was that Listen.com decided on that price simply because a Blockbuster video rental membership cost the same amount. At first, the Rhapsody catalog was limited to independent music companies such as the classical label Naxos. But, by July 2002, all the major labels had signed up to include their music in the service. Rhapsody soon had a small but very loyal cadre of early adopters.

As discussed in the download chapter, at the same time that Rhapsody launched, the labels were trying to regain control over their online destinies by offering services that emphasized downloads and included very limited streaming to counteract the effects of Napster. Universal and Sony launched pressplay in late 2001. For $15 per month, pressplay subscribers were able to download 50 songs, burn 10 songs to CD, and listen to 500 audio streams in low quality. The limited music selection certainly did not help to draw fans away from unauthorized services with their seemingly limitless catalogs.[xi]

But Rhapsody had music from all the majors by July 2002—almost a year before the iTunes Store launched—and this led the way to a successful download business. Yet while having a complete selection of music might have helped to compete with piracy, simply offering all those songs was not enough to make Rhapsody a success.

Cutting-edge
Technology

What prevented the streaming business, which has now proved to be so incredibly popular with music fans around the globe, from taking off sooner? What factors kept access to music as a service in a holding pattern for more than a decade? Rhapsody was another example of a "Minimally Viable Product" in the history of music formats. It certainly pointed the way to the future embodied by Spotify, but until technology advanced in several dimensions it was incapable of attracting a mass market.

Though Rhapsody did appeal to some early adopters, a majority of music fans were just not interested in streaming because of the limitations of the overall user experience. The ability to stream audio over the Internet was already in place. As we pointed out in Chapter 3, streaming versions of MP3 and AAC codecs were already developed to break up audio files into small packets that could be sent sequentially over a network and then reassembled at the receiving end. However, the audio files distributed by Rhapsody were all protected with digital rights management DRM technology, which restricted how the subscriber could interact with the music. The tracks downloaded to a personal computer expired after 30 days, and the rules prevented users from moving the songs to a portable music player and listening to them anywhere they wanted.

Limiting the experience of streaming to the desktop was particularly problematic. Music fans had become accustomed to listening to music on the go via portable cassette and CD players. Though the number of required steps introduced some friction into the process, Apple's solution that combined the computer-based iTunes Store with the iPod's portability let you load up your device and carry around "a thousand songs in your pocket."

Many of the feature limitations for Rhapsody were implemented at the behest of the record labels or due to weaknesses of the technology Listen.com was working with at the time.[2] Working around these constraints while still satisfying the label's demands required fundamental advances in technology to create a great mobile streaming experience. In addition, the typical consumer was not yet familiar with the paid-subscription model. iTunes was a record store on the Internet. Pandora was akin to radio. There was no clear analogy for Rhapsody. Netflix was still years away from beginning to shift from DVDs by mail to a streaming subscription model. Educating consumers on the value of this new model required a large marketing budget, and Rhapsody did not have the resources. Adding a mobile experience eventually enabled streaming to meet the expectations of millions of music fans and to achieve mass market adoption.

The smartphone in general, and Apple's iPhone in particular, brought a wide range of innovative capabilities right into the hands of billions of consumers. These powerful devices encompassed everything needed to make streaming services a great experiences, thus providing Spotify and its ilk with the runway needed to take off. App stores gave music fans an easy way to obtain and to pay for a streaming service as well as the means to update the service easily to offer new features. The touchscreen improved the user interface, which allowed subscribers to scroll through and select songs, albums, artists, and playlists much more easily than the iPod's scroll wheel. Every single day, 100,000 new tracks (worldwide) are added to the already enormous catalogs of tens of millions of songs available for streaming on these services.[xii] And unlike the complexity of the download era, a subscriber can access any of those songs by touching the screen of the device in their hand a few times.

The widespread availability of affordable high-speed Internet bandwidth was critical to the adoption of smartphones for communications and entertainment. In the Chapter 8, we observed that the explosive growth in broadband connectivity to the home in the 2000s let millions of music fans download entire albums in seconds rather than waiting more than 10 minutes for a single song to arrive on their PCs. The 3G cellular data standard was introduced in 2001; it offered download speeds of 5–10 megabits per second (Mbps). The 3G penetration rate was limited because of the costs of the associated data plans. In many cases, corporations covered the costs of their employees' data plans to enable e-mail connectivity on those then-ubiquitous Blackberry devices.[xiii,xiv] But average consumers chose to keep their wallets in their pockets or purses rather than making the move to mobile broadband. That is, until the iPhone swept in (followed closely by similar Android-based smartphones) and dominated the market for mobile devices. Apple's creation of yet another "must-have" device unleashed the desire among millions of users for broadband data on a mobile phone.

One might think that the uptake in mobile data by 2010 would have been sufficient to fuel the growth of streaming services from a technology perspective. The Celestial Jukebox, with a catalog numbering in the tens of millions of songs, sat in the cloud waiting for music fans to select a track to listen to and then have the bits stream directly to their smartphones for playback. Though 3G networks could support mobile Internet access that was fast enough for music streaming, performance was spotty and dropouts were frequent. Data plans often included caps on the amount of data that could be used each month, with hefty overage charges. Wi-Fi hotspots that are ubiquitous now were not yet broadly deployed. Having a slight delay in loading your emails or loading a webpage was annoying, but it did not completely undermine the value to the consumer. But if you were listening to your streamed music on the streets of NYC, heading down into the subway would simply break the connection. How could one charge $10 per month for an online streaming service promising access to any song at any time if the connection was incapable of delivering on that promise?

From an engineering perspective, the solution to this problem was obvious: make copies of lots of songs and store them in the device when connectivity was available and play them back when it wasn't. Storing copies of compressed music files had already been solved for the download era. The desire to broaden the distribution of purchased files beyond Apple had contributed to the decision to remove DRM, which reduced friction in the user experience. The labels had decided that allowing unfettered copying of songs that were already paid for was not without risks, but was, on balance, a good business decision. Yet that same decision did not make sense in the world of streaming. If subscribers were permitted to have copies of thousands of songs stored on their device, the service needed to ensure that access to those tracks disappeared when a user stopped paying for the service.

Fortunately, mobile phone designers, including Apple and Google, developed the capability in their platforms that enabled Spotify and other streaming services to cut through this Gordian knot. Though far less obvious to the user than a high-quality display or responsive touchscreen, the mobile platforms contained state-of-the-art encryption capabilities. A Trusted Execution Environment (TEE), a secure area on the main processor, was designed into most smartphones starting in the early 2010s. This hardware-based solution provided better security for passwords, cryptographic keys, and other credentials. They allowed the streaming companies to store music files securely and to meet the requirement that any such files would become unplayable should a subscriber cancel their service as well.

The tracks stored on the device were encrypted using a private key. That private key was stored in the TEE, and it was used to decrypt the music if and only if the device had a valid license from the service. Each month, when the user's mobile phone communicated with the service, it would check that the user had paid their monthly fee. If so, a new license was issued and stored securely in the device, thus renewing access for another month. If the subscriber stopped paying, the license eventually expired, and the key to decrypt the stored tracks was no longer valid.

Unlike the DRM originally used on downloaded tracks, users accepted this approach. The experience was consistent with their expectations. If they stopped paying for their wireless service, they expected their mobile phone to stop working, and it was only logical for the same to be true for their music. Given the negative reactions to DRM in the download era, it is not surprising that streaming services avoid mentioning those letters. But as David Hughes, the former CTO of the RIAA, said in 2008, "Any form of subscription service . . . still requires DRM. So DRM is not dead."[xv]

This solution was the final technology piece needed for a great streaming music experience on mobile phones. Fast wireless connections meant that music could be delivered in real time to mobile phones with streaming music apps ready to be accessed at the touch of a finger. The tunes stored on the device could fill in the gaps, enabling a seamless experience even when the network was unavailable or glitchy. And the labels' concerns about people continuing to have access to thousands of tracks without paying were alleviated.

Before we discuss the broad implications of this shift to streaming, it is important to recognize that this change is fundamentally different from the many format shifts that preceded it. Whether it was vinyl records or cassettes or CDs, each of these physical items contained limited amount of music. Fans acquired that music by paying a fixed one-time fee to purchase the physical carrier that held the songs from a record store. The physical embodiment of the music disappeared in the digital download era, but fans still purchased individual tracks or albums for a set price paid to retailers through a web storefront. Getting real estate on the iTunes home page was not all that different in practice from getting space on an endcap at Best Buy or Tower Records when it came to selling records. To be successful, artists had to create music that was good enough for fans to pay for. And music labels had to market that music to drive awareness and to convince consumers that they had to have a copy—whether on plastic or as a digital file.

The value of music streaming to the industry can be told through a few key statistics. In 2022, US recorded music revenues approached $16 billion dollars, and 84 percent of that total was generated by fans streaming songs. The total annual number of on-demand music streams of audio and video is now in the trillions. The seven-year run of increasing recorded music revenues fueled by streaming drove the value of song catalogs to new heights, with iconic artists from Bruce Springsteen to Neil Diamond to John Legend selling their rights for hundreds of millions of dollars. Universal Music Group, the largest major label, went public in September 2021 with a valuation exceeding $50 billion. Though still tiny compared to the tech giants, this represents an enormous increase in enterprise value over the past decade.[xvi,xvii]

It is impossible to understand the financial impacts of streaming without getting into the implications of service economics and how it differs from product business models. Fans in most developed countries pay the equivalent of $10 per month for unlimited access to all the tracks and albums in the catalog. For a streaming service, that means a subscriber who logs in can listen to any one of the many millions of available tracks. But unlike a product purchase, playing a particular song does not generate a direct payment to the rightsholders.

The following formula is a simplified version of how streaming services determine the amount of money that goes to the labels and artists for the music played:

$$\text{Net Revenue} \times \text{Share Percentage} \times \text{Pro Rata}$$

Net Revenue means the fees collected from paying subscribers each month, which are aggregated into a single pool of funds. **Share Percentage** is the portion of the net revenues allocated to the record labels and music publishers based on contractual agreements. The remainder of the net revenues is retained by the service to operate its business. The labels' share percentage is approximately 52 percent, and the publishers receive roughly another 10–12 percent. That resulting amount is then divided among all the labels based on the **Pro Rata** share of plays of tracks on each label recorded in the service that month. A play is tallied only if the track is listened to for more than 30 seconds. For example, if 25 percent of the total plays for the month were songs by Sony Music artists, then that company receives 25 percent of that label share along with a detailed data feed that includes the number of times each song was played, which Sony uses to calculate the ultimate artist payments.

The actual calculations are more complicated. Each streaming music service has multiple service offerings with different prices to consumers, such as student discounts and family plans. Prices also vary by country, and rates differ according to local economic conditions. For example, Apple Music is available in almost 170 countries; a music fan in Bhutan pays less than one in Boston. In addition, there is a minimum per-user fee, which ensures that there is a floor to the amount of money going to the revenue pool for labels. Adjustments for billing fees, sales taxes, annual subscription discounts, and free or reduced-price trials are factored in as well.

The approach just described lays out, in a general way, how the on-demand music streaming services calculate royalty payments for paying subscribers. However, Spotify is somewhat different, because unlike its competitors, it really consists of two closely coupled service tiers: the premium tier where users pay $10 per month (or different fees in other countries) and the free tier where users pay with their attention by listening to advertisements.

When one accounts for the revenues from both paid subscribers and free users, one can complete the calculations we've laid out and then derive an effective "per play" rate. That rate is a result of the methodology described and is not an input parameter to the royalty methodology. The effective per-play rate differs from month to month and from service to service. Furthermore, if users engage more with the service and listen to more songs, the effective per-play rate goes down. Recent estimates peg the Spotify per-play rate at $.0035 and the Apple Music rate at $.00675.[xviii] Comparing these rates is not particularly informative. Tidal may have a higher imputed per-play rate than either Apple or Spotify. But its smaller subscriber base means that they end up with far smaller total payments to labels and artists.

The lack of a fixed per-play rate and the declining effective per-play rate as the audience for streaming grows contribute to the frequent complaints about inadequate compensation from streaming. In a 2013 interview, Thom Yorke, the lead singer of Radiohead, colorfully described Spotify as "the last fart of a dying corpse."[xix] Taylor Swift took more direct action and removed her catalog from Spotify in 2014 because she felt the service was inadequately compensating artists, though she did return her music to Spotify in 2017. Her concerns were not limited to Spotify as she chose not to release her 2015 album on Apple Music for the same reason. When questioned at a conference in 2019, Jim Anderson, a former Spotify executive, described artists as "entitled" because the service was not created to make artists money. He went on to say, "I think Taylor Swift doesn't need .00001 more a stream." Needless to say, this sort of public posture has not exactly ameliorated performers' concerns.[xx]

The calculation of the pro rata share based on the aggregated plays of millions of users is perceived as unfair because the money paid by a subscriber who listens to music from a single indie artist alone does not directly benefit that artist. As an alternative, Soundcloud and Deezer are adopting a "fan-centric" model where the net fees paid by an individual are paid out only to those artists that they listen to. In July 2022, Warner Music Group became the first major label to agree to use the Soundcloud methodology to calculate royalties for its artists.[xxi] In early 2023, Universal Music CEO Sir Lucian Grainge stated that a new "artist-centric" scheme was needed for streaming payments and, just a few weeks later, his company announced they were examining alternatives with Tidal and Deezer.[xxii] Spotify has stated that they would consider changes but that they "require[] broad industry alignment."[xxiii] Without that, we can expect the issue of inadequate streaming royalties to continue to spark debate.[3] And Spotify's decision in March 2022 to spend an estimated $300 million on a sponsorship deal with the Barcelona Football Club does little to assuage artists' concerns about unfair compensation.[xxiv]

The mechanisms for determining payments have profound implications on the rest of the music business. If your company distributes music to fans, there are several ways to maintain and to improve your overall performance and your relative competitive position. First, you can improve your margins by decreasing the share percentage, that is, the proportion of net revenues contractually obligated to be paid to rightsholders. Second, you can use music's ability to attract users to bolster your other lines of business. Third, you can increase the monthly pool of revenues by growing the number of subscribers. The source of this growth could be people who already use another service and decide to switch, or people who have not yet made the leap to paying for access to music.

To reduce the costs of content, services can take the direct route of getting labels to accept lower payments, but such negotiations are always complicated and difficult. Like any other relationship between a "wholesale" supplier and the "retailer" that offers the goods to a consumer, there is a tension between the retailer wanting to reduce the amount it pays to its supplier for its "goods" and the supplier wanting to increase that same number.

The value of a streaming service is built on the premise that the monthly charge offers access to every song. And even though these catalogs now encompass over 100 million tracks, individual songs are not substitutable. If a fan wants to listen to "As it Was" by Harry Styles, one of the most popular tracks of 2022, there really is no other song that fulfills that desire. And, if a service lacks that song, any "Styler" (as his fans are known) is unlikely to feel their payment is worth it. Amazon took the approach of licensing a limited catalog with lower costs for its launch of Amazon Prime Music. The service was viewed as an added benefit to Prime subscribers, so a comprehensive music selection was less critical. However, when it decided to offer a separately priced premium service, Amazon Music Unlimited, it needed to license the full catalog in the same manner as the other streaming services, with similar economics.

But not all listening on these services comes from the most popular tracks on the *Billboard* charts. People often are satisfied with mood music for exercising or chilling out. There have been several reports that Spotify paid producers to create music for its popular Ambient Chill or Sleep playlists on a flat-rate basis. The artists for some of these tracks were obscure bands such as Deep Watch and Enno Aare. These musicians were so obscure that they had virtually no presence on any services other than Spotify. This strengthened the case that these so-called fake artists were being placed on popular playlists to attract listens that were financially more advantageous to Spotify than Taylor Swift songs or other major label content. Spotify has strenuously denied that it participated in such schemes, but concerns remain that this sort of behavior remains a tempting path to reduce royalties and enhance profitability for streaming providers.[xxv] And as we will discuss in Chapter 11, Artificial Intelligence will make it even simpler to generate content with a lower royalty structure.

Another way to reduce costs would be for a streaming service to integrate "vertically" and become a record label through ownership of a meaningful music catalog. It could then distribute that music with more favorable pricing. Though there have been recurring rumors of just such a major purchase, none of the streaming players have pulled the trigger.[4]

Direct payments to artists were a key part of the services pursuing "exclusives" in the middle of the last decade. A tried-and-true technique to attract buyers from the days of physical retail was to offer a product that could be found in your store and your store only. If Target had the exclusive version of Michael Bublé's Christmas album with bonus tracks, then his fans would be more likely to drive there to pick up the CD and fill up their cart with groceries and clothes for good measure.[xxvi] Not only were these exclusives intended to lower content costs over time but they also could convince users who already found sufficient value in streaming to defect from their current choice. Unlike the world of video, where the film and TV studios have divided their libraries among the various platforms, the music streaming services offered access to essentially the same catalogs. So it is logical that they attempted to take a page from the days of CDs to differentiate themselves through content exclusive to their service alone.

Apple Music, Tidal, and Spotify pursued these high-profile exclusives regularly. In 2016, Frank Ocean dropped not one but two new "albums," one audio and one visual (which was essentially a 45-minute music video), onto Apple Music and the iTunes store on consecutive days. However, these exclusives did not have a dramatic impact on adoption rates for the services. High-profile movies and TV shows have increased subscriptions for the streaming video services. But the content catalogs of these platforms number in the tens of thousands of items, compared to the tens of millions of tracks that were available through the music services even in the middle of the 2010s. Even the highest profile artist with a much-anticipated release may not make much of a dent overall.

Regardless, the major labels saw these exclusives as a threat to their relationships with artists. Not to mention that "cannibalizing" existing users to get them to hop from one service to another would not improve the health of the industry overall. This issue came to a head in August of 2016, when Sir Lucian Grainge, the CEO of Universal Music Group, banned streaming exclusives at the largest of the major labels. As Music Business Worldwide said at the time, "Universal has concluded that exclusive deals with single streaming services are bad for business."[xxvii] Since that announcement, all the major labels have largely abandoned exclusive releases as part of their strategy—although, as we'll see shortly, they continue to "window" releases on streaming services occasionally.

Although the services eliminated buying a label or negotiating exclusives as strategies, that didn't stop them from attempting to achieve more favorable terms for content. In 2018, Spotify tried again by announcing that it would license content from certain up-and-coming artists and legacy artists who had control of their rights.[xxviii] Artists could upload music to the service directly, bypassing labels and other distributors. These moves raised significant concerns at the labels. Daniel Ek, Spotify's chief executive, tried to assuage those fears during the July 2018 earnings call by saying, "Licensing content does not make us a label, nor do we have any interest in becoming a label."[xxix] That argument was less than persuasive, and Spotify abandoned its direct licensing efforts in July 2019 after what must have been very contentious discussions with their main content suppliers. The major labels had complained vociferously about the service competing with them directly.[xxx]

We've already mentioned that Amazon Music was launched to enhance the value of Prime membership for its most valuable customers. The margins for the streaming service on a standalone basis are a rounding error to Amazon in the larger scheme of driving profitability of their e-commerce business. Even its full-catalog Amazon Music Unlimited offer, which is priced at the same $9.99 per month as its competitors, costs only $7.99 if you're already an Amazon Prime member, or only $4.99 if you want the "single device" plan for your Echo smart speaker. Similarly, Apple made the vast bulk of its revenue from hardware products and has historically considered services such as Apple Music more as drivers of hardware purchases than as revenue sources in and of themselves. And Google, analogously, has viewed content services primarily as drivers of revenue from ads and user data.

Thus Spotify, unlike its largest competitors, was a "pure play" music offer for years after launch, with no other lines of business to supplement those revenues. To rectify this situation, Spotify added podcast playback functionality to its apps in late 2018; the vast majority of podcasts are available freely from podcast publishers to any app that wants to list them. By supplying both types of audio content through a single interface, Spotify embodies a simpler solution than Apple's two separate applications (Apple Music and Apple Podcasts). But they didn't stop there: Spotify invested upwards of a half a billion dollars acquiring several podcast studios and publishing tools as well as rights to individual high-profile podcasts. These acquisitions included Gimlet Media, Anchor, Parcast, and Bill Simmons' sports-related platform The Ringer. In May of 2020, Spotify licensed rights to the hugely popular Joe Rogan Experience podcast in a deal estimated to be worth over $200 million.[xxxi,xxxii]

In the aggregate, these deals cemented Spotify as a leader in the podcasting space, and Spotify is now the only meaningful competitor to Apple Podcasts in terms of user adoption. Spotify now describes itself as an "audio company" rather than one dedicated to music alone; the company has more recently started expanding to audiobooks as well. If Spotify users shift a significant amount of their listening from music to podcasts, it could impact their profitability in three ways. First, Spotify's current margins will improve because podcasts have a more favorable cost structure than music (at least for now). Second, Spotify should have more leverage in future negotiations with the record labels if they depend less on music for their success. And third, Spotify makes some podcasts they own exclusive or released first to their subscribers in the hopes of attracting additional customers.

Trying to lower content costs or enticing customers using a competing service equates to slicing the pie of total revenues differently among music rights holders, and that always leads to contention over who deserves a bigger slice. Focusing instead on increasing the overall size of that pie by growing the number of people paying aligns the interests of the services and the rights holders. To get more subscribers, the streaming companies use free or discounted trial periods to attract more people to try their services. In many cases, services use the negative option of charging the credit card number entered when the user signs up for the free trial to begin collecting payments automatically when the trial concludes. That avoids one more decision for the user to make, which reduces friction in the sign-up process. And, of course, in many cases users forget and simply fail to cancel the service before the charges begin. In addition, the services have negotiated lower per-subscriber prices covering family plans or university students to attract more price-sensitive users.

For the giant tech companies, the ability to leverage the advantages of their platforms is a key part of acquiring paying subscribers. When Apple finally launched Apple Music in 2015, four years after the launch of Spotify in the US market, it was able to market the new service to millions of loyal iTunes downloaders. The streaming application is also preinstalled on all iPhones, and Apple can position it prominently within the App Store. That leverage helped Apple Music to grow very quickly in the United States: in 2019, it passed Spotify in paying American subscribers, although Spotify has maintained its lead globally.[xxxiii] Not surprisingly, converting many downloaders to streamers led to Apple Music having a somewhat older demographic profile than Spotify: over half of Spotify users are aged 34 or younger, while that statistic sits at only 40 percent for Apple Music.

Google and YouTube can similarly leverage Android and the free YouTube service to promote its paid subscription option. Recently, Google invested $4.5 billion into Jio Platforms, the technology arm of Reliance, the Indian conglomerate.[xxxiv] The companies will collaborate on affordable smartphones, but Reliance is also the parent company of JioSaavn, a leading music subscription service in India. It would not be surprising if those new devices help to advance the growth of the content offering in markets where few can afford iPhones or high-end Android devices.[xxxv]

Though much of the press tends to focus on the competition between Apple and Google, Amazon, through its Prime Music offer, is not very far behind in terms of share of paid subscribers. With over 150 million Prime subscribers worldwide, it has a sizable addressable market for all its content offerings.[xxxvi] In November 2022, Amazon made every of the 100 million tracks in its music catalog available to Prime members as an additional perk, although the songs can only be accessed in "shuffle" mode rather than fully on-demand.[xxxvii] And it certainly helps when Amazon programs its market-leading smart speakers to ask users if they'd like to upgrade to their Amazon Music Unlimited services if they request a song that is not included as part of the basic Amazon Prime bundle. The power of voice interfaces to enable a superior music experience and Amazon's dominant share will be discussed in more depth in Chapter 11.

Marketing tie-ins with companies outside of the music space help to attract additional streaming users with discounts or complimentary offers as well. Such offers were quite popular in Europe and Latin America for years. The United States was somewhat late to the party, but this practice is quite common now. Verizon Wireless includes a free Apple Music subscription for its Unlimited data plan customers. Sprint, which is an investor in Tidal, bundles that service with its top plan as well. AT&T offers Spotify to its Unlimited mobile package customers as an "entertainment perk." Not all these offers are related to mobile services: for example, Spotify recently offered a $9.99 bundle that gave subscribers access to its service as well as the ad-supported Hulu video service.[xxxviii]

However, Spotify's most effective tool for driving paid subscriber growth is its ad-supported free tier. The users viewing ads are far less lucrative than paid subscribers. But the hurdle to get a music fan to try a completely free service is commensurately lower as well. From the time of its launch, Spotify argued that the free tier was the best way to attract users from piracy. It asserted that offering access with a better experience than unauthorized services would convince fans to give Spotify a try. And once those fans were in Spotify's marketing "funnel," they would eventually see the value in the service and decide to pay for the premium ad-free tier.[xxxix]

To say that the music labels, who had been damaged so dramatically by illegitimate services giving away their music, were skeptical about Spotify's free tier would be an understatement. In fact, Spotify's launch in 2008 was restricted to its home market of the Nordics because the labels were unwilling to risk broader licenses that could jeopardize their fairly robust download business. Spotify's success in its home country of Sweden, both in terms of attracting people to the free tier and in converting a significant percentage of those users to become paid subscribers, persuaded the labels to allow Spotify to enter other markets.[xl] Repeating those results in country after country gave Spotify the data to prove that its "freemium" approach did indeed reduce piracy and foster paid subscriptions.[xli]

Spotify's greatest hurdle was to agree on the terms that allowed them to enter the US market. According to some sources, Steve Jobs tried to block their entry into America; and the negotiations were difficult as the labels wanted to ensure that the free tier was restricted in ways that maximized the number of paying subscribers.[xlii] The data showed that a subset of users who were on the free tier for more than a year or two would still decide, after all that time, to take the leap and to start paying. Spotify's conversion rate, north of 40 percent in most markets, has shattered the expectations that the industry had for it in the early days.

America is the largest music market in the world, and the adoption of streaming in the United States contributes mightily to American services leading the world in market share (see Figure 9.2). In 2021, global music subscriptions climbed more than 20 percent year over year to almost 500 million, with Spotify representing more than 30 percent of all these subscriptions. Apple Music was second with a little over 15 percent of all subscriptions, and Amazon and Tencent Music tied for third place.

Yet as indicated by Tencent Music's position, focusing solely on the United States would be myopic when discussing the distribution channels in the age of streaming. The biggest players in the United States have global reach. For example, Spotify is available in 92 countries[xliii] while Apple Music services fans in 167.[xliv] The list of territories served includes countries such as Russia

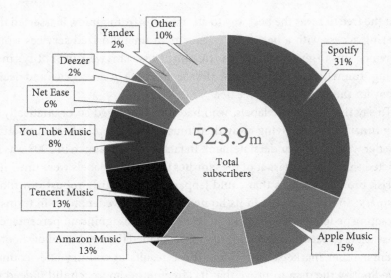

Figure 9.2 Global streaming music subscription share. © MiDiA Research. All rights reserved.

that have traditionally generated little to no revenues for artists and labels.[5] Deezer, which is based in Paris, beats them both by being active in over 180 countries. Deezer offers a free ad-supported tier similar to Spotify; it has over 20 million active users, with one-third of that total paying for the subscription service. All the global players are facing homegrown competitors in virtually every part of the world.[xlv]

This chapter began by looking at the IPO of Tencent Music based on its success in the Chinese market. China has over 700 million active users on its various music services. And China is not the only region with a service that is scaling up quickly to serve tens or hundreds of millions of streaming users. Over 300 million Indians enjoy streaming Bollywood music and international content on local services such as Gaana and JioSaavn.[xlvi] Anghami has 70 million users in the Middle East and Africa and was the first Arab tech startup to go public. In South Korea, Melon has over 28 million subscription users. Boomplay in Africa has 75 million subscribers.[xlvii] The average revenue per user may be lower in these markets, but as mobile connectivity improves and cellular data becomes more affordable, these markets have become significant sources of growth for the industry. The proposition of accessing the world's songs in exchange for a monthly fee clearly appeals to music fans regardless of geography and language.

The growth in these markets with low GDP and reduced prices is certainly going to be a big driver for future revenues. It has been somewhat surprising that the streaming services stuck with the $10 per month price point for so long, particularly in more mature markets with well-established subscriber bases. In video streaming, Netflix has raised its monthly rates several times over the past decade, although their recent subscriber declines suggest that they may have pushed too far. Spotify did "experiment" by raising the price in Norway by 10 percent, along with similar hikes for family and student rates, in July 2018. Wholesale streaming subscription revenue in Norway did increase, so it appears that the rate hikes did not increase churn significantly. In fact, according to a recent Polaris research report, the percentage of paying subscribers in Norway has increased from 50 percent to 55 percent despite the higher charges.[xlviii] Two years later, those same higher prices are still in place, suggesting that this is no longer an "experiment." And, in fact, Spotify has raised prices in over 40 smaller markets around the world. Similar changes have finally started to become the standard: in October 2022, the reference price for a music subscription began to move upward to generate more money for the entire streaming ecosystem. Apple led the way by announcing that it would increase its $9.99 monthly rate for an individual subscriber by $1 and its family plan rate from $14.99 to $16.99.[xlix] Just a few days later, Spotify CEO Daniel Ek declared that his users could expect similar increases in 2023.[l] And in early 2023, Amazon announced that their Amazon Music Unlimited subscribers would start paying an additional $1 per month in February.[li]

Consumers

Technology improvements embodied in the well-connected smartphone cracked the code in terms of enabling streaming services to meet the expectations of hundreds of millions of global music fans. Over half the populations in Mexico, Germany, the United States, the United Kingdom, and Sweden engage with paid music subscriptions. The top three reasons they do so include having no advertisements, the ability to listen to the music they want when they want it, and access to millions of songs.[lii] The expectations regarding the breadth of catalog available were established at least in part by the enormous selection of music on YouTube. Having any music video in the world playable on-demand for free, albeit with ads, meant that for many people there was simply no need to pay for streaming music. During the late 2000s, as we'll see in Chapter 10, YouTube was rapidly compiling—thanks to user uploads—a "music catalog" of tens of millions of tracks while the labels were lagging behind in feeding their catalogs even to download services such as iTunes.

Today you can pay for an enormous variety of services and goods by signing up for subscription services. Affordability may be an issue, given the panoply of services available, but it seems compelling for millions of consumers to subscribe to regular deliveries of razor blades, meal kits, or even clothing items. (Not to mention that every major media brand, whether it is HBO or NBC, seems to be launching their own new streaming video platform.) But when streaming music first arrived, the only consumption models for recorded music were physical products or radio. Persuading fans that they did not need to hold the music in their hands but could be satisfied paying for more ephemeral access was no small feat. The early streaming services, such as Rhapsody, simply did not have the marketing dollars or resources necessary to change consumer behavior. Spotify's free tier, along with the enormous unpaid media coverage they received were certainly key factors in establishing credibility for paying for music as a service.

Free trials and bundles with other desirable services could get people across the starting line and get them to give streaming music a try. But what ultimately persuades fans to pull out their wallets and hand over their hard-earned cash to subscribe? And what keeps them paying month after month? Fans clearly value the ability to select any song that they can think of and have it start playing immediately. But they also appreciate elements of the service or applications that go beyond that core proposition—elements that have become more and more important in differentiating one streaming service from another.

Music fans frequently prefer more of a "lean-back" experience, where the service selects the music, harkening back to the days of radio. But rather than being constrained by the limitations of a single broadcast channel (or even a fixed set of channels), streaming services have the ability to satisfy the tastes of virtually any fan. Subscribers can request music by any artist, genre, or decade. They can find music that is suitable for a long drive or a party. They may want music for working out or suitable for chilling at home.

The services can build personalized recommendations that their users really enjoy by relying on the data generated from each individual's interactions over time and marrying it with similar info from millions of others with similar tastes. Spotify's Discover Weekly playlist feature is perhaps the ultimate expression of this recommendation technique. The product of an internal hackathon at Spotify, Discover Weekly uses sophisticated data analysis to find new songs that a specific subscriber is more likely to enjoy. And if the subscriber skips one of those newly recommended tracks, the algorithms can use that information to make smarter suggestions the next week. Or the analysis can identify songs the user liked in the past and remind them to give that music another listen. The algorithms that generate these personalized playlists have become increasingly sophisticated over time and represent one of the first applications of artificial intelligence/machine learning techniques to the music industry; we will examine these technologies in more detail in Chapter 11. Based on the results, one would have to judge Discover Weekly to be a very successful use of these techniques: between July 2015 and June 2020, Spotify users spent more than 2.3 billion hours listening to Discover Weekly playlists.[liii]

One can get a sense of how music consumers value playlists by examining Spotify's statistics in even more detail. According to the company, its platform contains over 4 billion playlists in total.[liv] That number seems large, but if one considers it in the context of hundreds of millions of active users, it is somewhat less daunting. It is even more instructive to focus on the playlists that have the greatest number of followers. Twenty-four of the 25 most-followed playlists are "editorial" playlists that are created and managed by Spotify itself. Today's Top Hits has over 28 million followers, while Rap Caviar, the influential hip-hop playlist, has almost 17 million.[lv,lvi]

It is not surprising that having so many individuals following these popular playlists leads to greater listening time. Spotify-curated playlists constitute about one-third of the total time spent listening, with a little more than half of that dedicated to playlists that Spotify has tailored to each listener based on their past behavior. Just over another third of listening time is consumed by user-generated playlists. Which means that users are actively selecting individual tracks to enjoy for less than one-third of their time spent on Spotify.

Apple was late to the game in shifting from downloads to streaming, in part because of Steve Jobs's long-standing view that "The subscription model of buying music is bankrupt."[lvii] When it finally launched Apple Music in June 2015 in over 100 countries, it emphasized the hand-crafted nature of their service rather than the algorithmic aspects, a holdover from the Beats

Music service that Apple acquired (along with the Beats headphone business) and used to form the basis of Apple Music. The most hyped element of the new service was Beats One, an online radio station available around the clock. Apple poached DJ Zane Lowe from the BBC as the leader of a group of radio personalities who created programming for the station. Major music stars such as Elton John and Drake were also recruited to program other channels as part of the launch. Though they were called "stations," they were actually curated playlists of tracks to attract new customers.

As much as consumers listen to the playlists published by the services, many users want to play a more active role and create their own playlists for any occasion. To entice those users, the streaming providers make it easy to add tracks to personal playlists and to share those with friends or broader sets of listeners.[6] And once fans invest the time and energy to craft numerous playlists to enhance their experience, they are far less likely to jump ship to another service and then need to repeat all that work just to access those same playlists.[7]

The hurdle to convert users of the Spotify free tier represents an even greater challenge. If music fans enjoy the service and can access music indefinitely for free and listen to the popular podcasts published by the service, what would motivate them to pay? The answer is that the free tier is not identical to the paid service. Spotify degrades the consumer experience in several ways to make it less satisfying. The gaps between the free and paid tiers incentivize users to upgrade to the premium tier, and Spotify tinkers with those gaps constantly to improve its conversion rate even further.[lviii] For example, at this time of writing, free-tier users can't save tracks for offline listening and can only listen to certain playlists in order (others can be shuffled). Specific track selection is limited, as are skips per hour. These restrictions apply to mobile devices only; the full feature set (plus ads) is available to free-tier users on computers.

The same song catalog is available to the free and paid audiences, but with one key distinction. Although the major labels were adamantly opposed to exclusives, as we described earlier, they do have the right under the more recent contracts with Spotify to "window" new releases. That is, the labels can select certain new songs or albums to be playable by paid subscribers but not by free users for up to two weeks. The feature limitations and ads may not affect how much casual music fans enjoy the free version of Spotify. But taken collectively, they remind frequent users over and over that there is a better experience just on the other side of the paywall. Those nagging imperfections in the service help fuel Spotify's ongoing success in converting free listeners to subscribers.

Given the low revenues per user for those on the ad-supported tier, there is a temptation to clamp down on the free experience further to try to encourage greater premium adoption. Spotify has been able to demonstrate that such tactics can backfire. In 2011, for example, Spotify restricted ad-free listening in five European countries, including Spain, to satisfy the demands of certain rights holders. Individual tracks could only be listened to five times, and the total listening hours was capped at 10 hours per month for free users. Conversion rates dropped significantly, and the restrictions were soon eliminated.[lix] Instead of implementing drastic changes, Spotify's formula for success improves conversion rates via small, incremental shifts backed up by careful analysis.

On the other hand, windowing content yields positive results even in markets where paying for online music is a relatively new behavior. Tony Yip, Tencent Music's Chief Strategy Officer, explained that "approximately 10% of the streaming volume on our platforms" was of music windowed for premium users only. And he expected that this statistic would grow over time.[lx]

We discussed the long tail theory in Chapter 8; many viewed this as a law of the Internet rather than simply a hypothesis. But even with the increased selection in download stores, fan interest did not shift markedly away from the superstar artists who had dominated every format that had come before. The move to streaming, with its virtually limitless catalog available to any subscriber at the touch of a button, seemed like the perfect setup to drive a change in demand. However, the data showed just the opposite: 80 percent of the streams were coming from just 3 percent of the songs, while millions of tracks were never listened to at all.[lxi] The week after Drake released his *Honestly Nevermind* album in June 2022, the Canadian rapper accounted for one out of every 60 streams in the United States.[lxii] Despite the theories, the hits are still the hits, and artists still want to climb up to the rarefied air and join Drake at the top of the charts.

Moreover, recent data indicates that the hits fans are listening to are older than they used to be. According to MRC/Nielsen, album consumption of catalog music rose from just over 60 percent in 2018 to over 66 percent in mid-2021.[lxiii] The official definition of "catalog" includes any material released more than eighteen months ago. That includes music from one-name icons such as Elvis, Madonna, and Prince, but it also includes recent releases by currently active artists. Fans' interest in hearing these older songs over and over has certainly contributed to the interest in purchasing song catalogs at enormous valuations. This trend is fed, in part, by the methodology to calculate royalties—a single play of the Rolling Stones' first number-one hit from July 1964, "It's All Over Now," ultimately earns the same exact amount as a spin of the Stones' "Living in a Ghost Town," released 56 years later.

Of course, the desire to listen to more familiar music during the COVID-19 pandemic may have contributed to this growth. Furthermore, the early adopters of streaming tended to be younger than those older fans who have shifted to streaming more recently. The nature of the streaming experience and access to the complete catalog is certainly a major factor. Adele's release of the album *30* in late 2021, her first release in five years, encouraged many fans to go back and listen to her older material. And, of course, any Adele playlists will likely feature both the newest and the catalog material.

The enormity of the available catalog on the streaming services is certainly an attraction for many fans, particularly those with wide-ranging tastes. But some people might not want to pay the full subscription rate when their musical tastes are narrower. Or they might be willing to pay the same price if the service provided additional content geared toward their specific interests. Segmenting the market by offering niche services that encompass only a single genre of music could yield even more paying subscribers.[8]

When downloads dominated the music business, fans started to view their music collections in gigabytes rather than as numbers of CDs or LPs on a shelf. But when someone purchased a digital album or a track, they were making a decision to invest in that particular work. Buyer's remorse aside, once that investment was made, fans had a financial rationale to listen to the music they had acquired. When a user adds a track they hear on streaming to a personal playlist, they have a somewhat similar sense of "ownership." However, when a new song is played for them from the vast ocean of content in "lean-back" mode, they have no compunction about making a snap decision. The skip button on their app or a quick voice command to a smart speaker gives the user control. Like the station buttons on a car radio, the decision to move on to another song can happen in a split second. Streaming services and the artists themselves are constantly analyzing these decisions and reacting accordingly.

Creators

"Papa Was a Rollin' Stone" originated as a three-minute soul song recorded in 1972 by a Motown act called the Undisputed Truth. The Temptations' far more successful seven-minute version (itself a radio edit of a 12-minute album track) hit no. 1 on the *Billboard* Hot 100 charts and won three Grammys. *Rolling Stone* magazine rates it as one of the 500 Greatest Songs of All Time.[lxiv] The longer take begins with an instrumental introduction featuring organ, guitar, bass, and a hi-hat cymbal that ebbs and flows for more than four minutes before the Temps sing even one word. If the group were in the studio recording today, Motown founder Berry Gordy might insist on some very different choices. In particular, the titular chorus might have been featured much earlier in the song.

That's because the money collected by streaming services gets paid out on a pro rata share based on the number of plays each month. A play counts as part of those calculations if a user listens past the 30-second mark of the song. These may seem like fairly fine points when considering the billions and billions of tracks streamed overall. But they have far-reaching impact on how artists craft their songs and performances in the streaming era. Unlike for downloads, artists are making very different creative choices when crafting their songs and recordings to maximize engagement and connect with streaming listeners.

If a song you've never heard before takes a long time to get to the hook or simply has an extended intro, there is a good chance that you may simply hit the button to go to the next song. The terminology that captures this idea is "skip rate." Warren "Oak" Felder has written hits for top-selling artists such as Usher and Nicki Minaj. In a *Rolling Stone* interview in 2019, he said that the term was never mentioned in his 15 years in the business, but now it is "part of the conversation we all have as songwriters—'yeah we just want the skip rate of this song to be super low.'"[lxv]

To keep that metric as low as possible, musical artists want the song to connect with the listener as soon as possible, and to accomplish that they are moving up the hook or chorus to sit in that initial 30-second sweet spot. The hosts of the "Switched on Pop" podcast, which analyzes the structure of popular music, have even coined a new term for what they have observed: the "Pop Overture." They describe this trend as "a song, at the very beginning, will play a hint of the chorus in the first five to 10 seconds so that the hook is in your ear, hoping that you'll stick around till about 30 seconds in when the full chorus eventually comes in."[lxvi] According to Midia Research, the top 10 hits have an average intro of 7.4 seconds today versus just over 13 seconds 20 years ago.[lxvii]

Creators are modifying more than just the introductory sections of tracks for optimal performance on streaming. As discussed in Chapter 3, radio stations preferred shorter versions of songs to maintain interest. For streaming, every track that is listened to for more than 30 seconds counts as a play, but making it all the way through the song is a factor in future recommendations as well. As the Grammy-winning producer and performer Mark Ronson said in an interview in *The Guardian*, "All your songs have to be under three minutes and 15 seconds because if people don't listen to them all the way to the end they go into this ratio of 'non-complete heard', which sends your Spotify rating down."[lxviii]

Blogger Michael Tauberg examined the data in detail and observed that the average song length for the top hits has been declining since the turn of the twenty-first century.[lxix] From over four minutes at the turn of the century, the top tracks now are now more than a half minute shorter. He observed that the number of words in song titles has been decreasing as well. Examining the songs occupying the no. 1 chart position reveals an even more dramatic result: nearly two-thirds of the songs that achieved that lofty spot in 2021 (through August) were under three minutes long.[lxx] Ironically, these limited duration tracks would have fit comfortably on the early cylinders and phonograph records, whose length limitations (as we discussed in Chapter 2) constituted a major impediment to the artistic ambitions of artists of that time. The streaming payment methodology provides the incentive for these abbreviated songs: more short songs means more plays squeezed into any listening session with less likelihood of fans abandoning tracks before they complete.

Ironically, this shorter song approach has been complemented by albums that are getting longer in terms of the total number of tracks. In Feb 2018, the hip-hop band Migos had the no. 1 album in America. *Culture II* contained 24 tracks and lasted one hour and 45 minutes, which was almost double the length of their previous Grammy-nominated release. Many fans listen to the entire album from their favorite acts, at least the first time through, and the more songs on that album, the greater the income that is generated. *New York* magazine music critic Craig Jenkins said that Migos was "trying to game the

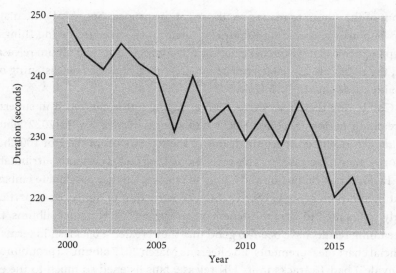

Figure 9.3 Average Song Length in Seconds for Top Hits:2000-2018.
Source: Medium
Credit: Michael Tauberg. All Rights Reserved

system."[lxxi] And Migos was not alone. Chris Brown's *Heartbreak on a Full Moon* in 2017 had 45 songs. Drake followed his 20-track 2016 album *Views* with *More Life* in 2017, which contains 22 tracks that Drake himself referred to as a "playlist."

In 2022, the British indie band Pocket of God took these trends to a new extreme when they released their album *1000 x 30: Nobody Makes Money Anymore*. The title said it all: the band was protesting inadequate compensation by offering an album comprising one thousand tracks of just over 30 seconds in length. The first song is titled "0.002," referencing the rate paid per song that results from the royalty calculations. The tracks on the album have been streamed over 600,000 times and, as a consequence, Spotify has modified its rules to allow short songs to be pitched for inclusion on their playlists.[lxxii]

And if you think of an album as just a different incarnation of a playlist, it is not surprising that the order of songs on the album will be designed to achieve more plays as well. Instead of sequencing the tracks to tell a particular story or to move through different moods and tempos, the likely hit single is getting placed first. Ezekiel Lewis, Executive VP of A&R at Epic Records, said, "people are definitely putting the focus tracks towards the front of the album to make sure those get the proper shot."[lxxiii] Some major hip-hop artists, including Kendrick Lamar and Drake, are taking things a step further and not even designating a "lead single" for their album releases. All the tracks are available at once on streaming, and the fans' listening behavior establishes the priorities.[lxxiv]

Combining these techniques with engaging music can result in superior streaming performance for tracks and albums. Taylor Swift's 2022 album *Midnights* occupied every single one of the top 10 slots of the Hot 100 chart shortly after its release.[lxxv] This record-breaking feat is certainly attributable to Taylor's musical talents and ability to engage with her passionate fanbase; but in addition, some believe that the construction of her songs is particularly well-suited to attract listeners on streaming.[lxxvi] For some albums, the streaming results have been so good that they created a backlash in terms of official chart measurements. Ed Sheeran's March 2017 album ÷ (pronounced "Divide") had 16 tracks in its UK release; fans listened so much to the entire album that the Official Chart Company reported that all those songs had made it into the Top 20. The industry was concerned that this outcome blocked a wider variety of music and artists from reaping the benefits of occupying the top chart positions. By June of that same year, the "Ed Sheeran effect" caused the UK industry to change the rules for positions on its charts. To prevent the most popular artists from dominating the singles chart with all the tracks from a single album, it was decided that an individual artist, regardless of the actual streaming numbers, could only have up to three of their most popular tracks in the top 100 at any point in time.[lxxvii]

Musicians who choose to create longer albums consisting of many shorter tracks, whether motivated by artistic or commercial considerations, have impacts beyond that individual project. The algorithms and curators responsible for improving playlists will notice the shorter tracks that are successfully crafted to be catchier from the virtual needle drop. The algorithms and people responsible will then move these tracks onto more popular playlists and place them in more lucrative higher-up positions. Given the dominance of playlist listening, this helps to generate even greater pro rata shares for these songs. The financial benefits will reinforce the behavior of artists and labels, and the cycle will continue.

Artists want to have songs that get maximum industry notoriety, whether measured by sales published in *Billboard* or by holding down a slot on Spotify's Today's Top Hits. The publicity is always a plus, but there is a lot of money at stake too. Complaints about inadequate compensation from streaming services notwithstanding, inclusion on Today's Top Hits means real money. A study by researchers at the University of Minnesota and the European Joint Research Centre found that being included on that very popular playlist resulted in 20 million incremental streams worth between $116,000 and $163,000.[lxxviii]

The streaming economy is not only leading artists to craft their songs and albums differently, it is also altering release strategies for new music. In general, the pace of releases has accelerated.[lxxix] Labels used to hold back on releases to attempt to maximize the physical sales of one album before the next one hit the store shelves (and hold back on single releases from albums to boost the sales of each respective single). In 2017, the rapper Future released two albums in consecutive weeks, and both of them hit no. 1. Brockhampton, another hip-hop artist, dropped three albums that same year. Yet in the attention-driven world of streaming, the numbers for the newest project are not all that matters. Every play counts in calculating revenues, whether someone listens to a newly released track or one from a decade ago. And if the new release reminds fans to go back and enjoy older music that they loved, so much the better.

Artists are also crafting promotional programs that drive incremental listening before the release of an entire album to enhance the playlist positions of songs on the album. For example, Mike Singer, a German pop singer and songwriter, invited fans visiting his website to listen to an older song from his catalog and to pre-save or pre-add his new album on their preferred streaming service. Lyrics for the new songs are released over time, encouraging more participation, and when enough fans join in, a portion of the album is released. The additional plays, saves, and adds should all represent positive indicators to the automated systems run by the services.[lxxx]

In Chapter 10, we will describe how the global nature of YouTube helps to increase the visibility and popularity of artists and songs such as Luis Fonsi's "Despacito" beyond the boundaries of its traditional markets. The same is true on Spotify, as Latin and K-Pop artists in particular are showing up more and more frequently in the Global Top 100. There might not have been adequate shelf space in physical retail to highlight these genres, but in streaming, there is literally a playlist for every taste.

More than 10 million music consumers follow ¡Viva Latino!, making it the third most followed playlist on Spotify; it highlights artists such as Bad Bunny and Ozuna.[lxxxi] This popularity has fostered more and more collaborations across genres as artists become more engaged with a broader spectrum of other artists. The creative impulse that drives musicians to create new and different versions of popular songs should not be discounted. But it would be naïve to ignore the commercial motivations that often factor in. A remix of a pop song that includes a bridge rapped by a popular hip-hop artist or a verse sung in Spanish by a Latin star means that this derivative track can be featured on a wider variety of playlists and appeal to the fans of the featured artist; it also increases the chances that such a track can appear in search results, as we discuss further in Chapter 10.[lxxxii]

As an example, Justin Bieber's song "Sorry" was released in October 2015; it soon topped the charts in 13 countries, including three weeks at no. 1 on the *Billboard* Hot 100. It has now been played over 1.7 billion times on Spotify alone. One month later, "Sorry (Latino Remix)" was released, featuring J. Balvin, the Colombian reggaeton artist, singing in Spanish. That version of the track appealed to a broader audience than the original while drawing fans to both versions; it racked up another 178 million Spotify plays.[lxxxiii] Lil Nas X's "Old Town Road" was the top song of 2019 amid controversy over whether the song fit the characteristics of the country genre.[9] Its success was reignited repeatedly by a variety of remixes as diverse as a more "authentically" country version featuring Billy Ray Cyrus and one featuring a yodeler.

Spotify CEO Daniel Ek explained in a 2020 interview that artists needed to change their approach to improve performance on services such as his. He said, "Some artists that used to do well in the past may not do well in the future landscape, where you can't record music every one to three years and think that's going to be enough."[lxxxiv] His remarks were viewed negatively by many artists who already felt that Spotify's payments were inadequate, and they expressed their sentiments via Twitter. David Crosby labeled Ek "an obnoxious greedy little shit," and Mike Mills of R.E.M. told Ek to "go fuck yourself."[lxxxv]

Music marketing executive Jay Frank laid out many of these same prescriptions for artists to be successful in streaming in 2009. In his book, *FUTUREHIT.DNA*,[lxxxvi] he accurately foretold the need to release more songs more often, to craft tracks with shorter intros, and to incorporate a variety of genres to broaden appeal.[10]

The Digital Millennium Copyright Act (DMCA), which we discussed in Chapter 8, provided the legal framework for many user-uploaded services, including YouTube, to thrive. The first service to offer music streaming from user-uploaded files ran into trouble because it ran afoul of those rules.

The beta version of a startup called Grooveshark was released in 2007 as a download store that charged $0.99 per song. But the three students at the University of Florida who launched the service pivoted once they had a large enough catalog of music and the appeal of streaming became clearer.

Grooveshark's pitch was straightforward: "Play any song in the world, for free!" That message resonated with music fans (as it had time and again in the digital era), and the service's user base climbed to a peak of 35 million users. But the company had no licenses from the major music labels, which brought lawsuits against them for copyright infringement. The concerns about the legality of the service extended to mobile app stores, and both Apple and Google removed the software. Undeterred, Grooveshark crafted an HTML5 version of its application, which ran in standard web browsers instead of as iOS or Android apps, enabling it to circumvent the app store bans.[lxxxvii] What they could not circumvent, however, was the evidence that Grooveshark employees themselves had uploaded tens of thousands of songs to ensure that the best tracks were always available for streaming. The DMCA shields services from liability only for their *users'* copyright infringements; the actions of Grooveshark's employees laid the company open to liability for direct infringement, making the DMCA irrelevant. Those actions led to a claim in the lawsuit for damages in excess of $17 billion. The case was decided in the fall of 2014 in favor of the record companies.[lxxxviii]

In a settlement with Universal, Warner, and Sony Music, the Grooveshark founders shut down the service in early 2015, erased all the music on their servers, and posted a formal apology for their actions on their website. They were required to urge Grooveshark users to take advantage of one of the many licensed services that pay artists and songwriters. The demise of Grooveshark took one of the largest free alternatives off the streaming playing field. Some price-sensitive users migrated to the free tier of Spotify or to YouTube to satisfy their music demands. Others undoubtedly valued streaming enough that they began to pay, helping to fuel the subscriber growth.

If running an unlicensed streaming service was going to carry substantial legal risks and the paid services were generating the vast majority of cash for the industry, then you can be sure that enterprising and amoral entrepreneurs were going to find other ways to skirt the rules besides infringing copyrights. If more listens and better playlist positioning mean a greater slice of the revenue pie, then that's where you will find the next crop of disreputable services. Just as Willie Sutton robbed banks because "that's where the money is," then creating fake streaming activity (that looks real) is where the money is.

In advance of Spotify's direct stock listing in April 2018, the company felt it was necessary to highlight this threat as one of the risks in its F-1 filing. It stated, "We are at risk of artificial manipulation of stream counts and failure to effectively manage and remediate such fraudulent streams could have an adverse impact on our business." There are several techniques that can be used to create popularity or to generate cash for music that has not engendered meaningful fan interest on its own. Spotify even offered some useful tips to potential scammers in its S-1:

> These potentially fraudulent streams may also involve creation of non-bona fide User accounts or artists. For example, an individual might generate fake Users to stream songs repeatedly, thereby generating revenue each time the song is streamed; or might utilize fake Users to stream specific content to increase its visibility on our charts.[lxxxix]

Given the risk of shareholder lawsuits, corporate filings tend to go a little bit overboard in terms of stating the risks for shareholders. Yet in this case, Spotify may have underplayed the severity of the problem. Two months before the direct listing, Music Business Worldwide (MBW) published a story explaining how a Bulgarian playlister had faked his way to millions in revenues.[xc] The article laid out in a step-by-step fashion how "Soulful Music" was able to get into the upper reaches of Spotify's top playlists. MBW found several indicators that someone was trying to game the system, including very few followers for the playlist, a large number of tracks just a few seconds longer than that important 30 second mark, and relatively few unique listeners per track, which suggests repetitive listening by bots instead of human users. Spotify, asked to respond, explained that it was investing in people and technology to identify signals that would help to ensure the accuracy of their results. For example, industry sources have stated that when a user plays a single track more than 10 times in a day, Spotify discounts any subsequent plays. K-pop supergroup BTS released the single "Butter" in May 2021; almost half of the more than 20 million plays of that track were eliminated from Spotify's official chart results.[xci]

One year after MBW's exposé, Richard Posen, founder of Hopeless Records, said in *Rolling Stone* that "My sources think that three to four percent of global streams are illegitimate streams. That's around $300M in potential lost revenue."[xcii] Today, if you type the words "Buy Spotify Plays" or "Buy Soundcloud Plays" into Google, you will get a long list of responses. The sites in that list are vying to be the "best" or the "cheapest" way to get more streaming plays. Some services unironically promise to help you "buy real plays and followers." And if you're willing to risk poking around the "dark web," you can purchase thousands of Spotify User IDs and passwords that can be commandeered to generate plays and cash by taking over accounts when they are not typically in use. This technique creates one more degree of difficulty in detecting bogus activity.

Scammers often piggyback on the popularity of more established artists to generate revenues or to create attention and interest. If you listen to the "This is Lil Loaded" playlist you end up hearing a bunch of songs by Wali Da Great. Wali's tracks have Lil Loaded listed as a "featured artist," leading to their inclusion on the playlist. But he is nowhere to be heard. The tracks were deliberately submitted with incorrect metadata to fool Spotify's systems and to garner attention.[xciii] Sometimes bad actors try even more blatant fakery. In June of 2020, the indie band TV Girl saw a newly uploaded track on their Spotify artist page. Their hard-earned fanbase of 119,000 followers were alerted to this new song, and Spotify added the track to the Release Radar playlist with over 1 million listeners. But the band had not created this new track. Not only did these plays pull funds into the pockets of the fraudsters, but the band's fans also complained to TV Girl that the quality of "their" music was slipping.[xciv]

Whether these services that boost popularity or plays artificially are strictly legal or not may be up to a court to decide. Regardless, the streaming services view them as clear violations of their terms of use. For example, Spotlister, which charged $2,000 and up to get songs onto popular Spotify playlists, was shut down because the service deemed it noncompliant.[xcv] In August 2020, German courts issued injunctions against five sites that manipulated streams to cease operations. The action was triggered at the behest of the International Federation of the Phonographic Industry (IFPI), the global record industry trade group, and the German national trade association BVMI.[xcvi]

These upstart "streamola"[11] fraudsters represent a significant threat to the trustworthiness and accuracy of streaming results and payments. But the infighting among some of the larger and more established entities in the industry over whether streaming services have obtained all the appropriate licenses has been an even larger issue.

It all goes back to those mechanical licenses created in the Copyright Act of 1909 to pay royalties to songwriters for piano rolls. The compulsory mechanical license allows a streaming service (in this case) to play any musical composition without asking for permission in advance, but until recently the service had to notify the owner(s) of that composition and pay them the royalties specified in the statute. If it couldn't locate the songwriters and music publishers who hold the composition rights, then it was allowed to file a form called a Notice of Intent (NOI) with the Copyright Office instead. The service had to do this individually for every track it ingested from record labels (or other sources, such as indie distributors).

But there was a problem with that: the service needed to know the identities of the compositions and the rights holders. Record labels don't necessarily include that information when they send their music to streaming services, so the services were on the hook to figure that out for themselves. This turned out to be a major headache for the streaming services.

When the major labels started pressplay and MusicNet, they worked with the Harry Fox Agency (HFA), then a subsidiary of the National Music Publishers Association (NMPA), to obtain mechanical licenses for the tracks they were offering. This arrangement resulted from the deal that the RIAA had made with the NMPA that we mentioned in Chapter 8. HFA had been the go-to source for mechanical rights clearance for decades, through the eras of physical recorded media; by the time interactive streaming services were ready to launch, HFA had amassed a database of information about the compositions being performed on millions of recorded music tracks and the songwriters and music publishers that owned the rights to them. And when Rhapsody launched with major-label licensing in 2002, it made its own arrangement with HFA to match recordings to musical compositions and clear the mechanical rights.

Rhapsody set a pattern that Spotify and most of the other Celestial Jukebox–type streaming services would follow in later years: instead of relying on labels themselves to clear mechanical rights for the music that labels sent to them, streaming services would engage HFA to match the recordings to compositions and clear mechanical rights. Another company called Music Reports Inc. (MRI), which traditionally cleared music rights for television, stepped in to compete with HFA in what was clearly going to be a highly lucrative market for these services. So did a startup company called RightsFlow, which Google ended up acquiring for exclusive use with its own music services, such as YouTube. By the mid-2010s, these rights-clearance services were processing tens of thousands of tracks per day for each of their music service customers—the vast majority of which were redundant (the same sets of tracks for each service). Yet none of these services had databases of rights owner information that were entirely complete, accurate, and up to date.

This situation continued without much complaint through the early 2010s while interactive streaming was only a small part of the market. But once streaming began to grow in importance, the rights ownership data problems rose in importance too.

It's important to bear in mind that matching recordings to compositions is often not straightforward. A classic singer-songwriter track like James Taylor's "Fire and Rain" is simple: James Taylor is both the recording artist and songwriter. You know who the songwriters are when you hear the Stones' "Jumpin' Jack Flash." But most of today's hip-hop, pop, and country songs have many different songwriters working with multiple music publishers; and occasionally a song will be released before they all agree on the "splits"— the ownership share percentages. There are old or obscure recordings where the songwriter credits are lost in the mists of time. And there are many other cases where composition rights holder information is missing or inaccurate due to various sorts of data errors that can creep in along the way.

Such errors and omissions are inevitable when that much data gets passed down the line from through multiple links in the music supply chain. For physical music formats, music publishers worked with record labels to figure out mechanicals.[12] But streaming services have had no direct relationships with music publishers, so they have had to rely on intermediaries such as HFA to figure out the ownership data after the fact.

So as streaming began to become the dominant source of revenue in music in the mid-2010s, more songwriters and music publishers began to notice that their mechanicals weren't being paid properly or at all, and the royalties involved began to matter enough to motivate them to do something about it. The situation came to a head in the mid-2010s, when songwriters and music publishers—some individually, some facilitated by the NMPA— filed lawsuits against Spotify, Apple Music, and other streaming services for unpaid mechanicals. Spotify settled the NMPA-facilitated lawsuit against it in 2016 for $30 million;[xcvii] the settlement covered the many publishers that chose to opt into its terms. But several publishers did not opt in and instead filed their own lawsuits. Within the next couple of years, representatives of dozens of songwriters of compositions recorded by Neil Young, Tom Petty, the Doors, Stevie Nicks, the Four Seasons, Thomas Dolby, Camper Van Beethoven, and many others brought their own lawsuits. The aggregate claimed damages went well up into the billions of dollars.[xcviii]

The industry had, of course, known about this problem since the days of MusicNet and pressplay in the early 2000s. The trade associations involved—the RIAA for labels, NMPA for publishers, and DiMA (Digital Media Association) for streaming services—made various attempts to solve it by updating the copyright laws. The fact that "phonorecords" in the streaming era are simply collections of bits transmitted via various internet and wireless protocols from cloud-based servers to smartphone applications makes the case that an update of the law was probably necessary.

One such attempt at legislative reform was the Section 115 Reform Act (known as SIRA) of 2006; Section 115 of the Copyright Act defines the compulsory licenses for making and distributing phonorecords. SIRA would have set up an infrastructure for mechanical licensing modeled on the one for performance licensing through the performance rights organizations (PROs): each streaming service could take a blanket license for mechanicals instead of having to license each composition individually, and an entity known as a "designated agent" would handle collective licensing and ensure that payments would be made to the proper rights holders. But the various factions involved couldn't come to agreement on various details, and the legislation failed; but the sense of urgency wasn't there yet in 2006.

That sense of urgency arrived with the rash of lawsuits filed—and the associated money at stake—in the mid-2010s, and the industry began casting about anew for solutions. The NMPA and DiMA ultimately arrived at a solution, achieved buy-in from the various industry factions, and presented it to Congress as the Music Modernization Act (MMA). Perhaps even more remarkable than the broad support across the industry for this bill was that both houses of Congress passed it unanimously in such a politically polarized era. The MMA became law in 2018.[xcix]

Like SIRA, the MMA created a blanket license for mechanicals that replaced the onerous track-by-track licensing requirement under the old scheme. This was a huge savings in administrative overhead for the streaming services. The MMA also implemented collective licensing for streaming mechanicals, but in a different way than SIRA contemplated. It created the Mechanical Licensing Collective (MLC), a nonprofit entity that would be designated by the Copyright Office, overseen by publishers and songwriters, and paid for by the digital streaming services. This meant that streaming services, instead of having to hire a service such as HFA or MRI to clear composition mechanicals for their incoming sound recordings, simply paid annual fees to an outside entity that would do this for all streaming services—and because the vast majority of this repertoire is identical for all services, this would also eliminate an enormous amount of overhead.[c]

The MLC managed to meet its launch deadline in early 2021, despite having to build out its systems on an aggressive timeline in the middle of a global pandemic. It chose HFA as its database provider. It is currently taking in play data feeds from music services, matching recordings to compositions, and paying the composition rights holders. The MLC needed to implement processes to ensure that inadequate metadata does not lead to a large pool of undistributed funds. To that end, the MLC started an educational campaign called "Play Your Part"[ci] to get music publishers to send it accurate and up-to-date rights ownership information so that they can be paid properly—something that many music publishers have never had to do before.

It is less clear how the next legal battle related to streaming will play out. Apple and Google's dominance of mobile phone operating systems via iOS and Android respectively mean that developers need to focus their resources on building for these two platforms to reach most smartphone users. For the vast majority of consumers, the App Store is the only way to install apps. But there is a literal price to pay Apple for this convenience that has streaming providers such as Spotify complaining. Apple charges a 15–30 percent commission on all subscription fees that come through its in-app purchase system. In addition, Apple's rules restrict what developers can tell users about other purchasing options outside of the app that could save money for consumers. Specifically, apps may not "include buttons, external links, or other calls to action that direct consumers to purchasing mechanisms other than the in-app purchase." Epic Games, the developers of Fortnite, one of the most popular games for mobile, sued both Apple and Google over their app store payment rules.[13]

Because of these policies, services like Spotify face a difficult choice. Either they charge a premium for purchases through the App Store, which places them at a competitive disadvantage to Apple Music, or they forego the convenience of the in-store purchase and require users to take the extra steps to pay them directly.[cii]

Complaints by Spotify and other developers of nonmusic services have persuaded the antitrust authorities in the European Union to announce, in June 2020, the start of a formal investigation of Apple's practices. The tech giant's response was not exactly conciliatory: "It's disappointing the European Commission is advancing baseless complaints from a handful of companies who simply want a free ride, and don't want to play by the same rules as everyone else." It probably won't be long before Apple faces similar issues in the United States. The House Antitrust Committee has been meeting with services such as ClassPass and Airbnb that are facing the same issue with Apple's fees and rules.[ciii] This fight will probably not linger as long as the legal issues created by other music formats, such as radio payments for artists. But the resolution is likely to have major ramifications on the streaming music leaders and their long-term profitability.

Conclusion

The shift from paying for products to paying for access has not been simple. This fundamental change required new strategies and approaches to be successful, but streaming represents a bridge to sustained growth after two decades of troubled water for the music industry. Meanwhile, the technologies that enabled this shift can also transport video along with sounds; and newer technologies enabled ordinary users to create not just copies of recorded music but music embedded into their own videos. In one sense, the resulting combination of user-created videos with pre-existing recorded music was an incremental extension of streaming music; but in other senses, it was the next major source of disruption for the music industry.

10

Streaming Video

Throw Away Your Television—Red Hot Chili Peppers

Video has become predominant as a means of promoting and distributing music. Yet as we'll see in this chapter, the music industry's ability to control and profit from music usage has diminished as video's prominence and ubiquity have risen.

As we saw in Chapter 6, MTV's heyday as an outlet for music videos ended in the early-to-mid-2000s as the network moved to reality shows and other types of programming. Yet even during MTV's peak period of influence in the 1990s, broadcast video had been promotional to music sales rather than a primary means of distributing music. Video products also started to become a means of music distribution in the 1990s: consumers bought VHS tapes and DVDs of music videos and concerts. Yet these constituted, at most, a minor portion of industry revenue, less than vinyl today.

Internet video started to become important in the music industry just after that time. It led to a quantum leap in the importance of video for music distribution. The inflection point came in the mid-2000s, when entrepreneurs figured out how to overcome three obstacles around the same time.

The first obstacle was the technology for encoding video and distributing it online. Digital video takes up an order of magnitude more memory than audio,[1] and consumer Internet speeds in the early 2000s just weren't fast enough to handle it. Streaming technology had eliminated the need for downloads, but it wasn't until that time that the codecs were good enough to stream acceptable-quality video over typical Internet connections. And consumer Internet speeds, as we'll see, began to increase rapidly with the acceleration of consumer broadband access in the mid-to-late 2000s.

The second obstacle was creation and production of video content. As we discussed in Chapter 6, artists and labels spent untold sums of money to feed the beast that was MTV; video production costs became major drains on release budgets, especially as fans came to expect lavish productions. The solution was simple, even if it wasn't one that artists and labels expected or

Key Changes. Howie Singer and Bill Rosenblatt, Oxford University Press. © Howie Singer and Bill Rosenblatt 2023.
DOI: 10.1093/oso/9780197656891.003.0010

even (in many cases) wanted: videos contributed by users. As we'll see, user-contributed music videos solved two problems at once: they were generated in extremely high volume at no cost to labels or artists; and they had a low-cost, DIY feel that—at least at first—suppressed fans' expectations of high production values.

The third obstacle was copyright law regarding user-contributed content. Napster may have shut down in 2001, but it led to many efforts to create content-sharing services that tweaked the Napster model in hopes of withstanding legal challenges. As we saw earlier, some—like LimeWire and Grooveshark—didn't succeed. But others did, and by the time entrepreneurs figured out how to thread the legal needle, the aforementioned technological limitations had been overcome, and so the focus of content sharing shifted from text and audio to video.

The resulting environment around 2005–2006, therefore, was one in which an Internet content-sharing service featuring user-contributed videos could flourish and grow to become a leading distribution channel for music. And that's exactly what happened. The race for domination was on, and there was one resounding winner: YouTube.

YouTube is approaching 20 years old today, but it is still the biggest recorded music platform in the world, video or otherwise. Yet YouTube didn't particularly invent new technologies. Streaming video had yet to reach the mainstream in 2005, but the codecs and other fundamental technologies had been in place since the late 1990s. It also wasn't the first video-sharing website. Of the ones that launched earlier, those that are still around today are Metacafe (launched July 2003), Vimeo (November 2004), and DailyMotion (March 2005).

Steve Chen, Chad Hurley, and Jawed Karim, all employees of the pioneering online payments service PayPal, actually started YouTube in 2004 as an online dating service, one that enticed women to upload videos of themselves. Finding too few women willing to make such videos (despite the promise of $100 rewards), they pivoted to general videos around May 2005 when the site went into public beta. The site's official launch was in December 2005, after the Silicon Valley VC firm Sequoia Capital made a $3.5 million investment in the startup.

Several factors contributed to YouTube's success, but—apart from the catchiness of its brand name—three stood out. The first factor was the "total product." YouTube did one thing, did it well enough, and was easy for anyone to use. YouTube was a place for video clips and only video clips; and it made it as easy as possible to upload, find, and view them online.

At that time, dealing with online video was not a simple or smooth experience for everyday users. Digital cameras were widely available at moderate prices, but most didn't shoot video yet. Consumer digital video equipment was divided between webcams and digital camcorders: the former were cheap, rudimentary, and tied to your PC; while the latter were expensive, bloated with features, challenging to use (the subject of many a joke at birthday parties and bar/bat mitzvahs), and used blank tape or disks. Typical personal computers of the mid-2000s had ample hard disk space for video, but it took expertise and effort to transfer video content from camcorders to PCs or Macs. Video editing software (such as Avid Media Composer) was in wide professional use but was expensive, required considerable skill and training, and couldn't run on everyday PCs. And smartphones—let alone smartphones that recorded video—had yet to exist.

YouTube cut through all that complexity. It accepted a wide range of file formats, codecs, and bitrates. It did as much processing as possible online and didn't encumber users with hard-to-use, hard-to-maintain desktop software.

It also developed partnerships with upstart electronics vendors that made cameras that were better suited to the task. The paradigmatic example was Pure Digital Technologies. In 2007, Pure Digital introduced the Flip Video, a line of basic plug-and-play pocket-size video cameras, with digital memory instead of tape and USB plugs; see Figure 10.1. You could shoot videos with the Flip Video, plug it in to your PC, and upload the videos to YouTube in just a couple of clicks. In other words, the Flip Video/YouTube user experience was meant to be as seamless as that of some digital cameras that had similar integration with photo-sharing sites of the time such as Flickr and Snapfish. Pricing for the Flip Video started at a reasonable $120, compared to well below $100 for webcams and well north of $500 for many camcorders. There was even a Flip Video camera with YouTube's logo on it. Pure Digital was acquired by network equipment giant Cisco in 2009.

The second of YouTube's critical success factors was network effects. As we saw in Chapter 8, Metcalfe's Law states that the value of a network was proportional to the square of the number of devices attached to it. YouTube

Figure 10.1 A Flip Video digital video camera plugged into a laptop computer.
Alan Levine, CC 0 (public domain) via Wikimedia Commons.

made its site more desirable by striving to get as much content uploaded to its
site by as many people as possible as quickly as possible. It made videos easier
to distribute by enabling users to embed videos in web pages, email messages,
blog posts, or anything else that used HTML, by providing embeddable links.
And it worked with Apple to produce a simplified mobile app—the first of its
kind—for the iPhone at the device's launch in 2007.

YouTube also showed videos at relatively low resolution compared to
other early video-hosting services, to increase ubiquity by trading off picture quality. Lower resolution meant faster uploads as well as smoother
streaming at lower Internet access speeds. YouTube chose the Flash video
format from Adobe, which was desirable at the time for its adaptability across
many different devices.[2] It also chose relatively low 320 × 240 pixel resolution, a quarter of the size of the VGA standard of 640 × 480 that just about all
computers of that time supported. New monitors in the mid-2000s typically
displayed up to 1280 × 1024 resolution, 16 times that of YouTube videos.
(YouTube increased its picture quality continuously over time; today it
supports up to 7680 × 4320, known as 8K resolution, the same as in cameras
widely used to shoot network television.)

The third success factor was external to YouTube: the steep growth of
broadband Internet access at that time, giving users enough speed to upload
digital video in reasonable timeframes as well as stream video with decent

quality. In February 2004, less than a quarter of US adults had broadband access through cable TV or phone lines (DSL). But by March 2005, this figure had risen to 30 percent, then to 42 percent by March 2006.[i] Meanwhile mobile broadband connectivity at speeds high enough to support streaming video didn't come until the early 2010s with the major mobile operators' buildouts of their 4G networks.[3] Without broadband access, residential Internet users had to contend with 56 kbps (or slower) dialup lines, which meant a few minutes of digital video took several hours to upload. Typical consumer broadband connections of the day reduced that time to a few minutes per minute of video uploaded.

All of these factors put YouTube on a jaw-droppingly rapid growth path, the likes of which the industry had never seen previously. Google acquired the company in November 2006; by that time—less than a year after its launch—YouTube had an estimated 50 million users worldwide and accounted for almost half of all video traffic on the Internet. (The price tag of $1.65 billion also caused jaws to drop, but no one has ever accused Google of overpaying after the fact.)

Of course, YouTube was not designed to be a music service; and as we'll discuss later in this chapter, it has had various phases of growing pains on its way to becoming the largest licensed music service in the world. Yet music was integral to YouTube from the beginning. Probably the most important video to appear on YouTube in its earliest days was "Lazy Sunday," a hip-hop parody music video that originally aired on NBC's *Saturday Night Live* (SNL) in December 2005. Several users posted unauthorized copies of the video to YouTube. It garnered over seven million views—despite the fact that the site had only officially launched two days before the clip aired on SNL.

By the end of 2006, the top 10 most-watched videos on YouTube included three music videos: two young comedians lip-syncing to the Pokemon theme song; a teenage Korean guitarist shredding his way through a rock version of Baroque composer Johann Pachelbel's Canon in D Major; and a DIY-style video of "Here It Goes Again" by the pop-punk band OK Go. The slickly produced music videos would come in time; but otherwise, these three low-budget clips encapsulated YouTube's appeal as a medium for music. Ironically, seven million views weren't quite enough to put "Lazy Sunday" in the top ten most-watched videos of 2006, though it came close. (The Pokemon theme song video garnered 18 million views.)

However, at the same time, many users started uploading videos containing commercially released music. We'll see shortly how YouTube addressed the inevitable copyright challenges, but for now, suffice it to say that the solution depended on another important technology: acoustic fingerprinting.

We first saw acoustic fingerprinting in Chapter 8, when the technology was used in attempts to block unlicensed content from being uploaded to peer-to-peer (p2p) networks. Several technology vendors had introduced acoustic fingerprinting solutions, and by the mid-2000s, Audible Magic had emerged as a de facto standard for copyright filtering applications. By 2005, the major labels began to accept its use in conjunction with licensed commercial music services.

One example of this was a p2p network based in Israel called iMesh. Like several other p2p networks in the wake of Napster, as we saw in Chapter 8, iMesh was sued by the major labels and lost. But unlike the others, iMesh worked out a deal with the labels to remain in operation while it transformed itself into a licensed service. The service that iMesh eventually launched was a file-sharing network that blocked uploads of copyrighted material identified by Audible Magic and allowed the uploads if Audible Magic didn't find a match. If a user searched for a track that wasn't in the fingerprint database, they could download it. But if a user wanted a track that was in the fingerprint database and paid a monthly subscription fee, they would get a DRM-protected file that only played on their PC. iMesh announced its first major-label license—with Sony BMG—in July 2005,[ii] though the new service didn't launch until September 2006.[iii]

YouTube emerged in the same timeframe. Bear in mind that in 2006, revenues from CD sales were plummeting from their peak in 2000, but CDs were still the dominant source of revenue by an order of magnitude over downloads. And interactive music streaming, available at that time through services such as Rhapsody and MusicNet, was a much smaller niche than downloads. YouTube represented another form of interactive streaming. So while YouTube was gaining enormous amounts of user traffic every month, it represented a music usage model that hadn't really caught on with the public yet.

This—along with a sense that file-sharing may have been more of a missed opportunity than the labels admitted publicly—may have led the labels to want to negotiate with YouTube, or at least to wait and see how YouTube could develop as a music outlet, instead of merely trying to sue it out of existence. At the same time, the latter strategy had its own challenges, as we'll see shortly.

Warner Music Group was the first to make a deal with YouTube; it did so in September 2006, a mere nine months after launch. In the deal, YouTube agreed to implement Audible Magic's acoustic fingerprinting system and to populate its fingerprint database with Warner Music's catalog.[4] Whenever a user tried to upload a video containing music from that catalog, YouTube would allow the video to go up on the site and would share a portion of the revenue from ads shown alongside the video with the label. (Other video-sharing sites such as DailyMotion still use fingerprinting simply to block uploads that contain music in their fingerprint databases.)

As for the other majors, Sony BMG Music and Universal Music reached deals with YouTube shortly after Warner Music did, but they were limited to catalogs of videos that the labels owned and did not license YouTube for user uploads of the labels' recordings.[iv] EMI cut a similar deal—known as a "whitelist" deal—in May 2007.[v] Warner, Sony BMG, and Universal all took equity stakes in YouTube around October 2006, even as some of them were filing lawsuits against other video-sharing services.[vi] The equity investments lent legitimacy to YouTube that helped it secure its $1.65 billion price when Google acquired it two months later.

As we'll see, Warner Music's deal became the archetype not only for other labels' deals with YouTube but also for countless other content owners' deals with user-contributed content services to come.

Meanwhile, music continued to be a major draw on YouTube. A 2008 study found that almost 20 percent of the 78 million videos—more than 15 million—on YouTube by then were categorized as Music (one of 13 categories at that time).[vii] To put that figure in perspective, the iTunes Music Store in 2008 had 6 million songs in its catalog.[5]

YouTube's domination of online music video held steady for a decade, even as the proportion of videos on the site in the music category declined. It kept original competitors such as Vimeo and DailyMotion trailing far behind and fended off numerous would-be startup competitors. Unlike those independent companies, YouTube benefited from several aspects of Google's technology infrastructure, such as its AdSense contextual ad technology, content delivery network, and immense cloud storage capabilities.

The first serious challenge to YouTube's music video supremacy[6] came in 2016 with the launch of A.me, a video sharing app from a Chinese startup called ByteDance. The app changed its name to Douyin and became incredibly popular incredibly quickly in China, amassing 100 million users in one year. In September 2017, it launched globally as TikTok.

TikTok claimed to have hit a milestone of 1 billion users in September 2021,[viii] although that number is in dispute: eMarketer put it at 755 million as of November 2021.[ix] This compares to YouTube's more than 2.5 billion and 422 million for Spotify (counting free subscribers) as of May 2022.[x]

TikTok's ultrafast rise, together with its origins in China, have led some governments to attempt to ban it as a security threat, given that China is known for its pervasive Internet surveillance activities. In 2020, President Trump issued a series of executive orders that would have banned TikTok in the United States if ByteDance did not spin off its US business to an American company. Oracle and Walmart, among others, were in talks to acquire it. At this writing, the US version of the app is still available and still owned by ByteDance, and President Biden has dropped the dispute, although attempts are being revived at various levels of government to ban the app; it's currently banned from devices owned by the federal government and several state governments. Meanwhile India and some other countries in South Asia have already banned it—allegedly out of concerns for its addictive behavior and lack of filters for sensitive content in addition to security and privacy concerns.

The simplest way to describe the difference between YouTube and TikTok is to say that YouTube was originally designed to be a video-sharing service that ran on web browsers on PCs and Macs, while TikTok was designed to be a video-centric social networking app that ran on mobile phones. YouTube videos can be of any length; and while TikTok videos initially were limited to one minute and typically in the 15-second range, the service has been increasing the length limit incrementally, to 10 minutes as of February 2022.[7] TikTok provides lots of tools for creating, editing, and adding effects to your videos on your phone, a la Instagram; YouTube doesn't (for most users).

Early on, ByteDance acquired another Chinese startup, a popular app called Musical.ly that enabled users to create music lip-synch videos on their phones. By August 2018 ByteDance had integrated Musical.ly's functionality into TikTok, and TikTok became primarily known for music lip-synch and dance videos.

TikTok appears unlikely to attract as large a user base as YouTube.[xi] Yet TikTok's revenues are growing much faster than YouTube's did.[xii] YouTube is certainly feeling the heat: it launched the TikTok-competitive YouTube Shorts feature in July 2021 after beta testing it in a few countries.

The most recent developments in Internet music video technology have been in the area of live streaming. Before the COVID-19 pandemic, Internet live streaming of musical performances was a small market and split into two distinct segments: big, expensive, professional productions featuring major stars; and small DIY facilities for everyone else. YouTube started experimenting with live streaming with a concert by U2 in 2009 using a third-party technical infrastructure. It began limited rollout of its own live streaming infrastructure in 2013 and eventually made live streaming available through its mobile apps.

A few small outfits provided live streaming functionality geared toward musical performances in the same timeframe. A prominent example was Livestream (formerly Mogulus), which hosted Internet-only concerts from the likes of the Foo Fighters starting in 2009. The company was acquired by Vimeo and renamed Vimeo Livestream in 2017. Facebook added live streaming to its namesake platform as well as Instagram in 2015 and 2016, respectively.

The advent of the COVID-19 pandemic in March 2020 led quickly to a parade of startup launches focusing on music-oriented live streaming: Mandolin, Veeps, Sessions, Bulldog DM, Dreamstage, and others. Online gaming platforms such as Twitch and Fortnite have also gotten into the act. Paid live streams are now an accepted part of the music industry. Although we aren't focusing on it any further in this book, live streaming is now a significant force in the industry and will continue to play a role now that the pandemic has faded into the rearview mirror.

YouTube met with roughly the same legal challenges that Napster faced, but it did so at a much later time. The major labels didn't sue YouTube as it became a huge draw for unlicensed content. But Hollywood did.

As we saw in Chapter 8, the Digital Millennium Copyright Act (DMCA) of 1998 established safe harbors for online services that limit their liability from their users' copyright infringements if they play by certain rules. One of these rules is known as "notice and takedown": online services must process requests (notices) sent by copyright owners to have them remove their content if it is there without permission. Another rule is that service providers must terminate the accounts of users who are repeat infringers.

By the time YouTube got started, processes for handling takedown notices had become established among online service providers, as were "three strikes, you're out" policies for terminating repeat infringers.[8] YouTube has a mechanism for processing takedown notices and a "copyright strike" repeat infringer termination policy. However, other aspects of the DMCA were less clear-cut regarding online service providers' responsibilities. The statute suggested that online services would not be required to affirmatively monitor their services for copyright infringements to qualify for DMCA safe harbors but that they did have some culpability through knowledge of infringements taking place on their services, known in legalese as "red flag knowledge." But as online services evolved, the boundaries among red flag knowledge, its legalese cousin "willful blindness," and affirmative monitoring became sources of legal uncertainty.

As we've seen, YouTube uses fingerprinting technology to help it determine when a user uploads a work that a copyright owner has claimed as its material. YouTube's legal position was (and remains) that it isn't legally *required* to use fingerprinting, because that would be tantamount to affirmative monitoring for copyright compliance. Some content owners were happy with neither this legal positioning nor YouTube's technological solutions after the Warner Music deal in 2006. Users found ways to circumvent Audible Magic's fingerprinting technology when they uploaded content to YouTube, such as by inserting a period of silence before the start of a song or shifting the song's pitch a little bit. And Audible Magic didn't work at all on video content (unless it happened to contain music that was in Audible Magic's audio fingerprint database).

Hollywood studios and TV networks in particular were not amused, even though at that time YouTube was limiting the length of uploaded videos to ten minutes. In 2007, the giant entertainment company Viacom—parent of MTV, as well as Paramount Pictures and Cartoon Network—sued YouTube, claiming a billion dollars in damages. Viacom's intent was to get a court to firm up online service providers' responsibility to police infringements on their networks.

But Viacom's gambit failed. The Second Circuit appeals court affirmed that YouTube had no obligation to monitor its network for copyright issues and sent the case back to the lower court. The case settled for an undisclosed amount and didn't go to trial. Around the same time, Universal Music Group (UMG) sued Veoh, another video-sharing site that launched about a year after YouTube. The results were similar; in addition, the judge in that case stated that the plaintiff had no right to demand—as UMG had tried to—that the online service use a particular fingerprinting technology.

While these lawsuits were being filed, Google replaced Audible Magic with its own content recognition technology, which it called Content ID. Content ID recognizes video as well as music; it is also more tightly integrated with Google's advertising technology. When a user uploads a video to YouTube, the Content ID system takes its fingerprint and looks it up in a fingerprint database, just as Audible Magic or any other fingerprinting technology would. If it finds a match, it gives copyright holders a number of options for actions that YouTube can take. Originally there were three choices: in addition to the ad revenue share option a la the Warner Music deal, the options were to block the upload or to track the usage statistics of the video for the copyright holder. Yet the ad revenue share option has become the overwhelming choice of record labels and other copyright owners. YouTube subsequently added a fourth option: to allow the upload but not allow users who qualify for monetizing their videos to share in the ad revenue.[9]

In other words, the Content ID revenue share scheme had become—as Google may have foreseen—a de facto licensing arrangement for music on YouTube before some of the major labels made actual licensing deals with the service. As we'll see, this arrangement has changed the fundamental financial dynamics of the music industry.

Yet although the labels mostly took the ad revenue share option, they weren't happy with certain loopholes in the Content ID system. Labels wanted more control over which user-uploaded videos could go up and which couldn't; for example, they didn't want user-contributed videos that cast artists in a disparaging light. It is possible to use the notice-and-takedown mechanism to have a video removed from YouTube, but as we'll discuss later in this section, users can repost videos immediately afterward. Users also have the option to issue counternotices and have the videos replaced. Users can easily claim that their videos are fair use,[10] and YouTube will leave the video up for two weeks before taking further action. Labels consider this to be unreasonable.

Like Audible Magic, Content ID originally recognized copyrighted sound recordings in user-created videos that contained them. But that process doesn't work when users upload their own cover versions of someone else's musical compositions. In that case, royalties are owed for the compositions; YouTube has to identify the compositions and figure out whom to pay royalties.

Automatic detection of cover versions of compositions—melodies, lyrics, and so on—is a much harder technical problem than automatic detection of sound recordings. And the solutions that exist are more recent. While acoustic fingerprinting technologies for sound recordings were first invented in the late 1990s and came to market in the early 2000s, cover detection techniques weren't even in the R&D stage until the mid-2000s. Starting in 2006, researchers have competed on song-cover detection in an annual conference called Music Information Retrieval Evaluation eXchange (MIREX). In the 2020 competition, the winners—a team from Peking University and Tencent in China—only got it right 84 percent of the time when asked to find cover versions of a given song in the test data.[xiii] Acoustic fingerprinting technologies generally achieve much better accuracy on sound recordings.

Since at least 2012, Google has been using Content ID to detect covers on YouTube.[xiv] Content ID's accuracy on cover detection is uneven but has likely improved over time.[11] Music publishers usually choose the Content ID option to allow uploads of cover videos but not allow user monetization. (This is appropriate for musicians who cover well-known songs to get exposure or share with their friends and family.)

YouTube may not be the only content-sharing service that attempts to detect covers of musical compositions, though it's unclear. SoundCloud, for example, does not publicize the ability to detect covers.

YouTube's origins as a user-generated content service make it a sort of catchall for music. The Content ID system gives YouTube an architecture for copyright compliance that could be described as "opt-out": copyright owners have to submit their content to Content ID for it to be flagged when someone tries to upload it. If someone uploads content that isn't in the Content ID database, then YouTube makes it available without restrictions (and doesn't share ad revenue with any labels). In contrast, services like Spotify and Apple Music are "opt-in": these services won't offer content unless the copyright owner (or appointed representative, such as a digital distributor like TuneCore or Symphonic) provides it. That's why YouTube is often a "music service of last resort" for fans of old or obscure music: there's no artist or label to either provide it to "opt-in" services or flag it on YouTube.[12] Conversely, there are virtually no artists anymore who distribute their music online but keep it off YouTube—despite the royalty disparity that we'll discuss shortly.

Another important implication of YouTube's "opt-out" licensing model is that it favors globalization. Licensing is inherently national in scope; artists are signed to contracts under national laws with labels that distribute music on a country-by-country basis. But a video uploaded to YouTube has global reach by default, and not one country's but many countries' licensing entities must choose whether or not to opt out. Later in this chapter we'll see how this has led to a class of global megastars that wouldn't be as possible—or as possible as quickly—without YouTube's opt-out effect.

TikTok also started out as an opt-out service, but it has changed to more of an opt-in model. At first, TikTok enabled users to add whatever music they wanted to their videos. But once record labels started expressing copyright concerns, it made users choose from a library of music tracks, although it has been possible for users to add any music they want anyway through various hacks.

The obvious resolution to this situation was for record labels to do license deals with ByteDance so that TikTok users could legally select the labels' recorded music as backgrounds to their videos directly within the app. Sure enough, between November 2020 and February 2021 the three majors each signed licensing deals with TikTok. TikTok has also launched its own licensed subscription streaming music service, called Resso, in India, Indonesia, and Brazil; it hopes to expand the service to other countries but has been getting pushback from the major labels.[xv]

As we write this, the opt-out model is under increasing legal pressure, especially in Europe. The European Union (EU) recently enacted a law, Article 17 of the 2019 EU Copyright Directive,[xvi] that imposes responsibilities on services like YouTube to take licenses to copyrighted material before making it available to users. Just how much responsibility—and what sorts of technological schemes will satisfy rights holders under the law—remains to be seen, especially since the law must be implemented in each of 27 EU member states according to their national copyright laws. But most commentators believe that it will result in services like YouTube being required to take more aggressive steps to block copyrighted content from being uploaded by third parties without permission.[xvii]

And in the United States, Congress is considering reforming the DMCA, in part according to recommendations from the Copyright Office after a multiyear study, which concluded that the DMCA, over twenty years of precedents set by litigations, has become tilted too far in favor of online service providers.[xviii]

One of the main provisions that copyright holders have been asking for in DMCA reform legislation is something they call "notice and staydown." The problem that copyright owners have with "notice and takedown" is that once you send a DMCA notice to have content removed, the same content can be reposted shortly afterward—a phenomenon that has come to be known as the "Whac-a-Mole" problem.[13] "Notice and staydown" is a proposed scheme in which once a copyright owner asks a service to take a work down, it should block all future attempts to upload the same work. While it's not clear how "notice and staydown" could be implemented as a practical matter,[14] it would have a huge effect on the content that services like YouTube can offer and the terms under which they offer it: it would move YouTube closer to an "opt-in" model while still offering content that no one is around to claim or wants to bother claiming.[15]

The effects of Article 17 in Europe could end up being similar, but it's too early to tell. At this writing, two US senators have introduced a bill called the Strengthening Measures to Advance Rights Technologies (SMART) Copyright Act that would update the DMCA by empowering the Copyright Office to impose requirements for technologies such as fingerprint-based filtering on user-uploaded content services. But the bill's future is uncertain, as it has no public support from the tech industry.

Finally, there is another copyright-related aspect of digital video services—whether opt-in or opt-out—that could change the dynamics of the music industry: synch licensing.

We first saw synch licensing in Chapter 6 in the context of music videos on television and in movies. As music distribution shifts toward video services like YouTube, TikTok, and all the live streaming services, synch licensing is becoming associated with an increasingly large portion of music usage. For Internet music videos, separate synch licenses are potentially necessary for both sound recordings and musical compositions. Synch licenses for the former are typically negotiated as part of agreements with labels.

Synch licenses for compositions are another matter. Recall from Chapter 9 that interactive streaming requires performance and mechanical licenses for compositions. Both of these are processed through collective licensing agencies, and both are typically subject to blanket licenses. This means that streaming music services need have no direct involvement with music publishers for licensing: they can pay performance royalties to performance rights organizations (PROs) like ASCAP and BMI, and they can pay fees to the Mechanical Licensing Collective (MLC) for mechanicals.

But composition synch licenses require negotiation with music publishers individually. There are no blanket licenses, no statutory rates, and few consensus royalty rates for synch. There are also no centralized licensing hubs or collective management organizations for synch licensing[16]—despite various startups' attempts to create them. This is at least in part because music publishers see synch as their last available point of control over licensing: they can determine whether each song gets licensed at all, to what services, for what video content, and at what rates.

Music publishers have long complained about having to play second fiddle[17] to record labels in digital licensing because they have been relegated to distant relationships with service providers. They will undoubtedly rely on synch licensing as a chance to improve their leverage, and this could affect the label-versus-publisher dynamics of the industry. However, because most of these newer video services are platforms for user-uploaded content, they are likely to be in for years of fighting with publishers over questions of copyright liability for service providers that are analogous to those that YouTube and Veoh faced.

After Warner Music made its deal with YouTube in September 2006, several years elapsed before YouTube garnered full-catalog licenses from all of the major labels. As we mentioned, the other majors made "whitelist" deals with YouTube later during the ensuing year that only involved their own music videos and did not cover user-uploaded content. Yet once YouTube had implemented Content ID, most record labels began registering their content in the system and received ad revenue shares. In other words, the labels may have had what lawyers call implied licenses even if they didn't have actual license agreements with YouTube.

YouTube eventually achieved formal license agreements with all of the major labels (as well as thousands of indie labels), which covered user uploads as well as terms other than royalty payments. The terms of these agreements are confidential, and in most cases it's not publicly known when those agreements were signed. But it's clear that by the time Spotify launched in the United States in July 2011, YouTube also had licenses covering virtually full catalogs from all the major labels.[18]

As YouTube continued to grow, some of the major labels got together in a joint venture to create a service called Vevo, which they called "Hulu for music videos" (referring to the video streaming service Hulu and its joint ownership by multiple TV networks). In reaction to their experience with MTV, the labels wanted to build a video service featuring their own content that they could control. The project started at UMG; UMG brought

Sony and EMI on board. They originally thought of building a standalone service to compete with YouTube—or at least acting like they were going to do that in hopes of gaining negotiating leverage against Google.[xix] But the service ended up being structured as a joint venture with Google. It would be a mechanism for feeding videos to and featuring them on YouTube, as well as showing them on a Vevo website, mobile apps, and embedded web players.

Vevo launched in December 2008. All of the majors except Warner Music Group (WMG) were involved; WMG chose to create its own channel on YouTube and to enter into a partnership with MTV on MTV.com. The labels controlled the content that was available on the Vevo website and mobile apps, which were also used as vehicles for sales of merch and music downloads on iTunes and Amazon Music. The same videos appeared on YouTube with a small Vevo logo on them. Vevo was mainly about negotiating higher ad rates as a single entity representing "premium music" versus the rates that each label or artist could get individually.

The strategy was a bit difficult to explain in an elevator pitch, but it worked. A year after its launch, Vevo was the most-visited online network in comScore's "Entertainment—Music" category, with over 35 million viewers in December 2009,[xx] though MTV had overtaken it by summer 2010.[xxi]

WMG finally contributed its videos to Vevo in 2016. By then, the labels had made renewed plans to build it out as a separate destination and a "life-style brand." To the extent the latter plans materialized, they did so as Vevo channels on the leading Internet TV platforms—Roku, Apple TV, Amazon Fire TV, and so on. These channels are all video equivalents of Internet radio stations: they are music video playlists focused on genres, moods, etc., with limited "skip" functions and ad breaks—or, for paying subscribers, no ads and unlimited skips. Otherwise, Vevo still distributes its videos on YouTube but no longer operates its own website (other than for corporate purposes) or mobile apps.

At this writing Vevo claims over half a million videos with 1.5 billion hours viewed per month.[xxii] In comparison, YouTube announced—back in early 2017—that it had surpassed a billion hours viewed *per day*,[xxiii] or about 20 times the viewership of Vevo. Data from 2019 shows that although the proportion of videos on YouTube in the music category has shrunk to 5 percent, 22 percent of video *views* on YouTube are of music videos.[xxiv] This means that YouTube had more than four times the current viewership of Vevo for music five years ago. YouTube has been the largest platform—video or otherwise—for music, by a wide margin, for several years.

Even so, YouTube's fit in the music ecosystem has been uncomfortable. As we'll explain later in this chapter, YouTube has had trouble building a compelling user experience for music fans. And many label executives have never been thrilled with the idea of an all-free, all-ad-supported music service, even leaving aside the question of royalty payments (which we'll also discuss later).

In addition, the YouTube user experience does not inherently funnel users toward big releases as that of Spotify and its ilk. For example, YouTube has no equivalent of Spotify's editorial playlists such as Rap Caviar; nor does Spotify's concept of influencer users with massively popular playlists have a real equivalent on YouTube. Far more people use YouTube for music listening than they use Spotify or Pandora, but the play counts of many hit songs on YouTube are proportionally lower than those on the other services. For example, Billie Eilish hits such as "bad guy" and "when the party's over" have gotten about two-thirds the number of plays on YouTube as they've had on Spotify; Drake's, Ariana Grande's, and Taylor Swift's numbers are similar.

YouTube has also had a challenging relationship with other outposts of the Google empire (though this is not at all unusual for large technology companies that have grown by acquisition). This has particularly been true with respect to the Android division. Google introduced the Android operating system for mobile devices in November 2007, a year after it acquired YouTube and just a few months after Apple launched the first iPhone. The first Android devices came out a year later. The idea of Android was essentially to do for smartphones and tablets what Microsoft did for PCs with Windows: create an operating system that would run on devices from a wide variety of manufacturers, as opposed to Apple's combined proprietary device and operating system offerings.

To compete with the Apple iPhone (and eventually the iPad), Google launched a set of apps and services for Android devices that were analogous to those available on Apple devices, such as iTunes, which by 2008 was offering downloaded movies and TV shows as well as music, and iBooks (now Apple Books), an e-book service launched with the iPad in 2010. Google launched a series of analogous apps under the banner of Google Play, its Android app store: Google Play Music, Google Play Movies and TV, and Google Play Books.

Google launched Google Play Music in 2011 as an iTunes-style paid download plus Internet radio service. In 2013 it launched Google Play Music All Access, an interactive streaming service to compete with Spotify. (It would be another two years until Apple launched Apple Music, its interactive streaming service.)

Google Play Music All Access was a much better-organized music listening experience than YouTube, but it didn't make much impact on the market. Google treated Google Play Music as more of a "checklist item" for its Android ecosystem than as a marquee offering, as Apple did with iTunes or Spotify did with its service; it devoted far fewer resources to design and marketing. Its listenership in 2015 was less than half that of Spotify and a smaller percentage of that of Pandora and iHeartRadio.[xxv]

YouTube and Google Play Music operated in separate silos of a large and fast-growing company. Despite YouTube's drawbacks as a music experience—and undoubtedly because it's free—YouTube's popularity as a music service always vastly eclipsed that of Google Play Music. At the same time, the major labels had been putting pressure on Google to take steps to steer users toward the paid subscription service, just as they have done with Spotify.

Google began a series of attempts at integrating the two services in 2014. This resulted in a series of confusing combinations of branding and technical features over a period of six years. The first try was YouTube Music Key, which launched in late 2014. For a $10 per month subscription, YouTube users got ad-free music videos and the ability to play the app in the background and save videos for offline playing. Google Play Music still operated independently, but its subscribers eventually got access to YouTube Music Key as well. Then in 2015, YouTube replaced Music Key with YouTube Red, which provided ad-free access to all videos, not just music, for the same $10 per month price. None of this was very successful: not only was the branding confusing but some labels refused to license music into the service.

Google tried again in 2018. By that point, interactive streaming had become the largest part of the music industry by revenue, and Amazon had emerged as a fast-rising competitor with Amazon Music. Google launched YouTube Music as a successor to Music Key. (It also launched YouTube Premium as a successor to YouTube Red at a higher subscription price. More branding confusion.) YouTube Music started out essentially as a paid-subscription, ad-free version of YouTube that attempted to impose some music-oriented order on the vast YouTube chaos, as we'll discuss shortly. Google took the final step in late 2020—nine years after the launch of Google Play Music—by transitioning its subscribers to YouTube Music and phasing Google Play Music out entirely.

The strategy finally appears to be working; YouTube Music is rising in pop-ularity faster than any of the previous attempts at paid subscription services did. For example, the 2022 Infinite Dial research study from Edison Research and Triton Digital shows YouTube Music leaping past iHeartRadio, Apple Music, and Amazon Music in monthly listenership. Only Spotify is more popular, at least in the United States.[xxvi]

The other major streaming music platforms have been adding video features recently. Spotify introduced Spotify Canvas in late 2019 as a way for artists to submit short video loops that play on artists' pages. In October 2020, Apple launched Apple Music TV, a channel on its Apple TV plat-form and mobile apps. Apple Music TV is a curated live broadcast stream of music videos and related content, such as artist interviews; it has more to do with differentiating Apple TV from competitors such as Roku and Amazon Fire TV than with the Apple Music service. Shortly after Apple Music TV's launch, Amazon began adding music videos to Amazon Music Unlimited, its paid subscription service.

And then there's Facebook. Facebook became the dominant social net-work in the late 2000s, overtaking the floundering MySpace. MySpace had focused heavily on music: in its mid-2000s heyday, it helped countless artists find and engage with fans. MySpace had actually launched the first free ad-based interactive streaming music service to be fully licensed by the major labels, the unsuccessful MySpace Music, back in 2008.

But Facebook did not focus on music in 2008. Facebook rose at a time when interactive streaming was promising but still a small market with many competitors. Facebook's initial strategy was not to launch its own music service but to integrate with everyone else's. It launched this strategy in 2011—the same year in which Spotify launched in the United States and YouTube achieved full label licensing. For example, if you integrated your Rhapsody account with Facebook, an item would appear on your Facebook page every time you played a song on Rhapsody so that your Facebook friends could see what you were listening to. It was a publicity bonanza for interactive streaming that likely helped bring about its "hockey stick" growth trajectory in the ensuing years.

Yet after several years of increasing engagement and Internet bandwidth, users began to post their own content with music in it to Facebook. Facebook had implemented a copyright filtering system using Audible Magic; more and more users experienced takedowns and got frustrated. After sev-eral years of studied neutrality, Facebook began to hire experienced music licensing professionals and engage with record labels and music publishers. Yet it wasn't obvious how Facebook—by that time a sprawling behemoth—should enter the world of licensed music services.

Video was where the opportunities for growth and differentiation were by the mid-2010s, so most of Facebook's music-licensing activity has been related to video content. In recent years, it has added a number of music video features, most of which are reactive to features already on YouTube or TikTok. Facebook also launched its own content identification technology, Facebook Rights Manager, in 2016 to supplement its Audible Magic implementation.

Facebook has launched a series of video features since then. It launched a streaming video service called Facebook Watch in August 2017. Then starting later that year with Universal Music Group, Facebook signed a series of deals with major and indie labels and music publishers to license the use of music in "social experiences" (user-uploaded content including video) on all of its platforms including Instagram and Oculus in addition to Facebook itself. In June 2018, it introduced Lip Synch Live, an obvious competitor to TikTok and Musical.ly. In August 2020 it released a feature that automatically adds music videos to artists' pages (unless they opt out)—in other words, a feature for turning Facebook's vast agglomeration of artists' pages into competition for YouTube. It also added a dedicated music section on Facebook Watch. And in September 2021, it launched Reels on Facebook, an offshoot of the similarly named service on Instagram.

YouTube's music licensing works similarly to interactive streaming services like Spotify and Apple Music, though YouTube has additional licensing wrinkles because it's a video service and because it accepts user-contributed content. Because it's a user-contributed content service, YouTube analyzes each video clip to see what copyrighted work it contains (if any) so that the correct rights holders get paid. As we discussed earlier, the Content ID system does the analysis. If a user uploads a file that Content ID matches with a sound recording, YouTube uses data in the Content ID database to help it determine whom to pay.

How do YouTube's royalty payouts to labels and artists compare to other interactive streaming services such as Apple Music and Spotify? It has been accused of paying royalties that are considerably lower than those services, which we discussed in Chapter 9. The music industry has adopted a phrase to describe this difference: "value gap."

"Value gap" originated in a 2015 report from the International Federation of the Phonographic Industry (IFPI), which then published a more detailed analysis in 2017.[xxvii] According to IFPI, the value gap is the difference between the royalties that content-sharing services pay to music creators and the royalties that they earn from paid subscription services. IFPI asserts that the value gap is the result of laws such as the DMCA that service providers rely on to avoid having to make licensing deals with rights holders before launching their services.[19]

YouTube, as the biggest music service in the world, was the service that IFPI has particularly called out here. As we saw earlier in this chapter, YouTube essentially backed its way into license agreements with record labels and music publishers by hosting user-uploaded content and avoiding liability in the courts through a DMCA safe harbor defense (and equivalents in other countries).

YouTube's position was that it had no legal *obligation* to monitor itself for infringing content uploaded by users, yet it was *willing* to identify user-uploaded content so that it could earn higher ad revenue by targeting ads to that content. To do that, YouTube needed record labels' help: to identify uploaded music, labels had to feed YouTube their content for use in its fingerprinting engine. So it was willing to share that incremental ad revenue with the labels. That was the crux of YouTube's original deal with Warner Music Group in 2006, which became the prototype for its other label deals.

This sounds like it would be a win-win for YouTube and the labels—but for two factors. First, from the labels' perspective, the resulting ad revenue has been less than YouTube would have to pay if the royalty rates were determined on the basis of "opt-in" licensing. The music industry's view is that YouTube's claims that it doesn't really have to do any content identification enable it to offer royalty payments on a "take it or leave it" basis; and consequently YouTube ends up paying lower royalties compared to "opt-in" music services. Moreover, because YouTube has the biggest music audience in the world, this drags down the royalty payments that labels can negotiate with other music services.

The other factor that mitigates the win-win aspect of the agreement for labels is that labels get less revenue share for user-uploaded videos than for their "official" videos—since, in many cases, a chunk of ad revenue for user-uploaded videos goes to the users. This puts the onus onto labels to create their own videos and upload them quickly. And that weighs against the original advantage of YouTube over MTV that we discussed at the beginning of this chapter: that labels can achieve scale economies in video production by offloading it to users.

For example, the biggest category of user-uploaded music videos in the early days of YouTube was lyric videos. These typically consisted of still images or plain backgrounds with the text of song lyrics on them. These were easy to produce and provided a service to users, so they became quite popular, especially when—as was often the case—they were among the first videos of songs to be posted.[20] A cottage industry of fast (and presumably automated) lyric video producers emerged. The labels eventually responded with official lyric videos, which tend to be more lavishly produced than user-contributed lyric videos, especially for big-name artists; yet these are still the exception rather than the rule.

The major labels' frustrations about the disparity in royalty payouts between YouTube and other services actually dates back much further than the IFPI's "value gap" argument: it dates back to 2008, when Warner Music Group was negotiating a renewal of its original license agreement with YouTube. The parties failed to reach terms, so in December 2008, WMG pulled its catalog from YouTube. Although the main digital music royalty benchmark at that time was iTunes downloads, WMG found that its ad revenue shares from YouTube even fell short of other ad-based online music services of the time, such as AOL Music and MySpace Music.[xxviii] The other major labels did not join in the boycott, however, and WMG negotiated a new deal with YouTube in September 2009.

Although music services' agreements with labels are confidential, various exposés over the years, based on artists voluntarily disclosing their royalty payments, have shown much lower royalty rates from YouTube than from opt-in streaming services. For example, a story published in the *Guardian* in Britain in 2015 indicated that an artist would have to get almost four times the number of plays on YouTube as on Spotify or Deezer to earn the same royalties, and almost ten times the number of plays on Beats Music (the precursor to Apple Music).[xxix] IFPI's value gap analysis in 2017 estimated that the worldwide music industry earns revenue per user from YouTube that is less than a twentieth of revenue per user from Spotify.[21]

In addition to the royalty rates themselves, YouTube's ad-based royalty structure makes it more difficult for labels to negotiate the kinds of rate structures they would like. The labels have evolved Byzantine rate structures with the opt-in services that depend on locations of users, minimum per-user fees, fan engagement metrics, the size of the label, stature of the artist, time of year, and other factors. If the revenue to be shared with a label starts with ad revenue earned from what could be several videos containing the same song submitted by users from anywhere in the world, in addition to official videos, labels have less control over the rate structure. In a paradoxical way, this is analogous to the labels' frustration with iTunes during the download era, when Steve Jobs insisted on fixing prices at 99 cents per track and wouldn't allow for variable pricing, as we saw in Chapter 8. Yet it's important to note that the foregoing only applies to "regular" YouTube and that royalty payouts for paying YouTube Music subscribers are in the same ballpark as Spotify.[xxx]

The music industry's approach to closing the value gap has been focused on changing laws so that services like YouTube are obligated to keep copyrighted material off their networks unless they have licenses for it, as we discussed earlier in this chapter. That's the intent behind the Article 17 copyright reform in Europe, which the media industry pushed for precisely because of the value gap. (Note that Europe's biggest native video-sharing service, DailyMotion of France, has long observed this approach.) It's also one of the media industry's main objectives in reforming the DMCA in the United States.

The value gap discussion pertains to all user-contributed content services, including audio-oriented services like SoundCloud. The negotiations that led up to Article 17 led it to include several exemptions for content-sharing services that weren't in the media industry's cross-hairs, such as personal cloud storage services and open-source software repositories. But the spotlight has always been on YouTube because of its enormous audience; so YouTube should serve as the yardstick for the music industry's efforts to address the value gap for the foreseeable future—although TikTok is also starting to raise concerns over royalty payments as it continues its meteoric growth.[xxxi] As is the case with the labels' deals with other audio streaming services, TikTok's royalty rates are confidential and vary according to several factors. The majors are even more dissatisfied with their payouts than they are with YouTube and have been pushing for higher royalties in contract renewal negotiations.[xxxii]

Consumers in the early 2010s were finally beginning to understand the value of interactive streaming, even though, as we've seen, it had been available with major label licensed music since 2002. Two distinct models of interactive streaming became popular. One is the paid-subscription, opt-in licensing model that provides a highly curated experience for music fans, as provided by Spotify, Apple Music, Amazon Music Unlimited, Deezer, and so on. The other is the YouTube model, based on user-uploaded content, free access, ad revenue, and opt-out licensing.

These two models lead to different consumer experiences. YouTube's barriers to consumer adoption are virtually nonexistent: you don't even need to register to use it, and free unregistered users have access to the full catalog with no restrictions. Music is available on YouTube that can't be found on the opt-in services, including old and rare music as well as music from all over the world.

On the other hand, it's fundamentally impossible—or at least extremely difficult—to create a music experience on YouTube that's as well curated, rich with information, and easy to navigate as in services like Spotify and Apple Music. The most obvious problem is that YouTube isn't just a music service; music exists on YouTube in a vast ocean of content, most of which has nothing to do with music. But even if YouTube were somehow limited to music videos only (whatever that means), it would still have an enormous problem with one ingredient that is absolutely essential in offering a curated music experience: metadata.

We've discussed metadata elsewhere in this book, but it's especially crucial to YouTube's challenges in building a successful music service. The simplest way to define metadata is as "data about data." In the music context, metadata includes basic factual information about recorded tracks such as artist, title, label, length, and release date, as well as more detailed information such as musician and producer credits. It also includes descriptive information such as genre, tempo, mood, and so on. A single music track can have hundreds of items of metadata associated with it.

Curation, search, navigation, and discovery are simply impossible for a music service without metadata that is sufficiently detailed, consistent, accurate, and up to date. Labels supply reasonable-quality metadata to opt-in services, and those services augment that with carefully maintained metadata that they create themselves or get from commercial third parties. But with user-uploaded content, the vast majority of metadata is nonexistent, minimal, inconsistent, or just plain wrong.

YouTube is considerably less compelling than the other services if you want to search and browse through music. It relies on artists to create and maintain channels, which we'll talk about later, but YouTube channels are inconsistent from one artist to another and typically limited in information. For example, channels enable artists to post links to other artists' channels to show relationships among them. But many artists don't use this feature, and even if they do, one artist's view of their relationships with other artists is not the same as that of the neutral and knowledgeable curators who maintain Spotify's "Fans Also Like" and similar features on the other opt-in services.

YouTube's search results are also not particularly geared toward music, though they do improve over time as YouTube gets more experience with your preferences and tastes. The results can include anything that matches the keywords you type in. For example, try typing "eagles" or "chicago" or "ice cube"—or "trap" or "drill" or "metal"—into YouTube's search box.[22] YouTube supports playlists, but they are general video playlists, not music playlists. Of course, some people like the potential for serendipity, but as a *musical* user experience, YouTube is kind of a mess.

In contrast, the opt-in services use metadata provided by labels, distributors, and third parties that enables a quality user experience. Each of these services has a "style guide" for label-submitted metadata as well as resources for cleaning it up. They have editorial staff to create experiences around music genres, including playlists, artist pages, and recommendations.[23] And it's not just a question of budget for editorial staff: deploying editorial staff to deal with a constant torrent of randomness from user uploads on YouTube is tantamount to staving off a tsunami with teaspoons.

As a result, YouTube and the opt-in services have pulled in different audiences, although they certainly overlap. Research from IFPI over the past several years shows that the percentage of consumers' streaming music listening through video services—mostly but not entirely YouTube—has declined gradually over the past several years as subscribership to services like Spotify (not to mention video services like Netflix) has grown. And as we saw in the previous chapter, there is also plenty of evidence that free tastes, such as on YouTube or Spotify's free tier, have led to paid subscriptions. In other words, music fans are seeing value in the curated experiences that the opt-in services can offer but YouTube cannot.

That, together with the increased revenue from subscriptions compared to advertising (not to mention licensing pressure from record labels), most likely induced Google to find a way to provide YouTube users with a smoother path to paid subscriptions and keep them within the Google eco-system rather than losing them to Spotify, Apple, Amazon, or Deezer.

As we mentioned, the result of this strategy was YouTube Music, which launched in 2018. Google's approach to creating YouTube Music was typically "Googley": it decided to rely on advanced technology rather than humans. Over time, YouTube was able to fuse the oceans of user-contributed content with the data that labels feed to Google Play Music to produce an experience that was music-first rather than video-first and offered a fair approximation to the highly curated experiences of Spotify and other services. It did so by using artificial intelligence (AI) and machine learning (ML) techniques—which we'll discuss further in Chapter 11—to normalize, clean, and wrangle the metadata. The user experience was a bit rough at first, but after a couple of years, it got closer to that of Spotify or Apple Music in terms of the accuracy and richness of the metadata.[24]

Interestingly, YouTube Music does not offer user-generated playlists or any other social features from the main YouTube app, though it does offer videos. It is an uncluttered, almost "purist" music experience, aesthetically more in keeping with Google's search engine than with YouTube itself.

While Google labors to create a true music app out of YouTube, its new competition is going, to some extent, in the opposite direction. TikTok, as we discussed, isn't really a music app—it is a social networking app that uses a lot of music. It uses music in two distinct ways: users take videos of them-selves (often dancing) that use music; or users who are musical artists upload short clips of their own music. An increasing number of established artists have their own TikTok feeds. And while more and more of those artists are posting short clips of their own as promotion for full-length tracks (whether on TikTok itself or elsewhere),[xxxiii] the bulk of activity for major artists on TikTok currently still consists of users posting clips containing their music.

And those users aren't necessarily posting clips with current music: TikTok has proven to be a potent way of revitalizing back catalog without involve-ment from artists or labels. One example of this was the astonishing resur-rection in September 2020 of Fleetwood Mac's 1977 hit "Dreams" in a TikTok skateboarding video by user Nathan Apodaca (a.k.a. Dogg Face). The clip went viral, which led to millions of streams of the song, thousands of paid downloads, and the song reentering the Billboard Hot 100. Two members of Fleetwood Mac even recreated the video themselves.[xxxiv]

But the result of such phenomena on TikTok is exposure and fame for the user at least as much as for the musical artist.[25] Some users try to convert a major artist's following into a following for themselves by posting videos with that artist's music and even using the artist's name in their accounts (for example, there are account names such as the.real.ladygaga, planet_doja_cat, and taylorswifttoday, which list their user names respectively as "Lady Gaga," "DOJA CAT," and "Taylor Swift"), although artists can apply for TikTok's identity verification which shows blue check marks by their names, and artists have other ways of promoting their music on the app. In general, the user experience on TikTok is of following users, not musical artists. This puts users in a more influential position than on YouTube or Spotify. Artist and label marketing teams are increasingly seeking out TikTok influencers to get them to post video about their artists, just as PR firms pay Instagram and Twitter influencers to post about consumer products, sometimes even offering them sneak previews of new releases before they drop.[xxxv]

With one exception that we'll talk about shortly, YouTube's influence on musical creative output has not been proportional to its user base. That's most likely because, as we've seen, Spotify and its ilk have user experiences that funnel listeners more toward big-label releases than YouTube does, resulting in proportionally lower play counts for those artists on YouTube. That, together with YouTube's significantly lower royalty payouts, means that artists and labels may be generally less interested in creating music "for YouTube" than for the opt-in music services.

Early YouTube successes such as OK Go and the SNL "Lazy Sunday" video fed the story that YouTube, like p2p and MP3s before it (see Chapter 8), was going to disintermediate labels and make it possible for anyone to be a star. As with digital downloads, the occasional exception does not prove the rule. Instead, and indeed as usual with these technologies, early exceptions have given way to instances where either the same old intermediaries figure out how to make the system work for their own purposes or new intermediaries are established.

YouTube has proven most useful to artist managers and label A&R people as a place to discover talent, though that talent still relies on those intermediaries to become successful. There has hardly ever been such a thing as a label signing a new artist and *then* the artist goes viral on YouTube; it's the other way around. There is no "formula" for making a music video that goes viral on YouTube, but as we'll see, labels and managers do various things to increase the odds.

Perhaps the archetypal example of this was the Canadian megastar Justin Bieber, who was "discovered" on YouTube in 2008 by powerhouse artist manager Scooter Braun. Braun got Bieber signed to Island Records later that year; the rest is history. Both Bieber and Braun will figure into the stories of subsequent YouTube sensations, as we'll also see.

Another example was a song sung in 2011 by a 13-year-old girl from Southern California. Her parents paid $4,000 to a small label in LA to write a song for her, make a recording of her singing it (with a heaping helping of Auto-Tune), and make a video of the recording for YouTube. The video went viral, thanks largely to activity on Twitter; and most of the reaction was negative ("worst song of all time"; "worst video ever made"). That did not stop Rebecca Black's song "Friday" from garnering 167 million views on YouTube during its first month, leading to an RIAA Gold certification and appearances on MTV, a Katy Perry video, and elsewhere. Black was exceptional in that she did not sign to a major label, but this was primarily because she was tied to a contract with the small label and could not get out of the contract despite years of legal wrangling.

But then those examples gave way to artists who were "discovered" on YouTube but were actually already stars elsewhere. This has been particularly true for artists from one country getting exposed in other countries with extreme rapidity, due to YouTube's global and opt-out architecture, as we discussed earlier in this chapter.

The first major instance of this came in 2012. As much as "Friday" was the pop-culture sensation of 2011, it was nothing compared to the video of a short, chubby South Korean rapper that was released the following year. Psy's "Gangnam Style" peaked at no. 2 on the Billboard Hot 100 and topped the charts in more than 30 other countries. By the end of 2012, it had become the first video to exceed a billion views on YouTube, a record it held for an incredible four years and seven months until it was surpassed by "See You Again" by rapper Wiz Kalifa. Even today it is the eleventh most viewed video of all time on YouTube.

To American fans, "Gangnam Style" seemed to come out of nowhere. Researchers analyzed its explosive growth on YouTube and found that much of its early spread was due, once again, to Twitter activity. But the reality was something different. "Gangnam Style" was hardly a fluke viral hit by an unknown independent artist from an "exotic" land. Instead, Psy was merely the first K-pop artist to break in the United States.

K-pop was, and is, a movement by a handful of integrated South Korean music companies—which run artist management, labels, music publishing, concert promotion, event production, merchandizing, and so on—to grow Korean pop music into a global phenomenon, an export for the country to go along with its massive exports of consumer electronics. K-pop began in the 1990s and expanded with help from the South Korean government, which was acting to coordinate the expansion of technology and content industries—in contradistinction to the United States where the two industries have often been at loggerheads. By 2012, K-pop had become a juggernaut not only in South Korea but in much of the Asia-Pacific region (Japan, China, etc.) and beyond. The United States was one of the last markets on Earth for K-pop to conquer, yet its conquest was foreordained. And K-pop was video-friendly by design.

Although Psy was not one of the top K-pop artists in Asian markets, he had recorded six albums on one of the handful of dominant K-pop labels (YG Entertainment), had won various awards, and had toured stadiums throughout the region by the time "Gangnam Style" was released. "Gangnam Style" paved the way for K-pop supergroups like BTS and Blackpink, who now routinely occupy high positions in the US pop charts.

Another example of an artist who exploded on YouTube but was already an up-and-coming star and benefited from the existing system also emerged in 2012: Canada's Carly Rae Jepsen. Justin Bieber heard Jepsen's "Call Me Maybe" on the radio in December 2011 while in his native country—where regulations require 40 percent of all music programmed on the radio to be by Canadians. Bieber tweeted about it; the song became a no. 1 hit and was the no. 2 song of 2012 (behind Gotye's "Someone That I Used to Know"). But once again, Jepsen hardly came out of nowhere: she had already finished in third place on Canadian Idol in 2007 and had garnered multiple Canadian Gold records. And her video went viral on YouTube in part because two existing superstars of the American label system—Bieber and his then-girlfriend Selena Gomez—appeared in it. Jepsen signed to Scooter Braun's SchoolBoy Records soon after "Call Me Maybe" became a YouTube sensation.

But the biggest example of YouTube's ability to convert regional into global stars so far has been "Despacito" ("Slowly"), by the Puerto Rican star Luis Fonsi featuring the rapper Daddy Yankee. The song was released in January 2017; a remix featuring Bieber (singing in Spanish) followed three months later. The song had peaked at no. 44 on the *Billboard* Hot 100, but the Bieber remix propelled Fonsi's original version to no. 1. Beyond the United States, the song (counting both versions) topped the charts in a total of 47 countries. As evidence of YouTube's vital role in creating that global mega-stardom: unlike the stars mentioned previously whose play counts on Spotify are greater than on YouTube, "Despacito" has, at this time of writing, gotten 1.6 billion plays on Spotify but over 8 billion views on YouTube. It was the most-viewed video on YouTube of all time for three years until it was unseated in November 2020 by the "Baby Shark" video—another product of South Korea, though not one associated with K-pop.

The appearances of Bieber on Jepsen's video and on Fonsi's remix were also examples of the most important way that Google and YouTube changed pop music creatively: artist collaborations, or collabs for short. While there are many artistically valid reasons for artists to collaborate with each other (or for managers or labels to have them collaborate), there are two reasons that have little to do with creativity. One is search engine optimization. A record with multiple artists is more likely to show up on more search results. This trend started in connection with Google searches for records in the early 2000s, but it increased once Google acquired YouTube in 2006 and applied its search-engine prowess to the service; music discovery on YouTube is based much more on search than it is on other services. The other reason is playlists: as we saw in the previous chapters, collabs tend to increase the number of playlists that will include a given track.

Many collabs involve rappers making guest appearances on pop records and being credited in the song title as "featuring" (or "feat."), so that both artists are more likely to show up in search results. This has not only fostered the crossover of audiences between pop and hip-hop but also undoubtedly helped usher in the present era where the two overlap almost entirely—that is, hip-hop *is* mainstream pop.

The first instance of credited featured rappers was in the new jack swing style that developed in the late 1980s as a fusion of hip-hop and R&B. "She Ain't Worth It," a 1990 hit by the Hawaiian star Glenn Medeiros, featured a rap from Bobby Brown. But other uncredited examples date back even further: the first was Grandmaster Melle Mel's opening rap to Chaka Kahn's Prince-penned hit "I Feel for You" in 1984.[xxxvi] Collabs and featured rappers on pop hits have become extremely common since then. As a measure of just how common, between a quarter and a half of the songs on the *Billboard* Hot 100 around this time of writing are pop songs with "featured" drop-ins (mostly rappers), multiartist collabs, or both.

Today most of the top music videos on YouTube are by major-label artists. At this writing, almost all of the top 10 music videos on the US YouTube chart tend to be on labels owned by one of the Big Three. As mentioned earlier in this chapter, labels and artists usually put up "official" videos for their releases; the vast majority of label releases today have official videos.

YouTube Channels enable artists to create more personalized presences there than on services like Spotify. Channels have evolved over time and currently include Twitter-like social media posts, merch stores, "about the artist" pages, recommended channels, and, of course, videos and playlists. Many artists post videos on their channels that aren't just music videos. For example, Cardi B's channel currently features videos of interviews, TV appearances, and so on; and her store sells T-shirts and jewelry. Lady Gaga's channel currently has content touting her makeup line and her charitable foundation, while her store sells vinyl, CDs, and cassettes.

As for TikTok, it is influencing artists' creative processes in numerous ways as its user base continues to grow. TikTok treats audio clips somewhat like hashtags:[26] it lumps videos together if they use the same audio, and it highlights trending audio clips for users. You can select an option to create a video with the same audio as the clip you're watching. Users can thus boost the popularity of their videos by choosing trending audio to go with them. This leads to a virtuous cycle that can give certain audio clips outsized popularity very quickly.

This has led artists to consider ways to create TikTok-friendly content. Some artists, as we mentioned earlier in this chapter, are crafting brief promotional videos of their songs to become trending audio clips on TikTok—sometimes because labels are requiring them to do so.[xxxvii] Short clips of songs can go viral on TikTok and lead the full-length songs to become hits. For example, a short clip containing the hook from the song "Bad Habit" by R&B singer/guitarist Steve Lacy[27] appeared in almost half a million TikTok videos on its way to reaching no. 1 on the *Billboard* Hot 100; the audience at a Lacy concert in October 2022 demonstrated that they didn't know the words to the song beyond those in the viral clip when they stopped singing along at the end of the lyrics that appeared in the clip. Another trend in this vein has been to create sped-up remixes of songs made for TikTok—which are also helping to push the songs up the charts.[xxxviii] And, consistent with the notion that TikTok is at heart a social network, pop/rock artist Gayle wrote the song "abcdefu," nominated for a Song of the Year Grammy in 2023, in response to a video that she posted on TikTok in which she asked for song ideas to be posted in the comments.

The next logical step is for artists to create musical short-form content specifically for TikTok (and/or YouTube Shorts, and/or Reels on Facebook or Instagram). Given that most TikTok videos are shorter than the 20–25-second average length of a pop song's chorus,[xxxix] that could lead to changes in pop song structures in the near future: choruses could shorten, or songwriters could craft songs that contain complete hooks within their opening seconds. Meanwhile, one sign of TikTok's movement away from the record label system is that its biggest current homegrown music stars (based on earnings), such as Bella Poarch, Dixie D'Amelio, and Loren Gray, have yet to make a dent in the Billboard charts.

Conclusion

Video has become an increasingly large part of music consumption as it shifts to new video services like TikTok and the live streaming platforms, and as the major social networks embrace music videos. At the same time, paid subscription services are also on the rise; and ironically, the growth in paid subscriptions has little to do with video. Even YouTube Music emphasizes audio and pushes video somewhat into the background. And services like Spotify, Apple Music, and Amazon Music use video in very limited ways.

The music industry has yet to encounter a music video service that large numbers of users will pay for directly. The sales of individual music video products (such as DVDs and VHS tapes) that we mentioned at the beginning of this chapter peaked in the mid-2000s—just before YouTube launched. They accounted for 5 percent of total industry revenue at that time and have decreased ever since; revenue from individual music videos is even more negligible now than vinyl was at its 2006 nadir. The paid subscription music video services that exist today have user bases that are tiny compared to paid subscription music (audio) services. Probably the largest is Qello Concerts, owned by the Canadian Vevo competitor Stingray; Qello's paying subscriber base was 70,000 in 2018,[xl] three orders of magnitude smaller than Spotify. Others serve niche markets, such as the classical-focused Medici.tv (owned by the French media group Les Echos-Le Parisien), with 20,000 subscribers as of 2020.[xli]

It is not as if there is no precedent for consumers paying for video services; users have paid for cable TV for decades and are now paying for the likes of

Netflix, Hulu, and Disney+ by the tens of millions. But the window of opportunity to charge mass-market consumers for *music* videos may be closed forever.

At the same time, the newer music video services are engaging hundreds of millions of users in ways that are drifting further and further away from the music itself. YouTube started out with user-contributed videos, but the much smaller number of artists' official videos now get the vast majority of views. But now TikTok is primarily about users' dances and lip-syncs; artists and labels have yet to find ways to establish the same primacy on these services as they did on YouTube.

In other words, from the artists' and labels' perspectives, audio services still rule. And a new breed of technologies and services is putting the focus back on audio, as we'll see in the next chapter.

11

Artificial Intelligence and Voice Interfaces

You Took the Words Right Out of my Mouth—Meat Loaf

Artificial intelligence (AI) is an often misunderstood term. That's not surprising, given that the term has been in existence for over half a century, and definitions have been in constant flux. Much confusion also stems from the entertainment business, though not from the music industry. Every movie fan is well aware that AI capabilities range from destroying humanity like Cyberdyne Systems' Skynet in the *Terminator* films to an empathetic operating system with the disembodied voice of Scarlett Johansson in *Her*. A formal definition of AI from 2018 is far less dramatic. It states that AI is "the theory and development of computer systems able to perform tasks normally requiring human intelligence, such as visual perception, speech recognition, decision-making, and translation between languages."[i]

Computer systems that emulate typically human skills are being applied to an ever-widening set of problems with increasing impact on our lives. We've seen AI advance from the fun and games of defeating the best human players at chess or Go to the life and death decisions required to drive an autonomous car or to help doctors identify cancer on scans of patients. Countless books explain the myriad technologies that are covered by the umbrella term of AI ranging from image recognition to machine learning (ML).

Data is the fuel that powers the training and improvement of AI algorithms. And data now pervades every aspect of the music industry, from the frequency with which fans select specific songs on streaming platforms to the magnitude of fans' engagement with artists on social platforms to metadata describing every aspect of a song from release information to mood. In some cases, AI models sit between fans and the music itself and are geared toward an improved experience or increased engagement. Other models focus on serving artists and industry professionals by improving processes, ranging from creating music to identifying unsigned artists with the greatest potential for success.

Key Changes. Howie Singer and Bill Rosenblatt, Oxford University Press. © Howie Singer and Bill Rosenblatt 2023.
DOI: 10.1093/oso/9780197656891.003.0011

Since the earliest days of recorded music, A&R executives determined which artists to sign to label deals guided by a combination of good ears and gut instinct. Seeing how an artist performs live and connects with an audience remains a key factor in those signing decisions. But now those emerging artists walk in the door with data that describes their existing fanbase and a track record of how they connect with their audiences. AI models can now evaluate mountains of streaming and social data to compare the profiles of new artists with others that have gone on to successful careers. For example, Sodatone, a startup based in Toronto, developed a measure called the Jump Score, which generates a normalized view of an artists' streaming and social activity that is predictive of future growth. Such models are continually refined by adding engagement data from newer platforms like TikTok and BandLab, and the accuracy of the predictions themselves provide additional feedback for improvement.

Signing artists with a greater chance of market success and avoiding those who are less likely to become stars increases label profitability. Warner Music Group found the Jump Score so helpful that it bought Sodatone to bring its expertise in house and to keep these insights out of the hands of its competitors. As WMG CEO Steve Cooper explained during a 2020 analyst call on the company's results, "We've doubled the number of new artist signings identified through our proprietary A&R app, Sodatone."[ii]

There are other examples where AI plays a role in today's music business, ranging from automated mastering of tracks[1] to prepare for release to deciding which album track should be promoted as the next single. Though these applications improve decision-making to improve revenues or reduce costs, we do not believe they will fundamentally alter the industry's dynamics.

However, there are two areas where it is already clear that AI will engender more transformative changes. First, the ability to understand human speech via smartphones and smart speakers offers a radically different user interface to music services. Second, AI tools capable of generating commercially and artistically viable compositions, lyrics, and performances are on the horizon.

Cutting-edge Technology

Soon after the invention of the first computers, it became apparent that they could be programmed to exhibit "intelligence" of the type normally attributable to humans. One of the most famous early instances of AI-oriented thinking is the Turing Test, invented in 1950 by the celebrated English mathematician Alan Turing, who broke the Nazis' secret Enigma code during World War II. In the Turing Test, a user interacts separately with a human and a machine using natural language; if the user can't tell which is the human and which is the machine, the machine can be said to be "intelligent." This test has stood the test of time, not least because it applies to all ways of interacting in natural language (typing, speech, and so on).

The term "artificial intelligence" was coined at a conference at Dartmouth College in 1956. But as the field developed over the ensuing decades, the definition of AI was something of a moving target; as a practical matter, it could often be boiled down to "Things that a computer can almost but not quite do right now." Several technologies that we consider mundane or trivial today were once lumped into the AI rubric, such as expert systems (systems that decide what to do based on a series of if/then rules) and knowledge representation schemes (templates for describing objects or concepts and relationships among them).

It's quite possible that the contemporary definitions of AI will have shifted beyond what they are in the early 2020s as you are reading this book. However, a few specific technologies that were developed some time ago and fall under current definitions of AI are particularly relevant to the music industry. These are ML, natural language processing (NLP), speech recognition, and speech synthesis. We'll describe each of these here briefly.

ML is a broad term that encompasses techniques for improving a system's knowledge or performance.[iii] The first ML systems were those that emulated neural networks in the human brain, such as the Perceptron, developed in the late 1950s by Frank Rosenblatt, a psychology researcher at Cornell.[2]

ML developed as a field during the 1960s and 1970s, but then it went dormant for a while because the techniques being discovered weren't producing sufficiently significant results on the computing hardware of the day. By the 2000s, however, as hardware grew more powerful by orders of magnitude and available to individuals, ML techniques became capable of real-world practical applications, and the field took off again.

In early ML experiments, computers were able to "learn" how to perform multi-step tasks, prove mathematical theorems, recognize certain types of objects in images, and so on. We're more concerned here with ML's ability to do things like classify data into categories, predict future data based on past data, or learn about users' behavior to improve responses to input. The deluge of data that digital music generates leads to opportunities to use a type of ML scheme called *supervised learning*. In supervised learning, an ML system is fed training data where the outputs are known. For example, there could be an ML algorithm for A&R that devises rules for predicting which independent artists might "blow up" based on their social media data. As training data, such an algorithm could take the numbers from Instagram, Snapchat, and TikTok of artists that became big stars and use that data to discern patterns that might apply to new artists.

NLP is another technology whose development began in the late 1950s. The basic idea of NLP is to build computer models for representing human language so that a computer can "understand" it well enough to do useful things such as obey natural language commands, translate to another language, and synthesize speech. Of course, NLP was seen as directly applicable to the Turing Test. One of the best-known early NLP experiments was ELIZA, developed in the mid-1960s by Joseph Weizenbaum at MIT, which simulated a psychotherapist in text dialog with a user (and caused many people to behave as if they were talking to a real therapist). Early NLP systems were confined to narrow areas of subject matter, such as placing telephone calls or making airline reservations, but as the field developed, they could be applied to domains that required broader vocabularies. The ubiquitous and unavoidable chatbots used in lieu of human customer service representatives today are direct descendants of this technology.

Speech synthesis technology generally developed in parallel with NLP. Early speech synthesis applications didn't require NLP; they were simply capable of converting text to synthesized phonemes. The first commercial products with speech synthesis appeared in the 1970s, including children's toys such as the Speak 'n' Spell, which voiced the letters of the alphabet, around 1978. Subsequent speech synthesis technologies have gotten asymptotically closer to creating output that sounds completely human (the Turing Test again!).

While speech synthesis doesn't require natural language understanding, speech *recognition* (generating text from human audio) does. Converting continuous spoken audio to text words that can then be processed by an NLP system so that the speech is "understood" is a major challenge. Even so, technology for understanding speech began quite early with systems that could recognize single words in narrow domains. Bell Labs, the formidable research arm of AT&T, pioneered the technology to help improve the efficiency of the phone company's nationwide network. In 1952, Bell Labs researchers built

Audrey, a computer system that could recognize individual spoken digits. Experiments in the 1960s were capable of handling distinct words in small vocabularies such as chess moves. By the early 1970s, systems were handling continuous speech with vocabularies of over a thousand words in broader applications such as database queries. As the use of personal computers exploded in the 1980s, speech recognition software packages were developed for them.[3]

The speech recognition systems of the 1980s were functional, but they required extensive training and noise-free environments, and they suffered from latency (the time lag between speaking and an action taken based on the words spoken). Mainframe computers enabled more sophisticated applications in the same timeframe: by 1992, for example, AT&T had deployed voice recognition capable of routing and handling more than a billion calls per year.[iv]

Speech recognition systems developed through the 1990s and 2000s were generally used in environments where lots of computing power was available. Yet the vocabularies they could handle were still limited by context. For example, when you talked to telephone voice-response systems of that era, the responses they understood had to be among lists of specific words.

This changed with the advent of smartphones—which not only had significant computing power onboard but could communicate with servers that had much, much more. The idea of a general-purpose voice assistant became possible. And the first one to gain widespread use, of course, was Apple's Siri. Siri, whose name derives from SRI (Stanford Research Institute), the source of the technology, was first released as an app for iPhones and iPads in 2010 and then integrated into the iPhone 4S in October 2011. Around the same time, Google introduced voice search—the ability for its search engine to take voice queries as input. The types of commands that both of these systems could understand were still limited, but the race to bring general speech understanding to mass-market consumer devices was on.

Finally, it's important to note that ML techniques are used to improve all of the above technologies—NLP, speech understanding, and voice synthesis. ML's broad applicability is one reason why many current definitions of AI are focused on ML-based ideas.

Speech recognition has fundamentally altered the experience of streaming music for fans. Streaming music services have evolved in various ways; smartphones with faster wireless connections accelerated their mass-market adoption. Spotify, Apple, and other competitors have made numerous improvements to their respective services; alternative payment plans for families have made them more affordable. Personalized playlists have kept fans engaged and less likely to terminate their paid subscriptions. But the changes wrought by speech recognition are much more significant. Any user can request a specific artist or song verbally; and then the service, far more often than not, begins to play the correct music after a minimal delay. The complexity of this task is daunting. The services offer music by millions of artists who perform tens of millions of songs with hundreds of millions of words in their titles. The words are spoken in dozens of languages by people with a variety of accents and vocal characteristics. Marrying speech recognition technology with ML algorithms to enhance performance enabled voice recognition to surmount these obstacles.

A variety of speech recognition startups such as Nuance Communications (a spinoff from SRI) implemented machine learning models to improve accuracy and performance. When it first introduced Siri, Apple did not apply the technology to make it easier to listen to a single song from a catalog of millions. The company had no need to do so, because it had not yet transitioned from selling track downloads to streaming songs (which Apple launched in 2015). Not to mention that smartphones were often used in noisy environments while headphones and microphones with noise cancellation were not yet ubiquitous. Those impediments compounded the difficulties of accurately recognizing the extremely large vocabulary required to operate a music service.

The quieter and more controlled setting of the home proved to be far friendlier for voice control. Amazon introduced the Echo smart speaker, powered by the Alexa AI service, for Amazon Prime Members in late 2014. When the device determines that the "wake" word of Alexa has been spoken, the rest of the spoken command is recorded. The multiple microphones in the device separate out the background noise to make that recording as clear as possible. The always-connected device sends the recording to the cloud, where Amazon Web Services' (AWS) processing power and memory dwarf what is available in the home. The request is processed and translated into text which can be used as input to the music service of choice which then streams the appropriate song back across the network to the smart speaker. This entire process is completed in a matter of milliseconds.

The Alexa service deployed within AWS is where AI comes into play. A large data set covering different voices, dialects, accents and languages was used to train the algorithm for accuracy. An internal testing team reviewed a small sample of the results and their assessment of what was actually said was fed back into the system to improve precision.[v]

Google, meanwhile, introduced the Google Home smart speaker in late 2016, a full two years after Amazon's launch of the Echo. It marketed and priced the device aggressively to catch up with Amazon. Google had introduced voice search a few years earlier, but it was only capable of passing commands to Google's search engine; the Google Assistant technology that powered Google Home (now Google Nest) devices was a two-way voice-response system like Alexa and Siri. Together, Amazon and Google effectively operate a duopoly in the smart speaker market; both companies license their voice-response platforms to third-party smart speaker makers such as Bose and Sonos, but not to each other or to Apple.[4]

Since the launch of the smart speaker, technology innovations have improved the performance of voice assistants on smartphones as well. Robust mobile data networks now connect to the cloud reliably when on the go, which enables access to expanded computing and storage. Headphones and earbuds equipped with active noise cancellation help to distinguish spoken commands from background sounds. In addition, it is easy to hook up your phone to take advantage of the microphones, speakers, and display when listening in your car.

The ability to deliver the right song in response to a voice query is inherently more difficult than providing responses to a text search. When you search for an album, song, or artist on the Spotify app, the service's response is a list of candidates akin to the pages of links in Google search results. In most cases, that list contains the item being searched for, and the user's click confirms that (and generates data to improve future searches as well). Providing a list of choices means that there are more opportunities to include the correct response even if the user misspells the artist's name or song title. With voice search, there is simply less room for error, as the use case requires the selection of a single track to play from the millions of options. And in many cases, those options can be tricky to pronounce (such as Ke$ha) or ambiguous given frequent changes to artist names (such as Sean Combs a.k.a. Puff Daddy a.k.a. P. Diddy a.k.a. Diddy).

The challenge of recognizing voice commands is even more daunting when you consider how the metadata related to music can be interpreted in a variety of ways. When using the word "Chicago," it could refer to a rock band of the 1970s or to a query about the weather in the midwestern city. And the word "jazz" could be a genre of music or the NBA team located in Utah.

Deploying voice control to millions of smart speaker owners provides the ongoing fire hose of data to keep refining the quality of the responses further. For example, when a user is dissatisfied with the song that begins to play, they may tell the speaker to stop and then issue a second somewhat different voice instruction to pinpoint the correct track. Each of those events creates useful information to help improve accuracy.

Using machines to perform music predates using them to recognize human speech. Alan Turing programmed a machine to play several songs, including "God Save the Queen," in the 1940s.[vi] AI has enabled computing platforms to create new music and not just render it. David Cope, a composer and former professor of music, began building an AI-based tool to write music in the 1980s that mimicked the compositional styles of Mozart and Bach. The software program, ultimately named Emily Howell, has released recordings of music for chamber orchestras and multiple pianos.[vii]

The successful implementation of AI across the music industry relies upon two critical success factors. First, it depends on a profusion of data related to music, artists, fans, and the engagement around music for developing and validating models. Second, the ability and expertise to develop AI models needs to be made available to companies and developers broadly.

Social media, e-commerce, and other online services generate detailed transactional and behavioral data across all forms of media including music. The evolution of music formats from physical products to downloaded files and now to streams of bits has driven the proliferation of data. In the 1980s and earlier, industry data was gathered by calling stores to find out which records were selling; as we saw in Chapter 7, this yielded limited and inaccurate results. The Soundscan era began in 1991 by reading the barcodes on CDs and other products at the cash register. That data provided much more meaningful insights about the business—including the surprising result that country and rap genres were far more popular than believed. Those Soundscan statistics covered the 1.2 billion units sold in 1999, with CDs accounting for 80 percent of the total. Industry revenues peaked that year at almost $15 billion and then started declining in terms of both dollars and units. But with the launch of the iTunes store and the popularity of the 99-cent download in the early 2000s, the number of transactions grew even though overall revenues continued their decline.

By 2008, the number of units sold peaked in the United States with total transactions approaching 2 billion. Detailed records of each of those sales sat in the databases controlled by Apple, Amazon, and others. Streaming now generates data on a scale that dwarfs even these numbers. The vast majority of the most watched YouTube videos are music videos.[viii] The number of songs streamed across Apple, YouTube, Amazon and the other major services in the United States alone blew past the one trillion mark in 2019.[ix] That total is five hundred times larger than the largest number of units sold ever tallied in a year—without even including other streaming platforms that license music, such as TikTok and Peloton.

Other useful song popularity data comes from non-royalty bearing events on other platforms. Shazam, the music identification application now owned by Apple, is used by more than 225 million people per month. A Pandora user giving a "thumbs up" or a Spotify user deciding to follow a specific artist or an Apple Music listener skipping a track at the 20-second mark are just a few examples of useful signals that illuminate consumer preferences better.

And that's not all. Music artists hold five of the top ten Twitter accounts at this time of writing, with over a half a billion followers in total.[x] Ariana Grande, Selena Gomez, and Beyonce collectively have more than a billion followers on Instagram.[xi] And we haven't even considered individual fans interacting with artist content on these social platforms by liking a particular Instagram photo or a Facebook post. Companies focusing on live performances, such as Bandsintown and Ticketmaster, have millions more entries in their databases covering interest in shows and purchasing tickets. The need to gather and analyze these enormous data sets covering fan engagement on streaming services and social networks has created the opportunity for a variety of companies to offer business intelligence to the industry.[xii]

This profusion of data about how fans interact with songs and artists is crucial in building models that are predictive of mass-market success. Creating music requires detailed information about the songs and performances themselves. There are many examples of companies investing in song analysis, although the initial applications are not aimed at generating new music. Shazam creates an audio fingerprint that uniquely identifies a track based on a wide range of audio characteristics. It works similarly to technologies for managing copyrights on user-uploaded content platforms, such as YouTube's Content ID system, which we saw in Chapter 10; but Shazam is optimized for identifying songs via smartphones' microphones in noisy settings.

Pandora used the Music Genome as the key to its recommendations for songs to be included on their personalized radio channels. As we saw in Chapter 3, the company hired musicologists by the dozens to listen to every track and detail a range of song characteristics based on their expertise. This yields excellent data, but the approach is simply not scalable to the tens of thousands of new songs added every day; so Pandora resorted to augmenting its team of musicologists with automated analysis techniques to make its music catalog competitive in size to other music services. The Echo Nest, a spinout from the MIT Media Lab, developed automated tools to analyze the audio and text associated with songs, including websites, blogs, reviews, and so on. In 2014, Spotify bought the Echo Nest to add to its engineering expertise in these areas. Now the technology examines every one of the 100 million available tracks in Spotify's catalog to determine audio attributes including beats per minute, length, key, "energy," and "danceability." These characteristics drive the Discover Weekly playlist mentioned earlier, as well as many other song recommendations on Spotify; they are accessible to anyone via an application programming interface (API) on the Spotify Developer platform.

The other important input to AI algorithms in voice-response systems is data about the music itself, a.k.a. metadata. Labels really want to make sure that when the user asks a smart speaker to play "some crunk," "that new Olivia Rodrigo song," "some 70s rock," or "some jazz with Wayne Shorter on saxophone," it selects the right tracks. In addition to information about the inherent characteristics of the music, the metadata needs to include information about genre, instrumentation, featured artists, release date, focus track,[5] and so on. We saw in Chapter 10 that YouTube used advanced ML techniques to wrangle discographic metadata from the vast ocean of user uploads to create a decent user experience in YouTube Music. But quality metadata that describes the music itself can't be determined through automated analysis; someone has to assign correct values for all that metadata so that the smart speaker can do its job well. That's a huge job.

Luckily, smart speaker makers agree that good metadata is important for producing the best results for users. So the technology companies have been collaborating with labels on a standard for metadata about music called Media Enrichment and Description (MEAD), which is part of a suite of standards[6] for communicating information about music among labels, music services, and other participants in the music supply chain. Such is the importance of the single-search-result smart speaker that it has labels working actively on metadata after decades of treating it as an afterthought.

It is not only the data itself that is being made more broadly available. Google and Amazon already enable many startups and developers to scale their businesses cost-effectively by accessing inexpensive processing and storage via their cloud computing infrastructures. That approach includes access to many of the AI models developed by the top-level technical talent recruited and funded by these tech giants. The applications for AWS' AI tools range from identifying fake accounts to improved forecasting. Google's Tensor Flow is an open-source platform for developing and training ML models that anyone can access via their browser. Relying on Tensor Flow, Google has created Project Magenta, which consists of an open-source library for ML that supports creators.[xiii] For example, AI Duet, which was created with Project Magenta, lets you play a few notes and then hear a response from an AI model trained using many examples.

Smaller AI startups often offer access to their platforms as well via open APIs. In May 2020, the Microsoft-backed AI research lab OpenAI released "Jukebox," which can create new music in the style of over 9,000 different musicians and performers. The breadth of artists being offered is impressive although the quality of the results remains somewhat uneven (at least so far).[xiv]

When one considers generating music using AI, there are a variety of use cases that could be pursued with varying degrees of difficulty. Most of these applications already exist, although the suitability of the music produced varies widely. For some of the "easier" applications, such as production music matched to YouTube videos or mood music for indie films with shoestring budgets, the AI-generated output already offers a satisfactory combination of quality and price. The results are also good enough to help artists who are seeking ideas or inspiration for new compositions. However, there is not yet a viable model for generating entirely new songs that are good enough to become popular hits.

The following list summarizes many of the relevant use cases for AI-generated music, beginning with ones that are feasible today because they build upon existing content and require the lowest amount of true creativity. The list progresses to those tasks requiring the most significant advances beyond today's capabilities because they require greater and greater artistic ingenuity and true creativity:

- Master and mix already created music;
- Act as an "assistant" for artists by suggesting compositional and lyrical elements;
- Separate a completed musical work into "stems" that isolate vocals and instrumental parts;

- Create "functional" production music that can be used for low-budget films, commercials, and user-generated content such as YouTube videos;
- Stream more engaging playlists through smoother transitions between tracks and announcements similar to professional DJs;
- Transform a performance of a song into a different style or genre, including altering the instrumentation;
- Write parody song lyrics for an existing song;
- Create instrumental ambient music;
- Perform an existing composition in the voice and style of a particular artist (including translating into another language);
- Compose a new composition in the style of a particular artist, composer, or genre;
- Create a new composition with an original melody and lyrics.

Technology advances that became available in the early 2020s made it clear that the average user will be able to use sophisticated "generative" AI tools, that is, tools that generate new content on their own in response to human prompts. Simply typing a descriptive text prompt provides all the information required for DALL-E to generate impressive art in the style of Picasso or any other artist, ChatGPT to draft a cogent answer to a question on virtually any topic, or Google's MusicLM to create songs in a particular genre using specific instruments. When one considers the breadth of these applications and the simplicity of voice and text interfaces, it's obvious that the implications for the rest of the industry will be profound.

Smart speakers are already a lucrative business for manufacturers. Even though they are often sold at deeply discounted prices, they engender loyalty and foster greater commerce. More than 35 percent of Americans 25 years and older, equating to more than 100 million people, own such devices, with Amazon leading in market share and Google in the number two spot. Many households now contain than one device.[xv] This is not merely an American phenomenon, as the number of smart speakers sold in China each year surpassed the United States in 2019.[xvi]

These products have proven to be a significant asset for the music industry. Smart speakers enable a wide range of capabilities, including web search, checking the weather, or setting a timer. But the number one reason cited by consumers for purchasing a smart speaker and the most frequent use is listening to streaming music.[xvii] Roughly 40 percent of users in the United States take advantage of that functionality every day.[xviii] So it is no surprise that almost half of smart speaker owners increase the amount of music they listen to. Moreover, almost 40 percent of smart speaker owners decide to pay for a music subscription service, which provides a significant boost to revenues. Amazon in particular has benefited from the popularity of smart speakers for music streaming, as we'll see shortly.

The current state of AI technology for music creation makes it more suitable for reducing costs than for generating additional revenues. However, the trajectory is clear and, as the technology matures, it will be capable of creating derivative works based on existing music or entirely new music that resonates with fans and earns substantial revenues. Today, artists can avail themselves of AI-powered tools to generate ideas for lyrics or instrumentation to assist in the creative process. The feedback from these collaborations will fuel the improvement of the ML tools to become increasingly self-sufficient.

The popularity of the ambient music genre on the streaming services means that distributors could use AI-generated music to reduce their costs of content and to improve their margins. It has already been reported that numerous "fake artists" have tracks on Spotify that have been prominently featured on these ambient music playlists and are garnering significant activity. These reports assert that the service has a special arrangement with the creators of these tracks to pay reduced royalty rates.[xix] Clearly, using AI models to generate content would be even more advantageous in terms of reduced royalty payments. Just the prospect of such activity reducing payments for "real" artists could lower operating costs and generate leverage for the streaming services in their future royalty negotiations with record labels. In November 2022, Tencent Music Entertainment announced that it had used AI technology to generate over 1,000 songs with replicated human voices and that one of those tracks had been streamed over 100 million times.[xx]

Though they are not yet ready to write a hit pop song, AI models can create "functional" music that is suitable for a YouTube video or a low-budget film. This foreshadows a major shift in the economics of production music. Drew Silverstein's background as a composer led him to found Amper Music in 2014. The company has developed an online portal, Amper Score, that anyone can use to create a piece of music designed to match a particular piece of video content. One can select the genre, mood, instruments, tempo, and the key moments in the video requiring emphasis. In a few seconds, the tool creates a new piece of music using Amper's proprietary library of millions of music samples covering an enormous variety of musical instruments. The musical selection can be modified easily until it meets the user's needs exactly. When the user is satisfied with the result, they can download a copy and obtain a perpetual license to use the newly created track for under $100.[xxi] In 2020, Shutterstock purchased Amper Music to complement its online image licensing business.

Amazon's Prime service launched in 2005 with expedited shipping for all purchases; soon after its launch, customers who subscribed were spending even more with the e-commerce giant. Amazon has continued to add items to Prime since then, making the offer more valuable for subscribers while raising the annual price too. Just a few months before the introduction of the Echo smart speaker, Amazon unveiled its Prime Music offer. This was an advertising-free streaming service that gave all Prime subscribers access to two million songs at no additional charge. Though that sounds like a large music catalog, it was far smaller than what Spotify was offering, which enabled Amazon to negotiate lower-cost licenses with the major labels. In addition, the number of songs made accurate voice recognition a somewhat less daunting task for the Echo speaker. Amazon certainly had the Echo speaker in mind when implementing Prime Music, though the two were not developed together.[xxii] Moreover, the millions of users who were soon interacting via voice created extensive data to improve the AI recognition models in the cloud. That helped to prepare for the 2016 launch of Amazon Music Unlimited, which offered access to a full catalog of tens of millions of tracks, matching the scale of the other major services. The Unlimited tier required an additional payment, but it was available to anyone, even those who did not subscribe to Amazon Prime.

This tight coupling of devices and connected service capabilities enabled distribution that has proved as valuable to Amazon as the combination of the iPod and the iTunes Store was to Apple a dozen years earlier. It helped to accelerate Amazon's growth in streaming music and position it among the leaders in streaming alongside Spotify and Apple. Amazon announced in 2020 that it had 55 million music subscribers worldwide, including both the Prime and Unlimited tiers, just behind Apple Music's announced numbers. And Edison Research's Infinite Dial, the independent consumer survey, ranked Amazon Music equal to or even ahead of Apple in its 2021 results.[xxiii] In other words, smart speakers were a "Trojan horse" that persuaded more consumers to pay for streaming music.

Meanwhile Apple, with its "closed" HomePod smart speaker platform, found its subscriber growth slowed down as Amazon's grew.[xxiv] This undoubtedly led to Apple's November 2021 introduction of a "Music Voice" plan to regain some momentum in the marketplace. The new offer costs half as much as the regular Apple Music service. It works only on Apple devices with the Siri voice assistant and does not offer some features, such as downloading songs for offline listening. And like Amazon's service, a trial of the service can be initiated by voice command alone, reducing the friction for new users.

The distribution channel for production music used in films, television or advertisements is quite different. For example, when an advertiser is seeking music for a campaign, the ad agency prepares a creative brief that traditionally gets sent to production music houses. The brief describes the product, target market, creative concepts, and key tags that convey the characteristics of the music they need. For example, a car manufacturer might want to highlight young people driving to the beach for surfing, and they want music that highlights summer, sun, sand, and fun—perhaps with a Dick Dale guitar vibe. Some production houses have launched online portals where buyers can search the catalog and purchase rights. The viability of AI-generated production music means that the customers can serve themselves. Production house employees can access an online portal that enables them not only to describe and to search but to craft the music they need in real time and then obtain the necessary licenses.

As we have discussed in previous chapters, experience shows that collaborations or remixes can broaden the appeal of a particular song. In the '90s, popular singles were remixed frequently to tailor the track for dancing in clubs or to fit different radio formats. Going back into the studio to rerecord the original version of a track to incorporate a Latin hip-hop artist or to add steel guitar and a fiddle to create more of a country sound can be an expensive proposition. Moreover, there is no guarantee that the investment will pay off in terms of increased listening or popularity.

Warner Music Group invested in LifeScore, an AI startup that adjusts music to different contexts such as exercise.[xxv] We can expect that this technology will creep ever closer to becoming a market reality in the near future; Korean researchers have already created an AI model to create a piano-only cover version of any popular song. AI models will lower the expense of creating more extensive variations of the same track, including shifting instrumentation, genre, tempo and even the language of the singer.[xxvi] Apple has already acquired a startup called AI Music that has announced plans to use AI to shift the style of existing music.[xxvii] Once the quality of such transformations is good enough and the costs are low enough, we can expect to see a proliferation of new versions of songs. These alternate takes will then be positioned on various distribution platforms and playlists that cater to different audiences or languages. Some will fail to catch on with fans while others will prove successful. The additional listening and popularity will then yield a greater share of royalties. The data resulting from both the successes and the failures will then be fed back into the AI models to improve the ability to craft ever more popular variations.

Taking this idea a step further, AI models will create versions of tracks that are even more finely tuned to a user's tastes beyond shifting to another genre or giving the song a more upbeat tempo. The services have the historical data on every listener's preferences and can determine what engages them the most. With lower costs and greater computing power, they will be able to stream truly personalized playlists that feature versions of songs matched to those preferences. If you want "more cowbell," that's what you'll get.

Radio program directors have long curated the list of songs to play to keep listeners tuning in. For streaming services, algorithms built using AI use your listening history and those of people with tastes similar to yours via collaborative filtering to personalize the songs recommended to each user. Collaborative filtering is a type of algorithm that compares your behavior and preferences with those of other users so that it can generate recommendations for you based on other users' behavior.[7] The better the recommendations, the more likely fans will keep listening and subscribing because they enjoy the service. Listener reactions to song recommendations, whether a "thumbs up" ranking or skipping a track quickly, generate additional signals to improve those recommendations. Spotify's popular Discover Weekly playlist is one such example where ML techniques automatically incorporate user reactions to improve the results over time.[xxviii]

AI models can improve not only the quality of each song selected for personalized lists but can also enhance the overall experience in ways that go beyond selection of music. Often, streaming services have mismatched volume levels and pauses between their songs and advertisements. Radio stations use people to solve these issues and to provide information and branding between the songs (which are often centrally programmed, given the corporate conglomerates that own many stations). The best DJs relate interesting facts about the band or the song while the intro plays and then "hit the post"—finish up just as the lyrics kick in. The streaming services had no cost-effective way to offer similar capabilities. Super Hi-Fi, a Los Angeles-based startup, uses AI tools to provide a comparable experience at a low cost.[xxix]

Shifting tastes in music point toward another way AI-generated music will play a role. Over the course of 2020, many people listened to more streamed entertainment to deal with the stress of the COVID-19 pandemic. Ambient music, as a genre, grew in popularity because as a background listening experience it provides a sense of calm or serenity for many people.[xxx] Ambient is a type of instrumental music that eschews traditional musical rhythms, structure, or melodies in favor of tone and atmosphere. Spotify playlists featuring ambient music, such as Deep Sleep, Peaceful Piano, and Deep Focus, collectively have over 12 million followers.

Compositional elements make the ambient genre particularly amenable to the current capabilities of AI models. Daniel Jeffries has used Google's Project Magenta tools to create ambient music; he explains as follows: "The hazy softness of ambient music gave us a little more leeway to screw it up just a bit but still have something that sounds wonderful."[xxxi] As another example, Mubert is a new service that uses AI to produce generative ambient music that streams royalty-free and is available via API.[xxxii]

Many artists change their names as their career evolves or opt for spellings that help them stand out from the crowd of artists (e.g., A$AP Rocky). While these choices complicate the tasks of recognizing and pronouncing names for voice interfaces, creators are making decisions about song titles that simplify things. The data from Spotify shows two distinct trends that both have ramifications for voice interfaces. First, song titles are getting shorter in terms of the number of words along with the songs themselves being shorter (as discussed in Chapter 9).[xxxiii] The process of recognizing each individual spoken word has an associated error rate, so fewer words means that there is a higher probability of getting the correct interpretation of an entire string of words. The context of an entire sentence can help to improve the accuracy of recognizing a longer string of words. Many song titles would fit that paradigm, but for every "Leave the Door Open" there is an "Ob-La-Di Ob-La-Da" or "Da Do Ron Ron." Second, though the titles are shorter, the size of the vocabulary used has expanded. More different words with distinct sounds means training over time will achieve greater accuracy.

AI systems can already draft simple news stories based on fact-based information, such as the statistical results of a sports event. The task of creating an article that clearly articulates facts is far simpler than analyzing the reasons the Lakers won't win the NBA title this year. Analogously, writing a piece of "functional" music that supports a mood or style with particular instruments is far less difficult than crafting a wholly original work that expresses sentiments and emotions of the artist and resonates with fans. That means that, at least for today, AI is more suitable as a collaborative tool than as an independent creative entity. AI tools can certainly make useful suggestions to a composer who is stuck coming up with a new chord progression or a bridge. Similarly, providing options for lyrics helps to trigger new ideas to a writer who is struggling to come up with the right phrase.

Several artists are already experimenting to create new works using AI models as partners for their creative efforts. Holly Herndon's 2019 album *Proto* features tracks that were created with Spawn, a piece of ML software. The avant-pop musician used Spawn to write music that was distinctly different from her previous works.[xxxiv] She also created a website called Never Before Heard Sounds (heardsounds.com) that features vocals by a model called Holly+ trained on Herndon's voice.[xxxv] In November 2022, Herndon released a new single performed by this AI model of her voice; a cover version of Dolly Parton's "Jolene." And she has made the technology open: anyone can upload an audio file to her site and get back a download of that same music "sung" by Holly+.[xxxvi] Grimes used AI technology to generate a "soundscape" in a smartphone app with original vocals and music that adapts to your current location and weather. It was designed to promote better sleep for children and adults.[xxxvii]

Not all artists are as sanguine about the prospects for AI-generated music. Many will view negatively even a simple admission that a computer could assist in the creative process—though it is worth noting that similar objections were raised when synthesizers and Auto-Tune were first used for producing music. Just as those innovations became commonplace and accepted over time, more artists will rely on AI-based assistants as part of their creative process.

One of the more problematic AI applications for society is creating deepfakes, which are synthetic images or voices that are designed to look or sound like a known person without the person's permission. In some deepfakes, the content shows an individual saying or doing things they never actually did. For example, the BBC posted a video showing Queen Elizabeth delivering an "alternative" 2020 holiday message to emphasize the risks of the technology as a tool to spread misinformation.[xxxviii] Kendrick Lamar deployed deepfake technology to morph his own image into a series of other famous people, from Kanye West to O. J. Simpson, in his music video for his song "The Track, Part 5."[xxxix] As the technology improves, it will become harder and harder to determine whether a particular statement or image is real or fake.

Given the vast amount of video of musical artists speaking, there is more than enough training material to create deep fakes showing them making controversial statements about politics or race that could complicate their career or damage relationships with many fans. Google's AI team has created a tool called Tacotron 2 which renders any text in a convincing human voice.[xl]

There is no lack of training material of rap performances either, so it is a short step to move from faked spoken words to a "counterfeit" musical selection. Jay-Z's voice and his vocal style are both distinctive and were used to train an AI model to imitate him. Though he has never rapped the "To be, or not to be" soliloquy from Hamlet or Billy Joel's "We Didn't Start the Fire," you can find YouTube videos of both faked performances.[xli] Given how close that song is to rap performance, these fakes are easier to create than a fully melodic performance. However, that does not mean that people are not trying to do exactly that. Using the OpenAI platform to generate a Frank Sinatra-like rendition of Britney Spears's "Toxic" is a bit more of a stretch in terms of the quality of the output.[xlii] Jay-Z and Frank Sinatra's estate will not view these appropriations of their musical personas positively, particularly when the new works were created with neither permission nor remuneration.[8]

But why stop at having a known artist "artificially cover" an existing song when an AI model can create a completely new track building on an extensive data set of previous performances and compositions? In March 2019, Google created a "Doodle" for its home page that honored Johann Sebastian Bach on the composer's birthday.[xliii] The user inputs two measures of notes, and using rules defined by over 300 Bach compositions, the AI algorithm crafted the appropriate harmonies in just seconds and played back the results. OpenAI has used its Jukebox tool to create country music in the style of Alan Jackson and pop in the style of Katy Perry by training its algorithms on other songs by those artists. The quality of the music produced by these tools is not great, but is better than it was a year ago and will continue to improve.

Several of the AI applications we've described, including varying the genre or tailoring a track to an individual user, clearly involve the creation of derivative works. The right to create derivative works is reserved to the creator under copyright law, so it requires the rights holder's permission for someone else to do that. However, for many other uses, AI is just the latest example of an innovation outpacing the law's ability to keep up.

Katherine Forrest, former US District Judge for the Southern District of NY, former Deputy Assistant Attorney General in the Antitrust Division of the US Department of Justice, and currently adjunct professor at NYU Law School, summarized these issues in her comprehensive lecture to the Copyright Society of the USA in November 2018. As she said then, "What is clear today is that AI is 'this' generation's challenge to the copyright law."[xliv]

Her assessment remains true today as many questions remain unresolved despite the steady progress of AI technology in generating music. For example, when an AI model generates a new piece of music, who owns the copyright? Is it the owner of the company that created the AI software? Is it the person using the AI tool and selecting the options and settings? Or could it be both, with varying degrees of ownership based on the level of decision-making by the person using the tool? Perhaps AI models should be treated as "contractors" that complete "works for hire"[9] with the rights retained by the person or entity who "assigned" the project. And when copyrighted works are used as the data set for training, is a license for those works required?

As AI becomes more capable, the complexities compound. Forrest posed the scenario of a "computer program that can ask other computer programs to assist it in analyzing creative works, and contributing something to the creation of a new one, and imagine that this process can occur incredibly with little or no human intervention." The resulting work would represent contributions from many different AI programs. Determining how ownership could be determined seems like a Gordian Knot.

There is one settled case that offers some narrow guidance on these questions, though it relates neither to music nor to AI-enabled tools. In 2005, a monkey in Indonesia took a series of selfies using a nature photographer's camera. The photographer published the photos in a book. The animal rights organization People for the Ethical Treatment of Animals (PETA) filed suit claiming that this action infringed on the monkey's rights under the Copyright Act. The court found that only humans can hold a copyright.[xlv] On a related question, the US Patent and Trademark Office ruled in 2020 that an AI may not be listed as an inventor on a patent.[xlvi] In February 2022, the US Copyright Office extended that same logic by ruling that an AI algorithm cannot be granted a copyright for its artistic creation.[xlvii] And if we accept that conclusion, is a new work created autonomously by an AI model even copyrightable? The Copyright Office has already published guidance stating that the answer to that question is "no," that works by generative AI technologies cannot qualify for copyright registration without substantial human input (of which a simple text prompt is not sufficient).[xlviii]

These are the sorts of questions that IP lawyers love to explore, and they have already been the subject of a great deal of legal scholarship and debate. The IP law community has taken an active role in convening experts to discuss the questions and in soliciting opinions from both the technology and creative communities. On February 5, 2020, the Copyright Office and the World Intellectual Property Organization (WIPO) held a symposium on the issues of AI and creativity. The panelists addressed such issues as the level of human interaction required to make an AI-generated work eligible for copyright protection and the rights issues associated with using copyrighted works to train AI models, as well as how these AI-related policies relate to the goals of copyright itself. If the law's protections are intended to incentivize the creation of new works, do AI models even require such incentives?

Also recognizing the importance of AI, the US Patent and Trademark Office solicited input on thirteen questions related to copyrights, trademarks, and other IP rights in 2019.[xlix] Not surprisingly, the responses to the questions exemplified the split between the creative and technology industries, with the former arguing for stronger protections of their intellectual property including the need to obtain licenses for training material. These processes will continue well into the future; the Copyright Office has been holding a public consultations on AI and copyright during 2023.

In the absence of definitive law, some AI companies are explicitly stating their treatment of copyrights as part of the terms of service to use their platform. They take the position that the entity creating and offering the AI software deserves a stake in the work product produced. For example, Amper Music's Terms of Service specify that the user assigns and transfers any and all rights to the music created to the company. The user receives a royalty-free license to use the music created in perpetuity, but the copyright belongs to Amper Music.[l]

We've already cited several examples of AI models creating music in the style of a particular artist or composer. That artist's catalog of music makes up the data set used to train these models. As expected, rights holders believe that such training requires a license, which conceivably could include approval of any commercial uses for the AI-generated content along with payments. In July 2022, all the UK bodies representing artists complained to the government about data mining[10] of music to create AI models without remuneration.[li] Certainly, any uses of the newly created content that relies on the name and image of the original artist without obtaining the appropriate permissions would probably be blocked.

Jay-Z's legal team chose to file DMCA takedown notices (see Chapter 10) to remove the YouTube videos containing AI-generated deepfake vocals rapping the Hamlet soliloquy and "We Didn't Start the Fire." Their claim was that "this content unlawfully uses an AI to impersonate our client's voice."[lii] Filing such a notice is simple, but in this case, YouTube rejected the claim and allowed the videos to remain available. Their decision may have relied on the logic that imitating someone's vocal mannerisms is not copyright infringement. Creative Commons offered the following view: "It is ill-advised to force the application of the copyright system—an antiquated system that has yet to adapt to the digital environment—on to AI."[11] The unidentified owners of the channel called Voice Synthesis that posted these videos to YouTube asserted that their videos are parodies, which are protected under fair use. Jay-Z's legal team could decide to push back on these theories and go to court to have their claims adjudicated, but, so far, they have not elected to do so. Although this example used Jay-Z's voice only, we can expect to see deepfake vocals performed by characters that are the product of computer algorithms as well. The K-pop group Eternity has already cracked the Spotify charts in Korea with eleven AI-generated members.[liii]

There are other possibly stronger legal arguments that artists can make with regard to these deepfake performances. The first involves impersonations of a musical artist without their permission and has nothing to do with whether AI was used to create the imitation. In the 1980s, Ford Motor Co. put together an ad campaign for its Lincoln brand to appeal to Yuppies that relied on nostalgia for several songs of the 1970s. The company approached Bette Midler's manager to request a recording of "Do You Wanna Dance?" for the ads and were refused. Ford liked the concept so much that it decided to re-record the song and hired a singer to imitate the Divine Miss M's style. The impression was so good that many people thought it was Midler herself singing. She thought that Ford should have taken her "no" for an answer and filed suit.

The US Court of Appeals for the Ninth Circuit overturned an initial lower court in favor of Ford. The higher court found that even though Ford did not refer to Midler by name, nor use her likeness in any way in the ads, it did misappropriate her voice, and it ruled that it is unlawful to imitate a famous person's voice for commercial purposes without their express consent. Artists will definitely use that argument when unauthorized deepfakes of their performances are exploited.[liv]

This rationale regarding the use of an artist's voice without permission may be viewed as a more expansive application of the right of publicity (another branch of law, separate from copyright). There is no federal statute protecting an individual's right of publicity, although there have been some discussions that such protections should be considered. Instead, many states offer legal protection of an individual's identity (Including name, likeness, and persona) from being exploited for commercial purposes without permission. Some states provide this protection for celebrities only, while others do the same for all individuals. Regardless, we can expect to see musical artists using the right of publicity to protect their rights in the age of AI deepfakes.

The legal framework for using copyrighted material as training data has not yet been clearly delineated. The technology companies do not see the need to obtain a license to train an AI model on a catalog of copyrighted songs and performances. They will argue that having an algorithm identifying characteristics and attributes contained in the originals is no different from a person listening to all of Taylor Swift's songs and then writing a new one in her style from the "lessons" they absorbed. If a portion of one of her songs was copied and reused in the new work, then the traditional remedies associated with copyright infringement are available. However, if an algorithm simply "listens" to her catalog and extracts features mathematically, in a manner akin to audio fingerprinting technologies, then tech companies will argue that the new song is not a derivative work requiring permission.[12] Instead, they will take the position that the law should treat the AI company and its model in the same fashion as any other Taylor Swift-inspired "wannabe" and therefore that the newly created work should be covered under fair use.

Interestingly, the first lawsuit filed alleging improper use of data for training AI models has nothing to do with what we typically deem the creative arts, such as music or photographs. Copilot is an AI-based tool that generates code to help programmers while they are writing it. It was trained using the extensive database of programs on the Microsoft-owned platform GitHub, and it offers to insert chunks of code taken from GitHub repositories. Although much of the code on GitHub is made available to others under open-source licenses, the parties filing suit claim that using it as training data violates GitHub's terms of service and that Microsoft has failed to provide the proper attribution to the creators.[13,lv]

In early 2023, two separate lawsuits were filed by visual artists and Getty Images (one of the largest image licensing services) against AI-powered text-to-image generators. The parties claimed that these platforms were using copyrighted images to train their algorithms without permission or compensation for the creators. The music industry will be monitoring the arguments and decisions in these cases carefully, as they could establish precedents that are likely to apply to AI-generated music.[lvi] As Michael Nash, Chief Digital Officer of Universal Music Group, stated publicly, "Unless creators are respected and fairly compensated when their works are exploited to train AI, the world's creators will suffer widespread and lasting harm."[lvii]

There are other scenarios that could make the licensing questions even murkier. What if the technology company does not disclose publicly which artist's catalog of music was used to train their system or simply applies the same methodology to the entire Billboard 200 to extract the key elements from all these songs? The nature of ML is such that the precise steps used to refine the models are unknown, and the resulting model is equivalent to a "black box." That is one reason that unintended biases can become embedded in AI models used for tasks such as approving mortgages or selecting job applicants. Therefore, reverse engineering a particular piece of AI-generated music to determine which songs were used to determine the parameters of the resulting model is very difficult, if not impossible. Given all these uncertainties, as commercial uses of AI music expand, we expect that questions of licensing music for the training of AI models and relevant ownership of the resulting works are likely to be debated in the courts for many years.

Consumers

As discussed earlier, fans with smart speakers take advantage of the friendly voice interface to listen to more music and often decide to pay for subscriptions. In surveys, almost three-quarters of smart speaker owners say they broadened their listening habits. Almost 40 percent of such owners listen to a more extensive music selection, around 40 percent discover more new music, and over 40 percent listen to more playlists.[lviii] Some of that variety is driven by the ease of requesting music via voice beyond specific songs or requests such as "happy music" or "most popular songs," as discussed above.

In terms of genres, country music has benefited the most from the popularity of smart speakers. Younger music fans moved to streaming first; that demographic group favored hip-hop and pop music. Amazon Prime customers were older with more established households that valued free shipping, possibly because they are not as mobile as younger people or live in more rural places. That audience included more fans of country music.[lix] Knowing their CD and download purchasing habits, Amazon specifically curated the type of songs that would appeal to them when licensing repertoire. It even negotiated an exclusive relationship to offer streams of Garth Brooks's music; and to this day, Brooks keeps his songs off other streaming services because of the presumably lower payouts.

In addition, voice control gives even young children the ability to play the songs they want to hear by simply asking Alexa themselves rather than needing their parents' help to enjoy music. That enables the youngest of music fans to boost the numbers for the songs they love to hear over and over again. Though we do not have the detailed data to prove the point, it is almost certain that kids played a significant role in making "Encanto" the most streamed album and "We Don't Talk About Bruno" the most played song in the first half of 2022.[lx]

When it comes to AI-generated music, rights holders and tech companies are likely to be at odds over rights and licenses, although as usual, most consumers will be indifferent to these squabbles. Regardless of the legal battles that might be underway, fans will listen to the music at issue if it appeals to their tastes.

Many people will view having access to additional, high-quality music "from" their favorite artists as a positive result if the quality of the

AI-generated imitations is good enough. That will be true whether those artists have chosen to stop creating new songs or have unfortunately passed away. There have already been tours featuring holograms of Roy Orbison, Frank Zappa, and Whitney Houston (backed by live musicians), supported by their respective estates, that were generally well-received and profitable. Though there was certainly a group of people who found the concept ghoulish and exploitative, ticket sales indicate that the many devoted fans welcomed this opportunity to see their favorite artists once again. Using AI models to add new songs and performances for those artists could well drive additional demand.

Technical standards will emerge that provide indications of the provenance of music. Some distribution channels will apply these standards to distinguish songs created or sanctioned by the artists from those generated by AI models. Some fans will care about the "authenticity" of the music associated with artists they support and will respect this distinction. They will make their service and listening choices in accordance with the artists' preferences. There will also be popular platforms that simply make everything available without indicating the source and then let users sort things out for themselves. Many people presume that if they can find a song on a platform such as YouTube, it must be legitimate. The processes for removal of contested AI-generated music will prove at least as frustrating for rights holders as they are today for other unauthorized content.

Many artists will eschew AI tools as part of their creative processes in much the same way that they avoid Auto-Tune. Experience shows that many fans will simply not care whether or not artists avail themselves of these new tools. And for the increasing number of people who are more than passive consumers of music and videos, they will add AI-powered algorithms to their own bags of tricks to make better and more interesting content. Consumers have already made it clear that they love easy-to-use tools that make it easier for them to express themselves creatively on platforms such as Snapchat and TikTok. In February 2022, Kanye West announced the release of his new album *Donda 2* on a $200 device called the Stem Player.[lxi] It will enable fans to manipulate the component elements of the song while listening. Users will be able to manipulate the stems created by AI models for other songs added to the device. This points toward AI enabling simpler and simpler ways for fans to customize music or to create new songs in the style of artists they love that they will then post for all to hear on social networks.

Conclusion

Unlike its portrayal in so many Hollywood movies, AI does not possess any malicious intent. It is a tool that can be used for good or for ill. The ocean of consumption-related data will continue to make voice recognition models easier to use and more accurate when determining the speaker's intentions. The availability of AI-powered models for generating music will unleash an enormous amount of creativity. It will empower individuals with abilities that they did not previously possess to make interesting and engaging music. Much uncertainty remains. But, as we've seen time and again, the uses of AI technology will have repercussions across the rest of the business.

12

Coda

Time After Time—Cyndi Lauper

For more than 140 years, technology and the music industry has been a story of succession. New formats enabled by innovation come to the fore, and the repercussions propagate throughout the business. Stepping through the formats in chronological order has allowed us to examine these impacts on each of them in depth through the lens of the 6C Framework. Now we'd like to alter our perspective and examine each of the 6Cs across the span of time. As you'll see, some different and useful insights emerge. As Mark Twain is often quoted, "History doesn't repeat itself, but it does rhyme." For example, "The music you want, wherever you want it" sounds like the marketing pitch for any number of today's streaming music services. In fact, this phrase was included in an advertisement for an early phonograph from a century ago.[i]

Though the circumstances are never exactly the same, common themes that echo through the decades merit examination. Moreover, these themes provide relevant lessons for other industries in dealing with their own disruptions caused by technology. We offer one such theme for each of our 6Cs here.

Cutting-edge Technology

Convenience Beats Quality—Across Time

Edison's phonograph used cylinders for recording music. Berliner chose flat discs to fulfill that function for his gramophone. These decisions created a conflict in the market that took years to resolve. Such rivalries of incompatible technologies are referred to as "format wars"; they recurred throughout

Key Changes. Howie Singer and Bill Rosenblatt, Oxford University Press. © Howie Singer and Bill Rosenblatt 2023.
DOI: 10.1093/oso/9780197656891.003.0012

the history of recorded music, including 45s versus LPs and 8-track tapes versus cassettes.

In each of these battles for dominance, one of the formats vying to be the winner held a clear technical advantage in what would seem to be a crucial characteristic: audio quality. However, even when the product provided superior sound, it did not guarantee victory in the market. Instead, consumers repeatedly chose convenience over quality as an even more critical success factor.

In general, cylinders provided more accurate reproduction of the original music than discs. That quality was uniform from the beginning to the end of each recording. For discs, the constant rotation speed meant that the stylus traveled a shorter distance over a given period of time as it made its way toward the center of the record, and with each diminution of distance came a corresponding reduction in sound quality. However, people found it far more convenient to play and to change recordings on discs. The Gramophone was designed to deliver entertainment only and didn't include any recording capability; this resulted in a less complex product that was simpler to use. The form factor of the disc also made it easier to identify recordings by reading the center label rather than trying to discern the far less legible text etched on the ends of cylinders. And storing discs in their sleeves took up much less space than stacking all those cylinders in their cardboard cases. All of that added up to a friendlier experience that proved crucial in winning the market-share battle. Even Edison eventually conceded and, despite more than a decade of championing the superior sound of cylinders, began to release music on discs.

The 12-inch LP provided better sound quality and longer playing time than the 78 record. With more than 20 minutes of playback per side, the LP could begin to address the requirements of lengthier classical repertoire with far fewer discs. RCA initially positioned its competing 45 format as suitable for the classical market as well, in part because it offered even better sound quality than the LP spinning at 33 rpm. But the 7-inch discs could only hold the same four to five minutes of music per side as 78s. To address this issue, RCA created an automatic record changer. But the convenience of a single disc providing over 40 minutes of entertainment with a single interruption to flip to the B-side carried the day—not to mention that classical concertos and most symphony movements could be heard without interruptions in the middle of the music.

Of course, the advent of rock & roll in the mid-1950s ensured the longevity of the 45, as its capacity was a perfect match for the music that millions of teenagers were hearing on transistor radios. Still, the revenues garnered from LPs have always dwarfed the dollars earned by 45s.

The technology story for the tape format represents the best example of a convenient experience winning out over audio quality. Reel-to-reel machines provided sound that was superior to 8-track tapes. But the simplicity of inserting a cartridge into a player and pushing a single button won over handling and threading tape. The introduction of the Compact Cassette brought a further degradation in quality that would eventually be offset by several innovations, including Dolby noise reduction and chromium dioxide tape. Once again, improving the user experience proved to be more important than the decline in audio performance: cassettes were half the size of 8-tracks and offered random access through fast-forward and rewind.

As we noted in Chapter 5, cassettes' convenience motivated the innovations that improved their sound quality. The same innovations made their way into 8-tracks: Dolby-equipped component 8-track recording decks and blank chrome 8-track tapes were both available. But even though both tape formats enabled recording in the home, consumers didn't embrace 8-track recording despite its potential for better sound quality because of the format's relative lack of convenience. Cassettes became the medium of choice for home recording—including recording music from the radio and copying LPs onto cassettes. So although record labels preferred 8-track as a commercial release format and tried to hamper the growth of cassettes by withholding their catalogs from the format in its early days, their convenient features proved irresistible, and the labels had to accept that reality. The cassette became the dominant tape format, surpassing even vinyl for a time in the 1980s and 1990s, despite the fact that many commercially recorded cassettes were duplicated cheaply and didn't sound very good.

As technology evolved to enable the distribution of music files across the Internet, the same themes recurred. The labels authorized limited experiments with startups, but they chose to work with companies like Liquid Audio and a2b music that implemented Digital Rights Management (DRM). The record companies viewed securing downloaded files as essential to deterring unauthorized distribution. Their partners had to deploy DRM that constrained how consumers could enjoy and share the music. Moreover, MP3 compression was included in software that made it simple to add any song to your library by "ripping" files from CDs without any restrictive usage rules. The AAC compression scheme used by a2b music provided better audio quality than an MP3 file of comparable size. But there was no way for users to create AAC files from their CD collections at that time. The virtually limitless catalog of MP3s unencumbered by restrictive rules provided the frictionless experience that trumped audio quality.

Convenience Beats Quality—Across Industries

Coffee is arguably a more essential consumer good than music. Certainly much of humanity can't function without that first cup in the morning, and for some of those people, the taste and quality of the coffee in that cup aren't very important, as long as it's hot and caffeinated. But just after the turn of the millennium, the proportion of coffee drinkers who cared about the quality, origin, and taste of their daily brew started to increase.

The result became known as the "third wave" of coffee. The first wave was the pure utilitarian stuff issuing out of tin cans, percolators, and urns in the mid-twentieth century. Pioneers such as Alfred Peet of Peet's Coffee and Tea in Berkeley, California ushered in the second wave in the 1960s by focusing on countries of origin and darkness of roast.[ii] Peet was a direct inspiration for Starbucks, which first opened in Seattle in 1971, went public in 1992, and became virtually synonymous with (and ubiquitous for) gourmet coffee to many people.

With the third wave of coffee in the 2000s came local chains of coffee shops that also sold beans into the home market. Companies such as Intelligentsia of Chicago, La Colombe of Philadelphia, and Stumptown of Portland, Oregon, expanded their businesses by selling carefully selected single-origin coffees and custom blends from fair-trade sources that they roasted for maximum flavor, and by charging premium prices. To brew those beans, aficionados also began taking home a plethora of coffee-making gizmos beyond the usual Mr. Coffee-style auto-drip devices: grinders, kettles, French presses, pour-over filter cones, stovetop moka pots, and all manner of espresso machines. By 2010, 25 percent of coffee made in American homes was "gourmet" coffee.[iii]

The problem was that getting the most out of those expensive artisanal beans involved technique, effort, and mess. John Sylvan and Peter Dragone, who had been roommates at Colby College in Maine, wanted to eliminate all that. In the mid-1990s they developed a machine that made it easy to brew single cups of the coffee of your choice without having to measure, grind, or clean anything—or commit to a full pot that would taste stale or burnt by mid-morning. You'd simply insert a pod in a slot in a brewing machine, place your mug underneath the spout, press a button, and get your coffee in less than a minute. The next person to come along would open the slot, throw your used pod in the trash, and start again. Sylvan and Dragone chose a Danish word meaning "neat" or "proper" as the name for their system, and in 1998—after six years of trial and error—Keurig delivered its first machines and K-Cup coffee pods to offices.

The Boston-based company produced its first models for home use in 2004 as the third wave was gaining steam.[1] Coffee for the K-Cups initially came from second-wave Green Mountain Coffee Roasters in nearby Vermont; Green Mountain would eventually buy the Keurig company. As sales began to take off, large food concerns such as Salton, Sara Lee, and Procter & Gamble began to introduce single-cup brewing systems, but Keurig became the dominant player.[iv]

As Keurig's popularity soared, other coffee producers began to obtain licenses to produce K-Cups of their coffees. When some of its patents expired in 2012, Keurig introduced proprietary ink-based technology to ensure that only those who took licenses from it would be able to produce K-Cups that worked in the brewing machines—a sort of DRM for coffee pods. (Like many DRMs, Keurig's was eventually hacked.)[v]

Keurig achieved an overwhelming leadership position in the single-serve coffee-maker market over other systems such as Nespresso (from Nestlé of Switzerland) and Tassimo (from JDE Peet's of the Netherlands). The Green Mountain Keurig company ultimately merged with Dr. Pepper Snapple Group in 2018 to form Keurig Dr Pepper, a publicly traded behemoth with a market capitalization not far off that of Starbucks. The company took in over $4.2 billion from Keurig machines and K-Cups in 2019.

However, Keurig had two "dirty" secrets. One was that K-Cups were wasteful and bad for the environment. The other was that the coffee just didn't taste very good. Any serious coffee fan will tell you that the most important route to a good cup is to start with freshly roasted beans and grind them just before brewing. K-Cups, filled with preground beans that had been sitting on warehouse and store shelves for who knows how long, could never compete. Wirecutter, the *New York Times*'s consumer product recommendation service, tested Keurig machines and found that they "brewed watery, flavorless coffee that paled against every other kind of coffee we've made at home. At its best, Keurig coffee tastes like diner coffee. At its worst, it tastes like hot brown water." One of Wirecutter's testers found that it "tastes like an ashtray."[vi]

Yet adoption of single-cup coffee machines rose steadily in tandem with consumption of gourmet coffee in the home. Coffee industry market research has shown that gourmet coffee consumption increased from its 25 percent share in 2010 to 61 percent by 2019. And throughout that period, ownership of single-cup machines—mostly Keurig units—increased to 42 percent in 2019 while drip coffee maker ownership slowly declined (though it remains the most widely owned type).[vii]

Single-serving coffee has begun to wane in popularity as other coffee trends, such as cold brew, take over. But many people still drink it, whether at the office or at home. And although most third-wave roasters do not sell their coffee in K-Cups, large producers of gourmet coffee like Starbucks and Peet's do. (And to address the environmental harm, Keurig now offers refillable K-Cups, and a few coffee producers sell compostable cups.) In other words, many consumers buy "quality" coffee despite the fact that the Keurig system does not do it justice—just as many music fans have been perfectly happy to listen to pristinely produced music tracks as easily downloadable, mediocre-sounding MP3s. Once again, convenience beats quality.

Tough Times Call for New Experiences—Across Time

As new formats emerged and dominated the record business, they paved the way for strategic decisions that maximized revenues and profits. The labels offered fewer singles to encourage increased purchases of more profitable CDs. Dividing streaming music revenues based on the pro rata share of plays led to huge deals to acquire the catalogs of iconic legacy artists and to signing new artists who already have millions of engaged followers on social platforms.

The most consistent theme, however, has been the industry's willingness to place significant bets on new products or business models only when its financial condition is at its most precarious. The Great Depression decimated the entire US economy, including the sales of phonograph records; this accelerated the declines instigated by the growing popularity of radio. The record companies cut prices, but that did little to turn the tide on declining sales.

Coin-operated or automatic phonographs that could change records were introduced in 1927. Bars and restaurants, reinvigorated by the end of Prohibition in 1933, purchased more than one hundred thousand of these "jukeboxes" annually by the middle of the decade. By then, jukeboxes and the record purchases to feed them accounted for one-third of total industry sales, and by the end of World War II, an estimated 75 percent of all records manufactured ended up in jukeboxes. Instead of constraining the flow of new music to jukeboxes to maximize sales to individuals for their home, record labels found an essential lifeline in the sale of one record heard by hundreds.

Decades later, at the dawn of the MTV era, labels had little interest in providing music videos to an embryonic cable business. The channel's business model of providing promotion rather than payments was a nonstarter for many label executives. However, the quarter century of rock-music-fueled growth was sputtering at the end of the 1970s: both units sold and revenues dropped almost 20 percent. Suddenly, the prospect of revitalizing sales revenues seemed more crucial than any remuneration for the videos themselves. That shift in attitude gave MTV the videos it needed to launch and ultimately to establish its own star-making power.

The profits of vinyl and cassettes made it difficult to make the leap to the CD given the significant investment required in new production capabilities. The same pattern held one more time when startups pitched labels on the coming wave of digital distribution in the 1990s when the CD was at its peak of revenues and profits. The music companies did deign to participate in some limited experiments, but the terms were designed to protect the existing business models rather than empowering meaningful online sales. Only a few songs were made available in a series of one-off projects. Even when they partnered with established technology companies such as IBM, they followed a conservative course. Rather than using DRM technology to provide user-friendly rules for the music, such as allowing several multiple copies of a song to be burned onto recordable CDs, the customer's flexibility was constrained.

Then along came Napster. The financial squeeze when industry revenues declined precipitously led to decisions that just a few years earlier would have been anathema to a business reaping enormous CD profits. Not only were the vast majority of albums made available for download, but every song on those albums was available as a single for the modest price of 99 cents.

The download business enabled by Apple's iTunes store and the iPod became a significant contributor to the industry's bottom line. But it never generated enough cash to replace the revenues from CDs as that product continued its decline. Once again, financial pressures provided the impetus for the industry to take a fundamentally different approach when Spotify launched in the United States in 2011. A free tier that provided unlimited access to the entire music catalog and served as a marketing funnel for paid subscriptions was no longer a nonstarter in licensing negotiations. More than a decade later, the streaming business, powered by a variety of global players, has brought top-line growth back to the music business. The valuations of the major record labels have reached heights that few, if any, would have predicted at the turn of the twenty-first century.

Jim Griffin, the technologist who persuaded Geffen Records to make an Aerosmith track available via a digital download in 1994, characterizes this as "Tarzan Economics."[2] Businesses need to let go of their current mechanism for making money, that is, the "old vine," at the right time and grab a "new vine." When a business relies on returns from its current model and the revenues from the new approach are insignificant with an unproven potential for profits, that shift requires a leap of faith that many conservative executives are loath to make (particularly when their bonuses depend on current quarter results). In the case of new music formats and the business models that accompany them, that old vine needs to be fraying visibly to make the case to let it go.

Tough Times Call for New Experiences—Across Industries

Publishers of college textbooks in the early 2010s found themselves in a state of diminishing returns from a business model that had served them well for many decades: selling books for steadily increasing prices to a captive customer base. Students had few choices when the professor assigned the intro physics or economics textbook. If they couldn't afford the $200 for the new book, they could try to find a used copy in decent condition (for not that much less than $200) or just try to do without.

The Internet chipped away at that model in various ways for some time. Online stores like Chegg and VarsityBooks made it easy to buy, sell, and even rent used books by simply entering your school and course number. Unauthorized copies became available online in PDF format if you knew where to look. A growing movement of academics started creating Open Educational Resources (OER)–digital text materials that were free and published under Creative Commons licenses[3] so that no one could restrict or profit from them. And more and more professors began to adopt free or cheap nontextbook curriculum materials such as websites and trade books (books that sell at retail bookstores).

At first, publishers tried to stave off these developments without altering the basic model. They tried getting textbook authors to release new editions of their textbooks more frequently so that the used older editions wouldn't be as desirable. The major publishers formed a joint venture called CourseSmart to publish e-book versions of their texts that students could "rent" for less money than buying print textbooks, but the products were mostly "shovel-ware"[4] that not many students wanted to use. Publishers attempted, in vain, to get copyright law changed to restrict reselling books. Mainly they just kept raising prices. As one example, the classic textbook *Economics* by Paul Samuelson dates back to 1948. It sold for $10 in 1969. Today, the book—now in its 19th edition—sells for more than $200. Even when adjusted for inflation, that's a threefold price increase.

As the effectiveness of these incremental strategies waned, the industry contracted through consolidation. Then in 2013, Cengage, one of the major textbook publishers, declared bankruptcy. That was the industry's "Tarzan moment." Cengage emerged from chapter 11 with a new model called Cengage Unlimited that is analogous to studio-run streaming video services such as Disney + and NBCUniversal's Peacock: digital materials at an all-you-can-read semester or annual subscription price. This was a risky move that the publisher wouldn't have attempted during the good (or even just-okay) times. It required major investment in technology and processes to convert print-oriented texts to "digital-first" materials that work well online. It also meant having to contend with authors who hadn't given Cengage permission to publish their materials in this way; a few of them filed lawsuits, which settled.

Early indications are that Cengage Unlimited is successful, attracting millions of students who save money while helping Cengage's bottom line; and other publishers—such as Pearson, the largest educational publisher—have launched similar plans. And the move to these digital-first models has another advantage: it's much easier for authors and publishers to keep online text materials up to date with incremental changes to digital content than to produce entire new print editions.

In the latest wrinkle in this scheme, the University of California at Davis, a large public university, is acting as its own distributor of text materials from educational publishers. Its Equitable Access program charges students a flat fee per semester for all their text materials. The scheme ensures that students who major in chemical engineering pay no more for their text materials than English majors, and publishers participate with the confidence that students are "buying new" instead of resorting to used textbooks or copyright infringement.[viii]

Artists Leverage New Formats—Across Time

Throughout the history of recorded music, artists followed their creative impulses wherever they led, crafting music that illuminated the human experience and connected with listeners. They accomplished that despite needing to change their output because of the evolving constraints imposed by the various formats. The constraint that had the greatest impact was time.

The capacity of cylinders and 78 rpm discs suited the parlor, operatic aria, and folk song traditions that had long existed when those formats were created. But artists working in other styles—notably jazz—shortened their performances in recording studios to fit, and the popular music styles that emerged in the 1920s and 1930s also conformed to the constraints on song length. Those three to four minutes circumscribed the "single" for more than a century. They became the standard length for radio stations programming the hits and for the rock & roll songs on each side of the 45. For works that required more time, like classical pieces or Broadway shows, the industry created the "record album" to provide a convenient way to purchase and to organize multiple discs.

When the LP provided room for longer recordings, some artists used the additional time simply to provide "more of the same." Others saw that format as an opportunity to create works that told a broader story, such as Frank Sinatra's 1955 album *In The Wee Small Hours of the Morning* or

Sergeant Pepper's Lonely Hearts Club Band by the Beatles a dozen years later. Though more music could be placed on each side of the LP, there were still technical limitations that affected the creative choices. A particularly loud song included at the end of the side increased the likelihood that the needle would jump out of the groove. And the final track on the "A" side needed to be sufficiently engaging to convince the listener that getting out of their chair to flip the record was a worthwhile endeavor. These constraints made the sequencing of the songs on the LP a critical part of the creative process.

Napster disaggregated the album into its constituent tracks for file-sharers, and Apple's iTunes store did the same for music purchasers. The one big hit song was no longer the driver to purchase the entire album, much to the detriment of the music labels' bottom lines. But it did mean that artists like Flo Rida could dominate the singles charts with far greater frequency than the album charts. And as streaming became the main source of revenues, artists began to craft releases with many more tracks of shorter lengths, each with the hook upfront to minimize song skipping, and to take advantage of calculating royalties using a pro-rata share of total plays. Throughout the history of recorded music, artists have altered their output to conform to each format's constraints and show off their creativity in the best way while maximizing potential revenues.

Artists Leverage New Formats—Across Industries

The press probably wrote more stories explaining how the Internet caused the music industry's precipitous fall than about any other business. However, the writers of those stories were part of another industry in the throes of a crisis caused by disruptive technologies.

The newspaper business was built on advertising. The revenues from selling papers defrayed some of the costs of running a newsroom, but they were far from sufficient. The daily editions that summarized the happenings in politics, the arts, and sports aggregated audiences of readers that were valuable to advertisers. The papers that served an individual metropolitan area relied on the ad revenues from that area's department stores, electronics retailers, or record shops, promoting their products and latest sale prices, as well as on classified ads for jobs, apartments, and a myriad of other goods and services. A few newspapers, such as the *New York Times, Washington Post,* and

USA Today attracted readers across the country and were able to supplement those local advertisers with a broader selection of national brands.

As the online audience grew, the newspaper companies built web-based versions of their newspapers, but they treated them as complements to their primary print business. Like the music companies, they viewed their digital businesses as sidelines rather than making them their primary focus. Like the textbook publishers we mentioned earlier in this chapter, they simply served up shovelware: HTML versions of articles on the same daily publishing schedule that had served them well for decades. They gave the news away for free in the hope of attracting enough eyeballs to generate revenues from the digital ads they displayed.

But the technology of the web provided capabilities that enabled alternative ways of presenting and monetizing the content that had previously been confined to print. Craigslist, begun as an email list in San Francisco in the mid-1990s, leveraged its initial success by replicating sites for other cities with minimal costs. Its text format was so simple, and the interface so easy to use, that their advertisers could post ads themselves, which kept operating costs extremely low. By capitalizing on these web capabilities and giving its service away for free to advertisers,[5] Craigslist became a behemoth that served almost 50 million unique visitors with more than 80 million ads each month across the United States alone, decimating newspapers' classified revenues.

Facebook's social network and Google's search interface, both supported by highly efficient online advertising, provided ways to connect with enormous audiences with appetites for information. That enabled sites that catered to specific niche audiences, such as inside-the-Beltway politics filtered through a specific ideological viewpoint, or celebrity fashion, or aggregated movie reviews, to draw enough geographically dispersed users and sufficient investment to fund their growth (if not profits).

These new players in the news business were not wedded to tradition; they changed the way they created content for the web. They abandoned the multiple reviews and editing passes required by newspapers as well as the entire concept of a daily schedule for setting type and printing presses. The story went up on the website as soon as it was ready, and then it was updated as new facts emerged or errors needing correction were found. Multiple headlines were published on the same story, and whichever one produced the most traffic was quickly adopted going forward. The most provocative headlines were often the most effective in attracting traffic even when they did not accurately represent the content of the story, giving rise to the term "clickbait."

News sites would emphasize pictures or videos as the main way to convey information instead of relying primarily on lengthy text stories with a few photos. Instead of stories built around a narrative, a collection of pithy sentences illustrated with photos related to a common theme drew many more viewers than wonky pieces about tax code changes. These so-called "listicles," perfected by sites such as Buzzfeed, featured headlines with numbers like "12 Extremely Disappointing Facts about Popular Music."[ix] All of these techniques were part of the search engine optimization (SEO) toolkit to help boost the stories to the top of Google's search.

Though creating content to attract clicks was a priority for sites like Buzzfeed and Huffington Post, it is worth noting that both of them supplemented these efforts with quality journalism; both have received Pulitzer Prizes for investigative reporting.

While many local newspapers cut back significantly on their staff of journalists or closed up entirely, the existing national papers used their larger addressable markets to adopt story-telling and money-making approaches more suitable to the Internet era. Rather than simply giving the news away and relying on advertising revenues to monetize that traffic, they have implemented paywalls that require paid subscriptions, typically after a set number of articles are read.

The *New York Times*'s implementation of a paywall led to significant growth in paid subscribers, reaching more than 9 million by April 2022 with overall revenues returning to growth after years of declines. It has also been able to make more varied offers that would have been impossible in the days of print. By creating separate subscriptions for crosswords and recipes, the *Times* has been able to monetize niche audiences by allowing its readers to purchase more limited access at a lower price than for the entire paper.

The new technology not only enables news organizations to provide access to their traditional content online, but it has also allowed them to expand the types of stories they tell. Podcasts, such as The Daily from the *New York Times*, provide journalists the ability to go deeper on the stories they present in print and online. In 2017, its first year of operation, The Daily grew to almost 4 million listeners each day; and it has consistently been ranked among the most popular podcasts.[x] Newspapers have also hired data journalists who are experts in visualizing complex stories with charts and tables. In print, they can produce interesting but static charts and graphs. That same information placed online can be interactive as the user selects and reconfigures the information with a few clicks. For example, rather than providing national or state views of the latest COVID-19 statistics alone, these data visualizations enable online readers to select the county they want to see, the statistics they are most interested in, and the time periods relevant to them. Not only have Internet technologies enabled news organizations to offer access using different configurations and business models, but they also allowed the nature of the content offered to change.

The Law Always Trails Technology—Across Time

Innovations in the music industry have often led to structural changes because of quirks or loopholes in copyright law. The speed of technology changes has increased constantly since the early twentieth century while the speed of changes to the law has stayed much the same; and the gap between the two has grown.

The first significant manifestation of that gap was the lack of copyright in sound recordings, which we discussed in Chapter 4. That gap wasn't closed until Congress passed the Sound Recording Act of 1971, which established federal copyright in sound recordings and likely contributed to record labels surpassing music publishers as the dominant generators of music industry revenue in the ensuing decade.

Yet the most longstanding manifestation of the gap between technology changes and the law has been in radio. As we saw in Chapter 3, when radio arose as a popular source of entertainment in the 1930s, regulations limited the ability of radio stations to play recorded music on the air. Those restrictions faded away when television emerged in the 1940s and live entertainers began fleeing radio for the new medium. From then on, laws and regulations had the opposite effect: they enabled playing recorded music on the air to become a highly lucrative and low-cost business.

Radio stations did not have to license the records they played for public performance, because there was no copyright protection for sound recordings. They did have to license the musical compositions being performed, but the law did not require stations to seek permission from music publishers in advance, and there was a competitive market for composition performance royalties after the establishment of BMI in 1939. But even the Sound Recording Act of 1971 did not extend copyright protection to radio broadcasts.

Although Congress established sound recording performance royalty schemes for digital radio in the 1990s, to this day AM/FM broadcast radio does not have to pay for the use of records on the air. The National Association of Broadcasters' success in fending off repeated attempts to establish performance royalties on sound recordings for AM/FM radio broadcasters has benefited the radio industry for nearly a century.

Copyright law's limited ability to respond to technological innovations affected the industry in a different way in the 1970s, when the convenience of tape cassettes motivated innovations that turned a format originally intended for voice recording into a high-fidelity medium for music. By the late 1970s, consumers could buy moderately priced tape decks and blank tapes and make copies of LPs that could sound almost identical to the originals. Copyright law forbade activities such as copying your friend's albums so that you didn't have to buy them, even as its applicability to other activities, such as taping your own albums so that you could play them in the car, was not entirely clear.

But the law wasn't effective as a tool against copying albums onto cassettes. As home taping rose and record sales began to decrease in 1979, the industry made a series of attempts to ameliorate its effects, including pushing Congress to enact a levy on blank tapes that would go to copyright owners. This failed, as did the media industry's attempt, in the *Universal v. Sony* ("Betamax") Supreme Court case, to find home taping of broadcasts to be a violation of copyright law.

As personal computer technology and online services began to disrupt the music industry in the 1990s, music industry lobbying forces tried more aggressively to ensure that copyright law kept up with technological developments. But even when the industry got Congress to pass laws that extended copyright protection in the Internet environment, technologists found ways around those laws.

The furthest-reaching example of this is the Digital Millennium Copyright Act (DMCA), which was signed into law in 1998. Its purpose, among other things, was to give the emerging online services at that time space to innovate without having to be responsible for their users' potential copyright infringements. Service providers could avoid that liability as long as they responded to takedown notices and kicked repeat infringers off their services. The idea was to strike a balance between the interests of technology companies and copyright owners.

Yet a seemingly endless procession of startups exploited one loophole in the DMCA after another. As we saw in Chapter 8, when Napster was found liable for the copyright infringements of its users due to its central database of file locations, several other file-sharing networks arose, such as Grokster and Kazaa, that were based on decentralized architectures with no single source of file location information. And when the record labels succeeded in shutting most of those down, along came BitTorrent.

BitTorrent is a file-sharing protocol, invented in 2001, in which all participants in a BitTorrent network send each other pieces of large files—such as audio or video files—in a carefully choreographed process that repeats until everyone has all of the files being shared. An update of the design of the BitTorrent protocol in the mid-2000s made it technically difficult to collect evidence of infringing actions. Under this version of BitTorrent, websites that list BitTorrent information, such as The Pirate Bay, do not actually point to specific content files, so that it's not easy to get the DMCA (and similar laws outside the United States) to apply to them. The one significant legal decision that the record labels used to their advantage against BitTorrent-related sites that were accused of infringement[6] was the Supreme Court's holding in *MGM v. Grokster* in 2005 that Grokster had "induced" infringement of copyrights, as we discussed in Chapter 8. The *Grokster* inducement theory of liability was invoked in later BitTorrent-related cases such as *Columbia Pictures v. Fung* in 2013, regarding the isoHunt BitTorrent search engine, which the movie studio won to the tune of $110 million in damages.

On the other hand, several other court rulings have expanded the types of content-related services that providers can offer and still avoid liability under the DMCA. We saw a couple of these in Chapter 10 involving YouTube and Veoh. And as we also saw in Chapter 10, the US Copyright Office recently published a study that concluded that DMCA jurisprudence over the past twenty years has failed to maintain its intended balance of interests between copyright owners and technology companies, and that the playing field is now tilted toward the latter. New legislation in the European Union is designed with the intent of restoring that balance, but it is too early to tell how successful it will be or whether the United States will enact similar reforms—or what new technologies will emerge that race ahead of the law yet again.

The Law Always Trails Technology—Across Industries

Many Internet startups live by the adage: "Ask for forgiveness; not permission." Launching services designed to exploit legal or regulatory loopholes has become an essential element of Silicon Valley culture. In music, that meant skirting the precepts of copyright law, but for others seeking to disrupt the status quo, it meant ignoring the constraints or financial impacts of the tax code or labor laws. The so-called "gig economy" relies on the ability to deploy software applications that match revenue opportunities with providers who are treated as independent contractors rather than employees. Such businesses not only avoid obligations around salary, benefits, and taxes but also often require those contractors to use their own assets—whether automobiles or rooms in their home—to satisfy the needs of customers.

There may be no better example of an upstart rule-breaker confronting a highly regulated industry than Uber and taxicabs.[xi] Innovation has played a role throughout the history of this transportation business. In fact, it gave rise to the very term taxicab. The hansom cab was a light horse-drawn carriage; its name was a shortened version of the French term "cabriolet." When a carriage was equipped with a "taximeter" that measured time and distance traveled, the "taxicab" was born. Overcharging for rides led to the imposition of a licensing structure for drivers. The pollution caused by cars proved less distasteful than what horses left behind, and automobiles soon became the preferred vehicle for taxis. The Great Depression led numerous unemployed people to seek work as taxi drivers, making it increasingly difficult for anyone to make a decent wage. To constrain the number of taxis permitted to pick up passengers, major cities, starting with New York, instituted a medallion system to authorize cars in addition to licensing drivers.

Over time, cities kept a tight rein on minting additional medallions. This drove enormous increases in prices.[7] Larger companies amassed the resources to own numerous medallions and then hired drivers who had to earn enough to cover their "nut"— the substantial upfront fees for each shift. The bureaucracy frustrated upward mobility for drivers and constrained the supply for passengers, creating the perfect conditions for a free-wheeling[8] entrant willing to defy the rules.

In 2009, Internet entrepreneur Garrett Camp, frustrated by the high fees to hire a private car, came up with the idea for a "ride-sharing" application. He was soon joined by Travis Kalanick, a serial entrepreneur who had built and sold peer-to-peer file-sharing and content delivery network startups. Kalanick became the public face of the new company and its aggressive take-no-prisoners ethos. "Ubercab" launched in San Francisco without any approvals from regulatory or government bodies. Despite offering only luxury car rides priced higher than taxi fares at first, the convenience and value of the service fueled rapid growth. Ubercab expanded to other cities and added lower-cost options by allowing individuals to use their own cars, subject to Uber's background check, insurance policies, and vehicle standards.

Cabs and their drivers had to follow the far more rigorous rules and licensing requirements that Public Utilities Commissions enforced in each city. And those institutions, prompted by complaints from the incumbents, pressured Ubercab (and its "fast-follower" competitor Lyft) to live by those same rules with a campaign of fines and tickets for the company and their drivers. Some cities, such as Portland, Oregon, simply declared such services illegal. Taxi drivers filed class action suits for unfairly taking their fares.

Uber was not deterred by any of these actions. Claiming that it was a technology company not subject to conventional taxi regulations, it rebranded as "Uber." It used some of its substantial venture capital cash to pay the fines. It developed software called Greyball that used data to detect when government officials were using the app to catch Uber and its drivers in unauthorized activities: actual drivers quickly canceled the officials' rides, while Greyball showed vehicles approaching on their phone displays that simply did not exist. If there were no rides, there were no violations to cite.

Lyft gained momentum by enticing riders with lower prices and allowing drivers to align with both services. Uber responded by creating software to create fake Lyft riders to gather data on the availability of their competitor's cars and drivers to improve their own service. In addition, the data it gathered surreptitiously identified drivers working for both firms who could then be targeted with special bonuses to become exclusive to Uber. These actions put Uber at legal risk for pursuing unfair business practices.

Expanding the number of Uber drivers increased the availability of rides, but it also created issues around passenger safety, as female passengers were sometimes subject to harassment or worse. In 2014, Uber added a surcharge of $1 on every trip as a "Safe Rides Fee." However, the cash was not used to improve safety in any way. Instead, in yet another case of unsavory practices, the half-billion dollars collected were simply added to the company's bottom line.

Uber was, for a time, the most popular download in Apple's app store. As part of its extensive data collection, Uber's software enabled it to identify individual iPhones even after a user deleted their Uber app, a practice that violated Apple's policies. Apple refused to approve an updated version of the Uber app unless it abandoned its intrusive practices. Not wanting to abandon the edge provided by the data, Uber crafted a devious solution to the dilemma: it retained the secret data collection code but created a "geofence" around Apple's headquarters in Cupertino. Within that area, any Apple employee running the Uber app would observe strict adherence to the rules with no problematic data collected. But if you ran the app outside of that region, all bets (and rules) were off. Apple eventually discovered the ruse, and CEO Tim Cook threatened Kalanick with Uber's complete removal from the app store. Uber complied, although the entire kerfuffle proved to be nothing more than a slap on the wrist.

One of the most successful elements of Uber's pushback on governmental efforts to rein it in was in the court of public opinion. It mobilized its riders, who found the service superior to conventional taxis, to put pressure on politicians. Uber obtained thousands of signatures on petitions that it could deliver to the steps of City Hall, with drivers and riders cheering it on. Ultimately, Uber's tactics prevailed, and it was able to expand its services in cities all over the world.

Many drivers appreciated the flexibility of scheduling when driving for Uber, but their contributions to the company's growth were not rewarded. Treating them as contractors who drove their own vehicles gave Uber the benefits of huge revenues without incurring the costs of salaries, benefits, or car repairs. In the face of mounting driver complaints about compensation, Kalanick famously said that Uber would be better off financially when it could replace the driver completely with self-driving vehicles.

Playing fast and loose with the rules did have consequences. The company's reputation took significant hits for its underhanded maneuvers (and its misogynistic workplace culture). When Uber went public in 2019, it was valued at over $80 billion, worth more than GM and Ford combined. Still, by 2022, even with the public exposure of all its questionable practices, the company's enterprise value declined only about five percent. Kalanick himself took a much greater hit as his investors forced him to resign as CEO for the company that he had propelled to market dominance. His bank account did not suffer, however, as his shares were worth billions after Uber's IPO.

Overall, one would have to conclude that "permissionless innovation" had proved worthwhile for Uber. And despite various current attempts to change labor, transportation, and other laws to address the behaviors of "gig economy" companies, the laws remain the same—for the time being.

Consumers

Fans Are More Tolerant than the Establishment— Across Time

Music listeners have repeatedly shown that popular tastes evolve over time and that they have a willingness, if not a desire, to connect with new genres and artists. These shifts have become even more pronounced since World War II and the rise of teenagers as a distinct demographic segment with significant purchasing power. Each new wave of teens want music and artists that represent their own particular generational concerns–and if their parents found that music objectionable, so much the better.

These new musical styles and genres were repeatedly brought into the world by African American artists. But the power structure of the industry held the mistaken and biased view that the majority of their audience simply would not accept these artists, so they deliberately limited the aperture for this material to reach the broader market. They chose to keep the Black artists in the background and placed their melodies and words in the hands and voices of white performers to improve the perceived acceptability to white fans.

The earliest recordings continued the minstrelsy practices prevalent in live performances of the day and offered "race music" with white artists using exaggerated Black speech patterns and demeaning language. Jazz evolved out of earlier forms of African American music and was refined by Black musicians in New Orleans. But the first recording of the genre featured the Original Dixieland Jass Band,[9] which was made up entirely of white musicians. Paul Whiteman became known as the "King of Jazz," while the arrangements for his orchestra of white musicians toned down the more improvisational elements of the genre to broaden its "mainstream" (i.e., white) appeal. Entrepreneurs created independent companies such as Okeh Records that, unlike the established companies, were willing to feature artists such as Mamie Smith and Louis Armstrong. Jazz performed by these and other artists was marketed to both Black and white audiences, and the establishment's limited viewpoint proved unfounded. Fans of all colors bought the records, and by 1928, Columbia Records purchased Okeh and its catalog.

Through the 1940s and into the 1950s, radio segregated music from African American artists on separate stations. The industry periodical *Radio & Records* did not even have a chart to report on the popularity of music from Black artists at that time, rendering it invisible to readers.

Early rock & roll music was widely viewed as a corrupting influence on young people, and the race of the founders of the genre contributed to that impression for many in white America. One of those founding fathers of rock, Fats Domino, released "Ain't It a Shame," a song he cowrote with Dave Bartholomew, in April 1955. Within a month, a somewhat sanitized version of the same song recorded by Pat Boone, now retitled as the more familiar "Ain't That a Shame," followed. One would be hard-pressed to find a less objectionable musical artist to white households than Pat Boone. His co-opted version gained national attention for the song (and publishing royalties for Domino). Yet fans proved to be more accepting than many expected, and Fats Domino's version outsold Boone's.

At the start of the music video era, MTV resisted playing videos by Black artists because they did not think they would appeal to its core audience of predominantly white rock fans. Michael Jackson's "Billie Jean" gave the lie to that perception after some arm-twisting by CBS Records resulted in a change of policy. The popularity of Jackson's videos and those from other Black artists demonstrated once again that fans' musical tastes were broader and more diverse than expected.

A few years later, the mainstream record business was uninterested in signing hip-hop artists when the genre emerged in urban Black neighborhoods. The view that this was not "real music" even held them back from offering "white-washed" versions. In this case, the technology available provided an alternative path to reach fans. The availability of recordable tape cassettes and, later, CDs, gave those artists a way, albeit on a limited scale, to manufacture and to distribute their creative works. Soon independent labels focusing on rap music provided the capital and infrastructure to expand. As the popularity of the new genre grew, the major labels did adapt and brought these smaller hip-hop labels into their corporate structures. However, the genre still received short shrift in terms of marketing and promotion until the birth of the Soundscan era. Having accurate sales data showed that rap (and country) were far more popular than the industry believed. Fans across the country—both Black and white—demonstrated their affinity for new genres born in the African American community despite the hurdles placed in the way.

Fans Are More Tolerant than the Establishment— Across Industries

Professional sports has a similar checkered history in terms of providing equitable opportunities for talented African American athletes to reach the broadest possible fan bases. Black baseball players were consigned to the Negro League for decades until Jackie Robinson broke the color barrier in 1948. For many years, successful Black college quarterbacks did not get the chance to play that most highly paid and publicized position in the NFL because the "experts" believed they lacked the necessary "football IQ." Instead they were "converted" to wide receivers or cornerbacks, where pure athleticism was deemed more critical. Once these players got the opportunity and showed off their extraordinary talents as quarterbacks, most fans had no issues rooting for them.

Professional basketball provides an excellent example of an industry restricting its talent from reaching the broadest audiences possible because of concerns over the acceptance of Black athletes and culture. Basketball can be played in relatively small spaces with a minimal investment in playing facilities and gear when compared to other sports, making it a perfect fit for urban communities. Those characteristics made these communities fertile training grounds for talented Black players as well as for the pioneers of hip-hop.

Black players were not accepted into the NBA until the early 1950s, and whites continued to dominate rosters throughout the 1960s. Over time, the racial mix shifted and, by the 1980s, African American players constituted the majority of NBA team rosters. The league placed a disproportionate amount of attention and promotion on the smaller number of white players, thinking that was needed to retain favor with their fanbase. For example, Larry Bird joined the league in 1979. His small-town Midwestern roots paired with his copious talents made him a perfect candidate for that spotlight. He eventually proved himself to be one of the greatest players of all time, but it is indicative of the sport's approach to race that, in the early part of his career, he was referred to as "The Great White Hope" of the NBA.[10]

By the late 1990s, hip-hop's cultural influence and importance to the music business was well-established. Around that same time, Allen Iverson entered the NBA with the basketball abilities to dominate any game he played despite being only six feet tall. He was selected number one in the NBA draft by the Philadelphia 76ers in 1996, and with his numerous tattoos and cornrows he resembled rappers in music videos more than superstar players of the day such as Michael Jordan. "Gangsta rap," which represented the milieu of street gangs and culture, was seen by some as promoting criminality, and Iverson's personal history gave people more evidence to paint him with the same brush: he had served time in jail while in high school over an altercation at a bowling alley, although the conviction was later reversed. On the basketball court, Iverson did not adhere to the unwritten rules that required deference to players like Michael Jordan. Iverson seemed to embody the very image that white ownership wanted to avoid for its majority-Black league. When he appeared on the cover of the NBA's magazine, they airbrushed the photo to remove his tattoos.[xii]

Another supremely talented player also entered the league in 1996, but in contrast to Iverson, Kobe Bryant came with a resume containing all of the establishment's preferred attributes. Bryant had decidedly not grown up "in the hood." He was raised in the affluent area of the Philadelphia suburbs known as the Main Line, and in Italy where his father Joe played professionally after leaving the NBA. Not many basketball prospects from the inner city spoke Italian fluently and played soccer. Despite strong grades and excellent SAT scores, Bryant decided to skip college and made the leap to the NBA directly from high school.

Dr. Todd Boyd is the Katherine and Frank Price Endowed Chair for the Study of Race and Popular Culture and Professor of Cinema and Media Studies at USC. He wrote that "Kobe Bryant has often functioned as the league's de facto White Man, in that his upper-middle-class status is more easily assimilated in the game's overall fabric than the hip hop-inspired narrative that Allen Iverson embodies."[xiii]

Though the league might have preferred Bryant as a more "acceptable" star, Iverson's success on the court made him a fan favorite. The hip-hop aesthetic that Iverson represented became an intrinsic part of the league. Rappers now headline the performances at the NBA All Star Game, and hip-hop music is played for the dance teams as entertainment in every arena. For a time, Jay-Z owned a small share of the Brooklyn Nets.[11] Despite the fears of white owner-ship, this shift has driven the league to greater heights of popularity with both white and Black fans.

Channel Control Is Elusive—Across Time

The music industry created retail channels in the late 1920s when record labels standardized on the 78-rpm disc. Once that happened, it was inevi-table that independent stores would appear that sold records from all labels. As we saw in Chapter 4, this in turn led to the proliferation of retail channels for physical music products throughout the latter half of the twentieth cen-tury, with all of their complexity: indie record stores, big discount chains, distributors, rack jobbers, and so on. It also led to the swift exit of record companies from the hardware business.

The reason why record labels adopted a standard format was simple: in-crease the size of the overall market by making it easier for consumers to buy more records. This is an extremely common and proven strategy in many markets, from tires to mattresses to plumbing fixtures. Yet in the vast ma-jority of cases, standardization comes with a tradeoff: suppliers of products into standards-based markets lose control over retail channels. Goodyear, Serta, and Kohler don't control Mavis Discount Tire, Mattress Firm, or Home Depot.

Control over retail channels amid format standardization became a per-ennial struggle for the music industry; the history of the industry is one of record labels' repeated and mostly futile attempts to take back elements of channel control. Antitrust law constrained record labels' ability to control re-tail channels in significant ways, so they resorted to other tactics that worked around the edges.

One of these tactics was selling directly to consumers through record clubs. This was moderately successful; but the labels had to cross-license titles to each other's clubs to compete effectively, especially against discounters like Sam Goody that had also built formidable mail-order businesses. Otherwise, the tactics that labels used to influence retail channels cost them money, such as giving away albums by lesser-known artists to get rack jobbers to place them at retailers and paying big retail chains for endcap displays in their stores.

When digital music emerged, the nature of labels' attempts to control channels changed. As we saw in Chapter 8, the big challenge in the late 1990s was to compete with free. The industry understood that any licensed channel for digital music would require the catalog of every label to have a chance of success. So the labels shifted from *format* standardization to *catalog* standardization, even as digital services proliferated that each had their own formats and apps. Catalog standardization meant making sure that as many licensed channels as possible had as much music as possible.

Antitrust concerns prevented the major labels from launching their own single service representing their full catalogs. Instead, independent digital music services flourished that all had full-catalog licenses from all labels. The first of these was the early streaming service Rhapsody, which garnered licenses from all of the (then five) major labels by July 2002, almost a year before Apple launched the iTunes Music Store. At the time, the majors viewed Rhapsody as a limited experiment, but in many ways, it became a model for services that would launch later on, such as Spotify.

Apple's control of music distribution grew and grew through the mid-2000s, despite various attempts by the labels to curb its growing market power. By 2008, it had become the largest music retailer in the world—of any kind. In doing so, Apple beat out technology stacks from other vendors such as RealNetworks, Microsoft, and Sony.[12] The labels' partnership with Amazon that did eventually eat into Apple's market share was more about retail merchandising and less about technology. The deal required the major labels to abandon their requirements for DRM, so that MP3 files purchased on Amazon could play on the then-ubiquitous Apple iPods. Amazon's entry into the market forced Apple to adopt the variable pricing that labels had sought. But otherwise the market didn't change much. Amazon's share of digital downloads never made it very far into the double digits; Apple continued to dominate until streaming overtook downloads in 2015.

The majors' other structural attempt to take back control over channels in the late 2000s was the launch of the streaming video joint venture Vevo in 2008. The original intent of Vevo, as we saw in Chapter 10, was to compete with YouTube and head off an Internet-age repeat of MTV's monopolization of music videos in the 1980s and 1990s. But while Vevo succeeded in drawing a lot of user traffic and helping the majors negotiate higher ad revenue shares, it failed as a YouTube competitor; on the contrary, it became primarily a vehicle for distributing official videos of major-label releases on YouTube. The labels' leverage against user-upload services like YouTube and TikTok is arguably even lower than with streaming services such as Spotify and Apple Music because, as we also explained in Chapter 10, they must opt out of allowing their content up on those services instead of controlling their access to it.

As streaming rose in popularity, labels attempted to exert control over the market by taking equity stakes in independent streaming services and by structuring complex royalty deals that favored their artists. Attempts to exert control by limiting catalog or granting exclusives were few and far between; and in 2016, Universal Music Group CEO Sir Lucian Grainge announced that the world's largest record company would no longer do exclusives, though the related practice of windowing (see Chapter 9) did continue occasionally.

In recent years, the strategy of at least some of the major labels, apart from the "value gap" legal strategy discussed in Chapter 10, has been to bulk up on as much catalog as possible to gain leverage in royalty negotiations with all digital music services. If this strategy succeeds, it could lead to further con-solidation of record labels as well as the Netflix-like possibility that digital music services will start signing artists themselves. At this writing, TikTok is making moves in that direction, such as hiring A&R staff.[xiv]

Yet that strategy is also reaching its limits, due to a phenomenon that has been building for the past few years: the sheer explosion of recorded music. Labels and artists are releasing music now at a rate of about 100,000 tracks *per day* to digital services worldwide,[13] a pace that is over 100 times that of record releases during the CD era.[xv] And the major music companies' collec-tive contribution to that number has been decreasing steadily; it was a mere 4 percent in 2022.[xvi] Even if the majors were to consolidate to a "Big Two" or even a "Big One," size of catalog is becoming less and less important.

The major labels have finally started to confront this trend. For example, in January 2023 Grainge accused "those committed to gaming the system through quantity over quality" of pushing "lower-quality functional con-tent that in some cases can barely pass for 'music' "[xvii] and called for the new artist-centric streaming royalty schemes that we discussed in Chapter 9, which would be likely to benefit "name" artists the most. It remains to be seen if such tactics will affect existing channel dynamics, especially with AI-generated music entering the mix.

Channel Control Is Elusive—Across Industries

Hollywood studios and television networks were able to watch the record labels suffer through the Napster era at a relatively safe distance: Internet access speeds and storage media in the late 1990s were not fast or large enough to handle digital video. (For example, it took roughly 10 hours to download a movie over a 56 kbps dialup line, and the resulting file would fill up the hard drive of a typical PC of that era.) So while they knew that video on the Internet was coming, they had some time to plan.

The major studios and networks tried to be more aggressive than the record labels in taking control of online distribution channels. The studios had bitter experience with the loss of channel control in the late 1940s, when the Supreme Court's decision in *United States v. Paramount Pictures* forced them to divest the movie theaters they owned. And the television networks were stymied in the 1950s by the FCC's regulations that limited the number of broadcast stations that a single company could own.

Hollywood's first attempt to control online channels was a digital download service called MovieLink, which was a joint venture of most of the major studios. MovieLink launched in late 2002, about a year after the major labels launched MusicNet and pressplay. It was the first Internet video service to offer licensed content from all of the major studios.[14]

MovieLink was never more than a moderate success, and its competition increased over time. By the mid-2000s, the video rental chain Blockbuster had expanded into online video, as did a few startups and consumer electronics retailers. The studios licensed their content to those entities, and for a little while it looked like services such as Blockbuster Online and Best Buy CinemaNow might be the future of video with ample major-studio catalogs of content for sale. Yet online movies and TV were slow to catch on. Downloading was still a clunky process, and few people wanted to watch movies on PCs. The resulting business that these services did was minimal.

The mood in Hollywood shifted in late 2005 when Apple launched video-capable iPods and expanded the iTunes Store to sell movies and TV shows. The studios saw that Apple was dominating the digital music world of the time with its tightly integrated, easy-to-use products, so they attempted to prevent it from doing the same thing in video. Their response was a technology called UltraViolet, the brainchild of Sony Pictures executive Mitch Singer.[15]

UltraViolet was a scheme that enabled consumers to buy video content online and have it play on a wide variety of devices while protecting it from rampant unauthorized copying. When you bought a movie or TV show from an UltraViolet-participating retailer in that retailer's format for playback on its compatible devices, the UltraViolet system would store a record of your purchase. This enabled you to go to another participating retailer and obtain the same content in that other retailer's format for little or no additional cost. You could also sign up for a free family plan that enabled up to five family members to play the content you bought on their devices.

UltraViolet launched in 2010, but it had trouble garnering interest from retailers: it prevented them from building "walled gardens" and constrained their ability to compete on features; and the technology infrastructure they needed to build to support it was expensive and complex. Apple didn't participate at all, nor did Disney: Steve Jobs was on Disney's board of directors, and the UltraViolet consortium's principal technology partner was Apple's arch-rival Microsoft. A few major retailers experimented with the system, but the only one that really participated was Walmart. UltraViolet shut down quietly in 2019.[xviii]

Yet as the industry transitioned from downloads and physical products to streaming, the studios did manage to recapture some measure of control over channels after all. When Netflix branched out from DVD rentals to streaming in 2007, the studios initially licensed their content to the service eagerly, as it promised to be a viable competitor to Apple. But it soon became apparent that streaming would eclipse downloading and grow to become a major mode of video consumption; and the studios began to fear that Netflix would dominate streaming video as Apple did downloaded music. So they took steps to prevent that from happening—steps to control distribution channels more tightly.

The studios saw that the record labels were licensing their full catalogs to a growing number of independent streaming services. They decided to do the opposite: they curtailed their licensing to online services and did not renew Netflix's licenses to large swaths of catalog content. And they began to launch their own Internet video services. The first of these was Hulu, which launched in 2008 as a joint venture of News Corporation (parent of 20th Century Fox studios) and NBC Universal; Disney joined the following year.

Hulu quickly overcame skepticism and derision from tech-industry pundits who figured that old-line Hollywood studios had no chance of success on the Internet.[xix] Hulu's rapid rise and Netflix's success led to a profusion of studio-owned subscription streaming services, including HBO Max, Disney+, Paramount+, Discovery+, and NBCUniversal's Peacock. These compete with independent paid streaming services such as Netflix, Amazon Prime Video, and Apple TV+, all of which started producing their own exclusive content.

In many ways, these services are the diametric opposite of the world that UltraViolet enabled. Each of them has its own walled garden as well as distinct content catalogs that include exclusives as well as on-demand offerings of the owners' movies and TV shows. Each is free to decide on subscription pricing, whether to run ads, and other features without worrying about its competitive position relative to other services with essentially identical content. And each has subscribers in the tens or hundreds of millions.[xx]

But the result of this strategy is not great for the consumer. You have to know which service carries the show or movie you want to watch, and you have to subscribe to that service. Then you have to select the service on your smart TV, set-top box, or mobile device and navigate its distinct user interface. This would be tantamount to knowing (or having to look up) which label the music you want to listen to is on, subscribing to that label's service, and firing up its app on your device, instead of just going to your choice of music services knowing that your music will be there.

That difference highlights the limitations of the studios' channel control efforts as more and more of them launch their own subscription streaming services. There's a limit to the amount of money that consumers will spend on subscriptions per month; and consumers are finding it increasingly challenging to decide which services to subscribe to, to contend with all those different user experiences, and to find the content they want. This phenomenon already has a name: "subscription fatigue." Aggregators and consolidation are inevitable; and the pendulum may swing back toward a market that looks more like on-demand versions of cable and satellite TV, with a mixture of paid and ad-supported free services—i.e., more like the music market that we know today.[xxi]

In fact, as we write this, there are already signs that the studios' and networks' stampedes into streaming are running into these limitations and slowing down. In 2022, in rapid succession, Netflix announced its first annual loss of subscribers in over 10 years; CNN shut down its subscription streaming service CNN+ a mere three weeks after launching it; and WarnerMedia (owner of CNN, HBO, and other properties) completed a merger with Discovery Communications, with staff cuts looming for all of them. And the Holy Grail of channel control continues to elude Hollywood just as it continues to elude the music industry.

Conclusion

The history of the recorded music experience is certainly a long and winding road. We've progressed from the indentations in a tinfoil cylinder to terabytes of zeros and ones stored in the cloud. Instead of placing a needle ever so carefully on the right spot on a record, music is now accessible by the touch of a finger on a powerful handheld computer or a few spoken words. Understanding how each of the advances in technology and formats came about is essential to understanding today's music industry. In his 2005 commencement address at Stanford University, Steve Jobs said, "You can't connect the dots looking forward; you can only connect them looking backwards." We think that we've done more than simply recite the history of recorded music formats. We've provided a framework—the 6Cs—that connects the dots and provides both a consistent way to examine that history and provides perspective about the changes yet to come.

There are two incontrovertible lessons that we can take away from our examination of the industry from the earliest phonographs to streaming services powered by AI algorithms. First, it is only a matter of time before some yet-to-be-invented technology changes the way that we experience recorded music again. And second, regardless of that experience, billions of people will be listening. The artist Moby said, "A great song is a great song, whether it's on vinyl or CD or cassette or reel to reel or mp3. Then again, that might be an overly optimistic view, but I do think that great music will transcend the medium in which it is delivered." We agree.

Afterword

Unchained Melody—Righteous Brothers

What's the next technology that will disrupt the music industry? As we write this in 2022, we're pretty sure of at least one word in one answer to that question: blockchain.

Blockchain adherents claim that the technology will disrupt many industries as profoundly as the Internet itself did, starting back in the 1990s. The amount of money, hype, and talent being poured into blockchain technology today has not been seen since the first Internet Bubble of the late 1990s; that alone virtually guarantees that the effects that the technology will have on various facets of life will be profound.

The music industry has been engaging with blockchain and related technologies for the past several years. Although the technology's impact isn't likely to be truly clear for a few more years, the contours of its likely effects on the structure of the industry are starting to come into view. We can suggest some directions that it will take, as startups, artists, and others experiment with it, and as the public starts to catch on.

The simplest way to describe a blockchain is as a database or ledger of transaction records, which is organized as a series of *blocks* of records that are linked together in a *chain*. The database has various special properties. One is that every entity involved in the transactions has its own complete, up-to-date copy of the blockchain at all times, and no single entity owns or controls it. Another is that it's only possible to add records to the database, not change or delete them. New records are propagated over the Internet to all copies of the database.

The first blockchain was created in 2008 by Satoshi Nakamoto, a pseudonym for a person (or persons) whose true identity (or identities) remains unknown to this day. It was used in the implementation of bitcoin, the first cryptocurrency. People involved in the field soon understood that the technology had many applications beyond cryptocurrency. Bitcoin uses one blockchain; just as there can be arbitrarily many databases (or database companies) in the world, there can also be arbitrarily many blockchains.

Several ancillary technologies have been invented to enable certain types of blockchain applications; these, together with blockchain technology itself, are collectively known as "Web 3.0" or simply "Web3." The term "Web3" reflects the notion that these technologies are bringing about a third wave in the development of the Internet, where "Web 1" was the original "Wild West" Internet of the late 1990s through early 2000s and "Web 2" represents the current environment dominated by tech behemoths like Alphabet (Google) and Meta (Facebook, Instagram).

The most important of these Web3 technologies for these purposes is smart contracts. A smart contract is a piece of code that runs on every instance of a blockchain whenever a new record is added to it. Smart contracts are so named because they are often used to implement rules of an agreement (contract) among parties in transactions. Certain blockchains, such as Ethereum, Solana, and Cardano, support smart contracts and are used in music applications.

Blockchain applications for music began to emerge in the mid-2010s. They have fallen into two categories, which we can refer to as B2B (business-to-business) and B2C (business-to-consumer).[i]

Many B2B blockchain applications in music involve using blockchains for rights administration and royalty transaction processing. The basic idea is to replace the complex, proprietary systems that exist within participants in royalty processes—labels, publishers, PROs, rights administrators, music services, and so on—with decentralized blockchains that store transactions and process royalties automatically, and that every stakeholder can access.

A paradigmatic example of this is royalty payments for music streaming. Each time someone plays a song on a streaming music service, that service needs to calculate and make a number of royalty payments. The record label should get a royalty for the sound recording, based on a rate that the label negotiated with the music service. The owners of rights in the composition being performed should get their shares of mechanical royalties, with rates set by law. The PROs representing those rights-holders should get performance royalties according to the blanket licenses that the music service negotiated with each PRO. And so on. The idea is that each time a song is played, the music service adds a record to a blockchain that indicates the identity of the song, along with other data indicating the type of use,[1] and a series of smart contracts executes to pay the royalties.

Such a scheme would have substantial advantages over the current status quo, where each music service has to maintain its own highly complex infrastructure for making royalty payments. It would reduce operating costs, not just for music services but for everyone involved. Because the vast majorities of streaming services' music catalogs are identical, this scheme would eliminate massive redundancies. And it would provide consistency, verifiability, and transparency for royalty transactions.

Yet this example is idealistic and currently unattainable, for a number of reasons. One is that blockchain technology at this time of writing is not capable of handling the billions of smart contract transactions per day that today's streaming volumes would generate. The fact that every new transaction must be propagated to every copy of a blockchain severely limits scalability. For example, Ethereum, the most widely used blockchain that supports smart contracts, can currently process between 10 and 20 transactions per second.[ii] A future version has been promised that will lift that number to 100,000, but even that is still not quite enough to support royalty transaction volumes for streaming music—which itself is growing over time.[iii]

Another reason is that the accuracy of transaction processing is only as good as the accuracy of the data that goes into it—the "Garbage In, Garbage Out" (GIGO) principle that data and technology people have long understood. This creates a decentralized data governance problem that blockchain technology by itself does not solve. Yet another reason is that it would require an unprecedented amount of highly detailed cross-industry cooperation required to implement such a scheme.

At least some of these problems are solvable, whether through technological innovation or through sheer effort and cooperation motivated by the potential benefits. Several startup companies are working on these types of B2B solutions, and pilot projects are under way. The Open Music Initiative, a standards organization working on metadata models and protocols that can be implemented on blockchains, created a blueprint for a blockchain-based solution to the streaming mechanicals problem that we discussed in Chapter 9—although that was sidelined with the passage of the Music

Modernization Act of 2018, which implemented a solution based on a traditional centralized database (the Mechanical Licensing Collective).

It is likely that the current crop of startups and pilot projects will lead to successful blockchain-based solutions for rights administration and royalty processing in smaller niche applications, where the number of stakeholders and the transaction volumes are low enough to be practicable. Already there are some implementations in areas such as royalty payments for radio airplay and synch licensing for films. A couple of startups have built blockchain-based techniques for achieving consensus on rights ownership data that ameliorates the GIGO problem. As these applications take hold and the scalability of the technology improves, the rest of the industry is certain to take notice and gain confidence in this type of solution, which could lead to adoption for broader use cases.

At the same time, various entrenched interests will impede adoption of this technology: because it requires such deep levels of cooperation among stakeholders to implement, a solution could fail if only one link in the chain refuses to participate. For example, certain entities have reputations for opaque "black box" processes for calculating royalty payouts; they will not be motivated to transition to technologies that emphasize openness and transparency.

A more recent wrinkle in these B2B royalty processing applications of blockchain technology is to extend it to consumers by enabling them to participate in royalty streams, as investment vehicles or as extensions of fan-artist relationships. Distributed autonomous organization (DAO) is a Web3 term for a business with financial rules that run automatically on a blockchain with smart contracts; DAOs are being set up to enable this scenario, so that fans get paid automatically, according to rules, when artists do. These are blockchain-based versions of current businesses such as Royalty Exchange that enable "retail investors" to invest in individual royalty streams.

But these B2B applications are virtually unknown outside of the industry. Far more attention—and hype—go towards B2C applications, which purport to bypass the entire industry infrastructure by using blockchain technology to sell music directly to fans. The buzzword that has been most frequently attached to this activity over the past couple of years is nonfungible tokens (NFTs). Unlike fungible tokens, such as cryptocurrency, which are interchangeable representations of directly tradeable assets, NFTs are representations of purchases of other types of assets that are not directly tradeable for one another. Put simply, an NFT is a record of purchase—of something—that is stored on a blockchain. That something could be a digital asset, such as a file containing digital music or visual art; or it could be a physical item. It could even be an experience, such as a backstage visit with an artist before a show. Or it could be a combination of those. In any case, the NFT is the record of purchase, not the item itself.

NFTs can be resold. NFT platforms like OpenSea, Nifty Gateway, and Catalog—there are dozens of them, with new ones appearing all the time—take commissions and allow creators ("minters") to set up resale royalties for themselves, so that no matter how many times an NFT is resold, the creator gets the royalty each time. NFT prices can be fixed or set at auction. For NFTs that involve digital music files or other digital assets, the digital content is typically not stored on the blockchain; it is stored "off-chain" on whatever storage medium makes sense.[2]

The first experiments of blockchain technology in B2C applications for music came in the mid-2010s. In most of these, you paid a small amount of money, and you got a digital music file with a record of your purchase of that file stored on a blockchain. The file was yours to do with as you pleased; there was no digital rights management (DRM) on it. This left many to wonder: putting all the hype around blockchain aside, how did this differ from purchasing a 99-cent download on iTunes? The answer was: not much that anyone could discern, certainly not enough to make it worth all the technological complexity and extra fees involved. The idea did not catch on.

But then the NFT phenomenon came along. The most important difference between NFTs and the aforementioned early experiments was that the number of NFTs available for a given work was limited, often to one, whereas this was typically not the case before. In other words, the salient point about NFTs was that they were intended to reintroduce the scarcity and collectability of physical media to the digital world.

The first instances of what we now call NFTs appeared in the mid-2010s. The term NFT came from a technical standard related to the Ethereum blockchain that was proposed in 2017 and published in January 2018.[iv] The first widely known NFT application was an online game called CryptoKitties that launched in 2017, in which players buy, "breed," and resell virtual animated cats, with purchases recorded on the blockchain. Something about

CryptoKitties appealed to the masses, and the idea of "ownership" of content that existed only in cyberspace took hold.

The first NFTs for music were launched around 2020; sales started taking off in 2021. According to Water & Music, a research firm focused on Web3 technologies in music, sales of music NFTs totaled less than $1 million per month until January 2021; then they spiked to a peak of $27 million in March, only to fall back to earth again by summer 2021. Sales of music NFTs have increased again, gradually, since then as more music-focused NFT platforms have launched. The majority of the several hundred artists who have minted NFTs thus far are not signed to major labels, and the most popular music genre is electronic. The most common release configuration is digital audio accompanied by visual artwork.[v]

One way of putting the NFT revenue numbers in perspective is to compare them to the music industry's main current source of revenue from physical objects: vinyl. The NFT market in 2021 was only 10 percent of the size of the US vinyl market by revenue.[vi,3] Water & Music's data shows that music NFT revenue in 2022 was about $96 million[4]—which is a 10 percent decrease from $105 million in 2021 and amounts to less than 8 percent of the $1.2 billion US vinyl market in 2022. In other words, at this time of writing NFTs' actual market impact is nowhere near the level of their hype. Yet these NFT sales figures are entirely typical of new technology adoption curves: huge hype-driven spike followed by steep plunge followed by slow, steady growth as the market settles on attractive value propositions.[5]

Another typical attribute of new technology markets is overcomplexity for the nontechnically savvy. This is certainly true of NFTs.

NFTs are not simple to buy. Even Coinbase, the well-known cryptocurrency exchange, says on its website that "NFT markets aren't exactly Amazon when it comes to ease of use."[vii] Once you have found an NFT that you want to buy, you have to determine which blockchain it's on, which dictates the cryptocurrency you need to use to buy it. For example, the majority of music NFTs are on the Ethereum blockchain and are typically purchased using Ethereum's ETH cryptocurrency. You may need to go to a crypto exchange (like Coinbase) that sells the cryptocurrency you want and buy some (or convert from another cryptocurrency). Then you need to make sure that you have a crypto wallet—an app, browser extension, cloud service, or hardware device—that's compatible with that cryptocurrency. Only then can you buy the NFT. And at each step of the way, fees may apply, including a "gas fee" that applies to Ethereum purchases to offset the electricity used to complete the transaction. That's one reason why fees for minting and buying NFTs have been quite high, often exceeding $100.

The process is similarly complex for sellers of NFTs, as it also is for artists who may want to participate in DAOs or other blockchain-based direct royalty schemes. The complexity is a real barrier to participation: it's worth noting that even today, SoundExchange—the sound recording PRO for digital radio that we saw back in Chapter 3—still holds millions of dollars in uncollected royalties on its books because so many artists have not yet provided even conventional payment details to it.

Of course, NFT minting and buying processes should get simpler over time and may well be much easier and cheaper by the time you read this. Service providers are already starting to appear that promise to make it easier for NFT sellers and buyers alike.[6]

Water & Music's data shows that the median price of a music NFT during 2021 fluctuated wildly and settled down in the $800–$900 range by the start of 2022. But by the end of the following year, prices had plummeted: the median price dropped below $40 by the end of 2022.

Yet waning interest immediately after the March 2021 sales spike is only part of the story. The developers behind Ethereum had been working for years to solve the problem of the skyrocketing costs of computing power and electricity required to validate transactions being added to the blockchain—which has caused serious environmental harm. In September 2022, Ethereum switched to a type of algorithm for validating transactions called "proof of stake" that requires far less computing power than the previous "proof of work" algorithm. The switch obviated the need for high gas fees; this made it worthwhile for creators to sell NFTs at lower prices. It remains to be seen where NFT prices will ultimately settle once fees become less relevant, but certainly there are plenty of music-related NFTs available at this time of writing for less than the typical price of vinyl.

This leads us to look at the music NFT market in another way as it moves into its next phase of development. Figure A.1 shows a classic hype cycle curve, including the number of artists minting NFTs and the total number of NFT campaigns launched each month from mid-2021 through the end of 2022. It shows a classic hype cycle curve, including an upward trend in both numbers that coincides with Ethereum's September 2022 switch to proof-of-stake. It's likely that this trend will continue as the market converges on pricing and release configurations for music NFTs that resonate with fans. Once that happens, we will see whether music NFTs grow to become a major

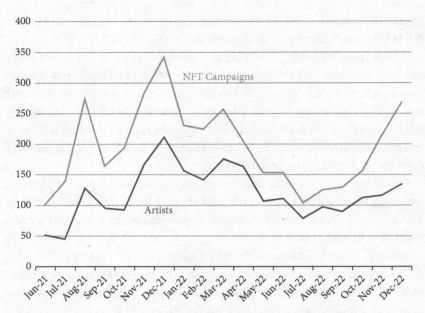

Figure A.1 2022 music NFT campaigns and artists. Water & Music.
Bill Rosenblatt.

music distribution format, like cassettes or CDs, or a small niche format that fades away over time, like PlayTapes or MiniDiscs, or something else entirely.

The notion of "music NFTs" has evolved beyond simply records of purchase of digital music files, although many of those exist. Artists are exploring various possibilities. One is to mint multiple NFTs for a given piece of music, akin to a limited-edition vinyl or CD release. This is a popular choice; the median number of copies of each music NFT at this time of writing is ten.[viii] Rapper Tory Lanez took this to an extreme in August 2021 by minting a million NFTs of his album *When It's Dark* at $1 each,[ix] and then, after the million NFTs sold out in less than a minute, minting a second batch of NFTs.[x]

Another possibility is to combine digital music with physical items, such as actual limited-edition vinyl or merch, or with artist experiences. The rock band Kings of Leon was an early NFT adopter, issuing a series of NFTs in March

2021 around their album *When You See Yourself* that included limited-edition vinyl and lifetime front-row seats at their live shows.[xi] Katy Perry auctioned off an NFT package that included the Golden Lion, a huge stage prop that she rode on in her 2015 Super Bowl halftime performance. (The package sold for $600,000.) In early 2022, John Lennon's son Julian auctioned off NFTs of some of his dad's guitars and items of clothing that John wore in Beatles movies, which sold for prices in the $10,000–$20,000 range. A startup called POAP (for Proof of Attendance Protocol) is building technology for POAPs (pronounced "poh-app"), which are NFTs that commemorate a fan's attendance at a concert or other event, like a digital ticket stub on a blockchain. The company announced a partnership with Warner Music Group in April 2022.[xii]

Yet other use cases lie in borrowing ideas from the larger and more active world of visual art NFTs.[7] So-called generative NFTs are those that use AI to create dynamic content that emerges or changes in real time according to a set of artistic parameters that could depend on the buyer as well as the creator. Generative techniques are making their way into music—along the lines that we discussed in Chapter 11—specifically for NFTs. Some musical artists are also selling NFTs for visual instead of audio content, such as Canadian singer-songwriter Shawn Mendes, who has a line of NFTs for 2D avatars that represent signature items such as his guitar and items of clothing.[xiii] And many audio NFTs also come with visual artworks, often created by noted artists and/or generative AI.

So what do fans actually get with NFTs, other than any physical items or experiences? That's a little hard to pin down. For NFTs on digital assets such as music files, in most cases, the purchaser doesn't get exclusive rights to the assets; they are usually not restricted with DRM or some other technological scheme, and they can be copied at will.[8] (One advantage of generative NFTs is that the content is not trivially easy to copy.) NFT skeptics often use the phrase "bragging rights" to describe what you get. After all, NFTs are really just publicly viewable entries in a database, as opposed to private purchase records stored by a traditional retailer; and they are verifiable records stored in your crypto wallet that you can show to anyone.

But there's more to it than that. Proponents of NFTs say that they enable artists to build more direct relationships with their fans. For artists, NFTs can be more personal in nature than mere music files; and the combination of high prices and complex buying processes means that, financial speculators aside, NFT buyers are likely to be among the most devoted fans. Yet the same has been said about various technologies—such as websites and peer-to-peer file-sharing—since the Web 1 era. It's not clear that NFTs will have more than those technologies' marginal effects on artist–fan relationships once the novelty wears off, prices and complexity come down, and the number of artists who use the technology increases. In addition, proponents' claims that NFTs eliminate intermediaries (such as record labels) seem dubious: the complexities of NFT commerce and the growing number of NFTs virtually guarantee that intermediaries will emerge, albeit most likely new and different ones.

The success of NFTs ultimately depends on their legitimacy as an "ownership" mechanism, that is, on the public's collective willingness to perceive these records in cyberspace as evidence of "ownership" or "collectability." In Chapter 4 we discussed how the desire for ownership has fueled the vinyl revival; it remains to be seen if NFTs satisfy that same desire. For digital music files, it particularly depends on fans' willingness to see them as indicia of "ownership" that they do not believe exist for the piles of encoded bits that they used to buy on iTunes. As NFT adherents like to point out, today's fiat currencies—no longer backed by gold or other physical assets—also depend on societies' collective willingness to believe in their value.

Ownership, of course, implicates copyright law. NFTs and copyright currently seem like two ships passing in the night. When you buy an NFT for a piece of music, normally you don't get the copyright to the musical work or the sound recording. In that sense, it's just like buying any other music product. But when you buy an LP or CD, you get copyright rights in that physical item, including so-called first sale rights—the right to sell, rent, lend, or give away the item as you wish. As we saw in Chapter 4, the law says that no such rights are inherent in digital files. And the resale royalties that NFT platforms enable could even be said to be at odds with copyright law if it were found to apply to digital files, because the doctrine of first sale dictates that the original publisher can have no involvement in further sales (or rentals, loans, etc.).[9]

Both creators and consumers have been uncertain about what content rights NFTs convey. Some consumers wonder why they should pay what may be inflated prices for things to which they don't have exclusive access (whether by law or by technology). And some creators wonder why they should trust this notion of "artificial scarcity" when it could reflect negatively on their reputations if it should backfire or evaporate.

Meanwhile, the current ferment of experimentation with NFTs is extending to their copyright law ramifications. A few people have engaged in boundary-testing projects, such as creating NFTs on works that are in the public domain or to which others own the rights. In perhaps the most brazen such scheme for music to date, a startup called HitPiece launched briefly in February 2022 with offers of unique NFTs of a large number of albums, though it had licensed none of the intellectual property associated with them—not the music, the trademarks, nor the cover images. After only a few days, the RIAA threatened a lawsuit and it shut down.[xiv]

On the other hand, lawyers are also seeing opportunities in the NFT world; they have started drafting NFT agreements that spell out rights for artists, sellers, and buyers;[10] and a growing number of entities are starting to mint NFTs that include contracts with such terms. As the stakes grow higher for NFTs, so does the need for clarification[11] and solutions to these copyright conundrums. Both will surely come in time, as will common understandings of what is and isn't permissible.[12]

Conclusion

The Web3 world is currently rife with complex technology, inconvenience, high expenses, exclusionary jargon, get-rich-quick schemes, scams, and fraud. All of these are obstacles to Web3's proliferation, even though—once again—they are also all typical of early-stage disruptive technology markets; this was certainly the case during the Web 1.0 era of the late 1990s. Yet some of the terminology has truly entered into the public consciousness. When television ads for NFTs air during the Super Bowl and the Olympics, it's certain that they are here to say. The music industry may not quite know what to do with them yet, and the arcane-sounding term "NFT" may give way to some other buzzword as the market converges on products and value propositions that resonate with fans and artists over the longer term. Technological and legal mechanisms that curb abuse are sure to follow, and pure financial speculators will continue to exit. And Web3 applications will become part of—and may well profoundly alter—the structure of the music industry in the years to come.

Notes

Chapter 1

1. Another music video sits at no. 1, but it would be difficult to describe "Baby Shark" as featuring major recording artists.

Chapter 2

1. The name "Graphophone" was trademarked, while "phonograph" is not.
2. In 1959, Mattel had far greater success with the Chatty Cathy doll. Pulling her string activated the mechanical playback of a low-fidelity phonograph record.
3. The Arcade, now a Hyatt Hotel, is less than a mile from another location crammed with music history: The Rock & Roll Hall of Fame.
4. Edison had considered the disc as an alternative to the cylinder, but he stuck with the latter because it provided superior sound.
5. "Gramophone" was originally trademarked in the UK but became a generic name in 1910.
6. Bell did eventually investigate the possibility of varying the turntable's rotation continuously to ensure a constant rate for the stylus as it moved toward the center of the disc. Though this was never implemented for the phonograph, the concept became an essential part of the design for Compact Discs in the 1980s.
7. Later versions of cylinders with harder plastic had the name of the selection included on the edge of the cylinder itself, though this was still more difficult to read than the label on the center of a record.
8. We think of shellac as a material used for wood finishing without regard for its origin. It is actually a resin secreted by female lac bugs found in Thailand and India.
9. The name "Victrola" was intended to evoke the most popular player piano of the day: the Pianola.
10. The word "orthophonic" means "reproducing sound correctly."
11. Consumers coined this phrase because prerecorded cylinders came in boxes that were similar in size and shape to canned foods. Almost 50 years later Billy Joel revived the comparison in his song "The Entertainer" and complained about the industry discounting his music like "another can of beans."
12. 3600 divided by 46 equals 78.26.
13. In 1927, the Victor Company introduced several models with an automatic changer that could hold up to 12 discs and provide an hour of semicontinuous playing time.

The least expensive unit cost $600 (or over $9000 today), so it was far from a mass-market product, though the technology established the foundation for the next generation of jukeboxes. VE-10-50 X. *The Victor Victrola Page*, http://www.victor-victrola.com/index.html. Accessed May 9, 2022.

14. In 1906, Sousa published a lengthy opinion piece in *Appleton's* magazine titled "The Menace of Mechanical Music," detailing his concerns.

15. Some theaters tried playing a record of Caruso singing to accompany the film, but keeping the two in sync was nearly impossible.

16. Though it took 70 years, Scott Joplin did eventually receive the popular acclaim he warranted, as several of his compositions were featured in the film score for *The Sting*, which climbed to the top of the Billboard Charts in 1974.

17. And, of course, the audience was not asked to distinguish between the artist performing alone and the recording playing by itself in a "blind" listening test. Such tests would come later on when the technology was more up to the job.

18. The purchase of automobiles made up half of that debt.

19. The same concept applies today to student discount plans for streaming services.

20. As we'll see in the next chapter, the term "race records" was used in the industry for decades until it was replaced by "rhythm & blues" in the 1950s.

21. The label was named to honor Elizabeth Greenfield who was born enslaved and became the best-known black concert artist of the nineteenth century. She was called the "Black Swan" in reference to the "Swedish Nightingale," world-famous soprano Jenny Lind.

22. This less-than-complimentary terminology lasted into the 1950s as well, when "country and western music" and subsequently "country music" became the accepted name.

23. For example, Santana's "Black Magic Woman" is arguably a better version than Fleetwood Mac's original. The same cannot be said for Pat Boone's take on Little Richard's "Tutti Frutti." Though in both cases, the covers outsold the originals.

Chapter 3

1. The NBC Symphony disbanded in 1954, but radio orchestras persist to this day in countries with government funding for the arts. In Germany, Sweden, the United Kingdom, Japan, and elsewhere, the orchestras of state-run broadcasters are among the finest in their countries.

2. Savage Beast Technologies was founded in 2000 to bring the MGP to market, its name inspired by the often-misquoted William Congreve line "Music has charms to soothe the savage breast." The technology was originally intended to assist retail stores in selling music before the company pivoted to streaming.

3. It wouldn't have made much difference. The band's follow-up album, *The Long Run*, wouldn't appear until September 1979, a full two years after *Hotel California* had faded from the charts.

4. These services originally employed rooms full of people, often college students, who would listen to radio stations and write down the songs they heard. Later on, acoustic fingerprinting technology (see Chapter 8) took over this task.

5. Classic Rock is a radio format that began as an offshoot of AOR and spread to dozens of stations nationwide in the mid-1980s through consultants such as Fred Jacobs of Jacobs Media. But Classic Rock never got its own chart in R&R, presumably because it featured older material rather than current releases.

6. Most trade magazines and tip sheets refused to publish R&B/soul charts or picks until then because, as they claimed, that part of the industry was too payola-ridden for the data to be trustworthy. Denisoff, *Solid Gold*, p. 260.

7. These regulations were quietly abandoned in 2009 by agreement between the NAB and record labels.

8. China was on this list until it passed legislation providing for royalties for radio play of recorded music, which went into effect in June 2021.

9. Plus Rep. Ted Deutch of Florida. Miami is another important center of music industry activity.

10. Some music publishers might disagree with this point; but as far as we know, it has not been tested in court.

11. A few ad-hoc solutions are being advanced among private parties. For example, Universal Music Publishing has offered a blanket license to its entire catalog to Wondery, a podcast publisher that is now owned by Amazon.

12. Industry gossip held that Davis was "thrown under the bus" for reasons that remain a mystery to this day. Sentiment was that Davis wouldn't have been fired merely for spending $94,000—on anything.

13. There was a sense in the industry that DJs on Black radio stations were more susceptible to payola because they weren't paid as well as their white counterparts.

14. Because it was hard for radio stations to buy shellac albums due to shellac shortages. Denisoff, *Solid Gold*, 221.

15. The FCC has five Commissioners who vote on regulatory matters. Typically, three of them (including the Chair) are of the party of the sitting president and the other two are of the opposite party.

16. Even this is a simplified example, because (among other things) it omits the roles of music publishers in PRO affiliations and splits. There are also some cases where the record is released but the splits are not defined or are in dispute.

17. Except small stations with low revenues, which need only pay nominal annual flat fees to SoundExchange.

18. Digital recording technology, which would make this type of process far less time-consuming, came a few years later.

19. "Like a Rolling Stone" wasn't the first song to be chopped into halves and pressed on two sides of a 45. Ray Charles's "What'd I Say" and the Isley Brothers' "Shout" both got the same treatment in 1959.

20. In the 2020 edition of Jacobs Media's annual TechSurvey of radio listeners, reflecting listening habits before the COVID-19 pandemic forced everyone to stay inside, 53 percent of respondents stated that all or most of their AM/FM listening

was in the car. For Gen Z and Millennials, the figure was 68 percent or more. Techsurvey 2020 Results, Jacobs Media, https://jacobsmedia.com/techsurvey-2020-results/. Accessed May 18, 2023.

21. In 1981, when the Rolling Stones released their *Tattoo You* album and embarked on a massive world tour, WYSP in Philadelphia played Stones music almost half the time during the run-up to the band's two gigs at JFK Stadium.

Chapter 4

1. Recording engineers eventually figured out how to extend the capacities of vinyl sides through severe audio compression that diminished sound quality. The likely longest LP and 45 sides were both prog-rock tracks from the mid-1970s. For LPs, Todd Rundgren's side-long epic "A Treatise on Cosmic Fire" clocked in at over 35 minutes on his 1975 album *Initiation*. For 45s, a 10 minute, 27 second live version of "Lunar Sea" by the British prog-rock band Camel was the B-side of their single "Another Night" in 1976.

2. The term "vinyl" likely arose as a short form of Vinylite, a name for polyvinyl chloride that was trademarked by Carbide and Carbon Chemicals Corporation, a subsidiary of Union Carbide.

3. Many old turntables had a fourth speed: 16. 16 2/3-rpm records were sometimes used to distribute prerecorded programs to radio stations and for audiobook recordings for the visually disabled. Old professional turntables with 16 speeds in college radio stations have served as perennial sources of amusement for late-night college DJs.

4. The name EP has been used since then to describe various other formats that are between singles and LPs in length.

5. Rosenblatt's first piece of "serious" audio equipment, a parental hand-me-down.

6. A fourth, Denon's UD-4, was introduced in Japan, Europe, and the United Kingdom.

7. The CD-4 quad system's requirement for phono cartridges with greater frequency response and lower tracking force led to improvements in cartridge design that made their way into standard stereo cartridges.

8. And of course there have been numerous innovations in turntable design over the years.

9. Those return policies weren't all bad for the labels. Occasionally they would manufacture and ship to retail many more records than they expected to sell, so that they could get RIAA Gold or Platinum certifications—and executives could earn higher bonuses—which were based on shipments, not sales, in the days before sales were measured with some accuracy. This gave rise to the saying, "Ship Platinum, return Gold."

10. See https://www.youtube.com/watch?v=SRjl_nIRSLk.

11. Ironically, Sony Music and BMG Music would end up merging—as would the two record clubs—in the mid-2000s.

12. Amazon is likely the no. 3 used vinyl seller. Amazon does not report used vinyl sales.

13. Some overlap exists between indie retail sales and online sales, because indie record stores sometimes sell their inventory through Discogs. This phenomenon increased when the COVID-19 pandemic forced brick-and-mortar record stores to close for a while—and coincided with a dramatic increase in RIAA-reported vinyl sales in 2021.

14. The right to resell digital files has been a hot topic of debate and the subject of a few noteworthy lawsuits, such as *Capitol Records v. ReDigi*, where the record company sued a startup that built a marketplace for "used" iTunes music files. ReDigi lost the case and the subsequent appeal.

15. Record Store Day (RSD) is an annual event that celebrates independent record stores. Hundreds of limited-edition albums are released specifically for RSD each year. Given that RSD started in 2007, just after vinyl sales hit bottom, it's often credited as a catalyst for the vinyl revival.

16. Those were the three best-selling albums on Discogs in December 2017.

17. Only one of the ten best-selling albums of 2022 on Discogs was a classic title (David Bowie's 1977 album *Low*, at no. 9); the rest were new releases.

18. That the album was available in several versions, including four standard versions and an exclusive version for Target stores, certainly helped boost this figure.

19. Outside of Western classical music, Indian sitar master Ravi Shankar released his first LP, *Three Ragas*, on the British label His Master's Voice (HMV) in 1956. "Raga Jog," over 28 minutes long, took up an entire side of the album. Ragas are largely improvised and can last for hours when performed live.

20. The *rotation* speed of a record is constant, but the *linear* speed is proportional to the square of the radius at any given point, so it decreases from the outer rim of a record towards the center. That's the reason why RCA's 7-inch 45s were designed with a large hole in the middle: so that the rotation speed toward the end of the side wouldn't decrease enough to harm the sound quality too much.

21. Not to be confused with Hipgnosis Songs Fund, an investment fund for song rights set up in 2018, which took its name from the design firm but has no relationship to it.

22. The first artist-owned label was Reprise, which Frank Sinatra launched in 1960. It wasn't a vanity label but one that Sinatra started himself after he became dissatisfied with Capitol. Reprise quickly became an important label with a big-name artist roster and was acquired by Warner Bros. in 1963.

23. This is an estimate; total annual revenue figures for music publishing from that period aren't available.

24. The eminent jazz critic Nat Hentoff testified at a 1961 Congressional hearing that "when [a jazz musician] performs on a record, his improvisation is what makes the tune quite a new one" and therefore that there should be no question of the performing artist's creativity.

25. Possibly because the labels knew that public performance rights in sound recordings were doomed to fail due to the radio industry's influence, as we saw in Chapter 3.

26. Under that standard, collections of hit songs performed by cover bands with names like The Realistics and Top of the Poppers, which were sold on late-night and UHF television in the 1970s, would have infringed copyright. Hallmark, Columbia House, and others put these albums out to capitalize on current hits by taking advantage of

compulsory mechanical licenses for the compositions and not having to pay the original artists' record labels.

27. Columbia eventually released most of the Dylan sessions—with The Band as backing musicians—as *The Basement Tapes* in 1975. Decca/London responded to the Stones bootleg by releasing an album of other performances from the same tour as *Get Yer Ya-Ya's Out!* in 1970.

28. ARMADA was eventually supplanted by the National Association of Independent Record Distributors (NAIRD) and then by the American Association of Independent Music (A2IM).

29. Lobbying around copyright law in the 1960s and 1970s was limited to industry "inside baseball" and was a much lower-key affair than it would become in the Internet era. The Copyright Office routinely puts out requests for input related to its studies on copyright law reform; in those days, the numbers of responses to those requests numbered in the low tens, while today they number in the thousands.

Chapter 5

1. Crosby sold one of his Ampex Model 200s to guitarist Les Paul, who used it to invent multitrack recording.

2. Studio recorders of the 1960s and 1970s typically used tape with eighth-inch track widths, such as 1-inch tape for 8-track machines and 2-inch tape for 16-track machines, as compared to four tracks packed into quarter-inch-wide tape (1/16 inch per track) in commercial prerecorded tapes.

3. For example, it wasn't until 1962 that Radio Shack's catalog listed any component stereo systems that included tape decks. Radio Shack's rival Lafayette waited until the 1970s when reel-to-reel had been superseded by 8-tracks and cassettes.

4. RCA introduced a quadraphonic 8-track cartridge format called Quad-8 or Q8 in 1970. Q8 was simply 8-track reconfigured as two sets of four channels instead of four stereo pairs. Q8 also predated the popular quad vinyl formats and faded away after a few years. Quad cassettes (four channels instead of two stereo pairs) were also attempted but never caught on.

5. For example, note the large hole in the upper right corner of the Fidelipac cart in Figure 5.2: this was for a pinch roller built into the player that would swing up into place when a cart was inserted. Each 8-track tape each had its own pinch roller, meaning that no such mechanism had to be built into players.

6. The slight taper at one end of the 8-track made it easier to determine which end to insert into the machine without having to take one's eyes off the road.

7. Another attempt at a commercial cartridge tape format was PlayTape, introduced in 1966. PlayTape was like a mini-Fidelipac, a small endless-loop mono cartridge meant for cheap portable players. A few thousand commercial releases were made in the format, but it never caught on, mainly because its 24-minute maximum capacity meant that it could never hold entire albums. PlayTape also met its demise in 1970.

8. Portable battery-powered 8-track players eventually appeared in the 1970s; they were never very popular.

9. Other Dolby flavors (Dolby C, S, and HX Pro) came later, but Dolby B has remained the most commonly used.

10. CrO_2 tape typically increases high-end frequency response by 2–3 KHz, so that, for example, a tape deck with 30–14 KHz frequency response with ferric oxide tape might offer response out to 16 or 17 KHz with CrO_2.

11. Other designs with enhanced sound quality came later, including "metal" formulations that used pure iron instead of iron oxide particles.

12. Howie Singer owned an Advent 201 tape deck. Bill Rosenblatt owned a pair of Advent Loudspeakers.

13. Including separate heads for recording, playback, and erase instead of a single head for everything, and a dual-capstan drive mechanism that kept tape speed more constant, minimizing wow and flutter distortion.

14. Such as proprietary noise reduction and tape bias settings.

15. The "Nak" became a status symbol for wealthy audiophiles. For example, in the recent HBO TV series *Vinyl*, about a record label in the 1970s, Nakamichi decks were ostentatiously mounted on the walls of both the label head's office and the living room in his palatial suburban home.

16. One more attempt at a new analog tape format came in the late 1970s: the Elcaset, created by Sony, Panasonic, and Teac. It looked like an overgrown cassette and contained one-quarter-inch tape that ran at 3.75 IPS. Its makers claimed sound quality equal to the best open-reel tape. But by that time, fine audio quality was already available from cassette decks that sold for half the prices of Elcaset machines; and record labels did not embrace the format for commercial releases. The Elcaset disappeared quickly.

17. Of course, a more complete explanation would take up far more space than it warrants here. Certainly recording your friends' albums so that you didn't have to buy them was considered unlawful. Also of note is the difference between US/UK law and Continental European law regarding so-called private copying; see footnote 22.

18. As we'll see shortly, the question of the legality of taping broadcasts at home was decided by the Supreme Court much later, in 1984.

19. In rough terms, this meant flat frequency response extending past 15 KHz, signal-to-noise ratio of at least 60 dB, and wow/flutter at less than 0.1 percent. By the late 1970s, those specs were widely available in midline cassette decks costing less than $300.

20. It was not the only one. Other likely factors included a long list of late-1970s superstar artists who didn't release new albums in 1979 (including The Rolling Stones, The Who, Queen, Fleetwood Mac, and many others), the Oil Crisis in the wake of the Iranian Revolution driving vinyl prices higher while depressing discretionary income, and the inferior audio quality of many commercial cassettes.

21. The decision in *CBS Songs Ltd v Amstrad Consumer Electronics Plc* was, in a way, a harbinger of the 2005 *Grokster* case in the United States, which we discuss in Chapter 9. The House of Lords held that Amstrad did not induce or incite copyright infringement and therefore was not liable for any infringements caused by its customers.

22. Some countries in Continental Europe had by then enacted levies on blank media to compensate for consumer copying, and eventually almost all of them did. But the law in Continental Europe is different from that of the United Kingdom. In Europe, unlike in Britain (and the United States), copying content for personal use is allowed without advance permission from copyright holders, although consumers are expected to pay royalties on those copies. So-called private copying levies are intended as mechanisms to ensure that such royalties get paid. See International Survey on Private Copying, Stichting de Thuiskopie and World Intellectual Property Organization, WIPO Publication No. 1037E/16, 2015. https://www.wipo.int/edocs/pubdocs/en/wipo_pub_1037_2016.pdf. Accessed May 27, 2022.

23. Consumer dual-cassette machines may have already been available in Japan when the Amstrad TS55 came out.

24. Actually, the case was appealed first to the Ninth Circuit, which reversed the district court; but then the Supreme Court reversed the Ninth Circuit on the relevant points.

25. Note that *Betamax* was concerned with home taping of freely available broadcast television, not copying of prerecorded tapes. Commercial prerecorded video tapes did not appear until after the original lawsuit was filed.

26. Fans of Frank Zappa will recognize this as an intended pun.

27. The increase in jazz releases on cassette was also surely due to the increasing popularity during the 1970s of jazz-rock fusion music that crossed over to the rock audience.

28. It is now known as CDSA (Content Delivery and Storage Association) and run by Guy Finley, Larry's son.

29. After the decline of cassettes, Moore moved on to CD-Rs, then to digital releases on various platforms.

30. Leaving aside that the parties may have taken place at venues that didn't pay performance royalties to PROs such as ASCAP and BMI.

31. The idea that a use of copyrighted material can be fair use if it is "transformative" comes from a highly influential 1990 law journal article by Pierre Leval, then a US district court judge. The article influenced subsequent court decisions about sampling, such as *Campbell v. Acuff-Rose,* discussed later in this chapter. Pierre N. Leval, "Toward a Fair Use Standard," *Harvard Law Review* 103, no. 5 (1990): 1105–36, https://doi.org/10.2307/1341457. Accessed April 4, 2023.

32. This could still require a license for the composition from the songwriter/music publisher, though not from the record label. In the case of "Planet Rock," Bambaataa and Kraftwerk worked out a royalty without going to court.

33. This behemoth was badged as the Audioton TBS9300, Dynasty HT-959, Elta 6930 (shown in Figure 5.5), ESC JC-2000, Helix Wheely 5000, International MS-959, Matsuki MS-959, Orbex MS-959, Shadow JB750, and Technidyne TD10000. See Wiki Boombox, Analog Alley, https://www.wikiboombox.com/tiki-index.php.

34. Raheem's boombox, a Promax Super Jumbo with dual cassette decks, is on display at the Smithsonian's National Museum of African American History and Culture in Washington, DC.

35. Sony also envisioned the use case of two people listening together. Early Walkman models, including the TPS-L2, had dual headphone jacks. They also had a HOT LINE button that would mute the music and turn on a built-in microphone so that the two listeners could talk to each other without taking headphones off. Sony removed these features in later models, but the use case was revived decades later in the age of earbud sharing.

36. An exception: Radio Shack, which called its product the StereoMate. Sony itself used the names Stowaway, Soundabout, and Freestyle in various countries before settling on Walkman worldwide.

37. Along with audiophile disc formats such as DVD-Audio and SACD.

38. Few of which mention *Guardians of the Galaxy*.

Chapter 6

1. Pluggers were known to bribe the store's salesgirls with perfume to push their tunes to customers—perhaps the first instance of "payola" in the music business.

2. Search for "Soundies" on YouTube and you will be able to watch performances by many of these artists.

3. Although the program gave the impression that the countdown was based on record sales, the final songs selected were under the control of the ad agency of the sponsor: Lucky Strike cigarettes.

4. Miller was a successful A&R executive and record producer who signed Johnny Mathis, Tony Bennett, and Patti Page, to name just a few. He loved pop but thought rock & roll was mediocre and famously passed on signing Buddy Holly, Elvis Presley, and the Beatles.

5. The night that the Beatles first appeared on Ed Sullivan, the variety show featured a musical performance from the hit musical *Oliver* as well. The original Broadway cast that night included "David" Jones as the Artful Dodger. Like so many other people who saw that Beatles performance, Jones decided that rock & roll would be his future.

6. Their hits included contributions from many of the top songwriters of the rock era including Carole King & Gerry Goffin and Neil Diamond.

7. QUBE was a bold early experiment in interactive television that presaged many later developments—including consumer privacy concerns that helped sink the service in the early 1980s.

8. This same pattern would be repeated with Apple and Steve Jobs after Napster's decimation of the business, to be discussed in Chapter 8.

9. Malone is now Chairman of Liberty Media, whose assets include Sirius XM Satellite Radio, Pandora, and part of iHeartMedia. See Chapter 3.

10. The baby boomers would eventually get their "own" music video channel when MTV launched VH-1 in 1985.

11. Young even wrote the song "This Note's for You" as a criticism of corporate advertising. Despite those sentiments, it won MTV's Video of the Year award in 1989.

12. You can search for and watch the video on YouTube, where it has 5.6 million views at this writing.
13. *Thriller* is the only album in history to sell more than 50 million copies.
14. History repeated itself almost 20 years later, when the AOL-Time Warner merger turned out so poorly that the company sold the then-struggling Warner Music Group to private investors who later made huge profits.
15. A summary of the use cases and payments for synchronization can be found in this Continuing Legal Education session at South by Southwest in 2014: Bob Donnelly, Danielle Aguirre, Kris Muñoz, and Andrew Sparkler Donnelly, "Flipping Publishing Micro-Pennies Into a Bucket," SXSW 2014 CLE, https://foxrothschild.gjassets.com/content/uploads/2017/03/Flipping-Publishing-Mirco-Pennies-into-a-Bucket.pdf. Accessed May 4, 2022.
16. In many other cases, rights holders have refused to entertain synch licenses on any terms at all. For example, the film *Almost Famous*, a paean to 1970s rock released in 2000, tried to license the ultimate 1970s rock song, "Stairway to Heaven," for the soundtrack, but Led Zeppelin refused. More recently, former Pink Floyd bassist/songwriter Roger Waters refused to license Floyd's "Another Brick in the Wall" to Mark Zuckerberg to promote Instagram.

Chapter 7

1. The other colors of the "rainbow" describe the later specifications for discs, including the writeable and rewriteable variations.
2. *Rashomon* is a 1950 psychological thriller by Akira Kurosawa known for its characters providing their different subjective views of the same crime.
3. You can listen to these recordings at the Smithsonian website: https://www.si.edu/newsdesk/releases/playback-130-year-old-sounds-revealed. Accessed May 18, 2023.
4. Higher sampling rates, larger sample sizes, and various sampling optimization techniques have been used to provide even higher quality digital versions in both optical disc and file download formats that appeal to audiophiles. For example, DVD-Audio discs contain audio that is sampled at as much as 192 kHz at up to 24 bits per sample.
5. Recall from Chapter 3 that FM radio sound quality doesn't quite have the frequency response range of LPs.
6. The Beatles were slow in making their music available in both downloads and streaming as well.
7. Another factor that led to *Thriller*'s phenomenal sales was its crossover appeal to white audiences, thanks in part to Eddie Van Halen's shredding guitar solo on "Beat It."
8. The title refers to Neil Young's 1972 song "The Needle and the Damage Done" about the perils of heroin addiction for musicians. Replacing "needle" with "CD" is a clever reference to the change in formats.

9. Young would be even more upset when the even poorer quality of the MP3 file came to prominence.

10. In fact, equivalents to this law in countries outside the United States are known as copyright exhaustion instead of first sale.

11. Japan never enacted similar legislation, allowing a CD rental business to become a thriving channel there for many years. However, the cultural norms there have discouraged unauthorized copying.

Chapter 8

1. File Transfer Protocol (FTP) is a standard for transmitting data files over computer networks that was invented in the early 1970s. It's widely used today, though not by casual users.

2. Integrated Services Data Network (ISDN), a telecommunications protocol created in the late 1980s, was about 50 times faster than the dial-up modems of the time. It was slow to take off and was eventually eclipsed by DSL and cable. Once broadband Internet began to catch on, ISDN became known as "It Still Does Nothing."

3. Audio File Size Calculations, *AudioMountain.com*, https://museumofportablesound. com/mp3/. Accessed May 23, 2022.

4. For example, a typical Dell desktop PC in 1995 included a 1 GB hard disk drive and sold for around $2,000, or $3,700 in today's dollars.

5. For example, Albhy Galuten, a Grammy award winning producer, inventor of the "drum loop," and technologist with numerous US patents, worked at Universal Music at that time.

6. This was an exemplar of Metcalfe's Law, a sequel to Moore's Law that states that the value of a network is proportional to the square of the number of devices attached to the network.

7. Some of the other major record labels engaged in their own trials, around the same timeframe, with other CD copy-protection schemes that were arguably less harmful to users' PCs; but the firestorm around the technology that Sony BMG adopted caused those efforts to be abandoned quickly.

8. Pun intended.

9. This wasn't the case in many other countries, which enacted levies (taxes) on devices with digital storage, including personal computers. See Chapter 5, note 22.

10. Copyright law doesn't require a plaintiff to prove actual damages, i.e., actual financial harm it claims to have suffered from the defendant's behavior. Instead, a copyright plaintiff can ask for statutory damages, which are amounts set in law rather than by economic damage assessments. At the time of the Napster case, the limit on statutory damages for willful infringement was $100,000 per copyrighted work (plus attorneys' fees); it has since been raised to $150,000.

11. The central directory indicated willful infringement, which could entitle the plaintiffs to higher damages. In addition, the court found that Napster's central directory

rendered it liable for so-called vicarious infringement, which essentially means "getting paid to look the other way."

12. Reciprocal, a Softbank/Microsoft funded start-up offering secure digital distribution services, was one of the companies that made such a proposal to Napster. Howie Singer was an executive at Reciprocal.

13. The highest damage award in a court case stemming from failure to qualify for DMCA safe harbors was $1 billion, awarded in 2019 in *Sony Music Entertainment et al. v. Cox Communications*, a case that the major record labels brought against Cox, a large cable ISP. At this writing, the damage award is on appeal.

14. Justice David Souter adapted the concept of inducement of copyright infringement from patent law, where it had long been established. A company can sell a product that infringes a patent when someone who buys the product uses it. Even though the user is the "direct infringer" (the one who is technically liable for patent infringement), the inducement principle makes it possible for patent owners to go after companies that "induce" users to infringe their patents.

15. There were two exceptions to this. Apple licensed the technology to HP, which released a line of iPod clones in 2004. It also licensed the technology to Motorola for use with Motorola's ROKR MP3-playing mobile phones starting in 2005. None of these was successful; the candy-bar-style ROKR was eclipsed by the iPhone in 2007.

16. The pioneering streaming service Rhapsody, which we'll meet in Chapter 9, acquired this version of Napster in 2011. In 2016, the company phased out the Rhapsody brand name and rebranded the service (yet again) as Napster.

17. For a detailed and dispassionate look at the history and technology of FairPlay from one of its engineers, see Rod Schultz, "The Many Facades of DRM," 2012. Available at https://web.archive.org/web/20150105090945/http://fortunedotcom.files.wordpress.com/2014/12/2012_misc_drm.pdf. Accessed May 18, 2023.

18. It is actually a gross overstatement to say that DRM for music has gone away. It has been eliminated for paid downloads, but all of the interactive streaming services, discussed in Chapter 9, use forms of DRM, including for "offline listening," a.k.a. tethered downloads. It is more accurate to say that a larger portion of recorded music industry revenue comes from DRM-based channels nowadays than in 2007. See https://copyrightandtechnology.com/2017/02/16/the-myth-of-drm-free-music-revisited/.

19. The album only content was often limited in time, and eventually all the tracks became available as singles.

20. The labels unsuccessfully tried to create an open standard for a similar enhanced album concept called CMX that would work on all devices including mobile phones.

21. The previous agreement between the companies had confined Jobs and Apple to use the Apple trademark for computer-related products but not for music, to avoid confusion with the music label of the same name founded and owned by the Beatles.

22. Superstar artists are sometimes able to negotiate rates as high as 25 percent.

23. As a matter of copyright law, a download purchase is a license, not a transfer of ownership as with a CD or LP. However, these cases turned primarily on language in the terms of contracts between labels and artists.

24. Neil Young later created his own high-resolution music player called Pono and an associated download store to create a superior audio experience.

25. Elaborate schemes were set up to steal CDs from factories before they were released to stores to ensure that the newest songs were available before the discs were even on a retail shelf.

26. Some of which were artifacts of tactics to evade technologies that detected unauthorized copies on the networks.

27. The methodology did not examine causality, and the correlation of interest in music could have provided the same results.

Chapter 9

1. Universal Music Group's IPO filing even went so far as to give "Music as a Service" the acronym of "MaaS."

2. For example, the early version of Microsoft's DRM that Rhapsody used for downloads did not support transfer of music files to portable devices.

3. For further details on possible shifts, see Howie Singer, "In 2022, 'Fan-Centric' Accounting Will Bring Emerging Artists More Money from Streaming Music," dot. LA, https://dot.la/what-streaming-music-services-pay-2656063221.html. Accessed July 17, 2022.

4. During the download era, Apple was rumored to be contemplating the purchase of a label, but that also never came to fruition.

5. The attacks on Ukraine have led many services to halt their operations in Russia.

6. You can find the *Key Changes* playlist for the song titles included as part of each chapter heading in this book at https://spoti.fi/3InaDsO.

7. Although, as often happens, friction in a user experience leads to opportunities for entrepreneurs. Startups such as SongShift and Soundiiz have developed tools for sharing playlists across music services.

8. In November 2022, Deutsche Grammophon, the iconic label owned by Universal Music Group, announced STAGE+, a higher quality streaming service catering to classical fans featuring audio, video, live performances, interviews, and other exclusive content. And in March 2023, Apple launched Apple Music Classical, a separate app from Apple Music for classical fans with over 5 million tracks in its catalog. As we explain in Chapter 10, classical music is especially attractive as a niche service because of its unique metadata requirements compared to those of mainstream services.

9. After an initial climb up the Country charts, *Billboard* reconsidered this classification and removed the song from that list, though it did not blunt its momentum on the genre-less Hot 100.

10. Frank was the Senior VP for Global Streaming Marketing at Universal Music Group. After his untimely passing at the age of 47 in 2019, *Billboard* recognized his thought leadership in digital music by creating an award in his name.

11. The forms of fraud we discuss here involve gaming the system to increase streams rather than the separate matter of giving financial considerations directly to streaming services (as payola did for radio stations).

12. When labels were reissuing albums on CDs in the 1980s and 1990s, they had to re-clear the mecha\nicals with music publishers. A backlog of uncleared mechanicals developed, which became the subject of lawsuits between labels and publishers that were eventually settled.

13. Epic Games prevailed over Apple at the district court level in November 2022; Apple is appealing. The case against Google is ongoing at this time of writing.

Chapter 10

1. As a rough rule of thumb, compressed music files take up a megabyte of storage space per minute of audio, while compressed video takes up a gigabyte per hour, both at decent quality levels. This means that video takes up about 16 times the amount of space as audio.

2. YouTube abandoned Flash around 2010 once the HTML standard began to incorporate video natively (HTML5).

3. The major mobile operators had completed their buildouts of 3G wireless by the 2007–2008 timeframe, as we saw in Chapter 9, but while 3G was fast enough to support streaming audio, it wasn't sufficient for most video.

4. As the technologist for Warner Music's strategy group, Howie Singer negotiated the specifics of this arrangement with YouTube.

5. Of course, this is not an apples-to-apples comparison. Many songs have multiple videos on YouTube, and many music videos uploaded to YouTube are not of commercially released music.

6. There are other highly popular apps that enable sharing of short-form video, such as Byte and the video features built into Instagram and Snapchat. But none of these particularly feature music.

7. YouTube had taken similar steps: its original length limit was 5 minutes, then 10 minutes, then all limits were removed.

8. The number three was never specified in law, but the baseball analogy had a certain ring to it and became conventional, if not standard, among online services.

9. YouTube users can earn ad revenue shares if they exceed certain thresholds of user video views and channel subscribers.

10. Fair use is an *affirmative defense* in copyright law—it's an excuse you give in court when you're sued for copyright infringement, and it's something that ultimately only a court can decide. There are many reasons why a particular use of content is or isn't likely to be fair use; for example, criticism and scholarly research are generally accepted as fair use. Further discussion of this is beyond the scope of this book.

11. Google has never entered the MIREX competition. In a much less scientific test, Bill Rosenblatt recently uploaded to YouTube a set of classic rock covers from an audience recording of a live performance by a band he plays in; Content ID flagged only a third of them. Yet when he uploaded studio recordings of the band's classic rock covers a few months later, Content ID identified all of the compositions correctly.

12. SoundCloud also fulfills this function, for similar reasons. But YouTube had a three-year head start on SoundCloud, so YouTube is used more often for this purpose, while SoundCloud is more popular for indie artists who want to eschew record labels and release their music directly to fans.

13. As mentioned earlier in this chapter, YouTube has a "copyright strike" system, in which it will terminate a user's account if videos the user posts receive three valid and unresolved takedown notices. This does not prevent other users from reposting the same content.

14. "Notice and staydown" is controversial, but the details—though quite interesting—are beyond the scope of this book.

15. The Copyright Office's study included several suggestions for DMCA reform, but "notice and staydown" was not among them.

16. Except in small niche markets. For example, WeAreTheHits.com has a library of a few million musical compositions that are fully precleared for use on YouTube. Musicians can post videos of cover versions of those compositions through WeAreTheHits.com and earn ad revenue shares (less WeAreTheHits.com's commission).

17. Pun intended.

18. It's worth noting that record labels were, at that time, still working feverishly to digitize their entire catalogs to make them available online. So the term "full catalog" was something of a moving target.

19. Laws in countries outside the United States vary, but "notice and takedown" is fairly common as a pragmatic implementation of some national laws, not to mention that it's easier to export takedown notice–processing systems around the world than it is to implement different systems that reflect the legal nuances in each different country.

20. Technically, lyric videos posted without authorization could be found to infringe copyrights in the lyrics. But there is no history of artists or labels suing individual users over lyric videos; at most, they use the DMCA process to have them taken down.

21. See the *Guardian* article cited in the previous sentence. This number could be reconciled with the data in that article by recognizing that YouTube pays out ad revenue shares to many independent artists that do not collect royalties through paid subscription services.

22. Typing "Arabian Prince" into YouTube brings up videos of Saudi Crown Prince Mohammed bin Salman as well as the hip-hop pioneer whom we interviewed for this book.

23. Services that focus on classical music expend even more effort on this to create and clean up metadata on composers, conductors, soloists, movements, and so on. One such service, Primephonic, was acquired by Apple in August 2021; Apple launched Apple Music Classical in March 2023 with Primephonic's metadata and editorial talent at the heart of the service.

24. YouTube Music still falls short of curated opt-in services in showing discographies of longtime artists such as Miles Davis and Elvis Presley who have large catalogs that are replete with reissues, special editions, anthologies, and so on.

25. For example, in Apodaca's video, he drank from a bottle of Ocean Spray cranberry juice; in gratitude, Ocean Spray sent him a brand new pickup truck loaded with Cran-Raspberry juice.
26. TikTok also has text hashtags that are similar to those on Twitter, LinkedIn, and so on.
27. Not to be confused with the late jazz soprano saxophonist of the same name.

Chapter 11

1. "abcdefu," the 2022 single by Gayle, was mastered with an AI-based tool called LANDR and nominated for a Song of the Year Grammy.
2. No relation to the author.
3. One of the early developers of speech recognition software for PCs was Ray Kurzweil, who also invented one of the first commercially available digital sampling synthesizers in collaboration with Stevie Wonder.
4. Accordingly at this time of writing there is no native support on Apple's HomePod smart speakers for Spotify or YouTube Music.
5. A focus track is akin to a single: it's the track from an artist's output that the label wants to push at a given point in time.
6. The set of standards is called DDEX (Digital Data Exchange). DDEX also includes standards for communicating more fundamental information about track releases from labels to music services and information about song plays and record sales in the opposite direction.
7. Collaborative filtering dates back to the mid-1990s, and a music recommendation system called Firefly was the first commercial application.
8. There is an emerging field of synthetic voices that imitate celebrities *with* their (or their estates') permission, so that their voices can do more without their personal involvement.
9. A *work for hire* is one that is created under contract to someone else, with the implication that the creator relinquishes rights to that work under copyright law.
10. Data mining is a process for analyzing large sets of data to extract patterns using statistical and other techniques. It is often used in training AI systems.
11. For further details on Copyright and Artificial Intelligence, see Briggitte Vezina and Diane Peters, "Why We're Advocating for a Cautious Approach to Copyright and Artificial Intelligence," Creative Commons, February 20, 2020, https://creative commons.org/2020/02/20/cautious-approach-to-copyright-and-artificial-intelligence/. Accessed June 2, 2022.11.
12. Some music companies have taken the position that audio fingerprints are derivative works for purposes of negotiations with fingerprinting technology vendors; but this theory has not been tested in court.
13. Notably, the lawsuit does not accuse the creators of Copilot of copyright infringement; it merely accuses them of violating terms of service, that is, of breach of license (contract). The plaintiff may have done this strategically so that the defendants cannot raise a fair use defense—which is possible under copyright but not contract law.

Chapter 12

1. Pun intended.
2. Will Page, the former Chief Economist at Spotify, used this phrase as the title of his recent book on digital disruption.
3. Creative Commons is a scheme for providing licenses to digital content that gives licensees rights beyond those normally granted under copyright law. Creative Commons licenses for OER typically allow a licensee to copy the content freely and merely require attribution of the content to its author.
4. "Shovelware" is text material traditionally published in print that is converted to a digital format "as is," with little or no reworking to make it digital-friendly. The resulting product is usually not a great user experience, especially on mobile devices.
5. Craigslist did eventually begin to charge for some categories of listings, such as employment opportunities.
6. There are myriad legitimate uses of BitTorrent. For example, several online game publishers use BitTorrent to distribute the enormous collections of software and media files that make up their games; Facebook and Twitter use it to distribute server software updates.
7. Pun intended again.
8. Pun intended again.
9. The group was later renamed to use the word "Jazz," reflecting a shift to the more recognizable terminology.
10. This term originated when segregated America and a biased press was searching for a boxer—any boxer—who could defeat Jack Johnson, who had become the first Black athlete to win the world heavyweight championship in 1908.
11. Jay-Z had to sell his ownership stake because he started a sports agency.
12. Sony Music was an exception to the rule about labels not launching their own formats and digital music stores—because, of course, it was a sibling to a consumer electronics giant. Sony made a couple of attempts to launch its own digital music technology stack and retail presence, often in partnership with other labels and electronics makers. None of these succeeded.
13. The number will surely be significantly higher by the time you read this.
14. Disney and 20th Century Fox did not participate in the joint venture but did license their content to MovieLink.
15. No relation to the author.

Afterword

1. Such data could include geography (country), type of user account (paid subscription vs. free), bit rate, and so on.
2. Another scalability constraint with current blockchains is that they don't have the capacity to store music or other digital content files themselves, although innovators are addressing that limitation too.

3. The RIAA's vinyl sales figures do not count some independent releases and are US only; Water & Music's NFT sales database does not necessarily track every music NFT ever minted but is not limited to the United States. None of these figures counts resales.

4. Although almost half of this is from a single NFT campaign by Snoop Dogg in February 2022, which netted over $44 million from 8,934 NFTs that sold for $5,000 apiece.

5. This curve shape is so common that the eminent technology market research firm Gartner calls it the Hype Cycle and has built an entire research methodology around it. See https://www.gartner.com/en/research/methodologies/gartner-hype-cycle.

6. In exchange for some combination of more fees or commissions, and/or with features designed to keep users glued to their services instead of competitors'.

7. The NFTs that have set price records have all been for visual artworks. At this writing, the highest price paid for an NFT was $91.8 million for *Merge*, a digital artwork by the artist known as Pak, in December 2021. In comparison, the most expensive single music NFT to date is one by electronic music artist 3LAU, which went for $1.33 million in March 2021.

8. NFTs with content access control technologies have begun to appear, though the purveyors of such technologies studiously avoid using the term "DRM."

9. Other countries such as the United Kingdom and France have resale royalties set in law, which apply to unique or limited-edition works of art sold at auction or by professional dealers. Attempts to pass similar laws in the United States have failed.

10. See for example "20 Questions: An Artist's Checklist for an NFT Pitch," https://musict ech.solutions/2022/03/01/20-questions-an-artists-checklist-for-an-nft-pitch/, from music tech attorney Chris Castle. Accessed May 17, 2023.

11. At this writing, the best explanation of the relationship between NFTs and copyright that we have seen is a piece by the noted Internet law scholar James Grimmelmann and two colleagues at Cornell University and the Initiative for Cryptocurrencies and Contracts (IC3); see James Grimmelmann, Yan Ji, and Tyler Kell, "The Tangled Truth about NFTs and Copyright," *The Verge*, https://www.theverge.com/23139793/nft-cry pto-copyright-ownership-primer-cornell-ic3. Accessed May 17, 2023.

12. The legal scholar Lawrence Lessig proposed a compelling framework for understanding how the forces of law, social norms, the market, and technology work together to regulate environments such as the Internet in his book *Code: And Other Laws of Cyberspace* (New York: Basic Books, 1999). This framework, which has come to be known as the Pathetic Dot Theory, will surely be used to analyze the progress of Web3 in the years to come.

References

Chapter 1

i   Thomas Ricker, "First Click: Remember When Steve Jobs Said Even Jesus Couldn't Sell Music Subscriptions?" *The Verge*, June 8, 2015, https://www.theverge.com/2015/6/8/8744963/steve-jobs-jesus-people-dont-want-music-subscriptions. Accessed June 28, 2022.

ii   "Nikki Sixx Quotes," *Inspirational Stories*, https://www.inspirationalstories.com/quotes/t/nikki-sixx/. Accessed June 28, 2022.

iii   Jem Aswad, "Global Music Biz Revenue to Double to $131 Billion in 2030, Says Bullish Goldman Sachs Report," *Variety*, June 14, 2022, https://variety.com/2022/music/news/global-music-revenue-double-goldman-sachs-report-1235293827/. Accessed June 28, 2022.

iv   Bill Rosenblatt, "The Short, Unhappy Life of Music Downloads," Forbes.com, May 7, 2018, https://www.forbes.com/sites/billrosenblatt/2018/05/07/the-short-unhappy-life-of-music-downloads/. Accessed June 5, 2022.

Chapter 2

i   Vinylmint, "History of the Record Industry 1877–1920s," Medium, June 7, 2014, https://medium.com/@Vinylmint/history-of-the-record-industry-1877-1920s-48deacb4c4c3. Accessed May 9, 2022.

ii   David J. Steffen, *From Edison to Marconi: The First Thirty Years of Recorded Music* (Jefferson, NC: McFarland, 2005), 23–25.

iii   David L. Morton Jr., *Sound Recording: The Life Story of a Technology* (Baltimore: Johns Hopkins University Press, 2004), 13–17.

iv   Steffen, *From Edison to Marconi*, 27–30.

v   Randall Stross, *The Wizard of Menlo Park* (New York: Broadway Books, 2007), 157–63.

vi   Emile Berliner and Frederic Wile, *Emile Berliner, Maker of the Microphone* (Indianapolis, IN: Bobbs-Merrill, 1926), 171–73.

vii   Morton, *Sound Recording*, 31–42.

viii Roland Gelatt, *The Fabulous Phonograph 1877–1977*, Revised 2nd Edition (New York: MacMillan Publishing, 1977), 82–86.

ix   Andre Millard, *America on Record: A History of Recorded Sound*, 2nd Edition (Cambridge: Cambridge University Press, 2005), 125–28.

x   "History of the Record Industry 1877–1920s."

xi   David L. Suisman, *Selling Sounds: The Commercial Revolution in American Music* (Cambridge, MA: Harvard University Press, 2009). 94–96.

xii   Millard, *America on Record*, 140–47.

xiii   Greg Milner, *Perfecting Sound Forever: An Aural History of Recorded Music* (New York: Faber & Faber, 2009), 58–60.

xiv   "New Music Machine Thrills All Hearers at First Test Here," *New York Times*, October 7, 1925, https://www.nytimes.com/1925/10/07/archives/new-music-machine-thrills-all-hearers-at-first-test-here-researches.html. Accessed April 4, 2023.

xv   "The History of 78 RPM Recordings," Yale University Library, https://web.libr ary.yale.edu/cataloging/music/historyof78rpms. Accessed May 9, 2022.

xvi   Millard, *America on Record*, 145.

xvii   Steffen, *From Edison to Marconi*, 48–49.

xviii   Clive Thompson, "How the Phonograph Changed Music Forever," *Smithsonian Magazine*, January 2016, https://www.smithsonianmag.com/arts-culture/pho nograph-changed-music-forever-180957677/. Accessed April 4, 2023.

xix   Morton, *Sound Recording*, 92–93.

xx   Morton, *Sound Recording*, 57–60.

xxi   Steffen, *From Edison to Marconi*, 52–57.

xxii   Millard, *America on Record*, 102–3.

xxiii   Mark Katz, *Capturing Sound: How Technology Has Changed Music* (Berkeley: University of California Press, 2004), 17.

xxiv   Suisman, *Selling Sounds*, 105–10.

xxv   Steffen, *From Edison to Marconi*, 165–73.

xxvi   Millard, *America on Record*, 69.

xxvii   Enrico Caruso Jr., Andrew Farkas, and William R. Moran, *Enrico Caruso: My Father and My Family* (Portland, OR: Amadeus Press, 1997), 354.

xxviii   Suisman, *Selling Sounds*, 136.

xxix   Stross, *The Wizard of Menlo Park*, 224.

xxx   William Ruhlmann, *Breaking Records: 100 Years of Hits* (London: Routledge, 2004), 23–24.

xxxi   John Cilia, "The Search For The Oldest Record Store in the World," *Trackage Scheme*, July 21, 2016, http://trackagescheme.com/the-search-for-the-oldest-record-store-in-the-world/. Accessed May 9, 2022.

xxxii   Gary Calamar and Phil Gallo, *Record Store Days: From Vinyl to Digital and Back Again* (New York: Union Square & Co, 2012), p 40.

xxxiii   Suisman, *Selling Sounds*, 183.

xxxiv   Morton, *Sound Recording*, 38–39.

xxxv   Milner, *Perfecting Sound Forever*, 39–43.

xxxvi   Milner, *Perfecting Sound Forever*, 3–7.

xxxvii   Suisman, *Selling Sounds*, 185–92.

xxxviii   Suisman, *Selling Sounds*, 101.

xxxix   "History of the Record Industry 1877–1920s."

xl   Steffen, *From Edison to Marconi*, 170–72.

xli   Caruso Jr., Farkas, and Moran, *Enrico Caruso*, 359.

xlii   "History of the Record Industry, 1920–1950s."

xliii   Millard, *America on Record*, 168–70.

xliv   Morton, *Sound Recording*, 98.

xlv   Steve Hawtin, "Songs from the 1900s, The World's Music Charts," https://tsort. info/music/ds1900.htm. Accessed May 9, 2022.

xlvi   Lyrics of "If it Wasn't for the Irish and the Jews," The Washington Square Harp and Shamrock Orchestra, https://wshso.wordpress.com/tunes/songs/irish-jews-lyrics/. Accessed May 9, 2022.

xlvii   Morton, *Sound Recording*, 60–64.

xlviii   Suisman, *Selling Sounds*, 138.

xlix   Kevin Park, *Music & Copyright in America: Toward the Celestial Jukebox* (Chicago: American Bar Association, 2014), 7–10.

l   *Stern v. Rosey* Briefs and Transcript of Record, Internet Archive, https://archive.org/details/SternvRoseyBriefs/page/n29/mode/2up. Accessed May 9, 2022.

li   Park, *Music & Copyright in America*, 21–24.

lii   Paul Goldstein, *Copyright's Highway: From the Printing Press to the Cloud*, 2nd ed. (Redwood City, CA: Stanford University Press, 2003), 42–44.

liii   Gary Rosen, *Adventures of a Jazz Age Lawyer* (Oakland: University of California Press, 2020), 35–68.

liv   *White Smith Music Publishing Company v Apollo Company. Legal Information Institute of Cornell Law School.* Accessed May 9, 2022.

lv   "Ends Price-Fixing By 'License Plan': Supreme Court Gives Decision for Macy's Against the Victor Company," *New York Times*, April 10, 1917, https://www.nytimes.com/1917/04/10/archives/ends-pricefixing-by-license-plan-supreme-court-gives-decision-for.html. Accessed May 9, 2022.

lvi   Suisman, *Selling Sounds*, 184.

lvii   Milner, *Perfecting Sound Forever*, 45.

Chapter 3

i   Marc Fisher, *Something in the Air: Radio, Rock, and the Revolution That Shaped a Generation* (New York: Random House, 2007), 11–14; Christopher H. Sterling and John Michael Kittross, *Stay Tuned: A History of American Broadcasting* (Milton Park: Routledge, 2001), 63, 72.

ii   Lawrence Lessig, "Laws that Choke Creativity," *TED Talks*, https://www.ted.com/talks/lawrence_lessig_laws_that_choke_creativity. Accessed April 29, 2022.

iii   Charles Fitch, "How FM Stereo Came to Life," *Radio World*, January 27, 2016, https://www.radioworld.com/columns-and-views/roots-of-radio/how-fm-stereo-came-to-life. Accessed August 3, 2022.

iv   "The Infinite Dial 2022," *Edison Research and Triton Digital*, http://www.edisonresearch.com/wp-content/uploads/2022/03/Infinite-Dial-2022-Webinar-revised.pdf. Accessed May 25, 2022.

v   Sterling and Kitross, *Stay Tuned*, 339–41.

vi   Peter Fornatale and Joshua Mills, *Radio in the Television Age* (New York: Overlook Press, 1980), 125–26.

vii   Serge Denisoff, *Solid Gold: The Popular Record Industry* (Piscataway, NJ: Transaction Publishers, 1975), 257–58.

viii   Paul Rappaport, interview with the author, October 2020.

ix   Denisoff, *Solid Gold*, 267–69.

x   Rappaport, interview with the author.

xi   Mark Hugo Lopez and Daniel Dockterman, "U.S. Hispanic Country-of-Origin Counts for Nation, Top 30 Metropolitan Areas," *Pew Research Center*, May 26, 2011, https://assets.pewresearch.org/wp-content/uploads/sites/7/reports/142.pdf. Accessed April 5, 2023.

xii   Subcommittee on Courts, Civil Liberties, and the Administration of Justice of the Committee on the Judiciary, House of Representatives, 95th Congress, Performance Rights in Sound Recordings. Washington, DC: US Government Printing Office, 1978, quoting Hearings on Economic Conditions in the Performing Arts Before the Select Subcommittee on Education of the House Committee on Education and Labor, 87th Cong., 1st and 2d Sess. (1961–62).

xiii   Fornatale and Mills, *Radio in the Television Age*, 13.

xiv   Performance Rights in Sound Recordings.

xv   Fisher, *Something in the Air*, 279–80.

xvi   "The Infinite Dial 2022."

xvii   Larry Miller, "Sync or Swim—Licensing Music for Podcasts." *Musonomics* (podcast), September 28, 2020, http://musonomics.org/sync-or-swim-licensing-music-for-podcasts/. Accessed April 29, 2022.

xviii   Interactive Advertising Bureau, "IAB U.S. Podcast Advertising Revenue Study: Full-Year 2021 Results & 2022–2024 Growth Projections," *Interactive Advertising Bureau*, https://www.iab.com/wp-content/uploads/2022/05/IAB-FY-2021-Podcast-Ad-Revenue-and-2022-2024-Growth-Projections_FINAL.pdf. Accessed November 29, 2022.

xix   Richard Neer, *FM: The Rise and Fall of Rock Radio* (New York: Villard, 2001), 31–32.

xx   Ronald H. Coase, "Payola in Radio and Television Broadcasting." *Journal of Law and Economics* 22, no. 2 (October 1979), 269–328.

xxi   Fisher, *Something in the Air*, 91.

xxii   Denisoff, *Solid Gold*, 276–278.

xxiii   Frederic Dannen, *Hit Men: Power Brokers and Fast Money Inside the Music Business* (New York: Vintage, 1991), 115–19.

xxiv   John Jackson, *A House on Fire: The Rise and Fall of Philadelphia Soul* (Oxford: Oxford University Press, 2004), 177–80, 191–94.

xxv   Neer, *FM*, 153.

xxvi   Dannen, *Hit Men*, 201, 206.

xxvii   Peter Boyer, "CBS Assails NBC News over a Payola Report," *New York Times*, April 3, 1986, https://www.nytimes.com/1986/04/03/arts/cbs-assails-nbc-news-over-a-payola-report.html. Accessed July 12, 2022; Dannen, *Hit Men*, 286–88.

xxviii   Penny Pagano and William Knoedelsleder Jr., "Senate Plans Record Industry Payola Probe," *The Los Angeles Times*, April 3, 1986, https://www.latimes.com/archives/la-xpm-1986-04-03-mn-2589-story.html. Accessed April 4, 2023; Dannen, *Hit Men*, 291, 302.

xxix   William Knoedelsleder, "$1 Million in Suspected 'New Payola' Is Probed," *Los Angeles Times*, December 22, 1987, https://www.latimes.com/archives/la-xpm-1987-12-22-mn-30675-story.html. Accessed April 3, 2023; Dannen, *Hit Men*, 296.

xxx   Dannen, *Hit Men*, 286–312.

xxxi   Lola Ogunnaike, "Record Labels Must Pay Shortchanged Performers," *New York Times*, May 5, 2004, https://www.nytimes.com/2004/05/05/arts/record-labels-must-pay-shortchanged-performers.html. Accessed April 4, 2023.

xxxii   Jeff Leeds, "EMI Agrees to Fine to Resolve Payola Case," *New York Times*, June 16, 2006, https://www.nytimes.com/2006/06/16/business/worldbusiness/emi-agrees-to-fine-to-resolve-payola-case.html. Accessed April 4, 2023.

xxxiii   Jeff Leeds, "Radio Broadcasters Agree to Fine over Payola," *New York Times*, March 6, 2007, https://www.nytimes.com/2007/03/06/technology/06iht-payola.4812569.html. Accessed April 4, 2023.

xxxiv   Elias Leight, "Want to Get on the Radio? Have $50,000?" *Rolling Stone*, August 6, 2019, https://www.rollingstone.com/pro/features/radio-stations-hit-pay-for-play-867825/. Accessed April 4, 2023.

xxxv   Greg Milner, *Perfecting Sound Forever: An Aural History of Recorded Music* (New York: Farrar, Straus and Giroux, 2010), 153–56.

xxxvi   Buck Owens and Randy Poe, *Buck 'Em!: The Autobiography of Buck Owens* (Lanman, MD: Backbeat, 2013), 141.

xxxvii   Peter Asher, interview with the authors, September 2020.

xxxviii   Milner, *Perfecting Sound Forever*, 129–32.

xxxix   Milner, *Perfecting Sound Forever*, 237–39.

xl   Milner, *Perfecting Sound Forever*, 284–86.

xli   Greil Marcus, *Like a Rolling Stone: Bob Dylan at the Crossroads* (New York: PublicAffairs, 2006), 141.

xlii   Jim McKeon, interview with the author, September 2020.

xliii   Jac Holzman, interview with the authors, September 2020.

xliv   McKeon, interview.

xlv   McKeon, interview.

xlvi   "Nielsen Report Puts Radio at the Center of the Audio Universe," *InsideRadio*, June 30, 2022, https://www.insideradio.com/nielsen-report-puts-radio-at-the-center-of-the-audio-universe/article_a3188d52-f7f1-11ec-8617-6b7586059cd3.html. Accessed January 30, 2023.

xlvii   Techsurvey 2022 Results, Jacobs Media, https://jacobsmedia.com/techsurvey-2022-results/. Accessed November 22, 2022.

xlviii   The Infinite Dial 2022.

xlix   "Network Radio Averaged 16 Minutes of Spots per Hour, as Rates Crept Up," InsideRadio, November 29, 2018, http://www.insideradio.com/free/network-radio-averaged-16-minutes-of-spots-per-hour-as-rates-crept-up/article_97ff6ae0-f3a8-11e8-b201-8770a1fdf2ed.html. Accessed April 29, 2022.

l   "What Do Ad Loads Look Like on Internet Radio?" *Marketing Charts*, https://www.marketingcharts.com/digital-66030. Accessed April 29, 2022.

Chapter 4

i   Robert Levine, "For the Record: How Vinyl Got its Groove Back—to the Tune of a Billion Dollars." *Billboard*, May 25, 2022, https://www.billboard.com/pro/vinyl-boom-analysis-for-the-record. Accessed July 21, 2022.

ii   Roland Gelatt, *The Fabulous Phonograph, 1877–1977* (New York: MacMillan, 1977), 290.

iii   Scott Thill, "1948: Columbia's Microgroove LP Makes Albums Sound Good,"
           Wired, June 21, 2010, https://www.wired.com/2010/06/0621first-lp-released/.
           Accessed May 22, 2022.

iv   Gelatt, *The Fabulous Phonograph*, 293.

v   Sean Wilentz, *360 Sound: The Columbia Records Story* (San Francisco: Chronicle
           Books, 2012), 127.

vi   Gelatt, *The Fabulous Phonograph*, 292; Jac Holzman, interview with the
           authors, September 2020.

vii   Wilentz, *360 Sound*, 171.

viii   Vinylmint, "History of the Record Industry, 1920—1950s," Medium, June 8,
           2014,   https://medium.com/@Vinylmint/history-of-the-record-industry-
           1920-1950s-6d491d7cb606. Accessed May 25, 2022.

ix   Gelatt, *The Fabulous Phonograph*, 295.

x   Peter Copeland, "Manual of Analogue Sound Restoration Techniques," *The
           British Library*. https://web.archive.org/web/20110409161239/http:/www.
           bl.uk/reshelp/findhelprestype/sound/anaudio/analoguesoundrestoration.
           pdf. Accessed April 29, 2022.

xi   Emory Cook, "Binaural Disks," *High Fidelity*, November-December
           1952, 33–35.

xii   Andre Millard, *America on Record: A History of Recorded Sound*
           (Cambridge: Cambridge University Press, 2005), 192.

xiii   Millard, *America on Record*, 212.

xiv   Gelatt, *The Fabulous Phonograph*, 317.

xv   Daniel Duggan, "Investor Buys Former Handleman Co. HQ in Troy for $3
           Million," *Crain's Detroit Business,* February 24, 2010, https://www.crainsdetr
           oit.com/article/20100224/DM01/302249988/investor-buys-former-handle
           man-co-hq-in-troy-for-3-million. Accessed May 25, 2022.

xvi   Denisoff, *Solid Gold*, 191–92.

xvii   Denisoff, *Solid Gold*, 194–98.

xviii   Denisoff, *Solid Gold*, 201–7.

xix   Denisoff, *Solid Gold*, 210–12.

xx   Russell and David Sanjek, *American Popular Music in the 20th Century*
           (Oxford: Oxford University Press, 1991), 86.

xxi   Sanjek, *American Popular Music in the 20th Century*, 130.

xxii   Sanjek, *American Popular Music in the 20th Century*, 129–30.

xxiii   Daniel Brockman and Jason W. Smith, "The Rise and Fall of the Columbia
           House record Club: And How We Learned to Steal Music," *Boston Phoenix*,
           November 18, 2011, https://thephoenix.com/Boston/music/129722-rise-and-
           fall-of-the-columbia-house-record-clu/. Accessed May 25, 2022.

xxiv   Sanjek, *American Popular Music in the 20th Century*, 130.

xxv   Denisoff, *Solid Gold*, 191.

xxvi   Sanjek, *American Popular Music in the 20th Century*, 144–45.

xxvii   Sanjek, *American Popular Music in the 20th Century*, 204.

xxviii   Sanjek, *American Popular Music in the 20th Century*, 217.

xxix   "A Short History of How Jukeboxes Changed the World," Rock-Ola. https://
           www.rock-ola.com/blogs/news/a-short-history-of-how-jukeboxes-changed-
           the-world. Accessed May 25, 2022.

xxx   David van Etten, "American Jukebox History." https://www.jukeboxhistory. info/. Accessed May 25, 2022.

xxxi   Van Etten, "American Jukebox History."

xxxii   James Mishra, "The Dark History of the Jukebox: How the Mafia Used Murder to Build Music Machine Empires," *Click Track,* May 15, 2020, https://www. clicktrack.fm/p/the-dark-history-of-the-jukebox-how. Accessed November 12, 2022.

xxxiii   Robert Shelton, "Happy Tunes on Cash Registers," *New York Times*, March 16, 1958, https://www.nytimes.com/1958/03/16/archives/happy-tunes-on-cash-registers-record-industry-sees-tape-and-stereo.html. Accessed April 4, 2023.

xxxiv   Associated Press, "Vinyl music gives record stores a boost in a digital world," *ABC News,* April 19, 2017, https://web.archive.org/web/20180207210919/ https://abcnews.go.com/amp/Entertainment/wireStory/vinyl-music-record-stores-boost-digital-world-46887652. Accessed April 29, 2022.

xxxv   Lyndsey Havens, "Why Did Vinyl Subscriptions Spike This Year—And Will It Continue?" *Billboard*, December 18, 2020, https://www.billboard.com/artic les/business/9501250/vinyl-subscriptions-spike-2020-bright-eyes/. Accessed April 3, 2023.

xxxvi   Bill Rosenblatt, "Vinyl Is Bigger Than We Thought. Much Bigger," *Forbes*, September 18, 2018, https://www.forbes.com/sites/billrosenblatt/2018/09/18/ vinyl-is-bigger-than-we-thought-much-bigger/. Accessed April 29, 2022.

xxxvii   2018 figures, eBay (used), RIAA (new).

xxxviii Amina Niasse, "Vinyl Record Sales Climb Just 1% After Years of Rapid Growth," *Bloomberg*, July 14, 2022, https://www.bloomberg.com/news/artic les/2022-07-14/vinyl-record-sales-climb-just-1-after-years-of-rapid-growth. Accessed July 21, 2022.

xxxix   Millard, *America on Record*, 209.

xl   Gelatt, *The Fabulous Phonograph*, 297.

xli   Daniel Shannon, "Sales of Stereos Are Less Sound," *New York Times*, May 23, 1982, https://www.nytimes.com/1982/05/23/business/sales-of-stereos-are-less-sound-as-audio-industry-s-markets-slip.html. Accessed April 4, 2023.

xlii   Aaron Perzanowski and Jason Schultz, *The End of Ownership: Personal Property in the Digital Economy* (Cambridge, MA: MIT Press, 2016), 90–97.

xliii   Dave Grohl, "A Statement from the Desk of Record Store Day 2015 Ambassador Dave Grohl," Record Store Day, https://recordstoreday.com/Cus tomPage/3882 . Accessed May 25, 2022.

xliv   "U.S. Year-End Music Report for 2022," Luminate, https://luminatedata.com/ reports/luminate-2022-u-s-year-end-report/. Accessed April 5, 2023.

xlv   Keith Caulfield, "1 of Every 25 Vinyl Albums Sold in U.S. in 2022 Was by Taylor Swift," *Billboard,* January 11, 2023, https://www.billboard.com/pro/tay lor-swift-vinyl-albums-1-of-every-25-sold/. Accessed January 31, 2023.

xlvi   Shelton, "Happy Tunes on Cash Registers."

xlvii   RIAA figures.

xlviii   Copyright law revision: hearings on H.R. 2223, before the Subcommittee on Courts, Civil Liberties, and the Administration of Justice of the Committee on the Judiciary, House of Representatives, Ninety-fourth Congress, 1976, https://archive.org/details/copyrightlawrevi03unit. Accessed May 25, 2022.

xlix   "SME and WMG the biggest market share winners in 2021," Music & Copyright's Blog, April 5, 2022, https://musicandcopyright.wordpress.com/2022/04/05/sme-and-wmg-the-biggest-market-share-winners-in-2021/. Accessed May 25, 2022.

l   Barbara Ringer, The Unauthorized Duplication of Sound Recordings (Copyright Law Revision Study No. 26) (Washington, DC: U.S. Copyright Office, 1961); Subcommittee on Courts, Civil Liberties, and the Administration of Justice of the Committee on the Judiciary, House of Representatives, 95th Congress, Performance Rights in Sound Recordings; Oman, Ralph (Register of Copyrights), Report on Copyright Implications of Digital Audio Transmission Services (Washington, DC: U.S. Copyright Office, 1991).

li   Performance Rights in Sound Recordings.

lii   Sanjek, *American Popular Music in the 20th Century*, 144.

liii   Sanjek, *American Popular Music in the 20th Century*, 142.

liv   Sanjek, *American Popular Music in the 20th Century*, 170.

lv   Stanley Green, Jukebox Piracy. *The Atlantic Monthly*, April 1962, 136.

lvi   Sanjek, *American Popular Music in the 20th Century*, 229.

lvii   "History of the Jukebox License Office," Jukebox Licensing Office, http://www.jukeboxlicense.org/history.htm. Accessed April 29, 2022.

Chapter 5

i   Friedrich Engel, Peter Hammar, and Richard L. Hess, "A Selected History of Magnetic Recording," https://www.richardhess.com/tape/history/Engel_Hammar—Magnetic_Tape_History.pdf, 2–3. Accessed April 29, 2022.

ii   Toby Mountain, "The Birth of Stereo Recording," Northeastern Digital, https://www.northeasterndigital.com/post/the-birth-of-stereo-recording. Accessed April 29, 2022.

iii   Engel et al., "Magnetic Recording," 4–5.

iv   Engel et al., "Magnetic Recording," 8.

v   "AMPEX Model 200/200A Tape Machine," History of Recording, https://www.historyofrecording.com/AMPEX_Model_200.html. Accessed May 25, 2022; John Leslie and Ross Snyder, "History of The Early Days of Ampex Corporation," AES Historical Committee, December 17, 2010, https://www.aes.org/aeshc/docs/company.histories/ampex/leslie_snyder_early-days-of-ampex.pdf. Accessed May 25, 2022.

vi   Andre Millard, *America on Record: A History of Recorded Sound* (Cambridge: Cambridge University Press, 2005), 201–8.

vii   Maxine Roth, "The Story of Music on Tape," *Tape Recording* (January 1968), 44–48.

viii   C. J. LeBel, "Tape or Disc?" *High Fidelity* (October 1959), 56+.

ix   Brad Hardisty, "The Reel History of Analog Tape Recording," Performer, May 4, 2015, https://performermag.com/home-recording/the-reel-history-of-analog-tape-recording/. Accessed April 29, 2022.

x   David L. Morton, *Sound Recording: The Life Story of a Technology* (Baltimore: Johns Hopkins University Press, 2004), 146.

xi   Roth, "The Story of Music on Tape."

xii   Adrian Wu, "Open Reel Tape—The Ultimate Analog Source?," Copper
           Magazine,   https://www.psaudio.com/copper/article/open-reel-tape-the-
           ultimate-analog-source/. Accessed April 29, 2022; David Sarser, "Tapes, Disks,
           and Coexistence." *High Fidelity* (March 1955), 44+.

xiii   "Audio Vendor Brochure and Manual," Cousino Inc., http://lcweb2.loc.
           gov/master/mbrs/recording_preservation/manuals/Cousino%20Univer
           sal%20Audio%20Vendor.pdf. Accessed May 15, 2022.

xiv   Eric D. Daniel, C. Dennis Mee, and Mark H. Clark, *Magnetic Recording: The
           First 100 Years* (Piscataway, NJ: IEEE Press, 1999), 98–99.

xv   Morton, *Sound Recording*, 158.

xvi   Daniel et al., *Magnetic Recording*, 99.

xvii   Morton, *Sound Recording*, 160.

xviii   Stereo Review, *HiFi/Stereo Review's Tape Recorder Annual 1968.*

xix   Neil Genzlinger, "Lou Ottens, Father of Countless Mixtapes, Is Dead at 94,"
           The New York Times, March 11, 2021, https://www.nytimes.com/2021/03/11/
           arts/music/lou-ottens-dead.html. Accessed April 4, 2023.

xx   Daniel et al., *Magnetic Recording*, 102.

xxi   John Komurki, *Cassette Cultures: Past and Present of a Musical Icon*
           (Salenstein: Benteli, 2019), 15.

xxii   Stereo Review, *HiFi/Stereo Review's Tape Recorder Annual 1968.*

xxiii   Daniel et al., *Magnetic Recording*, 103.

xxiv   Robert Angus and Norman Eisenberg, "Are Cassettes Here to Stay?," *High
           Fidelity* (July 1, 1969), 46–53.

xxv   Julian Hirsch, "Julian Hirsch Hits the Cassette Decks." *Stereo Review*
           (November 1970), 56–69.

xxvi   Julian Hirsch, "Advent 201 Cassette Tape Deck." *Stereo Review* (October
           1971), 40–42.

xxvii   Stereo Review, *Stereo Review's Tape Recording and Buying Guide 1974.*

xxviii   Sarser, "Tapes, Disks, and Coexistence."

xxix   Roth, "The Story of Music on Tape."

xxx   Stereo Review, *HiFi/Stereo Review's Tape Recorder Annual 1968*, 31.

xxxi   Arthur J. Zuckerman, "Copy-Cat Tape Decks," *Popular Mechanics* (October
           1983), 94+.

xxxii   Alan Sugar, *What You See Is What You Get: My Autobiography*
           (London: Macmillan, 2010), 205–8.

xxxiii   Clinton Heylin, *Bootleg: The Secret History of the Other Recording Industry*
           (New York: St. Martin's Griffin, 1994), 238.

xxxiv   Richard Harrington, "The Record Industry Goes To War On Home Taping,"
           Washington Post, June 15, 1980.

xxxv   Stereo Review, *Stereo Review Annual Product Guide*, 1982–1986.

xxxvi   Harrington, "Home Taping"; Heylin, *Bootleg*, 232–33.

xxxvii   Ralph Blumenthal, "Goody Chain and Ex-Official Are Sentenced in Tapes
           Case," *New York Times*, November 6, 1982, 29.

xxxviii   Bill Holland, "Audio-Only Home Taping Bill Readied on Senate Side,"
           Billboard, September 7, 1985, 1+.

xxxix   Barry Miles, *Zappa: A Biography* (New York: Grove Press, 2004), 332–38;
           Harrington, "Home Taping."

xl   Schwann Publications, *Schwann Record and Tape Guide*, November 1971.

xli   Schwann Publications, *Schwann Record and Tape Guide*, 1971–1978.

xlii   "Finley to Use 4 and 8 Track Units," *Billboard*, July 31, 1965, 3.

xliii   "ITA Takes Giant Steps to Push Quality Tape," *Billboard,* May 20, 1972, 37. Verna, Paul, "ITA at 25," *Billboard,* March 11, 1995, 73.

xliv   James F. Peltz, "Cetec Gauss Bets Standard Tape Can Survive Digital Threat," *Los Angeles Times*, August 11, 1987, https://www.latimes.com/archives/la-xpm-1987-09-01-fi-5454-story.html. Accessed April 4, 2023.

xlv   Jon Pareles, "Record-It-Yourself Music on Cassette," *New York Times*, May 11, 1987, https://www.nytimes.com/1987/05/11/arts/record-it-yourself-music-on-cassette.html. Accessed April 4, 2023.

xlvi   Simon Reynolds, *Rip It Up and Start Again: Postpunk 1978–1984* (London: Penguin, 2006), 196.

xlvii   Amanda Sewell, "How Copyright Affected the Musical Style and Critical Reception of Sample-Based Hip-Hop," *Journal of Popular Music Studies* 26, nos. 2–3 (2014): 295–320, 298, quoting producer Vinroc.

xlviii   Sewell, "Sample-Based Hip-Hop," 302–3.

xlix   Jeff Chang, *Can't Stop Won't Stop: A History of the Hip-Hop Generation* (London: Picador, 2005), 387–91.

l   Millard, *America on Record*, 211–12.

li   Shelton, "Happy Tunes on Cash Registers."

lii   Sam Goody ads in the *New York Daily News*, 1973–1981.

liii   Chris Willman, "Adele's '30' Has the Biggest Bow of 2021 With 839,000 Album Units," *Variety*, November 28, 2021, https://variety.com/2021/music/news/adele-30-biggest-number-one-album-year-1235120896/. Accessed April 4, 2023.

liv   See for example Iain Taylor, "Audio Cassettes: Despite Being 'a Bit Rubbish', Sales Have Doubled During the Pandemic—Here's Why," *The Conversation*, https://theconversation.com/audio-cassettes-despite-being-a-bit-rubbish-sales-have-doubled-during-the-pandemic-heres-why-157097. Accessed April 29, 2022.

lv   See generally Komurki, *Cassette Cultures*.

lvi   Komurki, *Cassette Cultures*, 69–75.

Chapter 6

i   Jack Banks, *Monopoly: MTV's Quest to Control the Music* (Boulder, CO: Westview Press, 1996), 41.

ii   William Ruhlmann, "Your Hit Parade: 1957 Review," *All Music Guide*, https://www.allmusic.com/album/your-hit-parade-1957-mw0000884963. Accessed May 4, 2022.

iii   Stephanie Nolasco, "Elvis Presley's First Appearance on the Ed Sullivan Show Remembered 64 Years Later," *Foxnews.com*, September 9, 2020, https://www.foxnews.com/entertainment/elvis-presley-ed-sullivan-show-anniversary. Accessed May 4, 2022.

iv   Banks, *Monopoly*, 61–65.

v   Robert Fontenot, "The History of American Bandstand," *Liveabout.com*, June 12, 2019, https://www.liveabout.com/american-bandstand-important-events-timeline-2523794. Accessed May 4, 2022.

vi   Craig Marks and Rob Tannenbaum, *I Want My MTV* (New York: Dutton, 2011), 20.

vii   "The Beatles," *EdSullivan.com*, https://www.edsullivan.com/artists/the-beatles/. Accessed May 4, 2022.

viii   Bill Roedy and David Fisher, *What Makes Business Rock* (New York: Wiley, 2011), 42.

ix   R. Serge Denisoff, *Inside MTV* (Milton Park: Routledge, 1988), 73.

x   Denisoff, *Inside MTV*, 45–46.

xi   Marks and Tannenbaum, *I Want My MTV*, 16.

xii   Banks, *Monopoly*, 67.

xiii   Marks and Tannenbaum, *I Want My MTV*, 27.

xiv   Banks, *Monopoly*, 36.

xv   Andrew Goodwin, *Dancing in the Distraction Factory* (Minneapolis: University of Minnesota Press, 1992), 58.

xvi   Denisoff, *Inside MTV*, 95.

xvii   Nick Rhodes, interview with the authors, November 30, 2020.

xviii   Banks, *Monopoly*, 36.

xix   Marks and Tannenbaum, *I Want My MTV*, 74, 102.

xx   Jordan Rost (Former Vice President of Research, Warner Amex Satellite Entertainment), interview with the author, January 13, 2021.

xxi   Marks and Tannenbaum, *I Want My MTV*, 130.

xxii   Banks, *Monopoly*, 78.

xxiii   "March 1982: 'I Want My MTV!' Campaign Launched," *Totally80s.com*, https://www.totally80s.com/article/march-1982-i-want-my-mtv-campaign-launched. Accessed May 4, 2022.

xxiv   Banks, *Monopoly*, 38.

xxv   Marks and Tannenbaum, *I Want My MTV*, 80.

xxvi   Greg Prato, "David Coverdale Tells the Story behind Whitesnake's Iconic 'Here I Go Again' Video," *Consequenceofsound.com*, March 13, 2019, https://consequence.net/2019/03/david-coverdale-whitesnake-here-i-go-again-video/. Accessed May 4, 2022.

xxvii   Jerry Casale, interview with the authors, January 10, 2021.

xxviii   Marks and Tannenbaum, *I Want My MTV*, 125.

xxix   Marks and Tannenbaum, *I Want My MTV*, XLIV.

xxx   David Benjamin, interview with the authors, January 28, 2021.

xxxi   Jim Impoco, "The Beatles Suck. Yeah, We Said That," *Newsweek*, February 3, 2014, https://www.newsweek.com/beatles-suck-yeah-we-said-227748. Accessed May 4, 2022.

xxxii   Denisoff, *Inside MTV*, 37.

xxxiii   Goodwin, *Dancing in the Distraction Factory*, 54.

xxxiv   Marks and Tannenbaum, *I Want My MTV*, 242.

xxxv   Denisoff, *Inside MTV*, 157–58.

xxxvi   Banks, *Monopoly*, 101.

xxxvii   Marks and Tannenbaum, *I Want My MTV*, 243.

xxxviii   Banks, *Monopoly*, 84.

xxxix   Michael A. Hiltzik, "Viacom to Buy MTV and Showtime in Deal Worth $667.5 Million," *Los Angeles Times*, August 27, 1985, https://www.latimes.com/archives/la-xpm-1985-08-27-fi-25404-story.html. Accessed April 3, 2023.

xl   Roedy and Fisher, *What Makes Business Rock*, 44.

xli   Roedy and Fisher, *What Makes Business Rock*, 40.

xlii   Marks and Tannenbaum, *I Want My MTV*, 564.

xliii   Bobby Owsinski, "The Streaming Performance Royalty Explained," *Music 3.0 Blog*, November 13, 2019, https://music3point0.com/2016/05/19/streaming-performance-royalty/#ixzz6souR0TTQ. Accessed May 4, 2022.

xliv   "'Start Me Up': the $3 Million Anthem That Launched Microsoft's Windows 95," *4As*, https://www.aaaa.org/timeline-event/start-3-million-anthem-launc hed-microsofts-windows-95/?cn-reloaded=1. Accessed May 4, 2022.

xlv   Banks, *Monopoly*, 106–8.

xlvi   Roedy and Fisher, *What Makes Business Rock*, 53, 134.

xlvii   Roedy and Fisher, *What Makes Business Rock*, 161.

xlviii   Chris Molanphy, "A Deal with the TV Gods," *Hit Parade* (podcast), June 18, 2022, https://slate.com/podcasts/hit-parade/2022/06/television-is-a-hitmak ing-jukebox. Accessed July 5, 2022.

xlix   Denisoff, *Inside MTV*, 117.

Chapter 7

i   Kees A. Immink, "The Compact Disc Story," *Journal of the Audio Engineering Society,* 46, no. 5 (May 1998): 458–465.

ii   Kees A. Immink, "Shannon, Beethoven and the Compact Disc." *IEEE Information Theory Society Newsletter* (December 2007), 42–46.

iii   Marc Finer, interview with the authors, December 10, 2020.

iv   Kieran Prendiville, "Tomorrow's World: The Compact Disc," *BBC*, February 24, 2015, https://youtu.be/bMp1pSVxoqw. Accessed May 23, 2022.

v   J. B. H. Peek and J. P. Sinjou, "The CD System as Standardized by Philips and Sony," in *Origins and Successors of the Compact Disc: Contributions of Philips to Optical Storage*, ed. J. B. H. Peek, J. W. M. Bergmans, J. A. M. M. van Haaren, Frank Toolenaar, and S. G. Stan (New York: Springer, 2009), 53–136.

vi   "Portable Music Players Enter the Spin Zone," *Wired,* September 10, 2009, https://www.wired.com/2009/09/1001first-cd-players/. Accessed May 23. 2022.

vii   "Play/Pause: A Look at 30 Years of the Compact Disc," *Business Week*, October 1, 2012, https://www.bloomberg.com/news/photo-essays/2012-10-01/play-pause-a-look-at-30-years-of-the-compact-disc. Accessed May 23, 2002.

viii   Luke Dormehl, "38 Years ago, CDs Rewrote Our Relationship With Music and Primed Us For 2020," Digital Trends, October 12, 2020, https://www.digita ltrends.com/features/how-cds-prepared-us-for-the-future/. Accessed May 23, 2022.

ix   Edward Rasen, "Compact Discs: Sound of the Future," *Spin* (May 1985), 28–32.

x   Steve Knopper, *Appetite for Self-Destruction* (Seattle: CreateSpace Independent Publishing Platform, 2017), 41.

xi   Ryan Waniata, "The Life and Times of the Late, Great CD," *Digital Trends*, February 7, 2018, https://www.digitaltrends.com/music/the-history-of-the-cds-rise-and-fall/. Accessed May 23.2022.

xii   Milner, *Perfecting Sound Forever*, 211–19.

xiii   Kara Swisher, "Circuit City Plugs into Visions of an Electronics Dream World," *Washington Post,* February 1, 1993, https://www.washingtonpost.com/arch ive/business/1993/02/01/circuit-city-plugs-in-to-visions-of-an-electron ics-dream-world/2f67d9fd-c21c-4931-99d3-1c3a13c8db43/. Accessed May 23, 2022.

xiv   Bob Harvilla, "How Soundscan Changed Everything We Knew About Popular Music," *The Ringer,* May 25, 2021, https://www.theringer.com/music/2021/ 5/25/22452539/soundscan-billboard-charts-streaming-numbers.   Accessed May 23, 2022.

xv   Dan Margolis, "Music to a Customers Ears: CD Buyers Can Hear Them First in Stores," *Los Angeles Times,* June 14, 1995, https://www.latimes.com/archi ves/la-xpm-1995-06-14-fi-13105-story.html. Accessed April 4, 2023.

xvi   Knopper, *Appetite for Self-Destruction,* 36–40.

xvii   Jon Pareles, "Now on CDs, First 4 Beatles Albums," *New York Times,* February, 25, 2002, https://www.nytimes.com/1987/02/25/arts/now-on-cd-s-first-4-beatles-albums.html. Accessed May 23, 2022.

xviii   Donald Passman, *All You Need to Know About the Music Business,* 10th Edition (New York: Simon & Schuster, 2019), 81–83.

xix   Jay L. Frank, *Futurehit, DNA* (Pennsauken, NJ: Futurehit, Inc, 2009), 98–103.

xx   Chris Molanphy, "Hit Parade: The War Against the Single," Slate Podcasts, September 29, 2017, https://chris.molanphy.com/hit-parade-the-great-war-against-the-single-edition/. Accessed May 23, 2022.

xxi   Knopper, *Appetite for Self-Destruction,* 42.

xxii   Neil Young, "The CD and the Damage Done," *Harper's Magazine,* July 1992, 23–24.

xxiii   Nick Rhodes, interview with the authors, November 30, 2020.

xxiv   Jac Holzman, interview with the authors, September 4, 2020.

xxv   Peter Asher, interview with the authors, September 27, 2020.

xxvi   Albhy Galuten, interview with the authors, December 12, 2020.

xxvii   "The Loudness Wars: Why Music Sounds Worse," *NPR,* December 31, 2009, https://www.npr.org/2009/12/31/122114058/the-loudness-wars-why-music-sounds-worse. Accessed May 23, 2022.

xxviii   Jane Birnbaum, "The Media Business: Without a Scratch, Used CD's Rise Again," *New York Times,* September 6, 1993, https://www.nytimes.com/1993/ 09/06/business/the-media-business-without-a-scratch-used-cds-rise-again. html. Accessed May 23, 2022.

xxix   Chris O'Malley, "A New Spin," *Time,* August 24, 1998, https://content.time. com/time/subscriber/article/0,33009,988955,00.html. Accessed May 23, 2022.

xxx   Chris Nelson, "Music Piracy Shifts to Recordable CDs, Record Industry Says," *MTV.com News,* August 19, 1999, https://www.mtv.com/news/g5btet/ music-piracy-shifts-to-recordable-cds-record-industry-says/. Accessed April 5, 2023.

xxxi   Eric Espe, "Music Industry Sees Threat in CD-copying Technology," *Silicon Valley Business Journal,* August 30, 1998, https://www.bizjournals.com/sanj ose/stories/1998/08/31/story4.html. Accessed May 23, 2022.

xxxii   Chris Nelson, "Recordable CDs Undercut Traditional Bootleg Market," *MTV. com News,* May 21, 1998, https://www.mtv.com/news/dsuz61/recordable-cds-undercut-traditional-bootleg-market/. Accessed April 5, 2023.

xxxiii   Barbara Fox Kraut, "The Audio Home Recording Act," *DePaul Journal of Art, Technology, and Intellectual Property Law* 2, no. 2 (Spring 1992): 38–40, https://via.library.depaul.edu/cgi/viewcontent.cgi?article=1495&context=jatip.

xxxiv   "About Piracy," Record Industry Association of America, https://www.riaa.com/resources-learning/about-piracy/. Accessed May 23, 2022.

xxxv   Stephen Labaton, "5 Music Companies Settle Federal Case On CD Price-Fixing," *New York Times,* May 11, 2000, https://www.nytimes.com/2000/05/11/business/5-music-companies-settle-federal-case-on-cd-price-fixing.html. Accessed April 4, 2023.

Chapter 8

i   "IBM PC AT," *Old-Computers.com*, http://www.old-computers.com/museum/computer.asp?st=1&c=185. Accessed May 23, 2022.

ii   Paul Resinkoff, "A Proposal to Build Spotify (from 1982)," *Digital Music News*, June 21, 2012, https://www.digitalmusicnews.com/2012/06/21/proposes/. Accessed November 26, 2022.

iii   Devon Schiff, "GO AEROSMITH: How 'Head First' Became the First Digitally Downloadable Song 20 Years Ago Today," *Vice.com*, June 27, 2014, https://www.vice.com/en/article/6vapxr/go-aerosmith-how-head-first-became-the-first-song-available-for-digital-download-20-years-ago-today. Accessed May 23, 2022.

iv   Stephen Witt, *How Music Got Free: A Story of Obsession and Invention* (London: Penguin Books, 2016), 6–17.

v   Jonathan Sterne, *MP3: The Meaning of a Format* (Durham, NC: Duke University Press, 2012), 117–129.

vi   Witt, *How Music Got Free*, 27–28.

vii   Ian Corbett, "What Data Compression Does to Your Music," *Sound On Sound*, April 2012, https://www.soundonsound.com/techniques/what-data-compression-does-your-music. Accessed June 7, 2022.

viii   Sterne, *MP3*, 232.

ix   Seth Mnookin, "Universal's CEO Once Called iPod Users Thieves: Now He's Giving Songs Away," *Wired*, November 27, 2007, https://www.wired.com/2007/11/mf-morris/. Accessed June 7, 2022.

x   Po Bronson, "Rebootlegger," *Wired*, July 1, 1998, https://www.wired.com/1998/07/newmedia-4/. Accessed June 17,2022.

xi   Jennifer Sullivan, "The Sound of Busic (sic)," *Wired*, February 26, 1999, https://www.wired.com/1999/02/the-sound-of-busic/. Accessed June 7, 2022.

xii   Barry Fox, "Out of the Bell Tower," *New Scientist*, May 6, 1995, https://www.computerhistory.org/timeline/memory-storage/. Accessed June 7, 2022.

xiii   "Rio PMP300," *Wikipedia*, https://en.wikipedia.org/wiki/Rio_PMP300. Accessed June 17, 2022.

xiv   Sam Costello, "History of the iPod: From the First iPod to the iPod Classic," *Lifewire*, January 12, 2020, https://www.lifewire.com/history-ipod-classic-original-2000732. Accessed May 23, 2022.

xv   Leander Kahney, "Straight Dope on the iPod's Birth," *Wired*, October 17, 2006, https://www.wired.com/2006/10/straight-dope-on-the-ipods-birth/. Accessed June 27, 2022.

xvi   Jennifer Sullivan, "More Popular Than Sex," *Wired*, October 14, 1999, https://
          www.wired.com/1999/10/more-popular-than-sex/. Accessed April 5, 2023.

xvii   Matt Flint, "A File-Sharing Timeline: From the Creation of MP3 to the Trial of
          The Pirate Bay," *The Takeaway*, April 17, 2009, https://www.wnycstudios.org/
          podcasts/takeaway/articles/10560-file-sharing-timeline-creation-mp3-trial-
          pirate-bay. Accessed October 15, 2022.

xviii   "RIAA vs Diamond Multimedia Decision," *Cyber Harvard*, https://cyber.harv
          ard.edu/property00/MP3/rio.html. Accessed May 23, 2022.

xix   John Borland, "Metallica Fingers 335,435 Napster Users," *CNET*, January 2,
          2002, https://www.cnet.com/tech/services-and-software/metallica-fingers-
          335435-napster-users/. Accessed May 23, 2022.

xx   John Borland, "Napster Boots Dr. Dre Fans From Service," *CNET*, January 2,
          2002, https://www.cnet.com/news/napster-boots-dr-dre-fans-from-service/.
          Accessed June 7, 2022.

xxi   Borland, John, "Judges Issues Injunction Against Napster," *CNET*, January 2,
          2002, https://www.cnet.com/tech/services-and-software/judge-issues-injunct
          ion-against-napster/. Accessed May 23, 2022.

xxii   David Teather, "Napster Wins New Friend," *Guardian*, November 1, 2000,
          https://www.theguardian.com/technology/2000/nov/01/internetnews.busin
          ess. Accessed June 7, 2022.

xxiii   Mike Bebel, interview with the authors, June 27, 2022.

xxiv   Brian Hiatt, "Napster Offers Labels $1 Billion in Licensing Fees," *MTV News*,
          February 20, 2001, https://www.mtv.com/news/5r4iyc/napster-offers-labels-
          1-billion-in-licensing-fees. Accessed April 3, 2023.

xxv   Ted Cohen, interview with the author, July 27, 2020.

xxvi   Jim McDermott, "5 Reasons the Major Labels Didn't Really Blow it With
          Napster," *Hypebot*, https://www.hypebot.com/hypebot/2015/05/five-reasons-
          the-major-labels-didnt-blow-it-with-napster.html. Accessed June 7, 2022.

xxvii   "Napster Settlement Offer Rejected," *CBS News*, February 11, 2001, https://
          www.cbsnews.com/news/napster-settlement-offer-rejected/. Accessed May
          23, 2022.

xxviii   Matt Richtel, "The Napster Decision: Appellate Judges Back Limitations on
          Copying Music," *New York Times*, February 13, 2001, https://www.nytimes.
          com/2001/02/13/business/napster-decision-overview-appellate-judges-
          back-limitations-copying-music.html. Accessed June 17, 2022.

xxix   T. S. Spangler, "Morpheus, Other File-Sharing Services Sued by RIAA,"
          ExtremeTech, October 3, 2001, https://www.extremetech.com/extreme/
          58270-morpheus-other-filesharing-services-sued-by-riaa. Accessed June
          17, 2022.

xxx   Eric Schumacher-Rasmussen, "Record Industry Sues Morpheus and Other
          Decentralized File Sharing Services," *MTV News*, October 3, 2001, https://
          www.mtv.com/news/gpun33/record-industry-sues-morpheus-and-other-de-
          centralized-file-sharing-services/. Accessed April 4, 2023.

xxxi   Matt Richtel, "File Sharing Sites Found Not Liable For Infringement," *New York
          Times*, August 20, 2004, https://www.nytimes.com/2004/08/20/business/tec
          hnology-file-sharing-sites-found-not-liable-for-infringement.html. Accessed
          April 4, 2023.

xxxii   "Web Music Sharers Under Attack," *CBS News*, July 14, 2003, https://www. cbsnews.com/news/web-music-sharers-under-attack/. Accessed June 7, 2022.

xxxiii   "Public Knowledge Responds to RIAA's plans to sue P2P File Traders," Public Knowledge *press release*, September 7, 2004, https://www.publicknowledge. org/press-release/public-knowledge-responds-to-riaas-plans-to-sue-p2p-file-traders/. Accessed June 7, 2022.

xxxiv   Gil Kaufman, "File-Sharing Networks Can Be Liable for Copyright Infringement, Supreme Court Rules," *MTV News*, June 27, 2005, https://www. mtv.com/news/n3nkvo/file-sharing-networks-can-be-liable-for-copyright-infringements-supreme-court-rules/. Accessed April 3, 2023.

xxxv   Josh Halliday, "Limewire Shut Down by Federal Court," *Guardian*, October 27, 2010, https://www.theguardian.com/technology/2010/oct/27/limewire-shut-down. Accessed June 27, 2022.

xxxvi   Fred Goodman, "MP3 Technology Poised to Redefine Music Industry," *Rolling Stone*, March 9, 1999, https://www.rollingstone.com/music/music-news/mp3-technology-poised-to-redefine-music-industry-97515/. Accessed June 17, 2022.

xxxvii   Jodi Mardesich, "How the Internet Hits Big Music," *CNN Money*, May 10, 1999, https://money.cnn.com/magazines/fortune/fortune_archive/1999/05/10/259548/index.html. Accessed June 7, 2022.

xxxviii Brett Atwood, "Capitol to Sell Digital Singles," *Billboard*, September 13, 1997. Accessed June 27, 2022.

xxxix   Jon Pareles, "Trying to Get in Tune With the Digital Age; Recording Industry Seeks a Standard For Distributing Music on the Web," *New York Times*, February 1, 1999, https://www.nytimes.com/1999/02/01/business/trying-get-tune-with-digital-age-recording-industry-seeks-standard-for.html. Accessed June 17, 2022.

xl   Goodman, "MP3 Technology Poised to Redefine Music Industry."

xli   Eric Scheirer, "The End of SDMI," *MP3.com*, October 15, 1999, https://web. archive.org/web/20000229055832/http://www.mp3.com/news/394.html. Accessed June 7, 2022.

xlii   "MusicNet Launches Battle for Fans," *BBC*, December 4, 2001, http://news. bbc.co.uk/2/hi/entertainment/1691108.stm. Accessed June 7, 2022.

xliii   Dan Tynan, "The 25 Worst Tech Products of All-Time," *PC World*, May 26, 2006, https://www.pcworld.com/article/535838/worst_products_ever.html. Accessed June 17, 2022.

xliv   Matt Richtel, "Plans to Sell Music on the Internet Raise Antitrust Concerns," *New York Times*, August 7, 2001, https://www.nytimes.com/2001/08/07/busin ess/technology-plans-to-sell-music-on-the-internet-raise-antitrust-conce rns.html/. Accessed June 27, 2022.

xlv   Steve Knopper, "iTunes' 10th Anniversary: How Steve Jobs Turned the Industry Upside Down," *Rolling Stone*, April 26, 2013, https://www.rollingst one.com/culture/culture-news/itunes-10th-anniversary-how-steve-jobs-tur ned-the-industry-upside-down-68985/. Accessed June 27, 2022

xlvi   Nathan Ingraham, "iTunes Store at 10: How Apple Built a Digital Media Juggernaut," *The Verge*, April 26, 2013, https://www.theverge.com/2013/4/26/4265172/itunes-store-at-10-how-apple-built-a-digital-media-juggernaut. Accessed June 7, 2022.

xlvii   Paul Vidich, interview with the authors, December 7, 2020.

xlviii   Jack Denton, "A Requiem for the Microsoft Zune," *Fast Company*, June 15, 2022, https://www.fastcompany.com/90761088/a-requiem-for-the-micros oft-zune-the-little-gadget-that-couldnt. Accessed June 27, 2022.

xlix   Saul Hansell, "Amazon Launches a Music Store, Not a Service," *New York Times*, September 25, 2007, https://bits.blogs.nytimes.com/2007/09/25/ama zon-launches-a-music-store-not-a-service. Accessed June 7, 2022.

l   Steve Jobs, "Thoughts on Music," Apple, February 6, 2007, https://web.archive. org/web/20071223160841/https://www.apple.com/hotnews/thoughtsonmu sic/. Accessed June 7, 2022.

li   Michael Smith and Rahul Telang, "Assessing the Academic Literature Regarding the Impact of Media Piracy on Sales," Carnegie-Mellon University,August 19, 2012, Available at http://ssrn.com/abstract= 2132153. Accessed May 18, 2023.

lii   Jay Frank, *Futurehit.DNA* (New York: Futurehit, Inc, 2009), 118–120.

liii   Maria Aspan, "For Shakira, First Came the Album, Then Came the Single," *New York Times*, June 6, 2006, https://www.nytimes.com/2006/06/12/busin ess/media/12shakira.html. Accessed April 4, 2023.

liv   "Ace of Base to Release New Album Worldwide," *The Local*, February 24, 2015, https://www.thelocal.se/20150224/ace-of-base-to-release-new-album. Accessed June 7, 2022.

lv   Yinka Adegoke, "Labels Bet on Flexibility With iTunes New Pricing," *Reuters*, April 8, 2009, https://www.reuters.com/article/us-apple-itunes/labels-bet-on-flexibility-with-itunes-new-pricing-idUSN0641102320090408. Accessed June 7, 2022.

lvi   "iTunes Store and DRM-Free Music: What You Need to Know," *Macworld*, January 7, 2009, https://www.macworld.com/article/1138000/drm-faq.html. Accessed June 27, 2022.

lvii   Adrian Covert, "A Decade of iTunes Singles Killed the Music Industry," *CNN Business*, April 25, 2013, https://money.cnn.com/2013/04/25/technology/itu nes-music-decline/index.html. Accessed June 7, 2022.

lviii   Michaels. Sean, "Most Music Didn't Sell a Single Copy in 2008," *Guardian*, December 23, 2008, https://www.theguardian.com/music/2008/dec/23/ music-sell-sales. Accessed June 7, 2022.

lix   Helienne Lindvall, "Behind the Music: Is the Long Tail a Myth," *Guardian*, January 8, 2009, https://www.theguardian.com/music/musicblog/2009/jan/ 08/long-tail-myth-download. Accessed June 7, 2022.

lx   "Madonna Swears at Music Pirates," *BBC News*, April 22, 2003, http://news. bbc.co.uk/2/hi/technology/2962475.stm. Accessed June 7, 2022.

lxi   Goodman, "MP3 Technology Poised to Redefine Music Industry."

lxii   Bob Tarantino, "The Ninth Circuit's Eminem License vs Sale Decision," *Entertainment & Media Law Signal*, September 9, 2010, http://www.entertai nmentmedialawsignal.com/the-ninth-circuits-eminem-license-vs-sale-decis ion/. Accessed June 7, 2022.

lxiii   Marc Hogan, "Universal Settles Influential Eminem Digital-Revenues Lawsuit," *Spin*, October 31, 2012, https://www.spin.com/2012/10/universal-settles-influential-eminem-digital-revenue-lawsuit/. Accessed June 7, 2022.

lxiv   Nick Rhodes, interview with the authors, November 30, 2020.

lxv   Lydia Warren, "Steve Jobs Listened to Vinyl at Home—Because it Sounded Better Than His iPod," *Daily Mail*, January 31, 2012, https://www.dailymail.co.uk/news/article-2094590/Steve-Jobs-listened-vinyl-home-iPod.html. Accessed June 7, 2022.

lxvi   Bootie Cosgrove-Mather, "Poll: Young Say File-Sharing OK," *CBS News*, September 18, 2003, https://www.cbsnews.com/news/poll-young-say-file-sharing-ok/. Accessed June 7, 2022.

lxvii   Andrew Everard, "Never Mind the Lack of MP3 Quality, Feel the Lack of MP3 Breadth," *What Hi-Fi?*, April 1, 2009, https://www.whathifi.com/news/usa-never-mind-lack-mp3-quality-feel-lack-mp3-breadth. Accessed June 7, 2022.

lxviii   "Where Do Music Collections Come From?" *American Assembly*, October 15, 2012, http://piracy.americanassembly.org/where-do-music-collections-come-from/. Accessed June 7, 2022.

lxix   Goodman, "MP3 Technology Poised to Redefine Music Industry."

Chapter 9

i   Maureen Farrell and Anne Steele, "Tencent Music Files for U.S. IPO," *Wall Street Journal*, October 2, 2018, https://www.wsj.com/articles/tencent-music-files-for-u-s-ipo-1538496869. Accessed April 4, 2023.

ii   Maureen Farrell, "Tencent Music Rises in Trading Debut," *Wall Street Journal*, December 12, 2018, https://www.wsj.com/articles/tencent-music-opens-higher-in-trading-debut-11544632668. Accessed April 4, 2023.

iii   Glenn Peoples, "Cloud Village Music Subscribers Grew 51%, Revenues Up 38.6% in Q1," *Billboard,* May 24, 2022, https://www.billboard.com/pro/cloud-village-q1-2022-earnings/. Accessed April 4, 2023.

iv   Andre Paine, "Tencent Music Paying Users Up 52% in Q2," *Music Week*, August 11, 2020, https://www.musicweek.com/digital/read/tencent-music-paying-users-up-52-in-q2/080734. Accessed June 5, 2022.

v   Dylan Smith," Tencent Music Subscribers Grow 50% to 42.7 Million—Wall Street Isn't Impressed," *Digital Music News*, May 12, 2020, https://www.digitalmusicnews.com/2020/05/12/tencent-music-subscribers-growth/. Accessed June 7, 2022.

vi   Shawn Knight, "Spotify Hits 205 Million Premium Subscribers, but Financial Losses Swell," *Techspot*, January 31, 2023. https://www.techspot.com/news/97444-spotify-hits-205-million-premium-subscribers-but-financial.html. Accessed January 31, 2023.

vii   Sven Carlsson and Jona Leijonhufvud, *The Spotify Play: How CEO and Founder Daniel Ek Beat Apple, Google, and Amazon in the Race for Audio Dominance* (New York: Diversion Books, 2021), 248–256.

viii   Ashley King, "For the First Time Ever, Annual Music Streams Top 1 Trillion—in the US Alone," *Digital Music News*, November 30, 2022, https://www.digitalmusicnews.com/2022/11/30/annual-music-streams-top-one-trillion-us-alone. Accessed January 31, 2023.

ix   Charles Mann, "The Hot New Bad Idea," *Inside Magazine*, December, 2000.

x   Chuck Melvin, "AT&T Creates 'Ultimate Jukebox' for Rock Hall," *Cleveland Plain Dealer*, April 1, 1998, 1F.

xi   Jim Hu, "Pressplay Comes to Life after Long Wait," CNET, April 14, 2002, https://www.cnet.com/tech/services-and-software/pressplay-comes-to-life-after-long-wait/. Accessed June 7, 2022.

xii   Tim Ingham, "It's Happened: 100,000 Tracks Are Now Being Uploaded to Streaming Services Like Spotify Each Day," *Music Business Worldwide*, October 6, 2022, https://www.musicbusinessworldwide.com/its-happened-100000-tracks-are-now-being-uploaded/. Accessed December 4, 2022.

xiii   Melanie Uy, "3G vs. 4G Technology," *Lifewire*, June 10, 2020, https://www.lifewire.com/how-fast-are-4g-and-3g-internet-speeds-3974470. Accessed June 5, 2022.

xiv   "3G vs 4G," *Diffen*, https://www.diffen.com/difference/3G_vs_4G. Accessed June 5, 2022.

xv   Matt Buchanan, "RIAA Tech Chief: DRM Not Dead, Will Become More Powerful than You Can Possibly Imagine," *Gizmodo*, May 8, 2008, https://gizmodo.com/riaa-tech-chief-drm-not-dead-will-become-more-powerfu-388648. Accessed June 5, 2022.

xvi   Andrea Bossi, "There Were More Than One Trillion Music Streams in U.S. during 2019," *Forbes*, January 10, 2010, https://www.forbes.com/sites/andreabossi/2020/01/10/over-one-trillion-music-streams-in-us-during-2019-record-high. Accessed June 5, 2022.

xvii   "Streaming Forward 2020 Report," *Digital Media Association*, https://dima.org/streaming-forward-report/. Accessed June 5, 2022.

xviii   "About Royalty Rates," *Trichordist*, 2021, https://thetrichordist.com/category/royalty-rates-2/. Accessed May 25, 2022.

xix   Stuart Dredge, "Thom Yorke Calls Spotify 'The Last Desperate Fart of a Dying Corpse.'" *Guardian*, October 7, 2018, https://www.theguardian.com/technology/2013/oct/07/spotify-thom-yorke-dying-corpse. Accessed June 13, 2022.

xx   Paul Resnikoff, "Spotify Executive Calls Artist 'Entitled' for Requesting Payment of One Penny Per Stream," Digital Music News, June 29, 2021, https://www.digitalmusicnews.com/2021/06/29/spotify-executive-entitled-pay-penny-per-stream/. Accessed June 13, 2022.

xxi   Shapiro, Ariel, "Warner Music Adopts SoundCloud's User-centric Revenue Model." *Verge*, July 21, 2022, https://www.theverge.com/2022/7/21/23272548/warner-music-soundcloud-user-centric-model-spotify. Accessed July 22, 2022.

xxii   Ben Homewood, "UMG and Tidal Plot New Streaming Model to Benefit Artists and Fans," *Music Week*, January 31, 2023, https://www.musicweek.com/digital/read/umg-and-tidal-plot-new-streaming-model-to-benefit-artists-and-fans. Accessed January 31, 2023.

xxiii   "Loud & Clear," Spotify, https://loudandclear.byspotify.com/?question=user-centric-model. Accessed June 13, 2022.

xxiv   Karl Matchett, "Barcelona Agree £235m Camp Nou and Kit Sponsorship Deal with Spotify," *Yahoo News*, March 15, 2022, https://news.yahoo.com/barcelona-agree-235m-camp-nou-204133143.html. Accessed June 7, 2022.

xxv   Tim Ingham, "'Fake Artists' Have Billions of Streams on Spotify. Is Sony Now Playing the Service at Its Own Game?" *Rolling Stone*, May 15, 2019, https://www.rollingstone.com/pro/features/fake-artists-have-billions-of-stre

ams-on-spotify-is-sony-now-playing-the-service-at-its-own-game-834746/. Accessed June 5, 2022.

xxvi   "More to Love: Target and Michael Bublé Reveal Exclusive Bonus Tracks on His New Album 'To Be Loved," *CNN*, April 24, 2018, https://www.cnn.com/2018/04/24/us/monkey-selfie-peta-appeal/index.html. Accessed June 5, 2022.

xxvii   Tim Ingham, "Yes, Lucian Grainge Has Banned All Exclusives. No, It's Not All about Frank Ocean," *Music Business Worldwide*, August 25, 2016, https://www.musicbusinessworldwide.com/yes-lucian-grainge-banned-streaming-exclusives-umg-no-not-frank-ocean/. Accessed June 5, 2022.

xxviii   Ben Sisario, "A New Spotify Initiative Makes the Big Record Labels Nervous," *New York Times*, September 6, 2018, https://www.nytimes.com/2018/09/06/business/media/spotify-music-industry-record-labels.html. Accessed June 5, 2022.

xxix   Colin Stutz, "Spotify CEO Daniel Ek Says Direct Licensing With Artists 'Doesn't Make Us a Label," *Billboard*, July 26, 2018, https://www.billboard.com/music/music-news/spotify-daniel-ek-direct-licensing-artists-not-label-earnings-call-8467283/. Accessed June 5, 2022.

xxx   Mark Mulligan, "Did July 1st 2019 Mark the End of Spotify's Music Creator Dream?" *Midia Music Industry Blog*, October 8, 2021,https://www.midiaresearch.com/blog/did-july-1st-2019-mark-the-end-of-spotifys-music-creator-dream. Accessed June 7, 2022.

xxxi   Jon Russell, "Spotify Says It Paid $340M to Buy Gimlet and Anchor," *Techcrunch*, February 15, 2019, https://techcrunch.com/2019/02/14/spotify-gimlet-anchor-340-million/. Accessed June 5, 2022.

xxxii   Ashley Carman, "Spotify Acquires Another Podcast Network to Keep Building Its Original Show Catalog," *The Verge*, May 26, 2019, https://www.theverge.com/2019/3/26/18282301/spotify-podcasts-parcast-acquisition-gimlet-media-anchor. Accessed June 5, 2022.

xxxiii   Kif Leswing, "Apple Music Has Reportedly Passed Spotify in Paid Subscribers in the US," *CNBC*, April 5, 2019, https://www.cnbc.com/2019/04/05/apple-music-has-reportedly-passed-spotify-in-paid-subscribers-in-the-us.html. Accessed June 5, 2022.

xxxiv   Manish Singh, "Google invests $4.5 billion in India's Reliance Jio Platforms," *TechCrunch*, July 15, 2020, https://techcrunch.com/2020/07/15/google-invests-4-5-billion-in-indias-reliance-jio-platforms/. Accessed May 23, 2022.

xxxv   Sankalp Phirtiyal, "Google Expands Jio partnership with Indian Smartphone, Cloud Tie-ups," *Reuters*, June 24, 2021, https://www.reuters.com/technology/google-says-cloud-partnership-with-indias-jio-boost-5g-plans-2021-06-24/. Accessed June 13, 2022.

xxxvi   Daniel Keyes, "Amazon Has Surpassed 150 million Prime Subscribers Globally," *Business Insider*, February 3, 2020, https://www.businessinsider.com/amazon-surpasses-150-million-prime-subscribers-2020-2. Accessed June 5, 2022.

xxxvii   Marissa Matozzo, "Amazon Announced a New Perk for Prime Members—Here's How to Get It," *Yahoo Life*, November 16, 2022, https://www.yahoo.com/lifestyle/amazon-announced-perk-prime-members-140028030.html. Accessed November 18, 2022.

xxxviii   Eli Blumenthal, "Hulu and Spotify Partner to Bundle TV and Music Streaming for $9.99 per Month," *USA Today*, March 12, 2019, https://www.usatoday.com/story/tech/talkingtech/2019/03/12/apple-looming-hulu-and-spotify-partner-9-99-streaming-bundle/3138377002/. Accessed November 18, 2022.

xxxix   Harry Guiness, "Spotify Free vs. Premium: Is it Worth Upgrading? Spotify Free vs. Premium: Is it Worth Upgrading?," *How to Geek*, April 27, 2018, https://www.howtogeek.com/350288/spotify-free-vs-premium-is-it-worth-upgrading/. Accessed June 5, 2022.

xl   Carlsson and Leijonhufvud, *The Spotify Play*, 54–66.

xli   Jacob Key (formerly VP Digital Strategy Europe, Warner Music Group), interview with the author, March 15, 2021.

xlii   Carlsson and Leijonhufvud, *The Spotify Play*, 100–104,172–73.

xliii   "Where Is Spotify Available," *Spotify*, https://support.spotify.com/us/article/where-spotify-is-available/. Accessed June 5, 2022.

xliv   "Apple Services Now Available in More Countries Around the World," *Apple*, April 21, 2020, https://www.apple.com/newsroom/2020/04/apple-services-now-available-in-more-countries-around-the-world/. Accessed June 5, 2022.

xlv   "IFPI Releases Engaging with Music 2021," International Federation of the Phonographic Industry, October 21, 2021, https://www.ifpi.org/ifpi-releases-engaging-with-music-2021/. Accessed June 5, 2022.

xlvi   Murray Stassen, "JioSaavn's Paying Subcriber Base Has Quadrupled Since Early 2019," *Music Business Worldwide*, May 28, 2020, https://www.musicbusinessworldwide.com/jiosaavns-paying-subscriber-base-has-quadrupled-since-early-2019/. Accessed June 5, 2022.

xlvii   Stuart Dredge, "African Streaming service Boomplay Now Has 75m Users," *Music Ally*, June 3, 2020, https://musically.com/2020/06/03/african-streaming-service-boomplay-now-has-75m-users/. Accessed June 5, 2022.

xlviii   Thomas Røssel and Camilla Louise Brandt, "Polaris Nordic: Digital Music in the Nordics," *Polaris*, January 2020, https://polarismusichub.com/wp-content/uploads/2020/05/Full_Report_Polaris_Nordic_Digital-Music-in-the-Nordics-2020.pdf. Accessed June 5, 2022.

xlix   Murray Stassen, " Apple Music Just Raised Its Subscription Price to $10.99 in the U.S. Will Spotify be Next?" *Music Business Worldwide*, October 24, 2022, https://www.musicbusinessworldwide.com/apple-music-just-raised-its-subscription-price-to-10-99-in-the-us-will-spotify-be-next1/. Accessed October 25, 2022.

l   Dylan Smith, " Spotify CEO Daniel Ek Confirms 2023 Price Increase Plans Following Apple Music Raises," *Digital Music News*, October 27, 2022, https://www.digitalmusicnews.com/2022/10/27/spotify-price-increase-2023/. Accessed October 27, 2022.

li   Simon Cohen, "Amazon Music Unlimited Is Getting More Expensive in 2023," *Digital Trends*, January 20, 2023, https://www.digitaltrends.com/home-theater/amazon-music-unlimited-february-2023-price-hike/. Accessed January 31, 2023.

lii   International Federation of the Phonographic Industry, "Engaging with Music 2022," https://www.ifpi.org/wp-content/uploads/2022/11/Engaging-with-Music-2022_full-report-1.pdf. Accessed November 28, 2022.

liii   Eammon Forde, "Spotify's Discover Weekly Has Driven 2.3bn Hours of Listening," *Music Ally*, July 20, 2020, https://musically.com/2020/07/10/spotifys-discover-weekly-has-driven-2-3bn-hours-of-listening/. Accessed June 5, 2022.

liv   Luis Aguiar Wicht and Joel Waldfogel, "Platforms, Promotion, and Product Discovery: Evidence from Spotify Playlists," *EU Science Hub*, June 5, 2018, https://joint-research-centre.ec.europa.eu/publications/platforms-promotion-and-product-discovery-evidence-spotify-playlists_en. Accessed June 5, 2022.

lv   "Today's Top Hits Is the World's Destination for the Very Best in Music," *Spotify: For the Record*, June 24, 2021, https://newsroom.spotify.com/2021-06-24/todays-top-hits-is-the-worlds-destination-for-the-very-best-in-music/. Accessed June 13, 2022.

lvi   Paul Resnikoff, "What Succeeds on Spotify's Rap Caviar—A Statistical Analysis," *Digital Music News*, August 18, 2020, https://www.digitalmusicnews.com/2020/08/18/spotify-rapcaviar-analysis. Accessed June 13, 2022.

lvii   Y. Heisler, "Steve Jobs Was Never a Fan of Subscription Music," *Engadget*, May 19, 2014, https://www.engadget.com/2014-05-19-steve-jobs-was-never-a-fan-of-subscription-music.html. Accessed June 13, 2022.

lviii   Madeline Buxton, "Spotify's New Free Version Is So Good You Might Cancel Your Subscription," *Refinery 29*, April 24, 2018, https://www.refinery29.com/en-us/2018/04/197232/spotify-for-free-upgrade. Accessed June 5, 2022.

lix   Adrian Pope, "Clamp Down on Free Spotify? Now is Not the Time for Knee-Jerk Decisions," *PIAS: The Independent Blog*, Undated, https://www.piasgroup.net/blog/clamp-down-on-free-spotify-now-is-not-the-time-for-knee-jerk-decisions/. Accessed June 5, 2022.

lx   Andre Paine, "Tencent Music Paying Users Up 52% in Q2."

lxi   Bobby Owsinski, "The Music Long Tail Might Not Be That Long After All," *Music 3.0 Blog*, November 13, 2019, https://music3point0.com/2019/11/13/music-long-tail-rebuffed/#ixzz6QtTtdmzJ. Accessed June 5, 2022.

lxii   Glenn Peoples, "1 in Every 60 U.S. Streams Last Week Was Drake," *Billboard*, June 28, 2022, https://www.billboard.com/pro/drake-honestly-nevermind-streams-marketshare/. Accessed June 29, 2022.

lxiii   Tim Ingham, "Over 66% of All Music Listening in the US Is Now of Catalog Records Rather Than New Releases," *Music Business Worldwide*, July 13, 2021, https://www.musicbusinessworldwide.com/over-66-of-all-music-listening-in-the-us-is-now-of-catalog-records-rather-than-new-releases/. Accessed June 7, 2022.

lxiv   Stephen Dowling, "The Most Iconic Long Intros," *BBC*, April 8, 2019, https://www.bbc.com/culture/article/20190407-the-most-iconic-long-song-intros-in-pop-music. Accessed June 7, 2022.

lxv   Elias Leight, "Think You Have a Hit? Make Sure It's the First Song on Your Album," *Rolling Stone*, March 7, 2019. https://www.rollingstone.com/music/music-features/why-the-first-song-on-the-album-is-the-best-803283/. Accessed June 7, 2022.

lxvi   Zachary Mack, "How Streaming Affects the Lengths of Songs," *The Verge*, May 28, 2019, https://www.theverge.com/2019/5/28/18642978/music-streaming-spotify-song-length-distribution-production-switched-on-pop-vergecast-interview. Accessed June 5, 2022.

lxvii   Mark Mulligan, "How the DNA of a Hit Has Changed Over 20 Years," *Midia Research*, July 13, 2020, https://www.midiaresearch.com/blog/how-the-dna-of-a-hit-has-changed-over-20-years. Accessed June 13, 2022.

lxviii   Alexis Petridis, "Mark Ronson: 'I Was Floundering. I Was Drinking Too Much and Giving Orders,'" *Guardian,* February 22, 2019. https://www.theguardian.com/music/2019/feb/22/mark-ronson-i-was-floundering-i-was-drinking-too-much-and-giving-orders. Accessed June 13, 2022.

lxix   Michael Tauberg, "Music Is Getting Shorter," *Medium*, April 27, 2018, https://michaeltauberg.medium.com/music-and-our-attention-spans-are-getting-shorter-8be37b5c2d67. Accessed June 7, 2022.

lxx   "Are Songs Getting Even Shorter in 2021?" *Hit Songs Deconstructed*, Undated, https://www.hitsongsdeconstructed.com/hsd_wire/the-short-game/. Accessed July 8, 2022.

lxxi   Neil Shah, "Migos Album 'Culture II' Tops Charts but Sparks Debate Over Its Length," *Wall Street Journal*, February 5, 2018, https://www.wsj.com/articles/migos-album-culture-ii-tops-charts-but-sparks-debate-over-its-length-151 7848564. Accessed June 7, 2022.

lxxii   Erielle Sudario, "Spotify Changes Playlist Rules Post Pocket Gods' Protest Album," *We Got This Covered*, May 23, 2022, https://wegotthiscovered.com/music/spotify-changes-playlist-rules-post-pocket-gods-protest-album/. Accessed June 7, 2022.

lxxiii   Leight, "Think You Have a Hit?"

lxxiv   Jason Lipshutz, "RIP Lead Singles: Why Hip-Hop Titans Are Dropping Full Albums All at Once," *Billboard*, June 21, 2022, https://www.billboard.com/pro/drake-future-album-release-strategy-hip-hop-singles/. Accessed November 1, 2022.

lxxv   Corinne Reichert, "Taylor Swift Album 'Midnights' Sweeps All 10 Top Spots on Billboard Hot 100," *CNet*, October 31, 2022, https://www.cnet.com/culture/entertainment/taylor-swift-album-midnights-sweeps-all-10-top-spots-on-billboard-hot-100/. Accessed November 1, 2022.

lxxvi   John Gapper, "Taylor Swift Is Perfect at the Three-Minute Spotify Song," *Financial Times*, November 25, 2022, https://www.ft.com/content/afdd5bfe-c5ae-411c-900f-8c5eab846944. Accessed November, 26, 2022.

lxxvii   "Official Charts Company Shakes Up Rules to Stop the Ed Sheeran Effect," *Guardian*, June 27, 2017, https://www.theguardian.com/music/2017/jun/27/official-charts-company-shakes-up-rules-support-new-talent-ed-sheeran-effect. Accessed November 1, 2022.

lxxviii   Wicht and Waldfogel, "Platforms, Promotion, and Product Discovery."

lxxix   Neil Shah, "Didn't Like That New Album? Another One Is Coming Before You Know It," *Wall Street Journal,* March 26, 2018, https://www.wsj.com/articles/didnt-like-that-new-album-another-one-is-coming-before-you-know-it-152 2076320. Accessed June 7, 2022.

lxxx   Ashley King, "German Pop Artist Mike Singer Uses 'Stream-to-Unlock' Trick to Boost Streaming Algorithms," *Digital Music News*, July 14, 2020, https://www.digitalmusicnews.com/2020/07/14/mike-singer-stream-to-unlock-campaign/. Accessed June 7, 2022.

lxxxi   "Spotify Flagship Playlist ¡Viva Latino! Hits 10 Million Followers," *Spotify: For the Record*, July 26, 2019, https://newsroom.spotify.com/2019-07-26/spot

ify-flagship-playlist-viva-latino-hits-10-million-followers/. Accessed June 5, 2022.

lxxxii   "Popular Music Is More Collaborative Than Ever," *Economist*, February 2, 2018, https://www.economist.com/graphic-detail/2018/02/02/popular-music-is-more-collaborative-than-ever. Accessed June 5, 2022.

lxxxiii   "Sorry (Justin Bieber Song)," *Wikipedia*, https://en.wikipedia.org/wiki/Sorry_(Justin_Bieber_song). Accessed June 5, 2022.

lxxxiv   Stuart Dredge, "Spotify CEO Talks Covid-19, Artist Incomes and Podcasting," *Music Ally*, July 30, 2020, https://musically.com/2020/07/30/spotify-ceo-talks-covid-19-artist-incomes-and-podcasting-interview/. Accessed June 7, 2022.

lxxxv   Lake Schatz, "Spotify CEO to Artists: 'You Can't Record Music Once Every Three to Four Years and Think That's Going to Be Enough,'" *Consequence of Sound*, August 1, 2020, https://consequence.net/2020/08/spotify-daniel-ek-artist-recording-comments/. Accessed June 13, 2022.

lxxxvi   Jay Frank, *Futurehit.DNA* (New York: Futurehit, Inc, 2009), 30–34, 105–110, 131–135.

lxxxvii   Joann Pan, "Grooveshark Circumvents Mobile Bans by Launching an HTML5 Player," *Mashable*, September 5, 2012, https://mashable.com/archive/grooveshark-html5-player. Accessed June 7, 2022.

lxxxviii Peter Kafka, "Grooveshark, the Free Music Service That Used to Scare the Labels Gives Up," *Vox*, April 30, 2015, https://www.vox.com/2015/4/30/11562064/grooveshark-the-free-music-service-that-used-to-scare-the-big-labels. Accessed June 7, 2022.

lxxxix   F-1 Registration, *Spotify*, March 31, 2018, https://www.sec.gov/Archives/edgar/data/1639920/000119312518063434/d494294df1.htm#rom494294_7. Accessed June 7, 2022.

xc   Tim Ingham, "The Great Big Spotify Scam: Did a Bulgarian Playlister Swindle Their Way to a Fortune on Streaming Service," *Music Business Worldwide*, November 20, 2018, https://www.musicbusinessworldwide.com/great-big-spotify-scam-bulgarian-playlister-swindle-way-fortune-streaming-service/. Accessed June 7, 2022.

xci   Murray Stassen, "BTS Set Spotify Record with 20.9M Day One Plays, but 10M Nearly of Them Are Discounted on Platform's Chart," *Music Business Worldwide*, May 24, 2021, https://www.musicbusinessworldwide.com/bts-set-new-spotify-streaming-record-with-20-9m-day-one-plays-but-nearly-10m-of-them-are-discounted-on-platforms-chart/. Accessed June 7, 2022.

xcii   Leight, "Fake Streams Could Be Costing Artists $300 Million a Year," *Rolling Stone*, June 18, 2019, https://www.rollingstone.com/pro/features/fake-streams-indie-labels-spotify-tidal-846641/. Accessed June 7, 2022.

xciii   Peter Slattery, "Scammers Are Gaming Spotify by Faking Collaborations With Famous Artists," OneZero, June 1, 2020, https://onezero.medium.com/scammers-are-gaming-spotify-by-faking-collaborations-with-famous-artists-42d127e370dc. Accessed June 7, 2022.

xciv   Landon Groves, "Hate Your Favorite Band's Latest Song? On Spotify, It Might Be a fake," *Input Mag*, July 17, 2020, https://www.inputmag.com/culture/spotify-is-letting-scammers-rip-artists-off-in-plain-sight. Accessed June 7, 2022.

xcv Bruce Houghton, "Spotify Cuts Off Playlist Payola Service SpotLister," *Hypebot*, March 19, 2018, https://www.hypebot.com/hypebot/2018/03/spot ify-cuts-off-playlist-payola-service-spotlister.html. Accessed June 7, 2022.

xcvi Tatiana Cirisano, "Record Industry Groups Take Action Against Fake Music Streams in Germany," *Billboard*, August 24, 2020, https://www.billboard.com/ pro/ifpi-bvmi-take-action-against-fake-music-streams-germany/. Accessed June 7, 2022.

xcvii Ed Christman, "Spotify and Publishing Group Reach $30 Million Settlement Agreement Over Unpaid Royalties," *Billboard*, March 17, 2016, https://www. billboard.com/music/music-news/spotify-nmpa-publishing-30-million-set tlement-unpaid-royalties-7263747/. Accessed June 7, 2022.

xcviii Sarah Jeong, "A $1.6 Billion Spotify Lawsuit is Based on a Law Made for Player Pianos," *The Verge*, March 14, 2018, https://www.theverge.com/2018/3/14/ 17117160/spotify-mechanical-license-copyright-wixen-explainer. Accessed June 7, 2022.

xcix Dani Deahl, "The Music Modernization Act Has Been Signed Into Law," *The Verge*, October 11, 2018, https://www.theverge.com/2018/10/11/17963 804/music-modernization-act-mma-copyright-law-bill-labels-congress. Accessed June 7, 2022.

c "About the MLC," *Mechanical Licensing Collective*, https://www.themlc.com/ our-story. Accessed June 7, 2022.

ci "How Can YOU Play Your Part™?" *Mechanical Licensing Collective*, https:// www.themlc.com/play-your-part. Accessed July 17, 2022.

cii Natasha Lomas, "Apple Pay and iOS App Store Under Formal Antitrust Probe in Europe," *Techcrunch*, June 16, 2016, https://techcrunch.com/2020/06/16/ apple-pay-and-ios-app-store-under-formal-antitrust-probe-in-europe/. Accessed June 7, 2022.

ciii Jack Nicas and David McCabe, "Their Businesses Went Virtual. Then Apple Wanted a Cut," *New York Times*, July 28, 2020, https://www.nytimes.com/ 2020/07/28/technology/apple-app-store-airbnb-classpass.html. Accessed June 7, 2022.

Chapter 10

i John Horrigan, "Home Broadband Adoption 2006: Part 1. Broadband Adoption in the United States," *Pew Research Center*, May 28, 2006, https:// www.pewresearch.org/internet/2006/05/28/part-1-broadband-adoption-in-the-united-states/. Accessed May 25, 2022.

ii Martyn Williams, "IMesh P-to-P provider gets Sony Music license," *PCWorld*, July 12, 2005, https://www.pcworld.idg.com.au/article/135515/imesh_p-to-p_provider_gets_sony_music_license/. Accessed May 25, 2022.

iii John Borland, "Legal P2P opens for business," *CNET*, September 26, 2006, https://www.cnet.com/tech/home-entertainment/legal-p2p-opens-for-busin ess/. Accessed May 25, 2022.

iv "Sony BMG Music Entertainment Signs Content License Agreement with YouTube," Sony Music press release, October 8, 2006, https://www. sonymusic.com/sonymusic/sony-bmg-music-entertainment-signs-cont

	ent-license-agreement-with-youtube/. Accessed May 25, 2022; Nate Anderson, "YouTube signs up Universal, Sony BMG, CBS, and . . . Google?," *Ars Technica*, October 9, 2006, https://arstechnica.com/information-technol ogy/2006/10/7935/. Accessed May 25, 2022.
v	"EMI Music, Google and YouTube strike milestone partnership," EMI press release, May 31, 2007, https://web.archive.org/web/20070602142911/http:/ www.emigroup.com/Press/2007/press38.htm. Accessed May 25, 2022.
vi	Andrew Ross Sorkin and Jeff Leeds, "Music Companies Grab a Share of the YouTube Sale," *New York Times*, October 19, 2006, https://www.nytimes.com/ 2006/10/19/technology/music-companies-grab-a-share-of-the-youtube-sale. html. Accessed May 25, 2002.
vii	Michael Wesch, "YouTube Statistics," *Digital Ethnography @ Kansas State University*, March 18, 2008, https://web.archive.org/web/20140723075938/ http://mediatedcultures.net/thoughts/youtube-statistics/. Accessed May 25, 2022.
viii	"Thanks a Billion!," *TikTok*, September 7, 2021, https://newsroom.tiktok.com/ en-us/1-billion-people-on-tiktok. Accessed May 25, 2022.
ix	"TikTok Users Worldwide (2020–2025)," *Insider Intelligence*, June 1, 2022, https://www.insiderintelligence.com/charts/global-tiktok-user-stats/. Accessed November 16, 2022. eMarketer explains that its methodology for counting users is more conservative than the methodology that TikTok itself used to generate its 1 billion estimate.
x	"About Spotify," *Spotify*, May 25, 2022, https://newsroom.spotify.com/comp any-info/. Accessed May 25, 2022.
	"Essential YouTube stats for 2022," *Datareportal*, February 23, 2022, https:// datareportal.com/essential-youtube-stats. Accessed May 25, 2022.
xi	"TikTok Users Worldwide (2020–2025)." eMarketer predicted in late 2021 that TikTok's growth will slow significantly starting in 2022.
xii	"TikTok Is Hitting Revenue Milestones at Lightning Speed," *Chartr*, June 29, 2022, https://www.chartr.co/stories/2022-06-29-2-tiktok-is-hitting-milesto nes-quickly. Accessed July 14, 2022.
xiii	MIREX2020 Results, *MIREX*, https://www.music-ir.org/mirex/wiki/ 2020:MIREX2020_Results. Accessed August 5, 2020.
xiv	Andy Baio, "The Tangled Issue of Cover Song Copyright on YouTube," *Wired*, March 5, 2012, https://www.wired.co.uk/article/cover-song-licensing-on-youtube. Accessed May 25, 2022.
xv	Jessica Toonkel, Anne Steele, and Salvador Rodriguez, "TikTok Parent ByteDance Plans Music-Streaming Expansion," *Wall Street Journal*, October 12, 2022, https://www.wsj.com/articles/tiktok-parent-bytedance-plans-music-streaming-expansion-11665602937. Accessed November 16, 2022.
xvi	Directive (EU) 2019/790 of the European Parliament and of the Council of 17 April 2019 on copyright and related rights in the Digital Single Market and amending Directives 96/9/EC and 2001/29/EC. Official Journal of the European Union, https://eur-lex.europa.eu/legal-content/EN/TXT/HTML/ ?uri=CELEX:32019L0790&rid=1. Accessed May 25, 2022.
xvii	See for example Bill Rosenblatt, "EU Article 13 (Now Article 17) Passes After More Changes, Making Copyright Filtering More Likely," *Copyright and Technology*, April 1, 2019, https://copyrightandtechnology.com/2019/04/01/

eu-article-13-now-article-17-passes-after-more-changes-making-copyright-filtering-more-likely/. Accessed May 25, 2022.

xviii   Maria Strong (Acting Registry of Copyrights), Section 512 of Title 17 (Washington, DC: United States Copyright Office, May 2020). For a brief summary, see Bill Rosenblatt, "Copyright Office's Section 512 Report Finds the Balance Askew," *Copyright and Technology*, May 26, 2020, https://copyrightandtechnology.com/2020/05/26/copyright-office-releases-section-512-report/. Accessed May 25, 2022.

xix   Shelby Carpenter, "Inside Vevo's Plan To Beat YouTube And Become The MTV Of The Digital Age," *Forbes*, October 9, 2016, https://www.forbes.com/sites/shelbycarpenter/2016/10/19/vevo-play-beat-youtube-mtv-digital-age/. Accessed May 25, 2022.

xx   "VEVO Was Most Trafficked U.S. Entertainment-Music Web Network in December 2009," Vevo press release, January 13, 2010, https://www.prnewswire.com/news-releases/vevo-was-most-trafficked-us-entertainment-music-web-network-in-december-2009-81347087.html. Accessed May 25, 2022.

xxi   Ethan Smith, "MTV Overtakes Vevo as Top Online Music Destination," *Wall Street Journal*, September 8, 2010, https://www.wsj.com/articles/BL-SEB-46396. Accessed July 25, 2022.

xxii   "The World's Leading Music Video Network," *Vevo*, Undated, https://www.hq.vevo.com/. Accessed July 25, 2022.

xxiii   Jack Nicas, "YouTube Tops 1 Billion Hours of Video a Day, on Pace to Eclipse TV," *Wall Street Journal*, February 27, 2017, https://www.wsj.com/articles/youtube-tops-1-billion-hours-of-video-a-day-on-pace-to-eclipse-tv-1488220851. Accessed April 4, 2023.

xxiv   "Music Became Even More Valuable on YouTube in 2019," *Pex*, June 4, 2019, https://pex.com/blog/state-of-youtube-2019-music-more-valuable/. Accessed May 25, 2022.

xxv   The Infinite Dial 2015, Edison Research and Triton Digital, March 4, 2015, https://www.edisonresearch.com/the-infinite-dial-2015/. Accessed May 25, 2022.

xxvi   The Infinite Dial 2022. Edison Research and Triton Digital, March 23,2022, https://www.edisonresearch.com/the-infinite-dial-2022/. Accessed March 25, 2022.

xxvii   "Rewarding Creativity: Fixing the Value Gap (excerpt from *Global Music Report 2017*)," International Federation of the Phonographic Industry, April 25, 2017, https://web.archive.org/web/20190221033533/https:/www.ifpi.org/downloads/GMR2017_ValueGap.pdf. Accessed May 25, 2022.

xxviii   Ethan Smith and Jessica E. Vascellaro, "Warner Pulls Music From YouTube," *Wall Street Journal*, December 22, 2008, https://www.wsj.com/articles/SB122980193788724073. Accessed May 25, 2022.

xxix   See for example: Stuart Dredge, "How Much Do Musicians Really Make from Spotify, iTunes and YouTube?," *Guardian*, April 3, 2015, https://www.theguardian.com/technology/2015/apr/03/how-much-musicians-make-spotify-itunes-youtube. Accessed May, 25, 2022.

xxx   Paul Resnikoff, "YouTube Music Says It Pays the Same Royalty Rate as Spotify—At Least on Its Subscription Streams," *Digital Music News*, October 9,

2019, https://www.digitalmusicnews.com/2019/10/09/youtube-music-prem ium-subscription/. Accessed May 25, 2022.

xxxi   Tim Ingham, "So . . . How Much Did TikTok Actually Pay the Music Industry From Its $4bn in Revenues Last Year?," *Music Business Worldwide*, July 14, 2022, https://www.musicbusinessworldwide.com/so-how-much-did-tik tok-actually-pay-the-music-industry-from-its-4bn-in-revenues-last-year/. Accessed July 25, 2022.

xxxii   Elias Leight, "TikTok Pays Artists 'Almost Nothing' in Music Royalties—And the Industry is Losing Patience," *Billboard*, November 7, 2022, https://www. billboard.com/pro/tiktok-pays-artists-little-music-royalties-insiders-fed-up/. Accessed November 16, 2022.

xxxiii Dan Whateley, "How TikTok is changing the music industry," *Business Insider*, July 7, 2022, https://www.businessinsider.com/how-tiktok-is-changing-the-music-industry-marketing-discovery-2021-7. Accessed July 14, 2022.

xxxiv   Rania Aniftos, "Here's a Timeline of the Viral 'Dreams' TikTok, From Cranberry Juice Gifts to Stevie Nicks' Recreation," *Billboard*, October 14, 2020, https://www.billboard.com/music/music-news/viral-dreams-tiktok-timel ine-9465600/. Accessed July 14, 2022.

xxxv   Whateley, "How TikTok Is Changing the Music Industry."

xxxvi   Chris Molanphy, "Feat. Don't Fail Me Now," *Slate*, July 31, 2015, https://slate. com/culture/2015/07/the-history-of-featured-rappers-and-other-featured-artists-in-pop-songs.html. Accessed May 25, 2022.

xxxvii Ashley King, "YouTube Music Exec Calls TikTok Short Videos 'Junk Food'— 'It Has to Lead You to Long-Form Content So It's Not Empty Calories,'" *Digital Music News*, July 8, 2022, https://www.digitalmusicnews.com/2022/07/08/ youtube-music-exec-tiktok-junk-food/. Accessed July 14, 2022.

xxxviii Elias Leight, "Sped-Up Songs Are Taking Over TikTok and Driving Songs Up the Charts," *Billboard*, November 10, 2022, https://www.billboard.com/pro/ sped-up-songs-tiktok-streaming-charts/. Accessed November 16, 2022.

xxxix   Tamas Bodzsar, "How Long Should a Chorus Be," *Songwriting Essentials*, Undated, https://www.howtowritebettersongs.com/how-long-should-a-cho rus-be/. Accessed May 25, 2022.

xl   David Farrell, "Stingray Buys Qello Concerts. Now No. 1 SVOD Supplier," *FYI Music News*, January 4, 2018, https://www.fyimusicnews.ca/articles/2018/01/04/ stingray-buys-qello-concerts-now-no-1-svod-supplier. Accessed May 25, 2022.

xli   Julian Clover, "Les Echos-Le Parisien buys into Medici.TV," *Broadband TV News*, February 25, 2020, https://www.broadbandtvnews.com/2020/02/25/ les-echos-le-parisien-buys-into-medici-tv/. Accessed May 25, 2022.

Chapter 11

i   Bernard Marr, "The Key Definitions of Artificial Intelligence That Explains Its Importance," *Forbes*, February 14, 2014, https://www.forbes.com/sites/bern ardmarr/2018/02/14/the-key-definitions-of-artificial-intelligence-ai-that-explain-its-importance/. Accessed June 7, 2022.

ii   Murray Stassen, "Warner Is Signing Double the Number of Artists via AI Driven Tool Sodatone," *Music Business Worldwide*, November 24, 2020, https://www.musicbusinessworldwide.com/warner-is-signing-double-the-number-of-artists-via-ai-driven-ar-tool-sodatone-than-it-did-last-year-now-its-hired-a-global-head-of-data-science/. Accessed June 7, 2022.

iii   "What is Machine Learning?" *IBM Cloud Education*, https://www.ibm.com/cloud/learn/machine-learning. Accessed June 2, 2022.

iv   B. H. Huang and Lawrence Rabiner, *Fundamentals of Speech Recognition* (London: Pearson College Division, 1993), 1–28.

v   Bernadette Jackson, "How Amazon Echo Works?" *How Stuff Works*, https://electronics.howstuffworks.com/gadgets/high-tech-gadgets/amazon-echo.htm#. Accessed April 4, 2023.

vi   "First Recording of Computer-Generated Music—Created by Alan Turing—Restored," *Guardian*, September 26, 2016, https://www.theguardian.com/science/2016/sep/26/first-recording-computer-generated-music-created-alan-turing-restored-enigma-code. Accessed June 2, 2022.

vii   Tim Adams, "Interview David Cope: 'You Pushed the Button and Out Came Hundreds and Thousands of Sonatas,'" *Guardian*, July 11, 2010, https://www.theguardian.com/technology/2010/jul/11/david-cope-computer-composer. Accessed June 2, 2022.

viii "List of Most Streamed YouTube Videos," *Wikipedia*, https://en.wikipedia.org/wiki/List_of_most-viewed_YouTube_videos. Accessed June 2, 2022.

ix   Andrea Bossi, "There Were More Than One Trillion Music Streams In U.S. During 2019, Record High," *Forbes*, January 10, 2020, https://www.forbes.com/sites/andreabossi/2020/01/10/over-one-trillion-music-streams-in-us-during-2019-record-high. Accessed June 13, 2022.

x   "List of Most Followed Twitter Accounts," *Wikipedia*, https://en.wikipedia.org/wiki/List_of_most-followed_Twitter_accounts. Accessed March 31, 2023.

xi   Linda Andress, "Top Instagram Accounts in 2023," How Sociable, January 24, 2020, https://howsociable.com/charts-instagram-top-accounts/. Accessed March 31, 2023.

xii   Rutger Rosenberg and Jason Joven, "How To Understand and Use Music Data Analytics Tools," *Hypebot*, Undated, https://www.hypebot.com/hypebot/2020/06/how-to-understand-and-use-music-data-analytics-tools.html. Accessed June 2, 2022.

xiii "Making Music and Art Using Machine Learning," *Google Magenta AI*, https://magenta.tensorflow.org/. Accessed June 2, 2022.

xiv   "Open AI Jukebox," *Open AI*, https://openai.com/blog/jukebox/. Accessed June 2, 2022.

xv   Smart Audio Report, *NPR and Edison Research*, June 17, 2022, https://www.edisonresearch.com/smart-audio-report-2022-from-npr-and-edison-research/. Accessed June 17, 2022.

xvi   Stuart Dredge, "The Future of Smart Speakers: How Voice Tech is Impacting the Music Business," *Midem: Music Industry Insights*, October 10, 2019, https://blog.midem.com/2019/10/the-future-of-smart-speakers/. Accessed June 2, 2022.

xvii James Shotwell, "36% of Americans Now Own Smart Speakers: Here's What That Means for Musicians," *Haulix*, February 26, 2019, https://haulixdaily.com/2019/02/smart-speakers-music-business. Accessed June 2, 2022.

xviii   "Smart Speaker Use Case Frequency," *Statista*, https://www.statista.com/sta
          tistics/994696/united-states-smart-speaker-use-case-frequency/.   Accessed
          June 2, 2022.

xix   Tim Ingham, "'Fake Artists' Have Billions of Streams on Spotify. Is Sony Now
          Playing the Service at Its Own Game?", *Rolling Stone,* May 15, 2019, https://
          www.rollingstone.com/pro/features/fake-artists-have-billions-of-streams-
          on-spotify-is-sony-now-playing-the-service-at-its-own-game-834746/.
          Accessed June 13, 2022.

xx   Murray Stassen, "Over 1,000 Songs with Human Mimicking AI Vocals Have
          Been released by Tencent Music in China. One of Them Has 100M Streams,"
          Digital Music News, November 15, 2022, https://www.musicbusinessworldw
          ide.com/over-1000-songs-human-mimicking-ai-vocals-have-been-released-
          by-tencent-music-in-china-one-of-them-has-over-100m-streams/. Accessed
          November 16, 2022.

xxi   Dmitri Vietze and Drew Silverstein, "What Makes Amper's AI Music Tools
          Different with CEO Drew Silverstein," *Music Tectonics* (podcast), March 25,
          2020,   https://musictectonics.libsyn.com/what-makes-ampers-ai-music-
          tools-different-with-ceo-drew-silverstein. Accessed June 2, 2022.

xxii   Eric Harvey, "How Smart Speakers Are Changing the Way We Listen to
          Music," *Pitchfork,* June 29, 2018, https://pitchfork.com/features/article/how-
          smart-speakers-are-changing-the-way-we-listen-to-music/. Accessed June
          2, 2022.

xxiii   The Infinite Dial 2021, Edison Research and Triton Digital, https://www.edi
          sonresearch.com/the-infinite-dial-2021-2/. Accessed July 17, 2022.

xxiv   The Infinite Dial 2021.

xxv   Murray Stassen, "Warner Joins $14M Funding Round in AI Music Start-up
          Lifescore," *Music Business Worldwide*, March 7, 2022, https://www.musicbu
          sinessworldwide.com/warner-joins-11m-funding-round-in-ai-music-star
          tup-lifescore-founded-by-siri-co-inventor-tom-gruber1/.   Accessed   June
          2, 2022.

xxvi   Salvatore Raieli, "Generate a Piano Cover With AI," *Medium*, November 10,
          2022,   https://medium.com/mlearning-ai/generate-a-piano-cover-with-ai-
          f4178bc9cb30. Accessed November 16. 2022.

xxvii   Phillip Tracy, "Apple's Newest Acquisition Could Mean Changes for Apple
          Music," *Gizmodo*, February 7, 2022, https://gizmodo.com/apple-ai-music-
          acquisition-1848496216. Accessed June 2, 2022.

xxviii   Sophia Ciocca, "Spotify's Discover Weekly: How Machine Learning Finds
          Your New Music," *Hackernoon*, October 10, 2017, https://hackernoon.com/
          spotifys-discover-weekly-how-machine-learning-finds-your-new-music-
          19a41ab76efe. Accessed June 2, 2022.

xxix   Sam Blake, "How LA-Based Super Hi-Fi Hopes to Change Streaming Audio
          using AI," *Dot.LA*, September 21, 2020, https://dot.la/super-hi-fi-2647727032.
          html. Accessed June 2, 2022.

xxx   Zoe Beery, "Your Most-Played Song of 2020 Is . . . White Noise?", *New York
          Times,* December 24, 2020, https://www.nytimes.com/2020/12/24/style/
          white-noise-ambient-music-spotify.html. Accessed June 2, 2022.

xxxi   Dan Jeffries, "The Musician in the Machine," *Google Magenta AI*, https://mage
          nta.tensorflow.org/musician-in-the-machine. Accessed June 2, 2022.

xxxii   Alex Bainter, "How Mubert (Probably) Works; Generative Music at Scale," *Medium*, August 29, 2019, https://medium.com/@alexbainter/how-mubert-probably-works-e44de23c45bd. Accessed June 7, 2022.

xxxiii   Michael Tauberg, "Spotify Is Killing Song Titles," *Medium*, March 23, 2018, https://michaeltauberg.medium.com/spotify-is-killing-song-titles-5f48b7827653. Accessed June 2, 2022.

xxxiv   Rob Arcand, "The Artists Using Artificial Intelligence To Dream Up The Future Of Music," *Spin*, June 4, 2019, https://www.spin.com/2019/06/ai-music-artificial-intelligence-feature-holly-herndon-yacht/. Accessed June 2, 2022.

xxxv   T. O'Brien, "Listen to an AI Sing an Uncanny Rendition of 'Jolene'," *Engadget*, November 2, 2022, https://www.engadget.com/holly-plus-holly-herndon-dolly-parton-jolene-ai-cover-204750236.html. Accessed November 3, 2022.

xxxvi   Holly Herndon, "Holly +. Holly Herndon," http://www.hollyherndon.com/holly. Accessed June 2, 2022.

xxxvii   Grimes & Endel, "Endel x Grimes AI Lullaby," Endel.io. https://ailullaby.endel.io/. Accessed June 2, 2022.

xxxviii   "Deepfake Queen to Deliver Channel 4 Christmas Message," *BBC*, December 23, 2020, https://www.bbc.com/news/technology-55424730. Accessed June 2, 2022.

xxxix   Winston Cho, "Does Kendrick Lamar Run Afoul of Copyright Law by Using Deepfakes in 'The Heart Part 5'?", *Hollywood Reporter*, May 12, 2022, https://www.hollywoodreporter.com/business/digital/does-kendrick-lamar-run-afoul-of-copyright-law-by-using-deepfakes-in-the-heart-part-5-1235145596/. Accessed April 5, 2023.

xl   Jonathan and Ruoming Pang Shen, "Tacotron 2: Generating Human-like Speech from Text," *Google AI Blog*, December 19, 2017, https://ai.googleblog.com/2017/12/tacotron-2-generating-human-like-speech.html. Accessed June 2, 2022.

xli   Tim Knowles, "To Be or Not To Be Me: Jay-Z Asks Big Question," *Times (London)*, April 30, 2020, https://www.thetimes.co.uk/article/to-be-or-not-to-be-me-jay-z-asks-big-question-hk6vffl0m. Accessed June 2, 2022.

xlii   Dan Robitzski, "Mind-Melting AI Makes Frank Sinatra Sing 'Toxic' by Britney Spears," *Futurism*, May 20, 2020, https://futurism.com/mind-melting-ai-frank-sinatra-toxic-britney-spears. Accessed June 2, 2022.

xliii   "Behind the Doodle: Celebrating Johann Sebastian Bach," *Google*, https://www.youtube.com/watch?v=XBfYPp6KF2g&t=104s. Accessed June 2, 2022.

xliv   Katherine B. Forrest, "Copyright Law and Artificial Intelligence: Emerging Issues," *Journal of the Copyright Society of the USA*, 65 (Fall 2018): 355–370.

xlv   Susannah Cullinane, "Monkey Does Not Own Selfie Copyright, Appeals Court Rules," *CNN*, April 24, 2018, https://www.cnn.com/2018/04/24/us/monkey-selfie-peta-appeal/index.html. Accessed June 2, 2022.

xlvi   Jon Porter, "US Patent Office Rules That Artificial Intelligence Cannot be a Legal inventor," *The Verge*, April 29, 2020, https://www.theverge.com/2020/4/29/21241251/artificial-intelligence-inventor-united-states-patent-trademark-office-intellectual-property. Accessed June 7, 2022.

xlvii   Kris Holt, "You can't copyright AI-created art, according to US officials,"
             Engadget, February 21, 2022, https://www.engadget.com/us-copyright-office-
             art-ai-creativity-machine-190722809.html. Accessed June 7, 2022.

xlviii   "Copyright Registration Guidance: Works Containing Material Generated by
             Artificial Intelligence," *Federal Register* 88, no. 51 (March 16, 2023): 16190–
             16194, https://www.federalregister.gov/documents/2023/03/16/2023-05321/
             copyright-registration-guidance-works-containing-material-generated-by-
             artificial-intelligence. Accessed March 31, 2023.

xlix   Dani Deahl, "The USPTO Wants to Know if Artificial Intelligence Can Own
             the Content it Creates," *The Verge*, November 13, 2019, https://www.theverge.
             com/2019/11/13/20961788/us-government-ai-copyright-patent-trademark-
             office-notice-artificial-intelligence. Accessed June 2, 2022.

l   Amper, "Amper Terms of Service," Amper. https://www.ampermusic.com/
             terms-2/. Accessed June 2, 2022.

li   Stuart Dredge, "UK bodies protest against unlicensed AI data-mining of
             music," *Music Ally*, July 7, 2020, https://musically.com/2022/07/07/uk-bod
             ies-protest-against-unlicensed-ai-data-mining-of-music/.   Accessed   July
             8, 2022.

lii   Bill Hochberg, YouTube Won't Take Down A Deepfake Of Jay-Z Reading
             Hamlet — To Sue, Or Not To Sue," *Forbes*, May 18, 2020, https://www.forbes.
             com/sites/williamhochberg/2020/05/18/to-sue-or-not-to-sue—-that-is-the-
             jay-zs-deepfake-question. Accessed June 2, 2022.

liii   Ashley King, "Virtual Characters Are Hitting the Spotify Charts," *Digital
             Music News*, July 21, 2021, https://www.digitalmusicnews.com/2021/07/21/
             virtual-characters-metaverse-spotify-charts/. Accessed June 2, 2022.

liv   Cecelia Hubbert, "Midler v. Ford Motor Company," *University of Denver
             Sturm College of Law*, https://www.law.du.edu/documents/sports-and-entert
             ainment-law-journal/case-summaries/1988-midler-v-ford-motor-co.pdf.
             Accessed June 7, 2022.

lv   Cade Metz. "Lawsuit Takes Aim at the Way AI is Built," *New York Times*,
             November 23, 2022. https://www.nytimes.com/2022/11/23/technology/copi
             lot-microsoft-ai-lawsuit.html. Accessed April 5, 2023.

lvi   Beatrice Nolan. "AI art generators face separate copyright lawsuits from Getty
             Images and a group of artists," *Business Insider*, January 19, 2023, https://www.
             businessinsider.com/ai-art-artists-getty-images-lawsuits-stable-diffusion-
             2023-1. Accessed January 31, 2023.

lvii   Michael Nash, "Something New: Artificial Intelligence and the Perils of
             Plunder," *Music Business Worldwide*, February 14, 2023, https://www.musicbu
             sinessworldwide.com/michael-nash-universal-something-artificial-intellige
             nce-and-the-perils-plunder/. Accessed February 15, 2023.

lviii   "Smart Speakers Driving New Music Consumption Habits, Says New
             AudienceNet Survey," *Music Business Association*, October 10, 2018, https://
             musicbiz.org/news/smart-speakers-driving-new-music-consumption-hab
             its-says-new-audiencenet-study/. Accessed June 2, 2022.

lix   Mark Sutherland, "Amazon Music Director Ryan Redington on Country's
             Streaming Revolution," *Music Week*, March 12, 2020, https://www.musicw
             eek.com/digital/read/amazon-music-director-ryan-redington-on-country-s-
             streaming-revolution/079179. Accessed June 2, 2022.

lx   Keith Caulfield, "'Encanto' & 'We Don't Talk About Bruno' Rule Luminate's 2022 Mid-Year Charts," *Billboard*, July 14, 2022, https://billboard.com/music/chart-beat/Encanto-we-don't-talk-about-bruno-luminate-2022-midyear-charts-1235114205/. Accessed April 5, 2023.

lxi   Richard Lawler, "Kanye West's $200 Stem Player will be the only way to get his next album, Donda 2," *The Verge*, February 18, 2022, https://www.theverge.com/2022/2/18/22940748/donda-2-stem-player-kanye-west-exclusive-music. Accessed June 7, 2022.

Chapter 12

i   "The Music You Want Wherever You Want It," John Okolowicz collection of publications and advertising on radio and consumer electronics (Accession 2014.277), Hagley Museum & Library, Wilmington, DE 19807.

ii   Amy Scattergood, "Artisans of the Roast," *Los Angeles Times*, October 25, 2006, https://www.latimes.com/food/la-fo-roast102506-story.html. Accessed April 4, 2023.

iii   This and all subsequent statistics in this section come from annual consumer surveys by National Coffee Association of the USA, the American coffee industry trade association. Gourmet coffee includes espresso-based drinks.

iv   Daniel McGinn, "The Buzz Machine," *Boston Globe Sunday Magazine*, August 7, 2011, http://archive.boston.com/business/articles/2011/08/07/the_inside_story_of_keurigs_rise_to_a_billion_dollar_coffee_empire/. Accessed April 4, 2023.

v   Josh Dzieza, "Keurig's Attempt to 'DRM' Its Coffee Cups Totally Backfired," *The Verge*, February 5, 2015, https://www.theverge.com/2015/2/5/7986327/keurigs-attempt-to-drm-its-coffee-cups-totally-backfired. Accessed June 2, 2022.

vi   Sabrina Imbler, "The Best Keurig Machine (But We Really Don't Recommend It)," *Wirecutter*, September 10, 2021, https://www.nytimes.com/wirecutter/reviews/best-keurig-machine/#the-drawbacks-to-keurig-machines-and-why-we-dont-recommend-them. Accessed June 2, 2022.

vii   National Coffee Association of the USA.

viii   Bill Rosenblatt, "Disruption Comes to Higher-Ed Publishing," *Publishers Weekly*, August 16, 2019, https://www.publishersweekly.com/pw/by-topic/digital/content-and-e-books/article/80947-disruption-comes-to-higher-ed-publishing.html. Accessed April 4, 2023.

ix   W. H. Powell, "Top 10 Greatest BuzzFeed Lists Of All Time," *Medium*, June 28, 2016, https://medium.com/@whpeezy/top-10-buzzfeed-lists-of-all-time-that-will-tickle-your-list-bone-until-you-have-a-listgasm-ffb1ce7cd52c. Accessed June 2, 2022.

x   "Podtrac Industry Ranking: Top 20 Podcasts, April 2022," *Podtrac*, http://analytics.podtrac.com/podcast-rankings. Accessed June 20, 2022.

xi   See generally Mike Isaac, *Super Pumped: The Battle for Uber* (New York: W. W. Norton, 2019).

xii   Dr. Todd Boyd, interview with the authors, November 1, 2022.

xiii   Todd Boyd, *Young, Black, Rich and Famous: The Rise of the NBA, the Hip Hop Invasion and the Transformation of American Culture* (New York: Doubleday, 2003), 150–61.

xiv   Tatiana Cirisano, "Is TikTok Becoming a Record Label? The Question Misses the Point," *MIDIA Research Blog*, May 18, 2022, https://midiaresearch.com/blog/is-tiktok-becoming-a-record-label-the-question-misses-the-point. Accessed July 14, 2022.

xv   Joshua Klein, "Robert Christgau: Christgau's Consumer Guide: Albums of the '90s," *AV Club*, March 29, 2002, https://www.avclub.com/robert-christgau-christgaus-consumer-guide-albums-of-1798193851. Accessed April 7, 2023. The estimate of 35,000 albums per year released in the 1990s works out to just under 1,000 tracks per days assuming 10 tracks per album.

xvi   "Top Entertainment Trends for 2023: What the Data Says, as Presented at SXSW 2023," Luminate, Undated, https://luminatedata.com/reports/sxsw-top-entertainment-trends-for-2023/. Accessed April 7, 2023.

xvii   Dan Rys, "Lucian Grainge Calls for 'Updated Model' for Music Industry: Read His Memo to UMG Staff," *Billboard*, January 12, 2023, https://www.billboard.com/pro/lucian-grainge-umg-full-staff-memo-2023-read-message/. Accessed April 7, 2023.

xviii   Bill Rosenblatt, "UltraViolet, Hollywood's Attempt To Control The Digital Video Supply Chain, Will Shut Down," *Forbes*, February 3, 2019, https://www.forbes.com/sites/billrosenblatt/2019/02/03/ultraviolet-hollywoods-attempt-to-control-the-digital-video-supply-chain-will-shut-down/. Accessed June 2, 2022.

xix   "Hulu.com Proves Victorious over Skeptics," *SFGATE.com*, December 23, 2008, https://www.sfgate.com/entertainment/article/Hulu-com-proves-victorious-over-skeptics-3257176.php. Accessed June 2, 2022.

xx   Samuel Spencer, "How Many Subscribers Do Netflix, Disney+ and the Rest of the Streaming Services Have?" *Newsweek*, May 11, 2021, https://www.newsweek.com/netflix-amazon-hulu-disney-most-subscribers-streaming-service-1590463. Accessed June 2, 2022.

xxi   Erik Gruenwedel, "Streaming Fatigue: Too Many Choices, at Too High a Cost?" *MediaPlayNews*, November 22, 2021, https://www.mediaplaynews.com/streaming-fatigue/. Accessed July 19, 2022.

i   Bill Rosenblatt, "The Future of Blockchain Technology in the Music Industry," *Journal of the Copyright Society of the USA* 66 (Spring 2019): 271–89.

ii   "Ethereum Transactions Per Second Chart," *Blockchair*, https://blockchair.com/ethereum/charts/transactions-per-second. Accessed July 17, 2022.

iii   MacKenzie Sigalos, "Ethereum Had a Rough September. Here's Why and How It's Being Fixed," *CNBC.com*, October 2, 2021, https://www.cnbc.com/2021/10/02/ethereum-had-a-rough-september-heres-why-and-how-it-gets-fixed.html. Accessed April 29, 2022.

iv   William Entriken, Dieter Shirley, Jacob Evans, and Nastassia Sachs, "EIP-721: Non-Fungible Token Standard, Ethereum Improvement Proposals, no. 721," *Ethereum.org*, https://eips.ethereum.org/EIPS/eip-721. Accessed May 28, 2022.

v   "Music/Web3 Dashboard," *Water & Music*, https://www.waterandmusic.com/data/music-web3-dashboard/. Accessed November 16, 2022; "Music NFT

Sales in 2021: What We Learned," *Water & Music*, May 6, 2022, https://www.waterandmusic.com/music-nft-sales-in-2021-what-we-learned/. Accessed November 16, 2022.

vi   Joshua P. Friedlander and Matthew Bass, "Year-End 2021 RIAA Revenue Statistics," *Recording Industry Association of America*, https://www.riaa.com/wp-content/uploads/2022/03/2021-Year-End-Music-Industry-Revenue-Report.pdf. Accessed May 20, 2022.

vii   "How Do You Buy an NFT?" *Coinbase*, Undated, https://www.coinbase.com/learn/crypto-basics/how-to-buy-nft. Accessed May 28, 2022.

viii   "Music/Web3 Dashboard."

ix   Jeff Ihaza, "Tory Lanez Released an 'NFT Album,' and Then Things Got Extra Weird," *Rolling Stone*, September 30, 2021, https://www.rollingstone.com/music/music-features/tory-lanez-nft-legal-questions-1233890/. Accessed April 29, 2022.

x   London Jennn, "Tory Lanez Says His NFT Album Is Reselling on a Secondary Market for $100k," *AllHipHop.com*, August 25, 2021, https://allhiphop.com/news/tory-lanez-says-his-nft-album-is-selling-for-100k/. Accessed April 29, 2022.

xi   Samantha Hissong, "Kings of Leon Will Be the First Band to Release an Album as an NFT." *Rolling Stone*, March 3, 2021, https://www.rollingstone.com/pro/news/kings-of-leon-when-you-see-yourself-album-nft-crypto-1135192/. Accessed April 29, 2022.

xii   Dylan Smith, "Warner Music Group Inks 'First-Ever Partnership' With POAP 'To Mint Shared Memories As NFTs,'" *Digital Music News*, April 14, 2022, https://www.digitalmusicnews.com/2022/04/14/warner-music-group-poap-partnership/. Accessed May 28, 2022.

xiii   Samantha Hissong, "Shawn Mendes' Manager Is Helping Launch a New NFT Marketplace," *Rolling Stone*, March 2, 2021, https://www.rollingstone.com/pro/news/shawn-mendes-andrew-gertler-nft-marketplace-sturdy-exchange-1135558/. Accessed April 29, 2022.

xiv   Kristin Robinson, "HitPiece Wanted to Make an NFT for Every Song—Only Its Founders Forgot to Ask Artists First," *Billboard*, February 2, 2022, https://www.billboard.com/pro/hitpiece-nft-every-song-artist-permission-founders/. Accessed June 5, 2022.

Bibliography

"3G vs 4G." *Diffen*. https://www.diffen.com/difference/3G_vs_4G. Accessed June 5, 2022.

"About the MLC." *Mechanical Licensing Collective*. https://www.themlc.com/our-story. Accessed June 7, 2022.

"Ace of Base to Release New Album Worldwide." *The Local*, February 24, 2015. https://www.thelocal.se/20150224/ace-of-base-to-release-new-album. Accessed June 7, 2022.

Adams, Tim. "Interview David Cope: 'You Pushed the Button and Out Came Hundreds and Thousands of Sonatas.'" *Guardian*, July 11, 2010. https://www.theguardian.com/technology/2010/jul/11/david-cope-computer-composer. Accessed June 2, 2022.

Adegoke, Yinka. "Labels Bet on Flexibility with iTunes New Pricing." *Reuters*, April 8, 2009. https://www.reuters.com/article/us-apple-itunes/labels-bet-on-flexibility-with-itunes-new-pricing-idUSN0641102320090408. Accessed June 7, 2022.

Aguiar Wicht, Luis, and Joel Waldfogel. "Platforms, Promotion, and Product Discovery: Evidence from Spotify Playlists." *EU Science Hub*, June 5, 2018. https://joint-research-centre.ec.europa.eu/publications/platforms-promotion-and-product-discovery-evidence-spotify-playlists_en. Accessed July 13, 2022.

Amazon, "How Does Alexa Work?" https://www.amazon.com/how-does-alexa-work/b?ie=UTF8&node=21166405011. Accessed June 2, 2022.

"American Jukebox History." *Jukeboxhistory.info*. https://www.jukeboxhistory.info/. Accessed May 2, 2022.

"Amper Terms of Service." *Amper*. https://www.ampermusic.com/terms-2/. Accessed June 2, 2022.

"AMPEX Model 200/200A Tape Machine." *History of Recording*. https://www.historyofrecording.com/AMPEX_Model_200.html. Accessed May 25, 2022.

Anderson, Chris. *The Long Tail: Why the Future of the Business Is Selling Less of More*. Westport, CT: Hyperion, 2006.

Anderson, Nate. "YouTube Signs Up Universal, Sony BMG, CBS, and . . . Google?" *Ars Technica*, October 9, 2006. https://arstechnica.com/information-technology/2006/10/7935/. Accessed May 25, 2022.

Andress, Linda. "Top Instagram Accounts in 2021." *How Sociable*, January 24, 2020. https://howsociable.com/charts-instagram-top-accounts/. Accessed June 2, 2022.

Angus, Robert, and Norman Eisenberg. "Are Cassettes Here to Stay?" *High Fidelity*, July 1, 1969, 46–53.

Aniftos, Rania. "Here's a Timeline of the Viral 'Dreams' TikTok, From Cranberry Juice Gifts to Stevie Nicks' Recreation." *Billboard*, October 14, 2020. https://www.billboard.com/music/music-news/viral-dreams-tiktok-timeline-9465600/. Accessed July 14, 2022.

Apple. "Apple Services Now Available in More Countries Around the World." April 21, 2020. https://www.apple.com/newsroom/2020/04/apple-services-now-available-in-more-countries-around-the-world/. Accessed June 5, 2022.

Arcand, Rob. "The Artists Using Artificial Intelligence To Dream Up The Future Of Music." *Spin*, June 4, 2019. https://www.spin.com/2019/06/ai-music-artificial-intelligence-feature-holly-herndon-yacht/. Accessed June 2, 2022.

"Are Songs Getting Even Shorter in 2021." *Hit Songs Deconstructed*. https://www.hitsongsdeconstructed.com/hsd_wire/the-short-game/. Accessed July 8, 2022.

Aspan, Maria. "For Shakira, First Came the Album, Then Came the Single." *New York Times*, June 12, 2006. https://www.nytimes.com/2006/06/12/business/media/12shakira.html. Accessed June 7, 2022.

Aswad, Jem. "Global Music Biz Revenue to Double to $131 Billion in 2030, Says Bullish Goldman Sachs Report." *Variety*, June 14, 2022. https://variety.com/2022/music/news/global-music-revenue-double-goldman-sachs-report-1235293827/#!. Accessed June 28, 2022.

Atwood, Brett. "Capitol to Sell Digital Singles." *Billboard*. September 13, 1997.

"Audio File Size Calculations." *AudioMountain.com*. http://www.audiomountain.com/tech/audio-file-size.html. Accessed May 23, 2022.

Austen, Jake. *TV a Go Go: Rock on TV*. Chicago: Chicago Review Press, 2005.

Bainter, Alex. "How Mubert (Probably) Works; Generative Music at Scale." *Medium*, August 29, 2019. https://medium.com/@alexbainter/how-mubert-probably-works-e44de23c45bd. Accessed June 7, 2022.

Baio, Andy. "The Tangled Issue of Cover Song Copyright on YouTube." *Wired*, March 5, 2012. https://www.wired.co.uk/article/cover-song-licensing-on-youtube. Accessed May 25, 2022.

Banks, Jack. *Monopoly: MTV's Quest to Control the Music*. Boulder, CO: Westview Press, 1996.

"The Beatles." *EdSullivan.com*. https://www.edsullivan.com/artists/the-beatles/. Accessed May 4, 2022.

Beery, Zoë. "Your Most-Played Song of 2020 Is . . . White Noise?" *New York Times*, December 24, 2020. https://www.nytimes.com/2020/12/24/style/white-noise-ambient-music-spotify.html. Accessed June 2, 2022.

Berliner, Emile, and Frederic William Wile. *Emile Berliner, Maker of the Microphone*. Indianapolis: Bobbs-Merrill, 1926.

Bernhard, Robert. "Consumer Electronics. Higher Fi by Digits: Digitally Encoded Audio Disks and Associated Playback Gear Promise Breakthrough in High Fidelity, Low Noise." *IEEE Spectrum* 16 (1979): 28–32.

Birnbaum, Jane. "The Media Business: Without a Scratch, Used CD's Rise Again." *New York Times*, September 6, 1993. https://www.nytimes.com/1993/09/06/business/the-media-business-without-a-scratch-used-cds-rise-again.html.

Blake, Sam. "How LA-Based Super Hi-Fi Hopes to Change Streaming Audio using AI." *Dot.LA*, September 21, 2020. https://dot.la/super-hi-fi-2647727032.html. Accessed June 2, 2022.

Blockchair. "Ethereum Transactions Per Second Chart." https://blockchair.com/ethereum/charts/transactions-per-second. Accessed July 17, 2022.

Blumenthal, Eli. "Hulu and Spotify Partner to Bundle TV and Music Streaming for $9.99 per Month." *USA Today*, March 12, 2019. https://www.usatoday.com/story/tech/talkingtech/2019/03/12/apple-looming-hulu-and-spotify-partner-9-99-streaming-bundle/3138377002/. Accessed June 5, 2022.

Blumenthal, Ralph. "Goody Chain and Ex-Official Are Sentenced in Tapes Case." *New York Times*, November 6, 1982, 29.

Bodzsar, Tamas. "How Long Should a Chorus Be." *Songwriting Essentials*. https://www. howtowritebettersongs.com/how-long-should-a-chorus-be/. Accessed May 25, 2022.

Borland, John. "Judge Issues Injunction Against Napster." *CNET*, January 2, 2002. https:// www.cnet.com/tech/services-and-software/judge-issues-injunction-against-napster/. Accessed May 23, 2022.

Borland, John. "Legal P2P Opens for Business." *CNET*, September 26, 2006. https://www. cnet.com/tech/home-entertainment/legal-p2p-opens-for-business/.   Accessed   May 25, 2022.

Borland, John. "Metallica Fingers 335,435 Napster Users." *CNET*, January 2, 2002. https:// www.cnet.com/tech/services-and-software/metallica-fingers-335435-napster-users/. Accessed May 23, 2022.

Borland, John. "Napster Boots Dr. Dre Fans From Service." *CNET*, January 2, 2002. https://www.cnet.com/news/napster-boots-dr-dre-fans-from-service/. Accessed June 7, 2022.

Bossi, Andrea. "There Were More Than One Trillion Music Streams In U.S. During 2019." *Forbes*, January 10, 2020. https://www.forbes.com/sites/andreabossi/2020/01/10/over-one-trillion-music-streams-in-us-during-2019-record-high. Accessed June 13, 2022.

Boyer, Peter. "CBS Assails NBC News over a Payola Report." *New York Times*, April 3, 1986.   https://www.nytimes.com/1986/04/03/arts/cbs-assails-nbc-news-over-a-pay ola-report.html. Accessed July 12, 2022.

Boyd, Todd. *Young, Black, Rich and Famous: The Rise of the NBA, the Hip Hop Invasion and the Transformation of American Culture*. New York: Doubleday, 2003.

Brockman, Daniel, and Jason W. Smith. "The Rise and Fall of the Columbia House Record Club—And How We Learned to Steal Music." *Boston Phoenix*, November 18, 2011. https://thephoenix.com/Boston/music/129722-rise-and-fall-of-the-columbia-house-record-clu/. Accessed May 25, 2022.

Bronson, Po, "Rebootlegger." *Wired*, July 1, 1998. https://www.wired.com/1998/07/ newmedia-4/. Accessed May 23, 2022.

Browne, David, "How the 45 RPM Single Changed Music Forever." *Rolling Stone*, March 15, 2019. https://www.rollingstone.com/music/music-features/45-vinyl-singles-hist ory-806441/. Accessed July 13, 2022.

"B.T Interview: Why Network Radio Must Adapt or Die." *Broadcasting, Telecasting*, October 31, 1955, 35+.

Buchanan, Matt. "RIAA Tech Chief: DRM Not Dead, Will Become More Powerful than You Can Possibly Imagine." *Gizmodo*, May 8, 2008. https://gizmodo.com/riaa-tech-chief-drm-not-dead-will-become-more-powerfu-388648. Accessed June 5, 2022.

Buxton, Madelien. "Spotify's New Free Version Is So Good You Might Cancel Your Subscription." *Refinery 29*, April 24, 2018. https://www.refinery29.com/en-us/2018/ 04/197232/spotify-for-free-upgrade. Accessed June 5, 2022.

Calamar, Gary, and Phil Gallo. *Record Store Days: From Vinyl to Digital and Back Again*. New York: Union Square & Co, 2012.

Carlsson, Sven, and Jonas Leijonhufvud. *The Spotify Play: How CEO and Founder Daniel Ek Beat Apple, Google, and Amazon in the Race for Audio Dominance*. New York: Diversion Books, 2021.

Carman, Ashley. "Spotify Acquires Another Podcast Network to Keep Building its Original Show Catalog." *The Verge*, March 26, 2019. https://www.theverge.com/2019/ 3/26/18282301/spotify-podcasts-parcast-acquisition-gimlet-media-anchor. Accessed June 5, 2022.

Carpenter, Shelby. "Inside Vevo's Plan to Beat YouTube and Become The MTV of the Digital Age." *Forbes*, October 19, 2016. https://www.forbes.com/sites/shelbycarpenter/2016/10/19/vevo-play-beat-youtube-mtv-digital-age/. Accessed May 25, 2022.

Caruso Jr., Enrico, Andrew Farkas, and William R. Moran. *Enrico Caruso: My Father and My Family*. Portland, OR: Amadeus Press, 1997.

Caulfield, Keith. "1 of Every 25 Vinyl Albums Sold in U.S. in 2022 Was by Taylor Swift." *Billboard*, January 11, 2023. https://www.billboard.com/pro/taylor-swift-vinyl-albums-1-of-every-25-sold/. Accessed January 31, 2023.

Caulfield, Keith. "'Encanto' & 'We Don't Talk About Bruno' Rule Luminate's 2022 Mid-Year Charts." *Billboard*, July 14, 2022. https://www.billboard.com/music/chart-beat/encanto-we-dont-talk-about-bruno-luminate-2022-midyear-charts-1235114205/. Accessed April 5, 2023.

Chang, Jeff. *Can't Stop Won't Stop: A History of the Hip-Hop Generation*. London: Picador, 2005.

Cho, Winston. "Does Kendrick Lamar Run Afoul of Copyright Law by Using Deepfakes in 'The Heart Part 5?,'" *Hollywood Reporter*, May 12, 2022. https://www.hollywoodreporter.com/business/digital/does-kendrick-lamar-run-afoul-of-copyright-law-by-using-deepfakes-in-the-heart-part-5-1235145596/. Accessed April 5, 2023.

Christman, Ed. "Spotify and Publishing Group Reach $30 Million Settlement Agreement Over Unpaid Royalties." *Billboard*, March 17, 2016. https://www.billboard.com/music/music-news/spotify-nmpa-publishing-30-million-settlement-unpaid-royalties-7263747/. Accessed June 7, 2022.

Cilia, John. "The Search for the Oldest Record Store in the World." *Trackagescheme.com*, July 21, 2016. http://trackagescheme.com/the-search-for-the-oldest-record-store-in-the-world/. Accessed May 9, 2022.

Ciocca, Sophia. "Spotify's Discover Weekly: How Machine Learning Finds Your New Music." *Hackernoon*, October 10, 2017. https://hackernoon.com/spotifys-discover-weekly-how-machine-learning-finds-your-new-music-19a41ab76efe. Accessed June 2, 2022.

Cirisano, Tatiana. "Is TikTok Becoming a Record Label? The Question Misses the Point." *MIDIA Research Blog*, May 18, 2022. https://midiaresearch.com/blog/is-tiktok-becoming-a-record-label-the-question-misses-the-point. Accessed July 14, 2022.

Cirisano, Tatiana. "Record Industry Groups Take Action Against Fake Music Streams in Germany." *Billboard*, August 24, 2020. https://www.billboard.com/pro/ifpi-bvmi-take-action-against-fake-music-streams-germany/. Accessed June 7, 2022.

Clover, Julian. "Les Echos-Le Parisien Buys into Medici.TV." *Broadband TV News*, February 25, 2020. https://www.broadbandtvnews.com/2020/02/25/les-echos-le-parisien-buys-into-medici-tv/. Accessed May 25, 2022.

Coase, Ronald H. "Payola in Radio and Television Broadcasting." *Journal of Law and Economics* 22, no. 2 (October 1979): 269–328.

Cohen, Simon. "Amazon Music Unlimited Is Getting More Expensive in 2023." *Digital Trends*, January 20, 2023. https://www.digitaltrends.com/home-theater/amazon-music-unlimited-february-2023-price-hike/. Accessed January 31, 2023.

Coinbase. "How Do You Buy an NFT?" https://www.coinbase.com/learn/crypto-basics/how-to-buy-nft. Accessed May 28, 2022.

Cook, Emory. "Binaural Disks." *High Fidelity*, November–December 1952, 33–35.

Copeland, Peter. "Manual of Analogue Sound Restoration Techniques." *The British Library*. https://web.archive.org/web/20110409161239/http:/www.bl.uk/reshelp/findhelprestype/sound/anaudio/analoguesoundrestoration.pdf. Accessed April 29, 2022.

"Copyright Registration Guidance: Works Containing Material Generated by Artificial Intelligence." *Federal Register* 88, no. 51 (March 16, 2023): 16190–16194, https://www.federalregister.gov/documents/2023/03/16/2023-05321/copyright-registration-guidance-works-containing-material-generated-by-artificial-intelligence. Accessed March 31, 2023.

Corbett, Ian. "What Data Compression Does To Your Music." *Sound On Sound*, April 2012. https://www.soundonsound.com/techniques/what-data-compression-does-your-music. Accessed June 7, 2022.

Cosgrove-Mather, Bootie. "Poll: Young Say File-Sharing OK." *CBS News*, September 18, 2003. https://www.cbsnews.com/news/poll-young-say-file-sharing-ok/. Accessed June 7, 2022.

Costello, Sam, "History of the iPod: From the First iPod to the iPod Classic." *Lifewire*, January 12, 2020. https://www.lifewire.com/history-ipod-classic-original-2000732. Accessed May 23, 2022.

Cousino Inc. "Audio Vendor Brochure and Manual." http://lcweb2.loc.gov/master/mbrs/recording_preservation/manuals/Cousino%20Universal%20Audio%20Vendor.pdf. Accessed May 15, 2022.

Covert, Adrian. "A Decade of iTunes Singles Killed the Music Industry." *CNN Business*, April 25, 2013. https://money.cnn.com/2013/04/25/technology/itunes-music-decline/index.html. Accessed June 7, 2022.

Cullinane, Susannah. "Monkey Does Not Own Selfie Copyright, Appeals Court Rules." *CNN*, April 24, 2018. https://www.cnn.com/2018/04/24/us/monkey-selfie-peta-appeal/index.html. Accessed June 2, 2022.

Daniel, Eric D., C. Dennis Mee, and Mark H. Clark. *Magnetic Recording: The First 100 Years*. Piscataway, NJ: IEEE Press, 1999.

Dannen, Fredric. *Hit Men: Power Brokers and Fast Money Inside the Music Business*. New York: Vintage, 1991.

Deahl, Dani. "The Music Modernization Act Has Been Signed Into Law." *The Verge*, October 11, 2018. https://www.theverge.com/2018/10/11/17963804/music-modernization-act-mma-copyright-law-bill-labels-congress. Accessed June 7, 2022.

Deahl, Dani. "The USPTO Wants to Know If Artificial Intelligence Can Own the Content It Creates." *The Verge*, November 13, 2019. https://www.theverge.com/2019/11/13/20961788/us-government-ai-copyright-patent-trademark-office-notice-artificial-intelligence. Accessed June 2, 2022.

"Deepfake Queen to Deliver Channel 4 Christmas Message." *BBC*, December 23, 2020. https://www.bbc.com/news/technology-55424730. Accessed June 2, 2022.

Denisoff, R. Serge. *Inside MTV*. Milton Park: Routledge, 1988.

Denisoff, R. Serge. *Tarnished Gold: The Record Industry Revisited*. Milton Park: Routledge, 1986.

Denisoff, R. Serge. *Solid Gold: The Popular Record Industry*. Piscataway, NJ: Transaction Publishers, 1975.

Denton, Jack. "A Requiem for the Microsoft Zune." *Fast Company*. June 15, 2022. https://www.fastcompany.com/90761088/a-requiem-for-the-microsoft-zune-the-little-gadget-that-couldnt. Accessed April 3, 2023.

Digital Media Association. "Streaming Forward 2020 Report." https://dima.org/streaming-forward-report/. Accessed June 5, 2022.

"Directive (EU) 2019/790 of the European Parliament and of the Council of 17 April 2019 on Copyright and Related Rights in the Digital Single Market and Amending

Directives 96/9/EC and 2001/29/EC." *Official Journal of the European Union*, May 17, 2019. https://eur-lex.europa.eu/legal-content/EN/TXT/HTML/?uri=CELEX:32019L0 790&rid=1. Accessed May 25, 2022.

Donnelly, Bob, Danielle Aguirre, Kris Muñoz, and Andrew Sparkler. "Flipping Publishing Micro-Pennies into a Bucket." *SXSW 2014 CLE.* https://foxrothschild.gjassets.com/ content/uploads/2017/03/Flipping-Publishing-Mirco-Pennies-into-a-Bucket.pdf. Accessed May 4, 2022.

Dormehl, Luke. "38 Years Ago, CDs Rewrote Our Relationship With Music and Primed Us For 2020." *Digital Trends*, October 12, 2020. https://www.digitaltrends.com/featu res/how-cds-prepared-us-for-the-future/. Accessed May 23, 2022.

Dowling, Stephen. "The Most Iconic Long Intros." *BBC*, April 8, 2019. https://www.bbc. com/culture/article/20190407-the-most-iconic-long-song-intros-in-pop-music. Accessed June 7, 2022.

Dredge, Stuart. "African Streaming Service Boomplay Now Has 75m Users." *Music Ally*, June 3, 2020. https://musically.com/2020/06/03/african-streaming-service-boomplay-now-has-75m-users/. Accessed June 5, 2022.

Dredge, Stuart. "How Much Do Musicians Really Make from Spotify, iTunes and YouTube?" *Guardian*, April 3, 2015. https://www.theguardian.com/technology/2015/ apr/03/how-much-musicians-make-spotify-itunes-youtube. Accessed April 3, 2023.

Dredge, Stuart. "The Future of Smart Speakers: How Voice Tech Is Impacting the Music Business." *Midem: Music Industry Insights*, October 10, 2019. https://blog.midem.com/ 2019/10/the-future-of-smart-speakers/. Accessed June 2, 2022.

Dredge, Stuart. "Thom Yorke Calls Spotify 'The Last Desperate Fart of a Dying Corpse.'" *Guardian*, October 7, 2013. https://www.theguardian.com/technology/2013/oct/07/ spotify-thom-yorke-dying-corpse. Accessed June 7, 2022.

Dredge, Stuart. "Spotify CEO Talks Covid-19, Artist Incomes and Podcasting." *Music Ally*, July 30, 2020. https://musically.com/2020/07/30/spotify-ceo-talks-covid-19-art ist-incomes-and-podcasting-interview/. Accessed June 7, 2022.

Dredge, Stuart. "UK Bodies Protest against Unlicensed AI Data-Mining of Music." *Music Ally*, July 7, 2020. https://musically.com/2022/07/07/uk-bodies-protest-against-unl icensed-ai-data-mining-of-music/. Accessed July 8, 2022.

Duggan, Daniel. "Investor Buys Former Handleman Co. HQ in Troy for $3 Million." *Crain's Detroit Business*, February 24, 2010. https://www.crainsdetroit.com/article/ 20100224/DM01/302249988/investor-buys-former-handleman-co-hq-in-troy-for-3-million. Accessed May 25, 2022.

Dzieza, Josh. "Keurig's Attempt to 'DRM' Its Coffee Cups Totally Backfired." *The Verge*, February 5, 2015. https://www.theverge.com/2015/2/5/7986327/keurigs-attempt-to-drm-its-coffee-cups-totally-backfired. Accessed June 2, 2022.

Edison Research and Triton Digital. "The Infinite Dial 2015." https://www.edisonresea rch.com/the-infinite-dial-2015/. Accessed May 25, 2022.

Edison Research and Triton Digital. "The Infinite Dial 2021." https://www.edisonresea rch.com/the-infinite-dial-2021-2/. Accessed July 17, 2022.

Edison Research and Triton Digital. "The Infinite Dial 2022." http://www.edisonresearch. com/wp-content/uploads/2022/03/Infinite-Dial-2022-Webinar-revised.pdf. Accessed May 25, 2022.

EMI. "EMI Music, Google and YouTube Strike Milestone Partnership." EMI press release, May 31, 2007. https://web.archive.org/web/20070602142911/http:/www.emigroup. com/Press/2007/press38.htm. Accessed May 25, 2022.

"Ends Price-Fixing By 'License Plan': Supreme Court Gives Decision for Macy's Against the Victor Company." *New York Times*, April 10, 1917. https://www.nytimes.com/1917/04/10/archives/ends-pricefixing-by-license-plan-supreme-court-gives-decision-for.html. Accessed May 9, 2022.

Engel, Friedrich, Peter Hammar, and Richard L. Hess. "A Selected History of Magnetic Recording." https://www.richardhess.com/tape/history/Engel_Hammar--Magnetic_Tape_History.pdf. Accessed April 29, 2022.

Entriken, William, Dieter Shirley, Jacob Evans, and Nastassia Sachs. "EIP-721: Non-Fungible Token Standard, Ethereum Improvement Proposals, No. 721." *Ethereum.org*. https://eips.ethereum.org/EIPS/eip-721. Accessed May 28, 2022.

Espe, Eric. "Music Industry Sees Threat in CD-Copying Technology." *Silicon Valley Business Journal*, August 30, 1998. https://www.bizjournals.com/sanjose/stories/1998/08/31/story4.html. Accessed May 23, 2022.

"Essential YouTube stats for 2022." *Datareportal*. https://datareportal.com/essential-youtube-stats. Accessed May 25, 2022.

Everard, Andrew. "Never Mind the Lack of MP3 Quality, Feel the Lack of MP3 Breadth." *What Hi-Fi?*, April 1, 2009. https://www.whathifi.com/news/usa-never-mind-lack-mp3-quality-feel-lack-mp3-breadth. Accessed June 7, 2022.

Farrell, David. "Stingray Buys Qello Concerts. Now No. 1 SVOD Supplier." *FYI Music News*, January 4, 2018. https://www.fyimusicnews.ca/articles/2018/01/04/stingray-buys-qello-concerts-now-no-1-svod-supplier. Accessed May 25, 2022.

Farrell, Maureen, and Anne Steele. "Tencent Music Files for U.S. IPO." *Wall Street Journal*, October 2, 2018. https://www.wsj.com/articles/tencent-music-files-for-u-s-ipo-1538496869. Accessed May 25, 2022.

Farrell, Maureen. "Tencent Music Rises in Trading Debut." *Wall Street Journal*, December 12, 2018. https://www.wsj.com/articles/tencent-music-opens-higher-in-trading-debut-11544632668. Accessed June 5, 2022.

Feigenbaum, Edward, Avron Barr, and Paul Cohen. *The Handbook of Artificial Intelligence, Vols. 1–3*. Los Altos, CA: William Kaufmann, 1982.

Ferchow, Davey. "How the DIY Cassette Movement of the 1970s and '80s Changed Music Forever." *Discogs Blog*, October 14, 2021. https://blog.discogs.com/en/how-the-diy-cassette-movement-of-1970s-1980s-changed-music-forever/. Accessed April 29, 2022.

"Finley to Use 4 and 8 Track Units." *Billboard*, July 31, 1965, 3.

"First Recording of Computer-Generated Music—Created by Alan Turing—Restored." *Guardian*, September 26, 2016. https://www.theguardian.com/science/2016/sep/26/first-recording-computer-generated-music-created-alan-turing-restored-enigma-code. Accessed June 2, 2022.

"The First Sony Walkman Goes on Sale." *A&E Television Networks*. https://www.history.com/this-day-in-history/the-first-sony-walkman-goes-on-sale. Accessed April 29, 2022.

Fisher, Marc. *Something in the Air: Radio, Rock, and the Revolution That Shaped a Generation*. New York: Random House, 2007.

Fitch, Charles. "How FM Stereo Came to Life." *Radio World*, January 27, 2016. https://www.radioworld.com/columns-and-views/roots-of-radio/how-fm-stereo-came-to-life. Accessed August 3, 2022.

Flint, Matt. "A File-Sharing Timeline: From the Creation of MP3 to the Trial of The Pirate Bay." *The Takeaway*, April 17, 2009. https://www.wnycstudios.org/podcasts/takeaway/articles/10560-file-sharing-timeline-creation-mp3-trial-pirate-bay. Accessed October 15, 2022.

Fontenot, Robert. "The History of American Bandstand." *Live About*, June 12, 2019. https://www.liveabout.com/american-bandstand-important-events-timeline-2523 794. Accessed May 4, 2022.

Forde, Eammon. "Spotify's Discover Weekly Has Driven 2.3bn Hours of Listening." *Music Ally*, July 10, 2020. https://musically.com/2020/07/10/spotifys-discover-weekly-has-driven-2-3bn-hours-of-listening/. Accessed June 5, 2022.

Fornatale, Peter, and Joshua Mills. *Radio in the Television Age*. New York: Overlook Press, 1980.

Forrest, Katherine B. "Copyright Law and Artificial Intelligence: Emerging Issues." *Journal of the Copyright Society of the USA* 65 (Fall 2018): 355–70.

Fox Kraut, Barbara. "The Audio Home Recording Act." *DePaul Journal of Art, Technology, and Intellectual Property Law* 2, no. 2 (Spring 1992): 38–40. https://via.library.depaul.edu/cgi/viewcontent.cgi?article=1495&context=jatip. Accessed May 23, 2022.

Fox, Barry. "Out of the Bell Tower." *New Scientist*, May 6, 1995. https://www.newscientist.com/article/mg14619764-400-out-of-the-bell-tower/. Accessed May 23, 2022.

Frank, Jay. *Futurehit:DNA*. Nashville: Futurehit, Inc., 2009.

Freeeman, Kim. "Classic Rock Thrives In 18 Months." *Billboard*, October 25, 1986, 10+.

Friedlander, Joshua P., and Matthew Bass. "Year-End 2021 RIAA Revenue Statistics." *Recording Industry Association of America*. https://www.riaa.com/wp-content/uploads/2022/03/2021-Year-End-Music-Industry-Revenue-Report.pdf. Accessed May 20, 2022.

Gapper, John. "Taylor Swift Is Perfect at the Three-Minute Spotify Song." *Financial Times*. November 25, 2022. https://www.ft.com/content/afdd5bfe-c5ae-411c-900f-8c5eab846 944. Accessed April 4, 2023.

Gartner. "Gartner Hype Cycle." https://www.gartner.com/en/research/methodologies/gartner-hype-cycle. Accessed November 18, 2022.

Gelatt, Roland. *The Fabulous Phonograph 1877–1977*. Revised 2nd Edition. New York: MacMillan Publishing, 1977.

Genzlinger, Neil. "Lou Ottens, Father of Countless Mixtapes, Is Dead at 94." *New York Times*, March 11, 2021. https://www.nytimes.com/2021/03/11/arts/music/lou-ottens-dead.html. Accessed April 3, 2023.

Goldstein, Paul. *Copyright's Highway: From the Printing Press to the Cloud*. 2nd Edition. Redwood City, CA: Stanford University Press, 2003.

Goodman, Fred. "MP3 Technology Poised to Redefine Music Industry." *Rolling Stone*, March 9, 1999. https://www.rollingstone.com/music/music-news/mp3-technology-poised-to-redefine-music-industry-97515/. Accessed May 23, 2022.

Goodwin, Andrew. *Dancing in the Distraction Factory*. Minneapolis: University of Minnesota Press, 1992.

Google. "Behind the Doodle: Celebrating Johann Sebastian Bach." https://www.youtube.com/watch?v=XBfYPp6KF2g&t=104s. Accessed June 2, 2022.

Google Magenta AI. "Making Music and Art Using Machine Learning." https://magenta.tensorflow.org/. Accessed June 2, 2022.

Green, Stanley. "Jukebox Piracy." *The Atlantic Monthly*, April 1, 1962, 136.

Grimes & Endel. "Endel x Grimes AI Lullaby." *Endel.io*. https://ailullaby.endel.io/. Accessed June 2, 2022.

Grimmelmann, James, Yan Ji, and Tyler Kell. "The Tangled Truth about NFTs and Copyright." *The Verge*, June 8, 2022. https://www.theverge.com/23139793/nft-crypto-copyright-ownership-primer-cornell-ic3. Accessed June 9, 2022.

Grohl, Dave. "A Statement from the Desk of Record Store Day 2015 Ambassador Dave Grohl." *Record Store Day*. https://recordstoreday.com/CustomPage/3882. Accessed May 25, 2022.

Groves, Landon. "Hate Your Favorite Band's Latest Song? On Spotify, It Might Be a Fake." *Input Mag*, July 17, 2020. https://www.inputmag.com/culture/spotify-is-letting-scammers-rip-artists-off-in-plain-sight. Accessed June 7, 2022.

Gruenwedel, Erik. "Streaming Fatigue: Too Many Choices, at Too High a Cost?" *MediaPlayNews*, November 22, 2021. https://www.mediaplaynews.com/streaming-fati gue/. Accessed July 19, 2022.

Guiness, Harry. "Spotify Free vs. Premium: Is it Worth Upgrading?" *How to Geek*, August 4, 2022. https://www.howtogeek.com/350288/spotify-free-vs-premium-is-it-worth-upgrading/. Accessed April 3, 2023.

Haliday, Josh. "Limewire Shut Down by Federal Court." *Guardian*, October 27, 2010, https://www.theguardian.com/technology/2010/oct/27/limewire-shut-down. Accessed June 7, 2022.

Hansell, Saul. "Amazon Launches a Music Store, Not a Service." *New York Times Bits Blog*, September 25, 2007. https://bits.blogs.nytimes.com/2007/09/25/amazon-launches-a-music-store-not-a-service. Accessed June 7, 2022.

Hardisty, Brad. "The Reel History of Analog Tape Recording." *Performer*, May 4, 2015. https://performermag.com/home-recording/the-reel-history-of-analog-tape-record ing/. Accessed April 29, 2022.

Harrison Tape Guides. New York: Weiss Publishing Corp., 1956–1976.

Harrington, Richard. "The Record Industry Goes To War On Home Taping." *The Washington Post*, June 15, 1980. https://www.washingtonpost.com/archive/lifestyle/1980/06/15/the-reocrd-industry-goes-to-war-on-home-taping/80be4100-3fa2-4f73-8999-1efb6dd282d9/. Accessed April 3, 2023.

Harvey, Eric. "How Smart Speakers Are Changing the Way We Listen to Music." *Pitchfork*, June 29, 2018. https://pitchfork.com/features/article/how-smart-speakers-are-chang ing-the-way-we-listen-to-music/. Accessed June 2, 2022.

Harvilla, Bob. "How Soundscan Changed Everything We Knew About Popular Music." *The Ringer*, May 25, 2021. https://www.theringer.com/music/2021/5/25/22452539/soundscan-billboard-charts-streaming-numbers. Accessed November 16, 2022.

Havens, Lyndsey. "Why Did Vinyl Subscriptions Spike This Year—And Will It Continue?" *Billboard*, December 18, 2020. https://www.billboard.com/articles/business/9501250/vinyl-subscriptions-spike-2020-bright-eyes/. Accessed April 3, 2023.

Hawtin, Steve. "Songs from the 1900s." *The World's Music Charts*. https://tsort.info/music/ds1900.htm. Accessed May 9, 2022.

Heisler, Y. "Steve Jobs Was Never a Fan of Subscription Music." *Engadget*, May 19, 2014. https://www.engadget.com/2014-05-19-steve-jobs-was-never-a-fan-of-subscription-music.html. Accessed June 13, 2022.

Herndon, Holly. "Holly +." *Holly Herndon*. http://www.hollyherndon.com/holly. Accessed June 2, 2022.

Heylin, Clinton. *Bootleg: The Secret History of the Other Recording Industry*. New York: St. Martin's Griffin, 1994.

Hiatt, Brian. "Napster Offers Labels $1 Billion in Licensing Fees." *MTV News*, February 20, 2001. https://www.mtv.com/news/5r4iyc/napster-offers-labels-1-billion-in-licens ing-fees /. Accessed April 3, 2023.

Hiltzik, Michael A. "Viacom to Buy MTV and Showtime in Deal Worth $667.5 Million." *Los Angeles Times*, August 27, 1985. https://www.latimes.com/archives/la-xpm-1985-08-27-fi-25404-story.html. Accessed April 3, 2023.

Hirsch, Julian. "Advent 201 Cassette Tape Deck." *Stereo Review*, October 1, 1971, 40–42.

Hirsch, Julian. "Julian Hirsch Hits the Cassette Decks." *Stereo Review*, November 1, 1970, 56–69.

Hissong, Samantha. "Kings of Leon Will Be the First Band to Release an Album as an NFT." *Rolling Stone*, March 3, 2021. https://www.rollingstone.com/pro/news/kings-of-leon-when-you-see-yourself-album-nft-crypto-1135192/. Accessed April 29, 2022.

Hissong, Samantha. "Shawn Mendes' Manager Is Helping Launch a New NFT Marketplace." *Rolling Stone*, March 2, 2021. https://www.rollingstone.com/pro/news/shawn-mendes-andrew-gertler-nft-marketplace-sturdy-exchange-1135558/. Accessed April 29, 2022.

"The History of 78 RPM Recordings." *Yale University Library*. https://web.library.yale.edu/cataloging/music/historyof78rpms. Accessed May 9, 2022.

Hochberg, Bill. "YouTube Won't Take Down A Deepfake Of Jay-Z Reading Hamlet—To Sue, Or Not To Sue." *Forbes*, May 18, 2020. https://www.forbes.com/sites/williamhochberg/2020/05/18/to-sue-or-not-to-sue---that-is-the-jay-zs-deepfake-question. Accessed June 2, 2022.

Hogan, Marc. "Universal Settles Influential Eminem Digital-Revenues Lawsuit." *Spin*, October 31, 2012. https://www.spin.com/2012/10/universal-settles-influential-eminem-digital-revenue-lawsuit/. Accessed June 17, 2022.

Holland, Bill. "Audio-Only Home Taping Bill Readied on Senate Side." *Billboard*, September 7, 1985, 1+.

Holt, Kris. "You Can't Copyright AI-Created Art, According to US Officials." *Engadget*, February 21, 2022. https://www.engadget.com/us-copyright-office-art-ai-creativity-machine-190722809.html. Accessed June 7, 2022.

Homewood, Ben. "UMG and Tidal Plot New Streaming Model to Benefit Artists and Fans." *Music Week*, January 31, 2023. https://www.musicweek.com/digital/read/umg-and-tidal-plot-new-streaming-model-to-benefit-artists-and-fans. Accessed January 31, 2023.

Horrigan, John. "Home Broadband Adoption 2006: Part 1. Broadband Adoption in the United States." *Pew Research Center*, May 28, 2006. https://www.pewresearch.org/internet/2006/05/28/part-1-broadband-adoption-in-the-united-states/. Accessed May 25, 2022.

Houghton, Bruce. "Spotify Cuts Off Playlist Payola Service SpotLister." *Hypebot*, March 19, 2018. https://www.hypebot.com/hypebot/2018/03/spotify-cuts-off-playlist-payola-service-spotlister.html. Accessed June 7, 2022.

Hu, Jim. "About Royalty Rates." *The Trichordist*. https://thetrichordist.com/category/royalty-rates-2/. Accessed May 25, 2022.

Hu, Jim. "Pressplay Comes to Life after Long Wait." *CNET*, April 14, 2002. https://www.cnet.com/tech/services-and-software/pressplay-comes-to-life-after-long-wait/. Accessed June 7, 2022.

Hubbert, Cecelia. "Midler v. Ford Motor Co." *University of Denver Sturm College of Law*. https://www.law.du.edu/documents/sports-and-entertainment-law-journal/case-summaries/1988-midler-v-ford-motor-co.pdf. Accessed June 7, 2022.

"Hulu.com Proves Victorious over Skeptics." *SFGATE.com*, December 23, 2008. https://www.sfgate.com/entertainment/article/Hulu-com-proves-victorious-over-skeptics-3257176.php. Accessed June 2, 2022.

IBM. "What Is Machine Learning?" *IBM Cloud Education*. https://www.ibm.com/cloud/learn/machine-learning. Accessed June 2, 2022.

"IBM PC AT." *Old-Computers.com*. http://www.old-computers.com/museum/computer.asp?st=1&c=185. Accessed May 23, 2022.

Ihaza, Jeff. "Tory Lanez Released an 'NFT Album,' and Then Things Got Extra Weird." *Rolling Stone*, September 30, 2021. https://www.rollingstone.com/music/music-features/tory-lanez-nft-legal-questions-1233890/. Accessed April 29, 2022.

Imbler, Sabrina. "The Best Keurig Machine (But We Really Don't Recommend It)." *Wirecutter*, September 10, 2021. https://www.nytimes.com/wirecutter/reviews/best-keurig-machine/#the-drawbacks-to-keurig-machines-and-why-we-dont-recomm end-them. Accessed June 2, 2022.

Immink, Kees A. "The Compact Disc Story." *Journal of the Audio Engineering Society* 46, no. 5 (May 1998): 458–65.

Immink, Kees A. "Shannon, Beethoven and the Compact Disc." *IEEE Information Theory Society Newsletter*, December 2007, 42–46.

Impoco, Jim. "The Beatles Suck. Yeah, We Said That." *Newsweek*, February 3, 2014. https://www.newsweek.com/beatles-suck-yeah-we-said-227748. Accessed May 4, 2022.

Ingham, Tim. "'Fake Artists' Have Billions of Streams on Spotify. Is Sony Now Playing the Service at Its Own Game?" *Rolling Stone*, May 15, 2019. https://www.rollingstone.com/pro/features/fake-artists-have-billions-of-streams-on-spotify-is-sony-now-playing-the-service-at-its-own-game-834746/. Accessed June 13, 2022.

Ingham, Tim. "Daniel Ek Says Spotify's Subscription Growth is Increasing But That's Not True in Monetary Terms." *Music Business Worldwide*, April 29, 2020. https://www.mus icbusinessworldwide.com/daniel-ek-says-spotifys-subscription-growth-is-increas ing-but-thats-not-true-in-monetary-terms/. Accessed June 13, 2022.

Ingham, Tim. "It's Happened: 100,000 Tracks Are Now Being Uploaded to Streaming Services Like Spotify Each Day." *Music Business Worldwide*, October 6, 2022. https://www.musicbusinessworldwide.com/its-happened-100000-tracks-are-now-being-uploaded/. Accessed December 4, 2022.

Ingham, Tim. "Over 66% of All Music Listening in the US Is Now of Catalog Records Rather Than New Releases." *Music Business Worldwide*, July 13, 2021. https://www.mus icbusinessworldwide.com/over-66-of-all-music-listening-in-the-us-is-now-of-cata log-records-rather-than-new-releases/. Accessed June 7, 2022.

Ingham, Tim. "So . . . How Much Did Tiktok Actually Pay the Music Industry from Its $4bn in Revenues Last Year?" *Music Business Worldwide*, July 14, 2022. https://www.musicbusinessworldwide.com/so-how-much-did-tiktok-actually-pay-the-music-industry-from-its-4bn-in-revenues-last-year/. Accessed July 25, 2022.

Ingham, Tim. "The Great Big Spotify Scam: Did a Bulgarian Playlister Swindle Their Way to a Fortune on Streaming Service?" *Music Business Worldwide*, February 20, 2018. https://www.musicbusinessworldwide.com/great-big-spotify-scam-bulgarian-playlis ter-swindle-way-fortune-streaming-service/. Accessed June 7, 2022.

Ingham, Tim. "Yes, Lucian Grainge Has Banned All Exclusives. No It's Not All About Frank Ocean." *Music Business Worldwide*, August 25, 2016. https://www.musicbusine ssworldwide.com/yes-lucian-grainge-banned-streaming-exclusives-umg-no-not-frank-ocean/. Accessed June 5, 2022.

Ingraham, Nathan. "iTunes Store at 10: How Apple Built a Digital Media Juggernaut." *The Verge*, April 26, 2013. https://www.theverge.com/2013/4/26/4265172/itunes-store-at-10-how-apple-built-a-digital-media-juggernaut. Accessed June 7, 2022.

Interactive Advertising Bureau. "IAB U.S. Podcast Advertising Revenue Study: Full-Year 2021 Results & 2022–2024 Growth Projections." https://www.iab.com/wp-content/uploads/2022/05/IAB-FY-2021-Podcast-Ad-Revenue-and-2022-2024-Growth-Projec tions_FINAL.pdf. Accessed November 29, 2022.

International Federation of the Phonographic Industry. "IFPI Releases Engaging with Music 2021." October 21, 2021. https://www.ifpi.org/ifpi-releases-engaging-with-music-2021/. Accessed June 5, 2022.

International Federation of the Phonographic Industry. "Engaging with Music 2022." https://www.ifpi.org/wp-content/uploads/2022/11/Engaging-with-Music-2022_full-report-1.pdf. Accessed November 28, 2022.

International Federation of the Phonographic Industry. "Rewarding Creativity: Fixing the Value Gap (excerpt from Global Music Report 2017)." https://web.archive.org/web/20190221033533/https:/www.ifpi.org/downloads/GMR2017_ValueGap.pdf. Accessed May 25, 2022.

Isaac, Mike. *Super Pumped: The Battle for Uber*. New York: W.W. Norton, 2019.

"ITA Takes Giant Steps to Push Quality Tape." *Billboard*, May 20, 1972, 37.

"iTunes Store and DRM-Free Music: What You Need to Know." *Macworld*, January 7, 2009. https://www.macworld.com/article/1138000/drm-faq.html. Accessed June 7, 2022.

Jackson, John. *A House on Fire: The Rise and Fall of Philadelphia Soul*. Oxford: Oxford University Press, 2004.

Jacobs Media. "Techsurvey 2022 Results." https://jacobsmedia.com/techsurvey-2022-results/. Accessed November 22, 2022.

Jafee, Larry. *Record Store Day: The Most Improbable Comeback of the 21st Century*. Los Angeles: Rare Bird, 2022.

Jeffries, Dan. "The Musician in the Machine." Google Magenta AI. https://magenta.ten sorflow.org/musician-in-the-machine. Accessed June 2, 2022.

Jennn, London. "Tory Lanez Says His NFT Album Is Reselling on a Secondary Market for $100k." *AllHipHop.com*, August 25, 2021. https://allhiphop.com/news/tory-lanez-says-his-nft-album-is-selling-for-100k/. Accessed April 29, 2022.

Jeong, Sarah. "A $1.6 Billion Spotify Lawsuit Is Based on a Law Made for Player Pianos." *The Verge*, March 14, 2018. https://www.theverge.com/2018/3/14/17117160/spotify-mechanical-license-copyright-wixen-explainer. Accessed June 7, 2022.

Jobs, Steve. "Thoughts on Music." *Apple*, February 6, 2007. https://web.archive.org/web/20071223160841/https://www.apple.com/hotnews/thoughtsonmusic/. Accessed June 7, 2022.

Juang, B. H., and Lawrence Rabiner. *Fundamentals of Speech Recognition*. London: Pearson College Division, 1993.

Jukebox Licensing Office. "History of the Jukebox License Office." http://www.jukeboxlice nse.org/history.htm. Accessed April 29, 2022.

Kafka, Peter. "Grooveshark, the Free Music Service That Used to Scare the Labels Gives Up." *Vox*, April 30, 2015. https://www.vox.com/2015/4/30/11562064/grooveshark-the-free-music-service-that-used-to-scare-the-big-labels. Accessed June 7, 2022.

Kahney, Keander. "Straight Dope on the iPod's Birth." *Wired*, October 17, 2006. https://www.wired.com/2006/10/straight-dope-on-the-ipods-birth/. Accessed May 23, 2022.

Katz, Mark. *Capturing Sound: How Technology Has Changed Music*. Berkeley: University of California Press, 2004.

Kaufman, Gil. "File-Sharing Networks Can Be Liable for Copyright Infringement, Supreme Court Rules." *MTV News*, June 27, 2005. https://www.mtv.com/news/n3n kvo/file-sharing-networks-can-be-liable-for-copyright-infringements-supreme-court-rules/. Accessed April 3, 2023.

Kawaida, Michael. "Mixtapes: A Brief History Of Hip-Hop's Ever Evolving Tool." *HNHH (HotNewHipHop)*, February 25, 2010. https://www.hotnewhiphop.com/mixtapes-a-brief-history-of-hip-hops-ever-evolving-tool-news.103882.html. Accessed April 29, 2022.

Keyes, Daniel. "Amazon Has Surpassed 150 Million Prime Subscribers Globally." *Business Insider*, February 3, 2020. https://www.businessinsider.com/amazon-surpasses-150-million-prime-subscribers-2020-2. Accessed June 5, 2022.

King, Ashley. "German Pop Artist Mike Singer Uses 'Stream-to-Unlock' Trick to Boost Streaming Algorithms." *Digital Music News*, July 14, 2020. https://www.digitalmusicnews.com/2020/07/14/mike-singer-stream-to-unlock-campaign/. Accessed June 7, 2022.

King, Ashley. "For the First Time Ever, Annual Music Streams Top 1 Trillion—In the US Alone." *Digital Music News*, November 30, 2022. https://www.digitalmusicnews.com/2022/11/30/annual-music-streams-top-one-trillion-us-alone. Accessed January 31, 2023.

King, Ashley. "Virtual Characters Are Hitting the Spotify Charts." *Digital Music News*, July 21, 2021. https://www.digitalmusicnews.com/2021/07/21/virtual-characters-metaverse-spotify-charts/. Accessed June 2, 2022.

King, Ashley. "YouTube Music Exec Calls TikTok Short Videos 'Junk Food'—'It Has to Lead You to Long-Form Content So It's Not Empty Calories.'" *Digital Music News*, July 14, 2022. https://www.digitalmusicnews.com/2022/07/08/youtube-music-exec-tiktok-junk-food/. Accessed July 14, 2022.

Klein, Joshua. "Robert Christgau: Christgau's Consumer Guide: Albums Of The '90s." *AV Club*, March 29, 2002. https://www.avclub.com/robert-christgau-christgaus-consumer-guide-albums-of-1798193851. Accessed April 7, 2023.

Knight, Shawn. "Spotify Hits 205 Million Premium Subscribers, but Financial Losses Swell." *Techspot*. January 31, 2023. https://www.techspot.com/news/97444-spotify-hits-205-million-premium-subscribers-but-financial.html. Accessed January 31, 2023.

Knoedelsleder, William. "$1 Million in Suspected 'New Payola' Is Probed." *Los Angeles Times*, December 22, 1987. https://www.latimes.com/archives/la-xpm-1987-12-22-mn-30675-story.html. Accessed April 3, 2023.

Knopper, Steve. *Appetite for Self-Destruction*. Seattle: CreateSpace Independent Publishing Platform, 2017.

Knopper, Steve. "iTunes' 10th Anniversary: How Steve Jobs Turned the Industry Upside Down." *Rolling Stone*, April 26, 2013. https://www.rollingstone.com/culture/culture-news/itunes-10th-anniversary-how-steve-jobs-turned-the-industry-upside-down-68985/. Accessed June 7, 2022.

Knowles, Tim. "To Be or Not To Be Me: Jay-Z Asks Big Question." *Times (London)*, April 30, 2020. https://www.thetimes.co.uk/article/to-be-or-not-to-be-me-jay-z-asks-big-question-hk6vffl0m. Accessed June 2, 2022.

Komurki, John. *Cassette Cultures: Past and Present of a Musical Icon*. Salenstein: Benteli, 2019.

Labaton, Stephen. "5 Music Companies Settle Federal Case On CD Price-Fixing." *New York Times*. May 11, 2000. https://www.nytimes.com/2000/05/11/business/5-music-companies-settle-federal-case-on-cd-price-fixing.html. Accessed April 4, 2023.

Lafayette Radio Electronics Catalogs. "Lafayette Radio Electronics." https://worldradiohistory.com/Lafayette_Catalogs.htm. Accessed April 29, 2022.

Lawler, Richard. "Kanye West's $200 Stem Player Will Be the Only Way to Get His Next Album, Donda 2." *The Verge*, February 18, 2022. https://www.theverge.com/2022/2/18/22940748/donda-2-stem-player-kanye-west-exclusive-music. Accessed June 7, 2022.

LeBel, C. J. "Tape or Disc?" *High Fidelity*, October 1, 1959, 56+.

Leeds, Jeff. "EMI Agrees to Fine to Resolve Payola Case." *New York Times*. June 16, 2006, https://www.nytimes.com/2006/06/16/business/worldbusiness/emi-agrees-to-fine-to-resolve-payola-case.html. Accessed April 4, 2023.

Leeds, Jeff. "Radio Broadcasters Agree to Fine over Payola." *New York Times*. March 6, 2007, https://www.nytimes.com/2007/03/06/technology/06iht-payola.4812569.html. Accessed April 4, 2023.

Leight, Elias. "Fake Streams Could Be Costing Artists $300 Million a Year." *Rolling Stone*, June 18, 2019. https://www.rollingstone.com/pro/features/fake-streams-indie-labels-spotify-tidal-846641/. Accessed June 7, 2022.

Leight, Elias. "Sped-Up Songs Are Taking Over TikTok and Driving Songs Up the Charts." *Billboard*, November 10, 2022. https://www.billboard.com/pro/sped-up-songs-tiktok-streaming-charts/. Accessed November 16, 2022.

Leight, Elias. "Think You Have a Hit? Make Sure It's the First Song on Your Album." *Rolling Stone*, March 7, 2019. https://www.rollingstone.com/music/music-features/why-the-first-song-on-the-album-is-the-best-803283/. Accessed June 5, 2022.

Leight, Elias. "TikTok Pays Artists 'Almost Nothing' in Music Royalties—And the Industry Is Losing Patience." *Billboard*, November 7, 2022. https://www.billboard.com/pro/tiktok-pays-artists-little-music-royalties-insiders-fed-up/. Accessed November 16, 2022.

Leight, Elias. "Want to Get on the Radio? Have $50,000?" *Rolling Stone*, August 6, 2019. https://www.rollingstone.com/pro/features/radio-stations-hit-pay-for-play-867825/. Accessed April 4, 2023.

Leslie, John, and Ross Snyder. "History of The Early Days of Ampex Corporation." *AES Historical Committee*, December 17, 2010. https://www.aes.org/aeshc/docs/company.histories/ampex/leslie_snyder_early-days-of-ampex.pdf. Accessed April 4, 2023.

Lessig, Lawrence. *Code: And Other Laws of Cyberspace*. New York: Basic Books, 1999.

Lessig, Lawrence. "Laws that Choke Creativity." *TED Talks*, https://www.ted.com/talks/lawrence_lessig_laws_that_choke_creativity. Accessed April 29, 2022.

Leswing, Kif. "Apple Music Has Reportedly Passed Spotify in Paid Subscribers in the US." *CNBC*, April 5, 2019. https://www.cnbc.com/2019/04/05/apple-music-has-reportedly-passed-spotify-in-paid-subscribers-in-the-us.html. Accessed June 5, 2022.

Leval, Pierre N. "Toward a Fair Use Standard." *Harvard Law Review 103*, no. 5 (1990): 1105–36. https://doi.org/10.2307/1341457. Accessed April 4, 2023.

Levine, Robert. "For the Record: How Vinyl Got Its Groove Back—To the Tune of a Billion Dollars." *Billboard*, May 25, 2022. https://www.billboard.com/pro/vinyl-boom-analysis-for-the-record. Accessed July 21, 2022.

Lindvall, Helienne. "Behind the Music: Is the Long Tail a Myth." *Guardian*, January 8, 2009. https://www.theguardian.com/music/musicblog/2009/jan/08/long-tail-myth-download. Accessed June 7, 2022.

Lipshutz, Jason. "RIP Lead Singles: Why Hip-Hop Titans Are Dropping Full Albums All at Once," *Billboard*, June 21, 2022, https://www.billboard.com/pro/drake-future-album-release-strategy-hip-hop-singles/. Accessed April 4, 2023.

"List of Most Streamed YouTube Videos." *Wikipedia*. https://en.wikipedia.org/wiki/List_of_most-viewed_YouTube_videos. Accessed June 7, 2022.

Lomas, Natasha. "Apple Pay and iOS App Store Under Formal Antitrust Probe in Europe." *TechCrunch*, June 16, 2020. https://techcrunch.com/2020/06/16/apple-pay-and-ios-app-store-under-formal-antitrust-probe-in-europe/. Accessed June 7, 2022.

Longdon, Victoria. "Why Is a CD 74 Minutes Long? It's because of Beethoven." *Classicfm. com*, May 3, 2019. https://www.classicfm.com/discover-music/why-is-a-cd-74-minu tes/. Accessed May 9, 2022.

Lopez, Mark Hugo, and Daniel Dockterman. "U.S. Hispanic Country-of-Origin Counts for Nation, Top 30 Metropolitan Areas." *Pew Research Center*. May 26, 2011. https:// assets.pewresearch.org/wp-content/uploads/sites/7/reports/142.pdf. Accessed April 5, 2023.

"The Loudness Wars: Why Music Sounds Worse." *NPR*, December 31, 2009. https:// www.npr.org/2009/12/31/122114058/the-loudness-wars-why-music-sounds-worse. Accessed May 23, 2022.

Luminate. "Top Entertainment Trends for 2023: What the Data Says, As Presented at SXSW 2023." https://luminatedata.com/reports/sxsw-top-entertainment-trends-for-2023/. Accessed April 7, 2023.

Luminate. "U.S. Year-End Music Report for 2022." https://luminatedata.com/reports/ luminate-2022-u-s-year-end-report/. Accessed April 5, 2023.

"Lyrics of 'If it Wasn't for the Irish and the Jews.'" *The WashingtonSquare Harp and Shamrock Orchestra*. https://wshso.wordpress.com/tunes/songs/irish-jews-lyrics/. Accessed May 9, 2022.

Mack, Zachary. "How Streaming Affects the Lengths of Songs." *The Verge*, May 28, 2019. https://www.theverge.com/2019/5/28/18642978/music-streaming-spotify-song-len gth-distribution-production-switched-on-pop-vergecast-interview. Accessed June 5, 2022.

"Madonna Swears at Music Pirates." *BBC News*, April 22, 2003. http://news.bbc.co.uk/2/ hi/technology/2962475.stm. Accessed June 7, 2022.

Mann, Charles. "The Hot New Bad Idea." *Inside*. December 2000.

"March 1982: 'I Want My MTV' Campaign Launched." *Totally80s.com*. https://www.tot ally80s.com/article/march-1982-i-want-my-mtv-campaign-launched. Accessed May 4, 2022.

Marcus, Greil. *Like a Rolling Stone: Bob Dylan at the Crossroads*. New York: PublicAffairs, 2006.

Mardesich, Jodi. "How the Internet Hits Big Music." *CNN Money*, May 10, 1999. https:// money.cnn.com/s/fortune/fortune_archive/1999/05/10/259548/index.html. Accessed June 7, 2022.

Margolis, Dan. "Music to a Customers Ears: CD Buyers Can Hear Them First in Stores." *Los Angeles Times*, June 14, 1995. https://www.latimes.com/archives/la-xpm-1995-06-14-fi-13105-story.html. Accessed April 4, 2023.

Marketing Charts. "What Do Ad Loads Look Like On Internet Radio?" https://www.mark etingcharts.com/digital-66030. Accessed April 29, 2022.

Marks, Craig, and Rob Tannenbaum. *I Want My MTV*. New York: Dutton, 2011.

Marr, Bernard. "The Key Definitions of Artificial Intelligence That Explains Its Importance." *Forbes*, February 14, 2018. https://www.forbes.com/sites/bernardmarr/ 2018/02/14/the-key-definitions-of-artificial-intelligence-ai-that-explain-its-importa nce/. Accessed June 7, 2022.

Matchett, Karl. "Barcelona Agree £235m Camp Nou and Kit Sponsorship Deal with Spotify." *Yahoo News*, March 15, 2022. https://news.yahoo.com/barcelona-agree-235m-camp-nou-204133143.html. Accessed June 7, 2022.

McCormick, Rich. "The Awesome 'Guardians of the Galaxy' Mixtape Will Be Released on Cassette." *The Verge*, October 21, 2014. https://www.theverge.com/2014/10/21/7026

095/guardians-of-the-galaxy-mixtape-will-be-released-on-cassette-tape.   Accessed April 29, 2022.

McDermott, Jim. "5 Reasons the Major Labels Didn't Really Blow it With Napster." *Hypebot*. https://www.hypebot.com/hypebot/2015/05/five-reasons-the-major-labels-didnt-blow-it-with-napster.html. Accessed May 23, 2022.

McGinn, Daniel. "The Buzz Machine." *Boston Globe Sunday*, August 7, 2011, http://arch ive.boston.com/business/articles/2011/08/07/the_inside_story_of_keurigs_rise_to_ a_billion_dollar_coffee_empire/. Accessed April 4, 2023.

McIntyre, Hugh. "Adele's '30' Was The Bestselling Vinyl Album Of 2021, Taylor Swift Rules With Several Bestsellers." *Forbes*, January 6, 2022. https://www.forbes.com/sites/ hughmcintyre/2022/01/06/adeles-30-was-the-bestselling-vinyl-album-of-2021-tay lor-swift-rules-with-several-bestsellers/. Accessed May 25, 2022.

Mechanical Licensing Collective. "About the MLC." https://www.themlc.com/our-story. Accessed June 7, 2022.

Mechanical Licensing Collective. "How Can YOU Play Your Part™?" https://www.themlc. com/play-your-part. Accessed July 17, 2022.

Melvin, Chuck. "AT&T Creates 'Ultimate Jukebox' for Rock Hall." *Cleveland Plain Dealer*, April 1, 1998.

Michaels, Sean. "Most Music Didn't Sell a Single Copy in 2008." *Guardian*, December 23, 2008. https://www.theguardian.com/music/2008/dec/23/music-sell-sales. Accessed April 4, 2023.

Metz, Cade. "Lawsuit Takes Aim at the Way AI is Built." *New York Times*, November 23, 2022. https://www.nytimes.com/2022/11/23/technology/copilot-microsoft-ai-lawsuit. html Accessed April 5, 2023.

Miles, Barry. *Zappa: A Biography*. New York: Grove Press, 2004.

Millard, Andre. *America on Record: A History of Recorded Sound*. Cambridge: Cambridge University Press, 2005.

Miller, Larry. "Sync or Swim—Licensing Music for Podcasts." *Musonomics* (podcast), September 28, 2020. http://musonomics.org/sync-or-swim-licensing-music-for-podcasts/. Accessed April 29, 2022.

Milner, Greg. *Perfecting Sound Forever: An Aural History of Recorded Music*. New York: Farrar, Straus and Giroux, 2010.

Mishra, James. "The Dark History of the Jukebox: How the Mafia Used Murder to Build Music Machine Empires." *Click Track*, May 15, 2020. https://www.clicktrack.fm/p/the-dark-history-of-the-jukebox-how. Accessed November 12, 2022.

MIREX. "MIREX2020 Results." https://www.music-ir.org/mirex/wiki/2020:MIREX2 020_Results. Accessed August 5, 2020.

Mnookin, Seth. "Universal's CEO Once Called iPod Users Thieves. Now He's Giving Songs Away." *Wired*, November 27, 2007. https://www.wired.com/2007/11/mf-morris/ . Accessed June 7, 2022.

Molanphy, Chris. "A Deal with the TV Gods." *Hit Parade* (podcast), June 18, 2022. https:// slate.com/podcasts/hit-parade/2022/06/television-is-a-hitmaking-jukebox. Accessed July 5, 2022.

Molanphy, Chris. "Feat. Don't Fail Me Now." *Slate*, July 31, 2015. https://slate.com/cult ure/2015/07/the-history-of-featured-rappers-and-other-featured-artists-in-pop-songs.html. Accessed May 25, 2022.

Molanphy, Chris. "The War Against the Single." *Hit Parade* (podcast), September 29, 2017. https://chris.molanphy.com/hit-parade-the-great-war-against-the-single-edit ion/. Accessed May 23, 2022.

Moore, Geoffrey. *Crossing the Chasm*. New York: Harper Business, 2014.

"More to Love: Target and Michael Bublé Reveal Exclusive Bonus Tracks on His New Album 'To Be Loved.'" *CNN.com*, April 24, 2018. https://www.cnn.com/2018/04/24/us/monkey-selfie-peta-appeal/index.html. Accessed June 5, 2022.

Morton, David L. "The History of Magnetic Recording in the United States, 1888–1978." PhD diss., Georgia Institute of Technology, 1995.

Morton, David L. *Sound Recording: The Life Story of a Technology*. Baltimore: Johns Hopkins University Press, 2004.

Mountain, Toby. "The Birth of Stereo Recording." *Northeastern Digital*. https://www.northeasterndigital.com/post/the-birth-of-stereo-recording. Accessed April 29, 2022.

"MTV News Interviews Sean Parker and Shawn Fanning," https://www.facebook.com/watch/?v=447955682687893. Accessed June 7, 2022.

Mulligan, Mark. "Did July 1st 2019 Mark the End of Spotify's Music Creator Dream?" *Midia Music Industry Blog*, October 8, 2021. https://www.midiaresearch.com/blog/did-july-1st-2019-mark-the-end-of-spotifys-music-creator-dream. Accessed June 7, 2022.

Mulligan, Mark. "How the DNA of a Hit Has Changed Over 20 Years." *Midia Research*, July 13, 2020. https://www.midiaresearch.com/blog/how-the-dna-of-a-hit-has-changed-over-20-years. Accessed June 13, 2022.

Music Business Association. "Smart Speakers Driving New Music Consumption Habits, Says New AudienceNet Survey." *Music Business Association*, October 10, 2018. https://musicbiz.org/news/smart-speakers-driving-new-music-consumption-habits-says-new-audiencenet-study/. Accessed June 2, 2022.

"The Music You Want Wherever You Want It," John Okolowicz collection of publications and advertising on radio and consumer electronics (Accession 2014.277), Hagley Museum & Library, Wilmington, DE 19807.

"MusicNet Launches Battle for Fans." *BBC*, December 4, 2001. http://news.bbc.co.uk/2/hi/entertainment/1691108.stm. Accessed June 7, 2022.

"Nakamichi's $1,100 Cassette Deck." *High Fidelity*. August 1, 1973, 33–35.

"Napster Settlement Offer Rejected." *CBS News*, February 11, 2001. https://www.cbsnews.com/news/napster-settlement-offer-rejected/. Accessed June 2, 2022.

Nash, Michael. "Something New: Artificial Intelligence and the Perils of Plunder." *Music Business Worldwide*, February 14, 2023. https://www.musicbusinessworldwide.com/michael-nash-universal-something-artificial-intelligence-and-the-perils-plunder/. Accessed February 15, 2023.

Neer, Richard. *FM: The Rise and Fall of Rock Radio*. New York: Villard, 2001.

Nelson, Chris. "Recordable CDs Undercut Traditional Bootleg Market." *MTV.com News*, May 21, 1998. https://www.mtv.com/news/dsuz61/recordable-cds-undercut-traditional-bootleg-market/. Accessed April 5, 2023.

Nelson, Chris. "Music Piracy Shifts to Recordable CDs, Record Industry Says." *MTV.com News*, August 19, 1999. https://www.mtv.com/news/g5btet/music-piracy-shifts-to-recordable-cds-record-industry-says/. Accessed May 23, 2022.

"Network Radio Averaged 16 Minutes of Spots per Hour, as Rates Crept Up." *InsideRadio*, November 29, 2018. https://www.insideradio.com/free/network-radio-averaged-16-minutes-of-spots-per-hour-as-rates-crept-up/article_97ff6ae0-f3a8-11e8-b201-8770a1fdf2ed.html. Accessed April 29, 2022.

"New Music Machine Thrills All Hearers at First Test Here." *New York Times*, October 7, 1925, https://www.nytimes.com/1925/10/07/archives/new-music-machine-thrills-all-hearers-at-first-test-here-researches.html. Accessed April 4, 2023.

Nicas, Jack, and David McCabe. "Their Businesses Went Virtual. Then Apple Wanted a Cut." *New York Times*. July 28, 2020. https://www.nytimes.com/2020/07/28/technol ogy/apple-app-store-airbnb-classpass.html. Accessed April 4, 2023.

"Nielsen Report Puts Radio at the Center of the Audio Universe." *InsideRadio*, June 30, 2022. https://www.insideradio.com/nielsen-report-puts-radio-at-the-center-of-the-audio-universe/article_a3188d52-f7f1-11ec-8617-6b7586059cd3.html. Accessed January 30, 2023.

"Nikki Sixx Quotes." *Inspirational Stories*. https://www.inspirationalstories.com/quotes/t/ nikki-sixx/. Accessed June 28, 2022.

Niasse, Amina. "Vinyl Record Sales Climb Just 1% after Years of Rapid Growth." *Bloomberg*, July 14, 2022. https://www.bloomberg.com/news/articles/2022-07-14/ vinyl-record-sales-climb-just-1-after-years-of-rapid-growth. Accessed July 21, 2022.

Nicas, Jack. "YouTube Tops 1 Billion Hours of Video a Day, on Pace to Eclipse TV." *Wall Street Journal*, February 27, 2017. https://www.wsj.com/articles/youtube-tops-1-bill ion-hours-of-video-a-day-on-pace-to-eclipse-tv-1488220851. Accessed April 4, 2023.

Nolan, Beatrice. "AI Art Generators Face Separate Copyright Lawsuits from Getty Images and a Group of Artists." *Business Insider*, January 19, 2023. https://www.businessinsi der.com/ai-art-artists-getty-images-lawsuits-stable-diffusion-2023-1. Accessed January 31, 2023.

Nolasco, Stephanie. "Elvis Presley's First Appearance on the Ed Sullivan Show Remembered 64 Years Later." *Foxnews.com*, September 9, 2020. https://www.foxn ews.com/entertainment/elvis-presley-ed-sullivan-show-anniversary. Accessed May 4, 2022.

NPR and Edison Research. "Smart Audio Report." June 17, 2022. https://www.edisonr esearch.com/smart-audio-report-2022-from-npr-and-edison-research/. Accessed April 4, 2023.

O'Brien, T. "Listen to an AI Sing an Uncanny Rendition of 'Jolene.'" *Engadget*, November 2, 2022. https://www.engadget.com/holly-plus-holly-herndon-dolly-parton-jolene-ai-cover-204750236.html. Accessed November 3, 2022.

O'Malley, Chris. "A New Spin." *Time*, August 24, 1998. https://content.time.com/time/sub scriber/article/0,33009,988955,00.html.

"Official Charts Company Shakes Up Rules to Stop the Ed Sheeran Effect." *Guardian*, June 27, 2017. https://www.theguardian.com/music/2017/jun/27/official-charts-company-shakes-up-rules-support-new-talent-ed-sheeran-effect. Accessed April 4, 2023.

Ogunnaike, Lola. "Record Labels Must Pay Shortchanged Performers." *New York Times*, May 5, 2004. https://www.nytimes.com/2004/05/05/arts/record-labels-must-pay-shortchanged-performers.html. Accessed April 4, 2023.

Oman, Ralph (Register of Copyrights). *Report on Copyright Implications of Digital Audio Transmission Services*. Washington, DC: US Copyright Office, 1991).

Open AI. "Open AI Jukebox." https://openai.com/blog/jukebox/. Accessed June 2, 2022.

Ottens, L. F. "The Compact Cassette for Audio Tape Recorders." *Journal of the Audio Engineering Society* 15, no. 1 (1967): 26–28.

Owens, Buck, and Randy Poe. *Buck 'Em!: The Autobiography of Buck Owens*. Lanman, MD: Backbeat, 2013.

Owsinski, Bobby. "The Music Long Tail Might Not Be That Long After All." *Music 3.0 Blog*, November 13, 2019. https://music3point0.com/2019/11/13/music-long-tail-rebuffed/#ixzz6QtTtdmzJ. Accessed June 5, 2022.

Owsinski, Bobby. "The Streaming Performance Royalty Explained." *Music 3.0 Blog*, May 19, 2016. https://music3point0.com/2016/05/19/streaming-performance-royalty/#ixzz6souR0TTQ. Accessed May 4, 2022.

Pagano, Penny and William Knoedelsleder Jr. "Senate Plans Record Industry Payola Probe." *Los Angeles Times*, April 3, 1986, https://www.latimes.com/archives/la-xpm-1986-04-03-mn-2589-story.html. Accessed April 4, 2023.

Paine, Andre. "Tencent Music Paying Users up 52% in Q2." *Music Week*, August 11, 2020. https://www.musicweek.com/digital/read/tencent-music-paying-users-up-52-in-q2/080734. Accessed May 25, 2022.

Pallante, Maria (Register of Copyrights). *Copyright and the Music Marketplace*. Washington, DC: US Copyright Office, February 2015.

Pan, Joann. "Grooveshark Circumvents Mobile Bans by Launching an HTML5 Player." *Mashable*, September 5, 2012. https://mashable.com/archive/grooveshark-html5-player. Accessed June 7, 2022.

Pareles, Jon. "Issue and Debate; Royalties on Recorders and Blank Audio Tapes." *New York Times*, November 21, 1985, https://www.nytimes.com/1985/11/21/arts/issue-and-debate-royalties-on-recorders-and-blank-audio-tapes.html. Accessed April 4, 2023.

Pareles, Jon. "Now on CDs, First 4 Beatles Albums." *New York Times*, February 25, 1987, https://www.nytimes.com/1987/02/25/arts/now-on-cd-s-first-4-beatles-albums.html. Accessed April 4, 2023.

Pareles, Jon. "Record-It-Yourself Music on Cassette." *New York Times*, May 11, 1987, https://www.nytimes.com/1987/05/11/arts/record-it-yourself-music-on-cassette.html. Accessed April 4, 2023.

Pareles, Jon. "Trying to Get in Tune With the Digital Age; Recording Industry Seeks a Standard For Distributing Music on the Web." *New York Times*, February 1, 1999, https://www.nytimes.com/1999/02/01/business/trying-get-tune-with-digital-age-recording-industry-seeks-standard-for.html. Accessed April 4, 2023.

Pareles, Jon. "With a Click, A New Era of Music Dawns." *New York Times*, November 15, 1998, https://www.nytimes.com/1998/11/15/arts/music-with-a-click-a-new-era-of-music-dawns.html. Accessed April 4, 2023.

Parks, Kevin. *Music & Copyright in America: Toward the Celestial Jukebox*. Chicago: American Bar Association, 2014.

Passman, Donald. *All You Need to Know About the Music Business*, 10th Edition. New York: Simon & Schuster, 2019.

Passy, Jacob. "How Spotify Influences What Songs become Popular (or Not)." *Market Watch*, June 18, 2018. https://www.marketwatch.com/story/how-spotify-influences-what-songs-become-popular-or-not-2018-06-18. Accessed June 5, 2022.

Peek, J. B. H. *Origins and Successors of the Compact Disc: Contributions of Philips to Optical Storage*. New York: Springer, 2009.

Peek, J. B. H. "The Emergence of the Compact Disk." *IEEE Communications* 48, no. 1 (January 2010): 10–17.

Peltz, James F. "Cetec Gauss Bets Standard Tape Can Survive Digital Threat." *Los Angeles Times*, August 11, 1987, https://www.latimes.com/archives/la-xpm-1987-09-01-fi-5454-story.html. Accessed April 4, 2023.

Peoples, Glenn. "1 in Every 60 U.S. Streams Last Week Was Drake." *Billboard*, June 28, 2022, https://www.billboard.com/pro/drake-honestly-nevermind-streams-marketshare/. Accessed April 4, 2023.

Peoples, Glenn. "Cloud Village Music Subscribers Grew 51%, Revenues Up 38.6% in Q1." *Billboard*, May 24, 2022, https://www.billboard.com/pro/cloud-village-q1-2022-earni ngs/. Accessed April 4, 2023.

Perzanowski, Aaron, and Jason Schultz. *The End of Ownership: Personal Property in the Digital Economy*. Cambridge, MA: MIT Press, 2016.

Peters, Marybeth. "Statement to Internet Subcommittee of the Judiciary Committee." *U.S. Copyright Office*. https://www.copyright.gov/docs/regstat031104.html. Accessed May 9, 2022.

Pex. "Music Became Even More Valuable on YouTube in 2019." https://pex.com/blog/ state-of-youtube-2019-music-more-valuable/. Accessed May 25, 2022.

Phirtiyal, Sankalp. "Google Expands Jio Partnership with Indian Smartphone, Cloud Tie-Ups." *Reuters*, June 24, 2021. https://www.reuters.com/technology/google-says-cloud-partnership-with-indias-jio-boost-5g-plans-2021-06-24/. Accessed June 13, 2022.

"Play/Pause: A Look at 30 Years of the Compact Disc." *Business Week*, October 10, 2012. https://www.bloomberg.com/news/photo-essays/2012-10-01/play-pause-a-look-at-30-years-of-the-compact-disc. Accessed May 23, 2002.

Podtrac. "Podtrac Industry Ranking: Top 20 Podcasts, April 2022." http://analytics.podt rac.com/podcast-rankings. Accessed June 20, 2022.

Pope, Adrian. "Clamp Down on Free Spotify? Now Is Not the Time for Knee-Jerk Decisions." *PIAS: The Independent Blog*. https://www.piasgroup.net/blog/clamp-down-on-free-spotify-now-is-not-the-time-for-knee-jerk-decisions/. Accessed June 5, 2022.

"Popular Music Is More Collaborative Than Ever." *Economist*, February 2, 2018, https:// www.economist.com/graphic-detail/2018/02/02/popular-music-is-more-collaborat ive-than-ever. Accessed April 4, 2023.

"Portable Music Players Enter the Spin Zone." *Wired*, September 30, 2009. https://www. wired.com/2009/09/1001first-cd-players/. Accessed May 23, 2022.

Porter, Jon. "US Patent Office Rules that Artificial Intelligence Cannot Be a Legal Inventor." *The Verge*, April 29, 2020. https://www.theverge.com/2020/4/29/21241251/ artificial-intelligence-inventor-united-states-patent-trademark-office-intellectual-property. Accessed June 7, 2022.

Powell, W. H. "Top 10 Greatest BuzzFeed Lists Of All Time." *Medium*, June 28, 2016. https://medium.com/@whpeezy/top-10-buzzfeed-lists-of-all-time-that-will-tickle-your-list-bone-until-you-have-a-listgasm-ffb1ce7cd52c. Accessed June 2, 2022.

Prato, Greg. "David Coverdale Tells the Story Behind Whitesnake's Iconic "Here I Go Again" Video." *Consequenceofsound.com*, March 13, 2019. https://consequence.net/ 2019/03/david-coverdale-whitesnake-here-i-go-again-video/. Accessed May 4, 2022.

Prendiville, Kieran. "Tomorrow's World: The Compact Disc." *BBC*, February 24, 2015. https://youtu.be/bMp1pSVxoqw. Accessed May 23, 2002.

Pteridis, Alexis. "Mark Ronson: 'I Was Floundering. I Was Drinking too Much and Giving Orders."" *Guardian*, February 22, 2019, https://www.theguardian.com/music/2019/ feb/22/mark-ronson-i-was-floundering-i-was-drinking-too-much-and-giving-ord ers. Accessed April 4, 2023.

Public Knowledge. "Public Knowledge Responds to RIAA's Plans to Sue P2P File Traders." Public Knowledge press release, September 7, 2004. https://www.publicknowledge. org/press-release/public-knowledge-responds-to-riaas-plans-to-sue-p2p-file-traders/ . Accessed June 7, 2022.

Radio and Records Music Airplay Charts. *Radio and Records*, https://worldradiohistory. com/Archive-All-Music/Radio_and_Records.htm. Accessed July 13, 2022.

Radio Shack Catalogs. Radio Shack. https://www.radioshackcatalogs.com/. Accessed April 29, 2022.

Raieli, Salvatore. "Generate a Piano Cover With AI." *Medium*, November 10, 2022. https://medium.com/mlearning-ai/generate-a-piano-cover-with-ai-f4178bc9cb30. Accessed November 16. 2022.

Rasen, Edward. "Compact Discs: Sound of the Future." *Spin*, May 1985. https://www.spin.com/2021/09/compact-discs-sound-of-the-future-2/.

Recording Industry Association of America. "About Piracy." https://www.riaa.com/resources-learning/about-piracy/. Accessed May 23, 2022.

Recording Industry Association of America. "U.S. Sales Database." https://www.riaa.com/u-s-sales-database/. Accessed June 7, 2022.

Resnikoff, Paul. "A Proposal to Build Spotify (from 1982)." *Digital Music News*, June 21, 2012. https://www.digitalmusicnews.com/2012/06/21/proposes. Accessed November 26, 2022.

Resnikoff, Paul. "Spotify Executive Calls Artist 'Entitled' for Requesting Payment of One Penny Per Stream." *Digital Music News*, June 29, 2021. https://www.digitalmusicnews.com/2021/06/29/spotify-executive-entitled-pay-penny-per-stream/. Accessed June 13, 2022.

Resnikoff, Paul. "What Succeeds on Spotify's Rap Caviar—A Statistical Analysis." *Digital Music News*, August 18, 2020. https://www.digitalmusicnews.com/2020/08/18/spotify-rapcaviar-analysis. Accessed June 13, 2022.

Resnikoff, Paul. "YouTube Music Says It Pays the Same Royalty Rate as Spotify—At Least on Its Subscription Streams." *Digital Music News*, October 9, 2019. https://www.digitalmusicnews.com/2019/10/09/youtube-music-premium-subscription/. Accessed May 25, 2022.

Reynolds, Simon. *Rip It Up and Start Again: Postpunk 1978–1984*. London: Penguin, 2006.

Richtel, Matt. "File Sharing Sites Found Not Liable For Infringement." *New York Times*, August 20, 2008, https://www.nytimes.com/2004/08/20/business/technology-file-sharing-sites-found-not-liable-for-infringement.html. Accessed April 4, 2023.

Richtel, Matt. "Plans to Sell Music on the Internet Raise Antitrust Concerns." *New York Times*, August 7, 2001, https://www.nytimes.com/2001/08/07/business/technology-plans-to-sell-music-on-the-internet-raise-antitrust-concerns.html/. Accessed April 4, 2023.

Richtel, Matt. "The Napster Decision: Appellate Judges Back Limitations on Copying Music." *New York Times*. February 13, 2001, https://www.nytimes.com/2001/02/13/business/napster-decision-overview-appellate-judges-back-limitations-copying-music.html. Accessed April 4, 2023.

Ricker, Thomas. "First Click: Remember When Steve Jobs Said Even Jesus Couldn't Sell Music Subscriptions?" *The Verge*, June 8, 2015. https://www.theverge.com/2015/6/8/8744963/steve-jobs-jesus-people-dont-want-music-subscriptions. Accessed June 28, 2022.

Ringer, Barbara. *The Unauthorized Duplication of Sound Recordings* (Copyright Law Revision Study No. 26). Washington, DC: US Copyright Office, 1961.

"Rio PMP300." *Wikipedia*. https://en.wikipedia.org/wiki/Rio_PMP300. Accessed June 17, 2022.

Robertson, Adi. "The US Copyright Office Says an AI Can't Copyright Its Art." *The Verge*, February 21, 2022. https://www.theverge.com/2022/2/21/22944335/us-copyright-office-reject-ai-generated-art-recent-entrance-to-paradise. Accessed June 2, 2022.

Robinson, Kristin. "HitPiece Wanted to Make an NFT for Every Song—Only Its Founders Forgot to Ask Artists First." *Billboard*, February 2, 2022. https://www.billboard.com/pro/hitpiece-nft-every-song-artist-permission-founders/. Accessed June 5, 2022.

Robitzski, Dan. "Mind-Melting AI Makes Frank Sinatra Sing "Toxic" by Britney Spears." *Futurism*, May 20, 2020. https://futurism.com/mind-melting-ai-frank-sinatra-toxic-britney-spears. Accessed June 2, 2022.

Roedy, Bill, and David Fisher. *What Makes Business Rock*. New York: Wiley, 2011.

Rogers, Jude. "Total Rewind: 10 Key Moments in the Life of the Cassette." *Guardian*, August 30, 2013, https://www.theguardian.com/music/2013/aug/30/cassette-store-day-music-tapes. Accessed April 4, 2023.

Rosen, Gary. *Adventures of a Jazz Age Lawyer*. Oakland: University of California Press, 2020.

Rosenberg, Rutger, and Jason Joven. "How To Understand and Use Music Data Analytics Tools." *Hypebot*. https://www.hypebot.com/hypebot/2020/06/how-to-understand-and-use-music-data-analytics-tools.html. Accessed June 7, 2022.

Rosenblatt, Bill. "Copyright Office's Section 512 Report Finds the Balance Askew." *Copyright and Technology*, May 26, 2020. https://copyrightandtechnology.com/2020/05/26/copyright-office-releases-section-512-report/. Accessed May 25, 2022.

Rosenblatt, Bill. "Disruption Comes to Higher-Ed Publishing." *Publishers Weekly*, August 19, 2019, https://www.publishersweekly.com/pw/by-topic/digital/content-and-e-books/article/80947-disruption-comes-to-higher-ed-publishing.html. Accessed April 4, 2023.

Rosenblatt, Bill. "EU Article 13 (Now Article 17) Passes After More Changes, Making Copyright Filtering More Likely." *Forbes*, April 1, 2019. https://copyrightandtechnology.com/2019/04/01/eu-article-13-now-article-17-passes-after-more-changes-making-copyright-filtering-more-likely/. Accessed May 25, 2022.

Rosenblatt, Bill. "The Future of Blockchain Technology in the Music Industry." *Journal of the Copyright Society of the USA* 66 (Spring 2019): 271–89.

Rosenblatt, Bill. "The Short, Unhappy Life of Music Downloads." *Forbes*, May 7, 2018. https://www.forbes.com/sites/billrosenblatt/2018/05/07/the-short-unhappy-life-of-music-downloads/. Accessed June 5, 2022.

Rosenblatt, Bill. "UltraViolet, Hollywood's Attempt To Control The Digital Video Supply Chain, Will Shut Down." *Forbes*, February 3, 2019. https://www.forbes.com/sites/billrosenblatt/2019/02/03/ultraviolet-hollywoods-attempt-to-control-the-digital-video-supply-chain-will-shut-down/. Accessed June 2, 2022.

Rosenblatt, Bill. "Vinyl Is Bigger Than We Thought. Much Bigger." *Forbes*, September 18, 2018. https://www.forbes.com/sites/billrosenblatt/2018/09/18/vinyl-is-bigger-than-we-thought-much-bigger/. Accessed April 29, 2022.

Rosenblatt, Bill, Bill Trippe, and Stephen Mooney. *Digital Rights Management: Business and Technology*. New York: John Wiley & Sons, 2001.

Røssel, Thomas, and Camilla Louise Brandt. "Polaris Nordic: Digital Music in the Nordics." *Polaris*. https://polarismusichub.com/wp-content/uploads/2020/05/Full_Report_Polaris_Nordic_Digital-Music-in-the-Nordics-2020.pdf. Accessed June 5, 2022.

Roth, Maxine. "The Story of Music on Tape." *Tape Recording*, January 1, 1968, 44–48.

Ruhlmann, William. *Breaking Records: 100 Years of Hits*. London: Routledge, 2004.

Ruhlmann, William. "Your Hit Parade: 1957 Review." *All Music Guide*. https://www.allmusic.com/album/your-hit-parade-1957-mw0000884963. Accessed May 4, 2022.

Russell, Jon. "Spotify Says It Paid $340M to Buy Gimlet and Anchor." *TechCrunch*, February 14, 2019. https://techcrunch.com/2019/02/14/spotify-gimlet-anchor-340-million/. Accessed June 5, 2022.

Rys, Dan. "Lucian Grainge Calls For 'Updated Model' For Music Industry: Read His Memo to UMG Staff." *Billboard*, January 12, 2023. https://www.billboard.com/pro/lucian-grainge-umg-full-staff-memo-2023-read-message/. Accessed April 7, 2023.

Sanjek, Russell and David. *American Popular Music in the 20th Century*. Oxford: Oxford University Press, 1991.

Sarser, David. "Tapes, Disks, and Coexistence." *High Fidelity*, March 1, 1955, 44+.

Scattergood, Amy. "Artisans of the Roast." *Los Angeles Times*, October 25, 2006. https://www.latimes.com/food/la-fo-roast102506-story.html. Accessed April 4, 2023.

Schatz, Lake. "Spotify CEO To Artists: 'You Can't Record Music Once Every Three To Four Years And Think That's Going To Be Enough.'" *Consequence of Sound*, August 1, 2020. https://consequence.net/2020/08/spotify-daniel-ek-artist-recording-comments/. Accessed June 13, 2022.

Scheirer, Eric. "The End of SDMI." *MP3.com*, October 15, 1999. https://web.archive.org/web/20000229055832/http://www.mp3.com/news/394.html. Accessed June 7, 2022.

Schiff, Devon. "GO AEROSMITH: How 'Head First' Became the First Digitally Downloadable Song 20 Years Ago Today." *Vice.com*, June 27, 2014. https://www.vice.com/en/article/6vapxr/go-aerosmith-how-head-first-became-the-first-song-available-for-digital-download-20-years-ago-today. Accessed May 23, 2022.

Schumacher-Rasmussen, Eric. "Record Industry Sues Morpheus and Other Decentralized File Sharing Services." *MTV News*, October 3, 2001. https://www.mtv.com/news/gpun33/record-industry-sues-morpheus-and-other-decentralized-file-sharing-services/. Accessed June 7, 2022.

Schultz, Rod. "The Many Facades of DRM." 2012. https://web.archive.org/web/20150105090945/http://fortunedotcom.files.wordpress.com/2014/12/2012_misc_drm.pdf. Accessed May 18, 2023.

Schwann Record and Tape Guides. *Schwann*. Boston: Schwann Publications, 1971–1978.

Sewell, Amanda. "How Copyright Affected the Musical Style and Critical Reception of Sample-Based Hip-Hop." *Journal of Popular Music Studies* 26, nos. 2–3 (2014): 295–320.

Shah, Neil. "Didn't Like That New Album? Another One Is Coming Before You Know It." *Wall Street Journal*, March 26, 2018, https://www.wsj.com/articles/didnt-like-that-new-album-another-one-is-coming-before-you-know-it-1522076320. Accessed April 4, 2023.

Shah, Neil. "A Chart-Topping Album Sparks Debate Over Length." *Wall Street Journal*, February 6, 2018, https://www.wsj.com/articles/migos-album-culture-ii-tops-charts-but-sparks-debate-over-its-length-1517848564. Accessed April 4, 2023.

Shannon, Daniel. "Sales of Stereos Are Less Sound." *New York Times*, May 23, 1982, https://www.nytimes.com/1982/05/23/business/sales-of-stereos-are-less-sound-as-audio-industry-s-markets-slip.html. Accessed April 4, 2023.

Shapiro, Ariel. "Warner Music Adopts SoundCloud's User-centric Revenue Model." *The Verge*, July 21, 2022. https://www.theverge.com/2022/7/21/23272548/warner-music-soundcloud-user-centric-model-spotify. Accessed July 22, 2022.

Shelton, Robert. "Happy Tunes on Cash Registers." *New York Times*, March 16, 1958, https://www.nytimes.com/1958/03/16/archives/happy-tunes-on-cash-registers-record-industry-sees-tape-and-stereo.html. Accessed April 4, 2023.

Shen, Jonathan, and Ruoming Pang. "Tacotron 2: Generating Human-like Speech from Text." *Google AI Blog*, December 19, 2017. https://ai.googleblog.com/2017/12/tacotron-2-generating-human-like-speech.html. Accessed June 2, 2022.

"A Short History of How Jukeboxes Changed the World." *Rock-Ola*. https://www.rock-ola.com/blogs/news/a-short-history-of-how-jukeboxes-changed-the-world. Accessed May 25, 2022.

Shotwell, James. "36% of Americans Now Own Smart Speakers: Here's What That Means for Musicians." *Haulix*, February 26, 2019. https://haulixdaily.com/2019/02/smart-speakers-music-business. Accessed June 2, 2022.

Sigalos, MacKenzie. "Ethereum Had a Rough September. Here's Why and How It's Being Fixed." *CNBC.com*, October 2, 2021. https://www.cnbc.com/2021/10/02/ethereum-had-a-rough-september-heres-why-and-how-it-gets-fixed.html. Accessed April 29, 2022.

Singh, Manish. "Google invests $4.5 billion in India's Reliance Jio Platforms." *TechCrunch*, July 15, 2020. https://techcrunch.com/2020/07/15/google-invests-4-5-billion-in-indias-reliance-jio-platforms/. Accessed May 23, 2022.

Sisario, Ben. "A New Spotify Initiative Makes the Big Record Labels Nervous." *New York Times*, September 6, 2018, https://www.nytimes.com/2018/09/06/business/media/spotify-music-industry-record-labels.html. Accessed April 4, 2023.

Slattery, Peter. "Scammers Are Gaming Spotify by Faking Collaborations with Famous Artists." *OneZero*, June 1, 2020. https://onezero.medium.com/scammers-are-gaming-spotify-by-faking-collaborations-with-famous-artists-42d127e370dc. Accessed June 7, 2022.

"SME and WMG the biggest market share winners in 2021." *Music and Copyright Blog*, April 5, 2022. https://musicandcopyright.wordpress.com/2022/04/05/sme-and-wmg-the-biggest-market-share-winners-in-2021/. Accessed May 25, 2022.

Smith, Dylan. "Tencent Music Subscribers Grow 50% to 42.7 Million—Wall Street Isn't Impressed." *Digital Music News*, May 12, 2020. https://www.digitalmusicnews.com/2020/05/12/tencent-music-subscribers-growth/. Accessed June 5, 2022.

Smith, Dylan. "Warner Music Group Inks 'First-Ever Partnership' With POAP 'To Mint Shared Memories As NFTs.'" *Digital Music News*, April 14, 2022. https://www.digitalmusicnews.com/2022/04/14/warner-music-group-poap-partnership/. Accessed May 28, 2022.

Smith, Dylan. "Spotify CEO Daniel Ek Confirms 2023 Price Increase Plans Following Apple Music Raises." *Digital Music News*, October 27, 2022. https://www.digitalmusicnews.com/2022/10/27/spotify-price-increase-2023/. Accessed October 27, 2022.

Smith, Ethan, and Jessica E. Vascellaro. "Warner Pulls Music From YouTube." *Wall Street Journal*, December 22, 2008, https://www.wsj.com/articles/SB122980193788724073. Accessed April 4, 2023.

Smith, Ethan. "MTV Overtakes Vevo as Top Online Music Destination." *Wall Street Journal*. September 8, 2010, https://www.wsj.com/articles/BL-SEB-46396. Accessed April 4, 2023.

Smith, Michael, and Rahul Telang. "Assessing the Academic Literature Regarding the Impact of Media Piracy on Sales." Carnegie Mellon University, August 19, 2012, https://papers.ssrn.com/sol3/papers.cfm?abstract_id=2132153. Accessed April 4, 2023.

Sony Music. "Sony BMG Music Entertainment Signs Content License Agreement with YouTube." Sony Music press release, October 8, 2006. https://www.sonymusic.com/sonymusic/sony-bmg-music-entertainment-signs-content-license-agreement-with-youtube/. Accessed May 25, 2022.

Sorkin, Andrew Ross, and Jeff Leeds. "Music Companies Grab a Share of the YouTube Sale." *New York Times*, October 19, 2006, https://www.nytimes.com/2006/10/19/tec hnology/music-companies-grab-a-share-of-the-youtube-sale.html. Accessed April 4, 2023.

"Sorry (Justin Bieber Song)." *Wikipedia.* https://en.wikipedia.org/wiki/Sorry_(Jus tin_Bieber_song). Accessed June 5, 2022.

Soundcloud. "Mastering on SoundCloud Powered by Dolby." https://community.soundcl oud.com/mastering-on-soundcloud. Accessed June 2, 2022.

Spangler, T. S. "Morpheus, Other File-Sharing Services Sued by RIAA." *ExtremeTech*, October 3, 2001. https://www.extremetech.com/extreme/58270-morpheus-other-file sharing-services-sued-by-riaa. Accessed June 17, 2022.

Spencer, Samuel. "How Many Subscribers Do Netflix, Disney+ and the Rest of the Streaming Services Have?" *Newsweek*, May 11, 2021. https://www.newsweek.com/ netflix-amazon-hulu-disney-most-subscribers-streaming-service-1590463. Accessed June 2, 2022.

Spotify. "About Spotify." https://newsroom.spotify.com/company-info/. Accessed May 25, 2022.

Spotify. "F-1 Registration." Spotify. March 31, 2018, https://www.sec.gov/Archives/edgar/ data/1639920/000119312518063434/d494294df1.htm#rom494294_7.

Spotify. "Loud & Clear." https://loudandclear.byspotify.com/. Accessed June 13, 2022.

Spotify. "Spotify Flagship Playlist ¡Viva Latino! Hits 10 Million Followers." *Spotify: For the Record*, July 26, 2019. https://newsroom.spotify.com/2019-07-26/spotify-flagship playlist-viva-latino-hits-10-million-followers/. Accessed June 5, 2022.

Spotify. "Where Is Spotify Available." https://support.spotify.com/us/article/where-spot ify-is-available/. Accessed June 5, 2022.

"'Start Me Up': the $3 Million Anthem That Launched Microsoft's Windows 95." *4As*. https://www.aaaa.org/timeline-event/start-3-million-anthem-launched-microsofts windows-95/?cn-reloaded=1. Accessed May 4, 2022.

Stassen, Murray. "BTS Set Spotify Record with 20.9M Day One Plays, but 10M Nearly of Them Are Discounted on Platform's Chart." *Music Business Worldwide*, May 24, 2021. https://www.musicbusinessworldwide.com/bts-set-new-spotify-streaming-record with-20-9m-day-one-plays-but-nearly-10m-of-them-are-discounted-on-platforms chart/. Accessed June 13, 2022.

Stassen, Murray. "JioSaavn's Paying Subcriber Base Has Quadrupled Since Early 2019." *Music Business Worldwide*, May 28, 2020. https://www.musicbusinessworldwide.com/ jiosaavns-paying-subscriber-base-has-quadrupled-since-early-2019/. Accessed June 5, 2022.

Stassen, Murray. "Warner Is Signing Double the Number of Artists via AI Driven Tool Sodatone." *Music Business Worldwide*, November 24, 2020. https://www.musicbusine ssworldwide.com/warner-is-signing-double-the-number-of-artists-via-ai-driven-ar tool-sodatone-than-it-did-last-year-now-its-hired-a-global-head-of-data-science/. Accessed June 7, 2022.

Stassen, Murray. "Warner Joins $14M Funding Round in AI Music Start-up Lifescore." *Music Business Worldwide*, March 7, 2022. https://www.musicbusinessworldwide.com/ warner-joins-11m-funding-round-in-ai-music-startup-lifescore-founded-by-siri-co inventor-tom-gruber1/. Accessed June 2, 2022.

Stassen, Murray. "Apple Music Just Raised Its Subscription Price to $10.99 in the U.S. Will Spotify be Next?" *Music Business Worldwide*, October 24, 2022. https://www.musicbu

sinessworldwide.com/apple-music-just-raised-its-subscription-price-to-10-99-in-the-us-will-spotify-be-next1/. Accessed October 25, 2022.

Stassen, Murray. "Over 1,000 Songs with Human Mimicking AI Vocals Have Been released by Tencent Music in China. One of Them Has 100M Streams." *Digital Music News*, November 15, 2022. https://www.musicbusinessworldwide.com/over-1000-songs-human-mimicking-ai-vocals-have-been-released-by-tencent-music-in-china-one-of-them-has-over-100m-streams/. Accessed November 16, 2022.

Stassen, Murray. "Still Convinced that TikTok Isn't Turning into a Record Company?" *Music Business Worldwide*, October 3, 2022. https://www.musicbusinessworldwide.com/still-convinced-that-tiktok-and-bytedance-arent/. Accessed October 5, 2022.

Statista. "Smart Speaker Use Case Frequency." https://www.statista.com/statistics/994696/united-states-smart-speaker-use-case-frequency/. Accessed June 2, 2022.

"The Steady Reach of Radio: Winning Consumer Attention." *Nielsen*, June 2019. https://www.nielsen.com/us/en/insights/article/2019/the-steady-reach-of-radio-winning-consumers-attention/. Accessed May 25, 2022.

Steffen, David J. *From Edison to Marconi: The First Thirty Years of Recorded Music*. Jefferson, NC: McFarland, 2005.

Stereo Review Stereo Buyers Guide, 1975–95. *Stereo Review*. https://worldradiohistory.com/Archive-All-Audio/HiFI-Stereo-Review.htm. Accessed April 29, 2022.

Stereo Review Tape Recorder Annual, 1968–79. *Stereo Review*. https://worldradiohistory.com/Archive-All-Audio/HiFI-Stereo-Review.htm. Accessed April 29, 2022.

Sterling, Christopher H., and John Michael Kittross. *Stay Tuned: A History of American Broadcasting*. Milton Park: Routledge, 2001.

Sterne, Jonathan. *MP3: The Meaning of a Format*. Durham, NC: Duke University Press, 2012.

Stichting de Thuiskopie and World Intellectual Property Organization. International Survey on Private Copying, WIPO Publication No. 1037E/16, 2015. https://www.wipo.int/edocs/pubdocs/en/wipo_pub_1037_2016.pdf. Accessed May 27, 2022.

Strong, Maria (Acting Register of Copyrights). *Section 512 of Title 17*. Washington, DC: United States Copyright Office, May 2020.

Stross, Randall. *The Wizard of Menlo Park*. New York: Broadway Books, 2007.

Stutz, Colin. "Spotify CEO Daniel Ek Says Direct Licensing With Artists 'Doesn't Make Us a Label.'" *Billboard*, July 26, 2018. https://www.billboard.com/music/music-news/spotify-daniel-ek-direct-licensing-artists-not-label-earnings-call-8467283/. Accessed June 13, 2022.

Subcommittee on Courts, Civil Liberties, and the Administration of Justice of the Committee on the Judiciary, House of Representatives, 95th Congress. *Performance Rights in Sound Recordings*. Washington, DC: U.S. Government Printing Office, 1978.

Subcommittee on Courts, Civil Liberties, and the Administration of Justice of the Committee on the Judiciary, House of Representatives, 95th Congress. *Copyright Law Revision: Hearings on H.R. 2223*. Washington, DC: U.S. Government Printing Office, 1976.

Sudario, Erielle. "Spotify Changes Playlist Rules Post Pocket Gods' Protest Album." *We Got This Covered*, March 3, 2022. https://wegotthiscovered.com/music/spotify-changes-playlist-rules-post-pocket-gods-protest-album/. Accessed June 7, 2022.

Sugar, Alan. *What You See Is What You Get: My Autobiography*. London: Macmillan, 2010.

Suisman, David. *Selling Sounds: The Commercial Revolution in American Music*. Cambridge, MA: Harvard University Press, 2012.

Sullivan, Jennifer. "More Popular Than Sex." *Wired*, October 14, 1999, https://www.wired.com/1999/10/more-popular-than-sex/. Accessed April 5, 2023.

Sullivan, Jennifer. "The Sound of Busic (sic)." *Wired*, February 26,1999. https://www.wired.com/1999/02/the-sound-of-busic/. Accessed May 23, 2022.

Sutherland, Mark. "Amazon Music Director Ryan Redington on Country's Streaming Revolution." *Music Week*, March 12, 2020. https://www.musicweek.com/digital/read/amazon-music-director-ryan-redington-on-country-s-streaming-revolution/079179. Accessed June 2, 2022.

Swisher, Kara. "Circuit City Plugs into Visions of an Electronics Dream World." *Washington Post*, February 1, 1993. https://www.washingtonpost.com/archive/business/1993/02/01/circuit-city-plugs-in-to-visions-of-an-electronics-dream-world/2f67d9fd-c21c-4931-99d3-1c3a13c8db43/. Accessed May 23, 2022.

Tarantino, Bob. "The Ninth Circuit's Eminem License vs Sale Decision." *Entertainment & Media Law Signal*, September 9, 2010. http://www.entertainmentmedialawsignal.com/the-ninth-circuits-eminem-license-vs-sale-decision/. Accessed June 7, 2022.

Tauberg, Michael. "Music Is Getting Shorter." *Medium*, April 27, 2018. https://michaeltauberg.medium.com/music-and-our-attention-spans-are-getting-shorter-8be37b5c2d67. Accessed June 7, 2022.

Tauberg, Michael. "Spotify Is Killing Song Titles." *Medium*, March 23, 2018. https://michaeltauberg.medium.com/spotify-is-killing-song-titles-5f48b7827653. Accessed June 2, 2022.

Taylor, Iain. "Audio Cassettes: Despite Being 'A Bit Rubbish', Sales Have Doubled during the Pandemic—Here's Why." *The Conversation*, March 19, 2021. https://theconversation.com/audio-cassettes-despite-being-a-bit-rubbish-sales-have-doubled-during-the-pandemic-heres-why-157097. Accessed April 29, 2022.

Teather, David. "Napster Wins New Friend." *Guardian*, November 1, 2000. https://www.theguardian.com/technology/2000/nov/01/internetnews.business. Accessed June 7, 2022.

"Thanks a Billion!" *TikTok*, September 27, 2021. https://newsroom.tiktok.com/en-us/1-billion-people-on-tiktok. Accessed May 25, 2022.

"The Inevitable Choice: The Victrola." 1919. David Sarnoff Library digital archive, (Accession AVD.2464.001), Hagley Museum & Library, Wilmington, DE 19807.

Thill, Scott. "June 21, 1948: Columbia's Microgroove LP Makes Albums Sound Good." *Wired*, June 21, 2010. https://www.wired.com/2010/06/0621first-lp-released/. Accessed May 22, 2022.

Thompson, Clive. "How the Phonograph Changed Music Forever." *Smithsonian*, January 2016. https://www.smithsonianmag.com/arts-culture/phonograph-changed-music-forever-180957677/. Accessed April 4, 2023.

"TikTok Is Hitting Revenue Milestones at Lightning Speed." *Slow Reveal Graphs*, November 13, 2022. https://slowrevealgraphs.com/2022/11/13/tiktok-is-hitting-revenue-milestones-at-lightning-speed/. Accessed April 3, 2023.

"TikTok Users Worldwide (2020–2025)." *Insider Intelligence*, June 1, 2022. https://www.insiderintelligence.com/charts/global-tiktok-user-stats/. Accessed November 16, 2022.

"Today's Top Hits Is the World's Destination for the Very Best in Music." *Spotify: For the Record*, June 24, 2021. https://newsroom.spotify.com/2021-06-24/todays-top-hits-is-the-worlds-destination-for-the-very-best-in-music/. Accessed June 13, 2022.

Toonkel, Jessica, Anne Steele, and Salvador Rodriguez. "TikTok Parent ByteDance PlansMusic-Streaming Expansion." *Wall Street Journal*, October 12, 2022, https://www.

wsj.com/articles/tiktok-parent-bytedance-plans-music-streaming-expansion-1166
5602937. Accessed November 16, 2022.

Tracy, Phillip. "Apple's Newest Acquisition Could Mean Changes for Apple Music." *Gizmodo*, February 7, 2022. https://gizmodo.com/apple-ai-music-acquisition-184 8496216. Accessed June 2, 2022.

Tynan, Dan. "The 25 Worst Tech Products of All-Time." *PC World*, May 26, 2006. https:// www.pcworld.com/article/535838/worst_products_ever.html. Accessed June 7, 2022.

Uy, Melanie. "3G vs. 4G Technology." *Lifewire*, June 10, 2020. https://www.lifewire.com/ how-fast-are-4g-and-3g-internet-speeds-3974470. Accessed June 5, 2022.

Van Etten, David. "American Jukebox History." https://www.jukeboxhistory.info/. Accessed May 25, 2022.

"VE-10- 50 X." *The Victor Victrola Page*. http://www.victor-victrola.com/index.html. Accessed May 9, 2022.

Verna, Paul. "ITA at 25." *Billboard*, March 11, 1995, 73.

Vevo. "VEVO Was Most Trafficked U.S. Entertainment-Music Web Network in December 2009." Vevo press release, January 13, 2010. https://www.prnewswire.com/news-relea ses/vevo-was-most-trafficked-us-entertainment-music-web-network-in-december-2009-81347087.html. Accessed May 25, 2022.

Vevo. "The World's Leading Music Video Network." https://www.hq.vevo.com/. Accessed July 25, 2022.

Vezina, Briggitte and Diane Peters, "Why We're Advocating for a Cautious Approach to Copyright and Artificial Intelligence," Creative Commons, February 20, 2020, https:// creativecommons.org/2020/02/20/cautious-approach-to-copyright-and-artificial-intelligence/ Accessed June 2, 2022.

"Victor, The World's Greatest Musical Instrument." 1903. David Sarnoff Library digital archive (Accession AVD.2464.001). Wilmington, DE: Hagley Museum & Library, 19807.

Vietze, Dmitri, and Drew Silverstein. "What Makes Amper's AI Music Tools Different with CEO Drew Silverstein." *Music Tectonics* (podcast), March 25, 2020. https://mus ictectonics.libsyn.com/what-makes-ampers-ai-music-tools-different-with-ceo-drew-silverstein. Accessed June 2, 2022.

"Vinyl Music Gives Record Stores a Boost in a Digital World." *ABC News*, April 19, 2017. https://web.archive.org/web/20180207210919/https://abcnews.go.com/amp/ Entertainment/wireStory/vinyl-music-record-stores-boost-digital-world-46887652. Accessed April 29, 2022.

Vinylmint. "History of the Record Industry 1877–1920s." *Medium*, June 7, 2014. https:// medium.com/@Vinylmint/history-of-the-record-industry-1877-1920s-48deacb4c 4c3. Accessed May 9, 2022.

Vinylmint. "History of the Record Industry, 1920–1950s." *Medium*, June 8, 2014. https:// medium.com/@Vinylmint/history-of-the-record-industry-1920-1950s-6d491d7cb 606. Accessed May 9, 2022.

Waniata, Ryan. "The Life and Times of the Late, Great CD." *Digital Trends*, February 7, 2018. https://www.digitaltrends.com/music/the-history-of-the-cds-rise-and-fall/. Accessed May 23, 2022.

Ward, Ed. *The History of Rock & Roll, Volume II, 1964–1977*. New York: Flatiron Books, 2019.

Warren, Lydia. "Steve Jobs Listened to Vinyl at Home . . . Because It Sounded Better Than His iPod." *Daily Mail*, January 31, 2012. https://www.dailymail.co.uk/news/article-2094590/Steve-Jobs-listened-vinyl-home-iPod.html. Accessed June 17, 2022.

Water & Music. "Music/Web3 Dashboard." https://www.waterandmusic.com/data/music-web3-dashboard/. Accessed May 28, 2022.

Water & Music. "*Music NFT Sales in 2021: What We Learned,*" *Water & Music*, May 6, 2022. https://www.waterandmusic.com/music-nft-sales-in-2021-what-we-learned/. Accessed November 16, 2022.

"Web Music Sharers Under Attack." *CBS News*, July 14, 2003. https://www.cbsnews.com/news/web-music-sharers-under-attack/. Accessed June 7, 2022.

Wesch, Michael. "YouTube Statistics." *Digital Ethnography @ Kansas State University.* https://web.archive.org/web/20140723075938/http://mediatedcultures.net/thoughts/youtube-statistics/. Accessed May 25, 2022.

Whately, Dan. "How TikTok Is Changing the Music Industry." *Business Insider*, July 7, 2022. https://www.businessinsider.com/how-tiktok-is-changing-the-music-industry-marketing-discovery-2021-7. Accessed July 14, 2022.

"Where Do Music Collections Come From?" *American Assembly*, October 15, 2012. http://piracy.americanassembly.org/where-do-music-collections-come-from/. Accessed June 7, 2022.

Wiki Boombox. *Analog Alley.* https://www.wikiboombox.com/tiki-index.php. Accessed May 3, 2022.

Wilentz, Sean. *360 Sound: The Columbia Records Story.* San Francisco: Chronicle Books, 2012.

Willman, Chris. "Adele's '30' Has the Biggest Bow of 2021 With 839,000 Album Units." *Variety*, November 28, 2021. https://variety.com/2021/music/news/adele-30-biggest-number-one-album-year-1235120896/. Accessed April 4, 2023.

Witt, Stephen. *How Music Got Free: A Story of Obsession and Invention.* London: Penguin Books, 2016.

Wu, Adrian. "Open Reel Tape—The Ultimate Analog Source?" *Copper.* https://www.psaudio.com/copper/article/open-reel-tape-the-ultimate-analog-source/. Accessed April 29, 2022.

Young, Neil. "The CD and the Damage Done." *Harper's*, July 1992, 23–24.

Zaleski, Annie. "35 Years Ago: The U.K. Launches the 'Home Taping Is Killing Music' Campaign." *Diffuser.fm*, October 25, 2016. https://diffuser.fm/home-taping-is-killing-music-uk/. Accessed April 29, 2022.

Zuckerman, Arthur J. "Copy-Cat Tape Decks." *Popular Mechanics*, October 1, 1983, 94+.

Index

For the benefit of digital users, indexed terms that span two pages (e.g., 52–53) may, on occasion, appear on only one of those pages.

Figures are indicated by *f* following the page number